ASTRO...
PLANET PERSONALITIES & SIGNS
Speak through Robert Shapiro

Other Books by Robert Shapiro

Explorer Race Series

1. The Explorer Race
2. ETs and the Explorer Race
3. The Explorer Race: Origins and the Next 50 Years
4. The Explorer Race: Creators and Friends
5. The Explorer Race: Particle Personalities
6. The Explorer Race and Beyond
7. The Explorer Race: The Council of Creators
8. The Explorer Race and Isis
9. The Explorer Race and Jesus
10. The Explorer Race: Earth History and Lost Civilizations
11. The Explorer Race: ET Visitors Speak Vol. 1
12. The Explorer Race: Techniques for Generating Safety
13. The Explorer Race: Animal Souls Speak
14. The Explorer Race: Astrology: Planet Personalities and Signs Speak
15. The Explorer Race: ET Visitors Speak Vol. 2
16. The Explorer Race: Plant Souls Speak
17. The Explorer Race: Time and Beyond

Material Mastery Series

A. Shamanic Secrets for Material Mastery
B. Shamanic Secrets for Physical Mastery
C. Shamanic Secrets for Spiritual Mastery

Shining the Light Series

Shining the Light: The Battle Begins!
Shining the Light II: The Battle Continues
Shining the Light III: Humanity Gets a Second Chance
Shining the Light IV: Humanity's Greatest Challenge
Shining the Light V: Humanity Is Going to Make It!
Shining the Light VI: The End of What Was
Shining the Light VII: The First Alignment—World Peace

Ultimate UFO Series

Andromeda: UFO Contact from Andromeda
Zetas, Hybrids and Human Contacts

Secrets of Feminine Science Series

Book 1: Benevolent Magic & Living Prayer
Book 2: Disentanglement & Deep Disentanglement
Book 3: Disengagement, Engagement & Connections

Shirt Pocket Books Series

Touching Sedona
Feeling Sedona's ET Energies

ASTROLOGY
PLANET PERSONALITIES & SIGNS

Speak through Robert Shapiro

© 2010 Robert Shapiro and Melody O'Ryin Swanson
All rights reserved.

No part of this book may be used or reproduced in any manner without prior written permission from the publisher, except in the case of brief quotations embodied in critical reviews and articles.

*   *   *

ISBN-10: 1891824-81-3
ISBN-13: 978-1891824-81-4

Light Technology Publishing, LLC
Phone: 800-450-0985
Fax: 928-714-1132
PO Box 3540
Flagstaff, AZ 86003
www.lighttechnology.com

CONTENTS

PREFACE *February 20, 2010* xvii
    Astrology and Astronomy Are One xvii
    What's Missing Is the Heart xviii

1. **ISIS AND THE SUN** *January 16, 2003* 1
    Like You, We Are All One 2
    You Are Cut Off from Your Energetic Support 3
    You Need to Use Your Creator Skills 5
    Orbits Are a Way of Welcoming 6
    Learn from the Beings Around You 8
    Planets Know Each Other by Feeling 10
    The Nucleus of My Personality Is Everywhere 11
    The Creation of a Trinary Sun 12
    It's Hard to Say How Long This Creation Will Go On 14
    Planets Were Attracted to This Solar System 15
    Venus Came Here First 16

2. **THE SUN** *January 17, 2003* 21
    Sometimes You Are Experiencing Opposing Feelings 21
    Creating Union with Different Parts of Yourself 22
    You Are Capable of Feeling More Than One Thing at Once 23
    Encourage Your Children to Retain These Capacities 25
    Find Adventure for Your Children 27
    The Light of the Sun Provides Continuity for You 28
    Planets Request Things from the Sun 31
    I May Be Called on to Stimulate You 33
    Sunrise Is the Most Balanced Nurturance You Can Experience 36
    Nothing Is Static 36
    A Single Sun Gives You a Continuity of Source 38

3. **THE SUN** *January 18, 2003* 41
    My Solar Flares Are Like an Exhale 41
    The Dimensions Available to Suns Are Infinite 43
    You Can Solve Things Here 44
    Only a Percentage of You Is Here 45
    Some of You Are Bringing More of Your Personality Here 48
    When You're Connected, Travel Is Not Quite the Same 50
    Not All the Planets Are Fully Engaged 51
    There Needs to Be More Heart and Spirit Involved in Your Technology 53
    Earth Is Expressing Itself in a Great Deal of Variety 55

    I Don't Consider You to Be an Individual 57

4. THE MOON *January 21, 2003* 61
    I First Established Myself around Oodoo 61
    I Will Always Radiate What Is Needed 62
    My Light Is Infused with Nurturing and Inspiration 64
    I Feel More Feminine 65
    No One Has Been Destructively Mining Me 66
    The Past Is in Motion 67
    What I Do Has to Do with Feeling 69

5. CHON-DEH, SUN HELPER *March 8, 2004* 73
    My People Focus Sun Energy 73
    We Help the Sun Support Unusual Life Cycles on Earth 74
    Your Sun Can Only Support Natural Life 76
    You Must Become Material Masters to Live a Natural Earth Life 77
    We Also Help Others on Other Planets 79
    Planets Thrive by Attracting Other Life 80
    On Your Home Planet, You Have a Natural Life Cycle 81
    Life Is Unending 83
    Enjoy Your Earth Experience 84

6. SATURN *May 28, 2004* 87
    It Is My Pleasure to Be Here 87
    Some Planets Encourage Individual Expression 88
    The Real Measurement of Time Is Experience 89
    Learning to Travel in Space and Time without a Vehicle 91
    Astrology Provides a Means to Understand Yourself 93
    You Connect to Certain Planets Before You Are Born 95
    Here You Can Learn Certain Information About the Unknown 97
    Three Additional Planets Are Available for You 98

7. SATURN *May 29, 2004* 101
    My Personality Was Formed Long Before I Became a Planet 101
    You Are Here to Learn Something New 103
    Use Physical Mastery to Discover a More Benevolent Astrology 105
    Using your "wand" (hand) to make choices: 106
    On Earth You Have the Joy of Discovery 108
    More Than the Planets Influence You at Birth 110
    I Am Allowing You to See More of My Personality 111
    My Moons Offer Me Support 112
    Planets Interact with You in Your Dreams 113
    Walk-Ins Work with Astrology Almost Identically 115
    Astrologers Can Help You Fill in the Gaps 116
    Walk-Ins: Discover Humor 117

8. **JUPITER** *June 4, 2004* 119
   Astrologers Need to Make a Felt Connection 119
   A Method for Establishing Connection 122
   Being Bigger Has Made Me More Durable 123
   You Must Consciously Choose My Energy 125
   We Appear in Ancient Writings as Inspiration 127
   Astrology Will Be Available When You Need It 128
   You Are Learning that Action Brings Consequence 129

9. **JUPITER** *June 5, 2004* 133
   Elsewhere Practically No One Has a Name 133
   Before the 1960s, ET Visitors Didn't Know Who You Were 136
   It's in the Nature of All Life to Respond Similarly 138
   Everything in Your Environment Affects You 139
   Heliocentric Astrology Is Not Yet Complete 140
   Soul-Centered Astrology Will Be Profoundly Helpful to You 141
   You Need to Consider the Distribution of What's Available to All Beings 142
   Connecting Benevolently to Jupiter 145
   Use Your Discernment 146

10. **PLUTO** *October 5, 2006* 149
    The Questions Must Be Focused 150
    Creator Liked My Universal Worldview 150
    When You Come Here, You'll See All Points of the Universe 151
    Everyone Exists All the Time, Everywhere 153
    Feeling Is Natural 154
    Spirit Beings on Pluto 155
    You Must Become Self-Creators 156
    Interacting with Feeling 158
    Creation Is Always Personal 158
    The Energy of Pluto Invites Growth 159
    In Sleep, You Return to Your Natural State 160

11. **NEPTUNE** *October 14, 2006* 163
    This Solar System Is Intended to Have a Significant Energy of Welcome 163
    I Am a Walk-In 164
    Many of You Will Move Underground 165
    Admiral Byrd Traveled to Another Vibration of Earth 167
    Antarctica's Ice Might Melt 167
    Individuality Might Not Prove to Be Viable 168
    There Are Ten More Astrological Signs 170
    New Sign: A Connector from One Sign to Another 171
    So Much Astrology Has Been Lost 173
    Astrology Offers Potential and Opportunity 175

12 ASTROLOGY EXPERT *November 3, 2006* **177**
    Astrology Is an Offering 177
    Complementary Influences Must Be Completely Compatible............................ 178
    Filtering Out Your Physical Recollections of Earth 179
    Astrology Guides You in How to Learn on Earth... 180
    Your Planet Allows for Resolution... 182
    You First Need to Learn About the Thirteenth Sign 183
    Don't Create a Hierarchy within Personalities.. 185
    Your Pathway Has to Do with How You Choose to Learn 185
    It Is Intended You Learn According to Your Sign... 187
    Walk-Ins Bring in a Slightly Different Influence 188
    Karma Is Basically About Lessons.. 189
    Astrology Is Becoming More Feeling-Oriented than Intended.......................... 190

13. VENUS *December 5, 2006* **193**
    Being Close to the Sun Amplifies My Influence 193
    There Is Less of an Impact on Mars 194
    Fifteen Percent of Earth's Population Will Move to Mars.................................. 195
    You Won't Dig into Mars for Mining or Building 196
    Earth Still Feels the Personality of the Planet Who Was Here Before............... 197
    True Love Is the Building Block of Life...200
    I Wanted to Develop Love in This Solar System 201
    There Are Many Ways to Study Love 202
    Your Cultures Are Experiencing a Warping of the Nature of Love....................203
    Desire Is a Direct Result of Earth Life 205
    Creator Apprentices Help to Bring About Resolution 206

14. VENUS *December 6, 2006* **209**
    You Are in More Than One Place Right Now 209
    Venus Personifies the Feminine.. 210
    Planets Have Guides and Teachers When There Is a Need 212
    I Support Love, but I Am Not the Source of It.. 213
    Mistakes Have Value 214

15. MERCURY *December 13, 2006* **219**
    I Influence Communication and Humor on Your Planet.................................. 219
    My Energy Has Brought Great Understanding to Earth 221
    You Are Influencing Your Guides...222
    Creator Is Fond of Resolving Problems 224
    My Personality Influences Your Personalities 226

16. MERCURY *December 14, 2006* **229**
    Your Souls Also Retrograde...229
    Support Me During My Retrograde Times..230
    Cars and Trains Are Living Beings 232

    Mythology and Astrology Are Interconnected 233
    It Is My Job to Inspire 233
    Contact Is My Overriding Principle 235

17. PLUTO *January 2, 2007* **239**
    As You Move Out Farther in Your Solar System, I Will Have More of an Influence 239
    Pluto's Energy Can Help You Become Unblocked 240
    My Job Is to Reveal 241
    I Accompanied Creator to This Space 243
    From the "Truth" to the Heart 244
    You Are Moving Toward Tolerance and Forgiveness 245
    Your Migration to Mars Will Influence Your Astrology 247
    You Have Fewer ETs Visiting You Now 249
    You Are Moving Toward Change in a Benevolent Way 250
    Move Toward Your Heart 251
    The Imprint of the Solar System on Earth 252

18. MARS *April 11, 2007* **255**
    Mars' Energy Has Nothing to Do with War 255
    On Mars It Will Be Easier to Solve Problems 258
    Planets Can Help with Temporary Personality Energies 259
    Mars Assists You in Childbirth 260
    Mars Creates Difficulty in Working with Others 261
    Stone Remains of the Previous Planet Could Change Earth's Structure 262
    Stick to This Solar System 264
    Humans Need Optimism 265
    I'm There in Your Rivers and When You Sneeze 266

19. MARS AND GRANDFATHER *April 24, 2007* **269**
    The Awakening Is Here 269
    Make Those Changes You Feel 270
    This Is the Next Step 271
    You Need to Become Your Natural Self in Your Physical Body on Earth 272
    You Are Going to Have to Use Your Physicality 275
    Astrology Can Be Immensely Helpful to Parents 277
    The Soul's Desires Are in the Cellular Structure at Birth 277
    There Is No Isolation 279
    Astrology Has to Do with Timing and Physical Place 280
    I Give You Clarity 282

**20. UNKNOWN PLANET TO STABILIZE
    EARTH'S ORBIT** *April 26, 2007* **285**
    I Am Here to Stabilize Earth's Orbit 285
    My Gravitational Pull Is More of a Repelling Energy 286
    Sirians on My Home Planet Need to Sleep to Support Me 287

  I Support Earth's Atmosphere to Keep the Water on Your Planet 289
  I Influence Contradictory Behavior 290
  Human Wars Have Stunted Your Technology...292
  The Sun Requested This Unusual Orbit..294
  Astrology Is Only Necessary When People Don't Know Who They Are 295
  Practice Being Grateful 296

21. PLANET AXIS May 5, 2007 299
  There Is a Timetable Involved on Earth 299
  You're Going to Need to Develop Interdependency..300
  You Need Each Other for Your Survival 303
  You Are Taking Over a Percentage of Everything Mother Earth Is Doing.........304
  My Energy Is Largely Involved in Balance 306
  By Uniting with Each Other, It Will Be Easier to Create......................................307
  Draw Energy from the Sun and the Planets...309

22. ISIS May 12, 2007 311
  Earth Struggles Are Wearing Down Mother Earth's Energy of Renewal 311
  Your Own Renewal Is Being Affected...312
  True Magic Will Help You Create Resources Beyond That Which Is Fixed................. 314
  Listen to Your Physical Body 316

23. ISIS May 12, 2007 319
  The Thirteenth Sign Has to Do with Communion and the
  Connection to All Beings 320
  Your Personality Traits Are Universal.. 321
  There Is Usually Compromise Between the Conscious and the Soul...........................324
  The Traits of Personality Have to Do with Spirit and Soul...................................325
  Many Teachings Are Prompted by the Desire to Create a
  Benevolent Human Society..326
  Past Lives Are Really a Means to Understanding One's Current Life.................328
  Mythology Is a Great Storehouse of Wisdom...330

24. URANUS May 26, 2007 333
  I Bring with Me the Capability to Receive or to Absorb...333
  My Tilt Absorbs Stresses on Your Planet Earth 336
  All Universes Are Benign 338
  Elsewhere I Am More of a Star System 342
  Your Mask Both Demonstrates Your Experience and Protects You....................344
  Use Astrology to Network 347
  Astrology Is Subject to the Individuals It's Trying to Help...................................349

25. SEEKER—MILKY WAY GALAXY May 29, 2007 353
  Your Actual Intention Here Is Not Just Creation 353
  I Am a Portion of Creator..355
  I Don't Always Feel You...356

Astrology Helps You Understand the Larger Concept of Yourselves 357
You Only See About One-Quarter of Your Galaxy 359
Everything Emerges from the Center of the Galaxy..361
Teamwork Has Everything to Do with Astrology on Earth 362

26. ASTROLOGICAL HISTORIAN *May 31, 2007*....................................**365**
The Origins of Astrology Were Derived on the Sea...365
Inspiration Is the Means by Which People Live 367
Historians Should have Cabinet Positions in Government..368
Astrology Needs to Focus on the Family..370
I Have Always Been Attracted to Developing Cultures 371
Astrology Must Have Heart 373
Astrology Allows You to Correlate Your Lives Beyond This Planet.................................375
Signs Are Based on More Than One Thing...376
Children Are Being Born Under the Thirteenth Sign...376
Certain Qualities Are Required to Be on Earth 378
Birth Astrology Applies to Walk-Ins..379
Astrology Is a Loving Offer to Human Culture 381

27. MOTHER EARTH *June 4, 2007* **385**
Unexpected Pain Is Telling You Something 385
Your Soul Does Not Suffer Pain 387
Earth in This Version Was Prepared for You by Creator 389
You Can Help Others Grow Beyond This Planet 390
Souls Must Have No Resistance...392
You Are the First to Successfully Engage the Explorer Race Theme 393
Astrology Was Given as a Gift..394
Earth Is Overbalanced to the Feminine 395
Quantum Mastery Gives You the Potential to Do Anything
Moderated by the Feminine 397
Your Mental Process Is Changing 398

28. MOTHER EARTH *June 7, 2007* **403**
War Is Really Difficult for Me..403
I'm Withdrawing Certain Support from You 404
You Are Expressing the Feelings of My Personality...406
Storms Are a Way to Disperse an Excess of Feeling 407
The Sea Gives Life to the Land...409
I Would Support a Benevolent Reduction of Your Population 411
Become Responsible for Re-Creating Your Existence 411

29. MOTHER EARTH *July 5, 2007* **417**
A New System Is Being Created Astrologically 417
Soon Misunderstandings Will End..418
Astronomy Is the Foundational Element of Astrology 419

    I Am Aware of Human Beings 421
    The Subconscious Is Entirely About Resolution 422

ASTROLOGICAL SIGNS

30. VIRGO July 28, 2007 .... **427**
- Virgos Have the Capacity to Inspire and Stimulate 427
- All Signs Need to Be Encouraged to Be Who They Are 429
- Astrologers Can Rely More on Their Capacity for Inspiration 430
- Let Astrology Be Flexible 432
- I Encourage the Developmental Capabilities of Others 433
- Remember, You Are Not a Fixed Sign 434

31. GEMINI August 1, 2007 .... **437**
- Recently You Have Felt the Overwhelming Presence of Impatience 437
- Animals Help Stimulate Your Natural State 438
- The First World Order Is Based on the Global Family 439
- Advancing Adaptability for Others 440
- Gemini Will Help You Connect More Strongly to Your Guides 442
- All Aspects of Astrology Are Useful 443
- It's Important for Astrology to Be Complimentary to a Child 445
- Geminis Can Help You Learn How to Be Flexible 447
- Astrology Permeates All Life 448

32. ETCHETA August 4, 2007 .... **453**
- Your Personalities Are All Rooted Back to the Twelve Original Families 453
- Many of You Are Reconsidering Who You Are 455
- The Thirteenth Sign Is Not a Replacement 457
- The Twelve Families Came from All Over the Universe 458
- I've Come to Observe You from Time to Time 459
- The Twelve Families Represent Personality Traits 460
- Be Aware of Your Sign and the Challenges Associated with It 462
- Until You Wake Up, You Will Be Driven from the Past 462
- I Am a Simple Student of Cultures 464
- Simplify the Conflicting Elements in Your Life 466

33. PISCES August 6, 2007 .... **469**
- Feelings Are the Root of Your Survival 469
- Pisces Has the Ability to Broadcast Energy of the Future 471
- Pisces Is Instinctual in Its Nature and Can Reveal the Unseen 473
- Astrology Is Affected by the Stars You Can See 476
- The Hidden Is Part of Life 478
- There Are No Secrets 480
- The Thirteenth Sign Will Be a Sign You All Assimilate 481

34. TAURUS August 29, 2007 .... **485**

How to Connect with Feelings Emanating from Earth	485
Your Astrological Chart Is Stored in the Spinal Fluid	487
Creator Created Certain Personality Types for Earth	488
Everything Broadcasts Feelings	490
You Are Part of a Larger Astrology	492
Taurus Has the Capacity to Affect the Taste of Things	494

35. AQUARIUS September 4, 2007 499

Animals and Other Life Forms Are Also Affected by Astrology	501
While You Are Emanating Energy, You Are Also Acquiring	503
Welcoming Has Everything to Do with Mother Earth	505
All Signs Are Balanced	507
Astrology Has Much to Do with Observation	508
Aquarians: Be Aware of Your Impulses	510

36. LEO September 5, 2007 513

Leos Can Initiate Personality Traits in Others	513
This Broadcast Energy Can Be Overwhelming	514
Don't Focus on Negative Traits	516
There Are Latent Traits that Will Be Revealed	517
Leos: Study the Cat	518
Your Body Is Your Greatest Teacher	519
The Signs All Offer You Different Possibilities	521
Astrology Is Becoming More of a Potential	523
Recognize that Your Broadcast Energy Is a Gift You Have to Offer	523

37. SAGITTARIUS September 6, 2007 527

Sagittarius Also Helps Improve Connections between Planets	528
You Experience All the Signs During Your Life	530
Sagittarian Influence Can Make it Difficult to Connect with Human Things	533
Your Earth Life Has to Be via the Focus of One of the Twelve Families	534
Those of the Thirteenth Sign Will Support the Rest of the Signs	537
Dogs Generally Preview Unexpressed Human Traits	538

38. ARIES September 20, 2007 541

Aries Teach Others through Their Dreams	541
Aries: Teach Your Wisdom	542
In Ancient Times, Astrology Was Considered an Art	544
Aries Will Easily Adapt to the Shift from the Mental to the Physical	545
Feelings Are the Physical Messages of Your Inner Body	547
People Choose Their Signs for Different Reasons	549
Your Sign Is Stored in Your Energy Body	550
Aries Energy Emanates from Andromeda	552
You Feel the Motivation	553

39. LIBRA July 28, 2007 557

    Whales and Dolphins Are Holding the Libra Energy for You 557
    The Libra Energy Will Support You 558
    Libra Has to Do with Balance 560
    All Traits Are Becoming More Accessible 561
    There's an Acceleration Toward Benevolence 563
    You Are Being Protected from the Extremes of the Past 566
    You Need to Let Go of Blame 567

40. THE 13TH SIGN *October 2, 2007* **569**
    The Thirteenth Sign Will Come to Be Known as the Peacemaker 570
    You Have Always Had a Thirteenth Sign 571
    More and More Astrologers Are Using Inspiration to Fill in the Gaps 572
    Your Prayers Have Not Gone Unheeded 573

41. CAPRICORN *October 27, 2007* **577**
    You Are Now Learning the True Lesson of Capricorn 577
    The Idea of Absolute Precision Has Tainted Astrology 578
    The Personality of the Signs Reveals Everything 579
    It's Natural to Want to Discover Every Possible Thing 580
    You Can Experience the Best from All the Signs All the Time 581
    Capricorns Have an Ability to See the Truth in Others 582
    This Is Advanced Astrology 583
    Don't Overlook a Planet's Appearance 585
    Enjoy Your Journey through Life 587

42. CANCER *October 28, 2007* **589**
    The Explorer Aspect of Cancer Has Been Lost Over Time 589
    This Is Your Third Time through Your Lives 591
    The Job of the Astrologer Is Literally One of an Alchemist 592
    Exploring Has Everything to Do with Subtlety and Sensitivity 593
    Cancer Stimulates Looking at the Known in New Ways 595
    Living on Earth Is All About Influence 596

43. SCORPIO *November 3, 2007* **599**
    It May Be Possible to Re-Create the Missing Links of Astrology 599
    The Connection to the Unifying Element Is Important 601
    Scorpio Can Leave an Imprint for Others to Follow 602
    Your Other Forms Have Helped You to See and Feel Life in Different Ways 603
    The Scorpion Has Nothing to Do with the Sting 605
    Astrologers: It's Important to Be Encouraging 606

44. THE 10TH PLANET *November 21, 2009* **611**
    Your Responsibility Is Going to Be to Guide Other Planets through Discomfort 611
    This Universal Project Will Help Everyone Achieve Growth Benevolently 613
    I Am the Planet of Your Combined Wisdom 614
    I Am Not Entirely Physical 616

    You've Never Known the Feeling of 100 Percent Accomplishment 617
    The Reward Is Being Able to Ask for the Wisdom 618
    Visual Arts Are Moving in a Cycle 621

45. THE 11TH PLANET *November 30, 2009* 623
    The Distant Past Is Being Dissolved 623
    Male and Female Roles Will Blend 625
    Most Veils Will Drop When You Become Enjoined with Your Full Spirit Being 626
    The Correlation between Planet Eleven and the Moon Is Significant 627
    My Favorite Is the Feeling between Dimensions 627
    This Will Help You Move More into Your Natural Roles 628
    Many Astrologers Are Spiritual Beings 630

46. THE 12TH PLANET *December 7, 2009* 633
    The Heart Energy and Feminine Energy on Earth Is Rising 633
    Creator Invited Me for My Masculine Energy 634
    I Help Bring You Balance 635
    The Twelfth Planet Has Everything to Do with the Past 636
    I'm at My Greatest Influence When Sunspot Activity Is at Its Height 637
    I'm Not Really in Your Visible Spectrum 638
    You Need to Bring Your Masculine Energy into Balance with the Feminine 640
    Your Physical Body Is Not Unlike a Planet 642
    Creator Never Asked Me to Be a Planet Permanently 643
    You Need to Consciously Make Life Better for Yourselves 644
    You Have to Be Aware that Everything Is Alive 645

47. TEACHER OF ASTROLOGY *May 31, 2002* 649
    Imagination Paves the Way for Change 649
    True Knowledge Is Always Flexible 651
    The Love-Heat Exercise 653
    The Value of Astrology Is Upon You 654
    Homework: Add Words to Your Love-Warmth Practice 655
    Cultures Have Risen and Fallen on Earth 657
    There Needs to Be Flexibility 658
    Love-Warmth Is the Foundation of the Natural World 659
    We Go Where We Are Needed 661

48. REVEALS THE MYSTERIES *January 15, 2003* 665
    The Sun Provides Mother Earth with Touch 665
    The Earth Gives the Sun a Sense of Purpose 666
    The Sun Is Foremost About Intimacy 667
    Planets in This Solar System Receive All the Touch They Might Need 668
    You on This Planet Are Creating Solutions 670
    Some Planets Came from Elsewhere to Support You 671
    Homework: Experience the Feeling of Timelessness 673

Light Technology Publishing Presents 5 New Websites!

lighttechnology.com

FREE DOWNLOADABLE CONTENT ON ALL NEW WEBSITES!

If you are not familiar with the concept that humanity is the *Explorer Race*, we recommend that you download the first chapter of the first book in the *Explorer Race* series at the website, ExplorerRace.com. This will give you an overview of humanity as apprentice creators who agreed to forget who they are while being trained in the creator school on Earth.

You can also download the first chapter of each of the books channeled by Robert Shapiro by going to the above websites.

PREFACE
Astrology Reclaims It's Heart

February 20, 2010

Astrology and Astronomy Are One

I want to talk to you today about the value and the science and the heart of astrology. Over the years, astrology has become split off from its original complete self. The complete self of astrology includes astronomy, but some years ago during the real dawning of science in terms of its popularity—taking it out from what was once considered a cultish phenomenon, really—science was looked at with suspicion. Historians know about this. Science and the intellect were once considered that because they were not in rhythm with the cycles of Earth that one might find in a more agrarian economy—farming, you understand.

Originally, astrology and astronomy were one thing. But as the interest in science grew more, with the astrologers' blessing, the scientific aspects of the pursuit of astronomy took place. For astrologers, this was of value, since there would be perhaps greater understanding of the stars, the planets and their positions and so on. So it looked good on the surface to astrologers. But as attention moved away within the historical context of the agrarian society and into a more technological and intellectual society, there was pressure—really, peer pressure at the time—to separate oneself as a scientist from what was then taken for granted, which were the cycles of Earth, meaning the seasons, the time to plant, the time to harvest and so on. This was so taken for granted that the connection to astrology was actually dismissed.

Astrology has everything to do in the beginning with planting cycles, growth: the best time to do this, the best time to do that, the cycles of the Moon and so on. Much of this is still in use today for the best results in many farms and gardens. So the pressure on the pursuit of intellectual and technological times pushed people further and further away from their roots in astrology and the cycles of Earth.

Thus what started out as something that the astrologers at the time thought would be wonderful, gradually evolved into something separate, almost like a breakdown in language. Many ancient religious books point to this, but historians understand that this has more to do with cycles of nature and social interactions with people. So what we have, then, are lost elements of understanding about the nature of the planets, the true nature of the signs, and the heart of astrology, which is the same as the heart of humanity and other forms of life. That is, the unique personality of each being

When you have a unique personality—as you all know, since you have personalities—not only are you able to function well but you demonstrate qualities that people like and, at times, don't like, just like you feel about them. So you are able to gravitate into groups because your personalities are complementary. It's really the same in nature. Even in the cycles of nature, such as when the leaves fall from the trees in preparation for the wintertime and the change of season, everything is in its own time, in its own place.

What's Missing Is the Heart

So what I am saying is that astrology and astronomy are one. The heart is astrology; the mind is astronomy. But you would not, in your own personality, separate your heart from your mind, would you? Maybe not intentionally. But if you look back in recent years, the pursuit of the intellect has often—though perhaps not intentionally—set aside the heart, and many times this has been detrimental in society. So some might say, "We can do this; we can make it," whereas those of the heart might say, "But what good is it?" or "It might do harm." I'm not here to indict anyone or to say something is bad. Certainly science has done wonders and improved the lot of most human beings. But there is still that need, that feeling, that something's missing, isn't there?

The thing that's missing is the heart. Since the heart is not always quantifiable in feelings, then science might address feelings as emotions in order to create a pseudo-scientific terminology that does not actually fit the personality of all beings. So I'm not blaming science. What I am saying is that science does not have to change its path so much as to simply become more inclusive, which I feel is in your nature. You've been looking for something, and this is it.

This book honors that pursuit of the lost heart. It demonstrates the personality of the planets, the Sun, the Moon, the signs. This is what has been missing in astrology, ever since the heart was set aside in favor of the mind. Over time, such knowledge and wisdom was relegated to the corners, to the top shelf—in other words, to places that got lost. This book brings all that back. It allows astrologers to feel the planets, to feel the Sun, the Moon and the signs. This is not to abandon the knowledge and wisdom they have now, but to truly include, to show, to demonstrate, to provide to those seeking astrological knowledge and wisdom, to provide the heart elements of personality.

Do you know that the basic personality types on Earth are exactly reflective of the personality types of the planets and even to some extent of the Sun and Moon, and certainly of the signs? If you know that, you realize that there is a correlation to the intellectual process, which is why astrology, astronomy, the heart and the mind can be at home together. These do not have to be separate pursuits.

When you read this book, know and understand this so that you can feel at ease and at comfort with what is actually and truly a natural process: The bringing together of the different parts of a family that took different trails but found their way home. This book is about home.

Astrology in your time has been popularized in newspapers and magazines for its entertainment value, but this is sort of a gentle way of suggesting that there is another way to look at things. The potential for understanding your lives and being able to make the most of your potential will be greatly expanded by what is offered in this new astrology book. Professional astrologers in time may absorb what is in these pages and some of them may just incorporate the new information into their readings for clients on the basis of their feelings and intuitions as well as their study.

There are many ways to understand your lives now. I'm not saying that astrology is the only way, but it is a way that is available and can be taken more seriously these days, especially with the addition of this material. I am hopeful you will enjoy it and put it to good use.

— *Grandfather through Robert Shapiro*

Sun Shining on Earth

ISIS AND THE SUN
This Solar System Is Welcoming

January 16, 2003

This is Isis.

I'd like to ask if, rather than having someone talk about astrology, I can talk to the Sun, to the Earth, to Mercury, to Mars. Is Robert able to channel these beings comfortably?

That's an interesting idea. I don't think it has to be either/or. But if you would prefer that the channeling be directly from the Sun and the others, we could perhaps do that.

I thought that the beings/planets could express their own personal feelings—because that's what we've done in all the other books; we've talked to the beings directly.

Remember, the whole purpose of this book is to talk about relationships. Earth relates to the Sun this way, the Sun relates to the Earth that way, and so on. The whole book is really about how the other planets and the Sun relate to Earth. Earth has the capacity to communicate and establish communication, but sometimes she needs more communication, more skills, and Mercury supports Earth with this. Astrologers have identified things like this because they were given a lot of training in the distant past. This isn't something somebody made up.

✷ ✷ ✷

You call me the Sun.

Welcome.

Thank you. What do you want to know?

First, can you tell me about yourself? Did you have experience before being the Sun in this solar system?

Like You, We Are All One

I have always been as I am now, sometimes bigger, sometimes smaller. I was not always here—suns have a way of traveling. When we are preparing to move from one place to another, we get smaller—you call it collapsing—and we usually go into a dormant state for a time and get cooler, although not cold. When your science people see suns do that or can perceive suns doing that, this means that that sun is getting prepared to move. People on planets around that sun would have already moved or passed on.

In other places, before I came here, I was a sun—we use the term "sun," okay?—maybe six, seven or eight times as big (this is in volume). This is the smallest I have ever been. I find that it is no different; big or small feels exactly the same to me. As suns, we do not measure our volume the way the physical perception of humankind measures us. Our volume is measured by how far our rays travel—that's how big we are.

Here at night, if it's very dark out, sometimes you can see the galaxy; you can see at least the swirls of your part of it. So you could go to the other side of the galaxy, and if you had pretty good vision, you would see other suns, and those suns, far past what a human can see, would see rays coming from the Sun in this solar system. From those suns' perception, that's how big the sun is. So as far as our light goes, that's how big we are.

Ah, and yours goes beyond this galaxy.

As do most suns'. I grant and acknowledge that your measurement of the Sun in volume is so big by so big, but our personalities identify our size based on how far our light goes. This is why all suns are joined all the time. We are one. We are just concentrated here—here is this sphere, very dense, putting out light. Far away by humankind's measurement there is another sun, but that sun is like part of my body. There's no difference. My light can go there, and that sun's light can come to me. It takes time in humankind's measurement, but in experience it is immediate, constant, always, so we are one sun.

When you hear this term "we are one," it's not always clear what that means. You can say mentally, philosophically to yourself, "We are human beings. We are obviously created by Creator. We are one," like that. But I am talking about something more than that. It is that way for me as the Sun, and when you are told you are one, it is the same way for you exactly. Just because you do not send off light the way a sun does, you still radiate. But your radiations that go out, that can be felt on the other side of the universe . . . of course, here on Earth there is a shield to keep these particular discomforting radiations from going out, but without a shield or, say, on another planet where the shield would not be necessary because their feelings are benevolent, what radiates are feelings for human beings.

So when you are told you are one, this means all beings who have feelings like you—because on your Earth you have beings from other sources you call animals and their feelings are the same. Fishes have the same kind of feelings. Granted, they don't always have your kind of feelings, but you have feelings in common. Plants have feelings. So on other planets where there isn't discomfort or unhappiness and all that stuff, then when you are told you are all one, that means you radiate, that all feeling beings radiate feelings. You are all one just the way we, as suns, radiate light. We are all one because wherever our light goes connects us to the other suns, so we are one, in fact. Does this help at all? Do you understand how you are all one?

You Are Cut Off from Your Energetic Support

It is different for you on Earth right now because you are in a school and experiencing discomfort, and you are temporarily shut off from feeling your oneness with all beings in your universe. They are shut off from feeling your feelings as well, but that is to protect them. It is also why life for you on Earth is so short, so you don't have to endure the suffering for so long. If you were born even in an identical body on another planet—there are other nearby planets where the body is almost exactly the same as yours, and there are other planets where the bodies are identically the same—you would not feel the same as you do on Earth. You would feel your oneness with other beings.

So you would live a lot longer.

You would live a lot longer—that is the main thing. You would live 1,200; 1,500; 2,000 years even by your calendar now, because that's how long this body is built to last—that long. But because you are cut off from that feeling of oneness here on Earth, to protect you somewhat so you can do your job as the Explorer Race and also to protect others so they do not feel discomforts when they are not prepared for that, you live only a short life here. Your body has to work *very* hard and you have to sleep deeply to live as long as you do because your body is cut off from itself.

Other beings are not other beings—they are all *you*. I have just as much energy from the other suns as I give them. The same is true for human beings. You are cut off from the support from the bulk of the energy you would normally have. So even given the discomfort, if you had that energy flowing in from all other beings elsewhere, you would still be able to live here 1,500 years perhaps if your life was pretty good. Even if you were having a hard life, you could live a minimum of 670 to 700 years.

In old civilizations on this planet before the Explorer Race, they did live that long.

It was suggested that people could do that, but life was much more gentle then. Granted, you sometimes had to work hard to get the things you needed, but there wasn't what I would call stress. So, yes, it was suggested in the old books that so-and-so lived 500, 600, 700 years. Well, that is normal. But now there is so much more of a shield to cut you off from the rest of your being, since there are so many of you here; the more of you here, the thicker the shield gets, and it cuts you off more.

That's why the shield protects the animal and plant people, you know. But that is also why you need to have so many different forms of life here. It is not typical on other planets to have so many plants of so many different kinds, so many animals of so many different kinds. But because you are so cut off from other life in other places, you need to have as much variety of life as you can have on this planet in order to live as long as you do.

This is because the emanations from the plants and animals sustain us?

That's right, because what you call plants and animals are life forms from other places, and that is also why those life forms (the plants, the animals) are not as durable here. On other planets where there is only benevolence, they also might live 1,500, 1,800 years, something like that. But here they live a much shorter time because they are cut off.

But they know they are your teachers, they know they are needed, and they are providing, just by being, a certain amount of radiated energy to you that supplements your being—meaning what you would normally be connected to without discomforts, without the shield. Their radiation supplements your being energy, so it's like a small microcosmic universe here behind that shield. Sometimes the shield is extended a little bit out.

Like when an astronaut goes out?

Exactly. An astronaut goes out to the Moon, or maybe pretty soon a physical astronaut goes out to Mars and perhaps you can even set up a colony on Mars. It won't be easy, but with worldwide support, you can make it happen. Of course, people on Earth will feel a lot of excitement, a lot of fun, and that will be a good thing. So the shield extends out a bit. But other than that, it is pretty close to Earth.

It's important to know these things because you are told things in philosophies and they become ideals to live up to: "I am one with you; you are one with me. We need to treat each other better." All that is true, but there is a physical aspect to it that is not always understood. That's why I am trying to talk to you about this, because suns are very concerned with the *physical* nature of things. That is why we foster and encourage *physical* things. We encourage life, because the nature of physicality in terms of relating how things are to you . . . we are more than that, but relating for the purpose of this talk to human beings, we foster and encourage *physical* life. That is the best way you can nurture each other and ultimately go through what you need to go through, learn what you need to learn, and acquire this and that experience—so that you can learn how to make this place, Earth, more benevolent on your own.

So that's one way, one thing you need to know, but also you need to want it, because right now different cultures think of benevolence as different things. You have to be reminded what is benevolent to all of you at all times. Mainly you need to know how and you need to want it, and you need to know how and want it all at the same time. It just takes awhile, okay?

You Need to Use Your Creator Skills

Creating benevolence on Earth is worth doing. When that happens, the shield will not be removed by Creator. Rather it will be up to you to remove it using the know-how you have and the desire to live in benevolence with yourselves and all beings. With that combination, *then* you will be able to remove the shield so you can experience universal life benevolently, but until that happens, you will not be able to remove the shield.

Creator expects you to use the skills of Creator to accomplish what you need. This is why you are put in a place that gives you the basics you need but where you are expected to create what you need other than that. That's why humankind is so inventive, so dynamic, all of these things—using Earth this way and that way. Ultimately, though, with many, many people living on Earth now, there's only so much stuff, so you think, "Well, maybe we can mine the planets." But it's a long way to go, a lot of resources used, yes? "How much can we bring back?" So there's not much urgency to do that.

Maybe you say to yourself, "What can we do to have more on Earth to take care of the people we have?" It doesn't make any difference if Creator is not going to come down, give a finger on the planet from the sky, like in the famous drawing (see Illustration 1), and say, "Okay, now you have everything you need forever." Then what are you going to do? The only thing you can do is to use Creator's skills that have to do with benevolence, magic, timing, desire, need—all these things. Real magic is based on allowing those who would normally come together to come together in that moment, to be whatever is needed for others and to be that for yourself. That's how all atoms, molecules, moisture, everything, how it all comes together to form a tree, which is natural. A tree is not here to learn anything; it's here to teach.

It works the same way with your physical body. It comes together because all those atoms and molecules at that synchronous moment desire—they say, "Let's do that. Oh, it feels so good to me to be next to this molecule." The

Illustration 1: Michelangelo's "Creation of Adam" on the ceiling of the Sistine Chapel.

atoms feel as feeling and knowing in the moment: "This feels so good to be next to this atom; I'm going to be next to this atom now for a while." You have many atoms, many molecules, and so on, and they all come together and form that body for a while or that tree for a while or that mountain for a while, however long. Someday the mountain changes, the atom frees itself up and says, "Oh, that was very nice. Now I'm going to go roll down here and maybe become something else or fly off and become something else."

Love brings it together, but there's attraction based on desire. That's why I mentioned to you before that you have to all *want* benevolence. There's desire—that is the basic coming together. I am together with all other lightgivers as a sun. I am a point of the lightgiver. We are all united as suns, as lightgivers, yes? I am but one of many, and wherever there is a sun in this universe, I am there also.

Then you don't get bored.

It's not possible. I am working all the time, but it is not a job. Think about it. Your body works; your heart is beating. It beats because in your body it performs that function. It wants to beat. That is why it exists in your body. It's not a job; your heart is fulfilled by beating. The blood moves around in your body because it is happy to be blood, it wants to do that. It is fulfilled doing that, and it serves you. This is an example in your terms of what I'm talking about. I want to be a sun; I'm happy to do it. It fulfills me to be a sun, and it feeds all life.

Orbits Are a Way of Welcoming

You are here to learn that first. You are getting there as a race of people—you understand, as human beings. In your normal state, you know all these things, but here you are cut off from that because Creator wants you to become like Itself. So first you experience a lot of chaotic things, how things don't work when they're not unified. But Creator decides to create for you a small place all with volunteers (all the plants, animals, the planet herself), a little universe in that sense—a planet as a universe where souls, personalities, can come and be human beings and learn in a place that won't affect the rest of the universe. Even if it goes bad, it will be isolated, shrunk down. If that happened, it would be isolated, shrunk down, made as small as possible, and gradually recycled.

You would be recycled, too?

I would be responsible for recycling if it went bad. In the past, where things like that have been tried and the planets got blown up with some kind of weapon or something like that, it is always the Sun's responsibility in that solar system to purify those bits and pieces left from that planet, even if they meander all over the place. Then my light goes everywhere in this universe, just like another sun's light goes everywhere, but it would be my work to purify that planet. It is Creator's work to look after your souls; that's not my work. Creator and Creator's friends, representatives—angels and everybody—look after all the souls of plants, animals, and so on, but my work would be to look after the planet herself, even if she's in bits and pieces all over the place. I have done this before.

Yes, with the planet here before this. Where are those bits and pieces?

Some of them have formed up around rings around other planets. The rings are actually identifying zones of attraction—not exactly gravity, just a stabilized orbit. So if there's a ring of bits and pieces of a former planet, sometimes just things that have floated in there, this tells you that this is a welcoming orbit. What this means is that until there are moons there, or satellites—you call them moons here on Earth—then this is defining an orbit that is available.

Maybe also someday, when human beings travel out from your planet and are colonizing other planets, you might be looking for a very stabilized place. Granted, where there are rings around planets there are too many rocks, and you can't have a big ship floating there amongst the rocks. But if those rocks are around that planet, then it tells you that there are orbits available like that around all planets, including Earth, which has welcomed the Moon with something like, "Here's an orbit. Come be here and you can orbit around and be comfortable." Other planets—Mars, Venus, Jupiter, all these places—have orbits and some have moons.

Someday you might create the big ships that can travel from here to there, but sometimes you might just want to have a ship that goes somewhere and stays there. People live on the ship and repair it if necessary, but eventually you learn how to allow the ship to be self-sustaining and it becomes like an artificial planet. People are happy to be there. This is not unknown in other places; I'm just mentioning it to you in passing because I think some of your readers might like that. So these orbits are available.

Now, as far as other parts of the planet, lots of those parts have gone all over the place. Most of them are still in this galaxy, but I have purified them all. Some of them have traveled all kinds of different ways. You are conscious of falling meteors, yes? Meteors are usually parts of other planets. Sometimes they are compositions, meaning they are getting ready to be moons. They might come together some, because some so-called meteors are *really big*. A lot of moons started off as just floating about in space like that, as bits.

We don't have to talk too much about the astronomical thing, but I like to talk about the orbits because the orbits are a way of welcoming, and I intend to relate this to the human being. Human beings are the same as planets. You are always what you see, what you experience in your world, everything you experience here, including what you can observe with your science. This all tells you something about yourselves. Science is right about that—that's what it's about.

So if planets have welcoming orbits, places where moons can orbit, it is the same with people. You are conscious of the application of that as a family. People come together and they have children or maybe adopt children, something like that. Then there are orbits. They have children, and it is the same thing for human beings. So what is this way for a planet is exactly the same for the human being.

Learn from the Beings Around You

That's why the planets express themselves this way, so human beings will understand the basics of creation and never get too far away from understanding that. Even if you are not of a scientific culture, you will still see how the animals are, how they give birth to their young. You will see how the plants are. Some of them give birth in open ways, where seeds fly off, go wherever they go, and are welcomed. The ones who were fostered and bloom were the most welcomed, whereas the ones who only bloom for a little while were only temporarily welcomed. After a while, maybe someone comes along, eats that plant—then it was welcomed only for a while.

So you notice that. If you are a culture without science, you still have observers, and the intention is to see how these teachers for you are examples of how they live their lives—not just so you can be imitative, because human beings are intended to be imitative here to learn your lesson, but also so that you can learn the basic rules. Now, there's a joke here, the house rules and the Creator provides so that you can say, "This is what Creator wants me to learn here. I am in a school and I'm surrounded with these overlapping examples, and many of them can be reduced to certain basic things. They have basic traits in common. If all these forms of life have all these basic traits in common, it is clear that I am expected to master those basic traits. Whatever else I might do here, I'm expected, as a human being, as a family, as a culture, to master the traits of these plants and animals we have in common with them."

That's why certain animals appeal to you more. People like dogs so much—they love dogs. Dogs love them and dogs have certain feelings, certain ways. Some people love cats, some horses, and so on. But all these animals, as you say, have certain traits in common with you. Figure out which traits you have in common. If you are attracted to this kind of species—you like cats, you like dogs, whatever—what traits do you have in common with them? If they live with you, they choose to live with you; it's not just that you capture them. Maybe you capture them in the case of a fish or a horse, and so on, but a dog or cat adopts you as much as you adopt them, unless you keep them chained up or locked in the house.

So first figure out what traits you have in common. You don't have to *be* a cat or a dog, walk around on all fours and all that, no. What traits do you have in common? There is loyalty, love, friendship, all these kinds of things. If these are things that are benevolent and feel good to you, probably you are meant to know more, to do more, to experience more of what that animal shows you.

Some of you don't have animals, you have children. Then, of course, you are more conscious of being aware of what you have in common with other people, so I'm not dwelling on that. Very often you might have someone who doesn't have children, doesn't have animals, but he or she might have plants. What do you have in common with the plants? Plants have feelings. You all have feelings in common.

Now, your dog might have some feelings that you don't have, might do certain things in ways you don't do. The dog doesn't use his front paws like hands to examine things the way you do; he uses his mouth. Well, you don't have that in common, so you're not expected to learn more about that. If you are expected to learn more about that, then the lesson will be made obvious to you in other ways.

We'll get to plants last so I can make my point. One thing we know for sure is that plants have feelings. Even your science has discovered that. If plants have feelings, then, "We're supposed to explore certain feelings we have in common." The plants and the animals are more pure in their feelings, and by "pure" I mean they are not burdened with the many feelings you have because they are not here to learn anything, because they are here to teach by being. So you can learn by observing them and paying attention to their feelings.

If they're not here to learn, they are here to teach, but they cannot usually speak to you in your language unless you have someone like this channel. Then what are you going to do? You observe them. How does the good gardener get the plants to grow? Just by giving fertilizer, watering, putting them in the sun? No. The plant will grow sometimes for the good gardener (you say "green thumb"), because the plant likes the person and the plant likes the person also because the person actually likes the plant as someone; the person talks to the plant. The plant doesn't need to understand your words but sometimes does. So the gardener gently talks and says sweet things, "Oh, you're so beautiful"—just like you might want to say to children to give them a good feeling about themselves. It's the same thing with the plant, especially when you grow plants from seeds.

The plant isn't here to learn anything, though. If it isn't here to learn anything, why is it here? It's here to teach. Pay attention to the plant's feelings, pay attention to the animals' feelings—pay attention to the feelings of those around you who are not here to learn anything. If they are around you or in your orbit, then you will find that your teachers are never very far away with what you are expected to do, what you came here to do, what you want to learn.

Planets Know Each Other by Feeling

Reveals the Mysteries [see chapter 48] said last night that there are orbits around you that establish homes for planets also.

What do you make of that?

It's the same thing.

Of course, it is the same. The planets are family; that's how I think of them. I don't call them the same names, but then we don't have names, we have feelings—meaning I have a certain feeling. To you, you experience me as "Sun," a word, but other cultures have different words, and you also experience me in other ways. You go out, you feel the warmth, "Ah, Sun." But to us suns, we have like a physical feeling, and I also experience the planets at their physical feelings. The way they feel to me . . . that is how I know who they are.

It's the same for you, actually. Say a mother is blind. She has her baby and you come over and bring your baby—maybe you and this mother are twins, but you can see, and you each have a baby born on the same day. The blind mom, she still knows her baby. If you as the sister give the blind mom your baby without saying one thing or the other, and she says, "Oh, so nice to see you, be with you," she knows it's not her baby. She calls your baby by name. She knows her own by feeling.

So we are not blind as suns or planets; we know each other by feeling. It's the same thing for human beings. You meet somebody you know you've never met before, and before you know it you are old friends already. You feel like you've known each other all your life. You know each other by feeling. Maybe you have known each other in other lives, maybe you will know each other in future lives, or maybe none of that. Maybe you have never met before, maybe you've never had past lives, future lives, but you know each other by feeling, not just compatibility.

This person is in your orbit, so there is feeling. We need to expand your concepts a little bit. Sometimes you really hit it off with someone, you really like him or her, but the relationship doesn't take. Perhaps this person is in your orbit, but you're not in his or her orbit.

I relate these things to you because, again, as a sun, as the planets here for you, we are not here to learn anything, but we are here to teach. So I am speaking to you on the basis of what you are here to learn. There is really no point in my talking about things that have no relevance to you whatsoever—it just puts you off the track. But I can talk to you for the rest of your life about things that have relevance to you. I'm not going to do that, but for the purpose of this book, I'm giving you some things so that you can see how the way I see things correlates with the way you see things, or perhaps to help you to become more conscious of things and look at things in a different way, maybe in a way that will help you to achieve some measure of fulfillment.

Have you ever spoken through a channel before?
Yes.

Many times?
More than once. How's that?

Does it feel comfortable? You're really there—I feel you, I sense you, you're totally inhabiting the body.
Good. Do you feel warm?

I feel wonderful.
[Laughs heartily.] My joke. That's a sun joke; I'm not making fun of you. I hope you don't mind if I make a sun joke.

No, you're wonderful.

The Nucleus of My Personality Is Everywhere

Were you created within this creation by this Creator, or did you come from someplace else?
The nucleus of sun personality—that we are all one—is common to all beings everywhere. So imagine Creator making this universe, yes? What did Creator make it from?

Himself and the energy that was in the space.

So the nucleus of my personality is everywhere. Creator could not "make" a universe without using what is. Creator wanted illuminated bodies of light we call suns, yes? The nucleus of my personality is everywhere, so it is available to Creator to create suns, like that. What if I told you it is that way for everything, for life that exists in other universes having no relation to this universe in any way? Still, the nucleus of all their personalities, of everything in every other universe, is here too. It's just not expressed because the Creator of this universe says, "No, this is what I want here, and if I ever want that other, then I have all that I need here in this universe because all that I need is everywhere in every universe, so this is very convenient." Creators don't talk that way, but if they were to, then they would say that.

It's a good concept, isn't it? It's very interesting, that. I might add, that's how on the smaller scale a being from another planet who may be very foreign to this planet, may be nothing like it, can come here. Even from another universe, some beings can do that, you know—travel from one universe to another. They can be here, they can function here, because the nature of their being, what makes them up, is here also, even if there's nothing like them here and they are just passing through. It is present in its potential, yes, but it is also present just because it is everywhere. So the statement, "Everything is everywhere," is true.

So where were you a sun before?

We'll keep it to this universe for this book, but I have been . . . see, sometimes suns move like I said before, but I have always been in this galaxy.

The Creation of a Trinary Sun

Suns, when they move, do not usually move vast distances. They will move someplace because perhaps a solar system is going to develop, perhaps for a reason. In this case, it was the Explorer Race, and so on, but other times it might be some other reason. Perhaps Creator wants to express something or maybe one of Creator's students wants to express something. They don't think like this, but I'll create that personality of human thought, okay? So they think, "What do I want to create? How many planets, suns, moons? I want a sun to be here that will welcome what I want to create."

So you are not going to sit there and say, "Okay, come on. Okay." It's not like that, because time doesn't exist for such creations. It could take a billion years in terms of your calendar, or it could take a second or less for that sun to show up, and it's fine. So where I was . . . I relate in terms of your measurement somewhat. It's kind of a spiral, yes, your galaxy. It's not quite like that. But then I did not travel too far.

Does it have a name we've ever heard of?

I don't think so.

Did that solar system just naturally finish, then?

No—other things are possible. That student of Creator had a sun there—me, yes? But at some point the participants on the planets . . . it's not a big solar system, about seven planets. There are all different cultures on the planets, but one goal was taught as an ancient lesson—not something you have to struggle with, but a goal. They were told, "Your goal, no matter the littlest child or most aged, is working together with everyone else on these planets. Someday it will be your job to create a trinary sun, and once you have accomplished that, you will know that you did it on your own when that sun becomes binary within the average half-life of an average being on your planet. You will know that you did it and it was not done by other beings." Some of them might want that proof; others don't need the proof. "You will know when the sun becomes binary, two suns."

So their job was not to replace; that would be tough enough. Their job was they all had to work together at the same moment. A long time, they worked on this. It would be hard to measure on your calendar year—their lives are longer than human lives here. But they worked on it for about a thousand generations and accumulated at the same moment on all planets. It became like a religion. They worked on it—I'm going to put it in your calendar terms—every day at the same time for a few hours, and it became something they did. It was wonderful; it was not terrible.

Different cultures developed different ceremonies. Some of them danced in order to do it, some of them were quiet and meditative, and so on, but they were all doing it their way at that time. One day, *poof*, there were two more suns, and they were all excited and happy, and then they waited. They figured they might have to wait the average half-life of the average being on those planets, so it would be a long time and some of the people on the planets weren't going to know. In that culture, they would know—they would die, they would go on and would know then—but many of the people would know. So someday, *poof*, two suns only, one of them left. Guess who it was, eh?

It was you.

What you would see is this: Instead of one sun in the sky, suddenly you wake up and there are three suns in the sky. You still have night and day because the suns are not on top of each other, but you are still orbiting around three suns, okay? It is all very benevolent, no discomfort, and there are a few other good things, a little more nurturing for life, and so on. But then what you see is one of the suns . . . this is not typical, suns usually take a long time to get smaller, colder. But because this student creator had informed his peoples that they would all see it in their lifetimes, a sequence of preparing to move was greatly speeded up. So over a half-life, an average half-life, they saw the process take place—that the bright light from one of the suns became less bright, less bright, less bright, like that. Pretty soon they just saw this kind of dark spot, and then that dark spot was gone. That's when we moved off, "Goodbye." Off I went to the next place I was welcomed—here. That's it.

Did you know in advance the situation, the Explorer Race story?

It was not necessary. What was necessary only was . . . this is how it works. In your case it was Creator (granted, with some assistance), in the other case it was one of Creator's students, but what they would do is, they don't "tell" Explorer Race this and that. They just emanate a condensed-like, capsulized version of all the feelings that will ever happen there in order to accomplish what they want the solar system to be. If those feelings are compatible with a sun somewhere, then that sun comes. They were compatible. I felt I was up to the task, but also they were compatible with me. It's like, "Oh, I can take that," or "I like that," so it was compatible. So I volunteered and went there.

The civilizations on those other seven planets, did they call forth two suns? Is that what happened? Did they manifest them?

No, it was their job to create a trinary sun. They knew it was their job to create it so there would be three suns in the sky, and then they would know they had done it because one of the suns would go away and there would only be two suns. That was that, and they could live, they could go on—they weren't done.

So they actually created them. They called them forth from the space because everything is everywhere?

Remember, that solar system was created by a student of the Creator, and students tend to teach things or pass on things or want their students to do things that are similar to what they are doing. First and foremost, the creator student's personality is that of a student, he or she wants the people, the beings on those planets, to be compatible. "How can I relate to these beings? The best way I can relate to them is that our basic personalities are very compatible. So I am Creator's student, they are my students, and we have in common right away that we are students."

And you both create.

"We both create," and so on. So a good creator tries to create beings that he or she is compatible with. Otherwise, if you create a being you're not compatible with, you're always going to be trying to change each other. Sounds familiar, eh?

It's Hard to Say How Long This Creation Will Go On

You had experience before this system. Are you considered a really experienced sun or a young sun?

All suns are one. No one sun is older, younger, more experienced or less experienced than the other.

So you all share the experience because you're one.

It's like this: Is this side of your finger more experienced than the other side?

Is it correct that you each have a unique personality in some way?

In my experience, there are only slight variables of difference, but because we all have certain qualities of our personality . . . as a human being, you don't show the same qualities of your personality to everyone you know, yes? Some person sees you this way, some person that way. It is like that. You could talk to other suns and they might demonstrate some other qualities, but these would simply be qualities I hadn't demonstrated to you when we were speaking, although I would still have them.

Well, I like what you're demonstrating: humor, charm, all that. So how can I relate to how long you've been here? Was this solar system created quite late in the creation?

You can't really say that. It's hard to say how long this creation will go on, because this creation is going to be taken over by another creator. When it's taken over by another creator, it will be a continuity. It won't be like, "Okay, that was then, this is now."

Let me rephrase: Zoosh said that the Explorer Race came into being when the creation was 98 percent complete.

The way I interpret that is not 98 percent done, but that 98 percent of what was intended to be here was here.

So this solar system was basically created because of the Explorer Race—is that your understanding?

I've never really considered it that way. But given what is going on, put in that light, I could see where you might say that. Perhaps that is so. There is going to be more. You are not here for so very long, you know. There is going to be more that goes on in this solar system when you have moved on.

There has been much, much, much going on in all the eons you've been here, right?

Yes, so I cannot say it was created only for you. But it *was* created taking your needs into consideration.

Planets Were Attracted to This Solar System

So how does creating a solar system work? You showed up and there were no planets here?

No planets.

You put out a call? There was a need? How did planets come?

I think planets were attracted—not by me, but I am a requirement. Planets need to have a sun to orbit around. So I do not put out the call—I responded to the call in that sense, yes? But they respond to the call, and then when they do show up, in one way or another, there are orbits for them to get established in on the basis of where they feel the most comfortable according to their feelings—or, as we say, personality. So they take up those positions and begin orbiting, and then the planet and myself decide over time, "Are we both most comfortable with you being in this orbit?"—meaning that there might be some fine-tuning. Maybe the orbit goes out a little bit farther, maybe it comes in a little closer, so there's a little fine-tuning that goes on because sometimes the planet needs to be a little farther away from me and at other times it might want to be a little closer, and so on. This is not so different from human being relationships with other human beings.

Do you come equipped with orbits? Do you create the orbits?

It is my job to create the orbits based on how I personally relate to that space. I arrive in this space I've been requested to be in, and I gradually, what I would call for the sake of your understanding, bloom, not unlike a flower. At first, it's very dark and condensed, and then I start to get warmer. If I were dark and condensed, and if you could get closer, you might say, "I'm using this instrument"—in your spaceship—"and 10,000 years ago one of our ships passed by and this sun was this temperature and now it's up a degree and a half." So you'd make a note, because maybe this is a phenomenon you don't understand. Possibly you don't know; you say, "Gravitational patterns, temperature getting warmer, no apparent change in astronomical influences. Maybe this heavy gravity object is a collapsed sun." By that time your ships are not affected by such things because you're not using propulsion—but that's another story. The main thing is that you take note of it. It's like that.

Over time, as you experience life now, I get warmer and warmer and warmer, and then there's a glimmer . . . it's like a crust on the surface, and then I break through that crust. I had been using that crust, you see, to travel through space. It's like a shell, but on the inside it is still hot, and as I break through, this not only brings more of me to the surface but light comes out—*poof*—and so on. Then gradually I take the form you recognize as the Sun.

In terms of our years from the time you got here, has it been a million, a billion?

It's not really measurable in terms of years, I'm sorry. But it was long before you got here.

Venus Came Here First

So can we ask, who first answered the call? Who showed up first?

Yes, Venus came first. They don't necessarily come on the basis of who's closest or who's farthest away, but Venus came first and Venus wanted to be nice and close, cozy. That was nice, because we both had a chance to begin the solar system and we were close in terms of physical distance. That was nice, I think, for both of us. So we had this chance to be nice and close. That was very good, and we established our orbits over time, and sometimes Venus wanted to be a little closer, other times a little farther away—very nice.

Then who came?

I think then Mercury came.

Can you give me the order, just for our interest?

You need to ask the name of the planet and then I'll say. No, that's not practical either. I'll say the names, and then if I leave somebody out, you tell me. So then it was Neptune, then Jupiter, then Uranus, then Mars. What else have I left out?

Saturn.

No. What else?

Pluto, Maldek, Earth?

That planet you call Maldek—I don't like that name. It's only a very temporary name. I think the name I would relate to it is Oodoo.

Okay, so was that the next one?

That was the next one, then Pluto, then . . . what about Mars? Did we talk about Mars?

You talked about Mars.

The last one was Earth

The original Earth?

No.

So at that time were the orbits in the same order they are now? Mercury, Venus . . . were they in the order they're in now coming out from the Sun?

Yes, the positions are the same. Oodoo was a very nice planet. But, you know, it's interesting. Even though Oodoo is not here anymore, Oodoo's personality is still here. Oodoo is not here physically, in terms of what you experience as physical, but at higher dimensions Oodoo is still here. I can still interact with Oodoo, and Oodoo with me, and that I like very much. Also, the rest of the family can interact with Oodoo. Otherwise, if Oodoo was totally gone, it would be too much terrible grief. It would be like a piece of my own self had been torn away. We couldn't have Oodoo disappear entirely—only part of Oodoo's personality disappeared. Someday Oodoo will re-form physically if there's space, an orbit. But if not, then Oodoo is just there in other dimensions and that will be okay.

Her remains are what we call the asteroid belt?

Partly, but other parts are all over the place. Make a note of where you are now. It's a long session. We'll stop today and continue next time.

That's wonderful. I'd like to talk to you some more. We're getting wonderful new information about how creation works.

I think it's good that you are pursuing this as an *Explorer Race* book, because then the book can be more intimate and relate to the other books. (It's all right, my making comments like that?) I think it's good. People are still interested in astrology, and they will be very interested in this. The planetary bodies are important to consider, and even some people interested in astronomy might have their philosophy expanded a bit or at least have their imagination stimulated, and that will help them in their fields as well. Good night for now. We will resume next time.

ISIS AND THE SUN • • • **19**

⊙ The Sun

THE SUN
Enjoy and Expand Your Capacity to Operate on Multiple Levels

January 17, 2003

All right, this is the Sun.

Welcome. To start with, you have such an interesting perspective. Can you give readers some guidelines as to how they can bring more of themselves into their bodies, because that is part of the expansion and the benevolence?

Sometimes You Are Experiencing Opposing Feelings

I have made some effort to show you how all beings are alike and specifically how human beings and myself have some similarities. I'd like you to consider that all parts of you within your own life—not the past or the future; that needs to take care of itself—are one team. It's not just your conscious and your unconscious, but things you do even at moments.

Now, some of you will be able to identify with this, having had similar experiences. Even at moments when you're very angry, you will notice that a part of you wants to laugh, and you might justify it in your own mind, saying, "This is ridiculous," or "As angry as I am, there's something very funny about this," and your mind attempts to try and rationalize why. In a moment of great anger, regardless of how justifiable the anger may or may not be, your mind says, "Why am I also feeling like laughing?" So that's the rationale that goes on, and you might or might not express that.

What I am suggesting is that your mind is attempting to catch up with something that is occurring. When you are very angry, there is another part of you that wants to come through to be humorous, not so much because the anger is wrong or anything like that. It's not that the humor part of you is in competition with the anger part of you, but rather that, because anger can be self-destructive—you could harm yourself, you could harm another, you could become distracted and do something unintentionally for that matter—it comes through by way of balance.

Now, the other is also true. There are times when you think something is hysterically funny and you might be in the midst of laughing while at the same moment being somewhat upset and agitated for no particular reason. Again, your mind will jump to try to rationalize a reason or to make sense of why this opposite situation prevails, and time and time again you might be able to allow your mind to just relax. Don't look for an answer. Again, it is an attempt by your body to be in balance. Sometimes you might be laughing so uncontrollably that the anger comes in, not to be expressed as anger simultaneously (because it's not easy to do that and maintain sanity), but to create a heightened sense of alert. It is possible also while laughing uncontrollably or becoming so filled with mirth that one might miss something or one might equally—say you're driving or something—do something because you're distracted.

So the anger is not the enemy; it is attempting to create balance. You won't necessarily feel it as anger, but you might feel it as being slightly disturbed or slightly annoyed. Yet at the same moment, something is so very funny that you want to burst out laughing or laugh uncontrollably for a time.

The reason I bring this up is that these are two examples of things that many, if not most of you, have had occur at least once and often more than once. There are other situations where you can think of having two intense feelings or more than two at the same time. It is not usually necessary to look for an explanation, although there may be times when an explanation would be valuable.

Creating Union with Different Parts of Yourself

The reason I bring this up is that here you have feelings that are paired with physical acts and that might even have thoughts. What I feel is that the important part of unity for you is not to unify with all your other lives that might be going on in some other time sequence but inside of the whole picture simultaneously—not that. It's too much to do that and would be unnecessarily confusing. I think rather that it's more important to imagine all these different feelings in a quiet moment: imagine humor, imagine intensity. Think intensely about something unimportant for a moment. What might be unimportant? Look at something not associated with your body that is nearby but which has no importance to your life.

For example, you might have an object . . . there's one I'm picking up here for the moment. Here is a pen that I'm holding. I take the top off the pen, look at the top of the pen intensely for a moment, and think whatever comes to mind looking at the top of the pen. This is not an object that is important in your life or is ever likely to be, but it does allow you to think intensely for a moment without thinking in ways that have anything to do with your physical body or your life. You can see how that can turn into worry. So what I'm suggesting is that you try to create union with the parts of yourself that you readily express on a daily basis, so when you do have simultaneous feelings that appear to be the opposite—something very funny and you feel also a little undercurrent of anger, or you're very angry in the moment with an undercurrent of humor—that you are not attempting to discipline yourself to be only one and not the other.

It is perfectly all right to have both of these feelings at the same time. It doesn't have to drive you crazy; it's not intended to be something challenging or maddening. But rather it is intended by Creator that you be able to feel more than one thing at once, usually to create a more balanced situation for you and not to create an urgent necessity to rationalize why.

There's entirely too much "why" in your civilization. Psychologists have put too much weight on "why" because it is such an early life experience, and given trends and psychological analysis over the past fifty to sixty years, the idea of what happens early on in life has taken way too much impact. Granted, it is important, but I feel that just because children say why, this "why" happens, not because they are learning how to rationalize, but rather because they are trying to make connections between what they feel in their state as children—not having a rationalizing mind, though they might have a rational mind. "Why" often comes up by the child in order to understand the physical world and how it works, not just the culture the child finds himself or herself in.

So what I'm suggesting is that it's important to exercise your mind in ways so that it can simply think about things that are essentially meaningless in your life. If you don't have a pen handy, you might have some small item that has a screw in it. Take a look at the top of the screw, or look at something that just happens to be present—not part of your body, not something you cart around. If it's a paper object, don't look at the words on the paper but look at the corner of a page, especially if there's nothing printed on it—like that. Your mind can springboard off anything. The important thing is to allow it to springboard off something you know is innocuous and essentially meaningless in your life.

You Are Capable of Feeling More Than One Thing at Once

The reason for this homework I'm giving you is that it's important to be able to feel apparently opposing feelings in the middle of an intense expressed feeling (such as anger where you're upset about something or humor where you're laughing uproariously about something), to allow the opposite feeling or another feeling that apparently has no connection whatsoever with the main thing you're feeling and expressing to be present without attempting to analyze it. One of the easiest ways you can do that is to begin to exercise your mind to think about things that are innocuous and not important. In this way, you remind your mind that it isn't only functioning in your body to analyze everything you think, say, feel, do, and so on, but also to simply be the observer of the innocuous as well as the important.

So you're saying that by allowing all of those parts of us to coexist at once, then more of this can become available to us?

No, I'm responding to your question. What I'm saying is that if you want to be able to enjoy life more, you have to be able to relieve yourself of the constant scrutiny that many of you are taught to place on your life in such a way as it will actually interfere with the enjoyment of life. Too many of you are literally taught that if you have an outburst of intense feeling . . . usually it's anger or humor or fear or any intense feeling that one might often have, annoyance and so on. It's important to think about it, in terms of not only whatever it was in the moment but what that means to you and so on, meaning excessive analysis. I do agree that it can be helpful to understand your personal motivation *if* you are having some difficulties in your life or you're undergoing counseling or you're simply trying to understand your life better for yourself. But I do not recommend it as something you do all the time.

In order to unify the parts of yourself to be able to feel more at ease with yourself and your life, you need to allow yourself to feel things that might seem to be opposing or might seem to be anomalous, which ultimately not only leads to your capacity to feel more than one thing at the same time but allows you to be more open to your future being. Your future being, or your future personalities as they are developing, will allow you not only to do more than one thing at once comfortably—and a lot of the youngsters are really being trained to do this now, not just by technology but simply by how life functions in their time—but also to feel at ease with it.

Right now it's demanding and a lot of people don't really like being forced to do more than one thing at once, but think about it. What if you were doing something and had the opportunity to feel an energy or a radiant friendship? How good is it to feel that you are with your friends or your loved ones, that you are doing something that needs to be done and you feel their companionship and support?

In short, I'm suggesting that the communion you once found on Earth between all peoples and that you still find between animals and plants is going to return not only through availability but necessity. That communion will often create within you as a communication something that will support what is going on for you in life. It will not supplant it, it will not be instead of that, but you might find something very funny while at the same time hearing a word from a guide or an angel or having a separate stream, you might say, of communication. This is all intended to prepare you for the multiple levels of things you now do unconsciously, to do them more consciously in the future—not necessarily in this life, but to prepare you and upcoming generations to do this in such a way that it feels natural, normal and easy.

Interestingly enough, most children are born with this capacity, but your current cultures do not condition you to accept or apply it. And if children do not apply the abilities they are born with in the first few years of their lives, it will become a dormant capacity rather than being something that is infused into your daily life. As a dormant capacity, it can still come up and be utilized later in life, but obviously if a child is encouraged to be able to feel more than one thing at once and utilize it in some constructive way in his or her life, then of course that child will be able to someday not only do different things simultaneously but do them in a way that works with you.

Many of you do that now. Very often you might be driving and doing different things with each hand and yet it performs a syncopated task. You might become more conscious of that when looking at a musician playing a guitar, for instance—strumming the strings or plucking the strings while operating on the frets with the fingers in another way. The main thing is that all of you are capable of doing more than one thing at once. You also need to know that you are capable of feeling more than one thing at once and, of course, being ultimately inspired by more than one thing at once. This will also prepare you to integrate into your life a greater capacity to understand your dreams, as well as to have multiple-level communications with more than one individual or being simultaneously, which you don't need to do now.

Encourage Your Children to Retain These Capacities

You do need to make it clear to your upcoming generations that the capacity they experience as a very young child—being able to talk to mom and dad in rudimentary words while at the same time communicating in a very complex and sophisticated way with their angels, guides, teachers, and so on—that this capacity can be utilized in life when they grow up. You're not going to be able to teach the child to do this because you do not, as parents, have those capacities yet, but you will be able to give the child permission to do more than one thing at once.

So when children say the little innocent things that they say very often, "Mommy, who was talking to me when you were talking to me?" as they get that capacity, you say, "What were they saying, dear?" "Oh, they were telling me a story." "How did it feel?" you ask. "Oh, it felt really fun and nice." "That was one of your angels, honey." You might say something like that rather than, "Don't pay any attention. It's just your imagination."

These things are not said by parents because parents are dull-witted but rather because it's the sort of thing they heard when they were youngsters. As you become more conscious that you are capable, that you naturally do these things, then it will be possible to talk to your child. They might not be sophisticated, but parents can often understand children's grunts and sounds before they become sophisticated words. Then the child is simply given permission to not only have these capabilities, which you have when you're born, but also to be able to express them in some benevolent way for themselves and potentially others as they grow up, simply saying, "Oh that's one of your angels or one of your loving guides, dear. That's nice." Then if the child wants to tell you what's said and it's benevolent and even exciting or fun, you encourage him or her if you can.

You might be doing other things, but try to listen or at least say, "Tell me while I'm doing this." This encourages the child to take that experience in and perhaps even give you a running narrative of what's being said. As long as it's benevolent, encourage it. If it starts getting nasty—not just adventurous, but nasty—then just stop for a moment and say, "Well, I'm asking that your angel or guide make this a benevolent story for both of us." But instead of just saying "benevolent"—you can't say that to a child—you could say "benevolent and fun," and the child will pick up the word fun and benevolent will go in and come up later. Psychologists will understand that this is a way of nurturing the psyche.

That way, when such things happen later in life, when people might hear words, and so on, they don't have to think they're going crazy. The words might be coming in benevolently from a loving guide or teacher. I grant that if you're hearing terrible things, such as "jump out the window" or "kill yourself," that you need to see a psychologist or a psychiatrist and that these things are not coming from a benevolent source. I don't want you to think I'm criticizing psychology or analysis, as I feel it has largely been very beneficial to your societies, but it's important not to analyze everything in every moment. I think there's been too much attention paid to doing just that for the average person. You must remember that you are a union of many simultaneous things.

The joy ahead is that we will become more conscious and aware of those capacities, right?

Let's not put it in the future. You are that now, and what I'm encouraging you to do with this homework is to exercise those capacities you now have so that you can feel at ease with them. That's what the homework is about, which allows you to feel more at ease with yourself. Many people are raised to feel ill at ease with themselves given different feelings or thoughts. It's important to allow yourself to feel at ease with yourself, recognizing that you are at all times a multiplicity of various things happening simultaneously. Even when you're a youngster, you know that you have feelings and thoughts and ideas and actions and all of that going on, and when you're young, it's confusing. But as you get older, you need to know that this is still true—it's just that you might not be conscious of them or there might be certain things you don't think about.

Find Adventure for Your Children

Perhaps that's appropriate to you as an individual, but there needs to be an exploration of your mind to allow it to think about things that may not appear to have any immediate relevance or value. Your mind needs to be free to imagine all sorts of things. That's part of the reason the younger generation is attracted to thinking things that might not be approved of by the older generation. It is intriguing, because generations in the past have been rebellious on the basis of actions, feelings, and so on, but the current generation coming up—not the youngest, but the teenagers and preteens coming up—is attempting to strike out and is expressing a degree of rebelliousness in a desire to *think* what they want. This is part of the reason that some young people—not all—are attracted to extreme things to think about.

Please be aware, parents. Don't assume that your children are in serious trouble because they are thinking something extreme. As long as their lives are otherwise going well, it's their way of exercising their minds. You don't have to send them off to the counselor or therapist. If they're taking action on those extreme things, that's another matter, and then such counseling might be useful.

Now, I don't want to sound mysterious. The reason I'm bringing this up is that some of these video games might seem to be very extreme, and I do not feel good about the violent ones, but the reason they exist at all—things do exist for a reason—is not to train a nation of children to become violent and antisocial but rather to encourage you to see past surface appearances in order to find feelings that need to be expressed in some benevolent way. I'm not recommending violent video games, but if your youngster is attracted to them for a time, then this is the best reaction I recommend by the parent.

Don't turn a blind eye, but do encourage your children or take them places, especially on vacations, where they can have some kind of wild adventures. You may not be able to do these things with your children, but you might be able to send them somewhere, if you can afford it, to some kind of an adventurous vacation (when vacation comes up, or even a weekend adventure) that is truly exciting: shooting the rapids, or if you live near the sea coast, then surfing. That's pretty exciting, perhaps sometimes a little more exciting than the participants want it to be. In short, if children are showing that they need to have more excitement in their lives, encourage them to make the excitement physical so that they do not do it strictly on the imaginative level. That's what I recommend.

If you do not have the money to do this, then find something you can do with your children that is exciting. If you're in snow country and they are young, then encourage them to take an old piece of cardboard and slide down the hill. It doesn't cost much, but it's pretty exciting, assuming they don't slide out into traffic . . . they might just bounce off a rock or a tree. I'm not necessarily encouraging that, but the thrill of it can sometimes be sufficient in helping the child to move past too much focus on extreme inner violence and to recognize that the inner violence is often a need by their physical bodies to be more active and adventurous on an external basis. Now, I grant that if they start to show violence, self-destructiveness or harm to others in any way, especially in some way that is not typical or normal for a child, then by all means walk quickly with them to the nearest therapist.

The Light of the Sun Provides Continuity for You

You are observing us, and you sort of looked into this a little more since we started to talk, but you don't normally, as you said, focus on beings on any one level on any one planet. You sort of radiate out to everyone in the same way, right?

That's true, but since we are having this discussion for the purpose of this book, I have taken a closer look, so to speak. Suns have a nurturing role, but we also have a role in the immediate moment. We must be in the present because our duties and energy are feeding the present. Yet what we do in terms of our impact on the present will evidence itself over time. Your plants and, to some extent, other life are fostered and nurtured by the Sun's rays—any sun's, yes? As a result, you have an opportunity to see and experience things on a level of continuity associated with what I'm involved in. This tells me that any change I might need to make for myself, I must do slowly, gradually, so that your experience of me maintains that continuity.

For example, you have seen and know about and to some extent have studied eclipses as a group of people, as a culture. One might reasonably ask, "Is this simply a phenomenon observable by science, or is there actually some purpose for an eclipse?" I will say that there is a purpose. In those moments of eclipse, my light is still shining and the eclipse is only observable in certain specific positions—meaning not just on your planet, but if one were to be in a place in space while the eclipse was going on (I'm talking about a natural one), one might conceivably be off the planet and still be in the path of the observable eclipse.

You might reasonably say, "Why? What's in it for me as the Sun?" And I would say this: First and foremost, eclipses do not happen instantaneously, though they could—meaning, why would I want to be unseen by you for a time? There's that. The other question is, "Why would I want to be unseen by some of you," meaning the observable path of the eclipse, "for a time?" This change in my demonstrated personality, you might say, is important because here you have something you can count on: the Sun. It's daytime, so the Sun must be out, something you can count on, on the basis of what you know and believe to be true.

You can even look at your artwork and other cultural remnants, and the Sun is a prominent feature. So you know the Sun's been shining for a long time, even though science and reason—if you like, common sense—tells you that. Here you can produce evidence to say, "Well, look, here's a painting done hundreds of years ago and the Sun was a prominent feature." So the obvious is provable, but in order that I do my part to acquaint you with potentials or greater depth of expression of my own personality, I need to show a different face to you rather than simply just being here or not. When I'm not here, it is nighttime. When I am here, I'm radiating and you know me as the Sun.

Granted, although some scientists might explore solar flares (as they call them) and all that, for the average person, as far as you know I am either here or not. But in the case of an eclipse, I am here *and* not. Therefore, I express more than one quality to you in that moment, giving you the permission to express more than one quality of yourself in the same moment, such as feeling humor and anger or anger and humor in the same moment.

That's a nice way to bring that together.

That's why I bring this up, because it is my job to provide continuous, dependable light and heat and nurturance and so on—things that affect you personally and intimately. But it is also my job, from time to time, to give permission by my demonstration and participation in this demonstration of showing you a completely different quality. After all, when suns go into that quiet stage . . . which you do not normally see, living on a planet in a solar system as you do, but that you will see when you are flying about someday as a culture, from planet to planet and solar system to solar system. You will see suns in a dormant stage. When you do and when you know that they're suns, the first thing that will strike people is that this thing looks an awful lot like an eclipse, except that there's very little radiated light around it. Now, that's a hint to astronomers looking at phenomena. I'm not going to talk about it, but some of you are observing phenomena, and I want you to understand that what you are seeing—in one form or another using your current science—is something in transition, not just something you're observing in that moment all the time.

Why do you, as Earth, see this eclipse only in certain places? That is because if you all on Earth saw the Sun eclipsed simultaneously at the same time—everyone everywhere—it would be too shocking, too frightening. The absence of that light and, most important, continuity universally on Earth would have an actual shock to the feeling bodies of all plants, animals and people simultaneously. But if this just happens to a small segment of the population—plants, animals, people—all the rest of the people seeing the Sun in its brightness are still feeling the continuity of life and they, by their feelings, support your feelings seeing the missing Sun or the absence of the Sun in the case of a complete eclipse.

The maintenance, you understand, the support of your fellow beings—and by fellow beings, I do not mean simply within a species, but all your fellow beings on Earth—supports that continuity. You must have that feeling of continuity in order to maintain life as an individual, to say nothing of life as a culture. That's the real reason why the eclipse is only seen in a narrow path—not only the full eclipse, but even a partial eclipse.

Do you have any feelings or sensations, or does anything change within you when your light is eclipsed like that?

But it isn't. It is only what you see. Once you're outside the boundaries of the eclipse, the thing that you see . . . well, you can do it for yourself. You can put your hand up in front of the light, and if you put your hand out far enough and move your hand, palm toward you, back and forth in the light, there is no particular difference. But if you put your hand up close to your face and move it in front of your eyes, then the light is temporarily restricted from you.

Now, this might seem quite obvious, but what I want you to do for fun and to observe yourself as a being is, when the light is here, in the light of day, I want you to move your hand back and forth in front of you at arm's length with your palm facing you, and you will feel the way you feel. Then move your hand up close to your eyes. It doesn't have to touch your eyes—I prefer that it doesn't—but move it very close and put your hand over both your eyes. You can do that—most of you can. I want you to notice that your body will immediately change feelings. Within you, you will notice that there is a physical feeling that changes immediately, and when you pull your hand away, you will over time—not instantaneously—return to the feeling you had before as long as there is no other stimulation. In short, you will relax.

This tells you that the light of the Sun does have a physical effect on you and that light being there when you expect it to be there maintains continuity. The Sun is out, there's light. The Moon is out, there's moonlight only; otherwise it's dark except for the stars, and so on. That continuity is critically important to sustaining life itself because it's dependable. It's a dependable quality of life, and even if you can't count on anything else, you know that when the Sun's out, it's light and when it isn't, it's dark.

There is a reaction in many people in the wintertime when they're deprived of the Sun for a long period of time—when it's dark all the time, when daylight is late and twilight is early.

That's why there's been a lot of experimentation in recent years with sunlamps, and so on, and shining lamps on different parts of the body, which I encourage. Not so that you have harm done to your body with too much light and burns, like sunburn, but try to experiment with these things. You can't capture sunlight itself, but the more lamp manufacturers experiment, the more they will be able to produce something that is similar—not the same, but similar—in its light-producing qualities to the Sun, if not similar in terms of the Sun's actual full impact on you.

This is a worthy experiment and will someday be considered part of a natural medical treatment, not only for people who are living in areas that are deprived of the major aspects of the Sun for certain parts of the season, but also for people who have a long sort of twilight without any great brightness. These sunlamp treatments might be just the thing to improve the quality of your life and support and sustain life while you are going through that particular season of the year. At such latitudes, bright sunny days do not occur for great lengths of time at all. So having such sunlight available, even in an artificial way, might be very supportive and nurturing to the physical self. Of course, when and if you can get away for a vacation, I always encourage people living in such places to go to places that are warm and sunny, and that will encourage life in general. You might want to do that anyway, but I also encourage it.

Planets Request Things from the Sun

As your rays go out and radiate all the way to the next sun and beyond, what is the mechanism by which information about your solar system comes back to you—the radiation from the planets and the beings on the planet?

Feelings. As far as I've been able to tell in my existence, feelings are universal and beyond. You might reasonably ask, "How do I know that they are universal and beyond?" The reason is that my radiations go out, not just in the form of light, but in general, my radiations go out. You know your scientists have observed that there are radiations other than light, other than warmth. My radiations go out and can actually go beyond what you might call this universe. As long as my radiations have been going out and sun radiations have been going out from this universe, the radiations have never encountered any place or condition where feelings were not the primary means of communication and were not the primary function of the expression of life.

Do any of the planets ever request anything from you beyond your radiated light? Do they ever need anything individual, unique or special?

Good question. Sometimes they will require some understanding, usually based on feeling, because their expressions physically in this solar system do not have ready access. For example, some of the more gaseous planets might not have a complete personal experience of physicality in all of its senses of contact. Occasionally, for instance—I think this happened recently—one of the planets was impacted by a heavenly body, and this was partly because the planet itself needed to understand what it was like to have a sudden, significant touch. Although this particular method is not something the planet would care to experience again in the near future, the planet now understands what that's like and can thereby understand you as individuals better, to say nothing of other physical beings who might suddenly, for example . . . this is something the planet didn't understand before. Say you are walking down the street and you don't see your friend come up behind you, but instead of your friend saying, "Hi, how are you?" he or she first slaps you on the back and *then* says, "Hi, how are you?"—unintentionally frightening and startling you.

Jupiter, as you say—the planet who was impacted—did not know what that was like. Now, there might be other occasions . . . by the way, I did not arrange for that to occur, but the planet itself asked (essentially they don't talk and it's not intellectual) if that would be available, and so on, and radiated feeling as a welcoming. Before that happened, I was attempting to show the planet, to the best of my ability, what it would be like to have such an intimate contact happen deeply. I did this by sending out a particularly strong flare in the direction of that planet, and the impact on the planet was a little more than usual. I think it was noted by your scientists sometime before that impact that the surface storm they observed showed signs of change. This, I believe, was the sign of impact, which may or may not be measurable by your instruments at this time, even in post-analysis.

So that would be an example. There are other times when the planets request something from me that may not be something they would normally request. I recall once one of the planets wanting to know more about the personal feeling of an eclipse, meaning was it possible for them to be eclipsed and feel something, feel different, just as you when you take your hand and put it over your eyes closely and the light is not present for a moment when it normally is. You feel different. If they, as a planet, cannot see me or feel me—meaning they experience a full eclipse of the Sun—how might they feel as a planet? So they have to have that experience where the entire planet would feel—without, of course, this being the case, no population on it, at least not in your dimension—and they've all had varying feelings. You might wish to ask them if they have ever experienced that and what it was like for them.

Then, conversely, you are totally self-sustained and I think you need nothing, but have you ever requested anything from any other planet?

In the sense that by creating welcoming orbits, I didn't *need* them to be occupied, but there was a sense of satisfaction and happiness as a result of them being occupied. I wouldn't exactly call that a need, but it's a cousin perhaps. It's rather like . . . how can we say? Perhaps you might prepare a pitcher of lemonade for yourself and your companion, but the pitcher is much bigger than either of you might need, almost as if to put out the feeling that if others care to drop by you have plenty. Often this will attract such a thing as an individual. Maybe a neighbor comes by or the postman comes by at the end of his route and, "Oh, sit down for a moment. Have some lemonade"—often a welcome treat after a long walk.

I May Be Called on to Stimulate You

The process of you being nurturing to all of the planets, including the beings on the planet, we have not identified. How much of what you send out can be identified? What portion on the Earth? Gamma rays, infrared rays, ultraviolet rays—you send out so much.

You have, of course, put your energy into what you can physically measure, but you haven't put too much energy into what you can spiritually measure. That's why I'm putting your attention on feelings, because there are times when you as the human race on Earth or perhaps other races that have existed on other planets—not so much races as cultures, populations—might need to feel something simultaneously or have a specific feeling made available to you simultaneously. If the stimulation or prompt is not available on your planet on an immediately universal basis, then something that is available to your planet—and of course, in the case of the Sun, it would be half of the planet roughly—I might be called on to do that. If it's an important thing, it would be sustained over, say, a twelve- to fourteen-hour period so that everyone on the planet would have an opportunity to experience it. So obviously we're not talking about an eclipse.

I haven't done that yet, but it is available, a prompt that might happen that cannot be missed. Now, I have to correct that slightly. By "everyone on the planet," I mean that it is obvious, that it is visible, okay? Of course, you don't want to look directly at the Sun for any length of time. But say, for example, there was something on the surface of the Sun that was visible. In the case of the brightness of the Sun, it would have to simply be the absence of something—maybe not a shape, as in the famous motion picture, but just like a spot that you could see with your naked eye. Just a quick glance at the Sun for a split second and there's a spot you could actually see rather than one that might be seen only through careful observation with scientific equipment.

I haven't done that. There's no reason to do that, but it would undoubtedly create certain feelings on the surface of the population of Earth, for example—since we're talking to the population. Now, as I say, I haven't done this and there's no reason to do it, but that would be something that might prompt a feeling quite significant to everyone on the planet—at least every human. I think the animals and the plants would not be too concerned. You might reasonably ask, "Why would such a thing ever take place?" and I would say the following.

This is not the only reason, but a reason might be: suppose everybody, every human being on Earth—at least most everyone—would need to have an experience that you could all relate to at the same time. For instance, the northern lights might be experienced by many, many people at the same time, although not everyone—or there might be some experience such as your recent comet passing by, which most people could see but not all, if not physically then at least through some news agency. But what if the Sun, viewable from all parts of the Earth (at least at any given point in the day), had a dot on it, and with a quick glimpse or with a dark-shaded tinted shield, you could all glimpse that for a time. Or even through a reflected image (you understand, an obscura), you might potentially be able to look at it for a longer period of time. What if you could all on Earth see this at the same time? Would you not all have a wide variety of feelings but also a shared common experience that was something different from what you normally share and don't think about?

Most of your populations have more in common than you have different, but you don't typically have a shared essentially simultaneous experience on a regular basis that you're conscious of. This alone might be a unifying factor that could be useful for this or that purpose. That's why something like that would take place—and it would not be threatening, though some people might feel it was, but it would just be one feeling of many. Everybody else for the most part would just say, "Wow. Isn't this amazing? Isn't it extraordinary? What does it mean?" In short, the world would be buzzing.

As we expand our awareness and move closer to a more expanded dimension, are we going to call on you to provide something more for us, or is it always there and we just don't know it?

I think you will probably want me to do more. Perhaps what you will begin doing is that you will ask for more of this ray or that ray that you feel is nurturing of life, or less of this ray or that ray that you feel might be difficult for life or might interact chemically with your planet in some way that is pro or con. You could also consider asking for something from me that you might not necessarily identify as something that is quantifiable—meaning science can tell there is more going on but cannot quantify it. You might wish for a demonstration of what that unquantifiable thing is, as long as that demonstration is benevolent. In short, it becomes a physical, spiritual phenomenon.

There might be times when you'll ask me to do things for which there might be a fairly immediately response. For instance, people often consider their Sun's rays to be healing, and in the past, even more considered that. You might reasonably request of the Sun, as a people or even as certain individuals:

LIVING PRAYER
"Might it be possible, Sun, to increase the quality of your healing rays?"

You might say this as a living prayer, but you can check the documents you've gotten about that. Now, this has been asked before, but I think the more you explore these benevolent ways of asking for things as you've apparently looked into and begun to look into, it might be possible to request— stated in the right way, in a safe way:

"I request that you might radiate something toward the surface of the Earth that could improve the quality of life in any number of ways."

I'm suggesting this as something you might try, even before science says, "There's all this stuff we know the Sun is doing, but we can't really measure or quantify it." They have actually said this, but it largely goes out to scientific journals or discussions between fellow scientists and doesn't percolate out much to the general public.

How would you describe the different rays that are available to ask for?

I don't want to do that. I want you to ask for your needs as a population in some benevolent way. I want you to ask for your needs to be served in some greater way by what I have to offer, and then you'll find out. Rather than my directing your attention toward something I can do, I'd rather have you direct your attention toward something you *need* and not assume I can't support that.

I don't know what you're looking forward to, but you're open to a closer interaction between humans and yourself.

But you see, I am providing those things now. It's just that you're not directing them toward what you could direct them toward or asking for there to be more. More isn't always enough. You might need to say:

"Would you attune it to the exact frequency or pulse that this object/thing/ feeling/person/place is open to, in order that we might get the most out of the supplementation you have to offer for our greatest benefit?"

Sunrise Is the Most Balanced Nurturance You Can Experience

I understand there is something special about being there when the rays of the Sun first come over the horizon at sunrise. Can you address that?

When you're experiencing that for the first few minutes or so, you have the nurturance of the evening, the dark, and the nurturance of the day simultaneously. So it is the most balanced nurturance you can experience. As long as you are calm and feeling safe and in a benevolent state of being—some people might say "meditative," but it doesn't necessarily have to be that—then you can take in the best I have to offer. That's the main thing about sunrises.

The more ancient peoples in more ancient cultures often knew this, and they would, you might say, greet the Sun. This has come to mean in some cultures . . . if they don't understand the full meaning of that kind of religious ceremony, as long as they have been educated thoroughly by their teachers, the practitioner knows that the greeting of the Sun has everything to do with their own physical strength, durability and endurance, to improve the quality and often the length of their lives. Of course, you don't want to extend the length of your life if the quality is not up to the standard you need; otherwise, it's just perpetuating suffering.

Does it matter where you are on the surface of the Earth? Are there some places that are more conducive to the benefits of the sunrise than others?

Well, yes. Obviously, the best place to do it is someplace where you didn't have to wear any more clothes than necessary—meaning, the more your skin is covered out of the necessity of the environment, the less you'll be able to take it in.

You take in the rays of the Sun on your skin?

Is that not obvious? Granted, there are other rays that are not just light, but since the question has to do with sunrise, you need to keep it to that point. But I think it's awfully easy in your civilization to become somewhat obscured by words and thoughts and terms and so on, and to overlook the apparent. I don't want to make it sound as if you're blind to the obvious, but it's sometimes important to remind you.

Nothing Is Static

Do you orbit or turn on your axis?

Let's not rule out that question. You might say, in the larger sense, the whole solar system orbits, since the galaxy is in constant motion. But as a planetary body, of course, it is difficult for you. In terms of spinning on the axis, I think your science has answered that, too. But in terms of an orbit, it is my job to establish orbits rather than to orbit around on my own.

There's something called a Central Sun in this galaxy that supposedly you orbit around. Do you move the whole solar system through space?

I don't proclaim to do that on my own. Motion is normal. Lack of motion is unknown to me.

Okay, but is there an orbit established by the center of the galaxy that is made available to you?

Now, you understand that because of the culture and the conditioning in which you live—which is another time and space question—the idea of a hierarchical situation, meaning the old gravity experiment where you hold a string and whirl an object around . . . that's one of those questions. I'm not going to say that there is a Central Sun around which I revolve. But I can see where that would be an appealing thought on the basis of a linear existence.

Then let me rephrase it, because all the ancient teachings are that there is a Central Sun. How can I rephrase it so you don't feel it's a time and space question?

Let me do it for you. All observation based on a fixed position is quantifiable by that fixed position's identification with life. That's a physical fact that applies, not only to physics and mathematics, but also to cultural relationships. Given that, then one might extrapolate from this that the communication from such a position would have built into it certain fixed ideas and ideals. Since life takes place in a certain way for all beings for a reason, the fostering of such ideas and ideals is benevolent because of where you are—literally physically, emotionally, feelings, spiritually, everything.

So if the ancients have said all of that, it is to your advantage to hear that, given where you are and what you are doing. Nevertheless, taken as a universal principle, given that you might be in any given place, someplace else doing something else, experiencing something else, you may not experience those thoughts and positions as a permanent fact of existence. I hope that's not too obscure.

Let me repeat what I understand. You're saying that just because they're in our legends and they came from other civilizations in other star systems, they were just given that because of the need for the Explorer Race to think there's more? You're saying that the solar system does not move in space?

No. I'm trying to come up with a question or an explanation that covers the universe. When you ask a question like that . . . you started off with a precept. My understanding is, you were talking about the center of the universe, yes? You said there is a Central Sun around which you revolve.

No. As far as I know, it's just in the galaxy.

Even so, I am trying to help you stretch beyond that. But I do not wish you to dwell on it, because what I have stated is that what you know, how you know it, what is fostered, what you experience, ad infinitum, is a function of the reality that Creator wishes you to experience when you are focused in any one given place or time, period. Therefore, it is not my job to alter that perception, but it is given to me to allow you to know that more exists, even though you may have been carefully acculturated to perceive life from any given connections—my word for continuity—so as to see your place in that life. Perhaps it's not good to go into this at this time.

Does the Milky Way galaxy move in space?

Everything moves all the time everywhere. Nothing is static. Even entrenched beliefs are not static, including my own. We need to be careful not to wander too far afield, since the book is intended to serve the population in a practical way. We can wander around philosophically a little bit, but we don't want to wander too far. I don't want to make your life difficult and complicated. After all, there is a reasonable length of time that we might talk, and of course, you have lots of other planets and personalities to talk to. We don't have to go on indefinitely.

A Single Sun Gives You a Continuity of Source

Many solar systems have two or more suns. Is there a reason why there's only one here?

Yes. I believe it was felt that, in order for you to be able to develop a consciousness that one thing follows the other, there needed to be a clear, constant evidentiary backed up by numerous examples of "one thing follows another." You can't have a situation where, say, two animals come together to support the creation of others, or two humans come together to support the creation of others, where you have a binary sun that seems to be doing . . . the suns are going to be in the sky doing the same thing: warming, lighting. It was seen to be necessary to have the reminder of one, giving you a continuity of Source—the Sun not being Source, but the Sun being a connection to Source, one planet upon which you are living, okay? So it's done symbolically as well.

You have been in that star system where there were two suns . . . ?

More to the point, I've seen and can see right now a solar system where there are five suns.

Really? What would be the advantage or reason for that?

I believe that because the cultures in that solar system have such a wide variety of expressed capabilities, they need to have a more supportive system to encourage such capabilities. They have five or six sexes, depending on how you count them. They have multiple-leveled experiences going on all the time. It would appear to someone from, say, your culture that their cultures in that solar system are overwhelmingly complex, and yet they experience them as something that is perfectly normal. They would find your culture to be exceedingly singular.

Is this across the universe, or is this somebody we might contact someday?

It is not likely that your culture will bump into them physically, but certainly in dreams and teachers, and in other universal contacts it's very possible—very likely, as a matter of fact.

In our science fiction, there is a theme that Jupiter will become a sun and then there will be two suns here. Is that in the future?

No. In your world there is an almost infinite variety of expressions of life. This is not typical to most planets, but your Creator desired you to have the gift of variety, as your Creator loves and cherishes that Itself. This is part of the reason your Creator wanted you to have a variety of appearances of people so that you would desire to know, "Where did all these fascinating-appearing people come from? There must be places, planets, where these different-appearing people came from."

In short, your Creator wanted you to have your imagination stimulated all the time so that you would look at the smallest things and the largest things (the skies, the heavens) with curiosity and fascination. This is so you would assume—in many cases, rightly so—that the variety you see and experience on Earth is but the beginning of the variety you will find on Earth as well as in the stars when you explore them.

It is my job to support and sustain your curiosity, your intimacy, your personal connection with each other, as well as to sustain and nurture your lives. In so doing, it has been, it is and I know it will be an ongoing joyful privilege. Good night.

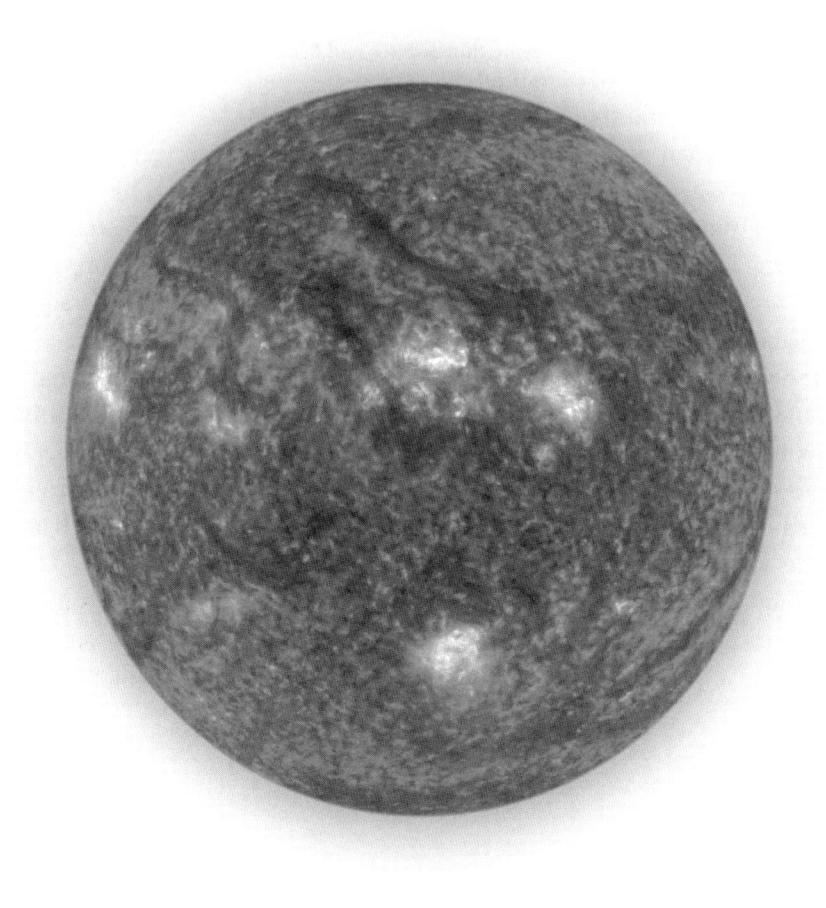

40 • • • ASTROLOGY: PLANET PERSONALITIES & SIGNS SPEAK

⊙ The Sun

THE SUN

The Nurturer of Life on an Intimate Level

January 18, 2003

All right. This is the Sun.

Welcome.

My Solar Flares Are Like an Exhale

When your energy flares out in a solar flare, what would we call that? Science calls that a hydrogen explosion. How would you characterize your energy in this dimension?

I don't think of anything I do as an explosion. There's no particular difference from your exhaling, so I might exhale. That's the way I might think of it. I don't characterize my energy in scientific terms, if that's what you're asking. If anything, I will tend to compare how I function with the way you function. Otherwise, it's not relevant to you.

Could you be more explicit as to the nature of the energy or the dynamic of it, how it works—because we could not live on Earth without your energy?

Well, energy radiates outward and inward at the same time. I think there's some understanding of that insofar as the research into fusion with your science people, though they are far from a practical model. But the main thing to keep in mind is that my radiation from my energy radiates from about the middle—you know, going in spherically from about the middle. It radiates in and then comes back to the middle of the planet. I'm describing only what goes on within your dimension, since that's how you framed your question. What goes on in your dimension is that the motion happens going in. For the outer part, all the motion is radiating out, but for the inner part, the motion goes in and out.

If we could perceive it, is it really hot?

Well, within the physical framework of your existence, as you know, friction causes heat. The high-speed motion of the physical mass going in and out at the same time consistently creates a lot of heat, but it's also very efficient. What science is curious about, from their perspective, is how this engine can continue to run with no apparent additional fuel.

Without running out.

That's their whole point. But it has to do with the fact that you are only seeing one small part of life. As long as science remains fixed on the notion that what you see here in your physical world is all there is, then they will never understand anything completely. But I'm counting on physicists to win them over eventually. They're getting there.

What would the fuel be, then? I mean, what comes in from other dimensions or other levels that keeps you going?

What keeps any atom going?

The desire to be.

There's that, but you can desire to be and you can continue to be in other forms. What I am saying is that in the physical world, you are conscious of things being born and functioning and then transforming.

So it's the spiritual complement, the immortal that . . . ?

Well, it's the aspect of existence without wearing out. Now, I've put forth the idea for you—in fact, how we function—that a change in appearance does not mean that something is dead. So in your space travels, once you begin doing that as a culture here on Earth, you will notice from time to time heavy gravitational bodies that aren't exuding any heat, though they may have a residual warmth that you can measure but that you can pass fairly close to—not anything that has major gravitational danger to you, but as you begin to travel in space, you will probably be warned off by other cultures that it's not safe to get too close. Those bodies will be suns in that dormant state, possibly prepared to travel.

Is that what we call brown dwarfs?

[Chuckles.] I don't keep track of your scientific terminology, just that your science is, perhaps appropriately, looking only at your own world. The science that is known to the general public, including perhaps the general educational community, is looking essentially at your own world and not really advancing itself in otherworldly phenomena, which would be more a secret science. But I'm not really talking to the secret scientific community, and this book isn't aimed at them.

The Dimensions Available to Suns Are Infinite

Can I ask how many dimensions you function in? I think there are thirty-three in the solar system—or do you encompass more than that? You probably don't like numbers.

No, though I will acknowledge that you have a society's attachment to quantifying things. I will just say that the dimensions available to us, to suns, are infinite. It depends where we are needed and, if we are no longer needed, where we currently are—and also, in some cases, if the dimensions as you call them are able to utilize what we have to offer within their experience. They might want something that is a component of what we are, but they cannot accept all that we need to be within that dimension in order to provide them the component they need, in which case they will need to get what they need from some other source.

So if I were able to go from the second to the thirty-third level (which somebody said that we had in this solar system), I would see you on every level, in every dimension?

Of course, it depends where you go. But if you are saying, if you stand in one place, do you maintain the same position? Of course, that's not possible, but for the sake of theory—then, no. When you change that kind of harmonic—or pulse or dimension—even if you could see, you wouldn't see the same thing. So it's not like dimensions are pictured in your society, where the higher you go, the more benevolent, or the scenery changes. It's not like that. But it is demonstrated to you sometimes that way because that is the most understandable way you relate to life when you are here. There are lots of dimensions where there is nothing to be seen at all, and therefore, it is not necessary to "see" as you understand seeing. Perhaps it would be feeling.

So you radiate out in some way on all the dimensions here in this solar system?

No. It depends what's needed. This is what you need here, so the Sun, as the nurturer of life on a sort of intimate level . . . this is what we provide here. That's what you need, that's what you expect, and that's what you require.

What about the next dimension? What is required there of you?

Whatever they need. It depends. Some places do not require light; some places do not require heat. But they might require a gravitational body at the center of their existence. Some places require only certain components of who and what we are. So the main thing is not to jump to conclusions. It isn't just that other dimensions of this solar system are where the physical rules are the same. The physical rules are not the same, and therefore, things might appear vastly different. One of the obvious differences is . . . let's just change the physical rules a little bit, just a teeny bit, not as much as it changes in other dimensions. But changing it a teeny bit, maybe the planets and the Sun would be much bigger or much smaller.

Oh, smaller! I thought of bigger, but I never thought smaller.

Why not? It's just changing things a tiny bit, maybe.

You Can Solve Things Here

Your imagination on Earth is going to use all the time at least some components of what you experience here, but you're not generally going to be able to imagine something that has no components whatsoever of what you have here. The interesting thing here is that you have more here than what is consciously perceptible, and that is because, at the level of sleep and dreaming (which you all do), it is quite clear that what you dream—which is often fantastic or at least recollected that way—is also here.

This is because you are here. Even though in your dream you may travel on the soul level, nevertheless, you are tethered here. So if it's available to you here, it is here. This tells you that there are exits and entrances to come and go, you understand? You travel on the soul level, but the soul is connected to the physical body as long as you are physical here. So that means that wherever the soul goes, whatever it does, is also here.

Otherwise, your soul, anchored to your body, could not go someplace that has qualities that are not here. From my perception, they are here. So your soul might travel through all kinds of dimensions, and the route might not be something you could find if you were wide awake. But your soul travels: it goes here, it goes there. In some cases, it doesn't go anywhere, but it simply accesses these things. That's because it's here, and it can do those things.

Now, that's an important hint, because your soul can do those things even though your mind, when you remember your dreams when you wake up, does not contain all the things that your soul did—or it might contain them in a sort of superimposed way or even a symbolic way in the case of, say, a nightmare. Nevertheless, because your soul can go places and do things—granted, much of which you don't recall—it's all available to you here, and that's the unexpressed potential of the human being in your now place. Just because it isn't expressed does not mean that you cannot access it at some point once you begin utilizing your full being here.

When you begin doing that (incrementally, of course), you will begin to change and resolve all of your difficulties and problems. It is intended that these difficulties and problems exist. Creator has set it up so that things have effects: You do something, this happens. You do something else, that happens. That's all intended, and very often the effects are good or benevolent, or they support you. But there are some things where the effects aren't so good and for which you have no cure.

Like cleaning up nuclear waste, right?

That's right. So you will have to become more of yourself in order to transform it or know how to transform it so that it becomes something, not only neutral that does not harm you or other forms of life, but it may even take on a form that you can again utilize in some new way that will support your life or the lives of other beings on this planet. That's intended, so you might say that's why some people get mad at Creator, because Creator allows human beings to do certain things. But that's because Creator is putting you into a position where, in order to resolve the apparently unresolvable, you have to become more while you're here.

But that's wonderful, because that says we can solve the problems we created without going off to the next dimension or somewhere to do it. We can do it here! That's a wonderful statement.

That's right—you can do it here. Of course, you'll pick up things in your travels in space, but you can do it all here. That's why it's a school—granted, an isolated school like a bubble—but it's all available to you. You will just have to be able to manifest and create on your whole level while you are here. You won't be functioning that way all the time all day, but if you can even go into that level for a few moments (things that you learn, benevolent magic, and so on), you can create huge changes: things that are not only going to affect you but could affect all life on Earth to bring about a better community and conditions for all beings.

So that's the route—benevolent magic? That's one of the ways there?

It's a step you are going to take to get there, because it helps you to understand that so much is available. There are so many beings totally prepared to cooperate with you to bring things about that in no way forces anybody to do anything but just tends to bring the parties together—including that which you call "things" together—that would happily do whatever it is that you want to come about. It may not happen immediately, it may happen over time, but it happens.

You are giving us little jewels of wisdom here. Suddenly so many things make sense.

Only a Percentage of You Is Here

What about your interest and activities? What percentage of your awareness is focused on this dimension? How much of you is free if you want to do something that's not involved with this solar system?

I understand what you're saying. Granted, it's not like this, but for the sake of giving you a figure that will cause you to say, "Well, all right, I understand that" ... and you want it in percentage, so we will honor that. It is 0.0000001 percent.

Oh, I see the zeros. [Chuckles.] You're going to run out of ...

I made a mistake. You can take off a zero there.

So what do you do with the rest of your awareness? [Chuckles.]

You have to remember: all suns are united everywhere. So I do not consider myself to be an individual. This tells you that if only that much of myself is here to do what I do here, I do not call myself an individual. All suns are united everywhere, so that which I am doing here, if you extrapolate that out, tells you how many suns there are in this universe. Mathematically, I just gave your mathematicians a formula by which they can figure out how many suns there are here in the universe. But I'm not going to do it for you.

[Laughs.] All right, we'll put that out. So what you are giving us is how much sun energy in this universe needs to be focused here—not how much of your energy, but how much of the total sun energy in the universe, right?

That which makes up my body here, which you see. I think your actual question may have been how much of that which you see am I actually focusing on your needs and the needs of this solar system. Is that what you were actually asking?

That's really closer to my question, yes.

So you would like a percentage figure for that also?

Well, if I can get it, yes. At the time, I was thinking that the Earth was where most of your conscious energy was focused, but I was incorrect. You keep everything alive, you know? Your energy is what allows sentient beings to exist in this solar system.

I'm going to write down something that isn't mathematical. I'm just going to write down something: so many zeros, okay? Zeds. My focus on Earth is 0.000000000000000006 percent. Is that good enough?

That's pretty amazing.

Can I tell you something? It only seems amazing, because you are speaking with your Earth personality as a human being. You consider yourself to be one. Now, I do not see you that way. I see you as being . . . let's just say you're a representative of the human race. Would you like your own percentage of how much of you is here compared to elsewhere as an individual, as a representative individual of the human race?

Yes, absolutely.

A reasonably representative individual, all right? I'm going to do the same thing I did on the last one.

Yes, with the zed, right.

This will help you to see why what you thought was so amazing in my comparison to myself is really not so amazing when you consider how much you are here as well. Human beings focus on Earth is 0.00006 percent.

Oh, I see. We're here three-quarters as much as you are. [Chuckles.] That's all we're here?

Think about it, though. I am not reacting to you on the basis of your time sequence. Did you want that? The time sequence would be different if we calculated where you are only in this moment that we're talking. Granted, moments move from moment to moment. But I'll write down another figure if you want: where you are as an average human being in this moment, how much of you is here. Granted, moments change, but . . . we have something now that looks a bit more like a percentage that you're used to.

Even so, you live other lives elsewhere simultaneously. You are in motion all the time, your heart field goes out, you are in motion, you are interacting—now I'm talking about in the body—with other beings in order to create what you are creating for yourself and what you are helping them to create for themselves and so on. So at any given moment, you are that much in your body. No, not at any given moment—at the moments we're talking about here. You are in your body to that extent. In this case, you are representative of the average human being on Earth.

Now, if we talk about, say, the average . . . well, let's pick animals who are house pets. For instance, the average family dog who likes to be with the family, and so on, might be maybe 3.7 percent. That's a dog, I'd better say an average dog—we'll do something else with that. Now I'll give you the average cat: the average cat may be 1.23 percent. Now, for the sake of comparison, I'm just going to use dogs and cats, if that's sufficient. I don't know if that makes any difference to you.

No, that's great. The average dog is at 3.7 percent, and the average cat is one-third of the dog! Why is that—because the cat travels a lot in other realms? Why is the cat here so much less than the dog?

A particularly spiritual dog would be able to do more, give more love. You see, the dog is very intimate: love, kindness, gentleness, concern, care. A particularly spiritual cat, for instance, while it might be loving, wouldn't show love the same way. Cats are more what I would call, not standoffish, but they would be able to travel in their physical bodies between dimensions. If they trust you, they might allow you to see that. Cats know and understand that they are teachers; they do not feel obliged to be nurturers. That's the big difference. They nurture you to the degree that they do simply because they have mastered giving by receiving. Dogs have also mastered that, but dogs are geared to be loving companions if they care about you that way. Cats know that they are here 100 percent to be teachers, especially spiritual cats. They know that, and they're teaching all the time.

Some of You Are Bringing More of Your Personality Here

You're there as the center of our solar system, and without you, we could not live here, we could not be here, correct?

Well, not in the same way.

What's the alternative? I thought it would be impossible without the Sun being here.

You'd have to live underground, artificially. Of course, there wouldn't be any plants. So here, it just depends. I can't rule out that there could be life. It might be in a ship. You know, same space.

We, this solar system, need your energy, and yet even though you're doing that perfectly, you still have all this time—well, you're not even in time—but you have all this opportunity to interact with everybody else in the universe, and you're not just totally focused here.

Yes.

That's what's so amazing. I mean, it seems like providing energy in a solar system would be a full-time job [chuckles].

Well, that's the reason I pointed out what you were doing. We need to expand your worldviews—and obviously expand the worldview of the reader—to understand that you're not here that much either. It's just that you have approximately that much of your self focused here in order to do what needs to be done.

How much of ourselves are we able to bring here?

You mean theoretically? That's a good question. I'm glad you asked that, because as you begin doing these things that we were talking about before—to solve the unsolvable—you will increase the percentage of yourself that is here. You have to remember that in order to do these things that are benevolent magic and so on, you will have to change. And each time you change to accomplish these things and become more like your total personality, you will bring more of your personality here to do that, even if it's just for those moments. When that happens, you will begin to feel more like yourself. If you felt kind of scattered or lost and you begin doing this kind of work, you will feel more like yourself, whether you're doing it for yourself or for others—as long, of course, as it's benevolent.

So as that happens, those figures change and you begin to acquire more of yourself that wouldn't feel safe to be functioning on the Earth as it is now, with your civilizations and cultures functioning the way they do now. But as you begin to utilize these capabilities and these capacities, you will of course be doing it to make your world—your family, your culture, your self, your life—more benevolent. As that happens and as the energy of that benevolence happens around and about you—because of who you are and what you are doing, how you are growing spiritually and so on—you acquire more of your self (maybe not there every moment, but at least when you are doing that). Repeatedly doing things like that along those benevolent lines will allow that "more of you" to feel safer here, and that percentage of you that is here—which will then feel safer to be here—will increase.

Of course, as that happens around the world, then the world changes—your cultural world, not the planet—and becomes more benevolent. More of the benevolent parts of all of you that are elsewhere that your soul travels to visit—they tell you that your soul travels to visit teachers, but it also goes to travel and visit other parts of your self—will feel safe to come here. That's when you'll begin to notice as a society that things are getting better, because everyone's doing these benevolent things in order to improve the quality of their own lives and the lives of others.

What occurs is that everybody begins to experience more of their natural benevolence. Then a lot of other things happen: the planet gets more mellow, things get resolved, the other cultures on other planets will gradually over time (as more of you gets here) feel safer to come and visit you again, may get permission to do so, it depends. A lot of things happen. I'm not saying that there's a real bubble around you here to protect you and to protect other cultures, but we can describe it as a barrier or bubble or veil or something. As you become more of yourselves and safer and more benevolent, that veil will get thinner, allowing you to travel more. How would you travel more? In ships? Not necessarily. What would happen is that your dreams would also become more benevolent and you would remember more.

All these things happen. There are a great many things that happen. I'm just giving you some guidelines so you can tell what's happening when it's happening. In the past, I think you've had people who have separated themselves from others, gone off into special spiritual places and have worked on that and worked on this so that they themselves, regardless of the time and culture in which they were living in these separate places, could achieve this—you know, in spiritual places or places where spiritual people gathered. But now that's really not the point. While some of that still goes on and maintains benevolence to a degree on Earth, these things need to happen from the greater population at large.

So we could hold twice as much of ourselves, ten times? Just a range, not precise, but if it's 1.76 now, we could hold 5 percent of ourselves?

No, it's like this. Remember how I described myself: I am one of many. But I am one of many simultaneously. You see me as one because you are experiencing individuality at the moment, but if you were to see me in my natural way—meaning that you could see to the ends of the universe—you would not see me as one. You would see me connected to all other suns. You would see the lines of connection, and some places it would just look like a mass with brighter spheres here and there. You would say, "Oh, those are suns," and so on—not exactly like a matrix, but more like a component, solid in places, more spacious in others, and so on. You are the same.

So while all parts of you may not be here in this physical place, you would be conscious of all parts of you, and all parts of you could freely communicate as all other parts of you are freely communicating now. Then you would have available to you all that you can do, plus all that you've learned here on Earth.

It sounds wonderful. No one has explained it quite like that.

When You're Connected, Travel Is Not Quite the Same

Do you travel on those lines between suns, or do you have another way to travel?

We only travel at all if we're no longer needed in a given place and we are needed specifically in some other place. That's only within your dimensional understanding of travel, and so on, but it's important to stay to that. So within that concept of "things move from place to place," then, yes—only under that circumstance. This gives you a hint about yourselves. Where you live now, things move from place to place, you could say. You travel, you go from place to place, but when you are totally connected to all portions of yourself, travel is not quite the same.

You would know what you are doing on the other side of the universe; you wouldn't have to go and check. You wouldn't just know it as something that you know about, encyclopedic, but you could connect with it as long as you were completely in the same benevolence as that other-side-of-the-universe place, just for this example. You could experience fully what's going on to the extent that it is compatible with your life from where you are. It would be the same from the other side of the universe. What you experience, as long as it's compatible with them, they could experience your life too.

Now they can't, because we're not being benevolent.

Well, you are in school and so they are missing you very much, just like you would miss something if some part of your body was missing and had always been there. You could compare that to someone who might lose a finger or something like that in life. It's traumatic and of course painful for you, but you never get over it. You always miss it. So they're looking forward to you being unified again. They feel it as if a part of themselves is missing. They know that what you're doing is important, but they can't wait for you to be whole again—from their perception.

Their perception, right.

Where you are, of course, you don't really know about that, but that's all right because you have enough to deal with. You don't need to deal with that.

But we still need to know these things for our future, that this potential is where we're going, right? We need to know this.

Interestingly enough, of course, it's also your past.

But when we get back to the place where the loop of time began, we'll be more, and because we have these ex— [gasps]. But they won't ever be able to share our experiences because it won't be benevolent!

They can only share it when it is completely benevolent.

Will we ourselves remember these melodramas?

Not the way you experience them, because once they're resolved, all of the energies that need to be resolved, all of the unresolvable things in other parts of the universe that you are helping to resolve, all that will simply be resolved and there will be no need to remember the struggle that went on. If beings remember struggling and sacrificing, there is a tendency to raise that struggle and sacrifice to something called glory.

[Laughs.] Yes, we do that.

Even though glory has its function where you are now, it has many times been the cause of great mischief.

Not All the Planets Are Fully Engaged

Do all solar systems look like that: a sun comes and then there's a call for the planets? Our science says the sun creates the planets—the debris goes around the orbits and it coalesces—but it's not true at all, right?

No.

So they all work the way this one does? A sun comes or a sun is there and calls planets, or there is a need for planets and then they come?

You are asking, "Where do planets come from," yes? Planets exist in other dimensions. So when planets come, they are welcomed because, "Here are the orbits; you can come and you can visit." They are already in existence in these other dimensions, so what we're really saying—if I were saying it, okay?—what is going on is that it's like there's this welcoming place. Granted, it's in this place of learning for a group called the Explorer Race, but there's this welcoming place, and the planets who already exist in other dimensions, if they wish to express themselves in this dimension . . . [snaps fingers].

They materialize.

Then they do. Of course, they don't come here on a whim; they know there's something major going on here. When that's done and the Explorer Race has moved off, if there isn't some other major reason to be here, they don't have to remain, or they can put—as it is on some planets—their expressions of themselves to less focus of concentration. For instance, Mars has got rocks and sand and water under the surface and, to a degree, a little atmosphere, and so on. So there's more of a little something that you could say, "Oh boy, let's go to Mars!" But other planets on the outer reaches in some places . . . it's not likely that you will be going there in the near future. So those planets do not have to put as much effort into being there and can just be gas clouds and less physical in nature. You see, they don't need to create something that you might visit or that you might even send a mechanical instrument up to land on, and so on, to explore, as I think there's been some effort to send . . .

Oh, to Venus?

Venus, yes. There's been some effort to send something there, too. Not that there's been much success, but there's been an effort.

So which planets, then, are fully engaged here in such a way that we could fully interact with them, besides Mars?

Well, I would say that, realistically, Mars is it for now, not counting asteroids. I think there will be a lot of interaction with asteroids, once you have gotten your mining that you can do in space up to speed. Say that an asteroid is passing by Earth and might be accessible. In the future, you might be able to have some access to it for reasonably maybe three or four days. If you are really serious about mining, you can get a lot done in three or four days and then it goes on. This is one of the reasons—not the only reason, but it's one of the reasons—that when these things tumble by, sometimes they look like someone's been digging in them.

Oh, because they have.

Yes, because they have. They go by and they have minerals that may be useful to some population, and the population says, "Okay!" Of course, if they have the capacity to travel at great speed or travel with it or have more advanced capabilities, they might be able to quickly take what they need and leave the rest. But nobody uses it for a dumping ground [chuckles]. Generally speaking, if you're that advanced in your space travel, you recycle everything. You don't dump anything.

Really. So Mercury and Venus, then, are also not formed in the way of rocks?

Oh yes, they have that.

But because they're too close to you, we wouldn't . . .

Well, it's not realistic. But that's why I say that when you go out to the further planets like Neptune, and so on, these planets do not require any great density (I think Pluto has some density). It's better for you to talk to them, but I'd say that, generally speaking, we're not talking about planets who are required to have density. For Mars, it is required.

Okay, so Mars, the Earth who was here before, whom you call Oodoo, and the record Earth, then, also had density?

They would be required to, because the chances of them having a humanoid population would be soon. It's not that many years into the future when there are practical colonies on Mars that the average citizen with a lot of money might be able to go there for a big expense, have the thrill of living on Mars for a few days, and come back. That will take a while, but there will be a lot of motivation to do it because there will be people who have the money and would love to go do it—a great adventure, a thrill! Of course, once there are more human beings on Mars, you'll be exploring. You'll find lots of very exciting things.

That's because we were there once, right?

Well, I don't think you'll identify with that. You'll say, "Someone was there," and "Isn't this fascinating?" but you won't identify with it having anything to do with your souls. You'll just say, "Well, there was this civilization here and look at this stuff! Isn't this fabulous?" So there'll be a lot of interest. Well, there's quite a bit of interest now.

What I want to say is that some planets may choose to have solid physical matter just because that's how they've decided to manifest themselves here in these welcoming orbits. But other planets, as I say, well, they're there, but you know, they're mostly gas, and so on. They don't need to be physical right away. When you begin exploring the planets as an Earth culture and go out farther and farther, the planets may or may not choose to become solid. It's up to them.

So what would you say is the purpose of the planets?

Well, a lot of the purpose, of course, is to attract you to explore the planets so that you don't become totally focused only on your own existence here. After all, there are people who look at the stars and say, "Aren't they beautiful?" and there are others who look at the stars and say, "What do we have to do to get there?" [Chuckles.] It's the people who are like that . . . that's what the planets are for, for you. They may have other cultures on them sometimes, but that's up to you to find out.

There Needs to Be More Heart and Spirit Involved in Your Technology

Are there other cultures? I'd have to go planet by planet and ask each planet, then, if there are other cultures in other dimensions?

They may or may not answer. After all, the whole point is to intrigue you. You're not going to say, "Oh boy, let's go to the Pleiades!" You might be thrilled and happy to meet beings from the Pleiades who can travel such great distances to visit you somewhere, but if you're going to travel somewhere in space—especially with the type of equipment you have now—you're going to travel to the places you can get to. It'll be quite awhile before you're able to travel in time effectively and safely. There will be a few experiments that will go wrong.

We've had some that went wrong, right?

I'm talking about experiments that people know about. I know part of the reason these unmanned vehicles are sent up now is to try things like that: "How fast can we make it go? Will it then travel through some other means that we know about?" and so on. Sometimes they just accelerate the vehicle as fast as possible to see how fast it will go and will the acceleration itself prompt it to go into another dimension, because the Einstein theory suggests this—that past a certain point of miles per hour, you can become something else. I think the formula's not quite complete, but it's all right to play with that.

It's been suggested that our math isn't quite accurate and that when we get that straightened out, we'll be better able to figure these things out.

There needs to be more heart and there needs to be more of the spirit involved. That's why the problems you have on Earth are much more urgent to resolve, because the means that you will use to successfully resolve them will require you to take these steps, to bring in more of yourselves, to use benevolent magic, to work with these benevolent beings who are available to you. Then, of course, you will learn that once you start building spacecraft, using that same kind of benevolence, you can then begin to discover and practically apply the capacity to travel by attraction.

Look at your typical rocket that sends some vehicle into space or astronauts into space. If you could illuminate all the space that uses a conventional engine and fuel, you could send a much bigger vehicle up with lots of interesting things and lots of people and with something teeny by comparison. Once you start doing that, the engine and the navigational equipment may not be much bigger than an average car. Eventually, you'll refine that down so that you can basically hold it in two hands. That's not untypical for many of the other vehicles that travel from many of the other star systems, but it will come in time in terms of practical application.

I'm not talking about experiments and the unknown denied by various secret groups here and there. I'm talking about what's practical and known and about welcoming the public and welcoming educators. As people have discovered quickly, the problem with developing things secretly is that you have to use only a teeny portion of the population involved. Very often, the people you really need are doing other things, but because the project is so secret, you can't really utilize anything that they're doing, except in some obscure way—meaning that they work on some tiny element of something that you take a chance and trust them to do, and that tiny element, while it's nice, if they were working on the whole project, you would be thrilled. So that's keeping your progress in those areas at a very slow pace.

Yes, but they have off-world technology to start with.

In some cases, yes, but there's not much they can do with it because they keep trying to do only physical things.

Right, when the off-world technology is beyond the physical here. [Laughs.]

Well, it has capacities beyond that, and the people who fly in it all have to be heart-centered if they want the vehicle to do something for them that the vehicle would want to do. If the vehicle doesn't want to do it, it's not going to happen.

Right. But these guys are looking for the nuts and bolts mechanisms.

That's all right for now. It's like a safety mechanism, and then they won't be able to find them, and that's good. But they'll be intrigued, and they'll want to know, and that's also good.

Earth Is Expressing Itself in a Great Deal of Variety

How many civilizations have you seen on Earth? Of course, there were two other Earths.

Well, you have to understand that I don't pay 100 percent attention to everything you're doing on Earth, so there will be times when you ask questions like that and I may not be able to answer.

Okay, but let's just talk about the first Earth. There was a wild battle there, and they blew it up—were you aware of that?

I'm always aware of what happens to the planets.

According to Zoosh, another loving planet was in this orbit, but it was too soft and vulnerable, so this planet, now Earth, traveled here from Sirius.

Yes. I don't see it as "travel," but I can see where it would make sense for you to think of it as travel.

Say how you would see it.

I would see it that this planet you now call Earth existed in Sirius and there was an orbit that was clean and available—cleaned out, you understand, everything ready for it. Not unlike the planets in other dimensions who came here to occupy those welcoming orbits, that other planet did too. That's how it could move swiftly and safely.

It moved in another dimension?

Yes. As your friend Zoosh likes to say, it took about . . . [snaps fingers] . . . that much time from there to here. Obviously, if it was moving in time and space, that couldn't really work, could it?

Is that correct? It moved in another dimension and then materialized here? Is that what you are saying?

It moved the same way the other planets who are here in this solar system manifested, as you like to say, in these orbits that were available to them—in the identical manner. That is why, if you went to that solar system (Sirius) to see if what you now call Earth was still there in the dimensions (as you are calling them) that it prefers to focus in, it's still there. If it chose to focus a version of itself in the third dimension (as you call it), well, it might be able to create another identical version of itself to be there. But that version of itself in the third dimension is here.

Thank you for explaining that. That makes so much more sense.

Yes. It's hard to picture a planet speeding through space [chuckles], whirling along, with water on it at that, to say nothing of some populations.

Somebody said that the Aborigines in Africa and Australia came with the planet?

Some populations trace their ancestry back to Sirius in that way, I believe. I think some of those populations are still in current existence on Earth here. There would be one or some others in Africa that are not 100 percent still here, but they have some representatives here in a fashion. There are a few others who don't really want that to be discussed.

Can you say why this planet was called to come here as Earth?

Oh, it wasn't that that planet was called; it was that the call went out.

And that planet answered it?

Yes, that planet answered it, and I believe that it is really quite a treat, wouldn't you say? Having a water planet here in this solar system? In this solar system, of course, it would be considered to be, well, just a wonder. One might go to other solar systems in other galaxies or even this one where all the planets—you know, one after the other—are water planets, and you wouldn't think anything of it. I mean, they're all wonderful; you'd enjoy visiting them. But it's quite startling to see a water planet within this solar system where the planets are not that way at all.

Therefore, it was felt that such a planet, with as much variety as well as potential for variety, with water and ice and hot and cold and all that kind of variety... I believe that Creator (being rather fond of variety Itself) perhaps felt that the Explorer Race would need to have the maximum amount of variety in order to foster, nurture and present the personality types that would be necessary to service the population as part of it, meaning to interact—different types, different groups. But in order to welcome those expressions of human beings who might very well relate their origins back to other planets, you would have to have certain weather conditions that might appeal to them as well. A rocky, dry desert planet, while it might appeal to certain cultures (what you see on Mars, and so on), would not appeal to certain cultures that are attracted to water, or ice, or steaming hot, or very cold, or volcanic or Earth motion—all of these things.

So you have here a planet that is expressing itself in a great deal of variety that would be considered welcome by races of beings who have direct corollaries on other planetary systems, in other star systems in some cases, and in other planets. So when you have an Earth citizen here, you might say, "Well, this type of citizen . . . it's not the individual—the individual is beyond classification as to a root to a specific. You understand that the soul is beyond simply being from here or there—but you might say that your expression in how you appear, that that cultural appearance might be traceable back to certain types of planets or solar systems or even galaxies, as you were talking about before in the case of the Aborigines going back further. But you might say that, in the case of certain appearances of people, their ancestors (if they wanted to visit their ancestors, in the case of those people you mentioned), that they would be from that planet and that star system.

Well, you could say that about other people, based on their appearances on this planet, that they would be from that star system or this star system. But the reason they felt welcome to manifest themselves here—or even come here with, initially, an expedition—is because they would find certain weather conditions that existed on their planet or from their culture or what they're used to. So they would feel welcome to be here and raise families here and eventually become a viable culture.

I Don't Consider You to Be an Individual

What about you? How did you feel when this planet came? What was your interaction with this planet?

Well, I felt that it was really a wonderful thing because it represented variety and beauty, but I don't like it any more than the others, if that's what you're asking. [Chuckles.] I like it just as much as the other planets and all that I interact with. I'm not clear what you are asking. You said, what did I feel about it.

I guess what we're looking for eventually are the feelings and the interactions between Earth and all the other planets and the Sun and the Moon. So maybe my question is, what do you give the Earth and what does she give you? What is the interaction?

No, it's not like that. I know that human beings think about that: a relationship, friendship. It's not like that with us. We are happy to be in the same proximity. Whether that proximity is so many hundreds of thousands of miles or whether it's on the other side of the universe, it's the same. It's still the same place. I am just as happy to be with planets on the other side of the universe as I am to be here.

Since all suns are one sun, you're with them, too. I understand.

For that matter, I'm just as happy to be with all planets in all universes in all existence everywhere. My likes and dislikes do not alter on an individual basis, because I am not an individual as you consider yourself to be in this moment. But I don't consider you to be an individual.

Well, I'll tell you. It sure feels individual here.

It does feel that way, and I understand (not on the basis of personal experience, but I understand) that it's very reasonable that you would consider yourself to be an individual. Of course, when you are asleep and dreaming, you know that you're not.

Oh, I'm looking forward to remembering that.

I'll give you an example. Have you ever had a moment when you felt totally united with any one being—a thing, a human, an animal—and you felt like there was no real barrier between you two?

Yes.

That moment gives you a way to understand what you normally feel like. But this a school. That's why Creator does not allow you to be here for too long—long enough, no longer. We're going to have to stop soon. It's been a long week for both of you, I think. I don't think we ought to run a full session today.

Let me just ask you your opinion about how to proceed. The idea that started all this was to get the more intimate aspects of astrology, because we were taught here that in our interactions with the planets, the planets have certain qualities. Mercury has the mind, Venus has love, and Saturn is a teacher.

But you see, we are doing that—because what you are getting is greater depth of personality. I feel that the advanced astrologer or various advanced astrologic teachers, and so on, could, if they chose, read this book and extrapolate further qualities that they might use to describe what the Sun and the planets are, and thereby be able to make more sense of an astrological chart. In that sense, they'd be able to create another level of an astrological chart or another way to express astrology, as to say, "Well, here's astrology based on the systems that I have been able to calculate from reading this book," which will come to be known by some term that the astrologers will use.

It will just give them another way to provide a reading or they might, if they feel it has enough value, just infuse it into what they normally do.

So from my perspective, what you were attempting to do in the beginning has simply expanded. That's all. You haven't deserted that; you're just doing more.

I like this a lot better.

I feel it's important for you to like it, and it's deeper while still serving its original purpose. We will resume the next time.

Oh, excellent! Thank you.

☽ The Moon

THE MOON
Nurtures and Inspires You

January 21, 2003

Greetings.

Welcome. Are you the Moon?

Yes. What would you like to know?

Everything. Tell me how you got to where you are now.

I First Established Myself around Oodoo

The Sun established a welcoming orbit around the former planet here, and I established myself there.

Around Oodoo?

Yes, and when Oodoo was no longer . . . there's some kind of a shield. Although the force, the feeling of the energy of Oodoo breaking apart, the unhappiness of it, did go through me, the physical parts didn't. So I remained in orbit for a time, but I do not know how long. There was something else I was orbiting—not Earth, not Oodoo, something else. It was very small in comparison to Earth, very small.

Like an asteroid, a piece of the planet?

No, it was not Oodoo. In my recollection of it, it was very small but strong. I think it might have been someone the Sun provided. It was about thirty feet across but located in the position of where the center of Oodoo would have been. It was very dense, had a very strong field. It might have been someone's sun requested to be there. You will have to ask the Sun.

We will later on.

For a time, I orbited around that. It had the same qualities of gravitational pull that Oodoo had, even though it was very small. I do not know how that is possible, but it happened. This happened for a while. Then in less timing—it was less than a second—there was actually a bit of overlap. The object and Earth were there slightly overlapped, and then the object was gone. It might have been a half-second of overlap and then Earth was there. Does that answer your question? Did you ask where I came from?

I said, "How did you get here?" and you answered.

That's how I got here.

That's a wonderful answer.

Perhaps it wasn't complete. I do have other versions of myself in other, as you say, dimensions. I have those, so in that way I got here the same way the planets did.

You materialized from the other dimensions?

Yes. On several of the other dimensions, I just look like a small planet but with no water.

No water on any dimension?

Not yet, but going around Earth like this, I've become accustomed to water and am considering creating a version of myself that has some water, but the water will not be very deep. In places there'll be maybe this much . . .

Six inches maybe, or four inches?

Yes, and I think I want to make it thicker than the water you have, maybe with more light in it—iridescent and thicker. It can be done, perhaps, with living beings in the water.

What level would that be in, what dimension?

What you would call the sixth. It will be nice. I don't think I'm prepared to do plants and water. My version of water is something that is more viscous and iridescent, but I'm not prepared to do plants yet. I like stone.

I Will Always Radiate What Is Needed

So what's the difference between a moon and a planet? You're as big as a planet.

A small one perhaps. There's no difference that I know of.

Just that a planet orbits the Sun and the Moon orbits a planet. Is that the only difference?

Yes, but in the case of your situation, you need to have something, someone, who is close enough and attractive enough to be inspiring, and also to at least dream about traveling to. So a moon is intended to inspire and encourage and all of those things for a people, for Earth people, who have such a destiny.

So you understand what the Explorer Race is?

A little bit. It is my job to nurture and inspire. That's what I do.

You do that very well.

Thank you.

Did you have experience anyplace else in the universe before this solar system, or have you always been here?

I believe I have been somewhere else. There is no residual of me there at the moment, so I am no longer there.

So all of you is here in this solar system?

In this area.

Does it feel different to you to orbit Earth instead of Oodoo?

Vastly different. Oodoo as a planet, for one thing, didn't have as many people on it. It didn't have as many plants. It was more reddish in color—the red having to do, I think, with the nature of the stone. There was some water but not a lot. It was much, much different going around Oodoo. Earth is feminine in her nature and does not require much feminine energy from me, whereas Oodoo required a lot of feminine energy. It was more masculine in its properties, so there was quite a big difference right there.

So you can choose the nature of the polarity of energy to send to a planet?

I don't send it, I just radiate it, and anything that happens to be along the line of my radiation will receive it, just as I radiate it in directions that I don't face. At any given moment, only half of me faces Earth, but I am radiating it spherically so it is going out in other directions. If that is of benefit to others, then that's good. I will always radiate what is needed in this case—as I said, what is needed for the planet Earth—and what is radiating elsewhere, they may or may not need.

Does the need of the planet pull the radiation from you? Is it something you do consciously?

Yes, I do it consciously. I do it on my own, and it comes from me and other expressions of me in other dimensions. I am not one moon here, I am one moon everywhere, and so whatever is needed might very well come from other parts. As your population of human beings gets bigger, sometimes there is more that is needed, and so I pull from other places where less is needed—not all of the places where I am, but if less is needed from certain places, then I pull from there.

So your identity is literally the core, the connection of all the moons that you are? You are the total of all of them?

No. I am one part of all of them.

So you're speaking now as the Moon in the third dimension?

Yes, your Moon. It would be irrelevant to do otherwise, wouldn't you agree?

I agree, but in your total beingness, you are all of that?

Yes, as you say.

My Light Is Infused with Nurturing and Inspiration

One of the things you do is you pass on the light of the Sun, but you do so much more than that, right?

The Sun can pass on its own light, you see, so I do not pass it on, though I understand what you're saying. I reflect it, infusing it with what I do.

Oh, it's reflected off you, but it also includes what you are.

It picks up what I do, and that light is what the Sun provides—not just the light, but the Sun's personality. It's that *with* my personality here, what I provide. You see, you need the Sun's personality, as well as its light and warmth. So when the Sun is not here, is not available for you—as you say, at night—you still need the Sun's personality. Granted, some of it comes through from the other side, passing through the Earth to where you are in the night, but what doesn't, then I reflect the Sun, adding my own personality to you.

What I add makes up for the Sun not being there. Nurturing and inspiration are helpful. Many of you sleep at night, and the nurturing and inspiration are helpful to your dreams. Those of you who don't sleep, you can still use the nurturing and inspiration, and often you'll look up and enjoy what is to be seen.

According to my education, when one has a sky to look up to where there are only stars—no moon though, just stars—one is more inclined to look toward the sky when there is a moon than when there are only stars. By looking toward the sky, you make contact with the greater portions of yourself consciously. You don't normally think about it, but when you look toward the sky, you relax, you're not in that moment having to do consciously, completely, with your own Earth personality. You expand in those moments usually, unless you are performing some immediate task and just glance toward the sky. You look toward the sky, and you relax and expand, becoming more of your total being.

You are likely to be looking toward the sky to see the Moon—where is the Moon that night? What about nights when there is what you call a new moon, no moonlight that you can see? People sometimes get a little upset or tired then, because there is no one reflecting the Sun to you. On such an evening, it is always best to do as little as possible. Don't make long-range plans, don't sign any contracts if you can help it that involve close scrutiny—don't do anything that requires exactitudes. It's probably not a good time to do diamond cutting unless you are an individual for whom that time is good (some people respond well to such time). In short, it's probably best to do simple things and get to bed as early as possible. Conversely, it might be possible to sleep very deeply, but dreams might be a little problematic—not always, it depends. That's not usually the case if you are in the countryside, but in cities it can be a bit much.

Nevertheless, my point is that on planets where there are moons that are regularly in the sky at night, it is much more likely that the population will glance toward the sky at least once every night than on planets where there are no moons and there are only stars. As beautiful as it is, one might not necessarily glance toward the sky without a moon. Every time you do that, even for a moment—ten seconds or more, five seconds in some cases, ideally seven seconds or more—you expand in those moments. You become more of your full selves. It is nurturing, it is enriching, and most importantly, it is revitalizing. So I believe Creator wanted me to be present around Earth so that you could have such revitalization, especially given the nature of your duties here, which are quite profound and far-reaching even beyond that which you do for yourselves.

So you consciously did not know that Earth was going to be placed in that orbit where that small, dense object was?

From my point of view, I was here for Oodoo, and then my role continued for Earth. The small object was there just to support my orbit so that the Sun didn't have to continue to support my orbit during the gap between Oodoo's presence and Earth.

When you orbited Oodoo, was it the same situation where half of you was shown to the planet and half never was?

It was the same.

Is there a reason for that?

A lot of it has to do with my own personal *restoration*. I receive a great deal of support and nurturance from the suns—you call them stars—at my other side, which you would call dark, but it is only dark in comparison to the reflected sunlight. It is not that dark. I take in a lot of support and nurturance from those physical bodies, those distant suns, and that's supporting me.

This is because you have to give so much to the Earth, because there are so many beings?

No, because many of the beings on Earth owe their spiritual and physical biological lineage to those stars. I have to take in and absorb energy from those places so that the energy I reflect and infuse with my own personality can be infused with physiologically specific and spiritually specific energies that will reach the variety of human beings on Earth, given your different star-system origins spiritually and, even as I said, to a degree physically. So there's a reason for everything, yes?

I Feel More Feminine

Say a little bit about your education. You said you were educated.

Yes, to perform the functions prescribed here initially for Oodoo, to be educated about their civilizations if the civilizations were learning anything. It's quite a bit different for civilizations that aren't really learning anything but are just going on, such as on your planet. The animals, although they might individually have to learn how to live, are not here to learn a lesson. That's what I mean by that. On Oodoo, it was like that. The populations were not there to learn a lesson, so it was quite a bit different. I was educated on how to provide benevolently for them, but for you, of course, it's much more.

You are here to learn lessons individually and as groups, you might say, physiologically speaking: racially, gender-wise, all of that. Then, spiritually speaking, there are some things associated with your kinship with a certain star system at any given moment that might change from time to time. Then, as the Explorer Race as a whole, you have all these other lessons, some of which are not even your own that you are resolving for others, so there's all of that. It's a lot. But my initial education, of course, was for Oodoo.

Then who educated you for the Earth?

You mean names?

Well, I don't know. Do you have spiritual teachers?

The knowledge is always present. I do not stop and ask them their names: "Who are you? Show me your ID." [Chuckles.] Pardon my humor.

I love it—you have a sense of humor. You are called Grandmother Moon by the native tribes. Do you feel more feminine than masculine, or is that their perception?

No, I do feel that.

You feel more feminine.

Yes.

I didn't think to ask the Sun. Evidently he is more masculine?

I think you will have to ask the Sun.

I will. So they're correct in perceiving your energy, then, because you've never been called Grandfather. It's always been Grandmother, right?

Yes.

No One Has Been Destructively Mining Me

Isn't there a lot of mining on what we call your dark side?

There has been. That is not usually ongoing. When that happens, it's usually some travelers going by who need something. Usually they take only what I can spare. No one has been destructively mining. Generally speaking, such things are not allowed. After all, one can take too much and things can be affected: orbits, and so on. That is generally not allowed, and most beings from other planets are pretty benevolent, but you do have times when groups will come and take a little something and perhaps leave something—a simple structure that they can utilize in the future should either they need to acquire more material like that or if others come along.

Since there will be an opening into my body there, the structure essentially covers the opening, you see, but the opening goes straight to the material that was needed—you understand, like a shaft. Therefore, anyone going by who might need a little of that material will, on the basis of being able to use instruments or feelings, essentially contact that thing that covers the opening and know what is there. That's why sometimes something is left, some simple structure.

So, yes, there are some of those structures on the other side. I don't think any have been allowed to be on the side that faces Earth.

They've been photographed, though. There are photos the government doesn't acknowledge that show huge craft and craters.

They don't acknowledge them, but they'd certainly know about them. I'm quite certain of that. They do, yes?

Of course they do. They just don't want us to know about them.

I wouldn't go that far. I think if they didn't want you to know about them, they wouldn't have made the pictures available.

I think they were made available before they realized what the pictures were. So there's no permanent base there? No ET culture that has a permanent base on the back of the Moon?

That's happened from time to time, but "permanent" is only a transitory term.

So you don't object to that.

No.

The Past Is in Motion

The astronauts who came from Earth didn't stay there long enough to have much impact on you, right? But you knew they were there.

I wouldn't call it much of an impact.

But they were there, right?

It depends how you figure time. Yes and no. You are changing dimensions, yes?

Yes.

Then yes and no. Do you understand why?

No.

If you are in 3.0 dimension . . .

Well, we're not.

There you are. If you were in 4.0 dimension . . . but you're not. You're in between. Once you're in anything past 3.33 or 3.34, then a lot of things having to do with the past are "yes and no." If you could conceivably trace—and you can't because of the populations on the Earth, where you've been and what you've done—but theoretically if you as an individual on Earth could trace your lineage back, say, 10,000 years, we would have to say that your grandfather who lived 9,000 years ago . . . I would have to give you the same answer. If you asked the question, "Did I have a grandfather on Earth who lived 9,000 years ago?" I'd have to say yes and no. It's not because it was a different level. It's because you're past 3.33, and anything past 3.33 into that mid-dimension range, you understand . . .

Then the past is re-created, discreated. We're connected to a different future. I understand.

Things are in flux, so all of that past orientation . . . that's why sometimes beings will say, "Well, this is the past," and you talk to other beings and they'll say, "Well, this is the past," and another being will say, "Well, this is the past," and you look at them and you say, "There's no comparison here." That's because everything is in motion. Perhaps it is that being's perception that that is the past, and maybe that was the past, and that being might have even lived that past, but that past is in motion. The true and most clear answer is "yes or no." It means yes *and* no, not yes *or* no. It's not yes or no; it's yes and no.

I see. I didn't realize that only thirty or thirty-five years ago things had shifted that much in that time.

It is not typical, you understand, for a planet to be in flux like this. It might happen if there was no surface population—that's not unusual. But for a surface population as complex and connected the way your surface population is, to be past 3.32 (but I'm going to call it 3.33) creates a lot of difficulty for historians and others to trace it. That's why I think, when they give you predictions about the future, the fact that any of those predictions come true at all is quite astonishing. There has to be a great deal of correlation between potential futures.

Picture for a moment multiple strands of yarn running forward. If they all run forward in direct straight lines, they don't touch each other. That means that any one prediction for the future would be very unlikely. But if we cross those threads and they touch each other and sometimes touch each other a lot, then you might have forty, fifty or even a hundred possibilities that contact each other. A prediction along that line might very well come to pass in part.

So our threads do intertwine and wind around and do all those things?

I don't like to say "intertwine and wind around." That makes it all sound like a big jumble where they all touch. They don't all touch, only some do. Predictions along the line where a lot of them touch in a given moment . . . and they're in motion all the time, they're not just fixed, so therefore at any given moment someone gives a prediction and says, "This will happen in the future:

five minutes from now, five years from now, five hundred years from now." If it comes to pass at least partially, you could automatically say to yourself, "Of the many futures, many of them apparently contacted in this area, and that's why this at least partially came to pass."

People are very attached to predictions for perfectly reasonable explanations. It's difficult to make plans if you don't know whether your life is going to be up or down or sideways or backward. It's nice to know that whatever it is that you are is going to be, at least in its basic delineations, that in the future. So people are highly desirous of at least basic predictions. I completely understand. Of course, being who you are, that is not always the case.

What I Do Has to Do with Feeling

So being the moon of a planet with this many people, some of whom trace their origin in other star systems, would be bad enough, but to have the Explorer Race here in the flux . . . your job must be incredibly difficult.

If I had to think about it, it would be, but I don't have to think. I can see from your perspective that this wouldn't seem to be so, but that is because you think to live. What I do does not require thought—it is feeling. With feeling, one simply is what one needs to be, no matter whether that is some simple thing or something highly complex. Feelings can do a multiplicity of things to the infinite in every given moment. Thoughts, on the other hand, become increasingly difficult to understand the more complex they get. That's quite a difference, wouldn't you say?

That's a big difference, but still, you have awesome potential. Let me rephrase that: Could any moon do what you're doing for the Explorer Race?

I cannot speak for all moons. I am an individual.

So it's different than suns—moons are individuals, okay. Since you don't remember where you were . . .

I remember. The other place I was? There is just none of me there anymore.

Was there any special training there or any special requirements?

There's always that.

Every place you go is special.

Every place I am present.

You're on all these levels, but since the Earth is here from Sirius, is she only on this dimension or is she on the other levels in this star system?

She's on a few—not all that I am on. When I look in this solar system in my various expressions in these, as you say, dimensions, sometimes I see Earth and sometimes I see Oodoo.

So she is in the places Oodoo isn't, then? Is that right?

Sometimes I don't see anything, but then in those places, I am not spinning nor am I orbiting. I am just there. This means it is a potential for something more to take place at some point, but it is not dormant, just not very active. But as I say, my education for Oodoo is helpful because Oodoo is still there in a lot of places. Looking at the variables, I'd have to say that Oodoo is present in perhaps slightly less of account (as far as places go) than Earth is. Earth is in a few more places than Oodoo, but in the majority of places, there's neither Earth nor Oodoo.

Of the levels of Earth you see, are there human beings or civilizations or cultures on those planets?

Oh yes, on some yes, but not like you, not the Explorer Race. Some of them would have to do with populations of long standing, and some of them, I would have to say, looking at them, are like populations one might find on Sirius.

We're going to have to come to an end for the day. I will be here for a while; I will be available for the next session. Good night.

Thank you.

THE MOON

A Depiction of the Sun

5

CHON-DEH, SUN HELPER
Focuses the Energy of Suns to Where It Is Needed

March 8, 2004

Greetings. I am Chon-deh.

Welcome

I'm here because I can supplement your and the channel's physical energy and also communicate. This may occur at other times in the future when the both of you are tired. I'm not a resident of your galaxy nor do I in any way ever come to visit. But my people are involved in the coordination of energies from what you call the Sun. I have come through today to provide this service that we do because the previous speaker asked, "Is someone available to give support and talk?"

My People Focus Sun Energy

As you all know as informed persons, there is more than one sun that illuminates and nurtures life. My people are involved in the focusing of sun energy, speaking in the terminology of distance, into units of physical stimulation and also in this case being different units of physical support. Most of the time the energy we send out goes to planets, not the residents, but in the past we have sent out energy to some dwellers on your planet: one you call rabbit, another you call earthworm. These dwellers had considered for a time to expatriate.

Leave the planet.

Leave the planet, yes. But we were asked by planetary advisers who consult on such topics—Earth advisories having less to do with the Explorer Race and more to do with Earth itself—to extend, if possible, the duration of those life forms' capacity to survive on Earth and to be compatible with energies that were incompatible with them. Frequency ranges that are created for the purpose of the support of the human race sometimes interfere with other Earth dwellers' means to survive. These frequencies are not intended to do that but are part of communication systems that replace natural communication.

You have capacity for long-distance communication without technology, but you as Earth dwellers now experiment with technology so that you can learn to understand the nature of communication. It is not that you do not have these capacities to communicate from afar, but these capacities are only practiced by a few, not many. I believe your civilizations are finding some interest in understanding communication through applications of science. So I understand that.

We do not look like you. You would not consider us humanoid, meaning generally approximating your appearance. But that is acceptable; we do not need to do that. Our planet has what you would refer to as light gravity. If you were capable of surviving on our planet, you would require considerable weight to hold you down to the surface. There's some gravitational pull, but it's minimal compared to what you are used to. The atmosphere would not support you, and generally planets where I exist are not meant for your visiting. You will not probably do that in your next hundred generations or so.

By then you will be completely at ease with forms of life that are completely unlike you. Children will have not exactly pets, in the sense of pet prisoners, but pets in the sense of visitors who are like protozoa—meaning children will be able to look at a slide, though it will not be in the constricted machine. It will be more like putting something up to the eye and being able to see in space in front of you a particle and communicate directly with that particle. Children particularly will find this fun and amusing, and parents will feel good about it because it helps prepare the child for the knowledge of the sanctity of all life and to appreciate that life is all around you, even if you do not see it with the eyes you are born with.

What do you look like?

That would be hard to describe in your terms. The most accessible description might be "light," but in multiple forms—meaning not a fixed parameter but light in a movable form. We find the arc shape particularly pleasing.

We Help the Sun Support Unusual Life Cycles on Earth

All suns are connected, so do you somehow move energy from one to the other? Is that what you do?

Not from one sun to the other, but we focus a sun's energy to go out over long spaces to where it might be needed. For instance, the sun you have here in this solar system, as you say, is intended to support natural life, which it does. But on your planet, life is not exactly natural.

Two dwellers on your planet—earthworm and rabbit, as you call them—found that the energies stimulated by your technological explorations were incompatible with them. The natural cycle for them would have been to depart. Such incompatible energies could develop by natural means—not specifically in this case, but it is possible that a volcano or a big storm could happen and life forms might be incompatible with that, and the natural thing to do would be to depart or, in some cases, to sleep deeply for a time until it goes by, as some dwellers do.

But in this case, life cycles of Earth dwellers are altered because unnatural life sequences are occurring on this planet in order for the Explorer Race, as you call yourselves, to learn and grow and provide what you will provide when you are a little further along. So there is some desire by the planet to have certain Earth dwellers here. The planet enjoys some things that the earthworm does and just likes them as people; likewise, the planet enjoys the rabbit and likes them as people. But they are also good in other ways for other beings—they are compatible and in some ways good for Earth-dweller humans.

So we help. Others help, but we help in this way. Your Sun does not support anything but natural life. Your Sun does not, then, support in many ways what happens on Earth. When things like this take place, where Earth would like earthworms and rabbits to stay or to have volunteers who will incarnate in that form on Earth, the Sun does not support that. Your Sun is not rigid, but it supports natural life. All suns do that. We know of a sun who would support that kind of volunteer earthworm soul, rabbit soul, that would come and live in an environment that is not quite as welcoming as they normally need, that's a little more hostile in terms of the type of nurturing they need to live a life on the planet. But for them to be here, they need to have certain energies from the Sun—if not this Sun, then another.

In order for that to take place, someone has to send units of support from another sun that can support life. We know how to focus this. In this case, the sun is in another part of this galaxy that you occupy, and we simply focus using techniques we have acquired. We focus and very precisely aim those energies so that they come to Earth and counterbalance the influence of the other energies—not completely, but sufficiently so that souls who volunteer to come to this more difficult place can live on Earth and be here—in this example, earthworms and rabbits.

So you do this in a way that's not technological but with your light, through your lightbeing?

We use a mechanism, but not as you understand machinery. There are no moving parts. It is something you might call spiritual, having to do with energies, but we know how to work with these energies, and they work compatibly with sun energy specifically. They are prepared to act as a temporary conduit for sun energy, and once they have delivered that energy, they continue on with their lives. But they volunteer this service of being a conduit, as you might call it.

Does this energy go through our Sun, or is it not related to our Sun at all?

It is not related, but your Sun recognizes that this is sun energy, so the Sun does not feel uncomfortable with it. The Sun recognizes that this energy is here to support unusual—that is the word I am looking for—life cycles on Earth.

Have you done this before for other beings here?

Yes, we have provided energy from other suns to Earth to support other life forms.

Can you say which ones?

Many.

For as long as this planet's been here?

For as long as the human race in the form of the Explorer Race has been here, but not immediately after you arrived. The Explorer Race didn't start using technology right away. We have supported many life forms whom the planetary consultants felt were still needed here and could live here—with some souls prepared to live here but requiring certain sun energy to do so to support their existence. So we are able to provide that for them.

I think that's wonderful. I had no idea this was needed or possible.

There's no reason for you to know because it does not require anything for the Explorer Race to do—or as you understand it, it does not require anything for human beings to do.

Your Sun Can Only Support Natural Life

Why can't our Sun support them? Is it a different frequency?

Your Sun, just like the sun in any solar system, will support, sustain and nurture life in its full and complete spectrum as it's expected to evolve—meaning what you call natural life. You understand "natural life," yes? Your people study natural life: the life cycle of a fruit fly, as you say, or the life cycle of a bobcat and all of these things. Well, you don't understand that too well because you've never lived with that being; it is hard to understand the life cycle of a stranger. But it is a little easier to understand the life cycle from a distance, and that is how your science works now, from a distance—meaning there is no intimate understanding of the life of a bobcat, but one might study bobcats from a distance.

Right. But what are some of the forms of life that are natural for this planet? Almost every form of life was brought here, wasn't it?

"Natural life" means natural life cycle. It does not exclude life forms that were brought here. Natural life cycle—not speaking for human beings, but speaking for other beings on Earth—would mean the cycle of life without any life-perpetuating external substances. For instance, human beings get sick or injured and seek medical treatment, but another Earth dweller living on the land gets sick or injured and dies. That's a natural life cycle.

Human beings who are sick or injured naturally want to help each other and use something that you create or synthesize from what is available. Natural life is not like that. This is not criticism but is just an observation. I do not place value on one or the other. but natural life . . . think of it. The Sun emits light and encourages plants to grow, yes? The planet spins, allowing for rest from the light during part of your light/dark cycle. The planet rests in natural life; plants rest. Some animals come out at night, and some come out at day—natural life. I do not know how to use other words to describe it. Natural life means that which lives on the land, sometimes under the land, maybe flies over the land, maybe lives in the water, but does not use any artificial means to perpetuate itself.

You Must Become Material Masters to Live a Natural Earth Life

Do we humans get the energy from Earth sources, or do we still get it from the Sun?

I do not know, since you do not live your natural life here. The natural life for a human being with your body, living in an environment that is ideal for you, is 700 to 800 years. But this environment is obviously not ideal for your bodies, so you are here on this planet that does not, for many of you, provide ideal circumstances. This tells me that human beings, as you know yourselves, are living an unnatural life on this planet. So you must be here to learn something—it is not natural otherwise. But other beings have been able to live in natural ways without needing technical support to stay alive. They don't put on winter coats, although sometimes they might grow extra fur, or if possible, they may fly someplace else where warmth supports and sustains life. You call that nature.

So this is not a criticism but strictly an observation that your form of life is not well adapted to the planet upon which you find yourself. You have had to adapt using artificial means, and this is to your credit, but it does not perpetuate your life to its capacity. If your physical bodies could live to be 600, 700, almost 800 years old, that tells you that there's a planet somewhere, probably many planets, where you could live a 600-, 700-, 800-year life without any artificial means and be nurtured by your surroundings. Then that would be your natural place to live.

Your Earth-human body has that capacity now. But your body takes many forms here: you are young and vigorous, then you get a little older and not so vigorous. Your life cycle is unnatural here. The environment of this planet does not nurture your life; it actually often challenges your life. You have to adapt and use artificial means to be comfortable. You have had to claim technology to support your life. Without technology, there is only one other way I know of for you to exist here on Earth, and that is to become a practicing material master.

You could have cities in very specific areas, and you as material masters could ask that conditions exist in those specific locations where humans live on Earth that are ideal for your body as it exists now. Maybe you have cities but only in specific areas, and let the rest of the planet be for other Earth dwellers. When you are material masters, the planet will respond and conditions in those locations where Earth humans live would become ideal. Then you will live your full natural life cycle and your Sun will support that.

Are you saying that now the Sun does not support humans? You have to help us?

We do not help you.

I'm sorry—you send energy to us?

We do not. But your Sun provides energy that supports and sustains unnatural life, meaning that the Sun in and of itself does not create an ideal environment on your planet for you—a survivable environment, yes, but not an ideal environment. Someday spiritual training not unlike what some you have received will support human beings to become material masters. A simple explanation of material mastery is *interacting in harmony with all life.* Then you are able to request lovingly and receive lovingly. That's the ideal situation for the human being Earth body as it exists—not as it could exist, but as it exists now—to be nurtured here.

Of course, this will stimulate you to ask yourselves, "Where is the planet that is our native planet, that will nurture and encourage us without us having to do anything?" Then you will begin the real exploration of space—no longer just going out to see what you can find. But it will require material-master individuals to feel the proper direction, to connect with the direction in a loving energy way: "Go this way, it feels better, not that way."

Navigation operates off of human feeling rather than only technology. Technology would be included, but the human feeling would be most important. "Oh, I feel good going this way," says the navigator. Other people on ship also need to be material masters, but navigators must be specifically trained for, "This way, not that," so to speak. Then the vehicle goes that way, and when you arrive, everyone is overwhelmed by a wonderful feeling of nurturing. Once you are assured that it is safe to go out, people run off the ship without even looking back to the ship for safety—they run off and are happy to be there. Everything you need is there; life support is nurturing. Everything is wonderful and fun. Then you say, "I am home." You find that home by feeling.

We Also Help Others on Other Planets

Now, I see that you are on this planet to learn something, and you are on this planet to discover how you can live more benevolently and beneficially by interacting with multiple teachers. Someday you will find your way, but we have not been asked to help you. We help others.

So you also help others on other planets?

If called for, yes. But your planet is the most frequent caller because of the unnatural situation that exists there. Yes, other times, on other planets, we help, especially if circumstances are out of sequence with natural existence. Usually in those cases, it is out of sequence only for a short time. With Earth human experience, it goes on and on, out of sequence generation after generation. But in other places, it might be out of sequence for a much shorter time.

What would cause that out-of-sequence situation on other planets: a calamity like a volcano or an earthquake or something like that?

Not necessarily any calamity—life beyond your learning environment does not much involve calamities. Calamity is something one experiences where you are, but it is not typical elsewhere.

So what would create an out-of-sequence experience on some other planet, for example?

An example might be, for instance, the birth of a planet at a distance, a star awakening, a new sun. These birth cycles happen. A temporary condition might be unexpected wave forms or light forms that have not quite learned how to go around in benevolent ways—meaning new suns are learning how and where to radiate. Or for instance, perhaps wave forms of that which produces sound or light are learning. They are young beings and need to have support that will allow them to find their way. They might be lost temporarily. It's not that they are unhappy or miserable; they just could be feeling better someplace else.

So we might focus the sun from their general home area toward where they are. Once they feel that, it's like, "Oh, *now* I can find my way." Or there might be other things that may not fit into the ideas you have and need to have on your planet. These are temporary situations, though—brief compared to sustaining Earth dwellers on Earth, which might go on for generations.

Planets Thrive by Attracting Other Life

So suns actually have to learn how to radiate and how to focus their energies?

Suns are not creators; they are beings like everyone else. They have a cycle of learning and even have a time of sleep, meaning they produce light, heat, and so on, for a given amount of their experience (the life cycle of a sun), and then they might get quiet and sleep for a time. They might even become another form of life once they choose to awaken again. Suns, when they experience sleep, often do not awaken as suns again. It is generally a one-time experience. One is a sun, and then one often chooses to be something other than a sun.

What would be an example of a being choosing to be something other than a sun?

Maybe after sleep time one might choose to be the core of a planet, which may form up around them. Planetary cores are often very dense and strong and very stable—planetary cores must be very stable. Many planetary cores I know of used to be suns. So you might say that a sleeping sun offers the potential for a planetary seed.

What about the core of our planet? Had it been a sun?

Yes, it had been a sun, but it remembers having been a sun so that at the times when it is entirely hot and molten, it feels completely natural. This is essential. Then there are other times, your scientists have noticed, that the core of the earth resonates a little differently. The core might not be as molten then—perhaps liquid, but not as hot. When any planet dies—and "dies" simply means sleeps; there's no death really—the core of the planet often solidifies. It does not become entirely cool, but it solidifies and remains warm should the planet choose to express sustaining life capacities—meaning become welcoming on the surface or slightly below the surface so that other life is attracted to it.

Planets thrive by having attractions for other life. Then the other life comes and the planet enjoys the other life and the mutual existence. The other life exudes something, perhaps feelings that the planet enjoys, and it is a mutually benevolent experience. Then maybe for this or that reason, the planet may wish to sleep. It often gives a long time of advanced notice that change is going to take place—sleep, maybe ice, something like that, giving examples you can identify. Then there's a long prediction of that change, so other life forms, natural life forms, know this is true and can choose then to incarnate elsewhere.

So life forms perpetuate, but possibly they look different because they adapt in appearance to other planets—sometimes, not always. On your planet, it is not unusual to find souls adapted in a different form than they might look in their home environment. But this is because volunteers of many Earth dwellers who come here are perhaps a bit more adventurous and prepared to enjoy different forms, at least temporarily during their life cycles here.

On Your Home Planet, You Have a Natural Life Cycle

I can really feel your energy; I'm kind of tingling all over. I like it.

We could support and sustain your life for the two of you. Your energies were not at their best before the session.

Have you ever done this before? Talked through someone?

Usually to other Earth dwellers or to other beings. We have not communicated through or to human beings before.

So there are many beings on your home planet or home place—there are many of you, right?

There are not too many in terms of your count. But we take up more space than you do.

You've always done this?

This is what we do, but we do not, as you say, live forever. I have been in existence . . . I will try to explain in terms of no time. I have been in existence before your Explorer Race arrived on Earth but not much before that. I will be in existence for a while yet. It is hard to describe our life cycle in your terminology; it's simply a long time.

But you have memories of having another experience before this one?

It is not necessary for us to have such memories, and they might perhaps be a distraction. We do not define recollections like that to support our lives, as we exist where we exist. We exist in our present and unified field of existence from the beginning to the end, and yet all of the beings where I reside do not consider previous life or what is to come. In my experience, these natural cycles are self-sustaining. They do not require my recollections or anticipations to be nurtured in their existence.

I understand: You just know that at some point you were something else.

We do not even think about it. Just as I think your people do not think too much about what you will be either. You are mostly struggling to survive while you are here. That is a main thing, because life where you are is not natural for you. You are not home, but you will find your own way there.

That's the first time anyone has ever said that. Thank you for that. I want to ask this again, even though I asked this before, but I wanted to make sure. Even though we are in an unnatural cycle, the Sun in this system does support our lives and our energies, right?

It supports you, but not in the same way that the sun in your home planet supports you. The sun there supports your life so that you can live, as you might say, the way the animals live on Earth. But nobody eats each other there—you just feel supported and nurtured. For example, you don't eat as much there because the sun's rays there support and sustain you. You are not like a plant, but you are supported and sustained there very much so from the sun. Instead of you picking an apple from a tree and eating it, there you might be able to go up to that tree and simply hold an apple—it might not be an apple, but you understand—up to your mouth and breathe, take a deep breath in, and it would be like food. You don't have to eat the apple; the apple does not have to be consumed. You are sustained simply by the energy of the apple.

You hold the apple, pull it toward your mouth without bending the branch too much. You hold up the fruit, take it to your mouth maybe or perhaps just a little distance from it, but the apple being cupped by your hand knows what is needed. Then you breathe. You take in big deep breaths, and that energy from the apple sustains you. Now, everyone doesn't line up behind you to take deep breaths from that same apple; they will go to other apples. The apple then will be released, go back up, and hang on the branch. It goes on with its life.

You do not have to eat, as you understand it, on your home planets. Here you eat, your physical body must do much processing of what you eat, and often you have complications from what you eat. There consumption is different. Sometimes you do take in food as you know it, but it is very easy to digest. Your digestion system has adapted a bit being here. When you are home, your digestion system will be returned to its normal way of being—"normal" meaning natural life cycle there at home.

For instance, certain organs will resume their natural size, which is much smaller. It will take awhile, but over time the intestine length will shorten by perhaps six and a half feet because not so much will be needed. Your heart will become a little smaller. Your physical stature will not be as tall, maybe just five feet, five feet two, something like that. Everybody will be pretty trim with no disease ever.

A natural life cycle means birth without pain: The baby is much smaller but comes out easy to nurture. Mothers will feed baby in the same way you do now with breast milk, but birth will cause no pain. Babies will be smaller and will not cause misery for mothers to give birth. When the end of your natural cycle comes, a person just gets tired, more and more tired, and feels like going to sleep. You lie down and go to sleep, and you don't wake up. It is a nice gentle passage of soul from one form to another. It's nothing like what you have here—no trauma, no accidents, no misery like that. Then you can pursue other endeavors.

Life Is Unending

Can't we learn now on Earth to adapt to eating less and living simply, and bring ourselves closer to that ideal?

You will have to adapt, perhaps because the environment can only provide so much. You have population increases, and you desire for your population to not only increase but to have an improved quality of life. Naturally, the knowledge and wisdom is needed by this population where you are to know, understand and embrace material mastery, so I honor these. You are putting out books like that which are very helpful. Someday also perhaps you can publish sound things [audio] that people can listen to.

Some people respond better to verbal sounds because their minds do not have the concentration to read and think. But those sound things do not have to be long; they can be twenty minutes, something like that. You might even have different things: They listen for a few minutes, stop, then maybe listen to music for a while. Some can only take so much life revelation at once.

In your future, not necessarily for what you will do, but someday people will take sound from speaking and add a little musical background. Perhaps the person will have a choice of music. I have observed while we have conversed that this is a popular fad now for your people, some of your amusements. But the ultimate application of these things you are providing to the human race to achieve material mastery by steps will be a visual presentation with all kinds of gestures. At some point you will have other means, you will have a whole arrangement like theaters have, which creates an environment that looks like plants, trees, what you call a theatrical effect. Then the speaker comes through with much hand waving [chuckles], a little more animated than my delivery.

Are there other ways of getting energy that we might not know about?

Well, I do not feel so much that I am a teacher but more that I inform you of things and occasionally make comments, not intended to drive you toward that, but just things that I can see. We help beings to live in environments that are not always the best for them. Since we need to understand the needs of those dwellers or those beings, we also have some necessary familiarity of who they are and what they might need. In conversations such as this, I have had moments where I could do more than one thing at once. I have observed your society somewhat, and I can see that your society hungers for this knowledge and almost as much hungers to be assured that existence on your planet has meaning and purpose beyond that which appears obvious. So I am happy to contribute in some small way to assure you that your life has infinite unending variety according to my brief experience.

"Ending" is a word in your culture, but in my experience, true ending does not exist. Something may stop for a time, such as a sun sleep cycle, but that sun as you have known it reawakens at some point, perhaps as a planetary seed. Then more grows or is attracted when that sun becomes prepared to be the core of a planet. This process is not unlike the process of a planet itself. It releases a feeling that attracts other material to come to be joined, and over time enough is there to look like a planet as you understand it. But there are other ways too—I only give you that as an example that life is unending.

[Chuckles.] This takes practice. I try to drink water through the nose—not his intention. The body you have is not like my own.

Enjoy Your Earth Experience

Perhaps that is enough. I could finish with flourish, but . . . you like humor? We like humor also. Humor, I have noticed, seems to exist everywhere, so you do not have to give it up when you move on.

I will finish then. Feel free to request me some time when you are tired. You will hear my voice maybe in your head. It might be something already said, it might be a recollection, but energy will be present. I cannot guarantee this every time, but if I am available, you might feel me a little bit. But don't use that as a substitute for rest.

Now I bid you good living in your temporary home. This is a good school home for you, but soon a bell will ring, and you will leave school and go on and enjoy life elsewhere. If you know that you are in school, then you know you won't be there forever. When your life cycle ends, you will go on to something much easier, but you will remain sentimental for quite a while and talk about your Earth experience, naturally forgetting discomfort because your next life will not have much experience with discomfort. So you will talk about Earth adventures sometimes to friends, and you will sometimes meet others who have lived here during a similar cycle.

In time, the memories will fade, and you will embrace life where you are as always. There are many of us in existence who support your life, just as there are those in existence who support our life. This is natural—each portion of life supporting the other is natural lives. You are a portion of natural life; you are just not home yet. But someday you will be and then life will be much more fun. For now, enjoy school as much as you can and someday things will be easier. Good experience.

CHON-DEH • • • **85**

♄ Saturn

SATURN

Reminds You of Your Purpose on Earth and That You Need to Serve Your Purpose

May 28, 2004

This is Saturn.

Welcome!

I will say that my job for the Earth human beings is to remind you of your purpose and why you came to Earth. It is not for me to know your purpose but rather to remind you at various times that your purpose needs to be served. Other than that, you will have to ask specific questions.

It Is My Pleasure to Be Here

I understand that because you're a gas giant, you're not fully incarnated here?

How did you get that information? Oh, I see—from your scientists.

It was something one of the other planets said. You're ensouling the planet Saturn. Have you ensouled other planets before this?

Nowhere in this realm, but I've had some exposure. I'm not comfortable calling it "ensouling." I understand your attempt to create a frame of reference, but I'd rather say that I'm the portion of the Saturn personality that can relate to you for the purpose of this book, exploring various elements of the astrologic and astronomic world.

That portion is a small portion of who you are?

It is that which is the most accessible for you. I see no advantage in attempting to communicate to you in the mathematical equivalent, for example.

What's the word instead of "ensouling"? What do you want me to use?

I have no problem with "ensouling," but "ensouling," for a human being, would always and only have to do with an agenda.

Ah! A soul purpose.

Yes. You don't come here without that. But it doesn't apply to a planet. It's not that I don't have a purpose for being; being is its own purpose.

So why are you here?

I don't know how to answer that question. Oh, you want to know if I am here for some reason of my own entirely separate from what human beings on Earth are doing. Is that what you are asking?

Well, yes. Were you asked? Did you choose? Why you, and why that particular form of planet?

These are questions human beings ask because you do not know why you are where you are because of your Explorer Race experience.

Our ignorance, yes.

I understand the framework of your question now. But I am here where I am because it is my pleasure to be here. When you have lives away from your school, then that will be your response as well. I grant that it is a generalized response, but it is . . . how can we say it? I feel hard-pressed to say I am here for this or that reason. I am not here to accomplish or gain anything that I don't already have. Is that helpful? Perhaps not.

Are parts of your personality available to us through what we see in this dimension and other parts of you available to other layers or levels of the Earth?

Yes, perhaps you could say that. Certainly the part of my existence that is in any way supportive to the human population on Earth would not be very helpful to you if you were a frog on Earth, but then frogs do not require my existence, though they might require the existence of water planets as a home source, you understand. But they would not, to give you an example, require my existence.

But the Earth and Mars are solid, rocky planets, whereas it was my understanding that Saturn wasn't as solid and physical?

It's like this: If there was fog in front of you but you knew there was a wall beyond the fog, you could, if you felt reasonably certain that it was safe, pick up a rubber ball and throw it through the fog and strike the wall. Maybe the ball would even come through the fog back to you, yes? I will say this. If you were—metaphorically speaking, but also in physical Earth terms—able to pick up a ball and throw it with the proper velocity (not something destructive) and strike Saturn, it would bounce back. In short, we're not speaking of something that does not have substance.

Some Planets Encourage Individual Expression

Can you tell me the purpose of the rings and what they're comprised of?

Their purpose is purely beauty. Scientists already have a pretty fair idea that they are comprised of bits of pieces of reflective and refractive matter, but they are purely an expression of beauty. They are beautiful, are they not?

They certainly are.

Many of the planets who revolve around your Sun are geared to inspire and support individualistic beauty and representations of life on Earth, to support and encourage people to be different in similar ways. By this, I mean that human beings all look one basic way, but you have people of different colored skin, different colored hair and so on.

Different shapes, different sizes, yes.

As well they have different personal desires to wear, for instance, this color of lipstick or that type of earring or different colors of garments. So the planets are essentially supporting and nurturing individual beauty as expressed through similar life forms. The planets are all similar in many ways, but they each look different in their own way.

What led you to show your beauty as the rings? Had you seen this somewhere else, or had you been this somewhere else? Or is it a common thing in other planets?

It is not unknown on other planets in other places. I had been aware of it someplace else—had seen it, as you say. But we planets do not see the way human beings see with eyes. So I was aware of it other places and I found it attractive.

The Real Measurement of Time Is Experience

The Earth has sent a spaceship out there that's going around Saturn and photographing it, and if I remember right, it's going to land on one of your moons, Titan. They want to know if the moons have ever had human life on them in the past.

You mean Earth human?

Well, human life.

I am not aware of any Earth human life having visited or set up an existence for a time. There have been other beings from other places who have landed occasionally just to rest, if their vehicles needed some repair, or sometimes just to explore.

But it's never had a civilization on it or a sustained community?

Nothing of any civilization that I'm aware of. There was for a short time a small underground repair facility having to do with ships from a distant planet, but a more benevolent surrounding was found by them. I think the cold was the problem.

What about your planet? Has there ever been life on this dimension, or is there life on other layers or levels of yourself, sustained civilization?

That is more than one question, so I will answer in a particular order. There is not at this time in your expression of existence where you are focused—I don't call that a dimension, but rather I call it a focus—any life that you would recognize on my surface or even underneath the surface. But if you're saying simultaneously to your focus of existence, are there other versions of myself hosting life, then the answer is yes. It does not . . . how can we say?

It has nothing to with us?

With you whatsoever. They are their own forms. They do not in that sense have any resemblance to you, they don't look like you, they don't relate to you, I don't think. They might not even be aware of you. So I'm not sure that is very helpful.

You said there is not now in our focus any life that resembles us. Has there been in the past?

You have to remember that your past is a very short run of time, because the past of the Earth that you occupy at the moment is very short. I'm answering when looking at the fact that your past is a very brief time. Earth is not in existence as you experience yourself in this time of polarities for very long. No planet could exist with polarities like what exists for human life—and to some extent for animal and plant life. No planet could exist like that for very long.

Can you give me any idea how long it has existed like that?

We do not use measurements. I will just say that no planet can exist with such polarities for a very long experiential time. I will say, on the other hand, that when your scientists, with the best of intentions, tell you that this piece of rock is so many millions of years old and all of that, that it is possible to create something that would appear to be millions of years old in your measurement of time. But it's also a measurement of experience when looked at in the broader context of a year. You can live a year and you can say, "I lived a year," but during that year you had a great deal of experience, did you not?

So in the larger sense, when you refer to years, you're talking about experience. It is possible to create something that might show itself in your current scientific capacity as being millions of years old while having had very little experience. The real measurement of time is experience. As I say, you can say, "I just lived a year," but that doesn't mean anything. If, however, you related to someone or kept some kind of record of what you did for that year, the description would be lengthy, would it not? That would be a description of an experiential year, having very little relationship to the actual measurement of time.

This tells you that it is possible—you might not understand this, but someone might—to create something that measures millions of years but has had very little experience in that time. This means that you could pick up a rock on the Earth as you now experience it and ask, if you could, for the rock to explain its experience. Unless its experience equaled what a rock, say, on another planet might give you, in terms of even a year, an experiential year . . . a year to a rock would be longer than a year to you. But say it related its experience. It would be vast, a great deal of experience on another planet, not in your school. A rock on your planet, however, no matter whether the scientist tells you it's so many millions of years old, would have very little experience.

This tells you that experientially your past is a very short time indeed. A rock is a frequent experience on Earth, yes? Everybody sees rocks; they're everywhere. But if a rock has had very little experience, then you know that no matter how old it is on the basis of how it can be dated, it really isn't that old, because its experience does not amount to much.

Here I'm trying to explain the difference between experiential time and calendar time, and also to explain how it is possible to create a planet—or a version of the planet, if you like—that offers a great deal of variety, offers all of the things that you experience in your school, but its existence does not go back very far. It can be measured and proven scientifically that a rock is, say, four, five, six, eight, ten, twelve million years old, just for an example. But if I ask the rock, "Tell me your experience," the rock proves to me that it has had, say, about 40,000 years of experiential time, regardless of how many millions of years "old" it might seem to be. So I am trying to explain the physics, the chemistry to a degree and the mathematics of the difference between your experiential Earth and, say, another version of Earth, or another planet somewhere that is not engaged in Explorer Race time.

Learning to Travel in Space and Time without a Vehicle

If one knows these things, one can learn how to travel in space and time with or without a vehicle. I gave that for those physicists out there who are attempting to understand the nature of velocity. Velocity can, for example, be utilized to explain moving from point A to point B, but if one wishes to travel great distances, one must use the means of measuring velocity. Even if you wish to go from A to B, you have to measure velocity from B to itself and include point A where you are.

So you have to be pulled from point B *to* point B, where you wish to go. You cannot push yourself. If you push yourself, you will leave from the place that has everything that is associated with that place (this is important for physicists). You will leave from point A, being your world, your time, your concepts, your experience, you understand? If you wish to go to point B, which might be on the other side of the universe, and you don't have an inexhaustible amount of lifetimes to get there, then the only way to get there is to utilize the means, manners, methods and existence of point B. You don't use your concepts, experiences of your point A. You use point B's concepts. Point B's concepts might not in any way be based on propulsion velocity. In fact, it is more likely that it will be based on attraction capacity.

With attraction capacity, one can move without a vehicle in order to explore whether such a place might be capable of supporting life as you know it, and also whether it might welcome life as you know it (or at least life as you know it that can be adapted to such a place). One travels to that point on the basis of given parameters that you are attempting to find or even on the basis of desired parameters—meaning descriptions of what you are hoping to find—even if you have no reason to believe it exists anywhere. In that way, you do not have the experience of any form of limit. You can see, you can examine, you can experience, but you do not bring any part of you that can in any way be damaged or cause damage.

This is what has been referred to by some beings through this channel in the past, I believe, as feminine science—having to do with attraction rather than propulsion. You must use the feminine exclusively to get there to observe, to see, and then have the means to describe it when you experience the end of that travel. This is for those of you who are working on long-distance exploration and wish to do so much more cheaply, and who would also like to be able to discover if is it worth your effort to send a mission (meaning will you be supported, and so on).

It is very important to understand velocity beyond the limit of propulsion, and yet your current theories, naturally, have to do with velocity based on propulsion. But as the feminine becomes more expressed on your planet . . . which is necessarily so, if for no other reason than with the overpopulation of human beings on your planet, the feminine must be more expressed. The feminine is more aware. It is conscious. It does not miss the obvious. I do not wish to sound that I am speaking from some point of superiority versus inferiority—nothing like that—but rather, the feminine must notice because it always feels.

So regardless of what is stated as theoretical thought or possible extrapolation, for example, the feminine has first and foremost to do with feeling and secondary, but compatibly speaking, also has to do with touch, meaning: "I feel; I touch." The two are compatible and support each other—given that it is not possible, utilizing feminine science or feminine capacities in this way, to avoid in any way the obvious. The obvious is something that can be felt, something that can be touched. There is no mystery about it; it's right there. But in your time of exploring possibilities, maybes, with the mind, if that becomes excessively the case (as it has been for the past few hundred years in your cycle of life on the planet), it is very possible to overlook the obvious.

Oh, thank you. Thank you very much. That was all unexpected, an extra bonus.

It is in my nature to be mathematical, but it is also in my nature to wish to explain in terms that many people who read this book will understand. Still, it is in my nature to desire to interpret mathematics, form (as you understand it), into applicable function in your time and, of course, in your place. What is most important for you to understand is that the rules you think apply in science are very limited concepts that are accepted because they are provable in your time—therefore, it is reasonable to accept them. But if you know, at least philosophically, that these rules do not apply in other places, it might be possible to explore these other places without having to bring your rules along.

If you bring your rules along, you will not see what is really there. That can be applied on a personal, individual basis on your planet from person to person now. How many people say to other people, "You just don't understand me"? They say that because the other persons are applying their rules of existence as they understand them, and they don't see you because they're not applying your rules of existence to you. It can be applied on a personal basis. You don't have to go to another planet to experiment with this.

Yes, but I've never heard it expressed like that. That's wonderful.

Astrology Provides a Means to Understand Yourself

Saturn is the teacher in astrology, right?

I would not stake that claim to that title exclusively. I think you will find, communicating with other planets and even systems, that they will have plenty to teach.

How did it happen that what you do is to remind people of their purposes?

It is my personality.

Ah! So astrology works on the basis of the planets' personalities?

That is my perspective. The attempt of astrology as it comes more into itself and comes more into its time of appreciation is to utilize the personalities of the planets (and to some lesser extent, the moons) to help an individual explore and understand the facets of your own personality on the basis of the concentration of the elements of your own personality when compared to the personalities we express. So it is a way—not the only way, but it is a way—to explore potentials for yourself so that you can discover where you might look to find hidden talents for yourself, where you might look to find strength, things you might do more easily, and where you might also look to discover why certain things are more difficult for you—and, if possible, that you allow those avenues to be explored by others who might have strength there.

You have seen clearly in your own societies as you structure them that some people do this and some people do that. Sometimes a person will do something, and he or she will seem to be very good at it. Other times another person will do that thing, and he or she might struggle with it. Perhaps that person doesn't have as much capacity on the soul level that supports the personality and the desire to do given things. This is not always associated with profession; it might more easily be found in the characteristics of personality. So astrology can be very helpful to understand the characteristic of your personality: where you might find your strength, where your talents might lie in general application, and what areas might be better for you to seek out and express to the best of your ability and to the best of your capacity.

So, of course, given that, it is very practical. One can work very, very, very hard and accomplish only so much in a given area, whereas another person who has capacity in that area might be able to work much less vigorously and gain more. This does not mean that you are stupid; rather, it means that your talents lie elsewhere. If you were exploring those areas, you might reasonably find that you might be able to work to a lesser degree and still be able to accomplish a great amount.

This is not Creator's way of saying, "You do this and you do that." It is rather Creator's way of demonstrating—speaking for Creator in this case—"I have put you all here on this planet to help one another. I did not expect you all to do the same thing. Therefore, I am distributing talents, abilities, desires, proclivities, and so on, among you in such a way as none of you have to do the same thing as others. In short, the whole of you makes up all that you need to do."

Therefore, Creator has made an attempt to provide you with various means to understand that what is available for one of you might be something different than what's available for another. These studies—astrology, for example—are attempts to make life easier; this is not an attempt to create a complication. Everyone does not have to understand it, but it is useful to understand at least your role, given the concept in teaching—to understand something about yourself and who you are and what you are and what might be easier for you to do.

A good astrologer may not be able to tell you what kind of job you ought to do, but he or she might be able to say that you will find this easier or you might find that more fascinating, and so on. These things are good to know, especially in this time of an attempt to receive higher education to prepare oneself as a student in college for a given career. But, in fact, if astrology were fully integrated in that, students might be able to avoid going into studying areas where their talents and abilities would not make that study easy for them.

So I am simply saying that for those of you who will probably have to do the study for future careers that will be demanded of you, many of your future careers are not laid out yet. A student says, "Well, I have four years or perhaps even six, and at the end of that six, I'd like to come out fully prepared for a job." Yet as many students know in your time, "How can I make my plan now for a job that doesn't even exist yet?" I will say, "Start with astrology to see where you might find your talents and abilities, as well as what you might find to be of interest to explore in this way," since Creator has given and nurtured this system over time and provided planets with personalities like myself. You might prepare yourself for the unknown career of the future.

Is astrology known on other planets? Is it used everywhere or just here because we are ignorant of who we are and what all of our abilities are?

It is more in use in a place such as this where you have hints available as to who and what you are. In a place where you know who and what you are, such a study would be something perhaps for a research student, someone who wishes to explore the capabilities of the study. But it is something that is more found in schools like this, to help you to the best of your ability.

Creator does not want to keep from you your talents and abilities, but because it's a school, Creator would like for you to demonstrate your personal interests and say, "Well, I will look here and see what I am likely to be good at, and I will then explore that area first. If I don't find something, then I will continue to explore the areas where I seem to have the most ability. If I still don't find something I'm interested in, perhaps I can at least do a job in those areas to make a living and to continue to explore other areas, and maybe I will find something that I'm interested in." That's largely what's going on now. People get jobs, but a lot of the jobs people get are very often in areas where they don't have talents or abilities, and they're more likely in that case to struggle in those jobs or even make mistakes that might be avoided by someone who had more talent in that area.

I'm not talking about brainpower; I'm just talking about what capacities you were born with. Astrology is intended to support you to find what you were born with, to see what works well and easily for you, and those ought to be the best areas in which to seek your employment, from my perspective.

You Connect to Certain Planets Before You Are Born

How does astrology work?

Let me help you. For your sake, I will apply my mathematical talk. I was giving hints about space travel, but it applies in many ways. If you say, "How does it work, being born and taking note of the position of planets? How does it work that way?"—it is the other way. Suppose you, as a soul, wish to come to this planet at this time and be a part of the Explorer Race and all of what they may do. You might say, "Well, I have an interest in doing this or that on this planet," and then your teachers might say, "In that case, we would like you to use all of the support that is available to you in this world, given that you will only have a short time there." Others have spoken to you about this as I am speaking to you now, that one does not live a life of any great length on Earth—a hundred years, generally, at the most. Occasionally people go past that.

So the teachers say to the soul, "You must use the support system that is available to give, to energize and to sustain the qualities within your soul as it expresses itself through Earth—meaning Earth life—that exist beyond Earth, because Earth is very complicated where you are going: many people, many things going on." Given the population of human beings of the Explorer Race on Earth, it is too much to expect Earth to support your personality's desires. But on other planets where the population is considerably less, if any, in terms of human beings, these planets can easily support the qualities that you wish to demonstrate and seek out in your soul's expression of Earth life. So you connect to those planets and places first, and *then* you are born on the Earth. That's how it works.

The planets themselves support qualities in the personal expression, the individual expression of personality, by any given life form on Earth. In this case, we are talking about human beings. So you as a soul, before your incarnation, even before the sperm has entered the egg—just in the talking stage [laughs]—connect with your teacher here, not having anything to do with your physical mother or father yet. You then go around and make your introductions, so to speak; you connect with these planets and other places referred to in the astrological realm of study. You connect to all of these places that will support your Earth personality. Then you wait until the mother, the father, the conditions, the time, the place, everything occurs that is ideal and synchronous to your capability, your desire, your connection—meaning what you want to do there. In order to do this, you will need to do it at a certain moment of measured Earth experience, also known as time, when the exact moment occurs. Then those are your parents.

You don't pick your parents; it's not like that at all. That has confused many researchers and has caused a lot of confusion in the exploration of past lives, and it has essentially made karma almost impossible to understand, except as a theory. I don't intend to go into an explanation of karma; I'm going to keep it to astrology.

That's completely opposite to what I thought. You make the connection and then wait for those energies to come into alignment and then get born. [Laughs.]

That's right. That supports and sustains your personality beyond Earth, so Earth is not forced to do that. Now, if we go back a little bit in time and there are, say, 30,000 or 40,000 people on Earth, then Earth herself can support each and every personality. But now, with millions, billions living on Earth, the planets must support the personalities. There are other influences that astrology uses, but I will just say the "planets" for the sake of simplicity.

Here You Can Learn Certain Information About the Unknown

How would people connect to you? What would they have in mind when they connect to you?

Well, pick up an astrology book yourself and read the qualities.

They're pretty accurate?

They're pretty accurate; I don't think I have much to add. I would guess that most people who connect to me, though, would have a desire on the soul level to have an inquiring mind. Not everyone is like that. Some people don't need to know more, or they are comfortable knowing what they know. But I think that is all well and thoroughly explained in most good astrology books. You understand, many astrology books are written for the public, but some are written for other astrologers, in which case there is considerably more detail. But I am feeling that the detail most books have right now is sufficient. Barring a more technical question, that's my answer.

Well, until I study a little more, you're not getting too many technical questions from me.

The advantage, however, of you asking is that we do not wander off in fields that are purely technical and of little or no interest to most people. So there is not a great disadvantage in your asking. I recognize that the original intent of this book was to support and sustain astrologers, but I believe the book has gone beyond that vision right now, which is why I gave you that answer about you asking questions. However, a good astrologer, someone who has been doing it for a long time, might come up with questions that you would find interesting.

If you do ask an astrologer to come up with questions, though, ask him or her to ask them in plain language. You don't want to require the reader to be an astrologer. A reasonable question from an astrologer might be, "How can we support the inquirer"—meaning whoever's asking the astrologer—"to know things about himself or herself for which we have no information." In this sense, there's a pretty good understanding of how Mars moves in its orbit, and so on, but there's very vague information about other planets. In short, the astrologer might ask, "How can we, on the basis of what we know, get more information that will help us to answer questions that come from what we might call the blank area of astrology, meaning what's missing?" And I will say, turn that around.

Rather than looking for information as you do now to answer the questions of the inquirer, study the inquirer's personality—find the portions of his or her personality that do not fit into astrology. You don't have to do this with all your inquirers, just the ones who pique your curiosity because they demonstrate something that is clearly not in any way directly aligned with the studies you've been able to accomplish, even if you consult with other people's expertise.

Working together as astrologers, you might accumulate characteristics that are not apparently supported by the literature and the research. When you have a body of these characteristics, it might be possible to use them as a means of identifying the planets or the astronomical entities that support these characteristics. Let me know if you have accumulated enough of these characteristics, and I will answer these questions directly.

I know some of you are attracted to certain names, but it is less important for you to have a name for an astronomical body than to understand that astronomical body's personality. Then you can have a means by which you can state to these individuals with characteristics for which you cannot provide the information they would need or require (or at least to assist yourself in understanding how to help them): "I can provide certain information about the unknown."

So you're saying that we have influences on the human-body energies from planets we're connected to, and that here on Earth we're not aware of these influences?

You cannot prove them scientifically. You can prove the existence of various planets in your solar system out to the point where you have the capacity to become aware of something, "Is this a planet? Is it orbiting?" and so on, such as in the location where you know the planet Pluto was essentially proven to exist. Did you know that that took place right where you are now in residence?

Yes, at Lowell Observatory here in Flagstaff, Arizona.

Yes, and it's quite famous internationally.

Three Additional Planets Are Available for You

You now have the capacity, with various instruments in space as well as instruments that are traveling out from your Earth, to discover other planets that might exist. So that is useful. Recently, I believe, it was celebrated that your space capsule, which you sent out in the Voyager series [launched in 1977], was leaving your solar system [in 1990]. I will say that Voyager has not left your solar system; it's simply gone past the uncharted.

Therefore, to the degree not only that scientific information might still in some diluted way be receivable, at least by other capsules moving in that general direction, and then relayed to Earth, it might also be useful for those of you who can relate to a portion of a machine—meaning those of you who are channels or psychics, as it's called—you might be able to familiarize yourself with some type of metal or combinations of metal or combinations of materials that are making up that space capsule and identify it. It's not an entity, it's not someone, but it is made up of the things that make it up, yes? You might be able to acquire information, riding along with those materials, about those other planets in your solar system, of which I am prepared to tell you at this time that there are three.

Well, why don't we just ask them to talk to us?

You might.

[Laughs.] That would be fun. You're from beyond this Creation, right? This universe? When did you become aware of yourself?

I have always been aware of myself. You understand, you are using time to identify personality, so the question, of no fault of your own, is limited to the constructs. Let's put into application what I've been teaching today and rephrase your question. Shall we? I will help you.

You were around; you were conscious before Creator came out to create this universe, right?

That's a good beginning. That was a good effort on your part, but let me help you. You might say, "In order to express the nature of your existence, can you explain how you assimilated your own personality characteristics?" See, that eliminates time. So I think that's a good question for tomorrow.

♄ Saturn

SATURN

Earth Gives You the Joy of Discovery

May 29, 2004

This is Saturn

Welcome.

My Personality Was Formed Long Before I Became a Planet

The places where the Explorer Race resides are many and varied and multifaceted. Therefore, I as Saturn must present a certain countenance in my nature to the Explorer Race as you send out your probes and ultimately send out your visitors to see what I'm all about (and all the other planets as well). So I must be able to reflect a face of myself to you that will make sense to you in your world of the moment, meaning at times gone by, simply by being something beautiful in the sky—"What is that thing with those rings? Isn't that beautiful?"—and then in images, as the world of science comes into play, having something that can send back pictures or that which can be converted to pictures and the greater detail.

Ultimately, as transportation over great distances becomes easier and quicker, I will need to express other qualities that will make sense to you in your situation: mentally, spiritually and as feeling beings. Therefore, as a planet I need to have that quality. But equally, since there are other beings in existence, in residence or sometimes even just passing by in other realms of presentation of myself—realms where the Explorer Race will not come, will not even visit, and really doesn't even need to know very much about—those facets of my existence will be meant to nurture, support and otherwise lend aid and comfort to those who will come and visit in those places.

In short, my personality was formed long before I became a planet, or at least since I have taken on the chore [chuckles] of being a multifaceted personality being with a vast capability for nurturance in its many faces and guises to multiple visitors, populations and even reacquaintanceship. This is my essential personality as you will find me. Now, you might reasonably ask—and you did— "How did you come to have this personality?" Well, I have described reasons why I have those characteristics already, but the core of my personality has to do with a desire to awaken and, in the case of some, to reawaken individuals, beings and groups of beings to their talents and abilities that will help them to benevolently create for the greater good of all beings.

Therefore, you can see how, with a personality like that, being a planet fits right into my general demeanor. On a smaller scale, you might reasonably find or from time to time meet human beings like that. Granted, they are human beings; they are not planets. But the fact that they have those qualities might mean that they have been in some other time or place a planet or they might be training to do that. Or they might be involved or will be involved or have been involved [chuckles] in some other activity that allows them to nurture and support benevolent creation in, by or for others. Perhaps I am biased, given my nature [chuckles], but I feel that these are worthwhile qualities to have.

You might also, living on your planet with many and varied life forms, notice these qualities in nonhumans. Some of you who work with the plant world have noticed these qualities in some plants; certainly fruit or food-bearing plants might be said to have these qualities. Think of it: An apple tree bears fruit that nurtures people, while at the same time it chooses to reproduce itself by placing its seed within that most attractive element of itself. Therefore, simply by being and by perpetuating its own being, it nurtures and supports.

There are also other types of beings. Many of you have plant friends, but many of you also have animal friends. You can think of many—a dog, a cat, a horse, even a bird—who have nurtured you and loved you and supported you simply because that's how they are. It is, I feel, a good way to be. So you are not held away from such sources of nurturance. Look around in your own world and from time to time glance in the mirror. Maybe you have qualities like that, too.

What was your experience before you expressed as Saturn?

You understand, I can only tell you what you can relate to—not only you as the speaker for the human race, but also what your readers and others can relate to. There's no point in telling you things that bear no point of experience ("bear" meaning carry, can weigh, can hold), so there are some things that have no point in saying. I will simply say that all life, without exception, has always existed, and the construct of time is essentially a means—not unlike a tool one might use to work on a vehicle or paint a house, and so on, work on a patient perhaps—to understand one or more elements of creation, which is why your question is naturally framed in that construct.

So I will answer your question this way, though it might seem to be oblique. When I answer questions in an oblique manner, this tells you that this manner of answering demonstrates my faith in your capability, not in your incapability. So even though my answer to come might not seem relevant, it will be relevant in time as you have experience.

Now, this is what I did before I became focused in my determination to maintain Saturn as an available being. [Laughs.] Before that time, I was in existence throughout all universes awaiting some means to express myself that would be of service. I might add that you all do this as well.

So there was a call or you felt a need and you came here?

Creator sent out a request, and since I exist everywhere as you do, that request was naturally felt by me. It felt like something that could be, for the most part, an enjoyable experience for me and also would allow me to express my core being in a benevolent way for all beings. [Chuckles.] One has to allow for the Explorer Race's sense of adventure and need to learn sometimes the same thing in many different ways—and sometimes even the same things the same way [chuckles]. Accumulation of experience is sometimes a good way to learn. Other times, as you know [chuckles], it's just annoying.

You Are Here to Learn Something New

The name "Saturn"—did you express that to the point that someone felt it and named you that, or did you channel it through someone in earlier times? How did we get that name?

It's purely a temporary name. I think you can look it up, where it came from, and so on. I do not call myself that, but for the sake of simplicity, I have no difficulty with that—how can we say?—sound.

You said that humans, while still in spirit, go to the various sources of energy and connect with them according to their plans or their purposes for their next lives. How do they connect, since they have nothing to connect to—they're a spirit? Does it go into the DNA? What anchors that on the planet? How does that work?

Did I not say that you are just like me? The way it works for me is the identical way it works for you, because you are not human beings. Yes, you are human beings at the moment, but you are more than that. You are your immortal personality. The DNA is simply an expression allowed and supported and nurtured by the Creator of this universe, but it is not the only way you do things. When you come to do something, to offer a service, to live, to experience life, you will have certain general things that you might wish to do, not unlike myself as I described it. You might have other things that you will simply allow for to support the things you want to do, especially given the wide variety available on Earth—perhaps a little wider than many might wish to experience other places.

Nevertheless, it is that you are determined to learn something new. Every one of you who comes here is overridingly determined to learn something new, and not just a new way of doing (though absolutely you are determined in that). That is why there is so much variety here, why things are unusual, why it is possible to learn something new or experience something new that is wholly individualistic to the life you have here, because Creator allows that. Of course, it might or might not in large part have any bearing on what you do away from here in other lives. But it will have at least a little and in many cases quite a bit—only in the rarest cases a great deal—to do with what you do elsewhere.

So the DNA is simply a means that is available, but it is not the only means. A smile is an expression on your face, yes? So is a frown, a studious look, an expression. This is a means of emanating your feelings, and it is also, intentionally or otherwise, a means to communicate, but it is not exclusive—meaning that those same feelings might exist other places, and in those other places, you may have some other form, some other body to express those communications to yourself or others. If the substance of life is different there, so be it. It is the means, it is the way you will express it.

Creator has set it up for human beings to be the form of your expression on this planet. It is purposely set up by Creator that for human beings, the body you reside in is delicate and necessarily requires you to go to great lengths in order to support your life here. Of course, like all beings who feel a sense of the briefness of life . . . on this planet especially, since you do not have the normal certainty of the continuity of life that you have everyplace else because you are here to learn and things must be different to support learning new things. What occurs as you go along in life is that you have opportunities to grow, to change, to acquire, to become and ultimately to terminate your life here in this expression. But, of course, life is permanent; you go on.

Creator has set up the human body here to be as delicate as possible but also as sturdy as possible within that delicacy, so you can be here at least as long as it takes for you to acquire some portion of your desire to learn something new. Some people might live just a few hours or a few days or a year or two or something like that; others might go on for many years, a hundred years perhaps, occasionally even more. But in most cases, you will live no more or less than it takes for the basic desire to learn something new to be accomplished.

There will be many other accumulations of wisdom and many other experiences for those living long lives, but sometimes it is not desired by beings to live long lives. Sometimes a short life will do, and that short life can accomplish a great many things for an immortal personality, Melody, such as yourself, and everyone else who's here on Earth. A short life can accomplish a great many things, especially if that soul has accomplished its basic purpose: it's learned something new. I'm saying this, not only to reassure those of you who have lost loved ones whom you perhaps wished could have been with you longer, but to reassure you that they have achieved their main purposes—to learn something new—and they also might have had the opportunity to pass on a little love and nurturance on their own just by being.

Use Physical Mastery to
Discover a More Benevolent Astrology

So an immortal personality chooses to come to the Earth. What are some of the places one can go to connect to energies? There are the planets in the solar system—what else?

Places—you mean geographical?

Well, let's call them beings. When someone connects to Saturn, he or she connects to you, right?

Well, to a degree perhaps.

So what is spread out on the table before a personality who is choosing to come to Earth, perhaps for the first time, and doesn't know the system? How is it explained to this immortal personality?

Melody, it could take months and months to say that. You want me to sum up months and months in a few well-chosen words? [Laughs.] I will do my best.

I would honor that, because I think we need a new understanding of astrology. I went and looked in a bunch of books today. Granted, mine are all pretty old, but they're pretty doom-and-gloomy.

Then perhaps you better look in some new ones that are a bit more cheerful.

Yes, okay, I will.

Don't just rush out and buy them. Go to the store and feel them, all right? Don't even look at the titles; just find the section and pull out the book in one part of the section. Say it's just a shelf—pull out the book on one end just enough so that you can touch it, so it's out about an inch from the shelf. Then pull the book out of the other end that ends the section. Take off your glasses and run your fingers very gently, using the wand. [See next page]

You can either touch the thin edge of the book with your fingers very slowly and notice where you get the most warmth, or you can move your fingers along the edges of the books, starting on the right side, moving to the left, and notice where you get the most warmth.

Using your "wand" (hand) to make choices:

The left hand is the wand because it is the receiving hand. (I know some people are left-handed and their right hand might be their receiving hand, but in reality the left hand is always the receiving hand and the right hand is the creating hand, the doing hand, even if you're left-handed.) By the feelings they get in their physical bodies, they know which rock gives them the greatest warmth, and that's the rock they can approach and ask, "Is it all right if I sit on you?"

A shaman will do that. The average person, however, can learn to run his fingers, his wand, over a wide array of things to see which one is right for him. This could be done in a supermarket. If you have a garden, you can go out and choose not only which ear of corn is right for you or your family that day but which plant wishes to offer it to you at a given time on any given day.

That personal feeling you get, the warmth within your body, tells you, yes, there is love for that today, right now in this moment, not an hour from now, not five minutes from now, but you'll have to do the experience with the wand again in an hour. Because plants, rocks, everything, have their own personal lives, five minutes from now they might be doing something else, just like a human might.

Left: Here is the wand, using the left hand.

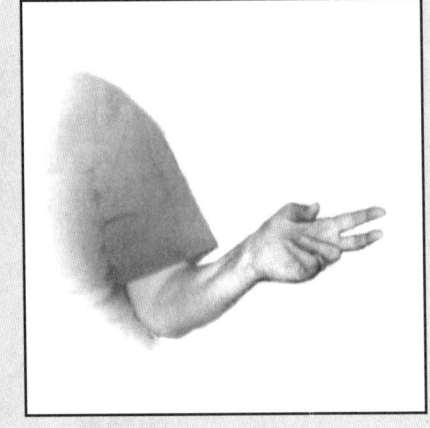

Right: Detail showing position of fingers for the wand.

Before you begin this, say to yourself (there may be other people present): "I would like to acquire," you might say, if you're purchasing a book, "books with a more benevolent outlook on astrology." That's all. Keep it simple. You can whisper, but say it out loud, like that. Then move your finger along there and see where you get the most warmth. If you get warmth from this, that or the other, then get all three. If you just get warmth for one, then pull that out and you can push the two other books back. Look at the book you pulled out and decide if it is something you wish to take home. But honor the system.

Your body will know more than your mind can ever know in this life. Your body is a portion of Earth and has accumulated experience. This is why sometimes you will feel warmth for something that has no rational appeal—because your body knows. Knowledge can be acquired gradually by beings who think as a primary means of moving forward in their lives. But physical knowledge, material-mastery knowledge, wisdom, can be expressed through your physical body, even with very little acquisition of mental growth.

So give it a try. I feel that would be the simplest way to assimilate books that might be more cheerful. Sometimes it might be written in a humorous fashion—it's good for you to expose yourself to more humor. Humor is the thread that supports and nurtures life to go on, even in the most difficult circumstances. Yes, it is love that holds things together, but humor is the thread that connects and unites and allows people to laugh about something that in its own right is not particularly funny. But given its commonality, its common ground with other human beings, especially if you are not having the experience but have had it, you can laugh about it. Sometimes you can even laugh about it when you're having the uncomfortable experience, especially finding it reassuring to know that you are not alone in that experience, that others are having it or have had it. Sometimes that can be very reassuring, even funny. That's what I recommend.

Know that I support completely your desire to put or at least supply another face for astrology. It is because we—speaking for the other planets and myself—feel that this has value that we have nurtured and encouraged you to allow the book to go beyond astrological interpretation and to show primarily the personality of the planets. The more experienced astrologer, and sometimes those who are simply learning astrology, might find this appealing because you can study about someone for a long time, but without actually experiencing that person, without meeting him or her, it's not that easy to know that person. It's like studying about what that person has done or reading a trail. You might draw certain conclusions about studying people's past activities, about what they might have been like, but that would be a best guess.

It is our intention in this book to demonstrate personality and characteristics of personality so that other qualities of the planets and other systems can be seen, felt or even inspired in the astrologer who is looking for something different to provide to those who inquire of them—or for that matter, even for the casual person learning about the system of astrology to understand that planets and bodies and groups of planets have something that is very similar to the human being, and that is personality. We are someone just like you—you are someone—even though we might seem to be *something*. Sometimes human beings respond to other human beings as if they are *something*. Those of you who have had this experience will know what I mean, and yet you know that you are *someone*. This book, in its largest sense, supports the knowing that you are someone, and it also supports the message that we are all someone.

On Earth You Have the Joy of Discovery

Can you give me the short tour of how one connects to these—I don't even know what to call them—energies, beings, persons, systems, whatever, to set up one's life?

You'll have to stretch because the answer is simple, not complex. You and everyone else reading this and everyone everywhere are immortal. You are connected in a profoundly intimate way with all beings everywhere at all times. Granted, on Earth you are not aware of that, but in almost all other lives, other places, as well as in the deep sleep state you experience on Earth, you are well aware of who everyone is everywhere and all of their qualities, because it is natural and normal to know that.

Think of it like this in the microcosmic sense: Your brain cells have different functions. Your scientists have been able to notice that if certain parts of your brain are stimulated that certain things might occur—so you might reasonably say that science backs me up on this. Your brain cells have different duties, and yet they all know that they are united and they have an intimate knowledge of all other brain cells. This is a demonstration on the small scale of how things exist everywhere.

The rules for being on Earth are that you are necessarily limited so that you will struggle against your limits in order to discover new things and new things about yourself. That's it in a nutshell. But in your normal state of being, when you are not in this school, in expressing your life either in a physical form someplace or simply existing beyond the parameters of a physical form, you know everyone and everything intimately. You know their personalities; you know everything.

It might seem strange to you now, but one of the most appealing things that your souls find attractive is to be able to come here to this place and experience ignorance where you don't know everything, because one thing that is clearly available here—and as far as I'm aware, almost nowhere else except as something to study before one perhaps comes here or simply to study as an anomaly—is discovery. On Earth, you can have the joy of discovery. You can discover something new because you are not aware of it existing, because you have, as your friend Zoosh likes to call it, the gift of ignorance here. That may seem to be a joke—your jokester friend Zoosh likes to kid around, which is good because humor is the thread, yes?

So your friend says that there is the joy of ignorance. Given that you know everyone and everything intimately everyplace else, the idea of having the capacity to be surprised about something or the capacity to not know something and then to desire to learn about it incrementally throughout the experience of your life here is so fascinating that many souls want to come here just to have that experience. They might enjoy it for a short time or a long time, but it doesn't start getting old [chuckles], as you might say, until late in life. Late in life, whatever that age might be for anyone, then you really want to experience the familiar. You want to feel at home, and then you want to be home. That desire gets greater, not lesser, so that your capability when death occurs is one that easily welcomes your angel or guide who comes to escort you home, and you are able to step out of your body and be home again.

So if you're from the other side of the totality and had never heard of this place, of Earth, you can instantly extend and feel and learn what you have to know to set up your life right away, become familiar with the beings and energies here—is that what you're saying?

There is no other side—totality is totality. If someone told you there is something beyond the totality, at which point you cannot be aware of the totality, that might have been an expression of his or her personality and I do not question it. But from my experience, everything is united everywhere. When one experiences a life of time and space as you experience here on Earth—so you can study things, measure things, enjoy incremental things, enjoy accumulations and so on—the idea of there being *more* is appealing. But the idea and the experience of there being everything everywhere united in the ways that are benevolent to you as an immortal personality everywhere is the normal state of condition in everything I've ever experienced.

So a soul comes here for the first time and is already connected to everything. Does it limit its connections when it comes here? How does the very art or science of astrology work?

A soul does not have to consciously limit itself. Most souls do not know how to do that. To consciously limit yourself would mean that you would then in the future know how to do that, and Creator does not consider that to be an advantageous circumstance. Rather, Creator considers that souls being unlimited in their capacity in all ways are perhaps a more benevolent expression of souls or immortal personalities (the names are interchangeable).

So you don't have to do anything as a soul. You simply come through what actually feels to you a lot like a membrane—even as a soul you have some sense of touch. It is not absolutely physical, but it is something you pass through, and you can feel yourself passing through it. When that happens, it is there for you, but you suspend a portion of your personality, which just remains beyond that membrane, to come here to this existence. By "coming here," I am not referring to a physical place so much but rather the rules set out by Creator and accepted freely by those who come to this creation where the Explorer Race is in residence. You accept those rules and you embrace them so that you don't have to change your immortal personality to be here. It works like that.

I understand that you're trying to understand how astrology works in a new way, but be aware that you don't have to work so hard, if you don't mind. I am not trying to stifle your curiosity; I just want you to know that you don't have to work too hard. We planets, speaking for myself, will try to show as much about personality as possible. It is very often the personality that will be helpful to the advanced astrologer and to the beginner as well. As far as reinventing astrology [chuckles], we don't have to do that. But by all means probe the places of your personal curiosity.

More Than the Planets Influence You at Birth

I'm still trying to understand how the connections are made that are considered the birth chart.

It is so simple—may I explain? As I've said numerous times, this is a place of time and space. You are born at a certain time . . .

In a certain space.

Specifically, you are born at a certain time, and space itself, with what it contains, is in a specific position at the time you are born. That's what astrology is about. You are born at a time, yes—the place where time and space functions—and at that time the planets are in a specific position. The fact that all other beings are in a specific position as well is also true, but that is way too vast of a subject to go into for this book (or any book, for that matter), because when you think of it in the larger picture, you could say, "The planet was in this position, was in this phase, and so on," but you might also reasonably say that at the moment of your birth, "The animal down the street was doing this, my neighbor was doing that, and all other beings, plants, animals, everything on Earth was doing certain things." A fixed thing, the moment of your birth does not happen at a precise second, but your birth is taking place over this time and all these beings are doing something during this time.

So you might say that astrology is an attempt to simplify and to provide general tendencies and, to the greatest of its ability, more specific possibilities of what you might experience, given the period of time of your birth. So astrology in that sense makes its best guess given the position of planets, which can be checked on. You can actually go to a book and say, "At such and such a time, at such and such a year, the planets were in this position," because these things are kept track of, at least to a point in your time of fairly accomplished astronomy. So that is good, but you cannot actually say, "And everyone on Earth was in *this* position." [Chuckles.] That's not reasonably available to you at this time, but it will be someday.

So someone is born on the planet and what all the other six billion people are doing will have an effect on his or her life?

Well, it always has an effect—everything is united with everything else. But it's not just what all the other people are doing; it's what every blade of grass is doing. It's what every atom is doing, what every molecule is doing. It's what everyone is doing. But we cannot expect astrology to serve all of that. If it did, it would be more of an explanation and perhaps even a revered religion, an ambition to which it really does not ambitiously strive toward, even though it has been used to support religions in the past.

Based on what you said, this is probably not accurate then, but a teacher in a class once said that if you could see spiritually, the horoscope would be imprinted on the back of everyone's body in the area of the heart chakra—if you had that kind of sight. Is that true?

No. I think you can dispense with that question. It was the person's . . . it is a metaphor, all right? Metaphors are not necessarily meant to be taken literally. You don't have to know about astrology to live. For those who wish to explore some of its more esoteric aspects, they can do that. It is hoped that this book will provide a valuable tool for those individuals, as well as being a different face of astrology for those who might wish to see it in a different light or even understand how very involved your loving Creator of this universe is in the tools and techniques He—or She, if you like—may foster support and nurture for your benefit in this school that you now occupy for this brief portion of your immortality.

I Am Allowing You to See More of My Personality

In the books I looked at today—and granted, these books are old—Saturn was the taskmaster, the keeper of karma. Like I said, it was kind of grim. But perhaps that was your face when we were in the loop of time. Are you showing possibly a different expression of yourself now as we move toward becoming our natural selves?

I am allowing you through this means—since you didn't start this book until recently—to simply see more of my personality, which was always present. Remember, I stated that in order to serve the Explorer Race's needs, I would need to present myself (as all planets would need to do) in ways that are in a timely manner, if I can use that pun—that which you believe and that which fits your current knowledge, wisdom and beliefs about yourself and your world. So I do not feel uncomfortable about that perception of myself by your astrology writers in times gone by, but not unlike other beings, there is more to me than meets the eye.

We have personality traits. Many people—you, Melody, as well as the reader—have personality traits that you do not demonstrate consciously to others in a way that allows or gives them permission to acknowledge those traits within you. Nevertheless, you are demonstrating those traits all the time unconsciously, and sometimes people will notice them and sometimes not. It is for me at this time, given the fact that you are doing this book through this channel, an opportunity to show more of my true nature.

That's exciting! So everyone can show more of his or her true nature than possibly what had been limited by our perceptions, our abilities to perceive it in the past.

Yes, and that is also the reason why you have been fairly dedicated to allow that personality to be shown in the transcripts and books, and so on, that you have published before. It's not just about the facts; it's also about the way the facts are presented.

My Moons Offer Me Support

Does the number of moons a planet has reflect its expression of personality or some need for its orbit or for whatever in the physical dimension?

Sometimes. This is a purely scientific answer, but sometimes if a planet's orbit or its balance is not working well, a body (sometimes called a moon or sometimes even a large asteroid) will migrate toward that planet to help stabilize its orbit and even its revolution on its own axis. This migration is done with intent: not somebody sending something to the planet to stabilize its orbit, but rather the exact being will come who is volunteering to stabilize the orbit or to provide stabilization to that which needs it.

Now, sometimes a planet will be perfectly stable in its revolution and its orbit, but owing to what is needed or is required of it—this would be your needs in the case here now of my version of myself that you are interacting with, otherwise known as "because of the needs of others"—there is a greater demand on what I must do or provide. There is even a speculation, you might say, given all of the potentials for your development in the future, as to what you might need and what I might be called on to provide. As a result of perceiving this need, I simply emanate a desire for an object, which you call a moon or even an asteroid, to come and stabilize itself in some way in my proximity so as to act as a balance: that I might be able to relax, let go of some of the things I was doing, and so the simple energy and support of that moon can take over and I can direct more of my energy to your needs.

However many moons you have—I think it's a lot—do they radiate your personality or do they express themselves?

That's a good question. They express naturally themselves, but they are influenced by me, just as you express your personality on Earth but you are influenced by your environment—influenced, of course, by the body you find yourself in expressing your personality, and of course influenced by your experience with other human beings, plants, animals, conditions of life and so on. So for them it is identical. Because they are in my environment, they will express their personalities as they are in cooperation with my personality.

Since they are here to perform a service for me, which I greatly appreciate, they will not only be supporting my balance but also something I perceive that I might need to do for you in the future. They will be taking on some duty that I might have felt was a distraction—meaning something I would normally do for myself or normally do for others, but because you might need more of my attention at given moments, that I would appreciate if they would take on that duty. It might simply have something to do with the physics of an orbit or a revolution on a given axis, but it would not have anything to do with a personality trait of mine, for instance.

Do you have moons on every level or only on the physical?

Meaning your physical?

My physical, what we see, yes.

No, I do not have this everyplace. Almost all other places there are no moons or asteroids that are required there. In other places, the demands on me are very gentle, and the places are gentle and benevolent, without polarity, and so on. Only one, maybe two others (it depends on how you count) have a moon that's just strictly for beauty.

Planets Interact with You in Your Dreams

How do you interact with humans? Do you interact on an individual basis or by exuding energy that they collectively need? Can you explain that?

To a degree, it is physical like that—simply my physical energy, which I think has been explained well in the past—but also to an extent as you can understand my personality that I'm trying to demonstrate here. But most of the planets—you will have to ask them yourself—will interact with you in a form in your dreams. A lot of what you need to do here on Earth (your desires, your means to express, your intentions and so on), that you talk about and work on at the deep states of your sleep as you would experience it physically, or simply when your soul can put more attention toward these consults with your teachers, spirit and so on . . . of course, when your body sleeps, that is possible. Then, very often the planets nearby in your solar system, who support you with the expression of certain traits and abilities associated with the position you were in when you were born, will be able to give you, support you and interact with you in your spirit form, in your soul, when your body sleeps in a way that you can then trigger when you reengage with your body fully, meaning when you wake up.

The nice thing about this, you know, is that you don't have to do it mentally. The exchange that takes place as you might remember in a dream, although it's unlikely, takes place spiritually. When your spirit is fully engaged with your physical body again—although there is a tether while you're out and about, so to speak—you go back in fully. The energy exchange will automatically trigger something in your physical body that will support, sustain and otherwise encourage your actions and reactions in life on the basis of those contacts.

I don't want to go into the whole physiological phenomena, because it is way too long and extensive for this book. But it's not unlike the way an athlete might train for some time to run a marathon race or to accomplish a goal—meaning that you have some idea of what might be expected of you, mentally speaking, and you physically train for it. In this case, spiritually speaking, there might be some potential for something that may occur or an opportunity that may be available. Therefore, it might be to your advantage to be able to express more freely certain energies that might support that opportunity. So in that sense, you might train.

How could that go? Let me give you an example. You might reasonably begin to feel a sudden interest in something that you had no particular interest in before. Let's say, in this case, since the nature of this book is astrology, you suddenly developed as a reader a sudden interest in astrology that you didn't really notice you had before and you begin to read about it—not just in the newspaper, which is meant for your sort of lighthearted reading, but more extensively you buy a book truly for your education astrologically. Of course, you're going to read about yourself, maybe you'll read a little bit about your friends and family, and you find it very interesting.

So you begin to develop an interest in something that you had no interest in whatsoever before, and even though you find it interesting, you don't see where it fits into your life. Then sometime later you meet someone who's very interested in astrology, and maybe that is what you have in common to talk about. Or perhaps you, with your new knowledge of astrology, meet two or three people, and you wonder which one would be the best for you. So you go to your astrology book and there it is—it says, "This one would be the best in the short run; that one might be the best in the long run." In short, you have a means of knowing beyond your own life experience and perhaps even beyond the wisdom of your friends and family. This does not mean you ignore them; it just gives you something else to consult.

Walk-Ins Work with Astrology Almost Identically

So this is all set up based on the immortal personality that creates the body. How do walk-ins work with this? Walk-ins come in with a different purpose, a different personality, a different everything. How do they work with astrology?

It's almost identical. For a walk-in, of course, you find yourself in something that was literally prepared for someone else. However, any time that preparation takes place for the soul who's involved in, not just initializing the body, but when the body is initialized—meaning prepared and all of the things that are prepared for your arrival as a soul—there is also (and this cannot be ignored) the potential for a walk-in to take place.

The walk-in can *only* take place, of course, if the initial soul chooses for whatever reason to walk out or to go someplace else, to continue life on someplace else. But also, the new soul coming in, in benevolent ways supported by Creator, must be comfortable with the creation of the previous soul. So you might say—and this is not an unreasonable observation—that the soul that left and the soul that came in must have a resemblance to each other that might not necessarily equal what you would call a physical resemblance, of course. But if you were able to see the soul that departed the body in its energetic form and see the soul that comes into the body in its energetic form, you would see something that is profoundly similar. So you might say—and how can we say this in a not entirely joking manner—that there's a family resemblance.

Therefore, the physical body that the walk-in finds himself in is adequate to his expression. It might not be as ideal as it would have been had it been the initialized physical body, but it's as ideal as it can be, given this manner of creation expressed in this form. It would be in that sense if you had, say, a twin brother or twin sister . . . and twins often do this, especially if they're identical. They sort of pretend to be each other sometimes just for fun. That's okay so long as it's done just for fun for a short time and then you tell the other person and no one gets hurt. But it is not that difficult for a twin to maintain that for a short time because there is not only a physical resemblance but some similarity in personality—not exactly the same, but some similarity. It is not unlike that in the walk-in situation.

So everything about the birth chart, then, is still applicable to the walk-in?

No, not everything. That's why the walk-in often finds the physical body not to be particularly expressive of his or her self. It is not at all unusual for the first year or two or three years of the walk-in to try to change the physical body in some way. Some people become more athletic, especially if they're younger. Some people put on weight, particularly if they're older. But there is a desire to allow the physical body to be more of the creation of the soul that walked in. So what is very often the case—say, seven or eight times out of ten—is some weight is put on, if only temporarily, to allow the new soul coming in to experience the simultaneity of creation that goes with the existence of being in a physical body, which is normally experienced in the case of birthing from your mother, as the soul is inside mother and the physical body is forming up in and around you.

Don't automatically assume [chuckles], if I might be humorous for a moment, that if your friend or neighbor or lover is putting on weight, then he or she is a walk-in. On the other hand, it is not unusual for a walk-in to do this. It does not have to be permanent. It's almost like you . . . the feeling is that you missed something, you see. You can't be in mom, so you grow, you might say, as an adult. Then when you feel more comfortable and compatible in your physical body and are familiar with it, you can, if you choose, re-form the physical body, if you have your physical health, in a reasonable way. You can perhaps re-form it in some other way: You can do some activity; you can change your habits. In short, don't feel that you have to be big to be a walk-in.

Astrologers Can Help You Fill in the Gaps

What method does a walk-in use in astrology to get the information he or she is looking for?

It is good to know the exact time of your birth. I do not know of any walk-in who knows that, so the next best thing is to know the exact day—although it is also very rare for a walk-in to know that. So the *next* best thing is to consult with an astrologer, one who is very experienced, who has worked with many clients (and this also applies to something else that I will bring up), and who can, on the basis of your birth astrology, by simply being with you for a time—it will probably take him or her a little time—observe you well and thoroughly through conversations, going to lunch, something like that. Take an astrologer to lunch, okay? [Chuckles.]

You might have to go to lunch, dinner. It might take time to get to know you, or he or she might be able to catch it right away—it depends. Then ask if your personality traits follow in the astrologer's experience with the birth chart, or if they might be an expression the astrologer would normally find with some other sign in the chart. This might also be a nice way to make a friend, and it could be a way to discover more about yourself. Remember, this is a planet where people not only serve one another all the time but you come here to meet people, to have experiences with beings who are having experiences similar to yours—not always, but very often.

Now, I wanted to tell you that there would be another application for this. There are some of you who are perhaps adopted or perhaps not aware of what time you were born or perhaps even what place you were born in. You can use this same method. You can talk to a well and thoroughly experienced astrologer who might be able to tell you, according to the birth chart, if not the exact time of your birth and perhaps not even the exact day, then he or she might be able to give you your basic signs on the basis of his or her perception of the personalities of human beings as applied to his or her chosen field. So you see how in this case, Melody, your question has served two purposes.

Walk-Ins: Discover Humor

If I might bring up something on my own that is really important for people who know they are walk-ins to do: Try to become familiar with the humor of the person in the culture you find yourself in. Read books, be with friends as you make them, enjoy your family to the extent that you can—in short, try to discover what humor is and how to react to it. Sometimes it will be obvious and it will be easy, but for others it will be difficult. Humor, as I said before, is a profound thread that will not only connect you to other human beings through shared experience but will often help you over the difficult times when you are feeling very strange in a place that does not have any landmarks that are familiar to you. This is a typical experience for walk-ins, even for those born naturally as well, if they haven't had a great deal of experience on Earth in your times.

Okay, this is pretty awesome. I'm out of questions, I guess.

Well, that's all right. There are other planets [laughs]. So on that note of shared wisdom, I will say thank you for your curiosity and thank you for being a good questioner and representative—albeit temporarily—of the human race.

I would like to talk to you again, but I need to learn more. Can I possibly ask for you in the future, maybe before we're done?

Certainly. Good night.

♃ Jupiter

JUPITER

Choose a Felt Connection to Jupiter to Experience Benevolence

June 4, 2004

This is Jupiter.

Welcome!

Let me stabilize a moment. All right, what would you like to say?

Well, we want to know as much about you as you would like to share with us.

You cannot know what I want to answer without asking questions.

Okay. What was your experience before you came and became what we call Jupiter?

I have always been Jupiter, just not in this environment you have required for your studies—you would say "in other realms" (perhaps you would say that), or "in other dimensions." But I have only recently been here in this place where your people are residing.

Oh, you mean you weren't in some other place in some other creation? You've been here, just not so that we could see you, not on this plane or this dimension or whatever you call it?

Exactly. That is not uncommon, I believe, with most of the planets. Perhaps some of them, as an exception, might have been elsewhere. This is what I am and who I am. I am appearing slightly different in other realms, but I am what you see here in this one.

Astrologers Need to Make a Felt Connection

You are supposed to be the most benevolent, wondrous source of energy and benefits—how did you choose that role? That's you expressing your personality, right?

Well, that is the personality aspect of myself as demonstrated through the subject matter you are exploring. I would not say that I whispered in too many ears how I would be that. But I can see how I might be considered to be that because of the original information, the inspiration that went to people who began writing about this every time they would connect spiritually, energetically, with the different planets that were known about then, or every time they were inspired to write about planets that were not even known about at that time, just believed to exist. They would feel very benevolent energy when connecting with me.

That is how much of the original feeling information was experienced by the human beings who wrote these things down initially. So I came to be known as being benevolent, not only because of how the people would feel when connecting with me, but also because of how their own lives would improve. You have to remember that these initial people who were being inspired—I think I will refer to them as scholars—had lives beyond their field of choice or the field that had been assigned to them, depending upon the lifestyle of the time.

But they could not help but notice that everyone who studied this and had the experience and had the ability to connect with me, how their lives would improve after this kind of felt connection. So a lot of the original material—in terms of "this planet is about this" and "that planet is about that"—was on the basis of people noticing not only how their connection was to the planet but how they felt, what occurred in their lives, and what occurred in the lives of the people they were interacting with. Or in the case of some situations, those in the court, for instance, who were involved with those they would be able to work for . . . many of the people who were able to write the material down—not just experience it, but actually write it down—or others who were able to make a record of it, were working for others so that they would not have to do what it took to stay alive.

So they would probably be working for a king or someone who was in charge of large areas or who was wealthy enough to support them?

Yes, they were working for someone who could support them, and as a result, the material got written down. But for years and years before that, going way back before people were writing these things down and were just passing information on from one to the other, this type of thing has been available. You only have the old documents in cultures of those who decided to or chose to make a record. Some of those are—how can we say?—shaded on the basis of current (at those times) political interests or religious interests.

So one does not always see the material from olden times in its pure state. That is why it is important, in every era, to encourage astrologers and those who study it (and even those who are interested in it) to make the spiritual connection, to be able to feel the planets and the signs and all that as a physical experience. That way they can either confirm the actual feelings associated with these places as something that is associated with their own lives, or they can say, "Well, I had a different reaction, and perhaps there is more to this planet than we have known about before."

I did not necessarily encourage that kind of study with all other planets. In that case, I will say if an astrologer is, for instance, struggling to keep something going or attempting to work out a difficult relationship with a person or even in a business, it probably wouldn't be a good idea to feel and connect strongly on a regular basis with Mars. It is the energy of Mars to seek quick and permanent solutions—permanent, of course, being fleeting. But in that sense, Mars might be considered to be somewhat impetuous. I am not judging Mars; I am just saying that the energy of Mars is resolution as swiftly and permanently as possible. So if you, as an astrologer, are working on something that is subtle that needs a great deal of time and effort to resolve, you might wish to study some other more benevolent (in terms of how you feel when you connect with it) planet or sign.

Such as yourself.

I am not saying that. I am saying that the astrologer needs to make the effort to make the felt connection—not just a mental connection, but a physical connection—to the planet or sign. Astrologers might, for example, if they meditate or do some other such thing, ask to feel to the best of their ability the feelings that are associated with the planet, constellation or sign they are studying. Astrologers can then go through the various planets and signs so they can find one that feels best to them. They can ask that, as they work with this and connect with it in that way, the effects in their life are not harmful.

After all, there are other situations, for instance, since I'm talking about Mars, that might make it beneficial to connect with Mars. Perhaps something needs to have a quick solution. Maybe it doesn't have to be dramatic, but it needs to be resolved one way or the other. In that sense, then, it might be helpful to connect with Mars, who can make actions and can encourage people and individuals to act when they have some sense of certainty as to how to act. The connection on a felt basis with Mars might give you the strength and encouragement to act. So Mars is not just something that would complicate your life. It can, in fact, provide the impetus that might be needed on a felt basis to support actions that need to be taken.

So that's my recommendation to astrologers, that they make it more personal, make it more physical—that they *feel* the place they are studying. When they find something that is compatible with them and their lives at that time, then that's what to study, that's what to consider. It is very important to recognize that some astrologers specialize in a given planet or sign and might write about it extensively. It is very important to realize that it is very possible—and many astrologers know this—that one might be at least temporarily affected by such specific courses of study.

Therefore, trust, if you would, that if there is someplace you want to write about but that place does not seem to be having a good effect on your life at that time, let somebody else write about that. It might be better for another astrologer to write about that and for you to find something that is more beneficial and benevolent in your life in general, as well as of interest to you to write about and connect with.

A Method for Establishing Connection

Are there any aspects of your personality that you will express now as we move into this expansion into our natural selves which haven't been written about in the past?

That's an interesting question. I did take that into account in the last answer, but yes, there is some of that. I might suggest that your readers in general make some effort to connect with myself on a felt basis if possible for them by whatever means they use, because it is possible that an infusion of my energy could be helpful. Let me give you a suggested method.

This is for people who meditate or have the capacity to feel energies, because simply looking at a picture of Jupiter is not sufficient. After all, the picture is printed on something. So the idea is, it is better to connect in terms of the personal. Of course, you cannot come here, but the connection might be that you would say out loud, for instance, "I am feeling"—you do not have to explain your life—"that a connection with Jupiter could be beneficial for me at this time." Then (even if you've seen a picture, that's okay, but don't look at one then) just close your eyes and ask to feel the feelings that you might have or to feel energies from Jupiter, and wait and see what you feel.

You might have a feeling of your own come up. If it feels good or you get warmth, something like that, then that's good. But if you actually get a physical feeling that feels good, you might then very carefully and very slowly begin to breathe in that physical feeling. Maybe if it's a pleasant feeling on a perimeter part of your body someplace, you can breathe in from that point. Notice, when you take the first tiny amount of breath, does it feel good in your body? If it feels good, take more breath. Try one or two or three breaths. If it feels good and continues to feel good, continue breathing in from that point.

The moment it no longer feels good or you feel no change, stop and just experience the energy. It will not come in to overwhelm you in any way; it will come in on the basis of whether it is compatible with your physical systems. But for you to invite the energy in, to feel the energy at some point on your body, and then to breathe in . . . I realize you do not have an opening, perhaps, in that part of your body, but picture or imagine that part of your body and breathe in as if you were breathing in from there while you breathe in your normal way. Then you can take in the energy that allows you to feel as a participant, which is very important for your people now, I believe.

This is a way that my energy can perhaps create a bit more benevolence in your life. It is very important for you to notice whether it feels good. If you breathe in and it doesn't feel good, then that probably isn't my energy. So you will have to experiment with it a bit. If it doesn't feel good, then immediately after you take another breath, blow out from that part of your body so you can expel it. Or if you do disentanglement, you can do that. But I'd recommend blowing out quickly. If you feel that the discomfort came in unintentionally and has settled someplace in your body, you can blow out (as you blow a breath out), but imagine it going out of that part of your body. These are old techniques that are well-established, I believe, in your societies, at least in some Eastern cultures, and are very useful globally to anyone who wishes to try them.

Being Bigger Has Made Me More Durable

At what point were you invited here? What was the situation when you descended to this physical reality or made yourself manifest here?

It was actually a request by the Creator of this universe—it was not done mentally, you understand, with words, but I will do my best to convert it to words—who essentially communicated the story about this whole Explorer Race. The Explorer Race needed to have, not only a planet, but also constellations and a whole external world—stars in the sky, everything—that they could relate to on a purely physical level in your particular environment and also to which and through which they could interact spiritually and mentally and everything else. It needed to be a representation of myself that would be durable, because things would happen because of their learning process that would not happen in other places—meaning there would not only be benevolence but there would also be action or activities that might be malevolent.

Most of the malevolence would be unintentional through ignorance, but occasionally there might be some malevolence that was intentional, so I would have to create some element of myself that would be durable while being able to express my personality. For me, that meant to be bigger. "Bigger" would be more durable, because I would have more capacity to deflect, if necessary, and also I had to be bigger so that the benevolent aspect of my personality could reflect to your planet and be seen. After all, I'm quite some distance away from your planet. In order to be seen, quite obviously I have to be big.

Was that at the beginning of this solar system?

It was not at the very beginning. That's an interesting question you ask, because as far as I know, most of the planets weren't here. Some of them were here, but quite a few of them came in on a similar basis as I did—at least, according to our communions, that is what I've been able to gather from them. They too existed elsewhere and formed up here for your experience.

So, no, I wasn't here right away. The experience of Earth and its citizens elsewhere did not require my presence right away. But—and this is perhaps going to surprise you—once my presence was urged by Creator, it was urged well before the time Explorer Race would be on Earth. So when I did initially create a version of myself here in this solar system, and more to the point, in an accessible space in your environment, I was not that big. I gradually got bigger over time as I began to realize the full impact of the Explorer Race dynamic.

So it's not really time, but for the sake of your reflection on what experience involves and how much experience accumulates in so much of a derivative (otherwise known as time), I will say that over about 50,000 years of your accumulated-experience idea did I get to be about the size I am now. This was my gradual assimilation of your needs and my needs in order to protect myself.

You had, of course, never experienced anything but benevolence, right?

Well, not before I came here. I was aware of one of the consultants whom I believe you have been exposed to before. Creator has a consultant . . .

The Master of Discomfort?

Yes. This was essential for Creator in order to build an environment and to invite (in some cases) environmental aspects—planets, circumstances, experiences, possibilities and so on—for the Explorer Race. I believe Creator needed a consultant along these lines to create the potential for growth and learning that comes about when there is some discomfort. So I was aware of that being, but it's one thing to be aware of it and another thing to actually be exposed to it here in your environment.

How do you protect yourself? Your energies ray out toward us, we connect to you . . .

Yes. When you think about it, that's strongly suggestive, is it not, that my energies come from within and go out—but spherically, not just in your direction. This is the case for all planets, and I might add, it is the case for all human beings as well. It is the case, for that matter, for all beings as far as I know.

Of course, when you are in an entirely benevolent environment, the radiation of your own energy is more associated with your wants, needs, desires and also what you can do for others: what are your talents, abilities, capabilities and so on. It will be almost exclusively that. Whereas in an environment like this, where there is polarity, then one needs to also radiate, for instance, strength, durability and endurance, capabilities that are beyond . . . how can we say? If you have a certain level of strength and you are in a dangerous environment, you might radiate even greater capacities of that strength than you might have accomplished in your short life as a human being, in this case. In short, you would try to walk down the street and look confident or even tough in order to deflect any threat. So what I do and what you do is very similar in certain ways, though I do not have to look tough, eh?

You Must Consciously Choose My Energy

So you radiate these energies. Does the quality of your energy change based on what you feel is needed, or is it sort of like a steady benevolence?

It's generally steady, but there are times when surges are needed, and there are other times now in your now time where surges cannot really get through to you. This is something that has to do with Creator's timing (I suppose I'd have to call it), in terms of what Creator desires you to do to take actions for your own growth, change and capabilities—which I'm sure other beings have spoken to you about at length. Therefore, I cannot on my own simply pulse out benevolent energy at a time when you might need it, such as in your current global situation. On the other hand, you can take action on your own, as demonstrated in the earlier part of our talk today. You can connect and breathe in my energy, which will be available for you. But you must be involved; it has to be something that you consciously choose to do.

In this way, my energy is not withheld, but you must be a conscious participant. This is what Creator desires for you so that you will be able to not only choose a more benevolent life but act on it in order to bring it about. Since Creator knows that all human beings, all planets, all beings in general radiate their experience—who and what they are—the more individuals who are choosing benevolence and connecting to beings such as myself and some of the other planets (to say nothing of other beings who might feel benevolent to you), the more you will bring that benevolence about. In the simple act of being, your energy does radiate out, and the more beings who are radiating out this benevolence, Creator feels, the more it will help to support other human beings on the planet who feel the need to have permission on a spiritual level, then on a feeling level, then perhaps on a subconscious level, and then on a conscious level, to take actions not unlike that for themselves.

What is the dynamic of you radiating energy to us? It's like we don't have the benefit of it—is that what you're saying?

Oh, no. There is some filtration that comes through, of course, and to a degree it has to do with the light reflection, the light waves. But there is some energy that comes simply from proximity, from being not that far away. Oh, I know that it seems far away in terms of miles, but in terms of a concordance of energies—meaning the energies from myself are in concordance with the energies of Earth—the human population is not so vast that that concordance is disrupted. But it *is* vast enough to where the human population has to give permission for the same degree of my energy to come through that has come through in past times when the population was less.

Now you have so many people that they have to decide whether they wish to have my energy come through in some way that is at least as great as it has been in the past. Perhaps if enough people make the connection in some benevolent way, such as suggested in this talk today, it might be possible to bring through more. But it will be up to you. Creator wishes it this way, and it is not for me to criticize that process.

Is this true of all the planets we know about and the ones we don't know about—no matter what their energies are? Is it true that whether it's Mars or Saturn or anybody, that their energies are not coming through to the extent they once did?

They're coming through. Please understand, it's not either/or. Their energy and my energy come through as well. It's just that if you want to experience the energy of a given planet for some energizing in your own life that would be beneficial . . . for one thing, as an astrologer you would know generally what the planets are associated with. But as a student of astrology or someone reading this book for the first time, you would greatly benefit from reading a well-written astrology book or two to have some familiarity with the literature as it has accumulated over recent times and then make the connection.

But the energy from the planets is coming in. It's just not coming in to the degree that human beings can get as much out of it as they used to, and that's because the energy that came in before was attuned to a given, fixed population on the Earth. So it would work without the people of Earth doing anything up to a certain range of human beings.

How many?

Oh, three or four billion, tops. But as it reached that number, it started to get to the point where it was necessary for people on Earth—and some spiritually educated people and cultures knew about this—to begin drawing the energy toward Earth. Now, I feel it's of value and I've been encouraged to spread the word about this a bit more so that others besides these few select individuals and groups around the planet—some who have been interfered with in recent years because of this or that battle—can now help them to bring the energy in. The rate of energy, the amount that flows naturally to Earth, has not changed. But the number of human beings . . .

Has doubled.

Yes, and who and what you are and what you are doing and all of the things you are doing have, as you say, doubled. Therefore, you need more energy—not the same amount. In order for there to be more, Creator has set it up in such a way as you need to act on your own and take responsibility at least in some small way for creation itself.

I understand. So if we do connect to your energy, does that mean that of the given amount we have more of it or that we pull more from you?

"We" meaning Earth, or "we" meaning human beings?

I'm sorry, human beings. If someone as a result of this connects to you and pulls energy into himself or herself, is that additional energy coming from you, or does that take some of what the limited amount is and bring it into that person?

Thank you. It brings in an additional amount; it doesn't pull on what is already here. Yes, very good question. Of course, because you are naturally radiating at all times, it will affect your life in some way. It will radiate in and around your life and what you do, and of course, it will also radiate out toward others in a benevolent way.

This is not something you can do only once; you can do it more than once. Perhaps you feel that another surge of that energy would be useful at some other time of your life—then do it again. Don't feel the least bit shy that this is something that you do once and that's it. You can do it more than once.

So you literally have an unlimited amount of this energy?

Well, let's put it like this: I have plenty more in reserve. [Laughs]

That is absolutely fascinating.

We Appear in Ancient Writings as Inspiration

Have you talked to humans through channels? Did the planets use this type of process at various times, in addition to what people felt? Was there also teaching?

If the culture made a space for it and there was somebody in the culture who could do it, then yes. We would do it if called upon. Usually we would not be called upon by name, but they might request "a being of benevolence who could improve the quality of the lives of our people," something like that. Then I might come through. That's how a lot of the original energy and wisdom about planetary bodies was originally researched by peoples in that way. Of course, when you go back far enough, one might find these researches in different dialogues, meaning that the culture might not refer to Jupiter in that sense as a planet. It might refer to some being who spoke through them.

If you went back as a historian or a researcher in these fields and you explored more ancient writings associated with religions and cultures from the past, you might very well find that when material was passed down this way and energies and so on—either through the so-called channeling process or what was known in times gone by as the inspiration process—that various forms of inspiration would happen. People would see visions or hear words or hear sounds, and sometimes these sounds would come through them in the form of language for others and so on, depending on how it was described. You would often find that various planetary bodies, as you know them to be today, would initially be described as some*one*, not some*thing*.

So it would just be different words. But if you had a capacity for understanding personalities, one could easily find—and I believe this may have been done in your documents and documentation by various individuals already, though you might have to search for the book—that, "In this culture such and such an energy was described by this word or by that word, and I believe," as the author might say, "that this refers to Jupiter and so on." Some of the more esoteric astrological writings have gone down these avenues as well, and they make very interesting reading for people who are researchers or historians in this field, although it is not necessarily something the average person would find interesting. But I feel that it goes to show how long such information has been available, how peoples have been inspired, and how the inspiration was able to help them in their own times, in their own way, within their own culture.

Astrology Will Be Available When You Need It

Is astrology only on this planet where we don't know who we are, as Saturn mentioned? How is it used on other levels where you exist? Are the energies worked with in the way they are here?

Astrology, as it is practiced here . . . the Explorer Race is exclusive to you. In other places, people do not need to be reminded of who they are, where they are from, why they are wherever they are, what they are doing, where they are going, and what they are becoming. They have that knowledge, or it is readily available, so it is something, as you know it and as you have known it, that is unique to this environment that you, as the Explorer Race, have here. It is a tool that you need, but also the Creator felt that it could eventually be used as a creator-school teaching tool, which as you can see from our conversation today, can be adapted nicely into your education as Creator has suggested.

So when we become a creator, unless we have other creator schools someplace, it's not going to be around very long, is it?

Well, it will be around, as you say it, as long as it's needed, and it will be available should the need arise at some other place.

That's amazing. It's so complex, and it's so precise, and it's so spiritual, mathematical—it's an amazing system! To have created it for just this one group, for the Explorer Race!

Yes, well, you needed it, didn't you? I think now more than ever, it is especially useful in understanding who to partner with romantically, but it is often overlooked as a source of who to partner with on a business level, except by the most successful businesses. The most successful businesses almost always use it, unless they are using some other form of spiritual inspiration. They might not necessarily discuss it openly, but if you're going to be successful, you need to take advantage of the opportunities that are offered to you and to know timing sequence.

Astrology is very good for when, and it is also profoundly good for who. In many cases, it can be very helpful as well for where and what. It is perhaps not as good for why, but why is, I can say, an open field—it is still accumulating why. I might add, this book is intending to add to why, who, where, what and all of that.

You Are Learning that Action Brings Consequence

What happened on your planet? A few years ago, something crashed into you. Was it a comet that hit you?

It was an object. It was an excitement, just the kind of thing I was warned about [laughs] from Creator—something to excite human beings. It isn't anything I invited, but it was very exciting for a lot of human beings.

What was the effect or result for you?

I would have preferred to not have had the experience; as well, that which was moving would have preferred to not have had the experience. On the other hand, it does give your human race on Earth pause to consider the possibilities of actions and their consequences. I think that since then there's been considerable more scrutiny toward looking at actions and their consequences globally. So, in that sense, it was a good example that science helped to show the world. After all, if there weren't telescopes and so on aimed in that direction, then as far as you knew, it could have happened not at all.

The whole point of it happening then was that you had the technology to show it. Granted, even though the scientists might have been excited and happy because they had something to see, they weren't of a violent nature themselves [laughs]. It was an unusual thing to see. One often studies it after the fact but rarely sees it happening. But from my point of view and from Creator's point of view, the whole point is that there are noticeable consequences when there is action. Look at your political climate now. There is a great deal of scrutiny going on in terms of noticing consequences.

Oh, absolutely. Everywhere—churches, prisons, politics, everyplace, yes.

Yes, older cultures have had this scrutiny for years, but your culture and your country is young. Although you are influenced by older cultures, you still, like any other, accumulate certain experiences on the basis of what you do as compared to what others have done.

I'm still not clear, though. Can you say what hit you?

I didn't say.

Can you?

I won't. I will simply say that it was not man-made. Is that not sufficient?

Yes, although I don't understand why, if it was a comet, you can't say so.

If it was, what's the difference?

Can we talk to you again?

Yes, as far as I know, we can resume the next time, whenever that might be.

Excellent. Thank you very, very much.

Be sure to do that connection to my personality and see if you can breathe the energy in for yourself. Remember, you must be able to notice in your own physical body what feels comfortable and what doesn't. So if you feel something, if you're breathing in from that point and you feel discomfort, then stop at once and try to blow out from that same place. Do you understand?

Yes. I was doing it when you were talking and it felt really good, so I'll do it again later tonight for a longer time. All right, thank you.

Good night.

JUPITER • • • **131**

♃ Jupiter

JUPITER

Helps You Move toward a Soul-Centered Astrology

June 5, 2004

Greetings. What would you like to inquire about today?

There seems to be a connection between Jupiter and Jove. Is there any connection between you and Jehovah?

Jehovah is the Earth name for God-deity, if that is what you mean. Of course, everyone is connected to Creator, but if you're talking about some individual who goes by that name, there's no more connection than I am connected to all beings.

Elsewhere Practically No One Has a Name

I think you said before that Jupiter was your name, or is that our name for you?

Your name.

You don't have a name?

Practically no one has a name, believe it or not. Names are vitally important where you are because as the Explorer Race you're studying the impact of one to another. Think about that. Your science essentially studies that and your actions as individuals are all about that, and even when one considers groups of individuals, one just adds the multiplier. So that's the main thing you are about, you understand? I think it is valid and useful to understand that, because if you look at your own life plus the lives of others, you could lay that right in there as a foundation block.

In other places, even on other planets who might have representatives who come to see you, names are not so critical. This is because there is no need to have any barrier whatsoever to communication. So on other planets, communion between benevolent beings would be the thing you seek. Often in your culture one seeks this in a lover relationship, but sometimes one finds it between friends and even sometimes with family members. Communion means that one understands quite clearly what others means when they are speaking (or even when they say a portion of a sentence), and sometimes one might understand their needs as well as their communication, even if there is nothing said. This might be a good working description of communion.

On other planets, then, where benevolence is the norm, one is not required to have any barrier up, either artificial (meaning something technologically stimulated) or personal (meaning some fear or some such thing). For instance, someone might come along and you wouldn't have to acknowledge that person by name. Think about it: When you acknowledge somebody by name, all kinds of characteristics, beliefs and experiences go with that name. It might even be the case that this is so for someone you've never met but you've heard things about him or her. Therefore, there is this whole list of qualities—real or imagined—that identify or function as an identifier for someone. If they are trusted, then communication at least can take place. If they are loved and deeply trusted, perhaps communion would be possible. But if they are unknown, then even if they don't have a name to you—meaning of course they have a personal name, but to you they are unknown—as an unknown you might consciously or otherwise ascribe a name to them based upon how you identify them.

In some cases, you would do that on the basis of their basic appearance—perhaps, as you might say, their nationality or some such thing. Or given that they have a similar nationality to you, for instance, you might identify them on the basis of what they wear, how they act, things like that. That will be very similar in description to the name reaction to you, meaning that you might react to them on the basis of previous experience with individuals you identify that way or on the basis of things you've heard—both worthwhile information, meaning truthful according to the person or persons speaking to you, according to their experience, or perhaps it is a misunderstanding, misinformation or even (intentional or otherwise) disinformation, meaning essentially a lie.

In other words, you have various agendas (which we need not go into) in terms of how you act or react on the basis of how you feel toward someone or something. But none of this applies on other places where there is benevolence. There a complete and total stranger might come up to you, and you are completely open to that being in communication and names are completely unnecessary.

This is why I mention that names, while they might very well exist, are not what I would call required. They are useful, of course, in describing or suggesting, or even in ceremonies or something official. But other than that, there is not a great deal that is required there. Even in many off-planet cultures, there is considerable knowledge and awareness of what one member of your culture or group might have said or communicated to some other group you are communicating with. So whether they talk to you about it or if they talk to another member of your crew or your group about it doesn't make much difference.

In short, what I am saying is that the names individuals have are very important to you on your planet but less so on other planets with other cultures—and considerably less so with beings who might be functioning as a conscious creator. I am not claiming to be a creator creating universes or multiple beings or anything like that, though I am a portion of this creation as you are. But I am involved in the creation and, at the very least, the maintenance of my own body as a planet. Therefore, I have quite a significant array of capabilities and I have no particular need—with the exception of the portion of myself that is potentially experienced by you, the Explorer Race, where you are living—to defend myself in any way. Therefore [chuckles], the need for a name, you understand, is not particularly necessary.

Now, I don't want to make it sound like you're the only people who have names. But I will say that names are very important to you to understand and appreciate, especially considering the fact that almost everyone—almost every human being and quite a few animals on Earth—are constantly thinking of your survival (you are thinking of it, or it is just below the surface). So I understand that names are vitally important to you so that you can *evaluate*. But other than your culture, you rarely find much attachment to names.

This is why in various reports of contacts over the years between human beings and extraterrestrials, almost the very first thing human beings will say after, "Where are you from?" is, "What's your name?" That's within the first two or three questions. Very often in the reports you'll read that the being who responds either says, "What's a name?"—and then the human being goes on, "It's a means to personally identify yourself," or something like that—or you'll often find that the being from another planet will be very vague about a name, not because that being's afraid of being indentified [chuckles], but rather because a name may or may not be a particularly important part of that being's identity culturally or personally. So for those of you who have had these experiences, don't feel that others are trying to hide their identity from you.

The other factor that very often exists when there has been a prolonged contact between an Earth person and someone from another planet, especially if the people from other planets may have (and this has happened in the past) some kind of a judgment that they're passing on you . . . not in a major way, but they may wonder why, for instance, your cultures are often violent or that there is violence whatsoever. This is because they do not know or they did not know for a while that you're accomplishing something here much more vast than what individual perceptions can detect, and the whole *Explorer Race* books and text and the other articles support the explanation of that. For those interested, you can examine that material.

Before the 1960s, ET Visitors Didn't Know Who You Were

In terms of the actual question/query of, say, an Earth contactee to some of these beings in the past, you might find that the Earth person said, "What's your name?" and then that person from another planet didn't answer right away and afterward might even have made—at some point, if they decided to share their name—the point of, "Why do you make such a big issue out of a name?" If you want to see examples of this, consult literature on the basis of contactees' reports, where the contacts themselves took place in the mid-1960s and before—nothing past that for the most part—regardless of when the publication took place. That actually shows a degree of judgment, but it also shows the ignorance that occurred mostly for some cultures that were in contact with you from the 1950s and before.

This was not the case for all cultures that contacted you from other planets, but it was the case for some. It was particularly the case for cultures that were very similar to you in appearance. Part of the reason they didn't know who you are and what you are doing here is that it was felt by Creator (and Creator's consultants and teachers and guides and angels and everyone) that because of the similarity—not only in appearance but, to a significant degree, biologically—there might be an actual biological (meaning cellular) identification process going on, even though the other planetary beings themselves might not be conscious of it.

So they were essentially protected from knowing who you are as these Explorer Race beings. This was necessary, not only so that they would feel good about who they are (protecting their identity in that sense, protecting their self-image), but it also was important because in contact with you—and there wasn't that much contact of beings like this with Earth people—it is possible for them (because you look so much like them, even though they might be highly technologically protected by various means of equipment) to become affectionate in some way toward you, to think of you as brothers and sisters, to think of you as like beings, only needing to be educated according to their philosophy and to understand whatever they believe. So because of this tendency that occurred from time to time, their contact with you was gradually weaned out. They were told only at the last moment (meaning around the 1960s) who you are and what you might mean to them in the long run, and they've been pondering this for a while.

An example of these people might be from the Pleiades, for instance. In places on the Pleiades, you could go and you would see beings from the Pleiades who, if a photograph was available, even a medical photograph . . . you could have a Pleiadian standing next to a human being, if possible, both facing you and then slowly turning to the side by quarter degrees or something like that, gradually turning around, and you would see no difference. From all outer appearances, the people would be identical. It was therefore considered to be useful and helpful to protect their self-image and to allow them time to assimilate what it meant that they would someday be in contact with you: that it wasn't for them to teach you, but rather for you to, not exactly teach them, but by your example to stimulate them to grow in ways that would be safe for them but would in time alter not only their culture but their perception of themselves as individuals.

Think about it; put yourself in their shoes, so to speak. Imagine that this is how you've been raised. Imagine you were suddenly told that in order for you to develop and come to be the beings that you *could* be, you would have to seriously consider—in time, through contact—emulating horses. Now, of course that is an extreme example; horses don't look anything like you.

But from their point of view, there was that difference in class and . . .

There was that kind of gap, that's right—and quite obviously emulating horses would not work for Earth human beings. It isn't that they thought so much less of you but that they had so much love for you as fellow beings, meaning you looked almost exactly like them, from their point of view, that they would want to . . . how can we say, in a term you can *so* easily identify with? They wanted to *save* you. Can you imagine, even for a moment, how shocked they were that it was really . . . ?

The other way around.

The other way around, at least to a degree. That requires some significant time for adjustment, wouldn't you say?

[Chuckles.] Yes.

So I thought that might be a little sidelight story to help you understand a name and what it's about.

Oh, that's excellent.

It's in the Nature of All Life to Respond Similarly

I have another question. A lot of our science-fiction literature assumes that in the future Jupiter will become a sun. Is there any basis in that? Do you know where that came from?

None whatsoever. It is purely an imagination that was generated by authors and then by other authors to suggest the possibility—purely imagination and art form.

Okay. The Moon sends its energy only toward Earth, the Sun in the center sends its energy out to all the planets, and you said that your energy was radiating out from the center.

If I might correct you, from my understanding, even if the Moon said it sends its energy toward you, that might be true in terms of the Moon's function with you. But from my experience with your Moon, it does radiate its identity from the side that does not face you. I think the Moon might have stated that the energy it broadcasts with *intent* is meant for you on Earth (and I would certainly agree with that), but it does broadcast a self-identifier beyond that. Now, please go ahead with your question. I just want you to understand the context—to put it in the fuller context, if you don't mind my saying.

To put it in context, if you were to approach another human being and you were to introduce yourself—"Greetings, my name is Melody," and so on—you would of course be projecting your identity, you might say, or at the very least demonstrating your identity to the person. Even though you were directing your communication to them and all that you wish to do with them toward them, your back (your shoulders, and so on) would still be projecting your self-identity.

Now, there's a reason I'm trying to say this: It's not as if you do not have the mental capability to extrapolate that toward yourself as an example, but it's very important to understand that certain fundamental facts, you might say, exist for all beings. I will give an example. Say there is liquid in a Petri dish that a scientist wishes to examine (I'm going to say "liquid" because it's the most easily understandable). Say the scientist puts a little swab of liquid—let's call it water—on a slide to examine under the microscope. Do you know that once the scientist begins to examine it, the molecules in that water all turn to face the examiner when that occurs?

It is interesting, because these are things you would understand. If someone spoke to you, "Melody, hello!" you would immediately turn to face him or her. If someone came into the room you were in and was staring at you, examining you, your natural reaction would be to look up and look back at that person. I'm mentioning this because it is important for you to understand that it is in the nature of all life to respond very similarly, at least on the physical plane that you occupy, to recognize and to learn the experience of one to another. The molecules themselves are quite well aware of one to another.

I think it's important for you to recognize this so you can realize that if I talk about the identity of the portion of the Moon that is not facing you (meaning not interacting with you), that it is still broadcasting its self-identity in the back of itself. When you look at the Moon and admire it, as you often do, or appreciate its light or even its energy, as some of you do, although you are seeing the portion of the Moon that faces you, you are of course also admiring the totality of the Moon, even though that portion is not a portion you normally see. By "normally," I mean you have the vehicles that have gone around the backside of the Moon and taken pictures, which you can identify, but it is not something you look into the sky and see.

Everything in Your Environment Affects You

Just as you radiate out in all directions (and let's say that all planets do), if you visualize the solar system and the planets going around, is there some sort of fusion or interaction between the energies of the planets that we get? As the energies from the planets radiate out in a circle or out from the center, do they interact with each other in some way that affects or influences us?

You mean, just by being, do they affect you? Yes. I'm glad you brought this up, because it's going to give me the opportunity to discuss something that you can apply to your day-to-day life, even in your homes. Everything in your environment, be it close by or be it at a distance, is actually in your environment. In this case, we are talking about planets that are at a distance, but you could say they're in your environment, because even though these planets we're talking about (including myself) are at a great distance, they are still in your environment, in the Explorer Race's environment. They are physical bodies—planets, yes—made up of substances not dissimilar to your own planet or atmosphere; that is why scientists can make good, educated guesses about what material they are coming into contact with. But it's also the simple mass of the planet, the size of it, its personality (as we're discussing in this book) and its foundational elements of personality that you as an immortal being—meaning a soul, a portion of Creator—might also demonstrate.

So, yes, the planets do affect you and your personality traits to a degree, but there are also many other subtleties involved here. Even the material you keep around the house—a couch, a chair, a book, to say nothing of a person or an animal—all of these things affect your personality traits, either encouraging certain traits to show themselves or perhaps even discouraging certain traits to show themselves. This is not counting the social interaction that you have between human beings and groups of human beings, animals and so on; just the physical matter in your proximity might very well affect your personality traits.

The planetary bodies then are, granted, ascribed to a degree in astrology with certain traits, but they're also ascribed specifically as having influences on human traits, since that is the whole point of astrology: to suggest who you are and to give you identifiers, according to planets or planetary groupings, as to who you are, what you are like, and how much of this you have, how much of that you have, and so on. These are the basics of astrology. So I'd have to say that that's true, as far as that goes. But what it doesn't take into account in the astrology most people are aware of—it does in some esoteric studies of astrology—is who your soul personality is and what your soul personality might wish to do. There are also other aspects of astrology that can demonstrate what you came here to do, why you are here, what you might choose to do.

Astrology is profoundly helpful in capabilities, meaning what you might find that comes easier to you. Therefore, if integrated into your society more in its precise way as it is used—when you were born, to the best of the ability of the physician to get it right minute-wise, and so on—this can be very useful and could help an individual, keeping him or her from perhaps choosing a profession, for example, that might be much more difficult for that person as compared to a profession that might be easier to study and so on. So I think it is worthwhile, but that perhaps is not the basis of your question.

Heliocentric Astrology Is Not Yet Complete

Well, I'd like to know more about that. You're saying that the astrology we know is based on the personality, but a heliocentric astrology is for the soul—is that right?

By heliocentric, do you mean Sun-centered astrology? Yes, and I understand that this is an attempt to understand the soul, but unfortunately it is not complete. The Sun, after all, while supporting life, nurturing life and so on, is more of what your soul might come here to do, but the Moon is more about what nurtures you to do that—and this has been discussed before, I think, so I won't go over it too much. I feel that in order to understand your soul's purpose, you have to also understand the tools and the energies you have available to sustain, to even maintain for a time, and to nurture one's own personality (on the immortal level or the soul level) and one's capability to contribute in some benevolent way that personality to one's self and others.

Therefore, in order for so-called heliocentric astrology to work benevolently and beneficially, the Moon will have to be taken into account and combined.

This may be done by some people; perhaps it's a ready being done and has been done by some. If so, I think that this would be a profoundly helpful form of astrology and can be done.

I know the standard frame of reference might be to look at the Sun as masculine and at the Moon as feminine, and I won't rule that out on the face of it, but I think it's important to allow that the Moon sometimes stimulates (so we can't say it's entirely feminine) and the Sun certainly nurtures (so it's not entirely masculine). Therefore, the traits I just mentioned, while they give these bodies a great deal more balance between masculine and feminine, also suggest their mutual compatibility.

So that's going to be my suggestion to astrologers: that heliocentric is not sufficient, but it's a good beginning. I believe those who have been working with heliocentric have noted that it needs something else. Include the Moon and I think you'll find what you're looking for. I know it doesn't actually work very well, because with the Moon, you're talking about orbits and timing, whereas the Sun is a constant. Nevertheless, try it and I think it will work pretty well. You can do it.

Soul-Centered Astrology Will Be Profoundly Helpful to You

One of the things I was looking for in this book was an expansion of the understanding of the personality traits of the planets, because humans are expanding, becoming more their natural self. So what would you say about the study of astrology as it is now? How can we add to that? Are there more planets who will talk?

I think there is a great deal of astrology that is studied and has been written about extensively that is not really filtered into the general public. Even books that are more advanced explorations of astrology—meaning more thorough, deeper—have not filtered out very much to the general public. Think about it: For most people in the general public who have any contact with astrology at all, it would be some notation in a newspaper or something like that. There needs to be a greater realization by the public, I would say, that while astrology cannot tell you everything that's going to happen in your life and in the future, it might make certain suggestions and allow you to become more prepared, utilizing the natural capabilities that you have based upon astrology's means of suggesting them and showing you that which you will be able to identify in yourself: "Yes, that's something I'm interested in," or "No, that's not something I'm interested in now."

What happens to the average person when he or she has an astrologer tell him or her about something? The astrologer will say, "These traits are associated with your sign," and then go into it and perhaps examine the traits more. Many times you will identify with that. For those of you who think that all traits are shared in all readings with all people, it's not true at all. Many traits are shared to a degree, but most of the traits associated with different signs are unique to those signs.

Another experience has to be understood. You might have some traits that you know about yourself now, but as time goes on, you may develop or become more interested in traits that you have later in life—though you don't know about them or think about them—or if something is added to the mix, as you were saying, meaning you are becoming more. You are becoming more of your greater self. In short, your immortal personality or your soul personality (those are interchangeable) is literally revealing more of itself.

Now we get to the crux of the matter, which is why I spoke at some length about the value of soul-centered astrology. I feel that that soul-centered astrology, using the Sun and the Moon, might be profoundly helpful in understanding greater portions of your soul personality that may be manifest now or may in time—on the basis of growth, change and (very important) adaptation to circumstances—just reveal themselves in the future. So if you're looking for a form of astrology that exists right now, this one would be worth exploring, especially for astrologers who have combined the Sun and the Moon. That type of astrology will not overlook your signs and all of this business, but the intent of that type of astrology is to add something else to the picture.

So if you're going to get a reading from someone who specializes in that, make sure you fit it into the overall picture of your astrological identity as you've understood it or into your astrological reading, as it's called. Don't just take it on its own, as something separate. It is not separate; it is something additional. I think that's very important, because there are some people who might wish to say, "Well, it's one or the other," but it isn't. I want to encourage astrologers to find ways (as some have in recent fictional books and so on) to integrate the value of astrology (especially at the deeper, so-called more esoteric levels) into the lives of the general public. If people are not going to be receptive to terminology, then use descriptive terms to describe the terminology. Don't be shy. I know there hasn't been much success with this being distributed to a wider degree in the past, but now is the time.

You Need to Consider the Distribution of What's Available to All Beings

The reason I am talking to such a wide array of topics today is that one of the things I know about, generally speaking, is the distribution of what's available to all beings. This is something that's a portion of my personality. That's why I made the comment about the other side of the Moon and compared it to the other side of your body, because it is easy to examine that which is seen. It is desirable, of course, to examine that which cannot be seen, and you've gone to some length to do that in these books. But it's also important to understand, whether something can be seen or unseen, how it moves about between people.

I want you to take that as a concept and think about it over the weekend when you have a moment. I want you to have time to think about it, and then for the next talk, let's continue a little bit talking about the distribution of this to that, if that is vast enough. I want it to be vast enough so that you understand. You've been asking about that a bit today, and I feel that it's important to continue to look at that. Look at it not only in its vastness—meaning planetary bodies and so on—but right down to the individualistic aspects of it: how it might apply to astrology, planets, planet personalities and so on. I can talk about that.

Can you talk more about that now?

I feel it's important for you to think about it and ask questions, because it's useful if you put some parameters around what specifically you'd like me to talk about in there. You understand, I do not wish to talk about it for the next three years [chuckles].

[Laughs.] All right—"distribution of this to that."

It won't be that difficult, because if you look at your life . . . even for an hour tomorrow, just look at it, everything. You feed the cats, yes? You give a certain quantity to this cat, a certain quantity to that cat, yes? That food comes from someplace, and it's managed and processed by someone and packaged by someone. This to that—do you understand? It's also the same thing for your food, as well as clothing, items.

What about personality traits? Have you ever picked up personality traits from someone? Quite obviously, people pick them up from their parents, their friends, their relatives when they are young, their schoolmates and so on. They might pick up a personality trait they hadn't demonstrated before, but was that personality trait there all along for themselves, being activated by somebody else? This is about things like that, see?

Distribution—think about it. Someone goes to a distant land in the past, maybe bringing technology. Granted, maybe in the 1600s you wouldn't think about what people had as technology, but say they go to a distant land where that technology isn't available and might be profoundly welcome—this to that. Things like that. Of course, many people on Earth are looking forward to benevolent contacts from extraterrestrials who will bring what they have to you—this to that. In most cases, they are quite conscious of not spreading too much of their energy to you in case it affects you in some way and being careful to not be exposed too much to your energy, because it might affect them. This doesn't mean that the products and services (and the knowledge and wisdom) they have cannot, in many cases, support who you are, what you are becoming, why you are here and, most importantly, what you need.

How soon do you see that?

Oh, I think it depends not on years at all. It depends on desires, and it depends on qualities being encouraged in the human being globally that are benevolent, including curiosity. Curiosity can be benevolent as long as people aren't encouraged, even in storybooks, to attempt to fly. That might make a nice story, but it is actually ultimately fear-based. You'd be surprised how many people it encourages to jump off bridges, not just because they are unhappy. I do not wish to blame the authors of these classic tales, which were intended to warn people about attempting things that were beyond their capabilities for safety's sake and so on. I know that it was well-meant. But it is more important to encourage the benevolent traits in people than to discourage the malevolent qualities. That is important, but it needs to be done while encouraging benevolent traits.

In short, your society has to become more benevolent and more caring about each other and everyone. Even though it looks right now like the opposite is true, this is not the case. If you asked every individual on the planet if they had the opportunity to say in just a few words what they would like, I think everyone would agree that they would like things to be better. Do you understand? You might define "things" differently and "better" differently, but you could say that they would like things to be better.

That would be the common ground, yes.

At the very least, they would like their lives and the lives of their families and so on to be more benevolent. I think everyone can agree on that. Since I feel [chuckles] that everyone can agree that they want things to be better, it is important to put energy into what everybody wants in some benevolent way. You are actually working on that. Some people are doing it now, and there is a groundswell developing toward that. Old institutions must be able to adapt; even if they are offering valuable services that people want, you must be able to adapt to being more benevolent and providing that which is more benevolent.

I know you're working on this, and I don't make any attempt to encourage you here to rush. I would rather that you go slowly, cover all the ground of any issue, be clear from one to the other what it is that you all consider to be benevolent, and work on that first to achieve it. In the process, you will probably be able to work out the differences that you have with each other to the degree of at least 80 percent.

Connecting Benevolently to Jupiter

I'd like to offer the reader a gift. You can, if you like—perhaps I have mentioned this before, but I'll elaborate—get a hold of a picture of how I look according to your vehicles that have flown by. You have had vehicles fly by; I've seen them go by. Use that if you like, but also in reading this material—understanding my personality a bit more and things that I feel are interesting to you, so getting a sense of me, if you would like—I would like you to think about me. Lie down sometime when you are completely able to, perhaps even before sleep sometime if you're not doing something else or before taking a nap, perhaps on a Sunday after church or after a meal. Lie down, and before you go to sleep, just picture me as you can, or having read this material, think a little about the material.

Just in picturing me and thinking about this material, if you can, ask me to connect benevolently to you, providing benevolence, generosity, wisdom, strength and a support for your depth of character and the qualities you would like to be aware of that are a portion of your own personality. Just say something like that before you go to sleep—and I have other prayers and so on. Say it either before or after sleep, depending on what feels right to you, and perhaps I will be able to impart that gift to you. You must say it out loud, however, in order for your body (not me) to know that this feels all right.

If at any time you're saying it out loud and it doesn't feel all right, don't assume it's you and don't assume it's me. It might be something in the environment, perhaps someone or perhaps some objects that are no longer a part of your life anymore but are in the place where you're lying down—this and that, maybe some stuff you intend to give away at some point, perhaps some stuff you've forgotten about in boxes. In short, there may be a little clutter here and there that might impinge on the effects.

It's always better when interacting with me—and really, to a great degree, with the rest of your life, meaning friends, family members and other human beings—to have only in your life what you are actually using or interacting with. It's easy to keep stuff around in close proximity to you (meaning in your bedroom or in your living room or office) that isn't really something that is part of your life currently. I would recommend that if you have an attic, store it in the attic or perhaps someplace over some portion of the house that isn't used that much or where people do not linger. If the basement is secure, you might put it there, or even a storage locker, if you have such things. This does not exclude it from your life, but it does recognize that it is not a part of your life now.

Other than that, if it feels good to make this comment, I will then to the best of my ability gift you with as much as I can and as much as is comfortable to you in that moment,. You may be aware of this to a degree when you awaken, or you might become aware of it sometime after you awaken, over time.

I feel it now—it's wonderful.

Use Your Discernment

Granted, you might very well be able to decide what is good in some ways for society, meaning violence by one to another is not good. But there are points at which your cultures make judgments that are too broad—meaning something is not right for you as a culture given, in many cases, perfectly reasonable explanations. For instance, since I'm using that, violence is not a good thing in your culture because it might very well—and usually does—harm someone and often things that you cherish, possibly even special things or special someones. So you can all pretty much agree that violence is not something you wish to integrate as a building block and cherish in your life or in your society—at least most of you.

There are other things you might wish to say are for you—and other things you might wish to say are *not* for you—but as a general rule, please don't in the future assume that if something is not for you that it is necessarily bad. Some things will require discernment to decide whether it is bad, meaning violence equals bad (I'm trying to be simplistic here so that you can agree on that). But in some cases—although this is not something I'm trying to encourage you to do—in some situations (I'm not trying to encourage you), you might consider violence to be good.

I'll give you an perfectly good example of this: If some object comes hurtling toward you—let's call it a hailstone, a big hailstone—if you're out in a storm and there are big hailstones coming, as big as golf balls, it is true that if you are wearing a hardhat as one might wear at a construction site, those hailstones will smash violently and be destroyed, and then melt when they bounce off your hard hat. That is violence, but it is perhaps a benevolent violence for you. Ultimately, because it is ice, it is not destroyed; its form is transformed.

This does not make it okay to shoot and kill, to maim and hunt your fellow human beings, and so on, but I am trying to suggest to you that it is very important, especially in the times you are living in now—where religions, philosophies, ways of being, attitudes, culture, conditioning and so on are coming under the microscope—to give yourself the mission to develop your discernment definitely. Also, give yourself permission when you read something or when you hear about something, to either use your discernment to say, "This is not for me," or to say, "You know, perhaps it is for others." Good night.

Good night. Thank you very much.

148 • • • ASTROLOGY: PLANET PERSONALITIES & SIGNS SPEAK

♇ Pluto

PLUTO

Expands Your Universal Awareness

October 5, 2006

I am the planet in your solar system that you have referred to as Pluto.

It is in my nature to observe from a distance and to consider whether the presented realities (what is seen) can represent the obvious, or whether there is more to be seen, felt and heard. That is my nature. I have experienced this orbit for some time, but my orbit has begun to change slightly. This is because there is another planet beyond that has begun to increase in mass.

You might not know this, but planets can grow. They are not just chunks of rock wobbling around in the universe. This planet is growing in terms of its overall size, and as a result, my orbit has been affected. I will wait for that planet to speak for itself perhaps, but for now I am available for your questions.

Does that other planet have a name we can ask for?

Just ask for the planet beyond Pluto, that's all. You understand, we do not call ourselves by the names you do.

How do you feel about our scientists calling you a planetoid instead of a planet?

I am not insulted. Whatever term they want to use is perfectly all right. They can call me an asteroid if they want to, but of course, I am what you would consider a planet, yes. But it really doesn't matter; it has perhaps been made too much of. Scientists have classifications, but a planetoid is still a planet. It's just another way of referring to a planet that has a dimension attached to it—"dimension" meaning size. But it is just a word. It doesn't change the fact that if you were walking on it, you would say, "Oh, well, this is a planet, quite obviously." Just like any other planetary body, it is a planet. Too much has been made about the reclassification.

The Questions Must Be Focused

I'd like you to tell our readers about yourself: how you got here, what your joys are. Do I need to ask them one at a time?

You always have to ask them one at a time. Do you know why? The reason you ask questions one at a time is that if you ask multiple questions, you are not focused. As the questioner, you must be focused upon what you are asking and you must actually have a desire to know what you are asking. If you have a desire to know more than one thing at once, you cannot hear the answer. We can answer more than one thing simultaneously, but you cannot hear it.

Therefore, the questions you ask—if you ask more than one—if you don't remember to go back and ask each at the time, you will have missed the other answers because they will be outside the range of your hearing. We actually answer all those questions. Say you ask three or four questions at once. We answer them all, but you only hear the answer of one. Then if you do not go back and ask those questions again, you and your readers will not hear those answers either.

It is your job, then, to be a lens. You focus. Try to retain your curiosity about whatever it is you asked. That's why writing down a few questions beforehand has advantages, so you don't have to think about what you're going to ask—even if it's something you would remember. Any time you are remembering another question while you are engaged in talking about the question you have just asked, immediately that answer begins to flow, so that information is lost.

You have to focus like a good lens. A good lens, when it is focusing, is focused only on one place and stays there. You know what I mean. When your eyes are working well, you hold a book up and you keep it in the exact spot, or perhaps you hover your head over the exact spot where you can see the print at its best. But if you pull back or you move too close, you cannot see it well. You must be the good lens: focus and stay focused.

Thank you. That's the best explanation I've heard.

Creator Liked My Universal Worldview

Tell me how you happen to be in this solar system.

A long time ago, before this solar system, I did exist, as we all do. I existed in many parts all over this universe—literally, as one might say poetically, scattered to the winds. I enjoyed that, because I was able to be many places at once and still be one personality. This is not unknown in the universe. But the Creator of this universe liked that view . . . you have something referred to as a worldview, yes? Creator liked what I had because I had a universal view and requested that I volunteer for a time—not permanently, but for a time—to be a planet in a solar system that He had special plans for ("He" being a term, but you could also put "She" if you like). Creator then went on to communicate—I'll say "say," but you understand that it's more than that—the plans for this solar system and the beings who would occupy the solar system, the Explorer Race and so on.

I felt it was a good plan and I would be happy to cooperate with it as long as I didn't have to have immediate contact with these explorers. I said that I would be fine having contact someday, but only after they had matured enough to be out in their solar system with the capacity to move beyond the immediate planet or two that they would like to explore. Even when exploring the immediate planet or two, they would still have a lot of their inner conflict, and I would like them to be past their inner conflicts by the time they got here. That's why I'm in my position.

I'm in a place where, when you get here as the Explorer Race, you will be well past your inner conflicts and will be devoted to seeking causes, cures and applications. I like that, because you will then be devoted to serving each other and experiencing what each other has to offer—meaning your born-to talents—and not demanding or commanding that everyone be the same, learn the same, and act the same, when you are not here to do that.

You are on your planet, as everyone is, to be unique, to have certain things you do well, and to do them well in a way that is unique to your own personality. If there is something that you do well and a few other people do it well also—meaning a talent, a natural ability—you don't have to all do it the same way. This whole thing that you are attached to right now, of everyone being the same, is an actual psychological outgrowth of wanting to fit in.

When you are young, you want to fit in, and now your entire civilization in the Western world and in the East as well is all about fitting in. So I think that I would be much more welcoming of you when you are your unique personalities and no longer something that is of only a few tones. I am going to welcome you when you can sing your full chorus.

When You Come Here, You'll See All Points of the Universe

How do you reflect what the Creator admires in you in this solar system?

Even though I am in this solar system and devoted to it, I am also able to be aware of everything going on in this universe as well. You will find that when you come here—and this is why you'll want to come here, you see—even if you are wearing an insulated suit to move about on the surface of the planet as best you can, that if you are here on the planet and even to a degree within, say, five miles of the surface, within five minutes you will begin to develop the ability to see (not feel, because you will be insulated from that) things in all points of the universe. At first it will come as many pictures, some of which will alarm you and others that will entice you. But in time you will be able to focus on this or that specific place, especially if you spend more time here.

There will be things that you will see that will be wondrous. If you have navigational instruments with you, you will be able to literally set a navigational course for those places. You may, of course, have to spend a lifetime getting there, but if you have already made friends with beings who can travel in time—and it is likely that you will have done so by then—you can move across the universe in a moment and get to that place in a form where you can interact with those forms of life there.

This may not mean that you will move across the universe in your physical body. That is actually the slowest possible way. The quickest way is to be in physical repose, where your body does not have to act or react to anything. I'm not talking about being in a comatose state or anything; I am talking about being in a completely quiet manner. You can be in a lighter form of your physical body and interact in that place that attracts you in a form that is comfortable for the beings in that place, and thus interact in ways that are comfortable to you and comfortable to them.

You might not know this, but that is how a great deal of interplanetary travel takes place when one decides that one does not want to use a ship anymore. Many of the beings who have visited Earth from other planets visit in this way, and they are able to fit right in and look just like any other human being, if they are visiting humans. Sometimes, if they are visiting what you call animals, then they look like one of them. They are able to look exactly that way, because it is in the nature of their form of travel that there is an adaptational process, where the closer you get to what you are interested in, the more you appear like that and the more you would be that. So those whom you are with in that place interact with you as that and you are able to interact as that yourself—all the while seeing yourself as you are on your native planet.

Therefore, you are able to be and to do what you do on your native planet, and you are also able to be and to do what that life form does on the planet where you are visiting. This is the way of planetary exploration for those who are beyond using ships. All of that will be possible when you come here, but you won't be able to get here until you are what I said you would be—not because I say it, but simply because you are in rapid transition toward that right now.

So because you can see to all points of the universe, then you're able to share that with the visitors?

It is not possible to be on the surface or even within, say, five miles of the surface without having that experience. So when you come, don't come with the idea that you are going to drill into the planet and see and do all this stuff. It is a place to come for visionaries, it is a place to come for explorers, and that is what you are. But it is not a place where you can do anything else.

When visitors, people from other planets, come here—even those who know what I am able to provide—they do not come *with* anything. They come, they land, or they sometimes hover. They experience that vision, and then they either go where that vision calls them, or they have the knowledge that they need. That's why beings do come here, and it is to their advantage that the planet is small. It can be found, you understand, I can be found, but you have to want to find me. [Chuckles.]

You have an eccentric orbit. Is there a reason for that? The others go around horizontally, and it's like you come up vertically?

I've said that: the planet beyond me. I am affected by the planet beyond me.

That much?

Yes.

Everyone Exists All the Time, Everywhere

Before you came to this Creator's universe, were you in another universe or in all universes?

No, I am using the word "universe" the way you use it.

But before you came to this universe, you already had this ability, right?

You want my recollections before this universe?

I understood that it was before this universe that you had this ability, and then the Creator asked you to come to this universe.

No. I was in this universe with that ability.

Ah, I see. But you had come from someplace else?

Everybody exists before everything. The best way to understood it is as a wheel or as a sphere. Everybody exists before everything, and yet if you exist before everything, how is that possible?

Tell me.

No, it is a question—it is the sphinx question, you understand? That means it is a question you are meant to ponder, not that I am going to answer. What would be your answer now?

I understand that there are periods of manifestation and periods of repose, and I don't know when the first one started, but before this current round of activity, we were all resting or unmanifest.

Yet you would be someplace, would you not?

We would be someplace, even though there were no manifest creations available out there to look at.

But that would be someplace. How could you be someplace before?

Well, there are pre-creation energies, there's more than one totality.

The answer is easier than you might think. *Everyone exists all the time, everywhere.* [Pause.] It is all about focus, like the lens. Picture a lens free-floating in space. The lens is part of space, so the lens is part of any given space it is in. If that given space is part of existence, then the lens is part of that existence. Yet depending upon what the lens is focused on at any given moment (it may be focused on this planet or that planet), the lens makes clear what is there for others to see. Is the lens that which it is making clear, or is it more than that? That is a hint that explains all creation.

Feeling Is Natural

How do you interact with other beings in this creation?

The closest thing that you can experience—and my answers must always be associated with what you can experience; otherwise it's completely irrelevant—is feeling. Feeling is a constant. For example, you might feel warm, and you feel warm even though there are other people on your planet in that immediate moment who feel cold. You are all one, you know that, and yet you feel warm.

What I am saying is that feeling is a constant. I am able to feel without harm to myself or others, and so I am able to feel what you or anybody else is feeling everywhere in the universe. This is typical when one is not experiencing life in the specific manner that you are experiencing it on Earth. You and others on Earth are learning how to be a creator, and you are well on down the road in that process—you are not just beginning. You are at the point where you are learning about how your creations are experienced by those whom you create, and the only way to do that is to be created by someone.

So you are experiencing life as an element of a creator. In this way, you can have every question come to the surface that anything or anyone you create would naturally have. Once you leave this process, you will be searching for the best and most benevolent answers to all of those questions. When you have those answers, then you'll be ready to take the next step in creator training.

If you weren't ensouling . . . how would you say it? Inhabiting that planet?

Not inhabiting—the planet . . .

So I could say you created that planet?

No. You could say that all the portions of this planet are identifiable as me. Even if you took a small part of the planet and took it over to the other part of the universe . . . someone who understands these things would say, "Oh, I know who that is!" Just as someone who is sensitive on Earth can be shown a stone and say, "Oh, I know who that is."

So you have a feeling connection to all the beings in the universe. Does it go further than that into communion with individual ones? What is the extent of your interactions beyond feeling?

Feeling is the one you can identify with and experience. But to give you an answer that will help mathematically, it is about one-tenth of 1 percent of my interaction with all life. It simply is that you have a limited experience of what you are able to do, so you are not overwhelmed by your natural talents and abilities on Earth and thus can experience life as the type of being—not the exact type, but the general type of being—that is your choice for the type of being you would like to create as a creator. What better way to understand the needs of those you will be supporting as a creator than to be one of them?

This is something that I recommend every child does, and when they are young enough they naturally do it. If they are around a dog or a cat they love and who loves them, they will naturally feel life as that dog or that cat. It is natural. The child will do that and sometimes even pretend to be that in a visual way: meaning crawl around, pretend to be a dog or a cat, much to the amusement of the parents. But the child has the capacity to actually feel like the dog or feel like the cat. In short, this is a natural ability you have.

Which we've forgotten as we grow up?

Well, you can still do it. Actors and actresses do it. You don't really forget it, you just set it aside, except for those who choose that as a profession and, by their very being, offer something you can all do, though perhaps not to the degree of professionalism by which they portray it.

Spirit Beings on Pluto

Do you have any beings on your planet? What type of life lives on your planet?

There are some forms of life. If you were here, you would say they are spirits, because they appear and then they are gone. But that is their chosen way of being. They do not wish to be in a given place for more than a moment. This makes them ideal, considering the nature of my being on the planet. They do not eat, they do not drink, they do not breathe as you understand it. But if you were here and were able to talk to one of them, you would see them and you would ask them a question, and then they would disappear.

If you stayed in your exact position to the best of your ability, they would reappear shortly thereafter and give you part of their answer. Then they would disappear, and then they would reappear and give you as much of the answer as you were able to take in, retaining the exact position you were in when you first asked the question. In short, they can find you as long as you appear to be who asked the question in the first place. But if you should move, even in the interim while they are gone, you would not find them appearing near you. [Chuckles.] This will be a bit of a conundrum, but I think if you can approach it in a childlike manner, it will be great fun.

Of course, they will have much to say, much to offer, and a great deal to advise you on while you are here, because the learning curve while you are here is quite prominent and you will not have to struggle. But it would be helpful to have an adviser or two.

To bring an adviser with us, you mean? Or would the spirits be our advisers?

The beings who are there. You would call them spirits, but of course, they live here. They just choose to be like that, as you might expect, since being here with who I am and what can be done here might very well prompt someone to be here and then be elsewhere.

You Must Become Self-Creators

So you have many focuses, right? Many levels of existence?

In my case, I have only a few. I am able to express what I am comfortable expressing in three or four. Earth is different. She needs to have a vast amount, because life with the Explorer Race upon her is so intense that she needs to have many other levels to maintain her personality and, to a degree, disseminate that intensity.

Almost to escape to, it sounds like!

[Chuckles.] Perhaps that is not so very untrue. When you have an intense day, you do the same thing, do you not? You change form. Changing form for the human being is a daily experience. Did you know that? You change form every single day when you sleep. You, your body, sleeps, but you, your personality, does not sleep. You change form into a natural state for yourself, and you travel, you go see friends, you experience your natural state of being, because you cannot be here constantly without sleep. If you are sleep deprived, ultimately death occurs, because your native spirit needs to be yourself.

Being yourself is not an option; it is a necessity. So changing form is a natural thing. In the larger picture, you might say, every day you change form into being the physical human being, and then when you are sleeping, you change back to being your natural self.

How long before we can consciously remember that?

You can remember it now—I just told you. I understand what you're saying, pardon my joke. You want to know when you can remember being your natural self. What's the advantage? If you remember that, why would you want to stay here as a human being and struggle? No one's going to want to do that until life on the planet is completely benevolent. Then you will want to do that, because it will be one more wonderful thing to do.

But since you are learning everything there is to know about that which you wish to create from the receiving end, not just the creating end, you will choose to create that benevolence yourself. After all, any creator is going to desire that who and what you create is able to do at least some of what you do and is able to bring about their own happiness in the case of something they have done that brought about sadness. So you must bring about your own happiness.

In other words, you must become self-creators. You in the smaller world, to a degree, create your life on a daily basis. Yet you need the assistance of others every day. Even if you think you are independent, you are always being assisted. You are assisted by other humans, by plants, by animals, by Earth herself, by the entire solar system and beyond. Many times you are assisted by those whom you don't know or never meet in human form or animal form, perhaps—and certainly when you eat, by that which you eat. So you are in constant contact with other life forms.

Thus, you create and re-create every day. This goes into a cumulative experience for you that you will examine once you have departed life on this planet. You will see, as a result, what you have contributed to your overall knowledge and wisdom, and to the overall knowledge and wisdom of all the beings of which you are a portion. Then you will either choose to go on and acquire more, or you will advise those who are going on to acquire that—meaning you will advise those souls who are coming to Earth to be born. What better adviser than one who has just left?

Than one who has experience, yes. So you only have a few levels of existence, and on one of them, those very fast-moving travelers live. Is there anybody else on any of the other levels?

Oh, yes, but mostly visitors. Not unlike your own planet, eh? Your own planet is packed with visitors, including yourselves.

What is your greatest joy in being who you are now in our solar system?

I am happy to serve this Creator, because this Creator has come up with something entirely new: the creation in which you know yourselves to be as the Explorer Race. But the new thing is how it will turn out, meaning that the inside-out apparatus is intended to create something new. Of course, it's really an aspect of benevolence that simply isn't seen very often. Still, it will be new to this universe and will allow you, as the Explorer Race, to create from a clean slate, while within is the entire creation made by this Creator.

Picture it as a marble. Inside the marble is the creation, which was created by this Creator, but you will be on the outside of the marble and that is where you will create. Then someday, when you choose to move on, to do other things, the universe will turn back to being what it was, only the creation of the Creator which you now know will be on the outside and your creation will be on the inside, awaiting the next creator-in-training. [Laughs.]

[Laughs.] Has that one been picked yet?

Why don't you ask them when the time comes?

Interacting with Feeling

How can humans now, stuck to our planet and not able to physically travel to you, interact with you in a way that is most benevolent for us and you?

Do like the child pretending to be the dog or the cat. First, imagine yourself as your favorite planet, whatever it is. If it is Earth, imagine yourself to be Earth in a completely benevolent expression of Earth, or if it is some other place, imagine yourself to be that. Imagine it in such a way as you can feel yourself in that spherical form. You will have to work up to that, because a sphere not only orbits but it also turns on an axis. But I don't expect you to be able to do multiple things at once.

Try to imagine it as a feeling, which is what the child does. Sometimes when the child is looking, staring at the dog or the cat or the bird who lives in the house with the humans, the child is totally being that, totally experiencing the feathers of the bird moving. The bird allows it, because the bird is feeling kindly toward the child. The same thing goes for the dog or the cat—they allow it.

Practice for yourself, if you wish. In a more simple way, you can find a tree you like, one which you feel affectionate toward and that is at least as old as you are. If you are a child, you can find a young tree. If you are older, find an older tree. Then imagine being the tree, and imagine it slowly and gradually so that you can gradually feel the trunk of the tree, the bark, the leaves, the Sun on the leaves, the rain on the leaves, all these different things—it may take more than one time doing this. That's a good beginning, so that you can work up to imagining yourself being a planet. Then someday you can imagine being other planets, and someday you might imagine being me.

[Laughs.] I'm just thinking about that, being everywhere at once.

Creation Is Always Personal

Have you been a creator?

I have not, but I am interested to observe the process. It is not something I choose to do. Of course, as a portion of creation I must say that I am a portion of Creator—I cannot say I am not that. But to be that exclusively, no. I am not that; I am other things. Of course, looking at it philosophically, which I must, I cannot exclude that I am a creator any more than you can exclude it. But in my understanding of the meaning of your question, how you mean it, then no.

It is an important point, though, that a creator must be able to identify with every single iota of what it creates as a personal point of oneself. So if I was the creator, my answer would necessarily have to be yes and no—meaning, yes, I am a creator, and no, I am Pluto, as you would call me. The creator would have to say, "Yes, I am a creator; yes, I am Pluto; yes, I am a cell on your fingernail," and it is personal. For a creator, I think you have to understand that every iota of what you create is personal, even though it may change form—which it always does. But it's always personal.

But there is this thing in this universe, where the Creator can't feel our pain.

But Creator has invited you here, and your job now is to feel that—not to suffer, but to be aware of that, so that when you become a creator, you will perhaps be a little more careful.

Not only careful, but able to feel if the suffering is there.

You will be a little more compassionate. The Creator of this universe is a wonderful being, but He/She would prefer that you be more wonderful. Every parent, if I might say, desires that his or her children be more.

The Energy of Pluto Invites Growth

How has it come to be that Pluto is considered a sign of challenge?

Might I say that the reason for this book is to reveal the personalities of the planets with as much demonstration of that personality as possible. This way, astrologers and others interested in such subjects can derive a greater definition of their chosen field and be able, as a result, to derive and extrapolate the influences not only of the planet, but the influences the other way: how the people affect the planets. So regardless of any ascribed value to the planets now, the purpose of this book is to help astrologers add to their field of wisdom and knowledge, so that they can add more to their knowledge—although, I grant that different astrologers will practice different aspects from this accumulation of material in this book.

I know that all the planets stand for something, and I am not in any way suggesting that astrologers are not profoundly helpful to those whom they advise now. But the purpose of this book is to give them more, because with the wisdom they have, they will be able to distill from what is being offered, not only more to understand the planets, but also more to know what to ask and how to inquire and how to prove, to their own satisfaction, that such representations might be so.

I'm curious as to how someone as wise and wonderful and expansive as you are is depicted in the charts as a darker influence?

But, you see, if you look deeper into astrology, you will find that it's not really that. That's on the surface. What it really means is a challenge. What is the purpose of challenge?

To grow.

That's right, growth. The long-distance runner will challenge herself or himself to run just a little more or run just a little faster or something like that, you understand. People challenge themselves all the time to grow. So the challenge does not have to be overbearing, but it is sufficiently present so that you must become more or you must discover something you can do. The challenge is only present when there is more that you can do—not when it is impossible for you to do more. It might simply be doing what you already do in a completely different and easier way. That's what it's really about. So if you look deeper and have the knowledge of astrologers who have studied the planets, that's the actual definition. It is only the surface definition—that it is a burden.

People who have the energy of Pluto, as you call it, are usually learning how to do something in a new way that will be simpler for them once they get good at it. Many times, though, they are learning how to do it in the way they were born to do it. Even though they've been educated to do things differently, their natural talents are usually those things that are the simplest for them to do.

Almost always, the energy of Pluto is to bring you back to your natural talents, which are always simple and easy for you to do. So even if you've become a profound expert at something you've learned, it doesn't mean you should discard that which you can do naturally and easily. That's a little clue, not only to support the astrologer's readings for people, but to remind people who are interested in these matters that it doesn't have to be as overwhelming as it might seem.

That brings up an interesting thought. Do you have a special relationship with humans who share your energy, partake of your energy, connect to your energy?

No, it is rather that you as the human being are choosing to have that connection in that moment with me. You understand, the decision is made on the soul level, not on the conscious-mind level. The conscious mind is what your physical body uses to conduct your physical life. But your natural life—which takes place when you are sleeping, in your natural form—that's completely different. Someday it will be very clear, but for right now, since you are in school, it is not always that clear. It will not be that long.

In Sleep, You Return to Your Natural State

We can't bring our physical bodies to you yet—do we come to visit you during our sleep?

Many do. That's when you discover that complications have a certain attractiveness. Sometimes, for those who have an attraction to what is complicated, they will attempt to play out that complication in their physical life—and that I do not recommend. It is one thing in your natural state to be challenged by the complicated, but it is another thing to draw complication to you in your physical life all the time. I don't recommend that. Generally speaking, simplicity is best.

We've been told that our planet has achieved levels of teaching all the way up to the quantum level of teaching, like a teaching master or a material master or a physical master. Do you have those abilities? Is that something you're interested in?

Remember, only one question. I will say—even though I'm going to give you a dual answer and you won't hear the other part—that I do not have a need to have all of those abilities, because you are not in occupation upon me as the Explorer Race. By the time you get here physically, you will be quite different than your now personalities. You will not be in inner conflict, for starters. So, no, I don't need that.

By the time we get there, will we still have physical bodies?

Oh yes, you will have physical bodies.

But much lighter and faster in vibration, right?

No. When I say it's lighter, I mean you are not burdened by inner conflict.

Oh, all right. So I missed the other half of the answer.

Just remember what you asked and ask it again. Some other time is all right. We're going to have to stop soon, because the channel has been going for a while.

This universe is almost over—have you considered what you might want to do when you leave here?

You mean, what do I want to do when I grow up? Why live in the future when the present is so interesting [chuckles]? That is simpler—much simpler.

Yes. You have so much wisdom.

You find that attractive in me because that is your natural state and one misses home. You all have that in your natural state. That's why sleep is so very important. Your body must sleep, and you equally must be yourselves. That is why you spend such a great deal of time looking to find yourself in your physical form. You cannot find yourself, but you can find things that are native to you, things you are good at, things you find amusing, things you find fascinating. All these things are part of you.

It's important to have humor and to be allowed to have humor. So even if you see children laughing at things that you feel are inappropriate or if a child sees you laughing at something they don't understand, laughter is less about what's being laughed at than the release in the moment of the happiness and joy that is felt by the physical body as food. Good night.

Thank you. Good life.

♆ Neptune

NEPTUNE

Radiates a Joyous Welcoming Energy

October 14, 2006

This is Neptune. What would you like to talk about?

Tell me why you were invited into this solar system.

This Solar System Is Intended to Have a Significant Energy of Welcome

This solar system is intended to have a significant amount of energy of welcome. It is necessary to have that kind of energy, not only to support the myriad of life forms originally on your planet, but also—given the lack of balance of the human being, which then affects all other species on your planet—there needs to be more of a physical feeling of welcome than might be present. It's hard to energize a sense of welcome on your planet because your planet is overwhelmed by what she has to deal with. So I am the one who transmits that to her core.

I have to transmit about four times the amount that is needed on the surface simply to stabilize your planet's orbit, since she needs to also feel welcome in that orbit and she doesn't usually, since it wasn't originally intended for her. So about half of what I transmit helps your planet, and then most of the rest of it percolates up to the surface to welcome forms of life as well as young souls coming in for the human being to stabilize the Earth population. Of course, many species are leaving the planet now, partly because of so many human beings being there, but this is expected given the natural growth of the human race on Earth. So that's what I do.

Does this energy of welcome come from you, or does it come through you from someplace or someone else?

It comes from me. When visitors, usually from other planets, come to this planet, they don't actually land as a rule, but they will sometimes hover surprisingly close to the surface—twelve, thirteen miles sometimes, that close. The refreshment of the energy that I broadcast is so strong that to get closer than fifty miles to the surface would naturally allow that energy to move through the hull of the ship, even if it's a solid vehicle, because the energy is compatible with all life forms. So sometimes these vehicles will come and essentially charge themselves up for an exploration of your solar system.

They usually only do this if they're going to come fairly close to your planet. I don't think there are many ships that come close to your planet anymore, but they'll come fairly close—perhaps somewhere between your planet and the Moon. They can be detected sometimes by your instruments, but most of the time they are not. They will visit Neptune first, to be charged up to withstand the energy being broadcast by the out-of-balance discomfort on your planet.

That's an unusual and wonderful thing. How is it that you are able to do that?

It is in my nature. When this solar system was created, several beings—if I may refer to other planets that way—were invited because of their qualities of transmission, meaning what they could transmit. I don't, of course, have to transmit this energy, but it is actually to my benefit to transmit it because there is so much of it otherwise and I have plenty, so I can share. When your solar system was being created, I volunteered to be the heart and soul of this planet while you, the Explorer Race, were in residence on your planet. When you are no longer in residence on that planet, I will perhaps choose to continue on where I was originally going. But I could stop—there wasn't any urgency to my getting there—so I did. I may continue on at some point.

I Am a Walk-In

Where were you going?

Well, I was going not quite to the other side of the universe to form up a small constellation there. I have had some experience with that, but I felt that it might be all right to be a planet one more time, especially in this situation in your solar system, because it represents a more extreme experience. It's not that I find that necessarily attractive, but it is possible, isn't it, when you form a constellation that visitors might come from some place whose energy is not necessarily benevolent. So I feel more prepared for that, should that ever occur.

So you've only been there since the Explorer Race has been here?

A little before that, in preparation.

What was in your orbit before that?

No, no, the planet was here—just somebody else, another personality, was present. But once it was known exactly what the Explorer Race would feel like and how that would affect the radiation of your planet, that personality preferred to be elsewhere, and I was available.

[Laughs.] So you're a walk-in!

In a sense, yes.

When you came to Neptune, was this water planet [Earth] here or was the previous planet in this orbit?

The planet you're on now was present.

I don't think we've explored your planet very much. Do you have a solid core?

You could land on the surface, but not everywhere. There is a surface. It's actually pretty dense, but no more dense than your own.

What about the atmosphere? Could we breathe it if we came to visit you?

No, but that's all right. By the time you get out that far in your explorations, I'm sure you'll have well-evolved breathing equipment. Plus, the suits the astronauts and the explorers will be using will be significantly abbreviated compared to what you see nowadays. Nowadays they are quite elaborate because they're really meant to provide more than what is necessary—meaning, just to be on the safe side.

By the time you get out exploring other planets, once you're, I would say, past Mars, you'll start getting help from others who travel in space. They will initially give you ideas of how you can create an environmental suit that is not exactly skintight but holds that promise. By the time you're out here around Neptune, maybe even by the time you get to Saturn, your cosmonauts will be wearing something that's almost skintight, but it will be very comfortable, very flexible, and will be fairly self-contained so that you do not leave anything on the planet and you also do not take anything in from the planet unless you choose to do so.

Many of You Will Move Underground

What would you like astrologers to know about your personality?

Well, I think I've already said that. The welcoming aspect is not necessarily something known by astrologers, and I feel that that is the most important aspect.

So if your energy was not being transmitted, Mother Earth's orbit would be unstable and we would not feel welcome?

No, it's not that polarized. It's just that you would not feel *as* welcome, and the orbit would probably be stable but Earth might wobble a bit more on her axis. That wobbling would not cause any disasters, but it could create some problems for you now that you have thin spots in the atmosphere.

What causes the wobbling on our planet now?

It is essentially caused by the species living on the surface being so out of balance. When you think about it, when people are frightened and upset, they tend to act in an agitated fashion. Then the planet herself feels agitated. Although she's not shaking with fear, that agitation must be represented by something that looks like a shake. Quite obviously, she couldn't shake or life couldn't exist—in that sense, in terms of existence, it couldn't exist comfortably—so she wobbles.

I feel that it's just a matter of time before quite a few individuals—more than now by a considerable margin—live underground. This isn't likely to come about as the result of any disaster, man-made or otherwise, but rather it will essentially come about simply because there are so many people on the Earth. Even though a great many of you can't even imagine the idea of living underground and not being able to look up and see the natural stars and other atmospheric conditions, you might be surprised just how many people will appreciate living underground. The number-one attraction will be stability, meaning that their lives will be very predictable and just as calm as they want them to be.

I do not think you will bring a lot of your current social architecture—meaning it's not likely there will be large gatherings of people rooting for this side or the other side, as in a sporting event. By the time underground civilizations are set up in such a way as to be attractive—sufficiently attractive to encourage people to be welcoming, you understand, of people moving there—there will probably not be competition as you understand it today, meaning businesses and governments and others will not be competing. There will be much more of a sense of cooperation.

That sense of cooperation is probably going to catch on in the underground levels of the civilization before it catches on in earnest on the surface. This will be necessary, you see, because the initial establishment of a comfortable underground civilization will require that everybody does something. Even though people will still be able to pursue their general careers, if there is little conflict, certain occupations will not be needed as much as they are needed now.

Disputes will probably not go to court; prisons will not be needed. There will be other ways of resolving situations, meaning that instead of sending somebody to prison as is done now, there will be an electronic means of altering personality and memory so that a citizen could be reformed on an electronic basis (I don't think it will be done surgically). That will be promoted initially, but then it will be seen that this is ultimately creating a conflict within the physical body, and the electronic medication—electronic energy influence—will be seen as something that is considerably more compassionate, meaning then that prison will be unnecessary. However, the persons being affected electronically will have their personality changed, and their loved ones won't like that. Yet after this they will be good citizens, they won't be involved in anything criminal, they won't be harming anyone, and so it will be a tradeoff.

Admiral Byrd Traveled to Another Vibration of Earth

We've heard a lot about Inner Earth, a hollow Earth. Can you tell me, do we actually have a hollow Earth, or is it molten core?

No, you do not have a hollow Earth. Oh, physically speaking, I wouldn't rule out there being a lot of liquid under there that's pretty hot, but you do not have what you call a hollow Earth, with civilizations living under there. Is that what you mean, a hollow Earth with many peoples living in there? Is that what you're referring to?

Yes. Supposedly Admiral Byrd . . .

You do not have that at the current focus of the planet you're on. However, in other focuses of the planet, yes, that does exist. When sensitive people have tuned in to that or felt the presence of that, that's at a different vibration of your planet, and the planet who exists in that orbit—if you don't mind, I'm just going to call it Earth—is at a different vibration of it. So, yes, that does exist, and that's what's actually being tuned in to. That doesn't rule out the fact that there have been underground bases by other civilizations, but I'm talking about a massive population. The massive populations would be at another vibration of the Earth.

What did Admiral Byrd see when he went into what he thought was a hole and went into this space where there was a civilization and a sun?

That was another vibration of this planet. That is why, when they flew up there, they were initially affected by this magnetic energy and they went through what they took to be the aurora borealis—which it might actually refer to in the documents, but the aurora borealis also has a veil-like effect—and they were allowed to see a higher frequency of the planet. So the reason no one else was able to repeat that experience is that we're talking about different physical areas.

The Admiral and his people actually saw what they say. It was real, but it was not this planet you know now. So you might say that they had an experience almost like flying into the Bermuda Triangle, but they were able to fly right out. It was a very important thing, because it allowed people to have hope that there was not only a more benevolent form of life available but that it might be freely available. Also, of course, no one was injured by the experience.

Right, and they were helped by the people there.

Antarctica's Ice Might Melt

What about Antarctica? Are we going to be on the planet when the ice melts? That's the site of ancient civilizations, right?

There have been civilizations there before. It seems likely that you will be on the planet. It's certainly possible that sometime within the next twenty years or perhaps less that all of the ice will melt. Initially, the rising water might cause a little displacement of some civilizations, but a lot of that water is going to go underground. It's not all just going to go straight to the surface water. Because of there being more rain in various places, it will also create a more nurturing environment for trees. This is absolutely vital for trees and bushes and grasses, and anything that exhales oxygen, and so this will be a very important factor.

It is not necessarily permanent that the ice will be gone. The ice on your planet has come and gone several times. It is not typical for your planet to ice over completely, but it has iced over quite a bit in the past, although I do not expect that to happen. It is, however, possible that when the Explorer Race leaves the surface of the planet—that will mean all human beings will be gone from the surface—the planet's surface might ice over a bit more, because those living inside the planet will, by that time, be totally self-sustaining, and it won't really make any difference what's happening on the surface. They will be able to survive and thrive. Also, if that should happen, it is very likely that there will be a significant amount of interactivity between extraterrestrials and those living inside the planet. The civilization inside the planet will be quite comfortable with people from afar, especially if those people look like human beings, which they will.

Will we find remnants of ancient cultures in or on Antarctica?

Given the weight of ice, you're not going to find structures, but you might find pictographs. That will be quite fascinating. You might find carvings in the stone that people may have made some time ago, not unlike what you find in readily available stone. That is going to truly fascinate scientists as well as laypeople.

Individuality Might Not Prove to Be Viable

If humans think about you or tune in to you, is that how humans can interact with you? Should they?

I see no reason to make an effort. You can if you like, but I don't see any point, because your planet naturally has a lot of the energy that I broadcast to it. So if you were to focus on welcome, of course you would probably be causing yourself to feel better and others around you to feel better perhaps, but it doesn't mean that you would be in any way connecting with my energy.

So you've been a planet in other solar systems, in other universes?

In this universe, mostly.

Do star systems get born, get created and die, like other beings?

Yes, but life is so long and there is no necessity to die, as you say it. What normally happens is a constant birthing from the center of the star system outward. This way all that the star system wishes to express can be continually created and it is not necessary to re-create other planets, other stars, you see? So as a rule, death as you understand it does not exist, though there might be some form of transformation.

Sometimes when your scientists perceive a hole in space or a dark star, as they call it, space, and all that is around it, is not being sucked into some unknown area, but there might be a fold . . . when there's a fold in space, it will look like that. It is essentially temporary, though such a temporary situation might last for millennia.

You are the planet, you are the life force of the planet—is there a being who is the star system?

Well, certainly—just as there's a being who's the universe, just like there's a being who's Creator as you know Creator to be. Everything is alive and everything has personality. The cells in your body each have their own personality. Needless to say, they are truly balanced and in complete cooperation.

So I can actually ask to talk to that being? How do you fit into that being? Are you part of that being, or is the being . . . ?

Everything is a part of everything else. There is no separation—it only appears to be that way in your now location. I am able to communicate, given the focus of individuality that you have there. But if you were in your natural state, it would be like a chorus. Right now you can experience me as an individual, because one of the great experiments that may or may not be successful on your planet is the current flirtation with the idea that individuality is a fact. But, you see, it isn't. It might seem to be, but cooperation and consciousness of one's fellow beings is the true fact, and that will come through your consciousnesses much more so as time goes on. It's happening now, and it's been happening for a while.

For example, many of you are having each other's dreams. Sometimes this is a little unsettling, but very often it allows you to experience things that are not you. As you are waking up they feel like you and you get confused, but when you are in a slightly deeper state—not the deepest level, but a slightly deeper state—you're very aware that you are having a dream of someone else and that the environment you're in is not your own environment. This is why it's attractive in your time to analyze a dream symbolically, because very often that is the only way to make sense of an otherwise frequently nonsensical environment.

You said this experiment of individuality might not succeed?

Oh, I don't think I said "succeed." It might not prove to be viable. Right now, individuality is not real. The children who are in your home at the moment . . . the very young one is crystal clear that she is in touch with other beings, though she may not be able to express it. She can feel it. She does not have a command of your language, nor is she entirely focused in her mind—therefore, the accepted forms of communication are not really open to her. However, if you were able to simply feel her energy, especially just before she goes to sleep and just as she's waking up, you might be able to have a sensation of environments considerably more vast than your own.

I look forward to that expansion. How long before the experience of individuality here will end? Will that last while we go out in spaceships to contact other planets?

That will last for quite a while, yes. At some point, it needs to become less so, however, because when one is focused on oneself only, even though you might very well love other people or even like other people, it is very easy to feel disconnected from people, say, on the other side of the planet who might need your assistance. But in an environment where you are much more aware, if something doesn't feel right in your body, the chances are pretty good—especially when one is younger and more vital—that this means somebody someplace else needs help.

There is still some sense of welcome for exploration, but it depends on how you treat the planets. Granted, civilizations that are a little less conscious of the embodiment of a planet having everything to do with everybody else will still be involved in mining operations and so on, but by the time you get here [to Neptune], it's not likely that you will be doing any mining. You will by that time have learned how to adapt materials to your own purpose, and much of what you do to survive and thrive will involve very little in the way of material.

It is interesting, because by the time you get here your population might easily be twelve million. There will be some stability efforts in population that will be successful without causing harm, and compared to the resources you are using now on the surface of your planet, even with that increased population you will probably be using about one-third to one-quarter of the resources then that you are using now.

There Are Ten More Astrological Signs

You're not a water planet?

I am considered to be associated with water.

I know, that's why I ask.

Yes. But I am considered to be associated with water, not because of being perceived to have water. You have to remember that we're talking about mythology involved here.

Is astrology something that was channeled even before the Explorer Race came?

No. I believe it was provided from ancient civilizations who came to your planet in vehicles many times, over and over, and contacted different civilizations at a time when they felt that the civilizations could either make a record of this wisdom or had a very good, reliable, repeated mechanism of teacher-to-student, so that it could exist. However, they were discouraged from giving too many details, because it would be very easy for it to become a religion and, hence, an authoritarian support system. You have to consider the possibility that if astrology as it was known in the past had become the core of a religion, then certain rigid structures might have suppressed the expandability of your own Earth culture. It was intended that your Earth culture have a chance to be flexible, and therefore, when there is too much rigidity, things happen.

I understand that the twelve signs represent twelve psychological types that are on the planet. So they have always been the same?

Oh, I think that's too simplistic. Psychological isn't complete. That is the mental way to say it, but it totally overlooks feelings. I would say that the signs that are known—there are more than twelve signs; there are at least fifteen signs—represent the natural outgoing expressions of some of the core personalities that are present in the human population on Earth. Did you know that there are about twenty-three personality types with dogs? Well, given a little time and given the recent arrivals that will be coming for the next ten, fifteen, twenty years, all of the new births and so on, you will probably assimilate your natural, native twenty-two personalities. So there are about another ten signs you don't have.

So unless we get these new signs out there, part of the population will not be represented or cannot use astrology?

No, they'll be miscast. But this is not because astrologers prefer to do that. Astrologers would love to have more information. That's why this book will be massive, you see? At some point it might be necessary to do a second volume where you give, not only channeling from the twelve signs that are present, but channeling from the other ten signs. See, there are some children who are coming who, no matter how good the astrologer or the really, truly specific capacities within astrology . . . which right now are down to the minute, but it might be possible to get them to the half-minute. But they will be a little stuck, you see?

Yes, because these people won't match.

Regardless of the timing involved, astrologers are going to notice people who seem to have predominant personality characteristics of more than one sign, and there's other stuff in there that no one even recognizes. Some of these people will be considered to be strange or odd, but they simply represent something else.

New Sign: A Connector from One Sign to Another

One of the most pervasive ones that has been around for a while now is a sign—you can name it something; we'll probably just give them numbers or something—whose predominant characteristic is a place between things, making them a connector from one sign to another, with the ability to demonstrate different personality types while maintaining one's own personality. So we're not talking about someone with a mental disease, but rather someone who is profoundly reflective, not only of what they are around, but of what they are around in other human personalities that needs to be exposed but which other humans are trying to hide.

These people, especially when they are children, will be acting out the unspoken in, say, their parents or grandparents. This will be initially misunderstood. Some of these children will speak languages from ancient times. So I'm putting child counselors on alert, here. Try to record it if children are speaking some language you don't recognize. Some of them will use hand signs and gestures because there are certain ancient languages that use hand signs and gestures, and it does not mean there's something wrong with the child.

Now I will bring to your attention this very important fact: There is a large group of youngsters coming along now who are generally referred to as autistic. These children are the leading wave of the children who will represent what I am talking about. I'm not trying to say that all autistic children are that, but at least 90 percent of them are. For those who want to help these children, first consult some astrologers and at least understand that there may be something going on that is not strictly psychological but is rooted in the feeling energy and can be most easily communicated by those who speak with inspiration.

So what do we do about the planets for these twenty-two signs, then? Are more planets going to surface?

No. The signs as you know them don't have anything to do with the planets. I am speaking what I can say. It might be helpful if you knew a little bit about astrology or if you had an astrologer as a consultant. It's important to bring these topics out, because with astrologers the unseen—which is what I am largely known for—can be seen when the time is right. That has always been known about me: when the time is right, the unseen is known.

But, you see, in the case of the unseen being known, it is almost always felt long before it is known and understood mentally. One does not have to trip over it mentally as an experience that you suddenly realize after the fact, when something uncomfortable happened. Rather it can be something you get feelings for, you understand the feelings, and you act on the feelings long before these feelings have to manifest into form and create events to bring something to your attention.

But it's only unseen because we're behind the veil, right? If we were on another planet, it wouldn't be so. That's why we have astrology—because we need that extra guidance, right?

It's helpful to have it. If you don't have that as a means of understanding things, astrology is one way, although there are other ways. But the advantage of having explanations, especially for the mental, is that for those who are involved in the mental, astrology is that, although feeling astrology is also very present. So those ten other signs are all about feelings, you see. The astrology of feeling is what's missing.

So that will only be those who will be coming? There's nobody on the planet now who has the energy of the new signs?
No, no. I already spoke about one.

Oh, the autistic, yes. But mostly it's the ones who are coming soon, right?
They're trickling in.

So Much Astrology Has Been Lost

So astrology was known in the past? Civilizations on this planet used it, and then they died out and it got pretty much lost, right? Did they know more about astrology in the ancient civilizations than we know now?

Oh, yes. A great deal has been lost over time, and that's why this book is important. We will not be revealing things that haven't been revealed before; we will simply be reminding the current generation of this wisdom.

So this is just getting back what's lost. Did they know the ten other signs also?
Oh, yes. This has all been suppressed or lost. It's not new—it's just that there are going to be a lot more of these people representing these ten other signs. They're really present now, but they're going to continue to come in. So without having the knowledge of those ten other signs, astrologers may not be able to be as helpful as they would otherwise choose to be.

Can you say what civilization was first given astrology?
None of them are on your planet now.

But we have remains of some of them, right? Buildings, buried stuff?
There are no buildings.

Is this because of the Ice Age and atomic bombs and wars and floods?
Well, most of it just has to do with something a lot simpler than that: trees and leaves. Do you know why? Leaves and twigs fall from trees, and there is other forest matter. Forests come and go, but what they do is that they build up soil—of course, there's volcanic ash too, but I'm talking about the buildup of matter on the surface of the Earth. Generally speaking, when archaeologists locate ancient civilizations, they dig for them. They don't just stumble across something.

But if we're coming to the end of the experiment now, why is it that you won't reveal what hasn't been revealed before—if it affects humans and if it would help humans?

It is not my job to do that. My job is to retain certain amounts of the unseen. It isn't as if there aren't other planets in the solar system who aren't going to talk to you. It isn't as if you don't have twenty-two signs waiting. My job is not to reveal everything all by myself. You know, it's important to know what's missing, not just on a speculative basis, but to know what's missing. It's not always easy.

Generally, astrologers who've been researching the topic for many years are much more conscious of what's missing or what is mysterious—meaning how you cannot explain certain actions. There has been a tendency to simply say, "Well, it's a portion of this and it's a portion of that," but it's not quite expressive enough. After all, one has the chart with all of the different segments, but if you added more to that chart, one would not only have more signs, but one would also be able to be significantly more accurate in predicting the future. If you could predict the future, not necessarily by events but by circumstances meaning, "This will happen, so it would be better to try this at this time," that kind of thing—then it would be possible to avoid many pitfalls and mistakes that are made now.

For instance, take a test flight of a new airplane. If astrology could say absolutely, without a doubt, that one day is better to test this airplane than another, a lot of people would be safer and there would be more success with products, just as an example. Of course, wisdom is not going to go away, but it would be helpful if grandfather or grandmother, when being with a child, would be able to know what to encourage—not what to discourage so much, but what to encourage in a child. The child is this or that sign, will probably show this or that tendency, so what do you encourage?

So with all the material on astrology that was lost—is some of it available on the planet now amongst certain groups and societies that suppressed it?

Yes, but it isn't complete. Even amongst those who have the extra material, it's incomplete, and I might add, because of competition, some have it and aren't sharing it with others who also have some extra, so it's a bit complex. That's why it's useful to put it out to the general public, if possible.

Yes, so everyone has it.

Although this book will be of interest to a wide-ranging group of people, I feel that astrologers will still benefit by this and will be interested in it. Granted, it might be of greater interest to younger astrologers (meaning newer in their careers) who are interested in expanding things beyond the obvious, but ultimately it will become something that is appreciated by a great many. That's the whole point of the book, although it might not be possible to put it all into one book. You want to get the planets in the solar system, for certain, and then we'll start on the signs: first the known signs and then probably the unknown signs. But it might come in a different order—I can't guarantee you the order it will come in.

Astrology Offers Potential and Opportunity

Are there other planets not connected to signs who send certain energies here that are needed for the Explorer Race who would like to speak also? Or is that irrelevant at this point?

I think we need to cover what has been mentioned, and if at the end of that you want to open up the floor, so to speak, then that could be done. But my feeling is that it would be best to cover the ground mentioned first.

You've been so helpful. I appreciate it so much, because this has been something that I felt I couldn't undertake. But now that I understand how important it is, we will do it.

Well, it's something that will serve a great many people, and it will have a fairly broad audience, and that's useful. As you know, many people who don't have any expertise in the subject at all are interested. So it is the hope of the planets and the constellations that knowing more about the subtleties as well as the drives that nurture, encourage and support your personalities will help you to appreciate the complexity as well as the symbiosis of your overall planetary expression.

The unknown, the unseen, is supported by initial feelings. It's important to be conscious of the feelings in your body. Sometimes, especially when feelings are closer to the surface—meaning physical feelings, you understand, that don't have any apparent causal factor from your inner body—these feelings are messages either from others or something associated with your own sign, even though it might be a portion of your sign that is not obvious to you.

What is known about each sign is what has survived. It is core material, but there is a surprising amount of core material that is missing. So pay attention to what you're feeling, as well as reading your daily astrology and keeping up with more details about yourself and perhaps your loved ones and even some workmates. These things are not rules; they are not meant to run your life, nor are they meant to restrict your life. They are meant to offer potentials and opportunities.

The purpose of this book is to add greater depth to the opportunities you have in life for happiness, for fulfillment and, yes, for cooperation with your fellow beings. Good night.

Thank you very much. Good night.

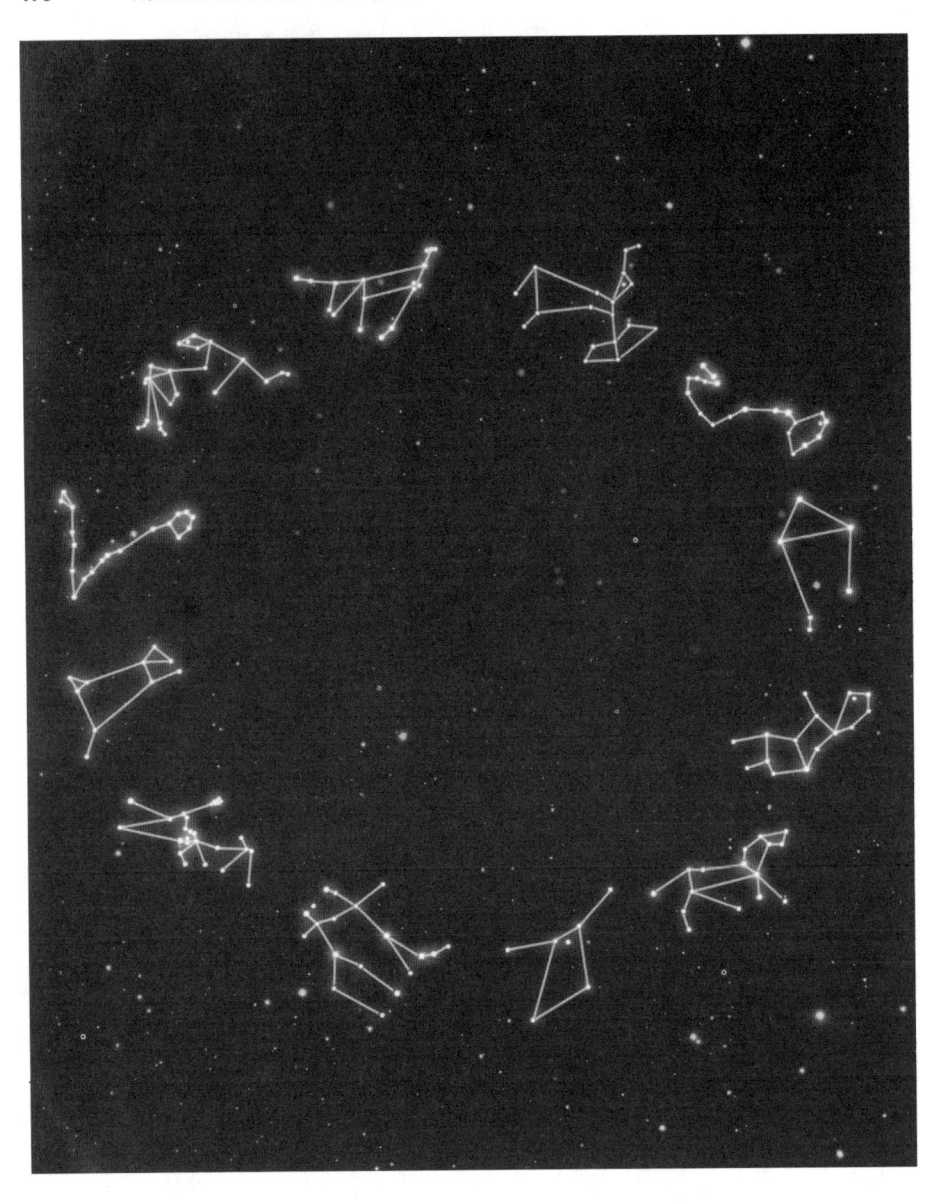

Astrological Signs

ASTROLOGY EXPERT
Astrology Has to Do with the Means, the Pathway, by which You Choose to Learn

November 3, 2006

I am an astrology expert.

Welcome!

Astrology Is an Offering

It is intended that you find your own way in this process. It is also intended that you do not have too much of a preconceived notion of it. The less you know about astrology, the better. This will enable you not just to fill in the gaps of what is known but to create something entirely new that might not be known, or might have been forgotten in the echoes of time, or might simply not have been provided yet.

So this is the guideline you requested. Don't be attached to hearing anything familiar. The way I see this book is that it is intended to inspire the astrology enthusiast, whether professional or amateur—to not just fill in the gaps, but to find new pathways that are complementary in this particular craft.

I use the word "craft" advisedly. Consider the artist making a pot or a cup or a plate. Of course, one must make it practical. It is intended to work and fulfill its function. But while doing that, why not add some beauty? Add something to improve the quality of life of the person using it, so that they might look at the design or the shape or the decorations and be cheered by recollections or reminders of the beauties of life.

That is the foundation of this book. So referring to astrology as a craft does not make it something that is occultish—meaning meant to be kept secret for only a select few—but rather it is more of an offering, something that is offered and available to all who have interest or even curiosity. That's what I recommend as your overview.

So maintain your personal curiosity about what this could be, what that could be, and understand that your bodies are made up of the planet you are living on. The other planets in this solar system are a combined total of what Creator desires for you, since it is understood that if even one of you sets foot on one of these planets or even the moons of these planets, that all of you are affected by it, even through the insulation of the garments. This combined quantity of planets is your first and foremost influence—perhaps you didn't know that.

You might be interested to know that it is not actually absolutely necessary to physically set foot on the planets. It is possible to imagine them and set foot on them in that way. It is also possible, for those who know how to do it, to use a touching capacity with the foot or hand or other at a distance, for that to be the means of contact. However, it would work differently this way. You would not be able to have the full influence of a physical person touching a physical foot (or hand or other) to the planet; you would have to have at least a hundred people doing what I believe your friends Grandfather and Speaks of Many Truths might refer to as *long touch*, in order for that to have an influence for all beings on Earth. Did you notice I said "all beings"? This does not exclude any being on Earth, you see.

Complementary Influences Must Be Completely Compatible

The acquaintanceship of the planets in your solar system with certain other systems is designed to act as *Complementary Influences*. Complementary Influences mean that these star systems are completely compatible with all of the planets in your solar system. Of course, as you look out in the sky, you can imagine the infinite possibilities simply by number, which you cannot really count, to say nothing of what you cannot see considering the distance. Complementary Influences must therefore be completely compatible with the substance of your planets: meaning the soil, the rock, the crust, the very body of the planets involved, to say nothing of the suns with your Sun. Since beings on your planet spring forth from the physical matter of your planet, then they must also have beings on those planets that spring forth, either from any of the physical matter of any of the Complementary Influences (star systems), or even from your planets in your solar system. So the compatibility factor is essential.

To a degree, these Complementary Influences might be seen as seasonings, meaning that instead of a seasoning that might be used in very small quantities in a food to create a subtle influence, this would be a more pronounced seasoning. Therefore, if we picked, say, Aquarius as a Complementary-Influence area of the sky, it would suggest then that this Complementary Influence is actually well and thoroughly advanced. All of the signs relate to the stars in your sky, and over time astrologers have made pictures out of them—not only to make it easier to locate these stars, but to make it more understandable to people who are more visual on the basis of their means to learn and assimilate such wisdom.

In order to be compatible, these Complementary Influences . . . let's look at it the other way, from the star systems that represent the signs looking toward your solar system that you now occupy. In order for a sign (I'll call it) to be compatible with your planets where you reside, including Earth, there must be a considerable amount of experience that has gone on for the individual souls to participate in, not only such a solar system as you have, but such a planetary existence as Earth.

Filtering Out Your Physical Recollections of Earth

Earth is unlike any other planet in this universe. It is a very advanced and hence profoundly challenging place to exist. Creator does not, as a rule, allow human beings to live past a certain point on your planet, so as to not overwhelm the soul with too much to resolve in, say, 10,000 experiential years after one's life there on Earth. Creator prefers the soul to have no more than 1,000 to 1,500 experiential years of existence after a life on Earth in which to come to resolution with all that you have retrieved from that Earth life. The retrieval process simply means that which is allowed for you to recall, not only as a mental experience (which is highly filtered intentionally), but as an experience where you would filter out some of the actual physical recollections. How does that work?

In the case of a physical recollection, one would not remember within the context of the experience the physical feeling. One would simply be able to remember, as a teacher might guide you, a certain feeling in your body and then bring that feeling of that moment into resolution. As an example, imagine an experience, just a simple experience: "I can't find a parking place." You get frustrated as around and around the block you go, and eventually you find a place, and then it takes you awhile to relax. That's a simple experience that a great many of you can identify with. I would say that just lifting out the aspects of feeling that a teacher or guide might work on with a soul who has moved off of Earth, there would be at least a hundred moments there where you could work on feelings.

The more intense aspects of the feelings would be too much to work on for a soul beyond Earth, but the subtle messages—which are what was intended to be noticed in the first place for the individual on Earth at that time—would be the most important aspects to notice. Therefore, to resolve those hundred or so subtle feelings before the feelings became overwhelming, to catch the attention of the person on Earth—that that person was frustrated or otherwise needing to do other than what he or she is doing, or to do it in a different way, which is more likely the case—would involve a signaling process.

So, one by one, those subtle feelings would be allowed for the individual soul beyond Earth to resolve, working with a teacher or guide or both—meaning that the student, the soul, might be advised by the teacher that, "Here's a feeling that your self felt on Earth in that life that was challenging, and it was a signal of an impending acceleration of that feeling." The teacher says to the student, "You do not have to work on the acceleration; you simply need to work on the ability to receive and the immediate understanding of what that feeling is. We have about a hundred of them, and it will take about sixty-five experiential years for us to work out that complete series of signals."

So it takes a long time. Then what would be felt, what the person would be allowed to feel, you see, in that life on another planet . . . that person would be allowed to feel something that would be the most subtle feeling you can imagine. Perhaps you can identify with this.

If you want to have a comparable sensation of that subtle feeling at the moment you are reading this, put the book down, take your hand, and very lightly touch the back of your other hand—either hand will do. The physical feeling is there, and you understand it. When you are doing that, though, you will have a very subtle feeling, most likely in the pit of your stomach or possibly somewhere in the general abdomen area.

You can do this several times over the period of an hour, so that your body knows that you are going to do it. Around the fifth or sixth time, when you notice that very subtle feeling in the pit of your stomach or abdomen area, then another extension of yourself—you could say a reincarnational life—would be working on that feeling. It is complicated, so I have attempted to provide you with considerable landmarks for you to understand the subtlety of the feeling that is worked on. The moments of extreme frustration, anxiety, upset, anger and so on—they don't work on any of that, because it's too overwhelming for them in their world.

Astrology Guides You in How to Learn on Earth

So what you have here, then, is a series of signs that you have in your astrologic that all have a complementary star system—and as I've explained the star systems to you, they are all in compatibility with Earth. This is why the whole recent string of books through this channel and through this publisher from this channel have been easing you very subtly from the mental in the beginning—to have an overview, a model of understanding of your universe and your existence—gradually toward feelings and feelings in physicality.

Astrology is entirely about physicality, feelings, subtle feelings, the heart's interaction with feelings, your heart's and feelings' interaction with all other beings, and your heart's interaction with all other beings, your planet and all other planets who are compatible with your planet. This is what astrology really is. For those of you who are experts in this area, you can see how that fits very nicely into the true overview of astrology, which for the greater part—including all that is known and remembered about astrology in your times, including that which is quite esoteric and not known by everyone—is truly meant to be a guide, a book of instructions on how to learn on planet Earth. It's not meant to offer how to live on planet Earth—that comes from experience and your culture. It is how to learn.

The entire reason your souls have the opportunity to come and learn is so that you can receive just the right knowingness through experience, so as to avoid making catastrophic errors. You see, as has been said in other books in this long series, the essential purpose of your existence here through the entire Explorer Race phenomenon is to eventually learn how to create on your own. After all, anything that is created by a creator has the opportunity and availability and even bias toward learning how to create itself.

Therefore, certain souls over time have been allowed to move along through various experiential cycles in order to learn enough about creation so that they might be allowed to become a creator themselves. But in order to do this, it is absolutely essential to be able to avoid catastrophic mistakes, because if you make a catastrophic mistake, it will undoubtedly affect others. If you are then distracted by resolving that mistake, your feelings as a creator will affect your entire creation.

This is why when people have moments of recollection of an encounter with Creator—in whatever form they see Him—they have what you call "after-death experiences," but then for some reason they are returned to physical life and can speak of these experiences. This is why, when they have met Creator, Creator was always exuding in great quantity absolutely loving energy, unconditional love, and that person having that experience was overwhelmed by it. This is essential. Imagine a creator who is distracted by having, if I might use the word, goofed up. If a creator had done that, he would be distracted all the time and would not be able to present that unconditional loving self to all those cycling through different forms of life, to say nothing of simply the benign and benevolent influence of the creator in its creation.

So it is to be expected in the creation process that you will have certain stumbles, that you will learn on the way. But you must be absolutely able to completely forgive, with unconditional love, your own stumbles, to trust that you will be able to work out those stumbles in a loving and benevolent way, and to never lose sight of the fact that you must be unconditionally loving at all times. So you can see why not only beings experience Creator that way (when they are allowed to have a so-called after-death experience) and live to tell about it, but why they also must absolutely have the ability to get catastrophic mistakes out of their system someplace where they are able to resolve them—or at least others are able to help them to resolve them in some way.

Your Planet Allows for Resolution

So you come to Earth where you are allowed to make catastrophic mistakes in the process of learning. A catastrophic mistake for an individual might be walking down the steps, tripping over something, falling down and injuring oneself—not dying, although that does happen occasionally, but perhaps injuring oneself for which one needs a considerable amount of time and adaptation, and must go through a great many feelings, both pain and more subtle feelings as well, in order to recover, and even then it might have some lasting influence.

In short, that would be an individual catastrophic mistake. Whereas perhaps on a smaller level, another form of a catastrophic mistake might simply be becoming distracted as one comes to the intersection when one is driving, and in the course of your distraction, you crash into other cars, causing injury or perhaps even death to others. This would certainly be a qualification for a catastrophic mistake that would have to be resolved in the best way possible by many others, including yourself.

I'm not here to present dismal scenarios to you but rather to suggest that your planet allows you in this advanced method of existence—it *is* advanced, believe it or not, on the learning level—to make catastrophic errors or mistakes and to come to creative and cooperative (working-with-others) solutions of some sort. This is why even in the best of times, whenever your planet is experiencing the greatest harmony between all species, all beings and so on, there are still mistakes being made. The difference is in how cooperative you as an individual are in bringing these mistakes to resolution of some sort and how cooperative others are with you in bringing about some form of regeneration or soothing application—in short, resolution.

So you can see how all of this is interwoven. Consider the way a cloth, a fabric, is woven—that is very much an example of life. To give you a little side story here, do you know that once upon a time the reason people with long hair braided their hair was entirely spiritual? It was to suggest the overlying/underlying, in-and-out, back-and-forth aspects and complements of life. A double braid would suggest you and another, a triple braid would suggest you and two others, and so on. But that is just an aside.

This book is not meant to go over ground well and thoroughly understood by professional astrologers and that which they would advise or write about for less-expert astrologers or perhaps even the hobbyist. It is intended to thoroughly reveal, to the greatest degree possible, that which has been either unknown or kept from you for some reason—or more likely, forgotten over time and, to a degree, never revealed. This way it is possible, especially for the expert astrologer, to see how it fits in. Keep in mind that the compatibility factor is greatly at work here.

Here's one last little treat for those expert astrologers who have debated this amongst themselves: They have wondered what astrology will be like when human beings travel at a great distance from this planet and are even beyond the capability to see the planets and the star systems that are of Complementary Influence. I want to give you a pleasant surprise. Yes, you will still have the influence of where you were born—of course, that goes without saying. But you will also derive the influence of where you are.

So if you are that far away from your own star systems and don't have the capability, even with instrumentality, to see any aspect of the star systems associated with your signs, the nice thing about this is that all these other star systems, all these other planets, even if they are not compatible, which is likely—meaning the physical makeup of the planet may not be entirely compatible with your own physical makeup—they will still on the spiritual level and to a minor degree on the feeling level influence your lives in a most benevolent way, because they will all be benevolent. That's a little treat for those of you who've been speculating on that.

You First Need to Learn About the Thirteenth Sign

Can you answer a few questions?

Perhaps. Not too many, because it is our intention for you to discover. After you have written this down and studied it, you will then have a means to know how to pursue your questions. That's why this is given to you specifically, but also to the readers, so they would have an understanding of the scope of this book—the intent, that is. So you can ask, yes, but if they do not fall under the general purview of what I have just stated, I may let you discover those in time, in talking to the various elements of your compatible influences here.

If there are twenty-two signs, what do we do with the 360 degrees? Do we divide it by twenty-two? Is the space for each even?

Twenty-two signs . . . you are getting that from . . . ?

Neptune.

Neptune said there are twenty-two signs? Perhaps he was referring to other subtle influences in your own solar system, or did he not explain it to you?

He just said that where we thought there were twelve, there were actually twenty-two signs, and we would receive them all. That's what I understood.

I understand. We will let the other planets reveal that as time goes on. I will simply say that it is not necessary to do any of that. I think that Neptune spoke a little too soon, there. It is not necessary to do any of that until you can clearly define the next sign. Right now, you have twelve you know about. You do not need to know any of that or factor it in mathematically—and you understand, mathematics is part of the foundational element to understand your world—until you know more about the thirteenth sign.

There is an aspect of mathematics known as fractions, yes? Fractions are always intended to be a predicting element, meaning if you are left with, say, ten and a quarter, you have to ask yourself, "Where are the other three-quarters?" "Ten and a quarter" means that eleven is on its way, mathematically. So don't be concerned if you are left with fractions.

Are there also twenty-two planets, then? One for each sign?

I will not say. I will simply say that Neptune was perhaps tipping the hat there a little too much. Or is it tipping the hand?

The hand, yes [laughs]. He was wonderful! He welcomed me to astrology. I wasn't interested until he talked. His energy was so wonderful, I felt that the whole subject welcomed me.

It is all right. I will simply say that it would involve more than influences in your own solar system, some of which are still arriving.

What about houses? Do the houses stay at twelve, or do they expand also?

They expand also.

It seems that astrology is 5,000 years behind. Do we need to get it up-to-date? It's like the people who knew how to keep it current haven't been around for 5,000 years or so.

It is partly intended to help the current professionals move it forward in time—and by "moving it forward in time," what is meant is, moving it forward past this time. So keeping it current is not sufficient. For astrology to function well, it must be located in the future, looking back into your now time. That allows it to have a purpose more than simply as a means of teaching and knowing how to approach one's lessons. It must have an anchor that draws one inexorably toward an outcome that would be desired by all beings. No one is excluded.

How many times have you heard that "no one is excluded"? No one would be excluded at all, you see, if the outcome was so pleasurable that everyone would enjoy it. So the purpose of this book is to allow astrology to anchor itself in a benevolent and intended and most certainly welcoming future.

Oh, that's wonderful.

Don't Create a Hierarchy within Personalities

What about humans? Somebody said one of the reasons you're giving this to us now is that beings are being born who will be core personalities of some of these signs we don't have. That seems to imply that when you first gave this information, there were twenty-two signs, there were twenty-two core personalities. Does that follow?

I understand the desire to use the term "core personalities," but I think one must be careful when using that term, because it would be very easy then to create a hierarchy within personalities. I will simply say that the twenty-two signs have to do with different pathways. That is a better way to look at it, simply because it might be very easy to break down the analysis of core personalities based upon signs.

I'll give you an example of that: You might put, say, twenty-five people in a room who are all the same sign, all born on the same day. Although there would be some vague similarities in their personalities, largely speaking those personalities would be entirely different. You would be hard-pressed to say, "Where is the core personality in all these beings?"

I see. So you can't call them archetypes either, then?

I don't think so. I think it's important to look at astrology as a means to learn and, since we want to root it in a benevolent future, as a means to guide. This then creates a most desirable future for everyone, regardless of religion or culture. There are certain meeting grounds for religion and culture—and philosophy, for that matter—that bear a considerable amount of agreement and to which, given all resolution, even the most arcane religion could agree.

Your Pathway Has to Do with How You Choose to Learn

Can you say more about pathways? Would these be pathways of experience to get to that benevolent future? How would you say it?

I would say the pathways have to do with the means you choose to learn. Say the sign would be Leo or Aquarius or Aries. These would all reflect a soul's . . . not a core personality's, you see, because you are all of these and more, but it is to reflect how you wish to learn in a given life. With the presentations of the astrological teaching path, you would have a certain desire or inclination to learn in a very specific way and be attracted to learning that way.

For instance, in one life you might be more studious and have a mental approach. In another life, you might be more physical and learn by what you do physically. In still another life, you might be very sensitive in your feelings and so on. So you would have different pathways in which you would learn what it is you desire to learn or what it is you need to know as an individual soul. Of course, there would be general things that you would need to learn, such as the ability to avoid catastrophic mistakes, as in my example before. But then there might be other things that an individual soul might desire to learn.

Since this planet does allow discomfort as a means to prompt or stimulate or remind one of the necessity to learn, perhaps one could come here as a soul with the desire to learn how to work with others. If you come in with a strong mental bias as a pathway to learn, you would learn how to work with others mentally. Perhaps you would have an endeavor in the scholastic realm or the philosophical realm of words. But if you come to learn things more physically, then perhaps you might be involved in some teamwork aspect or working with large groups of people to accomplish some physical outcome.

It is the pathway of learning intended to complement and to provide different ways of understanding. To suggest something you will all do someday together, no creator, even in its individual portions of itself (which in this case is all your souls coming together), can function in a complementary fashion if there are any portions of itself that are stubbornly refusing to move or to accept or to allow that all other portions of itself might be entirely right, might be entirely new, might be entirely loving—in short, might be entirely whatever. You cannot have a portion of oneself of a creator that is not welcoming, allowing, loving in a way that very broadly accepts all beings.

Therefore, as an individual soul you might come here to learn something that you already feel you know thoroughly, but your teachers or guides say, "Well, perhaps if you filter yourself through this sign . . ." You see, you are heading toward Earth, and you might have a planetary system that you wish to emulate in some way, perhaps by your appearance or perhaps by your root energy. But in order to learn what you desire to learn, you filter yourself through a sign so that your tendency or your bias to learn will be along that pathway. This allows you to perhaps learn one or more things about the thing you already know so much about. Perhaps you have almost all you need to know, but your guide or teacher says, "This influence of Gemini," for example, "will allow you to learn things from more than one point of view simultaneously."

Now, Gemini is intended to learn more than one thing at once simultaneously, or to be able to learn from more than one point of view simultaneously. This does present for Gemini a demanding learning cycle. Gemini and a couple of other signs who have complementary aspects to themselves do this. But in the case of Gemini, for example, Geminis must be able to accept in themselves that whatever they learn, even if they are absolutely certain of it or love it as it's happening, that there will be a complementary simultaneous learning that might present a different point of view and, most importantly, a different set of feelings entirely—which is what Gemini often stumbles over as a human being.

So for all you Geminis out there, in case you are reading this, do not be alarmed or upset or disappointed when you have two completely different sets of feelings functioning in your body in reaction or even in action (something you might do) to any and all situations. You will get through it, and generally you choose to filter yourself through the Gemini sign so that you can accelerate your capacity—when moving beyond the life here on Earth—to understand more than one situation that is going on at the same time around you from more than one point of view on a feeling level and be completely at home and comfortable with that. You can see how in diplomacy that would be a wonderful capability.

It Is Intended You Learn According to Your Sign

Is that how astrology works—the soul goes through the sign on the way to Earth and becomes imbued with that energy?

That is a way to explain it, but I am trying to explain things in a way that people can visualize, you see, as well as to suggest that this is something you just take on. I want to paint a picture with what I am saying, as well as to explain it in words. You can ask all of the individual beings you speak to about these things as well, as they may have more to offer. I am not here to answer everything; I am here to provide an overview.

So many things are intended to be complementary, to provide an influence and a subtle means of support as well. For those of you who are any sign, if you wish to know more about that sign in a comforting, nurturing way, I'm going to suggest you do something other than read about it. I'm going to suggest that you acquire, to the best of your ability—which might or might not be available, but many of your scientists have been taking pictures for years—pictures at a distance, telescopic pictures of the planetary groups or the star systems associated with your sign. You might not be able to get pictures of them all, but if you can get pictures, photographs—color ones or enhanced-color pictures—look at them.

Even if you cannot get these focused pictures, if you can, simply look at a photograph of the sign. Perhaps some of you will be fortunate enough to be able to look at the stars in the night sky. If you look at it long enough . . . don't stare at it so that your eyes are uncomfortable, but look at it. You can feel a physical sense of relaxation and nurturing, and you will also reinvigorate your personal enthusiasm on how to learn.

It is intended that you learn according to the sign, although you can have a flirtation perhaps and try to learn by the means and methods of other signs. There might even be times when it would be useful to do that. Check with your astrologer—he or she will tell you when those influences will be supportive of you. But your primary means of learning, by which you will most easily be able to learn, to assimilate, to grow and to become stronger, is to learn on your own pathway. Looking at that star system physically is best, but if that's not available, then the photograph would be helpful. If you can do that, you will feel great support and nurturance. Then go out and learn whatever it is you need to learn.

It might not involve resolution of any given problem, but whatever the problem might be, approach it to learn as your star system chooses to influence you to learn. In that way, whatever you are attempting to solve and the problems that life presents to you, you will be able to get what you came here to get. Do you see? You will be able to actually acquire the subtle awareness, the energy of, the means to resolve, and the complementary capacity to actually become this most benevolent portion of Creator.

What about the planets? Do we come through the planet who rules our sign the same way?

No, you don't have to, because if the planet is in your solar system, it is already entirely compatible with your planet. There is no planet in any solar system, regardless of how it got there, that is not completely compatible with all the other planets in that solar system—meaning that it would be able to present you with the energy of that planet if you're standing on any planet. So if you had the capacity right now to stand on Mars, Mars would be able to present you with Earth energy, because it is completely compatible with all other planets in this solar system.

It is important to remember that when I say "compatible," I don't mean they're going to just get along with these other planets. I mean that it has the capacity to present itself in energy—at least in portions of it, or sometimes in specific localities of it—with the energy of any other planet in the solar system. Your Earth can do the same thing. You could go places on your Earth that will feel very much . . . if you had been to Mars and stood on the surface, you would be able to walk or swim or visit perhaps even in the sky—not in a plane with a mechanism, but in some kind of a sail plane that doesn't require any sound, or not much to speak of—you would be able to visit some place on Earth or within the influence of Earth, such as in the sky, that will remind you exactly of the energy of standing on Mars. It's the same thing if you're on Mars.

Walk-Ins Bring in a Slightly Different Influence

Isis said something interesting long before this book was ever thought of. She said that you choose the place to be born, because the particles in that place become part of you. So different parts of the Earth have particles that are influenced more by certain planets and signs?

Well, certainly. Keep in mind that it was always intended that Earth receive particles from space. Earth has a massive quantity of material from space on its surface. Of course, the atmosphere is designed to filter out certain materials that are not compatible, that are simply traveling in space, and that is one of the vital aspects of the atmosphere. But you know this.

Yes. What about a walk-in? Does a walk-in continue to be influenced by the point of birth of the body it walks into?

Yes. I will not go into too much in terms of walk-ins, but since you are creating a book about the subject, I will simply say that the walk-in brings with it only a slightly different version of the influence. Of course, you rarely know the moment you walked in, in the same way that a doctor or nurse might write down the moment, to the best of their ability, when you were birthed from mother.

So you have your Sun sign, you have your rising sign, you have your moon—this is understood by astrologers. For the sake of a walk-in, you might have that as a distant influence. By "distant," I mean it would have to do with a personality that you bring with you. This can be noticed in a walk-in, some subtle differences in the personality of the individual. You see how they were before the walk-in and how they were after the walk-in.

So in this situation, the subtle influence of personality change could be understood by the expert astrologer on the basis of observation. Of course, it would be helpful if the astrologer had known the person beforehand. Another way to factor it . . . but this only works if you have noticed or believe you may be a walk-in, based upon the criteria you have for that. Anytime within a week or two is sufficient to grasp a subtle influence. You cannot, though, really—I am trying to talk around this carefully so as not to reveal too much at this time—use your own systems, your own astrology. Generally speaking, walk-ins never come from the system that is your own. They will come from an entirely different system. That is why they stumble through the first year or two of life here, because they are learning a new system. That's all I'll say about that.

Karma Is Basically About Lessons

Esoteric astrology relates to karma and reincarnation. I understand that we're not coming back to this planet again—what is that going to do to astrology?

Karma is basically about lessons. It is about the lessons you will have as a result of what you might have done in an individual life. It has been somewhat misunderstood in your times, however, because many times people do not understand that karma does not have to be an unpleasant thing. It might be a complement to your life; it might make your life easier. It might even, in some cases, make your life easier in a way that other people would look at and say, "Oh, that poor thing." But to you, as the individual, you find that most pleasant, most easy to learn, and it has benefits that are not easily noticeable to the eye of another. That's all I'm going to say about karma, especially since, on the greater level of the family of human beings, karma is no longer something you need.

Well, that's why I asked. Zoosh said we were through with karma. He said at least one person had experienced every single thing that we had experienced before coming into the loop of time—I think this was in 1998.

Yes, and that is why it's important to not just bring astrology into the present but to also help it to find its connection to that most-benevolent future, which will allow it to move you from karma to strictly . . . well, as some people might say, strictly to dharma.

That's good! [Laughs.] Did you give astrology to the humans on Earth who first received it?

No. I am here as an expert, not as a deity.

Well, you don't have to be a deity to have channeled through someone. How long ago was it first given to humans? What were humans doing then?

It was given in bits and pieces. No one person received it all, since it was understood that in order to get along on Earth physically, one would always need others. So it came to many different individuals over a considerable amount of time. That's why it is found in different formulaic expressions of itself all over the planet, in the fragments of it that have survived to this time.

Was it given to humans since they've been on this planet?

Oh yes, of course.

The other part of the ancient wisdom was given as the tarot. So is this going to relate to the tarot when we get all the information back, then?

It might. I am not an expert at that.

What about reincarnation? One of the predictive features of esoteric astrology is reincarnation, both past and future, and it's my understanding that we're not going to reincarnate on this planet. How do we deal with that?

It doesn't make a difference, does it? Wherever you exist, you will exist according to the functional aspect of that place.

Oh! Anyplace we choose to incarnate!

Astrology Is Becoming More Feeling-Oriented than Intended

I will make a closing statement now. In order for you to fully appreciate how to use this book, it is perfectly acceptable to use it as an inspiration of your own understanding of astrology. It is also perfectly all right to use it as a foundational element of an astrology that has not been widely distributed or disseminated yet. It is also acceptable to simply read it, think about it, and put the book down.

I would suggest, then, for the experts reading it, that you recognize that all astrologers in the future, including you, will be relying more upon your feelings.

I cannot say why. So don't get too attached to things written that suggest that astrology is something that is a task of the mental. You know, if you've been doing this long enough, when you are working with individuals, whomever they may be, you will have a considerable amount of intuitive knowledge—which is necessary, since very often they do not even know, much less remember, the answers to the questions you need to ask. So you have to feel. Feeling astrology is a little different, and it has to do with knowing your own feelings.

If you have not done so, try to identify your own feelings, even up to the point of knowing whether it is right for you to work with a given person. This way, even if that person is disappointed that you cannot work with him or her, he or she will find another who is more compatible. Compatibility is the cornerstone of astrology, because it has to do with how an individual lives his or her life, of how an individual and others live their lives, of how all individuals in group live their lives in the most complementary method possible. Good night.

♀ Venus

VENUS

Is an Expert at Intensifying and Applying the Pre-Existing, Everpresent Feeling of Love and Harmony

December 5, 2006

This is Venus.

Greetings! Welcome! Tell me about yourself.

Being Close to the Sun Amplifies My Influence

I was very attracted to the project here. Although the planets were largely set up—meaning preordained in a sense to be in certain positions—and I had never experienced heat to such extent, I felt that it would have value, being this close to the star called the Sun.

The previous experience I have in radiating the qualities that Venus is known for—and I feel astrologers have a good grasp of that—is in environments that were largely cool or cold. In such environments, there is a tendency by beings who live there to be more within themselves—if they are physical beings, you understand. At the very least, they might be bundled up. They are currently living in a cooler environment, and as such, one tends to experience a sense of greater retraction of one's auric field, at least when going from a warm house to the chilly outdoors. Still, one is highly attracted during that season of the year, or any time one might be cold, to warmth. Well, that point was not lost on me. So I came here largely to discover the effect of having a very strong support system to radiate the effect of my personality, besides what radiations I do on my own.

You understand that the Sun not only beams light but also many other waves—long waves, short waves and so on—that have a strong effect. They tend to wash over whatever is in their path and beam that out beyond. Earth is located in an environment that is far enough from the Sun that what is washed and beams beyond Earth—and by "washed," I do not mean only cleansed, but simply washed over as water might wash over a rock—is a little bit of everything that everyone experiences on the surface of the planet, plus the planet's personality herself. So for me, what I do is not amplified, but it has increased the effect simply because I am closer to the Sun.

So this is the new thing for me, and I am enjoying it. It is a way, you might say, of experiencing a greater sense of being influential. It is an interesting point, that. Picture for a moment a winter environment: People are cool in their houses, not as warm as they would like to be. But there is a gathering in the community, and aside from the interest people have in the event, they are also interested because the event is taking place in the most well-heated place available to the community—let's call it the community center—which is known for a good heating system plus two roaring fires and two very effective stoves. So the community turns out almost completely, trudging through snow drifts and freezing on the way getting there, just so one can experience that delightful warmth.

Well, that is not unlike what's going on for me and for the citizens of Earth. Of course, one has to recognize that while being here increases the closeness I have to the Sun, it increases the effect in another way. This is largely the case for all planets closer to the Sun. Speaking for myself and Mercury and so on, the impact of what we do is greatly amplified by the Sun's effect.

There Is Less of an Impact on Mars

That is suggestive, isn't it? If the effects of these inner planets are amplified by the support of the Sun impacting Earth, one has to wonder, what about planets beyond Earth? Well, I know there's a great deal of speculation by scientists and even normal citizens who have not studied the matter that there may have been some great and wonderful civilization on Mars. Although this was certainly true in the past, one finds the remnants of such civilizations on your own planet also.

Astrologers understand and define well in many books the impact of, say, Mercury and Venus on Earth and her citizens, so I won't go into that too much—that's already been done. But I will say that sometimes the impact on the people of Earth seems to be a bit overwhelming. In the case of Mercury, which has to do with communication and so on, people are constantly overwhelmed with the lack of communication and its impact on a personal basis, from person to person, to say nothing of its overall impact on your world's history. Also, one could reasonably say that misunderstandings about love, kindness, intimacy and so on, as is identified with Venus, also have an overwhelming impact on Earth and its citizens. Again, this can be charted not only in the outcome of one's personal life but in history as well.

Fifteen Percent of Earth's Population Will Move to Mars

So would there not be a better way to live as an Earth culture? Well, of course, one of the ways one learns about things is to be exposed to some long-standing and more intense impact of something, so that when one becomes exposed to something that is less of an impact, then one can accomplish it handily. An obvious example is to be a parent and raise children, and then when one is a grandparent and one's duties are not quite so intense, one often finds that one can be an effective temporary parent without being overwhelmed by a full-time job.

We then come to a seemingly logical conclusion that a very large contingent of Earth's population—not a half, not a quarter, but perhaps at some point 15 percent of Earth's population—will ultimately migrate to Mars when it is convenient to do so. There, the influence of Mercury will not be something that overwhelms you in communication, and the influence of Venus, where love is overwhelming—meaning that love is felt so intensely at times that it is overwhelming and also the misunderstandings about love can also be overwhelming—will be greatly moderated. Love will be present as a constant and easily felt and understood and experienced in the most benevolent way, and communication will not a problem and will be easily assimilated, with everyone being able to speak, know and understand the needs of others as they interact with their own needs. In short, as in my analogy from being a parent to being a grandparent, this is the intention.

You are in a school now on Earth—this has been taught over and over and over again in the Explorer Race material and others. This school, as many schools are, is overwhelming and intense, and there's not much escape. There are occasional intermissions—"occasions," one might say—but the school goes on. When one comes to the end of one's natural cycle, one is crystal clear that the intensity of the school has everything to do with the gradual migration of the culture to someplace where the impact of the greatest influences on all beings on the surface of the planet (in this case, meaning human beings) is greatly moderated—as will happen when one moves or develops a culture on Mars that is similar but much more benevolent than one experiences now on Earth.

While there are other impacts that have been discussed extensively in other *Explorer Race* books, the more personal impact on the souls who are either born on Mars in the culture that Earth citizens will establish there, or more to the point, who migrate to Mars and live there, is that that culture will be much more comfortable and easy to live with, even in the beginning when there is a certain amount of struggle to create a benevolent living circumstance. Children who are born there, and especially *their* children, will adapt to the thinner atmosphere and actually become strong and comfortable within it, and lifetimes will extend. But the pioneers will have their stories too—the pioneers being the incomers.

I just wish to give you an overview so you can see that my interest lies in the impact of things rather than in an analysis of the fundamentals of the things themselves. Now that you have an understanding of my personality, we can proceed.

It seems that you were asked to go to that particular position so that your influence and Mercury's would be the most intense for the humans in this school. Is that correct?

Yes, but I did not know that at the time. When Creator requested my presence there, Creator said that I might find the situation to be more interesting, more enlightening and more fulfilling—and this is the key to understanding my personality, when you consider the qualities of my personality that you are experiencing. Think about it: Love is certainly about fulfillment in its most benign stage, at least. So naturally I found that very intriguing. I cannot speak for Mercury, but I think that Mercury will have interesting things to say. I recommend that you request Mercury next time.

So I found it to be very fulfilling and I still find it to be that way. When someday this much of Earth's population moves on, I feel that there will be even greater fulfillment for me, personally speaking, because I will experience the fierce pride that a great-grandmother or great-grandfather might have for his or her children who are grandmothers and grandfathers [chuckles].

I will enjoy your culture blooming on Mars, and I feel that you will, as a culture, love Mars. Of course, there will be great appreciation and love for Earth, but Earth will gradually come to be considered a font of life, like a wellspring—revered, appreciated and loved. One does not play or bathe in the wellspring; one honors it and appreciates it. But one plays and bathes and consumes the outcome or the outflow, if you like, of the wellspring someplace else. That outflow of the wellspring will be consumed most comfortably and enjoyably for your culture, as you know your culture, but much more benevolently, you understand, on Mars.

You Won't Dig into Mars for Mining or Building

You might find that most of what you need to support your culture will gradually reveal itself once your culture is well-established on Mars. It will be unnecessary to mine Mars, to drill for water and so on. As a matter of fact, it is most likely that those in the social sciences—the anthropologists and the psychologists and therapists and so on—that these people will be much more influential on the culture of Mars, because much will be appreciated and known as a result of Earth history. There will be an overwhelming desire to avoid the mistakes encountered repeatedly in Earth history. Therefore, when developed on Mars, the approach (while being of Earth culture as you recognize it) will represent much more of the finer qualities of your culture and there will be less desire to make an impact on the planet.

So, for example, just picking something out at random, you will not find building foundations dug into the surface of the planet. Rather, you will find something that will look not unlike a skid plate—meaning the support for any structure will have metal supports and something that looks very much like a skid plate underneath that, so that the support for the structure is distributed the way it is in engineering when one has a flat object underneath a pier, for example. It will be distributed and be able to support a great deal of weight, but it will not be dug into the surface of the planet. This will allow anthropologists and archaeologists plenty of time to research former civilizations to discover what they have to offer to the civilization you will establish there and how it is complementary to your civilization. Digging in the planet, though, for establishing foundations and other mining purposes would only destroy the bulk of what there is to be found by archaeologists.

This has happened on your own planet, but this is a fait accompli that has already occurred. So it can be avoided. I believe that in space exploration so far by those who have gone to the Moon and so on, there has been an effort to not make such impacts, though I expect you will mine the Moon. Still, the impact of mining the Moon by your culture will underscore this determination by those who go to Mars to avoid mining Mars.

I thought there were already people mining the Moon who didn't want us there.

I am talking to the general public here, and I'm going to keep it that way. It's more important for this book, for my purposes, to talk about Earth culture and Earth people, not about who did what to whom. I must be strict on this point, because this book is meant to have a benevolent impact, to support astrologers and those who offer astrologers support, whether the astrologers be professionals, talented amateurs or simply interested parties. So I do not want to get off-track on that point. Also, you have explored this much more thoroughly in other books, so please excuse me if I will not discuss that.

There is a reason. Always know that when beings such as myself and others will not pursue an interest you might have that seems to be completely relevant in the moment, there is always a reason and the reason is good. I am saying this to you so that you will not feel offended.

That's all right. I just thought we were told not to go back.

Earth Still Feels the Personality of the Planet Who Was Here Before

When you first came here, was the planet we live on now here, or was the previous planet here?

The previous one.

The first one?

Yes. It was intended to prepare the space for your planet. Do you know that if you looked at that planet from a distance, it did not look anything like the planet you experience now? That's not surprising for scientists who have studied, at least through telescopes, the other planets in this solar system. There is no question that this planet looks decidedly strange—beautiful, yes, but it looks out of place in this solar system. This is understood and explored well in the other books.

The planet who was originally in that space was very different. For one thing, there was no surface water to speak of. If approached from a distance, the planet looked very dark. I do not mean "dark" in an abstract way; I simply mean that its appearance was dark. On the surface, the planet was very much made up of something you now search for on your own planet: coal deposits and other dark minerals.

It was not an easy place on which to live. As a matter of fact, the people who lived there were more than happy to migrate. They lived there, not because a culture developed naturally, but rather a certain amount of travelers would come by and stay and occasionally be stranded. So small cultures sprang up of adventurous personalities who wished to experience something for which they would not be required to live out their lifetime. Those who moved on were allowed to move on and were supported in moving on, and they were happy to go.

I'm sure you've heard many things about how this happened and that happened and so on, but the planet was always unstable. I remember the personality of that planet well. This might interest you, because there has been some latent impact on your own planet of that other planet's personality, but the personality could largely be referred to in this manner: nervous, with a desire to be elsewhere.

If you have ever been around a person like that, you get the feeling that that person is leaning away from you. In the beginning, there is a tendency to be insulted by that, but after a while, when comparing notes with others about this person, you realize that this is just his or her personality and it makes you nervous being around him or her. Think about that for a moment.

We know that this first planet migrated. People say it blew up, but there's another way to put that. Say you, as an individual, were feeling nervous—not because you were drinking too much coffee or anything like that, but rather because you were simply desirous of being many places and, as a single individual, you couldn't go many places at the same time. But what if you were in a different form? What if Creator came along, your guides (planets have guides, too) came along, and said, "It's possible for you to go many places at the same time, experience your personality and travel far beyond this solar system to experience whatever you like, wherever you want to go, and even to become a part of the cultures of other beings elsewhere simultaneously. In short, you can do a vast amount of things at the same time, enjoying them all as your own personality." Well, I can tell you that . . .

She was off and running, yes.

That planet was thrilled, and the idea of explosion was actually very attractive. So the bulk of the population—as you know surface populations to be and a few slightly under the surface—was allowed to move on, and the planet migrated. That is what I would call it, "migrated," because the only thing that can satisfy a personality like that is to do many things at once. You find that even peoples in your own culture who have that temperament are often very well suited in jobs that require them to do more than one thing at once. They can do more than one thing at once and actually are bored if there isn't more than one thing at once for them to do. So this is actually something that is found within your own culture.

The planet who used to occupy this space migrated really moments—I'm not speaking from the eons-of-time point of view; I'm going to use experiential time here, but it equates pretty close to time as you understand it—migrated about a day and a half before Earth arrived in this space. That was largely to keep the orbits of other planets and the welcoming orbit for a planet in that space—as third planet from the Sun—as stable as possible with a missing planet.

This had a side effect—there was no way to avoid it—which was that there would be some residual remains of the other planet's personality. That is why there has been some difficulty for Earth in maintaining her personality here. When at times she is tired and must take care of herself, there is a tendency for the old planet's personality to become more heightened. Thus, at these times the influence of the old planet's personality on whatever culture is learning on the Earth at that time—meaning, in your case, the human being—is greater. When Earth herself is more repaired or more comfortable, is able to do more for herself and others, then the impact of Earth's personality is much more the case.

When one looks back at the cycles of history that you know about—your own human history on the Earth—one finds then a rise and fall in historical intensity. One notices that Earth history might not be particularly noticeable for 100 or 200 years, during which time one might find that Earth herself was much more capable of serving her own needs and the needs of others. Whereas during times of great intensity in history, when there are a great many things happening, perhaps not so pleasant, one knows that Earth herself needed to look after her own needs and was less able to look after the needs of others. I thought you might find that interesting.

There was also a planet there for just a little while that I have been told was so gentle and so full of love. Did you see that planet?

Well, I think it was before my time here, but I believe that occurred before the other planet. I cannot say that for certain; I can only tell you that the planet who arrived after the other one migrated was Earth.

Oh, I see! Someone once said that sometimes even now souls come here thinking they're coming to that wonderful, loving planet that used to be in this space, and it's . . .

It's all gone, but it's available elsewhere.

True Love Is the Building Block of Life

Tell me about yourself. How does one become known for radiating love and warmth and affection and wisdom?

You have to understand that this is a natural state of Creator, of life. Without true love, which has absolutely no attachments whatsoever, it would not be possible for anything to find anything else with which it is entirely 100 percent compatible. True love is not just the building block of life. It explains how something can be found on the Earth—a structure apparently built by normal human beings—that has lasted thousands and thousands and thousands of years, and yet looks largely like other structures that are built in your time and don't last very long. One has to ask, "How is that possible?" It's possible because every element that is in contact with every other element in that structure is in true harmony with everything else it is touching. Therefore, there is a desire to remain in that position, because one and all are experiencing true harmony—in short, true love and attraction for all contacts.

This is the obvious building block of life. Even a human body or a body that is meant to be temporal . . . a deer, an ant, a spider, a cow, anything like that on Earth is meant to be temporary. They are not here to learn anything, you understand? But human beings are here to learn, and the best way to learn in such an intense environment is in a temporal way, meaning to have a structure or a vessel with which to gently hold your personality, though the effects of life on Earth are not always gentle.

Yet how does even a temporal vessel maintain its integrity? The only way it can do that, given that the temporal vessel is constantly retiring and being replenished (as in the cellular structure of the physical body), is that the temporal nature must be very much temporal—meaning that the atoms are not required to remain in total perfect contact with all other parts of your physical body at all times. There is a considerable amount of migration going on at all times, even in places where one might assume there isn't a great deal.

In the actual bony structure of your body, there is growth that takes place—from childhood, of course, the skeletal structure gets more prominent, gets larger. As one gets older, the skeletal structure begins to actually decompose within the body, supporting the termination of life. In short, there is constant motion. So it is a built-in factor of the human body that the temporal nature only requires that love and harmony exist between all cells, all atoms and so on within your body on a temporary basis. This means there is always the knowledge and wisdom for those forms of life that make up your own physical bodies, that they will very soon be able to migrate and find the places where they will be more comfortable. That is the nature of all temporal life.

In order for love, then, to function in such an environment, there has to be a greater sense of families of familiarity. In the case of families of familiarity, you will find on the surface of your planet—I'm taking into account, oh, say, 100 feet down from the surface as well—that all of that material on the surface and 100 feet down, give or take, will have at one time been involved in the body of a human being. Perhaps it is no longer in any way recognizable as having been involved in that body, but as a result of that accumulated matter, one then finds that in the actual soil in which food is raised, the mineralized soil is a general mix of about 20 percent—given the mining and digging on the surface of the planet now, becoming closer to 30 percent—actual matter of the Earth that has never been involved in the participation in a human being body. Almost all of the remaining matter is made up of that which has been involved in a human being body. So that matter is comfortable in becoming engaged again in some way, even fleeting, in a human being body.

Take a farm, any farm, and we'll say that on that farm broccoli grows, okay? The broccoli is growing in matter that was once involved in a human being body—at least 70 percent of that matter, perhaps 80 percent. Therefore, the food that is harvested and ultimately cooked and consumed by the human being is food that can assimilate into the human being body and is not repulsed by the personality of human beings in general, is not repulsed by its experience passing through the human being body. In short, it offers nutritional benefits because of its familiarity with the physiology of the human being. This is an example of love and temporal harmony.

These are all the civilizations that have ever been on this planet—not just the Explorer Race, but all of the eighteen civilizations that have come and gone represent that 100 feet of material that was once human?

All civilizations. I think it's more than eighteen, but I won't go into that at this time.

I Wanted to Develop Love in This Solar System

That was fascinating, but it really wasn't the answer to my question. There are these planets in our solar system, and you represent love and joy and all of the things that go with that. If all the planets have that as their core, can you say that you've chosen to focus on that—just as Mercury is focusing on the mind and another planet is focusing on some other quality? Or are you more of that?

Well, for one thing, I am not about joy but love. All of the planets—and we're talking about the personalities of the planets, you understand—have been recruited for their intense flavors of personality, which were intended to be in this solar system established by the Creator of this universe. So nothing is accidental. We were, in this case, however, recruited to be influential on what you have come to call the Explorer Race of beings. So, yes, I think I can speak for the other planets and say that, yes, we were recruited for our actual personalities.

But how did your personality get to be focused on love rather than one of the other qualities that the other planets represent? I mean, how did you get that way?

I know you want to know my history, so I'll give you a little bit, not all. As a result of my inception as a personality, I was introduced to this universe and experienced upon my arrival the awareness of its most elusive and desirable flavor—meaning that one could absolutely and with complete certainty be aware of how obvious love was present, and yet the intensity of love, which might be desired in heightened moments at times, was not to be found. It was rather a low murmur, as one might feel one's own heartbeat for a moment, and then it passes. The low murmur was a constant—a benevolent constant for sure—and yet I requested of the Creator of this universe that I be allowed to develop that most elusive and desirable quality so that it could be felt with a greater frequency by those individuals in this universe who might blossom as a result of that exposure. Creator said, "That's just fine, because I have a plan that would incorporate that exact need."

Of course, at that time—speaking about experiential time, of course—the Explorer Race was [chuckles], to use a contemporary term from your own culture, a twinkle in the supposed eye of the Creator and well off into the experiential future. But Creator certainly knew. He did not share that with me at the time, but looking back on it, it is a most cherished memory for me. So I spent quite a bit of experiential time acquiring different aspects of that most harmonious feeling so that I could become an expert, let's say, in its application and in the cooperative elements required to bring about any and all forms of resolution to the overintensity of love or of any other problem.

That took time. Once I was able to do that and was migrating around this universe, providing that energy where desired—only where desired, so that I was welcomed—Creator then came to me, so to speak, and said, "Would you like to participate in this project?" (Creator is everywhere in this universe, of course, but I'm putting it in terms you can understand.) I said, "Oh, yes," and here I am.

[Laughs.] Here you are!

There Are Many Ways to Study Love

How can we learn from you? How can we become adept at focusing love, at being love?

I will tell you, and it is something you already do. How often have you looked at the animals expressing love to their young and to each other? It is a fascination. Think about it. Let's go back before film to the visual arts: painting and so on. How often does one find the subject of painting to have something to do with affection (love, friendship, kindness), whether it has to do with humans or with animals? How popular are such paintings? Very popular indeed. So in your own contemporary times, how often does one enjoy seeing love and affection between the animals, the natural beings? It is so enjoyable that it is a theme in your visual arts that doesn't go away.

This is one of those studies you can do that puts a little distance between yourself and the actual participatory nature of love. I think it's important to look at the fact that animals will often show love (meaning nurturance, kindness, benevolence) in plain view of other types of beings, because there is absolutely no shame in it—just as a human mother will pick up her child and kiss the child and love the child in plain view, because there is no shame about that. Shame is perhaps one of the most conflicting of emotions, and it is entirely learned; you do not arrive with it. This is perhaps why therapy is so often found in your culture and needed, I might add, to help an individual understand his or her own behaviors—not just mentally, but as a good therapist might do through some form of performance, meaning acting something out in therapeutic ways.

So there is that form of study. But it is also important to take note of your own needs. Most human beings need to be affectionately touched many times a day, even if it is just a gentle hand on the shoulder or another form of affection, perhaps a hug between friends. Or there is even the great substitute that many human beings have found because of a lack of training in how to get along with other human beings: the beloved pet who loves you and who is very happy to provide affection when called upon or even from its own impetus.

In short, love in this form is the best way to study love. Study it on the basis of your own needs and be honest about these needs. Children are trained that affection is an award. This is unfortunate, and many parents have absolutely no awareness that they are actually training their children that way.

Your Cultures Are
Experiencing a Warping of the Nature of Love

Affection in a more healthy culture is a fact of life. It makes no demands, no one is forced into anything, and it occurs purely and simply as a part of life. As water forms a stream, it is in the stream of life. Yet when affection is denied for whatever reason—often for punishment, many times out of frustration—it builds up into intensities that often explode into uncontrollable acts. By "uncontrollable acts," I mean some terrible deed done from one person to another that the person doing the deed literally cannot control. Of course, there's a price to pay for all involved in such things. But for all parties involved in such terrible acts, even after life there is a long time, experientially speaking, of resolution and coming to terms with what you did or what was done, and that can be achieved.

So I must honor the fact that your cultures are experiencing, at times, a warping of the nature of love. Love has everything to do with absolute harmony, meaning a desire to be together for its own sake. Both parties and all portions of both parties desiring that is the true nature of love—meaning every portion of your physical body desiring to be with every other portion of the other person's physical body, in that sense. Or to put it into more easily understood aspects, why the walls of these ancient structures do not simply fall down the way the walls of your more modern structures fall down in time, no matter how well-engineered.

The true nature of love is harmony, and it is absolute harmony. But when it is warped or twisted, it becomes something else. This is perhaps not the best place to discuss such things, because they have been discussed so thoroughly and are so well-involved in therapies that are provided by your culture out of necessity, in order for the culture to simply remain on the planet.

If it weren't for therapists, most of your cultures would have died out a long time ago. Sometimes these therapists are trained and accredited, but most of the therapists on your planet do not have a piece of paper, have not had any formal training, and are simply known as friends and lovers and often pets.

I am making a point of saying that therapy is a valuable thing to pursue, because no matter how much intelligence a person has—and therapists themselves, to say nothing of psychologists or psychiatrists, are totally aware of this—no matter how much you know about something, this does not mean you have not sublimated that knowledge. You might be pursuing a pattern unconsciously to your own self-destruction, a pattern that you have a complete understanding for when you step back and look at it on somebody else. So therapy is a good thing. I have studied that, you know?

No—how did you get involved with that?

You cannot be love, you cannot emanate love, without completely understanding the resolution and the path to resolution of love that has been warped or twisted. Why do you think I've made a point of discussing this? And why do you think the ultimate driving force behind almost all people who learn to become therapists, and why those people stay with therapy, is a desire to provide love and the resolution of love in the most harmonious way to all they work with? I would like to give one little statement to therapists, though, and that is, don't work too much. Get involved in life more, find a hobby, have fun. It's too easy to become consumed by a desire to help.

Desire Is a Direct Result of Earth Life

How did you get to be known as Venus? Is that something we call you, or did you emanate that name so you would be called that?

Everything you call anything, in any of your languages, is a word or a sound—call it a sound—that your culture has created. So cats do not call themselves "cats," ants do not call themselves "ants," cows do not refer to themselves as "cows," and planets have other names.

Can you share yours?

It is a sound, "zh," like the very softest "j" sound, but continuously, like a hum. May I suggest something? I suggest that you ask all of the planets what their names are. Let them give you that sound. Someday it might be good, when you have the capacity, to release a sound device with those sounds.

That's a great idea, because when you said your name, I went mellow. How do we experience more of what you have to offer?

Why the desire for more? I'll tell you why; I'm going to answer my own question. On your planet, almost all human beings, at various times in their lives, want more. The desire for more is almost always a result of being denied the natural state of beingness of life. So one looks for more in the areas where one can receive more. If one can have more food, then one has more food. If one can have more excitement, then one has more excitement. This is desirable, you see? If one can have more adventure, then one has more adventure.

In short, the desire for more is a direct result of conditioned life here. Conditioned life on Earth is not at its perfect cultural state, so always know that any desire for more of anything is almost always a result of having that denied or subverted in some way in experiencing the culture of your own life as conditioned by others. This is not a criticism of you. You are a representative person asking these questions for yourself and for others, and I feel that the answer is important, so we do not stray too far.

You are asking, of course, how can one experience more benign and benevolent love? That is the source of your question. We have been talking around that pretty much for our entire conversation today, which we will continue next time. But the answer is not intended to be evasive. The answer comes in the actual things people can do. What is the point of giving you something that is abstract when the answer is essentially presented to you on a daily basis?

If you want to experience more love, then if you have a good friend, decide whether you feel safe and whether the friend feels safe in patting or touching each other on the shoulder or on the hand, or even giving each other a hug if both parties are comfortable in this. For those who do not have friends, then do what you can to develop friends. Find others like yourself and become friends. Find out what you have in common and pursue those traits with others. Friendships are great ways to develop the qualities you have within you that are part of your natural personality. If you pursue them with others, you will be supporting your own natural personality.

Watch out, on the other hand, for developing qualities within you that are self-destructive—meaning that are harmful to you or harmful to others and can bring about various warpages of love. For example, consider a loyalty to someone who is harmful or hateful, and that loyalty is so strong that you become harmful and hateful as well so that you can receive that person's love or admiration. That would be a warpage, you see? Whereas if you know and understand yourself (meaning you know there are certain qualities you have in your personality), then if you seek out other people who have those qualities, you will not only reinforce and feel legitimate in your own personality qualities, but you will also find people with whom you have things in common and you can do things that you both like. I think that's something you can do, and I would prefer to give things that you can do rather than something esoteric that seems separate from your life.

You're very practical.

Life on Earth—and Earth culture, of course—is about experiencing the qualities of your true personality as they can merge with the qualities of the personalities of others in the most benevolent way.

Never forget that. [Chuckles.]

[Chuckles.] Well, if Zoosh were here, he would certainly say that.

Creator Apprentices Help to Bring About Resolution

Since you've been here from the beginning of this universe, what is your opinion now, what is your feeling about the Explorer Race?

Well, not quite from the beginning—when I got here, it was already here. I feel it is a marvelous solution to what might appear to be an esoteric problem to other people. But if a creator does create a universe and then brings it to the point where the creator can bring it—you can only bring it to a certain point, because all that was desired to do has been done—the obvious thing to do is to leave someone in your stead, not only who can do more, but who can do more because they desire to do so. This means that those who are training . . . in short, the Explorer Race is ultimately training to become a creator as one participatory being.

Those who are going to take over as a creator, then, would have a vast amount of knowledge, wisdom and experience in bringing about resolution for the most minor to the most major situations that can be resolved, no matter what occurs in this universe—resolution that would be benevolent for all beings. That, of course, is exactly what you would want as a creator. This Creator of this universe is at that point and is already involved in a preparation of Its migration, since the Explorer Race is involved in the home stretch of its own acquisition of this wisdom and will ultimately become that creator. So everything is in motion for that transition.

As you discuss what we're going to do, what we've learned to do is what you've learned to do—bring it to resolution with love. So it sounds like you are going to be connected with us in the future, not just on this planet.

Do you think so?

Yes! [Laughs.] It sure sounds like it.

Maybe that's why I came in the first place.

Perhaps. That's a new slant on this. This is marvelous. Were you aware of the beings who are helping the Creator, like Isis and Zoosh and the friends of the Creator, before you came to this universe?

No, there was no need for that. I was in motion. I told you I wasn't going to tell you too much about my source being, but I'm telling you all you need to know.

You're connected to the Mother of All Beings, aren't you?

Everyone is.

Yes, but some . . .

No buts. [Chuckles.]

It just . . . it feels really wonderful. I'm so happy with this.

Well, you see, so much has been developed over the years by inspired astrologers, astrologers who have brilliant minds who can extrapolate for themselves as well that it is less necessary to bring out details and more necessary to bring out the feeling aspects of the personalities of these planetary bodies. In that way, an entire new avenue can be explored by the same brilliant and inspired astrologers. We need to give them credit for the capacities of their own inspiration so that they can continue to extrapolate based upon those very inspirations they have when stimulated by the personalities of those with whom they are fascinated. Good night.

Good night. Thank you, bless you. Thank you very much.

♀ Venus

VENUS
My Main Focus Is Assisting the Learning Curve of the Human Being on Earth

December 6, 2006

Greetings. This is Venus.

Welcome! I've been thinking a lot about what you said. You're the glue—you're the core around which the Explorer Race will coalesce?

Oh, I wouldn't say that. After all, you have your own motivations, your own purpose for being. But I understand the nature of your question. It is important, however, to grasp that love existed in this universe before I arrived. It is not possible to create anything lasting without love. Still, I was desirous of coming here in order to support, nourish and enrich those who might be under some level of distraction or strain—hence the obvious, the Explorer Race.

There was plenty of love that was needed for all places everywhere in this creation, but it wasn't working as well as Creator would have liked it to in the circumstances of the Explorer Race inclusion—meaning all that was involved with you. So Creator requested my presence to function with the innuendos, implications and broad variety of complexities, to support love insofar as the Explorer Race and, to a greatly lesser degree, a few other problem areas in this creation—which I will not comment on here because we're talking about the Explorer Race. This book, I believe, is for the human being on Earth, and the *Explorer Race* is the title of this lengthy series.

You Are in More Than One Place Right Now

Will you be with us as we as we integrate into one being?

I will be with you until you become completed in your temporary assignment as a creator—meaning that you are going to take over for Creator for a time, but after that you may or may not choose to stay together. So I will be with you until you become a creator in your own right, and then you will have integrated all that you need to proceed. But unless you specifically request my presence, I will move on. Understand, the planet itself will not move on, but my personality will move on. Your personality lives on regardless of whether your body does—it is the same with me.

I know that, but if we become the creator and you go with us, then you won't continue to be a planet?

I can be in more than one place at one time. So can you. You are in more than one place at once right now—I can prove that to you. When you are asleep, you join the other places you exist. But you are provided with a separation in subtlety, because when you wake up, you do not recall that entire experience and you refer to it as a dream. What you remember as a dream is some kind of scenario, yes, but you do not remember talking to your teachers and guides and so on. The dream, so to speak, is most often these days a training for you, which is why you do not see yourself in the dream as you are, because you are training to assist others. But you know this. I bring it to your attention so you can be reminded that you are also in more than one place at once.

Right, as is everybody.

Venus Personifies the Feminine

I've been doing a little research and you sort of gathered up all the good stuff. According to the books, you're the Goddess energy, feminine beauty—I've got a list of about twenty things here. Can we talk about some of them?

If you like.

Okay, let's talk about the feminine beauty and the Goddess energy. Since the whole idea of the Goddess energy is resurging on the planet now, this means that you are more and more involved, right?

Be alert to the fact that feminine beauty does not refer to physical appearance. Do you understand that? Feminine beauty refers to the heart of the feminine and her natural mysterious abilities, which are different than the masculine. One of the abilities is perception. The feminine does not perceive only what one can see or what one can think; the feminine perceives both the inner and the outer, meaning in layers. When human beings in your cultures have dreams and visions, this is an example of such perception, regardless of whether the person is masculine or feminine. So feminine beauty, then, does not refer to physical appearance.

I see. What about what we call the Goddess energy?

What you call the Goddess energy is an attempt, in literary terms, to refer to a more balanced perception of deity. Deities on your planet in the more predominant religions are masculinized, so it has been necessary by your cultures to create a Goddess energy to suggest that deity is also feminized. Any deity, of course, who exists on your planet is always balanced with masculine and feminine. Some religions have made more of an effort to suggest this, but other religions are stuck in an attempt to suggest that creation is a factor of authority and authority is often placed at the foot of the masculine, even though the masculine does not wear it very well—nor does anyone. Authority is always a factor of doubt or self-doubt.

I am not suggesting that people who are experts in something are associated with doubt or self-doubt. I am rather suggesting that the authoritarian function one finds in people who might, for instance, bully others or who might try to tell people how to do things even if they have no particular knowledge of how to do it—that this kind of authoritarianism has been identified as masculine, which of course it is not. So the term "Goddess" has been an attempt to put into balance the image one holds of any deity.

You're also connected with art and culture?

Yes. Again, these are things identified with the feminine, even though you certainly find the masculine involved with these things as well.

Also refinement. Now, that to me is one of the most beautiful qualities. It is not male or female; it's just like taking away the dross or constantly moving to a clearer state.

Well, no, not quite clearer—a more benevolent state.

One of the qualities I read about that you're associated with is one of human self-esteem. How does that come about?

It is an encouragement. Encouragement is the root of self-esteem. If one is not only encouraged to believe in the value of one's own life but encouraged when one demonstrates certain talents and abilities or is simply able to reproduce something that is desired or needed, then this helps any individual to feel worthwhile.

Empathy and compassion also seem to be connected with you?

Connected with the feminine. These are all qualities connected with the feminine.

Comfort and pleasure, I see. Creativity . . . that's not usually a feminine attribute, is it?

Well, I wouldn't go so far as to say it isn't. Creativity makes complete sense to identify with the feminine. Men do not give birth, so creativity is at its roots very feminine. Creator has allowed and deemed that only the feminine is trusted to give birth. Now, I grant that this is an old text, but it is an old text that has been removed from some of your most popular religious books. If that were added back into, say, the New Testament, then one might have an entirely different picture of the feminine.

But that's only with the Explorer Race. In other civilizations, giving birth is not limited to the female, is it?

Well, let's just say that other civilizations are not a factor in this book. This book is aimed toward people who don't know what they normally know when they are in other civilizations on other planets.

Right. Another interesting one was resources, that you have an influence over resources. A good Venus connection implies that a human has access to resources.

"Resources," in this case, does not refer to how much oil or gold you can get out of the ground. It does not, in that sense, refer to replenishment. "Resources" refers to connected communication, meaning how one is able to resource (or source, if you prefer) in a constant and revitalized way with all other beings—everything that has to do with the connection with all other beings. You understand, when I say "all other beings," I'm not saying "all other *human* beings." I mean all other beings period, *including* human beings.

[Laughs.] That's a lot of good stuff. It's probably obvious, but if you personify the feminine aspects, what planet in our system personifies the masculine? Mars?

You'll have to pursue that yourself. I think you will find that it is not Mars.

Planets Have Guides and Teachers When There Is a Need

Do you have any beings living on any levels of your planet?

There are a few living on a different level who require light to live and function with something not unlike photosynthesis. They do not eat nor drink, but they translate light into nourishment. Needless to say, they live on the surface.

You said that planets had teachers and guides—do you ask them for things? Do they bring things to your attention? How does that work?

Generally speaking, everyone has teachers and guides, including Creator. Generally, at this level, one asks for the cooperation of others to create or to support something that others are creating. By "asking," we don't pick up the phone and call. We just have a need, and when the need is present, then others do cooperate in that multiple-supported effort to assist others to create. Essentially, that's what happens.

So it's not conversational, as you might have a guide where it is conversational. Granted, it might not be the kind of conversation that you experience in your day-to-day life on Earth, but it would be something for which there were pictures, where all your senses would be used, plus a couple that you don't really have access to on the Earth. You would remember it, in the snippets in which you can remember, as something that felt like a mutual exchange. But since I am not here to learn, then it is more like an ongoing connection that is available and responsive if I have a need. Of course, for others, I am available to them if they have a need. So you might say that it's a mutual availability, in my case.

Is all your energy taken up with what you do in this solar system, or do you have time to keep up with your friends?

I can be other places if needed, but my main focus is assisting the learning curve of the human being on Earth.

The other planets in this system are doing the same thing. So do you have, like, teacher's conferences? Do you discuss certain things—not "discuss" as we talk, but do you interact with the other planets?

Yes, but it's more like a universal chorus. We are each doing what we do, and we don't have to sit down and talk about it. This is something that's comforting to the human being, because you feel isolated and that sense of isolation is always present—though perhaps less so in some friendly or family situations. But the reason that sense of isolation is present at all is because you do not have access to all you normally have access to in your usual state or condition. In this learning curve that you are involved in or finishing up with at this time, you don't have that access in the way you normally do, though you are regaining it slowly. But I do not have that sense of isolation, nor do the other planets.

Ah, that makes sense.

I Support Love, but I Am Not the Source of It

It's because we're physical on Earth that we talk about heart energy when we talk about love. But we have a feeling body with us here that's with us in other existences, is that correct?

Yes.

So what is it that you interact with when you radiate to a human?

Love. You refer to it on Earth as heart, but that is a word . . . it might very well be on other planets, of course, or even on Earth itself, but a stone has love, a tree has love, yet they don't have a heart as you understand it.

Yes. But that's why I'm asking. Do you radiate love and we feel it in every pore or in our feeling body? I don't know how that works.

You are easing around the idea that love comes from me.

I thought you radiated love to us.

Do you think love comes from me?

No, love is inherent in every particle and every . . . what we call space. It's everywhere.

Thank you. So I support love, but I am not the source of it.

How do you support it?

It's very hard to put into your words. I am able to provide certain moderating elements so that love is always something you are aware of. That's the best way I can put it in your terminology.

Can you say more about moderating?

I can't say much; it's hard to describe. If you had to describe what was in one cubic inch in front of your eyes, covering the entire spectrum of life and existence, how long do you think that might take you? This is something your guide says to you, you see? Of course, at that level you always respond, "Many lifetimes." So you're asking a question that requires me to describe something much larger than one cubic inch. It would take many, many lifetimes.

Do you have any trainees? Are you teaching anyone to do what you do?

Well, at a great distance, yes. Not in this universe.

Ah! So you have students someplace?

One.

Mistakes Have Value

What else is it that you want to say? I'm sure I've missed most of the important questions.

Oh no, you've asked all the important questions. I will say this: The purpose of this book is to provide you not only with a sense of the personality of the planets and the signs but also with a few details to understand the interconnectedness and the interactivity between these elements of your creation that allow you to function in such a precarious fashion and still have lives that are, most of the time, worth living.

The precarious fashion I am referring to is this completely unique situation in this place where you do not have full access to your total being. In all other places you have that access, and therefore, mistakes are almost unknown. Of course, you could say without being unreasonable that some mistakes are worth making. I'm not talking about catastrophic ones here, you understand. But simple mistakes that are repairable often lead to solutions that may cover a wider range of topics and circumstances than the solution originally was created to do.

So you might reasonably argue that some mistakes have value, and that is exactly what Creator feels. Creator felt that way sufficiently so that Creator asked for volunteers, and you all volunteered. I know it might not seem that way, but you all volunteered, not only to participate in the Explorer Race and all that entails, but you volunteered to experience a lesser degree of yourself. By "lesser degree," I'm not talking about something less than, but rather simply in quantity, a smaller focus of yourself that you could then stimulate. Of course, there would always be a magnetic attraction to reacquire, you understand, that you could stimulate to re-create yourself. But without having your normal state of condition whereas you would normally know all the things you have ever acquired in your life, to say nothing of all the valuable teachings you have ever received, you would tend to fumble around a bit in order to find what's you and eventually learn what is you and what really is of others.

In the course of this fumbling around, though, you would tend to discover, stimulate, create and re-create certain aspects that you had already done. Although that might seem pointless to those of you who are trying to accomplish something, the point is not what you are attempting to create, meaning the ultimate outcome—the point is the process. In the process, you often re-create sufficiently so that other solutions are found for long-standing problems, either for your specific personality—which is much more often the case—or in the universe in general.

So your whole point of existence here has to do with re-creation, rediscovery and ultimately solutions, many of which have nothing to do with you, the beings on your planet or this solar system at all. This is why almost everyone in the rest of this creation is well aware that what is going on in this isolated spot in this universe is the re-creation of life as you know it—meaning in other parts of the universe—in order to solve every known problem and to create a mechanism by which problems that may develop at some point can be solved.

If you know that about yourself, you will then feel better about what's going on here—not, of course, about the violence, war and all of that, but about the need to solve problems, which comes up almost every day for all of you. Understand that such creative efforts are only allowed to very specific individual personalities. Even though there were many billions more individuals who volunteered to try this, only those individuals who had had at least one life somewhere in this creation, and perhaps in other creations, of complete spiritual mastery about something—it may have been this or that thing—were allowed to come here, so that your soul or your immortal personality would have much greater depth to fall back onto given the circumstances of your life here.

Given that situation, you require a great deal of assistance that is not necessary in other parts of this creation. You require, in that sense, something to fall back on, systems of understanding your true nature, such as astrology or numerology or many other things, and the means to understand it pictorially, as one might find in tarot or some other means like that. So given these ongoing methods and manners that support your growth, change and accumulation of wisdom, you are encouraged by Creator and supported by Creator to create—in short, to learn how to create. That is why some beings refer to you as creator apprentices, because you must create, even as a child learns how to tie a shoelace. You must create, and it has to be beyond thought—it has to be physical actions. There have to be feelings, heart and soul in the creation, and what you create and cherish you often teach to others.

All of the planets in your solar system and all of the signs combine to support, encourage and nurture you while you travel through this learning curve on Earth. Granted, Creator does not expect you to live too long here, which is why your lives here are not very long. Compared to any life you might have in any other part of the universe, your life here is maybe one-tenth or one-twentieth or even less long. But in that life, so much is learned and acquired, so much is stimulated, that it often takes several lives beyond this point to work it out and understand what it all means, and to find a benevolent way to express it.

As each and every one of you learns as an individual, so much of what you learn is meant for other civilizations in other places. That is why very often when you come to the end of your natural cycle here and you are reincarnated after a time of completely learning and assimilating in benevolent ways what you learned here on Earth, you will choose to have a life someplace where . . . as a member of the Explorer Race, you acquired knowledge and wisdom on Earth, so you will choose to live on some planet in some culture someplace else in this universe that needs a problem solved that you solved in this Earth life. So never assume that your experiences, however odd, may go to naught. They will come to some benevolent outcome, even if it is in the far-flung reaches of space in this creation. Good life.

VENUS

☿ Mercury

MERCURY
Influences and Supports Both the Linear Mind and Vertical Wisdom

December 13, 2006

This is Mercury. Greetings.

Welcome! Tell me about yourself.

What do you want to know?

I want to know about you! What can you tell me?

What, do you want my name and address and how you can reach me? What do you want to know? [This being's energy is light and whimsical.]

[Laughs.] How did you happen to come to this solar system?

I Influence Communication and Humor on Your Planet

Well, Creator put out a call for personalities who would inhabit planetary bodies that would be a very specific and intense influence on these beings called the Explorer Race whom Creator has a great deal of love for. Given my position near the Sun, Creator wanted beings, personalities, who could not only be able to have the Sun's light and radiation streamed through them but could also complement the other planets. The planets beyond Earth, of course, are intended to have more gentle support. But the planets who are closer to the Sun and are washed over with the energy that really bathes the Earth—specifically, of course, Mercury and Venus—would definitely be the planets who were most involved in influencing Earth.

Creator gave Venus and me the choice: "Where do you want to go? What do you want to do?" Of course, I said, "Well, communication is my forte—if not necessarily in a multiplicity of languages, then at least in my capability to be forthright and, for that matter, also in my ability to be obscure while providing subtleties to lead individuals to the point." I must say, Creator thought that was amusing. I'm not sure I understood the joke, but since Creator thought it was amusing, Creator nominated me to personalize the planet—and that's really what beings do; it's not so much that we bring planets with us, you understand, for the planets might very well be there (and in my case, the planet was there, but it hadn't been personalized)—and to be prepared to emanate the maximum amount of my personality to make it available for the Explorer Race on Earth.

Creator seemed to particularly like the fact that I have a sense of humor. Creator specifically mentioned to me that one of the things that will allow the Explorer Race on Earth to get along in life, especially when faced with problems that might even be insurmountable, would be a sense of humor. If that was coupled with communication, I would not only be able to provide a vast array of humorous stories but also humorous invectives, humorous sayings and, yes, even humorous attitudes. I must say that I liked this. I consider it to be a bonus, and Creator apparently does as well. But also I believe it was Creator's clear choice that the people of Earth have not only the option to be humorous but the option to be humorous in many different ways.

So Creator understood that communication would eventually be a great challenge—which, as you know, in your time it is. But in the beginning, communication was very simple. Everyone "spoke" the same language, meaning communion was readily available. But once the Explorer Race arrived on Earth, you, of course, were not as equipped with your total being as other beings who occupied the Earth before you. These previous beings either were supported to move to other planets or were simply relocated in such a way as they would not interfere with your progress of solving the mystery of your existence.

So as you can see, Creator not only particularly wanted love and relationships to be highly influential on your planet but also communications and humor. I realize that I haven't exactly said where I came from, but I felt this preamble was important.

Now, I did not come from this creation, but Creator's request went beyond this creation quite naturally, as creators' requests go beyond their creations all the time. I was in another creation quite some distance away. In that creation, I was, you might say, an assistant—not exactly a creator, but more like an apprentice to a creator there. That creator had desired to create a creation that would allow all beings in the creation, whether they were planets or molecules or people such as yourself or anything, to be able to speak and think in whatever form they chose, but to have a very specific wavelength upon which they could all be in communion anytime they chose. So you can see that communication became something I had to learn about simply to assist that creator, and fortunately that creator also had a sense of humor.

You know, I cannot tell you how many times I have faced a conundrum for myself, and if it hadn't been for my sense of humor, I never would have been able to just go on and try to solve it. Imagine for a moment taking 1,000 or 50,000 years to solve something that's a conundrum. If you don't have a sense of humor, you're going to be crazy pretty soon. [Chuckles.] So by the time I was able to solve something, I had my biggest laugh, yes, but also it was a relief.

What often goes with humor is the feeling of relief. Sometimes when you laugh, you just let go of tension and you feel relief. Other times, the joke or the humor is so insightful that you feel relief because you got something that you couldn't get any way other than by laughing or seeing the subtle humor behind something. Oh yes, I feel that humor and communication go well in hand.

So when I became aware of the call that the Creator of this creation had put out, I felt attracted to participate. The being I was working with considered that it would be very good training for me to come here and participate during the time I would be influential here. At some point, this creation might become something that presents itself differently—certainly when the Explorer Race takes over and becomes their own creator, this will happen. So when I am no longer needed, perhaps somebody will take my place. Whenever that takes place, then I will probably return to my former position and continue with my work there, perhaps with a few more ideas, eh?

My Energy Has Brought Great Understanding to Earth

When the Sun streams its flow of energy toward us and carries your energy so that we feel it more intensely, does it change your energy or is it just like a carrier wave?

That's a very good description—it's more like a carrier wave. It doesn't change my energy. Interestingly enough, when Earth is, not directly, but pretty close to something that you would call alignment with the Sun's energies moving toward Earth, while this really rushes a great deal of my energy and the energy of my personality toward Earth, it actually heightens my sense of personality. For there is no amount of energy that simply runs out here. We're not talking about something that depletes and has to be restored over time. No, it actually heightens and creates a more specific clarification of my energy, since it will have to move these great distances and stream toward Earth.

I want to give you an example of what something might be that takes place during those times. One of the things that might happen is that some specific, perhaps even worldwide misunderstanding might be resolved. Oftentimes when my energy has been profoundly directed toward the Earth, great understandings have taken place. Either philosophies have been clarified or even, on some occasions, wars have been settled.

This does not mean that I have been in perfect alignment with the Earth at that time, speaking physically here, but very often the Sun will make an effort. The Sun seems to know. Perhaps all suns everywhere in this creation are specifically connected to Creator in some way beyond what the planets are—I do not know. I do think, of course, that it would be good for you to include the Sun in your book. Have you done that?

We've talked at length, but we might go back before we get all done and ask things that came up during the talks by other planets.

Very well. So when things like that have happened, I have noted at a distance—granted, I do not know your entire history—that there has been some genuine sense of a shift in consciousness that I can actually feel. I feel this has to do with a heightened physical energy of communication and the possibilities of communication, and often with a little humor thrown in as well.

It almost sounds as if you support inspiration as well.

I cannot say that I am involved specifically in inspiration per se. This is something more along the lines of Creator and those Creator has deigned to assign to this task. However, the means of communication of that inspiration to the individual and beyond . . . I feel I do have something to do with that.

So what happens when this energy streams into Earth and into humans, but then it keeps on going. Does it affect the other planets too, or does it just sort of dead-end into the Explorer Race people?

It is aimed specifically with an attunement, you understand, to the human beings on Earth, which we are calling the Explorer Race. It is aimed specifically at them. So anything that streams beyond that point will probably not really have much of an effect, other than to create a filter or spice so that on the other planets, when you visit them—as astronauts and so on, or eventually at some point when commercialization of space travel takes place for you—that energy will be available for you.

Oh, that's brilliant! Does it also work that way with Venus?

I believe so, yes. I believe all the planets affect all the other planets that way.

You Are Influencing Your Guides

Now, communication involves not just the mind, it also depends a lot on feelings. So you're affecting us on more levels than just the mental body, right?

Yes, but feelings are something that have to do with your physical self. Yet your capacity to understand what your feelings are, what they mean . . . that's where I come in. I understand that a lot of the work you are doing now with this channel and with your company is to instruct people on this topic, which has been somewhat misrepresented unintentionally in the past by others who did not realize that feelings were not simply something called emotions. There has needed to be greater clarity and a means to give the individual a more hands-on ability, so to speak, in the world of feelings. You are doing very well in such instructions.

We have the linear hard-drive, storage-type Andromedan mind, and we have been asked to infuse feelings into it before we give it back to the Andromedans. We also have vertical wisdom, where we know what we need to know when we need to know it, which we're only moving slowly into now. Your energy works on both levels?

Yes, it does. Vertical wisdom, of course, is your natural way of being, and you're moving slowly into it so that you can thoroughly complete all of the other tasks that have been entrusted to you. All this takes place while you are living your lives, of course, as well as contributing as much knowledge and wisdom and experience as you have to others who will perhaps pass it on to those whom they will be with at a later date.

You might understand this better if I elaborate. You as an individual will be working constantly with your guides, though you don't usually have an awareness of this. Your guides have to know and understand you thoroughly in your personality and, to a lesser degree, physically—because where they are, in their existence, they cannot really feel exactly what you are feeling or it might harm them. But they have a sense of what you are feeling so that they can be present and supportive in the lines of inspiration and in the other ways they can be.

What is going on, then, as you are easing in a general direction toward vertical wisdom, your native means of knowing, is that you are indirectly influencing your guides because they must learn about you. Think about it. These guides support you, and at some point you come to the end of your natural cycle here and you go on. But what do the guides do? Do they go on with you? Do they cease being guides? No. You move on to other teachers and so on, but the guides who have been training to interact with Earth people will move on and continue to interact with other people on the Earth.

So much of what you are learning allows the guide to become more thoroughly immersed and experienced in interacting with souls of beings who will inhabit physical bodies—in short, human beings on Earth. Thus, the inspiration and the subtleties of what you are learning, that they must learn in order to be of service to you, will be passed on to others. It is a way, you see, of sharing knowledge and wisdom, even that which goes beyond the individuals the guides might serve in the future. So it will be possible for guides, if they deem that it will have value to other beings, to offer inspiration at moments when it is needed that might not otherwise have gone to that person, because the guide itself or herself or himself—whatever you want to call them—has acquired this wisdom through the interaction of working with one human soul after another.

So where will these guides end up when there are no more humans on Earth?

Well, just because they have learned how to interact with humans on Earth as guides does not mean that they will simply cease to exist. They will go on to other places. In some cases, many of the beings who have been humans on Earth, when they live on other planets, will welcome a guide to interact with them whom they have experienced as a teacher/supporter, which is what a guide is on Earth. Other human beings who live on other planets who have never been to Earth might also welcome such a guide, even though the guide will have vastly more information, knowledge and wisdom than that being would need on some other planet. Think about it: In the future, the Explorer Race is going to do exactly what the name says—they're going to explore. They're going to go out to the other planets, they're going to love finding things, and these beings on other planets are going to meet them. What a wonderful thing, yes?

If you were born on another planet and someday met human beings coming from the Earth, wouldn't it be wonderful to have a guide who was once a guide to someone or many someones on Earth? Inspiration would be welcome for beings on other planets where these communications, messages between one's guides and teachers, are much more direct and much more available consciously—because they're not learning the way you are learning here. What a wonderful thing, to have a guide who could be much more forthcoming to prepare that being on that other planet in such a way as that being could hear it. It would be spoken gently, for instance, communicated with emanated feelings, colors and other phenomena. That being on that other place not only might be able to commune well with Earth astronauts but also might even be in a position that would be seen and understood by other beings in that civilization on that planet to be most particularly helpful in such communications. So that being might very well wind up being the diplomat or one of the diplomatic corps who meets, greets and interacts with Earth astronauts.

Creator Is Fond of Resolving Problems

Do you have beings of any type living on any level of your planet?

Yes. There are some beings living within the planet. Of course, they are in focuses I don't think you could see or interact with. Believe it or not, there are some beings who visit the surface of the planet. Some beings, of course, are not the least bit affected by very bright light and heat. Other beings actually thrive on it. Can you imagine that there are beings living on the surface of the Sun? It is true, of course; everything is alive.

Really?

There are other beings who visit the inner portion of the Sun. They are not affected in any way by the brilliant light—it is brilliant, you understand—and they are not affected, meaning harmed by, the heat. After all, such a thing is possible. So one finds a few beings who actually move about on the surface of the Sun. It's a little hard to describe them, but let's just say, from your perspective, that they're pretty sturdy.

[Chuckles.] But on your planet they're only in a higher focus? There's nothing in our dimension then, right?

That's right—and that's desirable, you see? (I think I can speak for Venus here as well, but you can ask her.) If the population were vast, it might very well unintentionally influence the people on Earth. It's one thing for the populations on other planets beyond Earth to be more thorough—if they have populations—because that isn't being washed over and sent downstream, so to speak, to the people of Earth.

Ah, yes—I hadn't thought about that. When did you get to your planet? Was this planet we're on now here, or were there previous planets in this orbit?

There was another here. But I got here pretty early, so I was able to settle in, so to speak [chuckles], before you came along. This was helpful, because it allowed me to see Creator's overall plan for you and to understand that that plan had purpose and means and, of course, intent, because one's intent might not always be only purpose.

Yes, a pretty outrageous plan, I'll tell you.

Well, it only seems outrageous because you're going through it at this point. But, of course, when you're done and you get to where you're going, you'll clearly see that it couldn't have been done any other way. Look at it this way, from Creator's point of view: How do you bring everything in your creation into balance and happiness when there are some beings in this creation who, in their own right, simply aren't happy? The people on Earth can completely and thoroughly understand this perhaps much better than beings on other planets. How can you make a moment of great suffering and misery happy? It takes awhile.

So Creator, you understand, loves variety and is also particularly fond of resolving problems. The Creator of this creation has even volunteered to resolve problems that can fit into this creation that really originated in other creations. That's why sometimes you as individuals will find yourself resolving something that doesn't seem to relate in any way to your life and doesn't seem like it even relates to anything on Earth that you know of. Occasionally these things happen, and usually they happen almost unconsciously. Sometimes they feel like insights; other times they just feel like puzzles. But sometimes a resolution can be a puzzle if it's something that's being resolved for another creation somewhere. What you consider a puzzle—meaning something you cannot resolve, where it's a conundrum and so on—might very well be considered an answer, because it is a stepping stone that leads to an answer that everyone knows how to get to, you see, in some other creation.

One thing that has become very popular in many of your cultures on Earth is puzzles: games, puzzles and so on. There is a constant search by many creative people in your cultures and on your planet to create the most difficult and challenging puzzles. Sometimes, through the assistance of computers or simply insights and inspirations, one comes up with puzzles that cannot be solved. One of the most common of these is tick-tack-toe, which cannot be solved under certain circumstances, and yet in another creation, it is considered the key to the resolution of a major problem.

That puzzle was created by your people, something that has nothing to do with this creation at all. I'm bringing it up because it has brought Creator such joy that you have been able to dream up something that has an insoluble portion of its personality—the game can be played, you understand, up to a point, but there is a point where it is insoluble. Creator loves that you created something like that, because that insoluble portion has, in fact, been the key to allow people in another creation to find their way through a problem of extreme difficulty. I might add that humor plays no small part in that.

Thank you for that—that's a new level of what happens here. It will be fun to get out and actually understand everything that happens here, instead of being in the middle of it.

You know, the funny thing is, once you do move to that point, it becomes an "Aha!" Once that "Aha!" passes—you kind of chuckle about it in your own way there—it then becomes an, "Ah, of course!" and the moment passes quickly. This is not to say that you won't love the moment, but it passes quickly and then: "Oh yes, of course."

Well, we're not there yet.

No, but you will all get there—that's guaranteed.

My Personality Influences Your Personalities

Let's just back up a little bit. You must have always been interested in communication, then, because that's what drew you to the other creator.

That's the interesting aspect. I wasn't that interested in communication, but I was interested in variety. I'm sure that's part of the reason I felt a sense of symbiotic connection with this creation, since your Creator is also keen on variety. It's just that my first stop, so to speak, before I came here was at that other creation. You can see how a being who's interested in variety would be very attracted to a creator's creation that involved such a massive amount of variety. So before I got to that creation, I was not focused on communication; I was focused on variety and humor. Interesting, eh?

It certainly is—that you were led there before here.

It certainly prepared me.

What about the variety on your planet, Mercury? What is your planet like? I don't think we know anything about it.

Well, it is made up of the same stuff as the other planets here. I wouldn't say that the planet itself is representative of my personality so much.

That's because it was there. You're like a walk-in.

[Chuckles.] Well, yes, you could say that. It was there, and I was able to personalize it. This doesn't mean it didn't have a personality of its own, but Creator requested that I personalize it with my own personality, given what Creator wanted to do.

How much do you participate in these waves of energy that come to humans on Earth? Is it just an automatic thing that happens?

Well, it is my personality. It's almost like asking, how much do you participate in your office or in a family group when you are being yourself? People are aware that you are present, and very often certain personality characteristics in them are heightened because you are present. I'm putting it to you like that, so it doesn't seem obscure.

Since my energy is present and it broadcasts to the Earth, it tends to heighten certain characteristics in the human beings on Earth, whom Creator refers to as the Explorer Race. Those characteristics that are heightened, of course, are the desire to communicate and specifically the desire to create as much clarity in communication as possible, which doesn't necessarily have to do with words. As you said yourself, it often has to do with feelings, it could have to do with touch, and it certainly has to do with art. Art is . . . say, a painting, for instance. It doesn't make any difference what language you speak. You might get many different things from it, and somebody else might get something else. In short, my personality is intended to be an influence that causes your personalities to act and react.

Well, what I was leading up to in my "how much do you participate in that?" was, what are your interests? What do you do to keep you . . . ?

Do you mean, how do I keep from getting bored? Let's talk about that tomorrow. Good night.

All right, we'll see you tomorrow. Thank you very much, this is fun.

Yes, we'll keep it that way.

☿ Mercury

MERCURY

My Job Is to Influence Energetically, to Inspire and to Stimulate Your Communication Skills

December 14, 2006

This is Mercury. Greetings.

Greetings! Welcome! Can we start by discussing what is called Mercury retrograde? When that's happening, if something can go wrong, it will [laughs].

Your Souls Also Retrograde

Well, you understand that all the planets retrograde, and it is a terminology that is designed to explain a different presentation of one's personality. Do you know that souls, individual souls in your bodies, also retrograde? You have times of the year when you need to rest, and during those times you are more able to serve your own needs and look after yourself.

If you can use astrology, your personal chart for you, a good astrologer can set up what amounts to a retrograde pattern. Now, it might be called something else; it might very well be called a time when you need to rest or something like that. I'm using a description here rather than a title. But it is really a time meant by the Creator of this universe that is intended for rest—meaning, not service.

Let's put that into a practical sense. If a person was perhaps working and had a family, then this would be a time from two to four weeks—maybe once or twice, more likely three times a year—when you would be off from work or you would be on light duties at work, meaning that whatever your duties normally were, you would do perhaps 20 percent of that. Also, instead of doing your duties at home, whatever they might be, other people would take over those duties and you would do maybe 10 percent of what you do at home. This would be the case for all human beings.

I'm bringing this to your attention, because human beings have, in your cultures, very often come to the conclusion that you must work, work, work all the time and that time off is somehow a luxury or an indulgence. Do you know that even in some of your biblical texts, it brings to your attention that time off is essentially important, even though it wraps it in the religious context of whatever religion we're talking about? But in reality, if Creator rested in the religious stories on one day, you are intended to rest on that day also. I do not wish to interfere with your religions, and I will say nothing more about that. But retrograde is a reminder that you must also rest.

Support Me During My Retrograde Times

So getting back to myself, speaking of the retrograde pattern, let's just say now that if I am resting during that time, then if you know as an individual (or as an astrologer or as an astrologic enthusiast) what Mercury does and more about Mercury's personality as I've attempted to present it here for you, then you can call upon your own spiritual acumen and see if you can support what Mercury does on your planet. Remember, you are the Explorer Race. You are learning. You are here to explore, you are here to try new things—"here," meaning on Earth—and you are also creator apprentices, so your jobs are often much more spiritual than the workaday world you live in.

So I would suggest that about three days before any Mercury retrograde—or any other planetary retrograde, if you're so inclined, but since we're talking about Mercury—starting about three days before and extending to two days after, add to your meditations or alter your meditations if necessary to feel most benevolently (in the most friendly pattern of feelings) all that Mercury does in the most benevolent way. That would be the feeling of easy communications.

You have all had the experience, perhaps, of talking to others where the conversation just flowed. They understood you, and you understood them. It was wonderful, even scintillating. Try to bring back the memory of that, if not the actual words, and feel those feelings of that wonderful conversation and how easy and comfortable it was. Just let those feelings flow through you and out into the environment.

Then you've also had times when perhaps you were driving and the traffic seemed to melt away in front of you and you could get from point A to point B, whatever that was, in the quickest, most smooth and perhaps most pleasant way. Perhaps you weren't driving; perhaps you were letting somebody else do the driving, see? Any number of things might be possible—in short, you had transportation that was easy and comfortable. Remember those times, if not the details of it, and ease into the feelings of it and just be in those feelings of ease and comfort in transportation, ease and comfort in communication and anything else that you feel Mercury might stand for—such as humor, which I've been talking about. You can all remember times when things struck you as funny. You don't have to remember what it was, but see if you can feel those feelings of good humor.

You don't have to do all these feelings at once; just go from one to the other and see if you can feel those feelings again. Then just allow those feelings to ease into your environment. You do not have to blow them into your environment, you do not have to direct them or send them into your environment—just feel them. All human beings are natural transmitters. Anything you feel is naturally broadcast into the immediate environment and loses some intensity as it moves on into the flow of life. So as it is with all transmitters, eh? Downrange from the transmitter, you don't pick up the signal very well, but close-up, it's loud and clear.

So that's what you can do, and that's what you're intended to do. Any time a planet goes retrograde and you feel its effects—and I know you feel the effects of Mercury retrograde, but of course there are other planets who go retrograde—then you take over their duties as best you can. It is not your job to be Mercury in your life but to just add that to your meditations, to your spiritual practices a few days before and a couple of days after and during the Mercury retrograde whenever it feels comfortable and easy. The whole procedure probably won't take more than two or three minutes, maybe five tops. That's what you can do.

That is brilliant. I never thought of it as you resting. It didn't occur to me that this was the meaning behind it.

It is a good way to think of it, though, isn't it? And it's a good analogy that human beings do that also. All beings do that, though some are more well-known for it. You know about the bear hibernating, but many life forms go into a form of hibernation during different seasons or molting patterns. Human beings also have that time. It isn't just sleep—that's not enough. That's essential, but there are other times when time off or reduced duties are important. It is rest and restoration. That is absolutely vital for all human beings. I cannot tell you how many mistakes human beings make, sometimes catastrophic, that affect a wide variety of people because you are work, work, working too much and you are not resting and restoring. It is absolutely vital.

Seek out your good professional astrologer to find out what times of the year are your rest and restoration periods. Astrologers, I know you can do this, and I feel it would be a great public service to offer.

We do feel Mercury retrograde more than we feel the other planets in retrograde, I think.

Well, it's different for different people. You'd have to ask the other planets or ask your friendly astrologer and see what they say. Some people might say that Venus retrograde might be a bit much also, but it just depends on your focus in life. After all, there are more pleasant aspects of Mercury retrograde. It is a time when it is possible to do things for yourself that are nurturing and helpful, and it may even be possible to bring things to completion that have only been begun but never finished. This is information that is well-known by astrologers, however, and I had this other information that I added so you would get a more complete picture.

Cars and Trains Are Living Beings

You mentioned transportation—in what ways do you influence transportation?

I do not influence transportation directly, but I influence . . . when you think about it, communication is the passage from one being to another. You have to keep in mind that everything is alive, even though you might not recognize it as a life form. Of course, you recognize animals and plants as life forms, but literally everything, the molecules, the atoms, they are all life forms, even when compressed or changed or altered into some form that suits human beings in your culture. So you might have an automobile, you might have a train, you might have a horse—all these things are alive. You are more conscious that the horse is alive, of course, but [chuckles] you are in fact moving in a living being, even though it is simply made up of mass forms of living beings—atoms, molecules, cells, in that sense—in a train or on a plane.

So everything is alive; every atom is alive. Everything is ensouled, and everything has personality. The reason the ancient structures that are still with you today have managed to maintain their happiness—meaning their ability to stay in one piece and essentially in the same piece, in the same form—is that the communication between the cells, between the atoms, is so simpatico from one to another that not only are they happy to be together but they welcome it. A scene put together like that does not go away any time soon.

Someday when your technology embraces this and involves this kind of spiritual work—and by "spiritual work," I do not mean working with ghosts; I mean working within the clear, loving spirit as intended by Creator on this planet and others—you might be able to work with that spirit, invite exactly what minerals and other items you wish to come together, and make products that will last forever. I grant that in some situations this is not needed or desirable, but there are some products where it would be very convenient for them to last forever, especially if they are not very accessible.

Mythology and Astrology Are Interconnected

Where did we get the name Mercury?

You'll have to look in mythology to find that. Just type "mythology" into your computer and you'll get that.

So humans name planets, then? I always feel when a child is born that the child sort of influences the parents in choosing his or her name. There's none of that with planets? There's just the arbitrary human designation?

No, but it does require going into mythology, which I really do not want to do in this book. I do recommend that those who are interested go into mythology and understand the nature of it. If you go into mythology, of course, you will understand some of the original meanings and purposes ascribed to planets, but the meaning and purpose came first, and the name came afterward. So in the times of mythology—that can be studied, you understand—you will easily find that the people in those times were inspired to know, not only what planets do what and why, but what names might be most comfortable and easily remembered. But you have to remember that, in those times, they were looking to deify these things, and that is why Mercury would be shown as the winged messenger.

Ah! So delving into the mythology of Venus and Saturn and Mars will bring us some of the original information that was channeled about the planets?

Well, it was inspired. Let's not say "just channeled," let's say "inspired," because inspiration is also a factor of human mythology. You beings are born profoundly receptive. Granted, your culture tends to defeat that quite a bit, but in some ancient times, if a child was noted to be highly receptive, if the parents and the culture were open to that, then these people were often allowed to function in a receptive mode during their lifetime and were essentially those who received inspiration and helped to guide the culture. Of course, the culture would have to be well-established to do that, because any culture that was not well-established would just be trying to survive. But cultures that were well-established were able to pursue these interests, and that's how a lot of this information was originally acquired—through inspiration.

I've always wanted to do a book on mythology through Robert.

If you did a book on mythology, you would constantly find references to astrology, because mythology and astrology are absolutely married. So doing this book is actually a nice preamble to that.

It Is My Job to Inspire

So you, as Venus mentioned, can be many places at once, right?

Yes, and in fact, everyone can. It's just that human beings on Earth are not allowed to do that so that you can create and re-create and all that other stuff that is printed well and thoroughly in the other *Explorer Race* books.

Yes. But what I'm leading up to is, then that allows you to keep looking in on the creator you were apprenticing, to kind of check on it, right?

There is no need to do that. One thing you must always do when you are involved, not only as a creator apprentice or even a creator assistant, but if you are involved in a creation such as I am here, working with the Creator of this universe, you must remain totally focused on what you are doing. Granted, during times when I am in retrograde and able to focus more on my own needs, then I might have a brief moment when I chat, so to speak, with my former mentor. But generally speaking, I am focused on my duties here.

That is so interesting that an apprentice creator is mentoring a whole planet of apprentice creators [laughs]. I see.

It seems to be simpatico, yes.

So we're only 6 percent or something of the total Explorer Race—were you here when the other 93 percent were here?

When they passed through here, yes.

Ah, so you have influenced all of them.

Well, we have all done that—all of the planets, the Sun, Creator, everyone here. Everyone is influential. On a smaller scale, of course, you are influential with the planets who revolve around you: in this sense, the other human beings, the animals, the plants. Everyone lives in their own solar system, just in greater or lesser size, volume. But if you look at any solar system—and this has been done, of course—it's really not that much different from the way an atomic structure is. This tells you immediately that it's been created that way. It's not an accident of science; it has been created that way because it is a message.

As above, so below.

Picture yourself as the sun of your own planetary system. If you are the sun, then it is your job to pay attention to the other human beings who are in your sphere of influence. You live with them, you shine the best light you can upon them, and you are hopeful that they are doing the same with you.

You've given us so many new ideas.

It is my job to inspire, is it not, and to stimulate your communicative juices so that they might flow easily from point to point.

You do it in such a juicy manner. [Laughs.] All right. Your energy comes here, but you mentioned earlier that you're not actually focused so much on the humans themselves and their culture. I mean, are you aware of what everybody is doing?

No, no, that's not my job.

That's what I thought.

My job is to influence energetically, but it is not my job to watch over you. I am not your fairy godmother, eh? [Chuckles.]

But you are aware of the current events?

Only broadly, but it is not my job to watch over you individually. You have guides, teachers and many others who do that—and, of course, Earth herself.

Contact Is My Overriding Principle

Venus talked about the population going to Mars. Will you continue to influence in the way you do now when a large group of humans goes to Mars to start a civilization?

Well, you have to keep in mind that if and when that takes place successfully, by that time you will be conscious as individuals of your spiritual duties, meaning that what you now call mystical or spiritual will become a way of life. You will not simply cede that to your religious practitioners to do for you. Yes, you will still have your religions, and they will be more benign, more nurturing. But you will be doing your mystical and spiritual duties—although they won't be mystical anymore, they will be known and understood. My energy will not have to be as strong, because you will be doing it and you won't need as much. So you can move a little further away, eh?

I see. So it won't be a civilization like we have now; it will be much more benevolent.

It has to be in order to live on Mars. Mars is not an easy place to live if you are upset or angry about something. But if you wish to build, to create, to establish long-lasting things, perhaps long-lasting cities that can function well and smoothly . . . if you know the how and when and who of welcoming materials to join other materials, as I've said before, you might just be able to put together a city that will last 1,000 years. Why just 1,000 years? Why not 10,000 years? Why not 100,000? There is no friction between atoms, cells and molecules if they want to be in contact with the other atoms, cells and molecules. If they want that, if they welcome it, if it is a joy to them, then friction does not exist. Think about that. Think of the effect of friction in your society. What if it didn't exist? [Laughs.]

Now, in your time you have a tendency—because you have been trained to do this—to look for what caused this or that. This is actually intended. Creator desires you to look for causal factors so that you can understand how this works and that works. But Creator does not desire for you to use that as a method to find blame. It's not about blame; it's about what works, why, and how you can encourage it and be encouraged by it to work better. What comes together and stays together because it's happy to be together? Don't try and force it to stay together if it completes that cycle.

Communication has everything to do with contact. If you understand that contact is the overriding principle of Mercury, then you will understand why your lives are so caught up in contact: how you get there, yes, how you communicate, yes, but what other forms of contact do you have? How do you touch and how are you touched, not just physically but also on the feeling level and certainly on the inspirational level? If you know and understand that, you will appreciate the Mercury energy in you.

You are here on Earth to be influenced by many things. Everything that you are here to do has a source of influence that stimulates and supports those desires within you. This system of analyzing, understanding and encouraging your application of those things whenever they come up for you is called, in this case of this book and this study, astrology. Astrology allows you to know, understand and, most importantly, solve, resolve and re-solve many different things in your life. Don't be attached to coming to completion with them in this life. Your job in this life is to make progress, to perhaps find some solutions, to help others to find their solutions, and working in concert, to maybe apply to one degree or another those solutions in practice.

Give yourself a chance to do that when the opportunity arrives, but don't, if you would, get attached to the idea that you're going to complete it. This lifetime for you all on Earth is about moving forward individually, in groups and globally to accomplish global needs such as communication, cooperation, benevolence—not in that order, but all together. Good life for you all. May it be so.

I really enjoyed this, thank you.

You are most welcome. Good night.

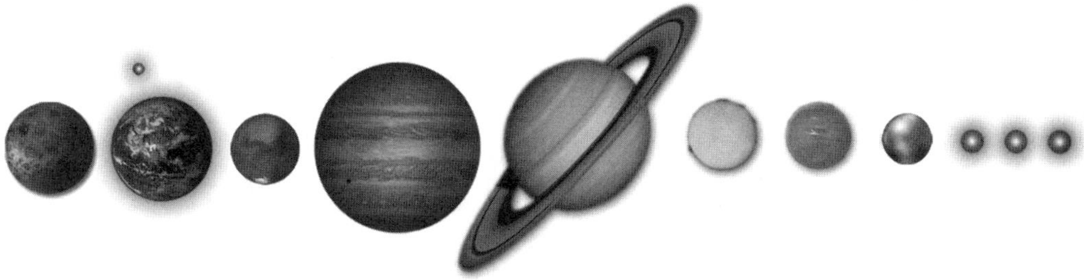

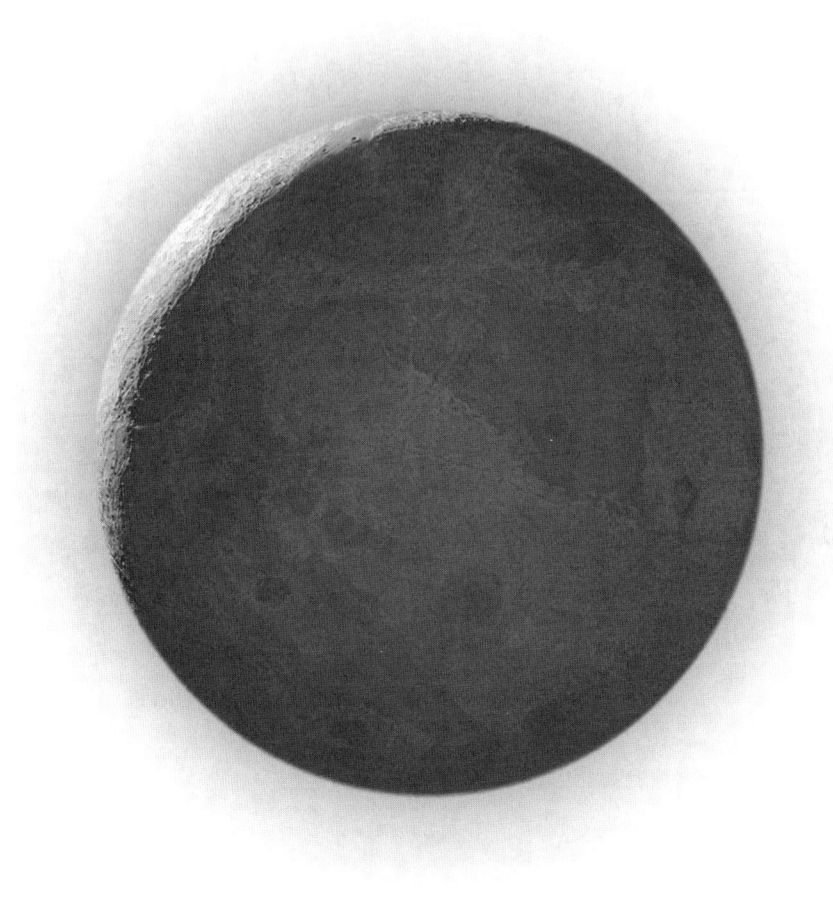

♇ Pluto

PLUTO

Helps You to Change and Get Past Your Limits and Blocks on a Personal Level as well as a Worldwide Level

January 2, 2007

This is Pluto, as you call me.

Pluto! Well, welcome! Tell me about yourself.
  You need to ask specific questions.

As You Move Out Farther in Your Solar System, I Will Have More of an Influence

What particular attribute or talent or ability caused the Creator to ask you to be part of this project?

That's a good question. Creator wanted certain personalities who could remain in reserve for influence as the Explorer Race started moving out and exploring planets. As you can see by your space projects thus far, you will travel someplace, explore it, and try to understand at least in a rudimentary fashion the way the planet or object functions so that you can set up a base, which is what's in the planning stages for the Moon and Mars and so on. Of course, you will be heading out from rather than in toward the Sun. By the time you get to the point where you're well-established on Mars and tentatively moving out a bit farther toward the idea of having a base on the next planet out, you will be feeling my influence more significantly.

Astrologically speaking, there is always a certain amount of influence, but that allows for relatively fixed positions of the beings involved—meaning the human beings and the planets involved. So these fixed positions would have to do with people who are basically on Earth. Just moving out to your nearby satellite, to your Moon, is not sufficient to change the positions.

Now, you might not grasp this in its subtlety, so let me explain something. If even a single individual of your species is exposed, say, to Mars and then travels back . . . by that time there will be travel that will move a little faster, but just fractionally faster. By the time you get ready to establish your base on the next planet out, you'll be moving very quickly indeed, with some assistance from afar. But to not get too off-track, when even a single individual gets closer and then returns to be amongst your peoples . . .

On Earth, yes.

. . . then that already has the effect, you see? It doesn't take the whole population; it doesn't even take five or ten. Just one gets it going. This will allow myself and planets beyond, for that matter—moons, and even to some minor significance some stars and their planets well beyond—to begin to have greater influence. So, of course, as you move out farther in exploring planets in your solar system, myself and one other object beyond me will have greater and greater influence.

Pluto's Energy Can Help You Become Unblocked

Creator asked us—the outer planets in the solar system—to be in reserve and said we would not really be required to do very much until you started to migrate closer to us. But then it would be very important to have the influence that astrologers have well and properly described to me, which is to bring about change where there has been truculence. In the case of this kind of change, it means not necessarily that which is uncomfortable but that which has been avoided or has been simply not detected due to various states of unconsciousness or a desire to keep something sublimated.

So being exposed to Pluto energy, even in places on the Earth where you reside, and moving into that energy is actually of value to people who feel blocked. If you feel blocked and you feel like something is keeping you from something, then it might be of value to go, at least temporarily (say, for three days) to someplace where, according to your astrologer, you will have strong Pluto energy. It doesn't have to be as intense as it gets but at least present. It is not always a wise idea to just plunge in with both feet. If you're not in a place where you have that energy or your chart has not progressed to that point, you might simply go someplace where the energy is more present and expose yourself to what can be.

Generally, what will come up are the layers of discomfort that you have pasted or even, in pastiche fashion, managed to use to cover and to disguise your discomfort. This is why it is so difficult for you as a race of beings to understand your own motivations, because very often you will have placed this disguise over the old hurt, and the old hurt will have been insulated—protected, as you say. But in the process, it will have been disguised so well that you will have forgotten why it was caused in the first place.

Many times these hurts happen in youth or in earlier years, so by the time someone moves into adulthood or even mid-adulthood, the original cause is forgotten. Sometimes the assumption is that some trauma has taken place and that the trauma was it, but that's not always it. Sometimes it's something very slight that pyramids, that gets more and more. But the nature of the pyramid, you understand, is not just the apex of the pyramid. The nature is that it gets more and more, and then you become less and less able to grasp it. So you begin to identify the cause of your pain with whatever is around you at the moment.

Pluto's job—I will speak of myself in the second person in this case, if you don't mind—is to get to the heart of the matter, to help you to be able to find as quickly as possible what it was that was causing your problem, or at the very least to help you to see, to literally almost trip over your own blind spot. It will be presented to you in some fashion where people might accuse you of being exactly what you are—and this is always a stunning shock, because it will often happen in places like that where people will make a casual offhand remark and it cuts you to the quick, and they usually have no idea that they're saying anything like that. They will assume you know this, and they will be commenting on it as if it were a personality quirk, assuming that you know it. Then you will go down the road and someone else will make that comment, and you'll be shocked and want to withdraw inside your shell. But if you know this is likely to happen, you see, then you will not be defensive about it, you will not be avoiding the possible growth implications.

My Job Is to Reveal

Now we come to why I, as Pluto, and the other beyond me are in reserve. Think about it. When your people start to migrate toward the outer planets and get more involved in the outer planets, and the whole human race on Earth gets excited about what's being discovered (Mars, for example, just to pick one out) and everybody starts thinking, there will be a lot of excitement and the energy of that planetary influence will be multiplied. You're going to want to have a civilization that's enthusiastic about that, that embraces that, and that manages to get past its own long-standing limitations: war, for example, or disease, or famine. You must be able to get by those kinds of things in order to embrace the excitement and happiness that await you with such planetary exploration. Therefore, these influences must be on a personal level for an individual, as well as on a worldwide level. [Tiger, the cat, meows here.] So says my assistant there, eh?

So if you know about this kind of influence and can go someplace on Earth where you have the Pluto energy and maybe some other energy accentuated in your chart during that time . . . so it doesn't hit you too hard when you first go to explore it consciously. There's a big difference between having it happen when you're not conscious about it and then you just get angry at the people speaking to you this way . . . "How dare you!" and that general feeling. [Chuckles.] There's a big difference between that and consciously going to a place where you have that energy and being open to how people are treating you, what the circumstances of your life are, what's different there from where you normally live, and what people are saying to you.

In short, this doesn't mean analyzing everything that everybody says to you, but it does mean paying attention, keeping a journal as well as a dream journal when you're in that location. If you keep that knowledge you've obtained by going to that area where you have more Pluto energy and bringing it back home to the place where you don't have any more than usual—especially if there's no particular and specific Pluto energy there other than the energy that radiates to Earth in the usual fixed-position influence—then when you're back home and things have calmed down and you're not in quite so sensitive or reactive a position, you can consider what it is that Pluto is helping to teach you and, more importantly, what Pluto is helping to reveal to you. This is because my job and the job of the planet beyond me (as well as that planet's other functions) is to reveal.

Think about it. In your biblical texts, even in your popular novels, why is it that people choose to read these things? Why do they gravitate toward them? The number-one joy of reading such things and other popular forms of media is the revelation that occurs. There is the story, and then there's the revelation. The whole point of revelation goes well beyond a single book that is influential in your religion today; rather it is to move to another plateau of your personal existence, which helps you as a culture move to another plateau of your worldwide existence.

Then when you as a planetary culture begin to migrate out to explore the Moon more thoroughly, to explore Mars more thoroughly, and so on, you can embrace the influences of the outer planets and will not take offense toward your fellow astronauts and fellow explorers when they make comments that might otherwise have seemed abrasive or insulting. You will recognize that, "Wait a minute—this is Pluto at work! Pluto is trying to help us get past our limits by helping us to feel our own personal revelation within." That's the number-one thing I'm doing here.

I Accompanied Creator to This Space

That's a fascinating ability—how did it start? How did you train, how did you get interested?

Before I came here, I was a student of the moments that cause change that is a benevolent influence. When you think about this on a universal level, not strictly being in this solar system, one finds it very fascinating, because you are able to study every other culture in this universe and figure out what was the moment that caused that culture to move beyond some long-standing limit that was holding it back from whatever zenith it has achieved at that moment. So I had studied that for a long time.

But way beyond this universe, because that's our problem in this universe, isn't it?

No, that's just your problem, really, in this immediate area. But the problem in this area is intentional, because Creator wants volunteers—which you all are, at least on a soul level—to come and study it, and to help others move beyond their limits, however minor compared to what you experience in this solar system. Although this might be true in the planetary cultures you will meet when you first go out for the first thousand years or so and explore, once you get beyond this immediate range of planets in your own galaxy, you'll find it less and less as a limiting factor and more and more as a simple factor of a planetary culture growing and changing and sometimes achieving an intended fork in the road—so that their culture can become either broader in encompassing its purpose or very often change its purpose toward something the culture itself finds more appealing.

So, generally speaking, it is possible to find such moments all over the universe, and this is where I've chosen to study. This suggests, does it not, that I have been one of the beings who has accompanied Creator to this space, and it has therefore allowed me to enjoy this since the universe began here. Creator, as you know—even to this day, counting time as a factor of influence—has always been one who enjoys variety and has not reproduced the same culture anywhere in any specific way. As you move through the universe, you will find life forms who look like you and life forms who don't. You will also find life forms who have a similar culture to you, one you can identify with on a personal level in all forms—meaning you will find that the predominant influence on a given planet with a *culture* that looks like yours, that the people themselves might not look anything like you. So with the culture that "looks" like yours, the culture itself might remind you so very much of home, so to speak, of the Earth, but the people themselves might not look anything like that. Whereas you might go to some other place where the people would look very much like your people on Earth and yet the culture will not in any way remind you of home.

So it will be that these cosmonauts, these astronauts who go out—including explorers, settlers and traders—will be constantly exposed to these odd juxtapositions of situation wherein one is always stumbling, as it were, over something that reminds you of home, and yet it will have great variety and great instinctive stimulation that is clearly something new. When you think about this as children of Creator—which everyone is in the universe, of course—then it does suggest that also at the core of your being you have a great love for variety. Needless to say, any soul who has volunteered to come to Earth at any time very specifically has a great love of variety. It may not always play out consciously as an influence in your life, but there is generally a great love of variety. Otherwise, you would not come to a planet where variety is so specifically brought to the fore as a heightened experience of a given life.

This is fascinating. It's like you're tied into the Creator's purpose, because Creator is trying to, as you said, get past all of those who have blockages in this universe and beyond. So your influence on helping us get beyond our blocks will then help us help everyone else—and your influence will be magnified a billion times.

Yes, but you understand, it's not something I am looking for. It is rather something that is happening in a timely fashion, because in order to help you come into your purpose and begin to apply it in influential ways beyond your own planet, you need to be able to take the incremental steps that allow you to do this.

From the "Truth" to the Heart

You might reasonably say, in an analysis of my position so far: "But how does that apply to the changes happening on Earth now that everybody is feeling?" Everybody is being—if I may use one of your old slogans, eh?—moved off the dime. Do you still say that?

[Chuckles.] Yes.

Everybody is being moved off the dime without any great apparent conscious desire to do so. But there is the rub, you see? Conscious desire. The desire is deep within you all. So many of you are really revulsed now by events in the world, many of which have happened in the past but you just didn't know about it. But in this day and age, where communication is more available, it is almost impossible, using your tools of networking—not only from your media broadcast, but simply from any research you might do—to avoid the conflicts and very often the unintended outcomes of those conflicts that are happening all over your planet. It is difficult to avoid being revulsed by that even in a single day, to say nothing of in a week or a month. Your souls have literally cried out, "Long enough!" to be rescued from that outer influence.

Think about it: How many times have you, as individuals, been in a position where you desperately asked for help in a situation and then you literally had to help yourself? Sometimes people get turned off to spirit as a result, but other times they realize that spirit is ready, willing and able to help, but you must make the effort as well, even if it seems to be a Herculean effort. I'm bringing this to your attention because my influence has a lot to do with that. It has a lot to do with what we do together—by "we," I mean everyone in this universe. Therefore, even if as a human being you have cried out to spirit for such a long time for help, at some point you start doing something. You as a planetary culture, the human race, have been doing "something" for a long time—it's just not always the right something. Very often what becomes appealing first is "the truth," and the truth can vary from individual to individual, to say nothing of from culture to culture.

The truth has been, for a long time, a very appealing goal. But nowadays, those who can step back from that for a moment—not into lies, but just step back—can look at the influences of the truth and see how this not only can be a stumbling block but can even be catastrophic. I'm not trying to suggest that truth in general is this. What I am trying to suggest is that truth has taken on a disguise, and that is a bit ironic, isn't it? But the truth has taken on a disguise in the form of this or that philosophy which claims to be the only truth or this or that religion which claims to be the only truth. There you have a menu, a recipe for impending if not actual disaster or catastrophe.

You Are Moving Toward Tolerance and Forgiveness

So what you as a culture right now are trying to do is to migrate away from "the truth" to the heart. This is something you all have in common. There are certain things that all cultures hold dear—the mother and her child, the love of a family, the love of a single individual with a cherished pet, lovers and so on, and on and on—things associated with the heart that your culture and each individual is moving toward. When you move toward that, you become tolerant of other people's truths—that's what happens first. But when you embrace the heart fully, that's when you are able to forgive other people for their truths. That's the next step you are ready to take: to embrace the heart more fully. You will be able to forgive other people for their truths very easily without any effort, no matter what harm they have caused in the past. That's very important.

That is why the past is anything past this moment. Initially, it will be the distant past, and then very quickly after that, it will be anything that happened yesterday or two hours ago. This kind of embracing is something that you, as a planetary culture, are moving toward even now. It is important for me to reveal this to you so you can understand that the outer planets' influence on you is becoming stronger now, not by anything we are doing—speaking for myself and the planet beyond—but rather by your own desire. You need to take an action; you are moving. Creator has set up our influence in this solar system so that when you make a move—even a small move on an individual basis or on a culture-wide basis—that the benevolent influences of the outer planets will help you to personally have the experience as you move toward the heart and away from "the truth" . . . that you will be able to feel a personal revelation and the joy of forgiveness.

It is an interesting thing, that. It's one thing to be forgiven by somebody else—you don't always believe it and it takes time to sink in by the way that person interacts and reacts with you. But, on the other hand, there is the joy of forgiving, because you can certainly let go of all the reasons and all the history—all of the magnitude, if you would—of what has been built up over time in your not being able to forgive any one person or even any one culture. Think about how many catastrophic things have happened historically simply because one culture was unable to forgive another culture, even though the individuals who caused whatever hurt to your culture, to your people, to your ancestors, to your grandparents and so on, may not even be alive anymore. To still be mad at that culture, even when you can step back from that "the truth" and say, "This is insanity! These are not even the same people!" . . . even then, you see, this is something that's remarkable.

So it is not only being forgiven and coming to believe it after a while as a result of the person who forgives you or the culture that forgives you, but it is the gift of forgiving that is so important. Then you can release that huge load that has, in many cases, been heaped upon you by well-intended parents and teachers and other individuals who influence you in your culture. You can not only let it go as an individual, but you can let it go as a culture. You can thus find, in that other culture that you used to resent and were angry at, not only what you have in common, but how you can truly complement each other. This is beginning to happen in many places on the Earth now as you are migrating past that singular devotion to any one version of "the truth."

Can we use the word "dogma"?

No, keep it with "the truth." "The truth" is so important—it spells it out. Think how many philosophies—not only developed by well-intended philosophers working together or through some personal revelation that they had, but developed by religions—that identify that what they are teaching is "the truth." Although perhaps individuals in that religion and even scholars in that religion might see comparisons in other religions or philosophies, they very often are devoted to the truth of their own. While that devotion can sometimes have offspring of wonderful moments in your own culture and sometimes even in others, it is the stumbling block of that truth—as it stumbles over somebody else's stumbling blocks—that almost always has been the cause of warfare that spreads well beyond that stumbling block. Think of all the unintended consequences that happen as a result.

What planet is the planet beyond you, which you keep referring to? What other planet?
I'll let that planet speak for itself.

Oh, all right.

Your Migration to Mars Will Influence Your Astrology

How will astrology change for humans when we're on Mars, then? Will we have to devise new calculations?

That is a very good question. For those who are actually on Mars, the astrology won't change in that sense. But you will have to take into account the outer planets slightly more. This will mean that astrologers will be able to say, "Well, now that the culture has migrated or stretched, you understand, beyond Earth . . ." Don't simply wait until there are 100 or 150 or 300 or however many people living on a constant basis on Mars. Understand that when even one or two or three are manning a small outpost there, this not only means that there is an outpost where there are some human beings beyond Earth, it means that your planetary culture has stretched to that point. That's the way to look at it.

So then you have to say that instead of your culture being of Earth as it relates to the other planets—Earth and to a degree your own Moon—as you move out to other planets, then Mars, you understand, and any satellites that it may acquire or have, are the center of your existence. You weigh a bit more heavily, as an astrologer, where the mass of your people are. But as time goes on and you begin to really acculturate Mars with your own cultured beliefs—and you have not only outposts but a developing culture on Mars itself—then you will say, "Well this astrology has truly changed," not just because of your relative position, but because of the influence of Mars as . . . what?

You can talk to Mars about this, but one of Mars' influences on you right now is that of adventure and adventuring. Now, this has been applied on your planet in ways that have very often been detrimental—meaning that this culture adventures into another culture and wreaks havoc in the process. You can imagine the outcome. But it is also something on a more positive level, where one discovers wonders and amazements, and the culture grows: "The creatures of the sea—how amazing they are. The top of the mountain—what an amazing view." In short, all adventuring is not so awful. Also, when done benevolently with the idea of discovering but not laying waste to the planets you are going to be exploring and the cultures you will ultimately be interacting with through space travel, adventuring can be thrilling, exciting and very much something of the heart. That level is very important.

So as you migrate out farther and stretch your culture, your astrologers will make allowances to include to a greater degree, as the center of the chart . . . you will move Mars a little bit more into that, you understand? By that time, there will be considerably more benevolence on your planet from one individual to the other and considerably more of a worldview, you might say—though your world will include Mars and, of course, the excitement about traveling and establishing communities on other planets and what they have to offer, what you might find there, who might help you and so on. It will be a wonderful time to be a person of your culture, because all beings in your culture are born with the joy of discovery encapsulated within them, which blooms every time you, as a baby or as a child, discover something that stimulates your happiness.

The first time you smell a flower . . . a flower is beautiful, but what about its smell? Oh, the look on a baby's face when he or she smells that! It's a treasure, isn't it? So you are born with that capacity, and that's why you are born with it—so that you will make the perfect explorer once you have well and thoroughly embraced the heart and moved beyond "the truth."

But look at the way it's set up. It's so fantastic, because when we get to Mars, the very adventure of Mars will help us go further.

That's it. All these things are intended, you see. Nothing is set up by accident in this solar system. As a good astrologer, you will be able to help to influence, to guide, and to feel quite a bit more appreciated. So for all of you astrologers who have been feeling unappreciated from time to time, outside from those who have embraced the study of astrology, I want you to be thinking very seriously about what you are writing—not just in helping others in your profession, but also be writing things about what you understand astrology to be. It is also very important to be writing questions. Leave your questions for future generations of astrologers, because as your culture embraces the heart and continues to move out and discover other planets and to feel the influences of the outer planets as a result, those questions will be vital in helping those people of those times to stay on course and to feel the influence of the astrologer's most benevolent guidance.

Sometimes, as you good astrologers well know, the astrologer's most benevolent influence is the questions you can give to the people who come to consult you—not just the answers. People comes to consult you because they want answers, but very often one of your greatest gifts is to give them a question that they can carry with them, that they can use to support their life and to ultimately support the discoveries they will make about their life in their culture, in their family, in their explorations and in their discoveries. Then when they experience the ultimate revelation of their life—and when your culture experiences the ultimate revelation—they will be able to see and feel the gentle hand of guidance, which you can offer, not only by offering answers, but by offering the best questions you have.

That's beautiful. I can think of a business: We should start an astrocartography program and then offer vacations for people in areas where Pluto's energy is strongest.

But not just that. It is most important, when you're going to do this consciously, to initially go someplace where Pluto's energy is only slightly increased and where you might have other energies that are complementary or allow you to take small steps. It's true that some people will want to jump in with both feet, but it is *always better* to take small steps, because very often when you jump in with both feet, you don't get it completely and then you spend some time recovering from that. It is not always the best idea to study something using the crash-and-burn system, as any skier can attest to: "Shall we start on the bunny hill, or shall we go right to the top and race to the bottom, and see how many pieces we arrive in at the bottom?" The crash-and-burn school is not always the best.

That's good! I can see how it wouldn't be.

You Have Fewer ETs Visiting You Now

I have another question, which you might not want to answer because it's maybe beyond the scope of this book. When one person goes to Mars and comes back, as you said, that affects the energy. What's the inadvertent effect of the sinister secret government going from Alpha Centauri to who knows where else and coming back? How did that affect energies?

I cannot really speak to that. You will have to speak to those beings who spoke to you originally about that. That is not my purview, to speak about that.

I just thought it would be sort of funny if they inadvertently helped us when they weren't trying to.

Now, here's an interesting sideline. What happens when people from other planets come to visit your planet? Perhaps they come to visit your planet because they feel there is some connection between your culture and their culture based upon the wisdom they have gathered. Does that connect you to their planets? It does, but usually only on a temporal basis—meaning for a length of time that may not ultimately have to do with your incremental steps toward self-discovery. It can unintentionally become a distraction, and for some time that took place and really caused, without that intention whatsoever, a distraction for your planetary culture.

There have been fewer and fewer contacts from other cultures that are related to your culture in some way, not because of methods of detection, as has often been discovered, but here is the real reason why: These other cultures have been informed that you are well and thoroughly on the path now to your own self-discovery, and such interactions, while well-intended, would actually be a distraction for you. Therefore, they are being told that when the time is right, they will be allowed to approach you again. As you move out from your current planet, discovering other planets, they will at some point be able to approach you again and offer their assistance—not only in traveling more quickly to other planets, but to help you discover things and perhaps provide you with vehicles that can move very quickly from your perspective at that point but which would be, from their perspective, a rudimentary space-exploration vehicle. It would be sufficient for your purposes without being too advanced, so that you wouldn't—how can we say?—jump too far and say, "Oh, dear," and have to recover from that jump. They will know your personalities by then. But for now they are holding back so they don't distract you.

Yes, because this was like an ET bazaar. The Zetas, the Pleiadians, the Andromedans, the Arcturians, the Orions, ETs from dozens of different sources—everybody was coming here.

Yes, because they all felt some sense of personal history or ancestry associated with you, something like that. They wanted to find out more about it, being curious like beings are. But then they were told by their teachers, "No, no, this is not the right time." So they are now holding back a bit, because they are enjoying from a distance your migration toward your natural capacities.

Ah, you are wonderful. You are giving us marvelous information.

You Are Moving Toward Change in a Benevolent Way

What happens when we get to your planet? By then we won't have any blocks, right?

Yes, because . . . think about it. If something has an influence to remove such blocks, or at least bring them to your attention so that you can do the work to remove them . . . initially moving grudgingly and then picking up more speed, dropping and shedding those old masks that you had to insulate and protect you from those pains and wounds of the past. Once you shed that and move on to a pathway for yourself that allows you to embrace forgiveness, to embrace the heart, and to move freely using your own capacities, then when you get even closer to Pluto, Pluto will simply help you to change as a culture and help you to welcome influences from far away, even if those beings look nothing like you.

Where you are now, in your now truth, if you saw those beings they would frighten you and you would react to them strictly on the basis of their appearance. But someday you will not have such reactions, nor will you have such reactions to other beings on your own planet. You will be able to receive the gifts of knowledge and wisdom that are available to you from, say, the beetles or the worms or the crocodiles. In short, from beings where you very often have a sense of revulsion or fear, you will be able to receive in a most benevolent way the gifts of wisdom they have for you, even though your interactions with them now are not always very pleasant.

Pluto and other outer planets will support you so that you can move more quickly as a culture toward that welcoming, toward that receiving, and toward change in a benevolent way. Change in a benevolent way . . . what might that be? A capacity to not only understand how a particular space vehicle travels but what you must be like in that vehicle in order for it to travel to a benevolent place. What if you were suddenly told that in order for you to travel in your car to the most benevolent place, the car itself must be constructed of only that which volunteers to be a car? And that you, while you are in that vehicle, must be completely at peace and in harmony with the harmony of the being of the vehicle—what if that was told to you?

Oh, right now that would be too much to do and to be, given your interaction with all the rest of society and your culture as it is. But in the future, that is exactly how vehicles will be. That which is utilized to create the vehicle will be only that which wishes to be that vehicle, and you will know it on the basis of your then understanding of all forms of life and the natural continuity between all forms of life, which is heart. That's why your move toward the heart right now is so vitally important, because it will help you to feel a connection between all forms of life. It will initially be between you and some other culture on the planet, another form of life that basically looks like you and basically acts like you, but these are incremental steps.

Someday you will be able to sit on a tree stump or perhaps on a rock and be surrounded by trees, birds, worms and ants—not all over you, but just nearby. They will come up and approach you, and you will certainly know what they are trying to say. You will have a grand old conversation with the littlest amongst you. Here you are, gigantic, towering over ants, and yet they have so much wisdom. They are a culture that goes back so very far, a culture that can, in small numbers, migrate or even stand at the opening of one of their homes—which this channel actually had the opportunity to observe once, so I bring that out for his sake—and by doing a special dance, even if there's not a cloud in the sky, they are able to bring rain, not as a spiritual phenomenon but as a physical phenomenon. Would that not be wonderful where famine and drought are the case? If these littlest beings could teach you how to bring rain to a drought area just by doing their rain ceremony in numbers, what a wonderful thing, eh? Why have drought if you don't need to? [To read more about this, see *Shamanic Secrets for Spiritual Mastery*.]

Move Toward Your Heart

What about you? Is that your main quality, or are there other side things that also . . . ?

Not really. All planets, I grant, have main qualities and generally have side qualities, but my side qualities really have nothing to do with you at this time.

As you migrate in your culture, as well as to some degree physically, then my side qualities may perhaps be of influence. But right now, because they have no influence, I'll not speak of them.

Will you continue with us as we unite into one being and become a creator? How long is your tenure here?

Well, once you are the creator, all you have to do is ask. At that point, you will simply know what you want, and you will also, like a good observer, take stock of what you have. You will poll the volunteers who are present to see who would like to stay and so on. That will come when it comes.

I see, I see. So your plans are open, then?

Yes!

So for those reading this now, if they have something they really want to change in their life, how can they take advantage of your energy, even if it's not in their chart in a prominent way?

How can they trace this energy? Always, now, for your culture: move toward your own heart. Begin speaking to your own heart as if it is someone. It is someone. All parts of your body are someone. Begin speaking to your heart. Start little groups, if you would, with others who are speaking to their hearts, and learn techniques that you each have developed in heart-speak. Eventually you may find that there are ways of employing heart-speak from person to person, as well as from an individual to his or her own heart. Some have already been developed and suggested, and you will find others. That's what I recommend you do.

The Imprint of the Solar System on Earth

That's about all I really have to say, so I will wrap it up here and simply give a closing comment, if that's all right.

Oh, please. You're wonderful. I just don't have any more questions.

That's understandable. For you all now, as you consider not only the astrological impacts of your relationships well beyond the planet but also the personal impacts of each other on your daily lives, it would be good to consider superimposing an imprint of the solar system on the Earth. Astrologers know and understand that this imprint is, in fact, a reality that they deal with on a regular basis in their own studies, in their chosen field, and in their perceptions of human beings at large.

Different human beings represent different planetary bodies and even different groups of stars, and therefore, they see you as being Jupiter or having Jupiter energy influence. But in the larger sense, they see the imprint of the solar system on Earth. They see the imprint of the stars on Earth. It is as if

Earth is a large and spherical mirror reflecting not only the daytime influences of the planetary bodies but the nighttime influences as well.

Consider that you all now are not only reflecting that as well—meaning, how does the Moon reflect on your surface, how do the stars at night or anything reflect on your surface—but also, how are these things coming to the surface within you as an individual? Factor this in, not only in your experience of astrology, but in your goals for planetary discovery for those who are involved in this. What is more desirable, and what qualities might you be experiencing more?

For those of you who are involved in planetary discovery or even in subplanetary discovery—meaning putting satellites in space—please make contact with good astrologers to improve the quality of your opportunities, success and goals. Also, as an individual citizen, please consult with whatever astrologer you find to be appealing to you as an individual—not just someone you have heard is wonderful, but someone whom you like, even if this person is a friend and a talented amateur. Talented amateurs, if they are wise, will always seek out teachers in their field who know more than they do, or who have had more experience and can guide them to the best question or the best advice.

In short, allow astrology to serve you, to support you, and to help you to find your own heart, your own purpose and your own ultimate question. Good life.

You are brilliant; you are wonderful. Thank you very much.

♂ Mars

18

MARS

Provides Energy so You Can Persevere until You Resolve Your Impossible Problems

April 11, 2007

Greetings. This is Mars.

Greetings! We've been waiting for you.

Yes! I have been waiting for you! It's the other way around.

Mars' Energy Has Nothing to Do with War

What were the qualities Creator saw in you that caused Him to invite you here and to this solar system?

Ah, what a good question. I believe what Creator might have seen within me is a certain invigoration that I have. I have a tendency to look at all things in terms of their possibilities rather than seeing the problems, and even if there are problems, to be able to work through those problems with a certain amount of strength and invigoration. This is what I feel the Creator of this universe felt good about with me, because He wanted the peoples who would perhaps need it (such as the Explorer Race and others) to have that capacity to move through something—or around something, if that would be better—regardless of how impossible it might have been or looked to have been to solve. For instance, you have some very serious problems in your culture right now, to say nothing of problems with your planet, and without the energy of Mars close by—and I am close by—without that energy I think you could just pretty well curl up your toes and say good night.

You're going to need to use the Mars energy to get through this, because, yes, magic's going to be helpful, but magic is something that is of a true nature. It is your natural selves. What you would call magic, meaning out of the realm of the ordinary in your now life—including benevolent magic and all of that—is really your true nature.

Your true nature, as it exists off the Earth, is something that is truly benevolent. On the Earth you are dealing quite constantly with things that are way beyond your capability and even desirability in your natural state. On the Earth you are expected to resolve things that have been largely irresolvable elsewhere, so you require an energy that goes beyond your natural being. I grant that sometimes this leads to problems, but it also very specifically leads to solutions.

How many times have you personally faced a problem that has appeared to be impossible on the face of it, but by trying this, trying that, and determinedly going forward, you have managed to resolve it? That's the Mars energy. Mars energy is totally misunderstood by a great many peoples. Many think it has to do with conflict and war and battle and all of that, but that's only one very tiny portion of the Mars energy. The majority of the Mars energy is, to put it simply, "I can get through this no matter what. That doesn't mean I'm going to knock everything down in my way"—that's not the Mars energy—"but rather, this is a very complicated path, but I can find my way through there without knocking anything down." That's the Mars energy.

How did you get that way?

I have always been this way. All the planets in your immediate environment—meaning in your solar system and, to a lesser degree, the planets in your galaxy—have qualities or at least, as you go further away from your solar system, nuances of qualities that make you up. You—anybody, any human being on Earth—do not have any personality characteristics that are not in some way a portion of these planets. Actual true personalities are very subtly different. Your nature as a being group, the Explorer Race, is to be totally cohesively connected, meaning you are fragments of one large personality that is completely calm and in agreement with itself all the time. But to come here and have the totally different personalities, even within the same family—regardless of the cultural elements of that family or of the society in which you are living—that requires for you a significant amount of influence from these large bodies of personality.

Think about it: As Mars I am a planetary body, but I am also a personality. Yet taken in comparison, my entire planet is my personality and my personality is in every grain of the planet. Compared to you as a single individual, that's quite a bit of difference in terms of size and just sheer mass. I am very far away from you, but in a larger sense, when you pull back and look at the solar system, Mars is pretty close to Earth. It can't be too close, but I have to be close enough. For all of those totally impossible-to-solve problems that exist elsewhere, that you could never solve in your natural state of being (nor would you be attracted to solve them), you must have someone like myself who would give you or make available to you the personality characteristics of simply not giving up until you managed to accomplish even some portion of what it is you're attempting to do.

But if all the beings out there are so benign and so cohesive, then were you created for this?

No, I have always been this. You understand, I'm not talking about the material, the mass of the planet, the things that make me up, but my personality. I have always been like this, including when I have been in other universes, and I have always been picked to be in universes where there was some kind of invigoration that had to be provided or there was some kind of a long-range problem that needed to be resolved.

You have to think about it now. With the Explorer Race, you have problems every day that need to be resolved and you need that energy to get you through that. But take a look at a more benign universe, for instance, one where there isn't this tumultuousness going on, as in this universe, where they would have eons to resolve something. Since the personalities of the beings in that universe weren't particularly interested in resolving something, they needed to have someone like me present so that when that resolution became urgent, they would have some energy source to draw on. I have always been like this.

Are there others like you?

Well, there might be, but I'm not familiar with them. I can't rule out the possibility, but not that I know of. How's that?

[Laughs.] What a fun thing to be! It makes you very desirable.

Well, let's put it this way: If Creator hadn't put out the possibility of inviting those personalities who chose to do something adventurous like having a life or two on Earth, if Creator hadn't wanted you to work on these difficult-to-resolve things, then I wouldn't be here. I am here only because you have that visited upon you, to do that. Even a child has to resolve things that are very difficult. The children in other benign places don't have to do any of that. Think about a child learning to tie his or her shoelaces—that doesn't occur anywhere else.

Or having to get along in school, or deal with bullies or personality conflicts, or learn two languages.

That's right—none of that exists anywhere else. But my energy is available for you to draw upon when needed. This is how people can become aggressive momentarily. Say the athlete has to run an extra mile on the track that day and hadn't planned on it; he or she has to pull up that energy from somewhere. It's a personality characteristic as well as being a physical energizing element of your own body. Mother Earth provides that physical energy. Of course, you have to work on it and build up your endurance and so on, but Mother Earth provides that. But in terms of the personality characteristic, that's where I come in.

How long have you been here in this solar system?

Oh, I came with Creator.

But this solar system hasn't been here since Creator came.

It's much older than you realize. Just because the planet you're on hasn't been here doesn't mean the solar system hasn't been hanging around. But I've always been here. The solar system is very old.

I didn't know that. Then how did you get so misperceived?

Well, I can't explain that. That's your job; you're a human being. I would say that I'm not really misperceived, though. I think the popular countenance of personality is to perceive me as a warrior—that's what's popular. But for those who are astrologers and understand the nuances as well as personality characteristics, they will tell you that Mars is not about war. This is overly simplistic. It would be as if to say that Jupiter is about riches—it's more than that. But there is a tendency by those who do not understand astrology very well to simply pull up a single word and brand one with that. I think you have this occur in your own lives, where individuals might be branded with a nickname that they're stuck with for their whole life, even though it does not describe them in any way.

On Mars It Will Be Easier to Solve Problems

Tumultuous events have taken place in this orbit in the solar system: we blew up a planet and brought another one in, and then this one we are on now. How does that affect you?

Well, no one who is a portion of a solar system likes to have another one of their members disappear. It was a shock, and it took some getting used to. It was quite a time of adjustment—in terms of your own time, oh, maybe 10,000 years after the disappearance before actually feeling okay.

Now we are on this water planet—you used to have water on your planet, didn't you?

Of a sort. It was not the same exact chemical formula that you have—it was a little thinner—but yes. You will probably find some of it still here, but in order to have the kind of water that you'll need when you set up your colonies here—which you will do, on the surface—you'll need to bring your own water. By that time—say, in fifty to a hundred years—you might actually be able to import the mechanism to create water. It's not exactly creating it out of thin air, but it's close. Also, by that point you might have trading going on with other beings who might consider providing you with mechanisms by which you can create what you need to survive.

So what happens when we are living on your surface and are so much closer to your energy? How does that work?

Well, it will be a lot easier to solve problems, but you'll have to be vigilant with the idea of disagreements and not let them go too far. Get used to saying, "Well, we don't agree on that, and that's fine." I don't think it's going to lead to pitched battles every day, but you understand, you will have more physical energy here possibly. So you'll be able to do more, and you also might find that certain of your personality characteristics are more out there—they will be more presented to the world.

Yes, exposed.

Well, it won't be so easy to keep what you might consider to be private. For instance, you might have a personality at your home versus your personality out in the world of work. Well, your home personality, which for many people might be much closer to your actual personality, would be your personality, period. So your actual qualities of personality would be presented to everyone. In other words, you wouldn't be able to fake it.

Planets Can Help with Temporary Personality Energies

So what you said earlier is, we're like a recipe, then? Humans on this planet are using the energies of all the other planets in this solar system?

That's how I see it.

So the soul sort of says, "I'll take a little of this and a little of that, and I'll need a whole lot of that"? Is that sort of how it sets up the life?

No. It would seem that way, but what actually happens is that you are born with a certain amount of receptivity, and when you are put in different situations, you have like a tap into, say, the Mars personality or the Neptune personality. In short, you have like an opening that you can use which will provide what might be considered latent qualities (as a psychologist might say) within you—which will provide a boost in those qualities to help you get through some aspect.

After that aspect of life, you might look back at it and say, "I don't know how I did that," because you won't recognize yourself in that moment, or friends and family might not recognize you. They might say, "I didn't know you had it in you!" or something like that, and normally, you might not have. But because the situation called for it, well, you were able to do it. For example—and I know this is going to get your attention—you have heard now and then about how the car slips off the jack and falls on somebody but doesn't kill him or her outright, and someone comes along and lifts the car up, and others help pull the person out from underneath it. When that happens, that's Mars at work.

But how do we tune our receptivity to these different planets?

I don't recommend it. I feel it's more important . . . you are on Earth to experience variety. There is variety, of course, in this entire universe because Creator is fond of variety, but Creator has gone out of Creator's way to create the maximum amount of variety on a single planet. Granted, you don't have as much as you once did, but you still have quite a bit of variety. Perhaps not in the predominant characteristics of your personality, but in personality characteristics that are temporary—such as needing a sudden infusion of aggressiveness, not designed to attack somebody but to get through something—to solve it you might call on Mars. You might call on Jupiter also, but it is not intended that you focus on these planets and pull them toward you all the time.

You are in reaction all the time. Your life is about that; that's why you're so receptive. You have to be receptive so that you can react. Many times, even if you are unable to solve something on your own, you might have others you can call on to solve it. But to simply deal with it, even if you can't solve it on your own, you need to have certain personality characteristics that you can call on that will amplify that quality within you temporarily. So I do not recommend that you try to focus on any given planet. You are here to experience the varietal possibilities of your own personality in reaction to the circumstances of your life.

Mars Assists You in Childbirth

There's a saying, "Men are from Mars, women are from Venus." So you're considered masculine, but you are obviously both.

I do not see it as a masculine/feminine thing, but it's understandable why it's considered that way, because doing things in the world, acting, taking action, moving . . . that does tend to be a masculine trait. But, of course, women do things in the world all the time. Most women could not possibly get through childbirth without Mars energy. Now, granted, the child is the gift, so I look at that as perhaps Jupiter energy and Sun energy also. But to just get through the experience of childbirth . . . without Mars, I don't think you could do it. It would be overwhelming. Every childbirth would be a surgical operation and you'd be unconscious. I'm not saying it's a bad thing for people who have that, but I'm saying that actually giving birth is so difficult.

Creator and I have had many discussions about this. The idea of giving birth to such a large child out of that small opening . . . I don't understand it.

What does He say in His own self-defense?

Creator has always said that it's up to you to use your magic abilities to change that into something more benevolent. My understanding of this, however, is that one person cannot do that. It needs to be a group experience. Everybody on the Earth, at some point, is going to have to do some kind of benevolent magic—it has to be true magic, at that—to resolve that so that babies are either born much smaller, or something changes. The physical and the plumbing . . . it's not right! Creator and I have chosen to disagree on this one.

Well, the human prototype for the Explorer Race was designed by others under the influence of Creator but not directly by Him, right?

That's right. In that situation it was understood that giving birth would be a simple operation. At that time, the baby a woman would have given birth to was a quarter of the size of the babies you're giving birth to now—meaning that you could stretch and the baby would come through. But now the baby is gigantic.

What changed? Why is it different now? How did we get so far from the prototype?

You'll have to talk to Creator about that. And perhaps you ought to, for this book.

Maybe we'll just kind of get to Him at the end. I have a book that says Mars is associated with the muscular body system, the gonads, the adrenal glands. Is each planet actually associated with a physical part of the body?

It could be seen that way, and I do understand why there have been those who would associate it with that, especially if they're involved in some form of the healing arts. Yes, I can understand that. But you have to look at it again. The muscular tissue and the reproductive tissue all have to do with what you do in the world and how you are perpetuated in the world. So I understand that, but there is another way of looking at the masculine. It's still focused in the masculine—meaning what you do as compared to the receptive—but even so, the masculine and the feminine are both receptive. They absolutely have to be.

Mars Creates Difficulty in Working with Others

I have a lot of Martian energy. I like where it says "decisive, freedom-loving and a pioneer."

Yes, that's very helpful—and you probably know this—but it does not make for an easy team player. Therefore, that's going to be your challenge. Your challenge is always going to be how you get along with others, how well you work with others. That will be your lifelong challenge, because it's physiological. It doesn't have anything to do with your soul, you understand—we're talking personally now. Your body was brought up by the soul that came in then; your body, your physiological body, was constructed around that soul. You have inherited that as a walk-in, and you cannot do anything about that. You can't change it, because that's your vessel. You can't say, "I want a new vessel." [Chuckles.]

[Laughs.] No, it's only due to this one that I'm here.

That's right. You have to be thankful, but you have to accept the vessel as it is. The vessel as it is, is the way you described it, but it doesn't make it easier to work in a team situation as you find yourself constantly in. Even with a pet. You have a pet dog or a cat or something who lives with you, and that's a team situation as well. The pet helps you, does things for you, provides certain things for you, but you also have to provide for the pet. It's a team on a small level. I'm not criticizing you. I'm saying that everything about your life has to do with a team, even in coordination with other things: driving a car, operating a boat. It all has to do with you in action with others.

So on other planets, all of that is taken for granted: this teamwork, this natural ability to get along with each other?

It's so taken for granted that it's not even considered as a part of life. No one thinks about it; there's no thought given to that at all. It's just natural. Just think of the natural things on your planet and in your culture. You don't think about them—they just are. I'm going to have to start speaking more quietly, because I can see that this channel's voice is getting blown out.

Yes, I can feel your natural energy and exuberance coming through. Were you one of the first ones here? Which planets were here when you took up your position?

No, no, we all came at once. We didn't all wander in, just show up, and say, "Where's the rest of the guys?"

[Laughs.] It's like a football team—they've got to all go out there at one time.

That's right.

Stone Remains of the Previous Planet Could Change Earth's Structure

Now, I'm not clear about this. Is the asteroid belt the remains of a previous Earth, or is it the remains of another planet who got blown up?

You know, this is largely misunderstood. Much of the so-called asteroid belt—and if you look closely at a lot of the planets, you'll find bits and pieces caught up in the midpoint of the planet's gravitational field—a lot of that doesn't have to do with any planet who ever got blown up, it just has to do with the collecting. If you were on that planet that's known for its rings . . .

Yes, Saturn.

You would find, in the midpoint of that planet, that the gravity effect was vastly different than in other places. Now, if you could go and spend time, perhaps a year or two, at the midpoint of your own planet, you wouldn't find that very much. Your planet is different. But other planets do collect that kind of stuff. One planet did blow up, but that's all. Just one.

The one who was in the position of this Earth.

That's right. A lot of that material went well beyond this solar system, but some of the smaller pieces did get collected. I believe that when you do go out and start looking closely at that material, you're going to find some interesting things. You might want to bring some of the material back to your Earth, but it's not going to be compatible with your Earth. Part of it is . . . how can we say? It would be like a seed. If you brought it back to your Earth and just let it even sit on the ground, it could change the structure of your Earth—because remember, some of that material was originally in this same space you now occupy. So it would be like a graft. If you brought it in, it would be like grafting something. Even if you moved the material, the stone, from sitting on the ground for a while, it would still have effects on the ground. That ground would never be the same.

Would that be good or bad?

It depends. For one thing, the planet who was here before this water planet was not a water planet. I would recommend that you examine things like that in space stations. Do so very carefully, because you must remember that even though you don't think of stone as having personality, it does.

Oh, I see! I missed that! So it could influence the personality of this planet!

That's right, to say nothing of its actual chemical makeup. It's about . . .

Being receptive.

That's right.

We were told that the being who is the personality of our Earth is a quantum master. To do all the things that all the other planets in this solar system have to do, to work with us, you all must sort of be in that league, aren't you?

No, Earth is unique. Think about it. Here you have a planet who existed in an entirely different part of the universe. I, for one, as a planet—not as a personality, but as a planet—could not possibly move from one part of the universe to the other. This is a planet who moved through time and space. It requires abilities far beyond my own physiological abilities to do that. No, no—Earth is unique.

Then when she goes back home, which she will . . .

But not for a loooong time. It doesn't even factor into your being in this universe. You'll be long gone as a people out of this universe before that takes place.

Ah, okay. I was going to say, it would leave a pretty big hole.

There won't be a hole; there will be something.

Yes, something else would come in to fill it, right.

Do you know what?

The original one might . . .

. . . might find a seed that could rebuild a planet who was here before. That's what you want to put there. You want a volunteer.

Stick to This Solar System

We haven't even gotten into the signs yet. Supposedly there are many more planets than we know about and many more signs.

I think that might be an unnecessary complication for the reader. From my perspective, it's enough to deal with day-to-day life. You want to enjoy a book like this because it might help to explain aspects of your day-to-day life. If you're going to be looking at signs that are only very obliquely involved in your day-to-day life, it might just become an unnecessary complication and I don't recommend that. You can if you want to, but I don't recommend it. If I were you, I'd just do the planets in the solar system and the signs themselves that are associated with the planets: Aries and all of that.

Do that, but I wouldn't go any further than that. For one thing, you'll have an encyclopedia when you got done, and for another thing, I think it's just realistically impractical. The people who are going to read this book are not just astrologers; they're going to be people interested in astrology and, in a larger sense, in influences on the human personality, which is basically what this book is about, from my perspective. Any overcomplication is just going to make it into an esoteric book. You don't want it to be esoteric; you want it to be reasonably grounded in life. The application of your personal life superimposed over the book will allow you to actually get something out of it on a personal basis, aside from professionals in the field.

But I do want that sensational thing of bringing some new planet out. I'm hoping we can do that. Let me ask you: You're connected with Aries—how does that work in your life? How did you get aligned with that?

You'll have to talk to the signs, and then if you want to come back and talk to the planets, that's okay. You have to have a working knowledge of their personality before you can actually phrase the questions.

But you can't just say, from your point of view, how you happened to be connected to that sign?

Yes. From my point of view, I'm not connected at all. But from Aries' point of view . . . you have to remember that these are all associations. But if you looked up into the sky and said, "Oh, there's Aries," Mars wouldn't be a part of it.

No, but theoretically as you move, at certain times you . . .

There you are, the keyword "theoretically."

Ah! So is it a metaphor to help us?

Ask me about myself. If you want to do signs, do the signs and then come back.

Okay.

Humans Need Optimism

So you have this wonderful active energy. Did you ever find yourself in a place where it wasn't appropriate?

No. I wouldn't be in a universe if I wasn't needed to be who I am.

But when you first became aware of yourself, you had to have been somewhere.

I've always been aware of myself. There wasn't a first—no first and no last. I understand your attachment to that at this time, in the cycle of your life, because you are functioning in what appears to be an open/close situation, but that is an artificial time-scape you are living in.

Yes, and I'm projecting that out on you. It must be wonderful to have that optimism and that sense of possibility.

I don't think it's possible for the human race to get along on the planet without having that available to them. You don't necessarily feel it all the time, but it's available to everyone all the time. I don't claim to be the only optimistic one, but it is a portion of that. It does make you a bit more optimistic to feel that you can get through something or that there's a good chance that you, with the help of others, can get through something or help others to get through something. That's a good thing, because there are natural things that come up which require efforts: "Oh, we're on this side of the chasm and we have to get to the other side. How are we going to do that? It's going to take us all working together."

Yes. We think we're so separate and isolated, and yet your energy contributes to our team-building too, doesn't it? To our unity?

Yes, you're actually attracted to functioning in a team. Look at most of your work situations: you are involved with others to accomplish a goal. This is not an accident. In your games, you're involved with others—the whole team thing just runs throughout your whole life. Even when you're in need and others are taking care of you, there's a team there. It's all about that, from my perspective.

Somebody said one of the things we had invented or discovered was hope. It was something we would give to other beings. So that also comes from your optimism and your energy—you're influencing it?

Partially. Others are, too. The main thing is that you must have hope in order to have the belief that if you can't resolve it today, with everybody working together, that maybe you'll be able to resolve it tomorrow with everybody working together. That's so important. Right now you find yourself a bit—how can we say?—scattered. You're not all working together as you will someday. But someday, when you're all working together and you each bring to the group situation your own unique talents and personality, almost all the problems on Earth from Creator's point of view can be solved by that method. Right now, you can only do so much, operating in smaller units, smaller teams. There are some things that cannot be resolved without everybody participating.

Everybody? All six billion of us?

Everybody.

I'm There in Your Rivers and When You Sneeze

We've touched on some fascinating parts of you. What are some other aspects of your personality that possibly are more subtle or lesser known?

I am influential in the meandering of rivers. Water, you understand, has a cumulative impact, but it also has the desire to go here and go there. Water as a substance does not like being restricted. Water finds it somewhat frustrating to not be able to travel up mountains, and this is why it has chosen to be on your planet, where it doesn't have to travel up mountains because it can evaporate and come down in the form of rain or snow and be on the top of the mountains. It can likewise be under the surface, in underground waters and lakes.

Water wants to be everywhere; it does not feel comfortable being restricted. This is why, when there are stones in creeks and rivers, the water rolls the stones along, because it wants to be inside the stones. It really has a personality of perseverance. So when it comes to the meandering path of rivers, I am there.

Well, I think that's really enough. Let's see. Okay, I'll give you one. I'm there when you sneeze. Certainly! It's an exhale; it's a physical, sudden act. It isn't something you think about, "Oh, I think I'm going to sneeze now." It's not a decision you make mentally.

I'm available to provide the excess energy impetus on a personality level, to not just sneeze—the physical body can do that on its own, of course—but to feel all right with the sneeze: "Oh, it's a sneeze; it's not a scary part of life." Remember, I don't claim to be some deity who is superimposed over everything and anything you do. All the planets are there, but I do not speak for all of them. I'm speaking for myself because that's who you're talking to. I might be there in a more pronounced way temporarily while you sneeze, but your physical body does it.

Yes, but as you said, you're there when a woman gives birth to a child, when a man runs a marathon, when he hits a home run, when he saves a buddy on a hill, when anybody goes beyond what a person thought she could do or what she usually does.

Oh, I don't claim that. I think you're ascribing a great many admirable traits to me.

Well, I just meant, when we go beyond what we perceive as our limits, then we call on you. That's what you said, right? Or do we draw on you?

Unconsciously. But, for instance, since you mentioned the idea of someone saving somebody in a brave situation, rescuing somebody off the side of a cliff, it's also Venus who's there—you know, love.

Yes, and Neptune welcomes. It's all of you!

Yes, everyone is there—it's a team effort. What more obvious example of a team would there be than a solar system? Planets traveling around each other? It's very much of a team.

♂ Mars

MARS AND GRANDFATHER

You Are Becoming Your Natural Selves in Your Physical Bodies on Earth

April 24, 2007

This is Grandfather. Greetings!

Greetings!

The Awakening Is Here

The awakening has proceeded along very nicely. Right now, you are experiencing the crest of the wave, but it is going to remain at crest for a little time. About 23 percent of people have woken up. This does not mean that they remember absolutely everything there is to know about their souls and their purposes for being here, but it is as if a series of veils has been removed from their sense of awareness. In recent times, because of this or that drama on the world stage—to say nothing of what's going on in people's private lives—there has been a tendency to remain in a fixed position, almost entranced, where one does not go forward or backward, or even from side to side. But this has been removed now, and the only delay for the others is that some people remain in a somewhat transfixed position, though the fog is gone, because there is a certain shyness to step forward.

So the experience for many people will have to do with seeing things that have always been there, but seeing them in a new way. I am not referring to, say, a plant that has always been fairly plain and is suddenly flowering. Rather, I am talking about something that looks exactly the same as it has always looked, but you see it in a new light. This is a very helpful situation, because in the past, there has almost always been a tendency to overlook the obvious. This is not a mental error but rather an experience of becoming accustomed to something and then becoming attached to your original perception of it. As you know, when you are attached to a perception, it is very easy to miss the changes that occur over time.

An example of this would be to see family members one has not seen for many years, and they react to you and you to them exactly the way you had the last time you saw them, even though there might be a considerable amount of evolution of personality, to say nothing of experience. This awakening, however, is something that affects your daily life, not those you see on occasion, so the tendency will be to see things as they really are, which in some cases might be a bit stunning but not exactly shocking. There will not be a possibility to delude one's self, to believe that something is other than what it actually is. For the most part, this is very healthy, because people will see that perhaps they are living in a situation that is really untenable or living in a situation that they had convinced themselves was something other than what it really is.

So I am not saying that marriages all over the world are going to break up, but I am saying that the tendency to drift off of one's path in life will become greatly reduced, and the tendency to move onto your own path, even though you might have to feel your way every step, will become a natural process. Since so many others will be doing it, there will be lots of jokes built up around it and shared experience that people will chuckle about, but there will also be a great deal of feeling that you are suddenly welcome. As you move down your particular pathway, you will be meeting people who feel good to you and who are happy to see you, and you are happy to see them. In short, you will be having experiences that actually reaffirm and cause you to feel welcome on the planet, rather than as a stranger in a strange land.

Make Those Changes You Feel

Any advice for people?

Yes. I'd say that, if this is happening to you, you don't have to make any sudden motions to do this or that, if you feel it is too extreme. But take note of things, and don't allow yourself to drift back into that cloudy, hazy situation where you don't choose to see something. You see, if you try to drift back into that because you don't like what you see or you regret the situation of your life, you will only become more resentful because you won't be able to be unconscious in that situation, meaning not aware of your surroundings because of a preferred delusion. You will perhaps be able to pretend, but it will build resentment within you.

If you can, if a move or a decision or a choice of life or a change in the way you are living your life or a change in where you are working, for example, if that feels like you must do it, then do. Look around. Make that change.

Gravitate toward something that feels good to you, that you will enjoy doing and for which you might actually be providing skills of your own personal ability—that which comes easy to you in a way that is not only good for you but might very well be good for others, because everyone does not have the same talents. Granted, some people have talents that are like your own, but not everybody. So that is my main advice. Once you feel and start to feel which way you need to go for your path, then begin to move down it. It will lead you to something more beneficial.

Is there a benevolent magic we can say to ask for that, the perfect path for us at this moment?

I would recommend a living prayer. You might say, for example:

> **LIVING PRAYER**
> "I am asking that when I am on my path now, that I feel in my physical body a very good feeling, warmth or relaxation, comfort, or something that feels like 'yes' to me, not just excitement, but something that feels like 'yes' to me, and I am also asking that others have this experience as well."

That's beautiful! What about the other 77 percent? What's the outlook? Soon? Eventually?

Soon.

How do you see this affecting the planet in the sense of strife and violence? Will we reduce that?

There is a good chance that on a per capita basis it will reduce. But those who believe in the value of such force might keep it up, because it is what they know. However, if we are talking about people who are drafted into armies or people who are even coerced into action, the tools of coercion may not work as they once have. Some tools of coercion have to do with lying, or let's just say, falsehood. Falsehood may not work as well because the people will be more perceptive, and while sometimes they will not be able to get out of a situation, they may find ways to decrease a violent action and turn it into a negotiation, which will be a step away from force.

This Is the Next Step

Is this a pattern that is set up? Is it in another few years that there will be a few more veils removed, or how does this go forward?

It depends on the experience of it. I see what you are asking: what is the next step? But this is the next step. I don't think we are talking about something here that is work. Rather, it will just feel natural. You will know by where you are going and what you are doing that something is for you, or conversely, you will know that it is for somebody else.

The reason I put it that way is because you won't necessarily judge what you are doing if you are off your path, because other people you talk to . . . for instance, you might talk about your job and be complaining about it, and other people you might know will say, "Gosh, I'd love to have that," you see. So it won't just be, "My employer is a rat." [Chuckles.] It will be something where you will become aware that you are simply in the wrong job and that others would love to do it. So you get on with your life and you find something that works better for you. It won't just be, "How much money can I make?" It might be, "How rewarding is this job? How much do I like it? How much do I look forward to going to work, as compared to hating every moment of it?"

I am adding this update today, with the assistance of the noble questioner, because it is important for you to feel encouraged. Many of you who read this or hear about this from your friends are shy to take these steps. I am not suggesting you take a step that resembles jumping off a bridge with a stretchy cord behind you holding on to you. Rather, I am suggesting that you consider a proportionate motion forward. You don't have to stretch with one foot while you keep the other foot exactly where it is, but if you are in some situation where you have lots of responsibility and you can't just bail out, so to speak, you can stretch out.

Do something different. Go someplace different. Start to expose yourself to other things, because there may be people, friends and opportunities waiting for you, but in order to accommodate that, you may have to try something new. Let it be something that is safe and enjoyable and benevolent, as far as you can tell, and allow yourself, even if you are shy, to see things as they are. If your friend says, "Oh, you must try this because it is so much fun," and it doesn't feel good to you, remember that when you've tried things before that didn't feel good, they didn't always work out. So if it doesn't feel good, allow your friends to experience it, if they wish, but you go on to what feels good for you. Good life.

❋ ❋ ❋

This is Mars.

Welcome! Welcome!

You Need to Become Your Natural Self in Your Physical Body on Earth

You said something that was so interesting—that we don't have any personality characteristics that are not in some way a portion of the planet's and the solar system's. That's incredible, but now as we open up to our natural selves, does that mean we've got to solve all the challenges we face using the energy of these other planets before we actually completely become our natural selves?

Yes, because you are here and you are, in fact, made up of the matter of this planet, Earth, which to some degree—because of meteorites, to say nothing of simple dusts that have infused this planet—does accommodate a certain amount of the atmospheric and also the energy of other portions of this part of the galaxy. So, yes, that is the challenge, you see. You're here, and you have been, essentially in terms of your natural personality, largely asleep. But now as you begin to wake up individually, you will find that you will desire to interact with the planet.

Things didn't work for you before because perhaps you were essentially lost, meaning that your natural native personality was not something you could actually feel or it was in a haze, lost in a fog, so to speak. But as you become more conscious of your natural personality, you find that you are very quick to notice that you are doing something that doesn't fit. You will want to begin to react to what is natural to you, so you will be drawn to places or people or things that will feel natural to you. Is that what you are asking about?

No. Evidently I wasn't clear. Unless we have resolved everything we have to resolve— which, looking at the planet right now, it doesn't seem that we are there yet—we are going to have to use the energies like strength and love and wisdom and generosity, all the things that the planets represent, for our benefit to resolve everything before we completely become our natural self.

But this is what I was saying, and I am tying in this last thing that was discussed.

Where Grandfather talked about the awakening, okay.

I am tying that in because it's important to recognize that nothing happens individually when it affects all beings. These are individual notes in a grand course, and that course goes on for some time. When you are fully awakened, you will actually be able to look back and see every single step, whether it is large or small, whether it happened to this group or that group. You will see how you got to your natural state from where you were. When you are in that process, you don't see it. However, you will know that what is going on for you now is that you are feeling your way physically.

For people who are totally attached to the mental and want to find their way by thought, they are going to stay lost. You are in physical bodies. This tells you right away that you are here to experience the physical and that Creator does not want you to ever lose sight of the fact that physicality is what this is basically about for you here. Of course, you have spirit and personality. Of course, you have guides and angels and all of that. But you wouldn't be in a physical body on a physical world that is alive (Earth is alive), you wouldn't be in that situation, if physicality wasn't the prime reason for you to be here now.

This tells you that you must use your physicality, not only to find your way, but to solve that which has been corrupted largely unintentionally by people who have been lost in a fog. As you find your way toward your full and complete natural being as a physical person, you don't have to rise up off the planet and to some other dimension of Earth. That happens naturally at the end of your natural cycle. You simply need to become your natural self in your physical body on Earth. When that happens, you will have a great many capacities that you actually have now but which you feel as a latent experience in you, where there is some occasional touchstone—meaning that you have some sense of who and what you are and what you can do, and then it is gone.

When you have that, you will be able to fix all the problems. You will be able to help Mother Earth restore all of her lubrication that she needs in her joints. Can you imagine for a moment if you had no viscosity, no natural lubrication in your own joints? As a person moves on in years, that natural lubrication gets a little bit gritty and you call this sometimes arthritis—speaking about that which happens to people sometimes as they get older because that natural lubrication in the joints that is there when you are young is no longer there. It is the same for Mother Earth. You will discover how to use what you would now call magic but what in your natural state you simply refer to as creation.

Does this mean you will suddenly become a creator, that which you identify Creator to be now? Not exactly, because you are not going to be creating universes with the intended responsibility. Rather, you are going to find that you can do quite a bit on your own, but you are also going to find that working with others is something that makes complete sense. You will have talents and abilities, and others will have other talents and abilities, and you will mesh finely. You won't bump up against each other, because you are not going to be lost, bouncing off of this and that, as you have been doing for a while.

You have come here very purposely as souls because you wanted a challenge, and what greater challenge can there be—which you can actually rise to—than to set things to right on this planet? Setting things to right does not mean enforcing a predominant philosophy or even enforcing a philosophy in your corner of the world that people in other parts of the world have not heard of. It doesn't have to do with forcing. You can force a machine, you can force things together in a machine, but the machine doesn't work too well, as any machinist or mechanic knows. You can, however, discover what naturally works in a situation, and it works so smoothly that it runs forever.

Mother Earth is an example of that. Her tendency is to run smoothly and to run forever, as it is with planets. You will become essentially a planet in practice, and you are becoming that now. Take note in your own personality when you see how others can do something better than you, and take note in your personality when your friends or others note that you can do something better than them. Then say, "Hey, when that thing comes up, you help me, and when my thing comes up, I'll help you."

Stay in touch with those people. You will notice that there is going to be a tendency to bind together in little groups until eventually you are all bound together, nobody trying to do what somebody else can do easily. Why work and slave at something that is not your natural talent when somebody else can make almost no effort and do it because it is their natural talent? Remember, you also have a natural talent. Very often people are unaware of this, because you have been so asleep.

When this happens and you are all together and functioning, you will be able to repair Mother Earth. You will be able to repair your societies and cultures. You will be able to repair your bodies. You will be able to repair your hearts and, yes, your psyches, because you will know what is natural for you as individuals, what is natural for you as groups and families. You will know because there will be no more lies. There will be no more fears, and people will know and understand who they are. You are very much in that process now. Take note when you have evidence of it.

Okay. You sound more like Grandfather than Mars—are you merged?

You cannot talk about a subject, as you started, that is so vital. You understand, the questions you are asking are almost exactly the same in both situations. You are asking about what to do, asking about the natural self, the natural being, are you not? "How are we going to solve the problems on Earth" say you, "in utilizing the energies of other planets?" Why does that not associate itself with the wake-up call?

You Are Going to Have to Use Your Physicality

Well, I guess what I was really feeling is that as we come into our natural selves, will we still need and be receptive to the energies of the planets and the solar system in the same way?

No. You see, the planet itself, Earth, has that attunement. Right now, because you are somewhat asleep, Earth has to do more, but as you are now beginning to wake up, in the early stages Earth will gradually pull away, you see, and you will be able to feel the energies that you need by moving toward Earth. In a way, it is like a dance. You will move toward Earth, and Earth will back up. By backing up, she becomes a desirable being.

Imagine a dance. Your partner is backing up, and you want to get closer to your partner. So in order to move forward, you must become more connected to Earth and you must become more of your natural self so that you can find Earth, you can feel Earth. Earth is connected in her true nature, her personality, to all the planets in this solar system as if they were members of her family. But in order to find your natural talents and abilities to do what you must, you are going to have to use the reason for being on Earth—you are going to have to use your physical bodies, you are going to have to use your physicality. That is why you are here. You are going to have to be yourselves, but you are going to have to be yourselves as physical beings made up of Earth.

Earth has all of these capacities, so Earth is going to step back and expect you to do things that she has been doing for you and for others, and you are going to step forward and do them. But as you step forward and do this, you are going to also be stepping away from the unconscious effect of the planets—myself and other planets. You are not going to need us to be supporting you unconsciously, because you are going to be actually moving toward the capacities of Earth. You are not living on my planet, my body. You are not living on Neptune. You are living on Earth. Earth has fantastic capabilities, and you are made up, literally, of the substance of her body.

She is a spiritual master, yes, a material master and more. What does that mean to you as a physical individual? Material masters who have achieved material mastery know who they are, where they belong, what to do, how to do it, and what is meant for others so that they do not attempt to duplicate something they do not do well. So you are literally working on material mastery as we speak. Once you accommodate that . . . this doesn't mean that once you are a material master you can conquer the world—that's not what it's about. It means that you know who you are and what you can do, and you don't try to do something that you don't naturally do well. Once you accommodate that, then you move on and work on other aspects of mastery that are available in the very blood and bones of your body, because you are made up of Mother Earth.

That's exciting! When we finished last time, you said that part of your energy went to enable humans to sneeze. I have been sneezing ever since you talked about it, and every time I do, I think about Mars. [Laughs.]

[Laughs.] Now I will make a comment on Grandfather's comment, if you don't mind. There is a certain amount of suggestibility going on here. If Grandfather or others talk to you about something that is going to happen, you are open. The energy is there, so it happens. But let me suggest something else: My energy also supports an awareness of what is natural in any given moment, what is rewarding, what is the best and safest path to take, and what is the most likely path to be personally rewarding—meaning how you can receive in a way that is benevolent for you and will cause absolutely no harm to anyone else because it is meant for you.

Astrology Can Be Immensely Helpful to Parents

So how, then, is astrology going to be important to us? Will it be as important as when we were unconscious?

It is going to be vitally important, especially around the time of childbirth so that people can understand what certain talents might be forthcoming from their young ones. Even before the child is born, parents need to have a general overview of what they can expect. Astrologers will be working overtime. There will have to be more astrologers, because those who are going to be parents are going to want to talk to astrologers and be advised how to interact with baby—what to encourage and not what to discourage—because, after all, a soul is born here. They will have to discover things for their own need—"This is for me; this isn't for me"—but there may be areas where you might wish to encourage the child, perhaps in the world of thought or the world of motion, dance, art, something like that.

In short, an astrologer can be immensely helpful to parents so they have some sense of what their child might have a tendency to do. There is going to be a major need for astrology and consulting. In other cultures on your planet, this goes on regularly, but in some of your Westernized cultures, you have moved away from that, not only because you are enamored with the world of thought, but you have also moved away to some extent from your religions. A lot of the religions owe their foundations, in terms of their practices (including some of their spiritual practices), to that which involves predictions and predictability based upon the Sun, the Moon and the stars. Many religions wouldn't like to admit that, but it is true. After all, before there was religion, there was the observation of nature and the simple fact that there was a Sun, there was a Moon, there were stars—and there was no question that those things seemed to affect life around you.

Some religions were obviously built up from that, certainly some philosophies. If you step back a bit, you could easily refer to astrology as a religion; it just has not sought to become one. I feel that this is one of its most definite aspects of grace, that astrology has not sought its own vain gloriousness. It has not sought to deify itself, and this is a good thing. As a practice, it has kept itself apart from that, so that it does not act as a divisive force but acts as a teaching and supportive structure. This way it is available to all.

I feel so good about everything you have said. I am just sitting here soaking it up.

That is quite all right. I do not require immediate reactions.

The Soul's Desires Are in the Cellular Structure at Birth

Would you be so kind . . . I have asked this a little bit before, but I always get the response that the astrologers already know this. Yet other people are going to read this book.

Yes?

When a child is born and is influenced by certain planets and houses and signs, is that imprinted on the child's energy body in some way? The soul sets out to do certain things, and to do that it needs a recipe of certain energies, so it chooses to be born in a certain place—is that right?

Yes. It is not necessarily a geographical place, though. The child might choose to be born in the most likely place where opportunities to experience what one desires as a soul will be present. So that's a place, but it's not necessarily a geographical place.

Then are those opportunities determined by the energies impacting the soul at birth?

Yes, so we are talking about physicality here. The soul's desires are actually in the cellular structure of baby at birth, and the memory of that remains, if not necessarily in every single one of those cells, then in some of them. The memory of that is infused at the very least as an echo in the cellular tissue, even up to the point of death by age. So that soul has those opportunities continuing to come up.

This also affects walk-ins, I might add. A sidelight here for walk-ins is that even if the walk-in experience takes place, there will be those opportunities that continue to come up, but the new soul simply doesn't take advantage of those opportunities because it no longer has that desire. So those experiences do continue to come up, but they might not cause you to trip over something, as it were—meaning the previous soul might have gone straight for that, whereas you will simply take notice of it and go on and do something else. But the opportunity presents itself, nevertheless, because of the memory of that original intent.

So where are the desires of the walk-in soul, then? They are not included in the original cells.

It becomes an overlay, very much like how you spread peanut butter and jelly on a piece of bread and it doesn't necessarily soak in. It is there for a while, but walk-ins don't necessarily say, "Okay, here is where I am and here is where I am going to stay." That is why, if you have a walk-in experience, it is not a guarantee that you are going to be there forever. Maybe somebody else will walk in. So it is kind of like peanut butter and jelly, if you don't mind my epicurean reference.

[Laughs.] Well, I would like to talk for years on that topic, but let's stay with the soul of the human born on Earth. The desires are in the cells—so how does that tie in with astrology?

You can go a little further. Where in the cells are they? Each cell actually has its own personality and its own persona. It may be hard to imagine that, but it really isn't that hard if you think about it. You are surrounded by other human beings who have their own personalities—you take that for granted. If you live with animals, it is quite clear that this cat has this personality and that cat has that one. It is the same with dogs and horses.

In short, beings you are quite well aware of all have different personalities, and you are used to that. It is a segment of life for which you have experience, but you personally have seen that the different planets have different personalities as well. You can extrapolate simply from your experience in life and your experience talking to the planets for the purpose of the creation of this book, but if that is true, one might reasonably extrapolate that everything that makes up everything else all have personalities and all function in concordance with some system whether recognized or not.

So within the cell structure, that is where it literally is. The personality of the cell gives it a personal bias toward or in some cases away from something, so that the literal cells of your body act or react when presented with certain situations. What action or reaction am I talking about? Well, of course, I am talking about feelings. I am not talking about something conditioned as in a smell, for instance, "Oh, that reminds me of . . ."—I am not talking about that. I am talking about a simple reaction to a nuance.

Say you are walking down the road and something happens, and you notice it because it has to do with the reason you are there on the planet in that body in that moment. Your other friends don't notice it at all: "What are you talking about?" "Oh, I've got to go over here." "What are you doing, where are you going?" In short, you notice it; the cells of your body notice it. You could hardly go on with your friends. Rather, you have to go over there, because over there is where your destiny lies.

There Is No Isolation

So that's our desire—now tie that into the planets. How do the planets affect these desires, and how do the desires affect what receptivity is for each planet?

That's easy. As I am talking about microcosms within your body, then there are also macrocosms. Earth has these certain predominant characteristics, and you and I have certain predominant characteristics, and having spoken to the other planets, you can see their characteristics. If that's so, then we are operating quite obviously in this solar system as a cohesive element. You might reasonably say, "But what about the other planets in the galaxy? What do they represent?" Well, of course, they all have personalities as well.

But which ones influence humans on Earth?

Every single one, just like humans on Earth and this solar system affect beings on the other side of this galaxy. There is no isolation.

Galaxy only? Not universe?

Oh no, it is the universe. I am just trying to keep it within an ability to imagine.

So what are the most prominent influences?

The most prominent influences, of course, have to do with the planet you are on, but the other influences might be ranked by, say, the planets in your solar system and then the planets in your galaxy—to say nothing of the suns, to say nothing of material simply floating around, to say nothing of life forms who might not have anything to do with planets. It is a universal course, but sometimes you have to step back and take a look at it from a distance.

This is the kind of thing you always do between lives, as you would say. When your physical body dies and your soul moves on, you always step back and take a look. For that matter, when you are in deep slumber, you step back and take a look. The reason you reawaken in the morning and don't simply say, "That's it; that's enough," is because you have seen it. You are reminded what it is all about, and you go back with joy. Granted, when you wake up you might not feel quite so joyous, but you go back with your soul, your personality, with joy to wake up so that you can get on with why you are motivated to be there. Every time you wake up from sleep, that is what is happening, because your soul, of course, does not have to sleep, but your body must.

Astrology Has to Do with Timing and Physical Place

So I know I have already, but I'm going to ask again. The desires of the soul are in the physical body, in every cell?

Yes.

So we are receptive to all these influences, but some of them we are much more receptive to. Do we shut off the ability to receive certain influences and turn up the ability to receive others?

You have to keep in mind that you live in a certain environment, do you not? So you are going to act and react on the basis of what's approved of. After all, when you are born, you do not have the same capacities you have when you are an adult. You have all of these abilities, but most often in your present-day cultures parents are not recognizing what the child is attempting to communicate. The parents are simply acknowledging that they have a new, rather helpless being who requires their full-time attention for everything, and so as a parent, you become the caregiver. In most cases, but not all, you don't necessarily recognize the brilliance or the wisdom of baby.

Right, but I am still trying to understand. A child is said to be an Aries, a Scorpio, a Cancer. What is the actual process of the baby being more susceptible to one set of energies from one planet over another?

That has to do with timing and, to a degree, what you might call geometry, the physical placement. You have desires as a soul, and therefore, you choose to be in a specific place where those desires can be fulfilled. So you wind up, say, for instance, in Madagascar, because those desires are most likely to be fulfilled in that environment with those parents and siblings. Therefore, the astrologer has the opportunity to utilize physical place and time in order to calculate what might be the most likely possibilities that will serve you and by which you can serve. So to a degree, it is somewhat mathematical. It has been built up over time from years and years and years and years of astrologers who have preceded you, if you are an astrologer, and amounts to accumulated wisdom—some of which might not fit if you are, say, born in St. Louis, Missouri, as compared to being born in Madagascar. But a lot of it will.

I understand the process astrologers use to create a chart, but I don't understand how the energies impact the child. Why is the child more receptive to one energy over another?

You are really asking about which comes first, the chicken or the egg. That is what you are really asking about, because you are really saying—correct me if I am wrong—is the soul the predominant influence, or is the soul simply influenced by where and when it begins? Are you not asking what comes first?

No. It's how. The soul has desires and it chooses a place to be born, so it is born at a certain time and place. But how do those energies impact the child? Is there something that draws those energies? Or is it just a matter of how the planets are moving around the Sun and the orbits and the energy that can get through to the Earth at that moment?

I think this would work better as an example. If you wanted to be a leader of an orchestra, but when you suddenly became conscious of yourself you were driving a truck, you would have to finish driving the truck before you could stop, get out, and go learn how to be an orchestra conductor. I know that sounds like a riddle, but the answer to your question on basic astrologic principles is a snap. You can look that up in a moment and read why and how astrology works. But if you are asking how you get from here to there, sometimes you have to take the journey, even though you may have an objective. If I cannot answer your question in a way that satisfies you, ask it again, talking to someone else. But before you do that, read the basics in astrology.

I am trying to understand how the energy comes from Mars, for instance, and then it's forever after that in your life and you are more receptive to that energy than possibly to another.

It is a menu item—a recipe, if you like. Your soul comes with certain desires, and therefore, the soul's desires require a mixture of certain influences in order to have opportunities. It's as simple as that.

That's making more sense. So we will leave that. I will be frustrating readers who understand astrology.

It's not complicated. Look at it as a recipe. If you want to make chicken consommé, for example, you will probably need a chicken.

[Laughs.]

I Give You Clarity

You are just a delight to talk to. You have been the most patient person. I have tried to ask some of these questions before.

It goes to show that my reputation has not entirely preceded me.

[Laughs.] No, you are far beyond your reputation.

Thank you. Now, given that, let me say this. Those of you who feel the need to have more strength and more ability to hear your own feelings, feel free when you see me in the sky—and a simple education from your local astronomer will help you to find me in your sky, for many of you (if not, you can imagine where I might be)—to simply breathe as you look at me. It might help you to feel a greater sense of your own physical safety and security. It might also help you to feel a sense of the value of your own personality, and it will also—and this is the nice thing—help you to be more clear.

It is a clarifier. It will help you to become more clear about what is your personality and what is somebody else's. Even though you might be living with friends and family and brothers and sisters and all of that, you will be able to see where they end and you begin. It is fine to have family and fine to have friends, but sometimes you must have your own personality so you know what is right for you. There may come a day when you will have to do something other than what everyone you know is doing. When that day comes, it might lead you to some benevolent place, and if that is so, perhaps you will find your way more easily. Good night.

Thank you so much. Thank you.

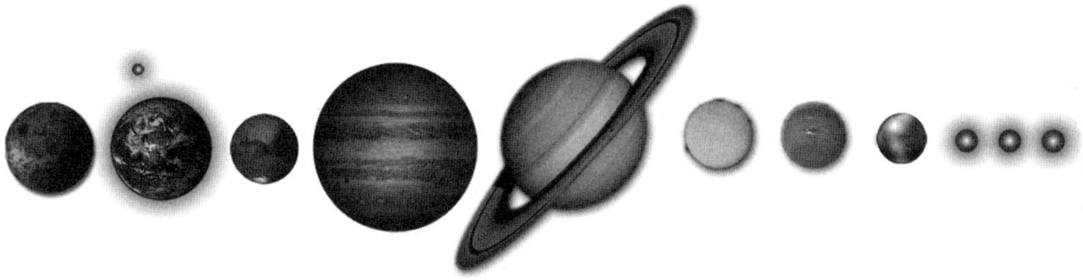

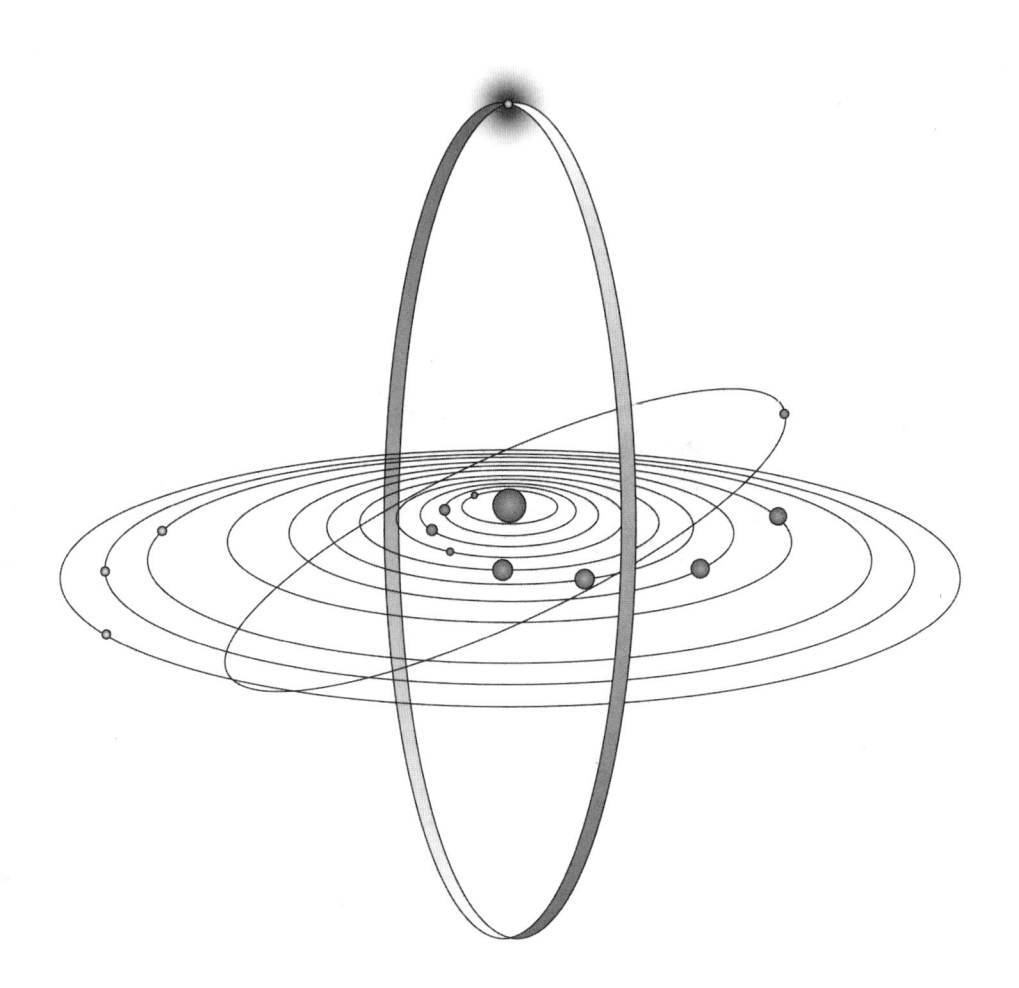

Unknown Planet to Stabilize Earth's Orbit

UNKNOWN PLANET TO STABILIZE EARTH'S ORBIT
Influences Your Out-of-Character Behavior

April 26, 2007

Greetings. Very well. I am a planet beyond the outer one you know of.

Beyond Pluto?

I Am Here to Stabilize Earth's Orbit

I am not certain how this will help your astrologers, since you cannot track the planet. It is very small, and only occasionally can you notice its presence (allowing for a very wide orbit) by subtle changes in gravitational fields that can only be observed sometimes. The physical mass would not seem to be very big, but in terms of gravitational mass, it's at least as massive as Saturn. This is why astronomers who have picked up this fluctuation have been unable to pinpoint a specific physical entity. In various observations, this has been assumed to be an anomaly. On the physical level it might appear to be, physically speaking, a small moon, but it is actually a planet. It has to be, since [laughs] a moon is a satellite of a planet, yes? So there are no moons around this one.

Have you been in the solar system since its beginning?

No. It was acquired when what you call Earth joined that solar system you are in on Earth. Then, within about ten years, I joined from the same place where that Earth planet was from, functioning as a counterbalance. You see, the Earth planet is not from your solar system and has great difficulty maintaining an orbit; it even wobbles a bit on its axis. So it requires a form of its own substance to be present, meaning from Sirius. But since you already have a satellite and do not need another moon—and because my gravitational field is so massive—it cannot be. There is not room for such a massive gravitational being in between Earth and Mars, and there's really no place else in the solar system. If I was someplace else in between, you see, I would affect . . .

The orbits.

Yes. So out here where I am [laughs], I'm less likely to cause any problems and can help Earth to maintain stability within its orbit.

How wonderful! Were you able to be closer to her in the solar system that you came from in Sirius?

Yes. In Sirius, I would have been, not the next planet out, but the planet past that. The orbits there are much broader and also the gravitational field is much less. But here, functioning in this focus—you say "dimension"—the gravitational aspect is much more powerful.

Why is your planet so massive? Is it because you didn't come from here?

Massive?

I mean the energy.

Good question. In Sirius, the planet, I would be much bigger. But here . . .

You are compressed. I see.

Yes, with no life as you know it on the planet. I'm just functioning to support Earth in a version of myself, but the version is still on Sirius, so it is like a personality. What I have here is a very small mass of compressed stone borrowed from space, enough to create a central core so that the gravitational field has something upon which to attach.

But in Sirius you have life on your planet?

Yes. There is much life and water, as you would recognize it, but not the color you have.

What color is it?

Sort of a rose color.

Will you go back when Earth goes back, then?

Yes, but that is a long time.

What a service!

It was necessary or Earth would not be able to maintain a stabilized orbit, at least as stable as it is.

My Gravitational Pull Is More of a Repelling Energy

Do you have an identity of any kind at all that . . . well, let's put it this way: will our scientists find you at some point?

They are already in observation of the gravitational field, but it isn't always observable. It's so far away from your planet! It is not a physical mass one could actually see.

How far are you from Pluto?

I do not know how to describe it, but about one and a half times as far as the average distance between planets.

What is your diameter, roughly? Can you talk in miles?

No, I will compare it. It's about one-quarter of the mass of your now Moon, but much more dense—*much* more dense!

If we tried to get close to you, would we get caught up in your field?

You cannot get close. My gravitational field is very powerful. I believe when you have sent out satellites . . . perhaps that was not your planet, but I recall a self-propelled satellite coming out. It greatly distorted that satellite's direction. Maybe that wasn't from your planet, but it was a machine and it happened to come near me. I don't know where it was going, but . . .

That's probably not where it went.

It was going someplace else.

[Laughs.] Are you pulling other things into your space? I mean, isn't there a lot of loose . . . ?

I would like to explain something here. You understand gravity to be that which holds something down. But this is a different kind of gravity, and perhaps I am using the wrong word. It is more of a repelling energy.

So it pushes away the stuff that normally would accrue?

Yes. This is why on the surface of the . . . I am going to call it a phantom planet, because this is something that scientists are loosely using as a term. Toward the center where the material is, there is gravity there as you understand it. But when you get out to the perimeter of where the planet would be—the actual size as it is in Sirius—there you have a repelling energy. This is largely because it is a broadcast current, not unlike broadcasting electricity, that is meant to be transmitted to Earth to stabilize Earth's orbit. I like the term "phantom planet," because a planet, after all, is meant to be someplace one might occupy, given reasonable conditions to support life, but I do not have that. I'm more like a living being supporting the living being of Mother Earth. I like the term "Mother Earth," and she does welcome life.

Sirians on My Home Planet Need to Sleep to Support Me

How much of your attention is directed here? Does providing this service take away from your performance on your home planet?

Yes, it does, and it actually affects the life forms there. Before this service was functioning, the average life form there would sleep for perhaps four or five hours in a given period of time—you would call it a day. Now it is closer to twelve hours.

Oh, because you can't give them that much support.

That's right, so they sleep more. Sometimes they sleep in two different periods of time, and sometimes they sleep for the whole twelve hours. They have enough food and water and all of that, but there is a certain amount of sustenance they don't get, so they are able to survive and thrive as long as they sleep. Their sleep is very deep. When they are in that sleep, they are able to support the planet itself through their cycle of breath. They become coordinated in a fashion, with so many thousands breathing exactly the same in the same moment, and that breath cycle supports the energy of the planet itself. This is not something done as a conscious act, but it is done unconsciously.

I was going to ask if they understood what they were doing.

No, they don't even know they are doing it.

How do they understand the difference in their sleep pattern, then? Well, it has been so many million years . . .

It has been so long they don't really think about it. It is just something that, as far as they are concerned, they have always done. But should things ever return to the previous situation, they will simply say [chuckles], "What's happened?" They have to sleep so much, they won't remember. Perhaps their teachers will tell them, but I do not know if they will.

What kind of beings are on your home planet?

Mostly beings who live in the water. There is some surface land but very little. Most of the land that breaks the surface of the water is considered to be a shrine, because everything else is water, the rose-colored water. Land that breaks the surface is, of course, under the surface as well. But very few beings go up onto the surface—meaning out of the water—and that is understandable, because they would not be able to breathe there.

Did Mother Earth have beings on her planet when she was . . . well, is she still there in Sirius? Did she leave, or is Earth a facsimile of her?

That is a good question. Earth as you know her here in this solar system is unique to this solar system, but there is also a sleeping version of her there in Sirius. You can see the planet, but it is asleep, meaning that the life forms that were once on the planet are no longer on the surface. There are a few, but they are under the surface, and mostly they are asleep. To put it in simple terms, there is a presence there, but the planet is not of life. She brought her life-giving and hosting capabilities to this solar system.

Look at how our experiment has affected others so dramatically!

But the experiment is not one of your own creation.

No.

You were invited to be involved in this experiment, and you, being somewhat adventurous, chose to cooperate in this experiment of the Creator of this universe. So you cannot really say you are in some way at fault.

[Laughs.] No, not at fault, but just appreciative!

I Support Earth's Atmosphere to Keep the Water on Your Planet

Were you invited to come here before Earth came to this solar system?

No, not before. I was contacted, that I might be needed, because water planets in this solar system did not exist when Earth arrived, though Mars once had water, as you understand it, and does have a form of water even today. But in their ancient civilization, they used the water much as your people are beginning to use your own.

For fuel.

But you will not end up like Mars. If you do, there will not be much life on Earth.

So you started to say you were invited here because Earth is a water planet.

Yes, and as a water planet, its outer shell is very often fully encased with its bodily fluid. You have bodily fluid, but it runs in encapsulations within your body. A great deal of Mother Earth's bodily fluid runs on the surface, so what you consider her surface is not really a surface at all. Her actual surface is the solid matter under the water, and if you calculated her shape without the water, she would not be as globular as she appears. So the water is kept in place because of gravity, yes, but also because there needs to be a spherical pattern.

It is my job to help support the gravity of Mother Earth so that the water, when it evaporates, does not keep going. Scientists consider that atmosphere does that, but what I do is largely support the atmosphere to keep the water on the planet. If your atmosphere thins too much, the water will escape. You know there are ice crystals in space, don't you? That is where they came from—planets lost their atmosphere, and the water just evaporated and was gone.

How do you do that?

It is hard to describe it scientifically, but it has to do with the capacity to have two different forms of gravitational fields functioning together: a counter-rotating pattern. So I spin on an axis one way, and my radiating field spins on an axis the other way.

Does this affect any other planets in the solar system?

No, because it is attuned to affect only Earth.

I Influence Contradictory Behavior

Are you influential in any way astrologically or energetically to humans?

I feel I am. I feel that the aspect of human beings that seems to run opposite to their own personality . . . at those moments, that's me! Think of human beings who are grumpy or grouchy, or who are people you wouldn't necessarily want to be around. Yet even those people have moments when they are kind and helpful and your best friend, and those moments are absolutely genuine. You might have other people who are kind all the time but express their kindness in a way that is completely unlike them.

So you know you have certain astrological signs that are considered to be dual signs, and there are other astrological signs that are not considered to be dual at all. But when a person who is of a sign that might be considered singular behaves in some fashion, demonstrating his or her characteristics, yes, but those which are entirely unlike his or her regular personality, I am most likely influencing that person.

Deliberately or accidentally?

No, it is not my intention; I am here for Earth. But your bodies are made up of Earth, so you are affected as well. It is not my intention, but it cannot be helped.

So how can astrologers figure you into the picture, then?

Speaking to astrologers, you might have to use the terms that I am speaking of when people behave in a certain fashion. Keep an eye on the news, and if you can chart unusual behaviors around the Earth, you might be able to get a pretty fair idea of my orbit. Don't assume. That is all I'll say to astrologers.

That's exciting. It is something totally new that nobody knew about.

Well, that's what you wanted, eh?

Yes, absolutely what I wanted. So you as a personality have always been in Sirius?

Yes, always.

Even though you've got a functioning planet there, there is a part of your energy here. Do you interact with the other planets in the solar system here?

No, and . . . I'm going to tell you something because I think I have put too much burden on astrologers, and I don't want to do that. So this is what I am going to say: Most of your planets are in orbit the way you understand, in orbit around the Sun and then moving out one after another in that same orbit. For the sake of simplicity, let's call that orbit a lateral orbit. What if there was such a thing as a vertical orbit?

Is that yours?

That's right.

Precisely vertical, or at an angle?

At an angle. If you want to know my exact orbit, then use the anomalous human behavior. But that's too tough, you see, even in your age of information, considering the level of anomalous behavior in general [laughs], so I want to give you at least a general area where to look.

So in your perception, how long have you been here?

About ten years after Earth got here.

Someone mentioned a figure of sixty-five million years, but with different focuses and things, I don't know that years relate.

I am comfortable with any estimate. As you said, with different focuses, then it depends.

You are in a different focus than ours in Sirius, right?

Yes, with Earth, even though she is asleep there.

What is putting some of your energy in this solar system taking away from you on your planet in Sirius?

Not that much, but as I said, it does affect life there. I might add that life there has stabilized at a smaller population level than it once was. It was not a die-off but simply over time a natural reduction in population.

That's because there wasn't the energy there to support more.

That is right.

Okay, but your personality, your interaction with the beings, with the other planets in your system, your joys, your whatever—is that diminished by having part of you here?

No.

Oh, good! Are there other planets between you and Pluto who affect us?

No. As I said, I am considerably farther away from Pluto, and even though I very rarely intersect or come close to intersecting Pluto, considering my orbit, I do come close occasionally. That is why Pluto has such an odd orbit, because when I come close occasionally, that creates a deflection.

I think they were looking for a satellite of Pluto. So beyond that, beyond you in the direction away from the Sun, are there any planets out there who would affect us? I am looking for any new planets we may have lost.

[Laughs.] You will have to ask for that next time.

All right. Is there any other way your energy affects us? You have two circling energies going in different directions and so we notice this in our selves, that we are acting in two different ways—then what?

Laugh it off. Many times in your cultures you grow attached to people being a certain way, and sometimes some of you find it difficult when people act differently—though sometimes those different actions can create a greater balance in their own personality. I would say, just be tolerant of it as long as it is not harming anyone or anything.

It doesn't sound like it goes that deep, that it is harmful to anyone.

I don't think so, because it is not actually meant for you but it just happens to affect you.

Right, it's a byproduct.

Human Wars Have Stunted Your Technology

Not having any life on your own planet, do you pay attention to the life on Earth, or is it really irrelevant to you?

When my orbit crosses near the pole, as you call it—the energy that goes through the center of Earth—not right over it, but when I get close to that, I am able to understand the hearts and minds of all those alive on Earth in that moment. That moment usually lasts awhile.

How long?

It's hard to say, but it lasts awhile.

Days, weeks, months, years?

Years.

So how often do you come around in your orbit, then? Can anybody relate that to Earth time?

No, not that I know of. I am struggling with your time as it is. It is not the years. I don't know—I don't function in your concept. So given the nature of counter-rotating gravitational fields, it tends to create the actual function of invisibility, meaning not simply being unseen, but actually not being present. Physical invisibility, if I can use that term, means not being present—having one's capabilities or senses present, but literally, otherwise, not being present. Whereas simply being unseen but being present, one has one's full capabilities. With counter-rotating gravitational fields moving in two different directions, most of the time I am not physically observable. I am invisible, but for those who can measure gravitational fields at a great distance, I can be observed.

This is just to support the scientists and astronomers who've noticed my presence there. Don't try too hard to find a physical mass. [Laughs.] I am not giving anything away here, but this is actually the technological means that one finds in transport vehicles to be able to travel great distances and be unobserved. The ships that do exist utilize this as technology. It can be artificially produced.

And we should take note of that.

Well, I didn't want to say that, but as long as you have.

[Laughs.] Okay, scientists, read this. We want to go to the stars.

I think this is not unknown in some of your scientific circles. I just want to encourage you that you are on the right track. I might add that as far as motivating force, it is not part of the actual travel but is a side effect. That's all I am saying.

Well, thank you. I am going to try this again. If a human lives a hundred years, do you think you would go over the planet more than once while that person was alive?

Yes.

Ah! But you don't know exactly how often, though.

I cannot say.

There have been eighteen civilizations, so as you feel the feelings of the beings as you go in your orbit, there must be a big variety, because they come and they go.

It is not just feelings; it's the ability to observe your cultures also.

Ah! So it's like a moving picture. You see it at all these different stages, different civilizations.

Well, you have to remember, I am only looking at it at times, because I am here for Earth and she hosts you, so that is part of her life. But I am not here to study you.

I am just saying that it must be interesting because it changes so much, doesn't it?

I wouldn't say so. In terms of the human population, I haven't noticed much difference in your ways. In the other nonhuman population, I haven't noticed much difference there either, except that there are not as many of them as there once were. But that has come and gone. There have been times in the past when the human population reached just about the level you have now as well, and it receded.

Do you know the cause of the recession?

Sometimes it was a natural phenomena of Earth, meaning too many people on the planet. Other times it was simply a migration. There have been civilizations that were much further advanced technologically in the past of your now civilization. Your now civilization has tripped over war, so to speak. If you hadn't gotten so engaged and enamored of war, you would now be 10,000 years beyond your current level of technology (using your years, if I may). So your thrill of war . . . though I don't feel it is very thrilling for those who suffer from it. But for those who do seem to like it so much that there is a desire to pursue it, your technology and other cultural aspects are backward as a result.

Your cultures would not be so backward had you not had your technology constantly smashed and pulverized, and your finest minds and hearts and souls eliminated. This is not to say that you don't have fine hearts and minds and souls now, but this war machine is self-destructive. It is a curiosity for a planet that is so welcoming of life to have such self-destructive beings upon her. My feeling is that this element of ignorance, of not remembering who you are, is the cause of it—because, of course, if you remembered who you were, you would never repeat the same mistakes. The Creator of this experiment, of which you are the result, seems to feel there is a purpose in it all, and it is not my job to offer opinions very often.

Where are you now in your orbit? Are you anywhere near us?
No.

We can feel an awakening on the planet. I am hoping it is better the next time you come over.
Yes, I believe it will be.

The Sun Requested This Unusual Orbit

Do you feel all by yourself with no beings on your planet?
Oh, it is not that way as a planet. There are other planets in the solar system. I am not alone.

Do you interact with them in any way?
Just the companionship of togetherness is adequate. But if you mean, do we sit around and tell stories? It is not quite the same as it is for humans.

[Laughs.] Well, at least if there is the feeling of companionship—that's important.
There is always that.

How is life different for you in this solar system in relation to the Sun than it is in your home solar system?
The reason I am moving in this anomalous orbit is a direct request of the Sun. The Sun here is not comfortable with my presence but is willing to accept it, considering that I am helping to stabilize Earth. If I do not travel in the type of orbits that the other planets do, it is because of my arrangement with the Sun—and, I might add, Earth's arrangement with the Sun, since I am here to support Earth. For that reason, I traverse the Sun in this unusual orbit, almost the opposite of what you have for your planet and the others. Then the Sun feels as if I am having the least effect possible on the other planets while doing what I do to support Earth. That is why I am in this orbit.

How interesting! That was negotiated before you came here?
Yes, but I felt that it was a request, not so much of a negotiation.

It doesn't affect your work, then? You can do it no matter what the orbit is?
That's right, and it seems like a good idea from my point of view too—if you want to call it an idea. Then I can do my work with the least amount of

distraction and I have the least amount of impact upon the other planets, although it does get a little bit of an effect sometimes.

How does he/she feel about that?
You will have to ask Pluto.

[Laughs.] Well, when we last talked to Pluto, I didn't know about this.
You can request Pluto again.

For the sun of the solar system in Sirius, where you and the Earth are from, does Earth sleeping and you being away part-time affect her in any way?
No, this is something we are doing here. There we are in our usual orbits.

Oh! As long as you are in your orbits, then that is what makes the world go round.
So to speak.

Astrology Is Only Necessary When People Don't Know Who They Are

You have a delightful sense of humor—this is a special treat.
Good.

I wish I had more knowledge of . . .
It is understood by myself and others that your lack of knowledge of the astrologic is to your advantage, because you really are coming into this with an open mind.

[Laughs.] That's one way to look at it: very open, empty.
I question whether you ought to pursue this any further. I really feel that the whole point of the astrology book is to understand your own planets in this solar system. It is up to you, but I would recommend you just stay with the planets in your own solar system. Don't go past that. Don't do the signs, don't do the houses, because then you are moving into abstract ideas. You are not talking about physical objects.

Let me ask you, is there astrology in Sirius?
Astrology is only necessary when people do not know who they are.

So it's only on this planet, in this solar system.
Well, it is considered an interesting part of Earth culture and might be studied as part of Earth culture in other places, and they might have their own ways of understanding things. But from what I know about human cultures, which isn't too much . . . [laughs]. I don't know if I can answer that, but if you are asking about how it is on Sirius, I think the teachings come from other directions and not from the understanding of the planets in the solar system.

That kind of thing is profoundly helpful for groups of peoples who don't remember who they are. Then such mathematical and accumulated wisdoms are helpful to remind you enough of who you are so that you don't work too hard to be something else. I still feel it is too much of a strain on a soul to not remember who they are. If you didn't sleep, you would all be insane.

Yeah, that's what we've been told.

I don't mean an insanity that one can live with—I mean impossible insanity. You couldn't live with it. You'd all be committing suicide.

But it's almost over. So there's a light at the end of the tunnel.

Yes, fortunately.

Can you tell me if there are any other planets? You said there are none between you and Pluto. Since you've got a bird's-eye view there of everything, are there some on the other side of Pluto that might affect us?

You will have to ask next time.

You don't want to give anybody away?

No. I am not here as a spy in the sky. I am not looking around to see who might be gaining on me.

Well, I don't know what you need. Couldn't we bribe you or something?

What have you got?

What have I got? Well, I can come back after I leave here and say hi or something like that.

We will talk about it then.

Oh, I love your sense of humor!

Practice Being Grateful

Is there anything you want to tell us that I haven't asked about?

Yes, I will close. When you find yourselves behaving at times completely out of character, know that this has largely to do with me. Learn how to use it to your advantage. An example of behaving out of character might not simply mean that you are behaving outrageously; it might very well mean that you suddenly for no explainable reason can do something that is very difficult for you to do otherwise and do it well. Then the moment passes and it is not there anymore. Don't just regret that it is not there anymore and you no longer can do that thing well. Be grateful for that moment, that gift.

One of the things that's missing in your lives these days, so very much, is a sense of gratefulness for the happy moments in life. The experience of being grateful and appreciative actually feeds your soul. Your souls are eminently grateful to have lives, to be born on the Earth, and those first few months of your life here are experienced much of the time as being grateful. That's what creates vitality between the heart and soul. So if you wish to revitalize your heart and soul, practice being grateful. Have a most benevolent good life.

Blessings to you! Thank you. I enjoyed your visit.

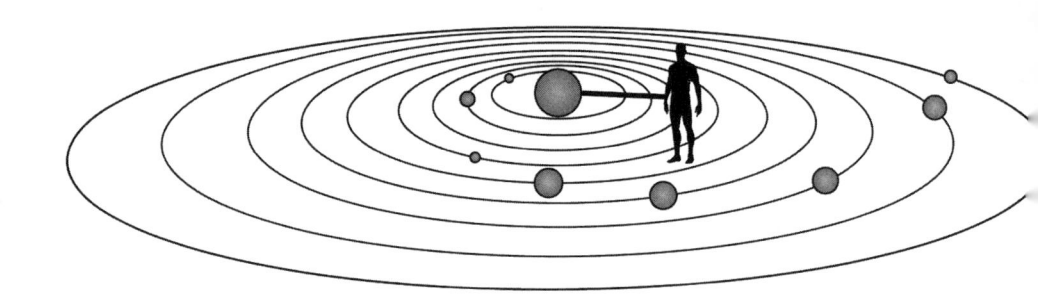

Planet Axis

PLANET AXIS
Learn How to Tap into the Energy of the Solar System

May 5, 2007

Greetings. No name for now.

Welcome.

I will comment on your concern about people's exhaustion [Melody and Robby were talking about people being exhausted before the session started]. There is a situation now on Mother Earth that is of long standing. You have been told repeatedly that you, as the Explorer Race, will have to take over some of her duties that she was serving for you and other beings on the planet. You have perhaps thought this meant that you would have to only, or exclusively, learn things, and then as you learned them you would apply them.

There Is a Timetable Involved on Earth

What you may not have realized is that there was a timetable involved and certain things would simply occur. Imagine a timer, where you have a cake in the oven and the timer rings, and that tells you to go over and check the ingredients and see if they are ready to come out. A timer rung recently on Mother Earth, and what happened is something automatic. The automatic thing that is taking place is that all beings on Mother Earth who are not a direct portion of her body—meaning not her mountains, not her rivers, you understand, but all beings other than that (trees, bushes, flowers, animals, insects, humans) are automatically involved in taking over certain portions of her works.

This does not require that you learn anything, but it will require that you begin to function in the way a solar system functions. Most solar systems are entirely interdependent. That means that there is a sun, as you know, and planets and often moons, but they are not individuals. They are a unit, and they operate as a unit.

Human beings perceive themselves as individuals, and that would be a normal intellectual assumption. But, in fact, all human beings on Earth are a unit, and the only way a unit can continue with people dying of natural and unnatural causes on a regular basis is for the birth cycle to continue to expand, meaning that more people are born than are dying. But that can only continue to a finite time, and then there needs to be a change wherein human beings draw on other sources of energy than simply increasing their number.

After all, much of this that needs to be done must be done by human beings now, because some human beings, or some industries employing human beings, are reducing the number of other animals and plants. Whole populations are being reduced in the forests and in the seas, oceans, inland seas, to say nothing of insects and natural wild plants, what you might call weeds. These are all disappearing, and that is because of humans needing more places to live.

Now, I am not here to judge you. Rather, I am here to say that given the decrease in the plant and animal population, and fishes too, that this just automatically signs you up for doing more. How will you do more when you cannot continue to increase the birthrate? The planet can only support so many, even with the best of technology, and I grant, technology is continuing to improve but not necessarily to create the most wholesome food. Still, you will resolve that in time.

You're Going to Need to Develop Interdependency

This is what you must do. I am not commanding you, I am not saying you have to volunteer—I am saying it is a fact. Mother Earth recently let go of another 4 percent of what she was doing, and you as human beings have automatically taken over 3.5 of that percent, because the plants and the animals really can't take over much more than they already were carrying. For many of you, you have felt this as a direct drain on your physical systems, and it has been hard for those who are stretched in terms of your physical capability, as it has caused a drain on you directly.

I am going to recommend that you do something on a daily basis, and it will carry you over for a time until you are able to do the thing that you need to do. Here is the simple cure that will carry you over: When the Sun is out—even if you use illuminating and it is cloudy, you can tell at least roughly where the Sun is—then what to do is to go outside. You really need to be outside to do this.

Look toward the sky where the Sun is. Obviously, if it's bright sunlight, you close your eyes, and while looking toward the sky with your eyes closed—either standing or sitting, it makes no difference; you can even be lying down—breathe in deeply, looking toward the Sun, and gradually release the breath. Take about ten or twenty breaths like that, not rapidly, just slow deep breaths at a pace that is comfortable for you. This will automatically increase your energy level, and it can be done at the rate of ten to twenty breaths three times a day, if you wish. It doesn't have to be, but it can be up to three times a day.

This will help to tide you over, but you will need to develop something like solar systems and you are going to need to develop interdependency. This is true in a business sense right now. You have interdependency, and in terms of the wheel of life, you have it as well, but in order to truly function, you are going to have to do something that you are already doing but are largely unconscious of. You all take and give energy to each other from yourselves. You might in that sense be around someone who has lots of energy and you are tired, and you will automatically . . . it is not a conscious thing, but rather your body was set up to do this. You will automatically retrieve energy from that person who has an abundance of it.

This is not something that is done with or without permission. You are made up of Mother Earth's body, and Mother Earth functions as a unit with the solar system, to say nothing of the galaxy and the universe, but I am keeping it simple here in the solar system. If you are going to do this—and you do it all the time; it is just part of the function of human beings—it would be good to begin to do it consciously. I recommend that you make an effort over the next few weeks. Don't wait. Make an effort to get involved with groups of people. They can be like-minded, where there are things you like to do together, common interests. That is fine. It doesn't have to be that way, but it might be easier. It can be a family, it can be friends, or it can just be people who have an interest like you do. Do that thing with the Sun.

After you do that, then be quiet for a moment: ten, fifteen, twenty breaths. You can decide beforehand. Then stand in a line and reach to the person next to you. Using your right arm, touch that person's left shoulder, on down the line—just a single arm touching the next person's left shoulder straight on down to the end. Then breathe normally for about five breaths, or three if it is not comfortable. If it is very uncomfortable, stop immediately, whoever feels that discomfort. This is training to learn how to become consciously interdependent instead of simply giving energy or receiving energy from others. You are made up of Mother Earth, as I said, and this is a natural human trait.

In order to assimilate these time quadrants—meaning the timing when Mother Earth gives over to you so that you must do what she has been doing—you will have to develop this kind of teamwork. It cannot be done under demand, meaning someone orders you to do it with a group of people. That won't work. It has to be with people you are comfortable with. It doesn't have to be twenty people. It can be three people—that is a good group. Or there can be ten people, there can be a hundred people, you understand? I would recommend at least three. You can stand like that, and it will help.

Learn to train that way. You can't, of course, orbit around each other, and it is not necessary, but you can stand that way and breathe. Learn to do that, because there will be times when there won't be any Sun out, all right? It might be at night when that happens, and you could be very exhausted indeed unless you can get up, stand with two other people, or maybe you will be at work (you might work at night). Stand with a few other people. Do the breathing. You will feel better. It is really making something conscious that has been happening for a time.

Will you say who you are?
Later.

So the level of energy that we are contributing now is going to increase?
Yes, but it will happen with these timing situations. It is like a calendar, you see—that is a good way to say it. Suddenly a date or a time will come up, and *click*, it will automatically happen. You will generally know when it happens because you will probably feel tired, but you now have something you can do to help you to get over that. You must learn to consciously be interdependent this way, or you will get more and more tired and you just won't be able to do much. You see, if you had many, many more animals and many, many more plants, it would just barely affect you at all; you would hardly notice it. But because the plants and the animals are so greatly reduced, then it comes to you.

It won't happen constantly—we are not talking about something that will develop every week—but when it happens, you will notice it. The reason I say you will notice it is that each individual will have moments when he or she is tired unexpectedly, but when everybody seems to be unusually tired, then you know that one of those moments has occurred. You don't really need to know exactly when. You stabilize energy like that, you work in groups, you breathe, and you become conscious of doing what you have been doing, meaning giving energy by taking energy. There may be times, you see, very often when no one has a lot of extra energy to give, and then everybody gets tired. That is what is going on now, see? So you can supplement it with the Sun.

There is another thing you can do. There is something you are going to need to learn how to do. You are going to need to learn how to tap into the solar system itself. Earth is tired because of all the mining and because of the balance of life being changed on the planet. Other planets, moons and certainly your own Sun are not so tired. So here is the secondary thing you can do, which I feel in the long run will be also very helpful. You can connect on a meditation, if you like, or in that other way I described with the Sun, and then over time with practice you can gradually add in the other planets in your solar system.

Obviously, you don't have to add in Earth, because you are on Earth and your physical bodies are made of that, but you can start with the Sun. Don't worry about the moons. Work your way out so that you are able to eventually, when you are breathing in that Sun energy, breath it in while you are united with the other planets in your solar system. That will give you about three times as much energy as you get now by breathing in the Sun energy, and when you get good with the groups you are joining, if you would, that will increase it to four or five times as much. A small group will bring it up to about four times, a big group, five times, and it will give you a lot of support. For people who have a lot of energy, you may not be able to take the five times as much, but for people who don't have much energy, the four or five times as much energy would be a big help.

You Need Each Other for Your Survival

We are just contributing to Earth's energy—she is just using our energy?

Mother Earth does not perceive any differences between her physical body—meaning her soil, her water and so on—and your bodies. It is all on loan to you, you see, including the trees, the fish, the insects, all animals, all life. It is all on loan, and when your spirits move on, your bodies return to the Earth, and this is the way she likes it. So that is an answer to your question, eh?

Right, but as she perceives our body as her own, is she drawing energy from us just like we are drawing from each other?

No. She is letting go of certain duties; she is not drawing any energy from you. You are taking over those duties. It isn't something you can classify, saying, "Oh, what are we doing? Are we now causing the planet to orbit differently?" It is not like that. It is everything that she does. You are taking over a percentage of that.

What percentage?

I think I will not say, other than what I have said. I don't want you to be frightened. It is just important that you recognize how vital it is that you cooperate with each other and that you get past your differences with each other. It is absolutely true that regardless of race, religion and anything, you are going to need each other to survive. I am not talking about someone growing food and somebody shipping food; I am talking about living.

So we need each other for our survival?

Yes, but you can start small. It is necessary, however, and would be very valuable to increase the group size. Can you imagine? Right now, you might have 40,000, 50,000 people at a sporting event, even more. They are all involved in roughly the same thing. There is a form of unity there. What if you set aside in that sporting event one minute to do that thing with the Sun? I am not saying that is going to happen now. I am saying it is possible to be united with other people you don't know and have never really met. You all do something for about ten seconds, twenty seconds, thirty seconds, a little more, and you feel tremendously invigorated.

What I am saying is that you don't have to know the people. You don't have to know how different you are, and you don't have to know how similar you are. Proximity is a factor, and you won't always have to put a hand on each other's shoulders. That is just to train. Eventually, when you get to know that feeling, then you don't have to touch each other. That is an advantage too, because then you could globally be united with people on the other side of the world, if you are so inclined.

The whole point is to get to operating as a unit. Once you are operating as a unit, even for minutes a day like that, you will recognize immediately when there is something wrong in the human chain of life. You will recognize that some part of the human chain is suffering and needs support. You will just know it, and you will lend that support because it is good for everybody. Yes, it is good for those who need the help, and yes, it is good for everybody. This is actually going on unconsciously for you now, but it needs to be conscious so that you can get past your battles with each other and get past the desire to have. It is good for everybody to have, and a great deal can be done toward that.

You Are Taking Over a Percentage of Everything Mother Earth Is Doing

So this thing that we are doing unconsciously, is it during the day, during the night, all the time?

All the time. Your bodies are doing it.

Our souls are doing it even when they are traveling at night? Or are our physical bodies are doing it, not our souls?

Your physical bodies and your souls, when your souls are in them. Do you understand? That is a unit, but when your body sleeps, most of your soul is not present there. There is a tether. Your physical bodies do this all the time; it is part of life. I am not talking about something radical. This is just a simple fact.

So it has always been part of our life but on a much tinier scale?

No. It's always been part of your life, period. This is very simple. You are not aware of it, but this has always been: this is a given, it's a factor. You don't have to learn how to create union. You have union now. You just need to become conscious of it. That is all.

We are tired because we are taking on duties from Mother Earth that she used to do? Now we are doing them?

That is right.

Are we doing them twenty-four hours a day?

As a unit you are, but of course, when you are asleep you are not doing it. But when you are asleep, other people are awake.

"As a unit," meaning as if we had one soul, all humans having one soul?

No, "as a unit," meaning all human beings. You are turning this into a soul thing. I am talking about your physical bodies. Your physical bodies and your souls are a fact, but you are separating this and I am not. I understand, but it is important at this point to understand that Mother Earth does things not only that you are aware of, that you can analyze, that you can consider scientifically, but a great many more things that you are not aware of.

Those are some of the things that we are doing, that our bodies are doing?

No. You are taking over a portion of *everything* she does, no exceptions, from the most obvious to the least obvious. You are not taking over things on a piecemeal basis.

Is that "taking over" going to increase the percentage of what we do?

Yes, it will increase, but it won't go to a higher percent. It will just increase to a point.

I have no more questions, because I don't exactly understand what it is that we are doing,

Think for a moment of some of the things Mother Earth does. What does she do? You don't have to think too hard.

Well, she provides our atmosphere, everything that is here: the oxygen, the food, the growing cycle, the energy for everything on her surface.

That is fine, and there are a great many more things that even science is not aware of. You can accept this, yes?

Yes.

You are taking over a percentage of everything that she is doing.

Which allows her to take care of herself?

That is right.

It is either that or we have to all get off the planet, right?

I wouldn't go that far. I would say you would need help from others, but you have to remember that you are here to train on how to create, and this is an opportunity to create. One of the things that creators, even creator apprentices, must do is that they must absolutely, positively know how to cooperate completely. Right now, you are fingers—don't try to be thumbs. Your thumbs don't try to be fingers. You walk on your feet, not on your hands. Do you understand? There is cooperation in your bodies individually. You might see athletes playing a game of some sort, and each person has their position and they play that position, but they don't play the other person's position.

So you understand cooperation and teamwork. On a team like that, individual differences, religions and points of origin are forgotten during the game, and one plays the game with a certain amount of joy. So I am not talking about something you can't do. You do it now, and you know how to do it in ways that are cooperative, so you don't have to learn something entirely new. You just need to expand what you are doing now and move beyond your differences so that you can all live and thrive. The whole point is thriving.

My Energy Is Largely Involved in Balance

I am the energy that functions as the axis in all the planets in this solar system. So my energy is largely involved in balance.

That's totally new: energy that functions as the axis. Do you make all the planets go around?

No. Since the planets go around, they have a buildup of energy in the axis. You understand, "axis" is an artificial concept. There is an energy in that pole-to-pole area, and that energy becomes concentrated over time and has a certain personality. Even though planets are different, that energy and its personality are associated with who and what I am.

Do we interact with you, then, on this Earth in any way?

Of course. You are on a planet with an axis.

So unconsciously we do something with you, or to you, or for you?

No, not really, other than the fact that you are of Earth. I feel that a great many of you do not think of yourselves as being of Earth, but you are, from the perspective of all the other peoples of the universe—which are too great to put a number to, eh? You are Earth people, and you will always be that to the others. And if all of these untold numbers can perceive you as one group, perhaps you can begin to perceive yourself that way.

That is beautiful.

You might go to other planets and see people who come in a variety of different appearances, and you would say, "Oh, they are like that, too," meaning that you have a certain variety of appearances given the fact that you all basically look the same. This is not unusual in the universe. One finds it.

We are told how unusual and different the Earth planet is. If your energy is the axis of all the planets in this system, does her energy feel different to you than that of Mars or Saturn or the other planets?

Yes.

In what way?

It feels more active.

Even in her tired state right now?

Yes. It requires a tremendous amount of energy, and Mother Earth pulls on the other planets all the time, but it isn't enough. Now she is going to require you to take over some of her duties for a time so that she can rebuild herself, and she will also require that you assist in that rebuilding at some point to learn magic in the true sense, meaning the benevolent sense, and help her to replace her veins of coal,

And oil.

And oil and everything she uses in her body. All that you are using, you must someday replace, and it can only be replaced when you are residents on this planet—meaning you cannot go to some other planet and get it and bring it back and put it in Mother Earth, even if you had the capability.

Oh, we have to create it?

You will have to replace it through magic, otherwise known as creation. You have the capabilities to do this now, but you must remind yourselves how. Since you are living on a physical planet and since you are cut off from the bulk of your knowledge and wisdom of who you are when you are conscious, thus you must learn slowly. That is why so many teachings have been going on in the pages of your magazine about magic. Remember always that magic is benevolent. The kind of magic I am talking about is benevolent to all beings all the time—that is why it works. Everyone embraces it, because it is good for everyone. No exceptions. That is the kind of magic we are talking about here. It can be done.

By Uniting with Each Other, It Will Be Easier to Create

Does your personality derive only from the activities in this solar system, or do you have memories of other places?

I don't have memories at all. I am always in the present moment. That is why, in order to produce this kind of communication, it is difficult—because I am speaking in a sequence but I am always and only in the present.

I see. So does each planet produce the energy to make the planet go around its axis?

Each planet, aside from the way the energy is produced for it to spin, builds up through the simple spinning a concentration of energy in its center.

Assuming it spins on a reasonable axis, meaning without too much wobble, then that energy will build up along that, pole to pole. As it builds up over time, I become associated with it.

Is that buildup of energy used for something? Is it used for something else?
It has to do with creation. That is why I am teaching you here how to unite with each other, so you will be able to more easily create.

We can create with that energy in the axis, or the energy in the axis creates something?
No—the "no" is to the first part of your question. You must learn how to create on your own, you must learn how to create on an interdependent basis with each other, and you must learn how to create in absolute benevolence for all beings. You must identify all beings as all life from the tiniest to the largest and all that makes up everything in between.

So does the energy in this axis just stay there, then? Is it necessary to keep the Earth spinning, or what is it used for?
Your question does not relate to the reality, but if you have something that is in perfect balance and it is spinning, it will spin forever. It is in its nature that that energy builds up physically. I do not create the axis in any planet, but the energy that builds up has certain familial qualities from planet to planet, and once it establishes that quality, then I am there.

What do you do?
You think of yourselves as who you are by what you do, eh?

Yeah.
I exist.

And if you weren't there . . . ?
If I wasn't there, the planets would continue to spin and all would be the same.

So then why are you here?
Why are YOU here? Do you understand? If you question creation on the basis of "why," you will necessarily create levels of qualification. If you remove "why," you will accept all life and regard it as beauty. Qualification, and thus ranking, all stem from "why." "Why" is a temporary question for you as a soul.

Only on this side of the veil, right?
On this planet, because you don't remember who you are. But when you are other places where you do remember who you are, "why" does not exist. You might explore "what," but you never explore "why." You accept, appreciate, honor and value, and "why" doesn't come into it.

See, another aspect of "why" that comes about as a result of ranking is justification. There is a great deal about "why" that is not so good, even though it can be interesting. I will simply say this: I have volunteered this information today, not because of any personal quest to do so on my part, but simply because I am available and others are busy.

Draw Energy from the Sun and the Planets

So you can feel us too from where you are? You can feel our energies? You feel everything?

Insofar as you are a portion of the planet. I do not make the effort to contact you as you would understand contact.

How long has this energy depletion of the Earth been going on?

Oh! Several thousand years, but not anything that Mother Earth could not handle in union with the other planets in the solar system. But since you have been increasing your number and having greater and greater impact on Earth as a planet, then it not only gives you the opportunity to do what you came here to do, meaning to create, but it goes beyond opportunity and becomes essential for your survival. The main thing you have to do that has been difficult for you to do and continue—not just do once, do for a moment, but to do and stay with it permanently—is to completely cooperate in a unified fashion in a way that is benevolent for all beings, as much as you can create that.

This is not an authoritarian society, not a commanding, demanding society, not a hierarchical society, but everyone doing what they can do for each other because it feels good. This requires love and it requires compatibility, and most of all, it requires balance. That is why I am here to talk. It is all about balance. So you see, this is something that is happening, and I am simply here to let you know and to give you advice on what you can do. It is good to train now, you see, because as it happens again and then again and then again, you will be ready, and after a while, you will be "Oh," and you can handle the whole thing in a few minutes because you don't have to go to a stadium.

You don't have to be with others in physical proximity once you learn how to do this. It doesn't matter where they are, any place on the Earth. Everyone will suddenly notice that they are having that feeling, and, "Oh, this is what we have to do now." You just get into the rhythm of breath with each other, and then you draw energy from the Sun and the planets—much as Earth does, much as happens in any solar system, much as any creator's apprentice needs to learn how to do—and you become a portion of life, rather than apart from life. You join the life function. You train to welcome all life, and before you know it, all life upon the planet welcomes you. Good night.

Thank you very much.

An Active Volcano

ISIS

Mother Earth's Pain Is Also Your Own

May 12, 2007

This is Isis. Greetings.

Isis, welcome! Can you add to what the Axis said last week, because it wasn't very specific.

Earth Struggles Are Wearing Down Mother Earth's Energy of Renewal

There are other goings-on as well. All of the struggles all over the Earth between peoples fostered by years of cultural struggle—which involves religion and philosophy and nationalism, as well as other things people know about—are wearing down Mother Earth's energy of renewal. Renewal is a fact of life for Mother Earth. You are aware, of course, of the seasons, and if there were no other demonstration of Mother Earth's feelings of renewal, the seasons alone would be a sufficient message that renewal is what she is all about. Souls come to this planet because, not only do they wish to learn something or participate in the Explorer Race experience, but also because they desire within their own immortal soul structure a form of renewal, any form. In some cases it is something major, in other cases it is something very slight, and everything in between.

So renewal is an important cornerstone of Mother Earth's personality. But with all of the struggles and the pollution that do not really have to take place . . . the pollution because technology, as well as people's desire to eat natural and live natural, can really eliminate at least three-quarters of the pollution, if only you were prepared as an Earth society to live in balance. I think it might take a generation to get fully engaged, but it could happen—by "generation," I mean twenty years. I would say that the primary challenge, then, is wars and the hatred that comes about as a result of wars and other violence. This creates an artificial renewal, one that is based in discomfort.

As a matter of fact, even jokes have been incorporated. In some places in the world, they have fires and floods and violence, and they have decided that that is a form of seasons, but it is a season of discomfort. So what you have now are decreased expectations of happiness and increased assumptions of discomfort. These kinds of things tend to lead to cynicism, and cynicism almost always is the accepting of the very worst. I realize it is a battle for you now to not be cynical and it is a belief by many people that being optimistic is bordering on being Pollyanna-like.

But there is a lot to be said for the character Pollyanna—a famous story, you know. Optimism can actually change the creation of your life. I am not saying to ignore things for which caution is to be taken, but when you are on your own, I am going to strongly recommend every day that you strive toward the physical feeling—as much as you can muster in your body—of optimism. It is very important, because it will have a cumulative effect that can decrease the continuing cycle of destructive creation and expand a natural cycle of renewal in the most benevolent way. Mother Earth requires—not just needs, but requires—your cooperation in this matter so that as many beings as possible can live benevolently on the planet.

So that is what I want to bring up, because while the other being had much to say that was of value, it is important to understand the cause, and this is the true cause over which you have something to say. I grant that the causes in Mother Earth's body are real, but you have some influence with your own world, your own culture, your own societies, and to put it more simply, yourself, your friends, your family. If you want to do something that is challenging and fun, get together with some friends and practice being optimistic. You can have a lot of fun with it, and I recommend it as an amusing activity. Try to keep it as benevolent as possible.

In this way, the core of Mother Earth's personality, which is love—and since you are made physically of Mother Earth, that is also your core—is replenished by love and is founded on love, even though it might not always be obvious. Therefore, optimism is the personality of love, and if you can be optimistic, you might just encourage and support your own natural renewal based on love.

Your Own Renewal Is Being Affected

Can you be more specific about what our bodies are doing that the Earth is not doing anymore?

Yes. You have seasons of your own, you know. You are born, you are a baby, you are a child, yes? Then you have your years where you are developing your personality, your body is growing and maturing, and so you are a young adult, yes? Youth. Then you become a mature adult and you pursue things adults pursue. Then you become elderly and you get along as best you can [chuckles] and prepare, at some point, for your passage to your natural state. So you also have seasons.

If you recognize that everything that goes on here on this planet is totally correlated to everything else, you will recognize that renewal, which has to do with the seasons—which has to do with Mother Earth, which has to do with you—is associated with your physical bodies as well. Since you must renew through your sleep cycle, through eating, and yes, to quite a degree, through the experience of dreams that can renew your psyche, your own renewal is being affected because Mother Earth must take care of her own self more so now—because of ongoing wounding. You cannot have explosions all over the planet (especially in wars) and poisons and other things meant to harm people without also harming Mother Earth, no matter what the cause.

Sometimes you believe, in your cultural practices or even in your technology, that some of this explosive stuff is a good thing. For example, building dams might often involve explosive charges to change the pattern or flow of water and also to cover land with water and to move stone. It is easy to forget that the stone one blows up or pulverizes is part of Mother Earth's body, and the expressions of her physical body in mountains, lakes, rivers and so on, are all part of her self.

You would recognize that in a physical person: you have arms, legs, your body, your face and so on. If there is an accident and you have a cut, then you have a scar. You see that on the physical body, and you say, "Oh, what happened?" or something like that. "Are you all right?" But because Mother Earth is so massive, it's very easy to just blow up some rock that is in your way in order to create a road or a dam (just for example) or move that rock out of its way, out of the way of progress. But it is like incising a cut, and it takes such a long time for Mother Earth to build up her body in the form of stone that she is wounded for a long time.

Just because you do not feel her pain—as you do not feel the pain of other people—does not mean the pain does not exist. This is vital for you to understand, and if Mother Earth has enough pain—and she has pain all over her body now, due to mining and drilling and construction, wars and explosions, pollution and so on—if she has enough pain and you are sharing her duties, then you have difficulties as well. Remember, Mother Earth does not differentiate between her physical body and the physical bodies of all beings on the planet, including human beings. If she is suffering, then you are, to a degree.

This is not vengeance on Mother Earth's part. She sees your bodies as extensions of her own, because the only part of you that is immortal and ongoing is your soul, but your physical body is entirely constructed of Mother Earth's body, and that is how she sees it. It is one of the reasons she loves you, because she sees you as a portion of herself and it is healthy to love one's self. So this is the cause.

What you are doing is experiencing a cycle. When your physical bodies have pain or disturbed natural rhythms, such as sleeping or eating at different times, or being able to concentrate and not being able to concentrate at different times—some people even have circadian rhythm changes, body changes, where the breathing is different, the heart rate is different and so on—what happens is that your body immediately goes into a cycle of healing. For example, some people might get an extra cold, something very uncomfortable but that you get through.

That cycle of healing not only helps you, it helps Mother Earth, for Mother Earth herself is in a cycle of healing. As long as she is able to maintain her own cycle of healing, so you will be able to maintain it as well. I think those of you who can read between the lines there might wish to take note of that.

True Magic Will Help You Create Resources Beyond That Which Is Fixed

Think of all the many things that Mother Earth does, her functions—I think this is largely available in science. Understand that you as a human race are providing fully 3 percent of your own energy—some people more, some people less—to contribute to the function of Mother Earth. On the one hand, this allows you to learn things that a creator might need to know, though mostly you are doing it unconsciously. On the other hand, it is draining your own energy because of that necessary contribution, and that is why many of you are tired all the time. Of course, there are other contributing factors—stress, decreased oxygen level and so on—but that is also added into the picture.

Do you see that in going forward a larger percentage of our energy will be needed and we just have to learn to deal with it?

I see that if you are going to have a population of Earth people, you must have a world government, a world-governing body, that is centered in love, not in authoritarianism. There needs to be a centeredness in environmentalism as well. There are a fixed amount of resources, as economists might say, but all human beings, having lived immortally, have accumulated a great many capacities that you are not using very much. That is why, as the other being indicated, there has been so much stress on magic—and true magic at that, which is benevolent for all beings—so that you can learn to create resources beyond that which is fixed.

After all, one might reasonably say, "Well, you are burning all the oil. What happens when it is no longer relatively easily available?" Well, there are a lot of products made out of oil that you will have to get along without, and it won't be easy to get along without them. So one of the obvious things to do is that you need to get past the internal combustion engine, and I think that is possible without having to give up private transportation. It won't be easy, but it can be done. Largely it can be done through the creation of electricity that does not involve the consumption of fuel as you understand it, other than water, wind, sun and things like that.

This can be done. It doesn't have to be done exclusively on a small scale, but it can be done on a small scale as well as on a large scale. I realize that many industries are playing catch-up on this, but they will catch up, and there is a lot of pursuit of that in various countries that do not have much in the way of resources—or would become too impoverished if they acquired those resources that are readily available. But they may have a lot of wind and sun, or they may have a lot of flowing water. In short, wind is going to be the big wave for the future. A lot of electricity can be produced by wind. Mother Earth is happy to share her electricity with you; she just doesn't want it to come about as a result of draining her physical body of fluids, which she actually needs.

You are advocating water as the movement of water to create power, not breaking down its component parts, right?

Correct, and I am also specifically advocating wind, since the technology to create power, as in wind generators, is readily available and is being put up by many companies in many places. This can be done on a small scale, as it has been for years, and it is being done on a larger scale and can continue to be done on a larger and larger scale. I would say, without too much effort in terms of technological growth (as compared to technological application), that this can be accomplished and can literally take over about 60 to 90 percent of the world's energy needs. The rest of it will be accomplished by the process of technology moving forward and the technology you have requiring less demand on resources.

What about nuclear power plants? Do you see them as benevolent?

They have the potential to become benevolent, but right now they are problematic. It is possible to build a nuclear power plant that is pretty safe, and there are some outstanding examples of those in existence, but there are also a lot of accidents that occur in the plant and releases into the atmosphere that go unreported for obvious reasons by a corporation. So I would say, given the proliferation of nuclear power plants—which is considerably more so than people think about, because many of them are in existence on a small scale— the technology is sorely wanting, and it is causing problems. But I am not going to say too much more about that. I will say that I would like to see that replaced, but I am not going to push that too hard for now.

Listen to Your Physical Body

So we are going to continue to be tired until we become benevolent? Is that the way it looks?

No, I think that is excessively simplistic. I think it's important to begin, and you will find that just beginning will be helpful because your body needs to have physical evidence that you are doing something that is healthful for your physical body. In short, you need to listen to your physical body—pay attention, rest when you are tired, and so on—not just exclusively control the symptoms. Yes, of course, you want the pain removed and you want to feel better, and yes, modern medicine is a great boon to your cultures. I am not saying eliminate it. I am saying, "Yes, take what you need to decrease the pain, but also pay attention." Pain is a message from your body.

Okay. I didn't understand that feeling her pain was helping her.

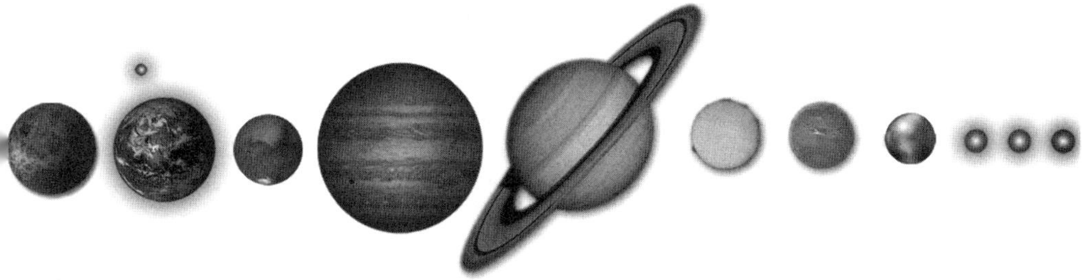

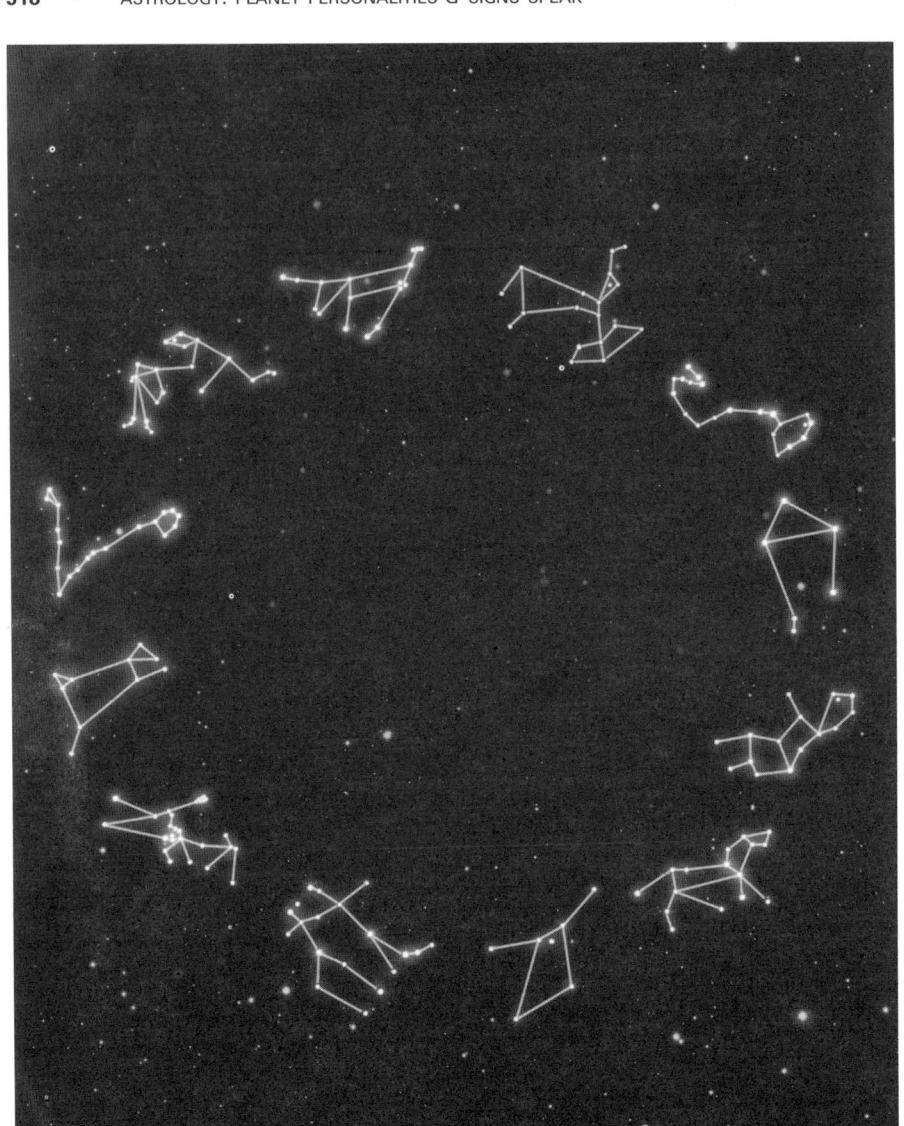

Moving Toward the 13th Sign

23

ISIS

You Are Moving toward the 13th Sign and a Connection to All Beings

May 12, 2007

This is Isis.

Does another planet want to speak?
You mean the planet beyond Pluto?

They promised us another personality type, the thirteenth personality, and that implies a planet with those qualities.
Not necessarily. There is another way. How about the combined soul of all the planets?

Oh, like an über-oversoul? [Laughs.]
Not exactly. Have you ever noticed the situation that takes place where you have individuals and you meet them one at a time, maybe over coffee or something like that, and they have their own unique personalities. Yet you get two or three of them together, and the individual personalities are altered—not just to blend as a group and become more cohesive, but the personalities themselves are altered, the way they express themselves. So while the planets stand on their own with their characteristics, there is also a unified—not an over-, not a boss—expression of personality. That is the other sign.

Does it have a voice?
I am not sure that it can speak in verbal terminology, but I will speak for it the best way I can.

The Thirteenth Sign Has to Do with Communion and the Connection to All Beings

When the elements of personality of all the planets together are combined, then you have the thirteenth sign. But, you see, we are waiting for that, because all the other planets are in balance. The beings—the spirits and so on, and various beings who exist on those planets—are in balance with that planet, but here we have a planet (Earth, yes?) and there are beings on the planet who are not in balance.

So why do we not have the thirteenth sign? We are waiting for you human beings to assimilate your true natures to enough of a degree—meaning get started with it, become committed to it, desire your true natures, demonstrate that desire, and don't backslide, if you can help it. Then you will begin to see the thirteenth sign.

The thirteenth sign has to do with community, it has to do with communion, and it has to do with a connection to all beings. How might that be demonstrated in personality? Someone who has this sign would likely be what I would call a hub, and other people would revolve around him or her. I am not saying these people would necessarily be leaders, but you might have a group of people who don't quite get along very well, and one or more of these people in that group—with totally opposing points of view, politically or philosophically or whatever word you wish to use—would be able to find their common ground because of the personalities of these people, not because of their persuasive arguments. That would be useful, eh?

That would be incredibly helpful. How will that express on the astrological chart, then?

People will be identified by long-standing professional astrologers as this type of personality, because they are naturally that and they don't have to discipline themselves to become that. In this case, birth time will not be a factor. So one might be a Leo or an Aquarius, for example, and still be that thirteenth sign. That will be helpful because time as you know it in terms of your measuring device is not going to change much—not to say that there aren't other ways of measuring time, but it is not going to change much insofar as it affects the astrologic (and I use that term for a reason: "astro-logic"). But it is not going to affect that.

So astrologers who have the capacity to make their best, not assumption, but their best evaluation of people's basic signs and general astrological profile just on the basis of communion—talking to them and noticing them, observing their habits and so on—if you can do this 60 percent of the time or more, you will have a pretty good ability to spot that thirteenth sign. Remember, people showing the traits now and then won't be it, because you all have that capacity. But people who show their capacity as part of their natural way of being and who always return to it, even though they might temporarily adapt to something else, they are it. They will be associated with another sign, but they will have that aspect that is predominant in their personality.

But if there is no timing to it, then how will astrologers plot it at birth? They will have to wait until the person grows up?

They will just have to be around that person. You can spot it with a child.

Yes, but most astrologers aren't around the people they do charts for, are they?

Well, I think it can be done. You could have an astrologer, or one who has experience and has that capacity. They could come for a visit, be around your child for a week or so, or you could go visit them and they will have students. It will get popular, this kind of training to be able to observe, and you astrologers will probably be able to develop programs of training for yourselves so that you will be able to spot people's signs. Many of you can already do this, just from a lifetime of experience, and you will be able to train others to do this. It is a good growth cycle for your profession. I think you will find that it will involve, very often, visits to somebody's household, or they may visit some academy that you have, and it might be possible to, even in three or four days, spot such a trait.

So when the Earth and its inhabitants are striving for balance . . .

And are committed to it—not necessarily achieving it. It will be in place when everybody is committed to it and you are not backsliding, not very much anyway. Individuals might backslide a little bit but then be urged onward by their fellow citizens. Then it will become more obvious. It is with you now. It is just a subliminal trait, but it will come to the surface and be noticeable.

So all of the planets, then, including the Earth, will contribute to this unified field, or overtone, or higher octave?

It is a combined energy, as I said before. You have a few people in a room, you speak to them individually or you relax with them individually, and they demonstrate their individual personalities. But you get them all around a table talking about something, and you will see a change in their personalities. It is the same with planets, especially planets in the solar system. They have their own unique personalities, and all the beings on the planet have personalities in concordance with the planet's personality. But the combination of all the planets' personalities is also present.

Your Personality Traits Are Universal

I was talking to an astrologer the other day, and she said that all professional astrologers know there is a thirteenth sign. She said it is the spider—the arachnid, I think she called it. Is there anything you can say about that?

They already know about it. They have assigned that particular creature to it because of the many legs and the idea, you see. The "many legs" thing is appealing.

So that is the same thing you are talking about, then?

Yes, it is. It is not associated with another planet, though I appreciate those who would say that it is. If it were associated with another planet, you see, you would have to wait and wait and wait to get really clear data on that, and you would still be stuck with, "Oh well, what about the time?" "What about the birth?" In short, you would be stuck. Why wait? It is with you now. You understand that I am referring to the way astrologers might see this. They might see it associated with a planet, and I am saying it isn't.

Okay. But a soul, an immortal personality, decides to be born here with that personality trait, then?

Yes, and you might see it sometimes, but it would come up like a wave and then be immersed in other traits of personality that might be considered more predominant—say, a Sun sign or rising sign or something like that. But this other is very present; it just requires a greater degree of global, cultural balance. You are all being backed into a corner on that anyway, because in order to survive as a global society, you must decide you are that. You can't have little fiefdoms all over the place and pursue that, no matter how well armed you are. At some point, Mother Earth will say, "That is enough of that." And why do that again? You have done it before. There is no advantage. Then you would just have to start all over again.

When babies are born, there has to be something in their DNA, in their magnetic field, there has to be something imprinted at that moment so that even though they move all over the globe, they are still affected by certain energies that the person sitting next to them isn't. What is that process or that imprinting, or whatever it is?

It is based upon the exact position of all the stars and all the planets at the moment of birth. It is universal. You say, "Even though they move all over the planet, they still have those same personality traits." You are right, and I would take it beyond that. If you could travel in a ship to another galaxy, they would still have those personality traits. Time and space don't make any difference in terms of those personality traits. When you are born, you take on a photograph. See it as a visual.

You can literally, and an astronomer can do this if it is known . . . the exact moment of someone's birth. . . you understand that some of that is a bit best guess. When can you say is the exact moment of birth? When the child first begins to emerge from mother, or when the child has completely emerged from mother? That is really up to the doctor or midwife. Nonetheless, glossing over that for the moment, if you get that time, you can then ask an astronomer what were the exact positions of the stars in that moment or you can look it up for yourself, because that kind of material is available if you have the capacity to know—the exact position of the stars, not only the planets associated with astrology, but all the stars in the universe. An astronomer could tell you the answer in the known scientific, observable world.

But you know it goes farther than that. You have to remember that this is a creation by a creator who is a magical being indeed. Every grain of sand, every step by an animal, every stroke of a fin or a fish in the sea, every breath of every human, every breeze that touches a leaf—in short, every single thing in that exact moment of birth—is in a position. It is that, all of that and more, that defines unequivocally every single nuance of personality, whether expressed in the lifetime or not. It is there, and it comes up at different times in different places according to different situations in different conditions. That is as brief as I can put it.

But on some level, then—whether it is in physical matter or in spirit or in some energy—that is imprinted on that soul, right? For this life only?

Yes. Well, it is not imprinted on the soul, because when the soul leaves . . . so I am not going to agree with that. I am going to say not imprinted, period. Drop that word, because that is the kind of word that creates hierarchical truths. You must let go of the idea of hierarchy. An atom, an elephant, a mountain, a human, a deity—they are all the same. You must recognize mentally the components of hierarchy. Look up "hierarchy" sometime. Read what it says. Then consider not only what it says, but consider what the components are that make up hierarchy, and you will discover how very easy it is to support that idea. That idea is at the core of almost all human struggle. Think about it. I think I can make a pretty good argument for that.

That photograph, then, at the moment of birth, is somehow, in some way, attached to that human for the duration of his or her life?

No. I am just not going to allow you to get away with that, because you want to have a very simple thing. I am giving it to you as an analogy, the photograph. It is true, but I am giving it to you as an analogy because you want a formula. You want to be able to do something, even though you don't call it this. What you are really asking for is a means of classification.

Well, how does it work, then?

I am not saying it doesn't work that way. I am saying that I won't give you a means of classification. Look around; look at history, hmm? Do you think the classification of human beings has been at fault for a lot of situations in history? Yes, I don't want to give you something that is classification, because you and

I are not alone in this conversation. It will be printed and possibly more. We are not just sitting around talking on the street corner here.

There Is Usually Compromise Between the Conscious and the Soul

There is something that happens to that human that is different from every other human, then.

Yes. That is why I put it to you like that: the position of all things in that moment. When you consider the variables beyond number in the universe, the position of all things in the entire universe, how many variables do you think might be involved there—beyond number, yes? There is the position of all things; there is plenty of room for every single being in the universe to have a different position of all things when they are born. But if you are asking, "Is that person's personality a direct result of the position of all things?" or, because you haven't said this, "Is the position of all things a reaction to the presence of the soul?" then we come back with, "Which came first, the chicken or the egg?" You have to remember, you are dealing with a profound, spiritual magician, with Creator. Creator loves variety and believes in completion, whole things—season and cycles. When you have a being like that with that kind of personality, there is not going to be anything extraneous—nothing.

That brings up two questions. First, if it were possible for two souls to be born as a human at the same time in the same place, it would still be the personality—the immortal personality—that would decide which of those traits to express in this life. I mean, there would be a difference because of the incoming personalities, right?

That is right.

The second thing is, there is then a progressed chart as you get older. Is that based on your actions in this life, or is that another extension of geometry?

No, it is based on potential, on potential pathways—meaning that the astrologer will say, "Well, this is likely to happen." But what the astrologer is really saying is, "These are opportunities, and they present themselves." From the astrologer's point of view, even if something appears to be unpleasant, the astrologer would see that as an opportunity for growth or, at the very least, an opportunity to see how you would react to this unpleasant thing.

So the astrology is an overview, giving you advice on what may happen, what could happen, depending upon what pathway you choose consciously *and* unconsciously—not "or"—because the unconscious is often used (and I will use it this way for the moment) as a parallel to the soul's intent and purpose. But at the same time, the conscious is also functioning. So there is more than one, and it is not a battle; it is usually a compromise. The soul wants to do this, the conscious awareness wants to do that, and you meet somewhere in the middle—or one expresses more than the other and sometimes within the same sentence. You know, people can sound contrary. They might say, "Well, it could be this or it could be that," and you might have huge differences—this as an example.

Are you saying that the soul is expressing part of the sentence and the conscious personality the other part?

It is possible. It is a little oversimplistic, but I am trying to give you something you can understand within the context of the mass of variables as stated before. But it isn't anything simple. It is not like, oh, you are born and there is a stamp on your soul, and that is who and what you are because all of that is a mass of variables. Depending upon what happens where and when, and how you feel in that exact moment—in short, all kinds of other variables that occur for you within you and all around and about you—you might express this, that or the other.

You consider that the conditioning humans get as children is in the conscious part of the mind, is expressing consciously, then?

Not necessarily. The parents might just as well be affected by their soul's purpose. No, I don't think it is entirely conscious. Some of it is.

But what I am saying is, all the unconscious is not the soul. Some of the unconscious choices can be based on conditioning, right?

I would say that is more subconscious. But I don't want to get overly psychological here because there is not a direct correlation. We are just creating one for the moment in order to create definable dirt roads, if not paved ones.

The Traits of Personality Have to Do with Spirit and Soul

When the child is born, is this imprinted also into the child's DNA as far as what potentials will be allowed to express?

No. DNA has nothing to do with it. What I am saying is that even when you are able to understand DNA as far as you will ever be able to, you won't find the traits of personality in there. The traits of personality have to do with spirit and soul, which are real. It is not something that is defined by religion only. It is real. Religion is an attempt to understand it, but it is not creating it.

Let me ask this just a little differently, then. The soul has a definite purpose. It arrives on the Earth at a certain time. But doesn't it then program the DNA for its purposes, allowing certain traits to be there and making inactive certain other possibilities?

No. Given the variables, the soul functions as well as it can within the expression of the physical self that it becomes. One of the challenges of souls here—and it is set up by Creator that way—is that you accept the cards you are dealt (as people might say in contemporary society today) and you express that personality as best as possible given those cards. Given that, the soul is not programming the DNA, nor is the DNA programming the soul. They both have to learn how to get along together, and they do.

In this way, the soul at the very core of its physical being—since you are talking about DNA—must, as an absolute requirement, create. Creation is a requirement of all souls here. You must create. You must cooperate in the creation going on with you, and you must allow it. If you fight it, well, you are going to have a short life. Souls sometimes do fight it, and they have a short life. However, this is not the only reason souls have short lives; I don't want to leave that as a suggestion.

So you are saying that the souls who create the body have to create it with what's been dealt by the parents, then?

And Earth and Creator and everything else.

But still, I mean, one child is born with autism, one with Down's syndrome, and one is a brilliant chess player. That is part of the personality, isn't it? Or is that part of the challenges?

The expression of the personality. A child can be born without legs, okay, and another child can be born without legs. Do they have the same personality?

But does the soul choose that?

The soul can be open to that, but a soul doesn't say, "Okay, I want to be born with nine fingers and eleven toes." No.

But does it say, "I want to be born with Down's syndrome or autism"?

No, but the soul might in this case say, "I'd like to experience and learn more about _____." Since you have picked Down's syndrome, for example, Down's syndrome might be a way that creation says, "Uh, there is a way you can do that. Try that this time." You have to remember, a soul might not get what it wishes to get in that particular created life. The soul may not get it all in that one life. Maybe it will have Down's syndrome in one life; maybe it will have something else in another life. Maybe the soul will be perfectly healthy in another life, but it will be running through variations of life expression in order to get whatever it is the soul is in pursuit of. You don't necessarily get it in one roll of the dice—since I'm using gaming as an analogy today.

Many Teachings Are Prompted by the Desire to Create a Benevolent Human Society

Well, I used to think that humans had many lives on Earth, that they reincarnated frequently on Earth, but then Arcturis threw me sort of a curve ball a couple of years ago when he said that in the past 5,000 years no immortal personality has been born more than once.

That is right. It is not typical to have lives on Earth in any event, because the simple math of it is omni present, isn't it? Think of all of the uncountable numbers so high, places one might be born in this universe and the desire to learn this or that as a soul. Why would you be born on the same planet over and over again, really? [Laughs.] It is laughable.

But that was all part of the ancient teaching, the wheel of karma, that you were here until you perfected yourself.

I am not trying to put down a worthwhile teaching. You only have to understand, what was the reason behind that teaching? The reason was to create a more benevolent society. Those who believe in that teaching today—that is the motivation behind the creation of it. It was a beautiful creation; I am not putting it down. Many philosophies and analyses within philosophies are all prompted by the same desire: "How can we take this chaos that we are living in," (say, before that philosophy is present) "how can we take this unjust world and all of these struggles—how can we create a philosophy or even a religion by which people live on a day-to-day basis? How can we create it and encourage people to live more benevolently, to treat their fellow beings more benevolently and kindly? How can we do that?"

Well, that's a real good way, and there have been lots of others and there are still others coming up. They are coming, so to speak. There are lots of ways, but they are all motivated by the same reason. "How can we treat each other better? How can life be better? How can we get along together? How can we enjoy each other's company? How can we enjoy each other's cultures and so on? How can we be safe together and live happily?" That is what all that is about, and it is good.

So is the concept of reincarnation, then, true universally, that we reincarnate over and over all over creation but just not over and over on this planet?

Well, for starters, you are bumping up against time. Incarnation is true outside of the context of time, you see.

Right. We incarnate all over the universe.

No, you, no . . . okay, I'll allow that. [Chuckles.] You incarnate—meaning you focus your attention some place and you live there—but in the larger sense of yourself, you are everywhere at once.

Beyond the confines of Earth. Well, not consciously on Earth.

No, including that. There are portions of you now in some other part of the universe that are totally conscious of your Earth life.

Would they please step up and talk?

[Laughs.] Well said.

So let's explore this a little bit, because one of the esoteric principles of astrology is karma and reincarnation.

Yes, because contemporary astrology—meaning astrology for the past 5,000 or 6,000 years—is a figment of the global culture of the past 5,000 to 6,000 years. So you have to consider your history, what has occurred during that time, to the best of your ability to know that. Of course, since written documents haven't been around for too long, then a lot of history is just based on your best guess—with some scientific support and, of course, inspiration, which is what we are involved with now.

Well, if we do not reincarnate on Earth, then that teaching was just an attempt, as you said, to create order out of chaos?

To create benevolence, not order. It is very possible to create order that is not benevolent. It has been tried, and history is almost exclusively about that, to create a shove toward a desire that you live—as part of your daily life and, ideally, totally—benevolently for yourself and benevolently with others. Period. They are not bad, and they are also, for the most part, motivated through inspiration, which is the wellspring of Creator.

Past Lives Are Really a Means to Understanding One's Current Life

I think Arcturis said that seventeen people plus three more had actually reincarnated on this planet in the past 5,000 years.

Yes, but only for very pressing reasons.

So people who remember their past lives . . .

That has been taught. We've talked about it extensively. Those lives are in the soil. Those lives, if they existed . . . let's just say "if they existed" for the sake of simplicity, because a lot of those lives are based on others' inspiration, if you are going back a few thousand years. You might reasonably remember that you had that as a past life (and many people might remember that they had that as a past life). How is that even physically possible, ruling out the soul aspect?

Well, think of all of the cells, to say nothing of all of the atoms, of that person. It is all in the soil. It is all in the wind. It is all in the air. It is possible within that context, but if you are talking about 10,000 people were one being on a soul level, then maybe not. But then again, all souls are united, so why not? You understand, I am not here to fault other philosophies or means to understand creation, but I am here to remind you that it all stems from one desire.

What desire?

To get along with each other.

Okay. I know that some of this is reiteration, but I wanted it in this book.

Yes, that is good.

I appreciate the clarity and the answers to my questions.

I feel astrology has a really good potential—and you understand that there are different forms of astrology, but just astrology in general—of being a unifying source of interest all over the world. So this book can contribute to a greater understanding, not only by professional astrologers, but by those who are interested in it as a hobby, and I want to encourage that. I am not saying to replace your religion or philosophy or understanding of culture with it. I am saying, consider adding it to your overall body of individual, cultural knowledge: to understand who you are, where you are from, why you are here, what you are doing, where you are going, and what it all means.

So those who use astrology to find past lives, and those who experience past lives and facilitate past-life research, are they doing something cathartic for the discomfort on this planet? Is there some purpose for that?

Yes, I think their purpose is primarily based in a means to understand the conditions of one's current life. I am not creating an explanation here; this is well understood. Past-life regression is a valuable means of therapy to understand potential motivations that are under the layer of conscious awareness, so it can be highly useful. It is just important not to become attached to the individual personalities and to pursue them as if it was a matter of record. It is better to understand those individual personalities of the past as defined by the person working with you or, say, the therapist working with you on that, so that you can understand your current life and perhaps broaden your options to pursue, to create a more benevolent lifestyle. That is the purpose of it, as far as I can see.

But you are saying the person having that regression didn't really have that past life.

I am not saying that. What I said before wasn't strictly an illustrative point. If a being existed . . . and we know they do, eh? You exist, do you not? Are you alive? Answer.

[Chuckles.] Exuberantly so, today.

So how many atoms do you have in your body? How many cells? You understand, you don't have to answer that, but at some point, when you move on, that will be distributed for a time in the ground and eventually—or even perhaps sooner, not later—in the wind. You will become part of the soil, part of the Earth, and at some point perhaps part of the stone, the expression of Mother Earth's body. So it is possible to have a personal identification, because maybe one of the atoms in your body today was in somebody else's body in the past. As a matter of fact, I would find it highly unlikely if it wasn't.

You follow that thread back and it connects, because it is part of your currently expressed personality. What therapists do—the past-life therapist—is they take into account, not only your desires, but also your problems and your difficulties, and they follow those threads back to another life that had that in some way as well. You can understand your life on the basis of having another portion of life added, almost like a dotted line between those two lives.

You might conceivably go back farther and discover several lives, all having a certain sequence of events that correlate to your present life, and that is the whole point of it. It is not intended to show you how you got here. It is really intended—and the past-life therapist understands this—to offer alternatives and suggestions, something you can do that might be fulfilling and something you may not have to do because perhaps you have already done it. It is all intended to be incorporated in an overall therapy to improve the quality of your life. I do think there is relevance in therapy and counseling in general. I would like to see it included, because it does allow people to see a bigger picture. Nevertheless, it has taken awhile for it to come into contemporary therapy. I think it has relevance, though.

Mythology Is a Great Storehouse of Wisdom

There are other planets astrologers use, such as Chiron. There is a new one called Eris. Are there other planets who have personality characteristics that are part of us whom we haven't talked to yet?

Yes. If you wish to get some general ideas from your astrologer about Chiron and the others, it is possible to add those to the book, but I wouldn't go too much beyond that. Part of the reason, I think, is that Chiron is largely accepted by astrologers to be relevant—and the book is intended to appeal to as wide an audience as possible.

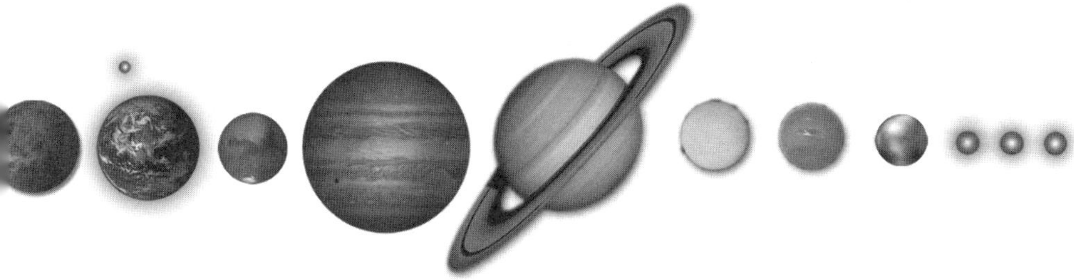

⛢ Uranus

URANUS

Accentuates Your Ability to Perceive on a Deeper Level—to Plumb the Depth of Your Capacities

May 26, 2007

Hello?

[Long pause.] Uranus.

Welcome!

Greetings. I am having to adjust my energy for the comfort of the channel, so wait, please. [Pause.] Very well, we can continue now.

I Bring with Me the Capability to Receive or to Absorb

What special qualities and gifts do you have that caused the Creator to invite you into this experiment?

I believe that the Creator of this universe requested my presence because I was able to absorb. You refer to absorption in the form of listening or taking in on your planet, where there are so many different songs and calls from different species as well as conversations and communications from different human beings, to say nothing of sounds the planet makes herself. I believe that Creator invited me in because of my ability to absorb—to take in, to receive, to be a witness, you might say—without adding anything of my own. This quality is something that I also have distributed throughout the other planets simply by my presence and the radiations from any planet that would naturally be environmentally ensconced within any solar system.

You often find that, regardless of what call or sound is being made, what words are being said, that ultimately what creates true communion, or at least communication, is someone being able to listen, to do more than hear—to listen and respond physically, or to have feelings that are attuned sufficiently so that the communicator's words (or call, or sound) have an effect that is not only based upon the sounds. Sometimes you, in conversation, may get a feeling about what somebody else is trying to say, though they might not have the right words to communicate their position or their desire.

Equally, in the animal world, sometimes one or more animals might be radiating a feeling, and other animals might respond simply on the basis of that feeling. Hunters in the animal world often focus on someone or something, either what they are hunting, or if they wish to be less visible, less apparent, they will sit near something and try to blend their energy with that so that their thoughts or feelings are not felt by the prey. In short, it is necessary to have the capability widespread, affecting all forms of life, to receive or to absorb. That is why I am here.

You have always been that way?

Yes, I am [chuckles] a good listener, eh? So in this situation where I must respond more, communicating to you in this way, it is a bit awkward. But I will do my best.

Ah! That is why you didn't volunteer before.

Yes.

Well, it is interesting, because traditional astrology calls you the one who stimulates newness and creativity and unusual, new things.

Well, this might be considered a new thing, then, eh? It's really so much the case that the ability to perceive is critical in your now time. On your planet, you have many different languages, and within those languages there are dialects, and even within those dialects there are nuances based upon an individual. An individual might speak the same line or phrase, and another individual might speak that same line or phrase, and it might have an entirely different meaning. There could be irony. There could be keywords. There could be meanings known only to the individuals of that group. In short, without people or beings there who understand the feelings the person is radiating or the desire to create communion, it is very easy to misunderstand.

In these times, so often even the people who are attempting to parley differences between one group or another will have misunderstandings, simply based upon their own knowledge and wisdom or simply because they do not have a clear understanding of the multiple meanings that a given word or phrase might have, and they don't factor for that. This is why there are more people now who are, as you say, waking up to your capabilities to understand communication beyond the words only.

There are youngsters who are being born now with those abilities, and those abilities are less likely to be grossly sublimated, as your cultures have generally discouraged such perception—not all cultures, but many in your time of the intellect. These youngsters are coming up now, becoming more communicative, "growing up," you say. As a result of more adults having this capability coming more to the fore in their consciousness, you will have many more individuals amongst you who would be considering that there may be more meaning to what was said—or more meaning to simple sounds filled with feeling, or more meaning to the unspoken—than was heretofore considered.

Ah, so your energy radiates that ability to perceive on a deeper level, then.

It helps to accentuate that quality, which you naturally all have as souls. But given the filtering that takes place because of the purpose of the human race on Earth at this time, you are expected to be able to plumb the depth of your capacities, even without much encouragement to do so and very often, in various cultures that are all over the planet, with no encouragement whatsoever, just based upon cultural differences.

So it is necessary now, given the mass of humanity and the many different desires of peoples across different cultural spectrums, that such energy—such capability, which you are really born with—be accentuated and brought to the fore so that you can have genuine communication, even in situations where peoples speak different languages or come from different cultures. One of the most critical problems that's not often recognized in your cultures is that people who speak the same language often mean things completely different when spoken, and sometimes this can lead to strife. Very often, after the fact, people realize that they were using the same words or the same general conceptual wordage but the meaning was vastly different. Given the urgent desire of individuals to communicate and to be understood in their communication, this has been creating problems.

Also, of course, many animal species are leaving the planet now. Some of them do not feel welcome or, in many cases, they are being eliminated unintentionally: such as with overfishing, for example, or fishing for a particular species, which may cause the death of other species, though not intentionally, just simply done without regard to the sanctity of life. This is not because the people fishing are evil, nothing like that, but because efficiency has been given more credit, for some reason or many reasons, than the honoring of all life forms.

Again, here you have a situation where life forms are attempting to communicate to human beings, but while there is no shared language, there are shared feelings. Many times, the hunter and the hunted feel a sense of shared feelings.

It is important, even if you are hunting or fishing, even if you are in battle, to pay attention to the feelings of those with whom you conflict. It may be that they are attempting to reach out to you, and it may be that opportunities for peace or harmony are being missed. Pay attention.

But you see an increasing tendency in humans to be aware of and accept and honor their feelings, so we are moving into this, right?

I am seeing this occurring. Not seeing it—I am *aware* of it occurring more frequently. But I am not saying that this is happening across the board on a percentage basis per individual; I am saying that this is happening with some individuals. Do you understand?

Yes. So can we look forward to that being more common in ten years, a hundred years or two hundred?

I think you can look forward to it becoming more prevalent, yes, but it often starts with the youth. It is, again, starting that way globally with youth. That is why it is important for you to be able to communicate. You have many tools like that now that allow it, that make global communication much more possible, at least if not perfectly, then in different forms.

My Tilt Absorbs Stresses on Your Planet Earth

You have an unusual angle, a tilt on your planet. It tilts at 98 degrees from the axis, which means that one pole is in darkness for twenty-eight years and then the other pole.

What this means is that when you consider the nature of my personality as I have described it, you might reasonably say that my personality is profoundly feminine, and that is true. That tilt in the axis simply has to do with my personality, and the axis tilt may be considered by those on your planet as something that is going to happen to all planets in this solar system, given a propensity for stresses in this solar system to reverse themselves. The stresses right now are overwhelming for your planet, and I have absorbed some of that so that your planet does not have to tilt over like that, you see?

When a planet is a bit overwhelmed, the tendency is for the planet to reverse poles. There has been a suggestion by some of your scientists and intellectuals that this pole reversal would take place without the planet actually moving, but the pole reversal takes place by the planet literally turning on its axis, you understand? If that happened to you now on your planet, there would be great suffering, loss of life. So given my nature to absorb, I have taken much of that, since my planet does not have life on it as you know it. I can tilt like that and cause no loss of life. If your planet were to tilt like that, there would be great suffering.

I remember in the seventies that this was the main topic of New Age conversation—that the planet was going to tilt on its axis.

Well, it is not entirely untrue, but that tilting will happen *very* gradually. It is possible that it will happen so gradually that the bulk of your population will be able to emigrate before that. You might say that many animal species and plant species are doing that now, leaving the planet and not just disappearing, you understand? So, given that, it might be possible that, considering the time involved, you will be able to emigrate. Of course, you won't go in vehicles—it would be too many vehicles—but you will develop a way or you will be assisted from populations from other planets.

So you see that in our future, then?

Well, it is necessary. Your planet has been injured, and when she is injured like that . . . she is such a vital planet, you understand? She always does what she must do to survive, which would be much more in electrical fields (thunderstorms), much more in earthquakes, fires, floods, volcanism—in short, things of life. When your athlete runs a mile, there is a tendency to breathe differently at the end of that mile, isn't there? One pants and sweats and all kinds of things. Your body leaps into a faster rhythm, and planets do that, too. When they leap into a faster rhythm, though, given the nature of all the beings living on their surface—and to some slight degree, under the surface—they are all affected, sometimes not in very pretty ways. So until you are able to emigrate en masse, including species of animals and plants who wish to emigrate, then for a time I will be able to absorb.

How amazing!

It is sufficiently complex that it was difficult for me to find the words to put it into. But as you know from the communion from other planets, it is important to make this understandable and not try to speak in other languages, eh? [Chuckles.]

Yes. Is anyone else in the solar system absorbing this? Are they all taking on a little piece or what?

They are all taking on bits, but because it is my entire focus, it may very well be one of the main reasons Creator has asked me to be this close in proximity to your peoples: kind of to back up Earth.

How does your planet tilting affect Earth?

I use the example of the runner, because the runner is doing something. The runner is doing something he or she wishes to do, let's say, as an athlete. So if the planet Earth must respond because she is injured, she is going to do something—she is going to create a motion. When she creates that motion, you see, she must breathe differently, so to speak, in comparison to the athlete; she must sweat differently. She must be different. She must become more vital. She must become more active in her respiration, in that sense.

That is where we get the typhoons and hurricanes and earthquakes and floods?
Yes, she is normally like that. That is part of her life cycle. She tries to keep those away from impacting human populations so much, but the more the human population grows, the more you are likely to be in a situation where you will be affected by that. You will be close to the shoreline or you will be on some island that might normally be receiving such a storm, but without a human population and without an animal population and plant population who can somewhat protect themselves or at least survive such a strike from a storm, then there is suffering.

I still want to learn about the tilt. Does that tilting away allow part of you to recover?
It is like a stress. If you put stress on something, it bends.

Ah, I see. Are the rings that you have there for a purpose?
They don't really affect my being. I think it is just the result of the concentration of gravitational forces there. If your planet had strong enough gravity, you would probably develop that, too. I think that with an observational platform far enough away—perhaps set up on another planet—you might be able to observe, in the case of Earth, a beginning of such a phenomenon for Earth. But, generally speaking, the more complex life forms there are on the surface and the more liquid water there is on the surface, the less likely one would have rings like that, because those kinds of rings often mean that the planet is reaching out beyond its own surface to accommodate life of various types.

From our perspective as planets, stone is life. After all, we are that. But given the nature, quality and variety—quality in terms of depth of capacities—that you find on Earth even now, and given the amount of water that you find on Earth, what you might find as rings of her materials associated with other planets are greatly expressed on Earth by water and wind cycles: rain, lightning, water vapor and so on.

All Universes Are Benign

You are considered the planet that is the ruler of Aquarius, which is the New Age. Everything changed. How does what you said tie into that?
You understand that I and the other planets, if I can speak for us all here, are not here to comment on your system of astrology. We are here to share our personalities so that astrologers can more easily interpret a broader range of characteristics and qualities associated with us. In the past, for astrologers—going back to the beginning of it to the degree I can perceive it, which is dimly—the system was given by stellar travelers to various tribes of peoples on the planet, and it has been reinforced over time with means not unlike the one we are employing now: various means of inspiration. But there has been much

lost, given the fact that many cultures did not have a written language and there was no means to pass on the material—or the means that existed disappeared for one reason or another, weather not being the least of them. So it is important to have these constant reminders of the personality of the planets so that astrologers can incorporate those concepts, rather than my commenting on your current understanding of the astronomy-based personality system.

Where were you before you came to this solar system?

I was in persona in another universe, as were many planetary personalities. But your Creator made the intention of this universe known, and several of us, while not removing our presence from other universes, were prepared to re-create a portion of our personal identity in order to participate in this universe.

So you are still there also?

Yes.

Does how you express here interact with or affect the you in the other universe?

It's exactly the same. When a personality goes anywhere, that personality does not change, especially if that personality is not here to learn anything. Your personalities appear to change because you give stress to different qualities of your personality at different times of your life, but the core of your personality does not change and is recognizable from life to life. This is how you might meet someone whom you know you have never met and you feel an instant friendship toward him or her. Or conversely, at times you take an instant dislike to somebody you have known or been in conflict with in a life before, and no amount of reason or logic helps you to understand why you don't like this person or why you like that person. In short, my personality has not changed. I am there as well as here.

How does what you are there . . . it is a benign universe, right?

All universes are benign. I realize that may sound strange, but you have to understand that your universe is benign. You can disregard a great deal of the tales that have been told to help you understand that what is going on in your part of the universe is something that is an anomaly. It is an anomaly that is allowed in this universe because your Creator is attempting to create something that is wholly unusual, meaning not in the norm for this universe.

Therefore, it is like a bubble that exists on your planet and to a limited extent beyond your planet in order to create a sense of continuity of understanding of your personalities as human beings so that you can understand your imbalance and create a desire toward your natural state of balance. In other words, Creator has put you into a situation where you feel uncomfortable to see how long it will take you to be comfortable, and you must do this on your own. Needless to say, only souls and personalities (interchangeable) who are reasonably advanced are allowed to participate in this.

I know it sounds like I am saying there is no suffering in your universe, but outside of the context of your existence and the means that is being used to help you to move and create a benevolent existence where there isn't one now, your universe is benign and benevolent, everywhere. But you are in school, and your school creates an artificial premise for you to solve, just as the teacher in one of your classrooms might go up to the blackboard and write a complicated mathematical problem and challenge the students to come up one after the other to propose their solution. It is not enough to sit at their desk and say, "Well, why don't you try this?" or "How about trying that?" They have to come up in front of the class and demonstrate their solution, even if it is wrong. They have to be prepared to be wrong. They have to be able to live with the possibility of being wrong and seeing the results of that wrongness. In short, it is a demanding test.

The test happens outside the boundaries of the actual universe, which is why the beings who have come from other planets to visit your planet must go through an extreme version of passage. They must come in highly shielded vehicles, and sometimes it takes them years—even as you would understand years to be—to get to their homes. They might have to go through a considerably longer process to get to the point where they actually can live in their homes with the other citizens. In short, it is a big, big deal, if I can use that term, and you don't get that many travelers. It is very much simpler for star travelers to go from one group of planets to another group of planets anyplace else in this universe.

Therefore, in order to come to your planet, there has to be a really very good reason. There has to be more than their own needs, more than their own desires and curiosity. It has to in some way bear to your advantage or bear to the advantage of populations on the Earth (not necessarily human) to come to this planet. Not much is allowed through as a result. In this way, Creator isolates you and the existence of you in this universe, through that . . . how can we say it? Like a skein, a web.

A veil.

Yes, a veil, a curtain. Then the universe is not affected by your existence. But because you have that separation from the universe and you can feel it, you have a drive to find the resolution so that you can rejoin the universe physically. That is why, even if you do nothing, even if you have no thoughts to do that—if you are asleep, if you are unconscious—the planets themselves, the portion of space, the living tissues of your own body, have a desire, a yearning that goes beyond any ability to control it by your souls, to rejoin that part of the natural universe. This is what causes the emotion toward that.

In order to do that, you have to desire it: to desire happiness, peace, compatibility, comfort, interchange with all life species as equals, which exists everywhere else in this universe. You are being tested to see: Can you create it? Can you create it as one group of peoples? Can you join with the other natural beings on your planet, all the different varieties of different life that are still in existence on your planet? Can you feel what they feel when they are at peace with their surroundings? If you can all feel that feeling at the same time, you will accelerate rapidly into that natural space of benevolence and join the rest of the universe. It is that simple.

For someone who doesn't speak much, you are pretty eloquent.

I am taking advantage of the opportunity.

[Laughs.] So what is your opinion of this experiment?

I can see that it has value. Creator is in a position where Creator desires to clone Itself, but rather than simply clone Itself, It desires to accumulate volunteering personalities from beyond this universe—which is where you all are from, because after all, this universe is fairly young, as universes go. Instead of cloning Himself, which He could easily do, Creator has decided that It would like to acculturate (you know, as one might acclimatize) these personalities to see if they can be a creator and be tested—go to school, as it were, creator school—and become a creator.

Of course, of all of the uncountable numbers of souls and personalities everywhere, only volunteers happen that way. Only volunteers who would be willing to go through the stress and strain in such a school, to say nothing of the struggle, are included. No one is included without their permission. Therefore, many have accomplished it. They are going through the school and are waiting to see who else will join. At some point, Creator will simply say, "Okay, that is it." She doesn't really talk that way, but I am putting it in your language: "Okay, that's it. That's enough that we need." And with a slight inclusion of Creator's infusion, a new creator will be born, and thus you will go on and do something else, eh?

But until that time, you will be given every opportunity to join the universe as benevolent beings through your own action. That is why you are surrounded with all these different forms, so that you can in peace connect with them in their peaceful feelings. Recognize that feeling within yourself: achieve it, grow it, spread it, speak of its value, if it feels to be of value to you. When you have decided that you will all do that in any given moment, suddenly in that moment—for it does not require a passage of time where you resolve this anomaly of space that is your school and rejoin the natural, benevolent universe—you will do it.

That sounds wonderful.

Elsewhere I Am More of a Star System

Now, how does this some of this apply to you? You have essentially cloned part of yourself from where you are permanently to be here?

I have re-created that. I am, what you would refer to in that other universe, more of a star system. So to simply be in this universe is not difficult, for here I am only as a planet and there I am a star system: many planets, many suns, many other that I really cannot describe, because there is no word for the feelings of it, no means to put it onto the printed page.

Are you saying that, in addition to the personalities of the planets and the suns in your galaxy, you are sort of an all-encompassed personality enclosing them, encompassing them?

Well, yes. All star systems are like that. In your own, even in where you are now, you are a portion of the personality of the star system in which you are engaged—a star system, I might add, that has an overall personality, even considering your isolation. Picture yourself like a patch, as it were—a transparent patch in your own star system—but you are associated with the general personality of your star system, which is loosely referred to in the rest of the universe as "the Seeker."

So there is a being out there I can talk to?

The personality would be loosely referred to as "the Seeker," because in that way, they don't call themselves "the Seeker," you understand. Yet that is the nature of their personality, and thus in your language they would be identified as "the Seeker."

[Laughs.] So I can ask to talk to that being. There is a being there?

Yes.

Oh, thank you. I didn't know that. So you are a huge star system. Does it have a theme?

You know very well what the theme is. Creator asked me to come because of my personality. What I am here, I am there. I refer to your personalities as having certain qualities and traits in your core, but they have to be in your core, because they are masked. You understand that the nature of the masking of your civilization on Earth is so that you cannot too easily solve the problem. But if one does not have to have that masking, one is what one is. That is why beyond the veils of living on the Earth—when your life comes to an end and you go beyond the veil and you are released from the masking—you can relax into your own native personality and then it is there. It is present. There is nothing masking it. You know it, it knows you, and all others can see you and feel you for who you are, and there is no disguise. You don't have to explain yourself; everyone understands you. I am there what I am here.

So would I choose to have a life in your star system to become more perceptive?

I think that you would not do that necessarily. You wouldn't have to go that far. Why would you have to do that? If you wanted to do that—you picked "perceptive" just as an example, I am assuming—if you wanted to become more perceptive, then your own personality . . . which is sufficiently perceptive I would say, but you are just not aware of it because of the masking. But if you wish to become more perceptive, you might go to someplace within this universe to become more perceptive.

Then why would a soul choose to have an incarnation in your star system?

For the same reason anyone would choose, because of any number of a myriad of desires, period. You wish to be in form, so you would have an ability, you would have a capacity to know where you might wish to be in form. You might simply wish to be in form where you have been in form with friends before—friends, family would come to bear there quite a bit, not because of obligations, but because of desire, happiness, because you wish to be with your friends. That is just one of a myriad of possibilities.

You wouldn't necessarily just go wherever you need to go in order to become more and greater and more wonderful, with more abilities [chuckles]. You have those abilities now; you are just not aware of them. You accept certain limits to come to this planet and participate in this experiment that Creator is involved in. You accept those limits for a duration, not forever. Then at some point you say, "Okay, enough of that." So your body returns to the Earth and you go on. You go on with your core personality and all those limits are gone. You are just not on Earth anymore.

So what about you, then? How are you able to absorb this discomfort when you are by your very nature so benevolent?

I do not absorb the discomfort; I absorb the stress. Stress where you are—using the term of "stress" in your common vernacular—would be in its nature uncomfortable, but look at stress in another way. Say you have a piece of wood, a branch growing on a tree. You might push on that branch, not for the purpose of breaking it or causing harm, but as the wind might push, touching the leaves, and it would bend. It would be that kind of stress: physical stress, not a discomforting stress. I absorb some of the physical stress upon Earth so that Earth herself can function. I realize this sounds like I don't care about you, but I am doing this for Earth as a planet. I am supporting Earth, the planet.

I understand. So does this cause any repercussion in your star system? Is there any feedback or anything? Or is it totally separate?

Completely. It's absolutely insulated. I might add that from what I have heard, so to speak—felt, been aware of—other creators made it very clear that in order to do what the Creator of this universe wishes to do, there would have to be considerably more insulation of this entire universe (even though it is only a very small portion, infinitesimal) that you occupy for this experiment to become a creator on your own capacities, for creator school to happen. Creator school, so to speak, happens normally in other ways, but this Creator [chuckles] of this universe has a reputation, you might say, of being a bit impatient. That is a kind of a joke that we like to kid with the Creator, but the Creator of this universe usually responds by saying that Creator perceives Itself not as being impatient but as being efficient.

Your Mask Both Demonstrates Your Experience and Protects You

[Laughs.] So it is my limited understanding that in order to come here, we have to assume the soul of the Creator like a glove. I have asked, but no one has told me yet, do we get to keep this experience, or will the Creator keep it? Does that relate to you also?

That is more than one question there.

Do you have to take on an aspect of this Creator, like something around you, to come here?

No.

No, okay. Well, then, it is not relevant. We do, right? Humans do.

At your core, no, but coming out from the core of your being—as if to compare to a solar system or an atomic structure—you might take that on as a temporary mask so that you can deal with the constructs of this universe. But given that you are immortal, that you have existed before this universe and, should this universe ever move on someplace else, you will exist after it—but outside of the context of time, at the very least you are immortal—your core personality is in no way affected by that mask. You are who you are and recognized, but when you are within the conceptual and the physical demonstration of the existence you are in now, you will take something on that will give you the capabilities to deal with what is here. This will also, at the same time, shield you from your full range of capacities and capabilities, because if you had those, you would instantaneously transform—not only for yourself, but for others, since your native core personality would not consider the suffering to be consistent with benevolence to all beings and you would, as an individual, instantaneously transform it.

Right, and then there would be no experiment and no awesome result when we succeed.

So there is another stress that exists within you. Almost all of you at one time or another—or at many times—feel a great sense of inner conflict. Even to do something simple like eat a steak or pull a vegetable up out of the ground for the purpose of consumption, there is a struggle within you to do that. It is seen most often in the very young—you know, when you are close to your core personality, without having donned many of the garments of personality that you will use to engage this temporary experience. So the inner conflicts that you will feel are almost always based upon your core personality's existence and the garments of personality that you don to function here.

See, there's always been this thing about what we are told, which to me is so conflicting. We are told that we are immortal, that we are these great vast beings, that we know as much as anybody we talk to through this channel—except when we are here. Yet we get this teaching that the soul is so innocent that we have to have all these guides and teachers, and the soul makes decisions and frequently makes bad decisions, and it doesn't feel discomfort—and it's learning and all that.

This is not in conflict when you consider it, because in order to function here, you see, you have to have that mask. A mask, you understand, is two ways. In this sense, it is not a mask to disguise you from others, but it is a mask to present you to others. It is a mask that forms into different shapes over time that demonstrate your experience—not only in your life here, but your experience in using the tools of life here. Others perceive you in that way, but at the same time you are not perceived by others as who you really are, so your native core personality is protected by the mask as well. So this is not in conflict, though it seems to be. How you can be these great and vast beings and yet need all these guides and teachers is the essence of your question.

Yes, absolutely.

You are being insulated and protected so that the core of your personality is not damaged in any way from your experience here. But at the same time, that insulation and protection goes both ways, so that what's being instructed for you is not your core personality. These guides and teachers are not instructing your core personality; they are instructing the mask. The tools that you use, the outer personality that you use in order to get along in this world—that's what we see as the instruction.

That is a part of Creator?

Well, in the larger sense, yes. That system wasn't invented by Creator, but that is the means by which Creator has chosen to protect you while at the same time giving you options and alternatives—in short, inspirations that you might get along in this world with the tools that are available to you beyond the kind of teaching you might get from other human beings who are experienced in this world. Sometimes you will need inspirations that have to do with your native personality, your core personality, which has to do with certain traits in your core personality.

Your basic personality traits are allowed to function in your outer personality that you use to deal with this world, but it is a one-way transmission. It comes out, but nothing goes in, so you are protected, you see. It is like a light bulb. The light bulb has a current that runs through it—the current in this case being your soul—and light emerges. The light radiates beyond the perimeters of yourself, beyond the perimeters of the bulb, but it does not absorb light that it might be exposed to.

Brilliant. Your clarity is so appreciated; you ought to talk more often.

[Chuckles.] It is my job to talk for this book, so enjoy it while you can.

[Laughs.] How do we as immortal personalities, then, keep the richness and the joy? I mean, there are difficulties and there are struggles and discomforts, but there is also a tremendous joy to being on Earth: the mountains, the air, the water, the flowers, the animals, the people. How do we take that with us? Does it all get absorbed into that piece of the Creator, that mask?

Oh, I think there is a misunderstanding here. The mask is not something that you necessarily cannot have access to. It is just that once you are in your core personality and no longer need to be insulated and protected—which as you now live, can only happen at the point of your death or before your life on Earth, or when you all choose to re-create, as I mentioned before, and you rejoin the universe in your natural states—you will be able to experience the memories, should you care to, of that benevolent experience that you refer to, the happiness of family and friends and beauty.

You will be able to do that, but it will be filtered through that skein that allows only that to come to you which is in complete balance and comfort with your core personality. But you are not going to experience the suffering, the pain, the wounding, the grief. You are not going to experience that, because that is a portion of the tools and abilities, the compassion and so on of this existence that Creator has created for you to learn, this school. But it doesn't go to you; that suffering does not go to you. You will not have access to it beyond here—nor will you need it, nor will you desire it. But you may simply have the lessons.

How can I describe this to you? You come here. You have all this capability, all of this vast wisdom. You don't *have* to learn what you are learning here. You are not learning anything in this creation that you don't already know. But given the mask, you have to remember, why are you here? You are not here to learn in creator school; you are here to volunteer for the experiment, which *may* result in some of you becoming a creator but does not require that all of you do that. No one is being drafted here. It is not like you come here and you flip your coin and you take your chances. It is not like that. You always have the capacity to participate beyond what occurs in this experiment or resume your life cycle wherever you are, as whoever you are.

But as the humans who choose to come together to become the new creator as one being, there will be some awareness of the experience, right?

Yes, there will be that recollection of the errors made.

How not to do it again.

Yes, exactly—how to do it, how not to do it. Yes, there will be that, because you will have lived through something that exposes you to a "do not do this again" lesson in no uncertain terms. You understand, away from this creator school, you know immediately if something is not for you because it doesn't feel good, all right? It is all about feelings. That is what balance is all about. If something doesn't feel good, you don't judge it, you don't say it is bad. You just are aware that it is not for you, and you turn and go some other direction, or you don't do that—or in short, you do what feels *good* to you because it is in balance with you. If something doesn't feel good to you and it is not in balance with you, it is not for you. It is very simple. You don't rationalize it; you don't reason it out in your mind. There is not analysis. You just do.

Other life forms living on your planet are like that also, given that they have to adapt to living in the circumstances of your planet. But the human being is here to participate in that creator school. The animals, the plants—they are not in creator school. They are here to help, to be available, to be at peace in various moments. So many of you may have seen, say, a snake or a spider—or a deer, or a bear, or an elephant, or a dolphin—at peace, relaxing, enjoying life as it were, maybe in some cases sunning themselves, just being, just existing. The feelings that they have in that moment, those feelings are the exact feelings you might have in your core personality at any given moment. In order to be at peace like that in your core personality, if you can share their feelings, if you can relax and just be relaxed with them in their feelings, you will feel a sense of native personality: your core personality and their core personality totally in being.

So this is often why spiritual teachers will go out into the woods or will go out to sea or something like that (paddle out to sea somehow), so that they can be at ease with life forms who are at ease with their own form. One does not always find that in the culture of human beings because you are in school, and the rules in school are completely different than they are in your natural life.

I understand. But they say we come here to learn. We come here to learn certain things, but we don't?

I am not saying; I can share only my perception. I do not claim to be a creator.

Use Astrology to Network

The whole purpose of astrology, I thought, was to set up certain scenarios so that while you participated in the experiment, you also got an accelerated learning on some issue or theme, like maybe patience or something.

You are really asking a question based upon the perception of a system, any system. You could ask a mechanic, "How does an internal combustion engine function? How does it deliver energy?" Do you understand? You are asking a question about a system that exists. But I'll give you this, okay? If you are asking, "How does the immortal personality acquire the experiences in life that can be analyzed through the tool of astrology?" then I would simply say, they don't take into account the tool of astrology at all, because you are looking at it from the wrong angle.

It is rather that the tool of astrology helps people who are functioning in life to understand how they might more easily function in life and to deal with what may come, and perhaps to bring about a more desired result for themselves and perhaps others. That is how it works; it is not the other way around. The soul doesn't make a choice on the basis of astrology. The soul makes a choice on the basis of the general personality desires of what it may wish to do in that life, which can then be assisted by studied individuals in this case having to do with the study of astronomy as applied to personality characteristics and, to a degree, predictability.

Predictability in this sense, however, is based upon the motion of planets. So if you didn't have the motion of planets, you wouldn't really be able to have predictability. The predictability is flawed, but it is intended to give you some sense of what you might encounter. It's more geared and structured to give you a greater sense of understanding of common traits of your personality that you might find with other people who are similar to you, who might also have common traits of personality, which might then automatically give you somebody you could talk to and say, "Well, this is how I solved this, but now I am facing this. What did you do to solve this?"

So you might talk to others who were born at the same date and time, roughly, as yourself. That would be a good way to network: "What did you do about this?" and then they say, "Oh, nothing, I haven't faced that before." Then they may ask you, "What did you do about this?" "Oh, this is what I did." And they might say, "Oh well, some of that might work for me, but then it doesn't fit because of this and this and this." In short, you might be able to give each other suggestions.

That isn't used as often as is desirable. People are seeking out astrologers to help them to understand themselves and their place in life and their possibilities and so on. But one of the things of astrology that isn't being used as much as it could be is to simply be able to network with other people who are in very close similarity with you, so you can develop sort of an encyclopedia of "how I did it because it works for me," based upon people with your similar personality traits. That's possible to develop in your time, much more so than it has been in the past because of information technology, and I would like to suggest that people get on with doing that.

Now, I know there are some projects involved here, but I think it could be done much more broadly and efficiently—not to create an absolute authority of how to do something, not to reject other approaches that might be done by people of other signs or birth dates, but rather to suggest that this solution might be in greater compatibility with you. If it worked well for this other person, though he or she might be completely different than you, living in a different culture, it might at least give you something that you might wish to try in some form. I am not saying it is something that you could set up. What I am saying is that astrologers might wish to, not do that exclusively, but help others to set up something like that.

Astrology Is Subject to the Individuals It's Trying to Help

I am still left with the question of how does one person being born in a certain place and who then moves on over the planet—where is that imprint on them that makes them susceptible to those energies and not to all the other energies being radiated at them?

Well, that is because you are still asking the question from the wrong perception. You are asking the question as if they were subject to astrology. They are not. Astrology is subject to the individuals it is attempting to help. That's the way to ask the question. Souls come here to experience something. Astrology was developed and passed on through inspiration, as mentioned before, to astrologers here so that they could help people to find themselves and to find the quality and the traits of life that they are achieving unconsciously, to help make that conscious.

Astrology is meant to help people. People do not seek out astrology. Astrology is something . . . picture a society, with people moving, families coming and going. Then take a grid, and the grid is called astrology. You can adjust that grid by placing it over the people, not binding them to it. It is purely transparent. They walk through it, they walk around it, but you can place it over them, like you might put a grid over an eyepiece looking at the sky so that you can understand, "Oh, there is the Pleiades. Oh, there is Orion." Do you understand?

This is a grid you might look at from a distance, not participating in the human race, and say, "Oh, there is somebody who is a Leo. There is somebody who is an Aquarius." You have to ask the question from that point. If you are asking, "How is it that people seek out experiences unconsciously that are associated with the astrological profile?"—they don't. The astrological profile is attempting to understand why people seek out such experiences, you see? That's where your question couldn't be answered, because it was the wrong perception.

As it was from the wrong end of the telescope.

Right, turn it around. I am going to have to finish up here, so let me say this: I salute you and your desire to support astrologers and the astrologic community. I am hopeful that the wisdom keepers of astrology will be able to assimilate this material in some way that will help them to have greater depth and to provide the skills and teachings to other astrologers that they might help people more. It is my intention and the intention of other planets to speak in this fashion so that your own personality characteristics and traits can be more easily understood through that system of astrology. With that salute and the doff of my non-planetary hat [chuckles], I will simply say good night. May you have the most benevolent lives in your experience, astrologically and otherwise.

You are wonderful! Thank you. Thank you very much. Good life.

URANUS • • **351**

Milky Way Galaxy

SEEKER— MILKY WAY GALAXY

Like You, Seeker Expands to Be in Contact with More

May 29, 200

This is Seeker.

Welcome!

Your Actual Intention Here Is Not Just Creation

To understand the term "seeker" in your language, you just need to know basically the definition, but in my case the definition would apply to the expansiveness. You can tell, basically by extrapolation—but to a degree from your national aeronautic space people—the shape of your galaxy. This shape in my case—adding to the definition of "seeker"—means "that which expands to be in contact with." So it is not so much about "looking for to find," but rather "to expand to be in contact with."

I will explain further. The space that is beyond this place in the galaxy—and which is about one-third as great as the space taken up by the galaxy—is the space I am attempting to contact. It has to do with the effect of the coordination allowing the purpose for your planet and you on the planet to fulfill your total intention here. The intention of the Explorer Race has been well explained in previous books, but your *total* intention here is not only to accomplish the purpose of the Explorer Race and to become a creator and all of that, but it is also to prepare you for the creation that you will begin from nothing, or as much as nothing exists as a concept in your own place of choosing.

When you do that, you will have to have all of the experience you are going to have in this universe, plus the motivation that you will have after you are replaced as the creator of this universe—and that motivation will simply be a feeling of being incomplete. That feeling is going to come about because you are going to be essentially inheriting a universe, but it will not be one of your own making. So it will be like you are going to be in a management position, but you are not going to be an entrepreneur, so to speak—though business has nothing to do with it, but I am using that as an analogy.

So your actual intention, then, is not just to create a universe. Before you came here to be a part of this universe, you didn't have that intention, but your actual intention when you came here was to be inspired to do something. Very often, travelers who keep on traveling are looking for the inspiration to do something, but if they don't get that inspiration, then they move on. That is your purpose here, to get that inspiration, and this you will complete and move on to the place where you will create your inspired universe.

Help me to understand the terms. When Uranus said a star system, I thought he meant this Sun and these local planets. Are you saying that you are the personality of what we call the Milky Way galaxy?

Yes. My primary location is at the center where the opening takes place—"opening," in this sense, meaning the creation level, motion outward and beginnings of. It is believed by Uranus and the other planets that a certain amount of connection to your galaxy would be helpful for astrologers: an overall acquaintanceship of the greater personality. I grant that I must speak in general terminology so that there is not a confusion applied to your particular solar system. Given that, I will tend to speak in generalities, because if I talk about things that are well past your solar system, it would be easy to apply that to your own astrology, and it doesn't exactly fit. So generalities will cover your participation in the solar system . . . pardon me, in this galaxy.

So just to make it clear, then: Uranus is in his universe also the personality of a galaxy?

No. Uranus is a planet in your solar system.

Yes.

Period.

Yes, but in his total beingness in another universe—he is something else, right?

Oh, I see—beyond, yes.

Yes. So is he a star system there or a galaxy? Those words get confused when we talk to beings from beyond the planet.

What do you mean by a "star system" and what do you mean by a "galaxy"?

A star system is this local system: one sun, ten, twelve planets, whatever. A galaxy is you, a Milky Way galaxy.

I cannot say what he is. You would have to ask him yourself. But it doesn't really make any difference, because the whole point of the book is about your solar system.

I Am a Portion of Creator

Are all of the personalities incarnating in this galaxy looking for something beyond—something more, something we call a seeker?

No. It is rather that everyone is open to that. That is all, but it doesn't mean that you are all seeking. However, you can see in the case of the Explorer Race, the people on the planet Earth, that seeking and exploring are certainly part of your personality. But I wouldn't say that the personalities of individuals, much less planets in the entire galaxy, are as involved in that concept as you all are. The reason you are so attracted to that concept, of course, is that you don't remember who you are for the most part, but that is changing gradually.

So how does it work? You staked out the real estate for this galaxy, and then you created the suns and the star systems?

You understand, that is four questions, and the first one is no. You want to ask them one at a time. It would be better, because you started out with a presumption that is false.

You are the personality of this galaxy. So what does that mean?

The presumption that was false was that I had staked out this space to build this galaxy. That is not true. The personalities that would be a greater portion of Creator—sort of a combined, collective personality—are feeling the space that is the most welcoming, not unlike the way a seed blown from a dandelion might find its welcome space to grow and thrive. It is the same way. The concepts that are at the smallest level (picking the dandelion as a good example) and at the largest level (universes, galaxies) are exactly the same. There is no difference. This is intended, because while the Creator of this universe does love variety, Creator is also fairly organized and is a believer in Its own concepts and carries them out repetitively because they have proven to be of value. So I, if I might say that about myself, felt most comfortable in the space in which the Milky Way galaxy, as it is charmingly called, is now in occupation. We can go from there now.

Thank you. So you felt comfortable here, and other beings came to create within this space, or you asked them to come? How did your galaxy get populated?

It is the same again as the dandelion, with the planets, with even the individuals. Think of the myriad places, beyond count, where you could be in this universe, and yet you are exactly where you are, and this is not an accident. There is no random. "Random," granted, is a word in your vocabulary, yes, but that is the extent of it. Random does not exist. Everything is specific and intentional, and while random might seem to exist, in the big picture, it doesn't. So I did not invite so much, but rather all that which is in its greatest compatibility and also feeling the most welcome arrived here, as with other galaxies. That would include the birth of any individual soul on any individual planet, not unlike your own, and a myriad of others. You would feel the most welcome here to do what you came to do, regardless of the way you arrived here.

Were you invited to come here by this Creator? Or are you a part of this Creator?

I'm a portion of the Creator.

What would be the next grouping beyond the galaxy? Would that be constellations? Or is that just something we have called them?

That is right. Let me put it like this: I consider Earth to be a portion of my being. I do not consider Earth to be something separate from me that just happens to be encompassed in me.

So the analogy would be that I am one being, but the cells of my "me," my body, while separate, are part of me—something like that?

Yes, very good.

I Don't Always Feel You

What percentage of time has the Explorer Race been here compared to the time that you have been here in this space?

Oh, a moment. [Pause.] Maybe one-millionth of a percentage is my best estimate.

If the Earth is part of you, do you feel the discomfort?

I am somewhat insulated from that. Creator has set this up—this whole concept of the Explorer Race and where you will explore until you are totally and completely remembering who you are—as something that is . . . how can we call it? It is not exactly an interloper, but imagine a cell. Imagine you were growing a sixth finger on your hand. You might see little stubs come along for a few generations, and then gradually something would evolve that would be a sixth finger. I am not saying this is happening, but suppose it were. It is like that. You are involved in this galaxy—not conceptually, but physically you are involved. Yet everywhere you go, everything you see, everything you do—in short, all that you experience on a sensory basis—is completely insulated and protected from everything else in the galaxy (and universe, for that matter). So while you are safe, you also are insulated and protected in such a way as everyone else is safe.

So given that, I do not always feel you. Other dimensions of Earth and the other places where you might go—say, the Moon and so on—I feel, but I do not feel where you are. Creator has created a veil, a series of veils and shields, so that I do not feel it. After all, if I did feel it, then everybody else would feel it too, and that is not good. You are here to learn something that you will share with others in the way that is most benevolent, but you are still learning it. Until you actually can put it into practice safely for all, then I must not feel it, because what I feel is available for all the beings on all the planets in myself to also feel. It is not something that everyone will feel, but it is available in the spectrum of feelings, you understand?

So what is your opinion of this? Were you asked permission before this experiment?

Keep in mind that I am a portion of Creator's personality, so permission was not necessary.

So do you have a good feeling about the project?

Yes, I do. I feel it is worth trying. There is no guarantee it will work, but it is looking pretty good in terms of being successful.

Well, it is pretty high stakes. If it is not successful, it's my understanding that the Creator has agreed to be discreated. This is like a high-stakes poker game, isn't it?

Well, it is not that high of a stake, even if one goes into retirement for a time. The universe is not simply going to disappear; someone else would take it over. Another creator would take it over and would alter everything so that everything is benevolent, and that would take a little time. Of course, most everything in this universe is benevolent, but just you and where you are and what you have influenced would have to be transformed. That would take a little time, but it would be done. It is not a disaster.

As you know, the Creator of this universe-to-be would essentially be asleep for a few, if I might coin the term, *universal years*. A "universal year" would be from the point of creation to the point of some radical change—meaning something major happening to that universe. It would be a single year in that sense, so beyond number in terms of years. Creator would be asleep for a few universal years. That is the worst that can happen to the Creator of this universe—it would be a long nap.

Well, we are going to make it.

Astrology Helps You Understand the Larger Concept of Yourselves

So astrology was given to the human population of the Explorer Race because we didn't know who we were, as sort of a guidance system?

That's right. It was given to you so that you would understand the larger concept of yourself—so that you would not only look to the Earth and to each other, but you would also, quite obviously, look up. You would see the stars. It was given to you so that you would not just wonder about the stars but recognize that you have a place in the stars and that the stars truly have a place in you. In this way, you are able to accommodate your total being beyond the planet, and of course, you are drawn there inexorably. You want to go and see. You want to explore, of course. So, yes, it was given as a means to help you find the greater you and to support your time of doing without such knowledge of yourself.

So astrology on other planets is available as guidance, but there it is just another tool?

It is not needed on other planets, because if you know who you are, you don't need to have a system to discover who you are.

Ah, excellent! I don't think I've ever gotten anybody to say that before.

Well, that is really the essence of all the systems given to people here. It's simple in that sense, because the core of astrology is not about what's going to happen in the future. The core is, "Who am I?" When that is not needed, then it is simply something that is used elsewhere.

That goes also for numerology and tarot?

That's right. All kinds of systems like that, including the I Ching and so on, are all based upon, "Who am I?" and thence, especially in the case of I Ching, "What might I expect as myself?"—because with the I Ching, one does have contact with something. The whole point is contact, and then you have a display afterward, not unlike with tarot, where you have contact with the cards. I might add that those who are very good at tarot might at times have the person they are reading for lay out cards. This is intended to create a personal contact.

You started out by saying that you had contact with a third of the galaxy and you were trying to reach out to the rest of it?

No. I said that I am attempting to expand this galaxy into a space beyond this galaxy that is about one-third as big as it. This helps you to feel a greater sense of who you are, while at the same time allowing those who have free passage and can travel in the galaxy a greater opportunity to travel, to do more, to be more, and to discover more. The desire to discover and travel is fairly consistent amongst all beings in this universe, but it is not necessarily something they wish to do. Very often it has been done in the past by some civilizations, but also very often there is a need to remain closer to home.

I am sorry, but I am somewhat constrained to talk too much, because I do not wish to speak of matters that are not of my personality, nor do I wish to speak of things that are of my personality that do not directly affect you. If I do that, then I just confuse the whole point of this astrology book, which is the personality of the planets. By the way, that is the title of the book: *Astrology: Planet Personalities and Signs Speak*. The fact that I am in there too is just a bonus.

[Laughs.]

But it is a small bonus, because my personality . . . you are getting maybe about one-third of 1 percent of it so that I do not confuse the astrologers.

Is it like you have a house and you buy some more land outside what you already have—not that you expand the house, right?

Exactly.

Okay. Well, I think it is a big bonus [chuckles]. I didn't consider that we would even be able to do this for this book.

You Only See About One-Quarter of Your Galaxy

You said that your energy is available, that it radiates. How do we use your energy on this planet?

You don't, because you are insulated and protected—meaning, you are veiled. You don't actually use the energy of the galaxy you are in. You see a version of the galaxy, but the version you see is within the context of the actual size of the universe. It is about one-quarter the size of everything. There is a distortion somewhat built in so that you cannot see everything—even if you had a telescope to see the end of the universe, for example, you couldn't—but you see in comparison to the size of everything else. This is what you see. You see something that is about one-quarter of the size of what it really is. In other words, the galaxy you are in now that you charmingly refer to as the Milky Way is about four times as big as you can see—and photograph, I might add.

The point of that is?

To make available to your ability to see only that which has the resistance to not take in your simple capacity to view it. Picture this: You are walking along on a country road, and you suddenly get the feeling that someone is looking at you. You are not uncomfortable with that because there are plenty of friends around there, but you are slightly uncomfortable because you don't know who it is—like that. So it has to be those who can accommodate being seen without being uncomfortable for being seen, which is roughly 25 percent. So you don't see it all.

Is the veil around the solar system or around the Earth?

The veil is around every place you can go to and see.

I thought we felt the energy from the other planets. Are we veiled from them as well?

Everything that you can see from a distance, even as a concept, you can think about, you can imagine, you can have feelings, so there is a veil there, too. What you see—you understand, not all of you see it, but some of you do—is then veiled and not entirely what is there. But as far as the true dense veil, the densest veil is around Earth and the Moon, only places you have actually put your feet on.

So when we see pictures of Mars, we are not seeing what Mars really is until we get there?

No. Double no. What you see is real for you, period. It is going to get too complicated. Let's not go there.

The question had to do with, if we are veiled and if astrology is feeling the energies of the planets—being stimulated by strength and by courage and by love—how do we feel them through the veil, then?

It is like this: You can see your fingers, yes? You can have a sense of the personality of yourself, yes? But are you familiar with the personalities of every single cell in your finger? Of course not. You don't need to be. It comes to that—you don't need to be. The planets have spoken and given you their personalities, and that is for the purpose of the astrologers, but it is not their job to reveal the secrets of the universe. Their job is to do as much as possible toward revealing their true personalities for the purpose of allowing astrologers to add that, to the best of their ability, to their astrological applications. But the planets—and myself, for that matter—do not feel an obligation to answer "keys of the universe" questions.

However, to give you the simple answer to what you are saying in terms of the veils: Everything that you can see, can do, and can sense, has a veil to some extent protecting the rest of the universe from your capability to touch or your capacity to sense. It is necessary. If you look through a telescope and can see Orion—the galaxy of Orion, eh?—you think about it. You make up stories about it; you have experience with it. If you are a reasonably receptive being on a planet in Orion, you are going to feel that.

So there has to be a veil, and you have to see only what is comfortable for Orion to allow you to see—which is, in the case of Orion, maybe ten percent. So you don't see it all, but when you get to the point where you are completely benevolent, then you will see it all and you will understand why you didn't see it all before. I will give you an example: You might have an adventurous personality as an individual. You might wish to ride on a roller coaster or walk across hot coals without getting burned. But you wouldn't expect a baby to do that, okay?

So how much of the energy of Venus and Mercury and Saturn and Uranus and Neptune are we actually feeling, then?

You are feeling all of it that is comfortable to you. Nothing has changed from what I have said. Nothing! Nothing has changed from everything you have heard before for the purpose of this book. Nothing has changed at all. You and I are off on this tangent at the moment, but everything I said doesn't change anything. We are just moving the veil up a bit more.

What would be more appropriate to talk about then for this book?

Well, you understand, I have already spoken it. My comments here are really somewhat superfluous for the purpose of the book.

But it adds incredible understanding to people who want to know how it works and who they are.

Yes, but it doesn't really apply to the book at all, other than the slightest explanation of who I am in my personal level. But the more we talk, especially with all these other things we have been saying for the past twenty to thirty minutes, we are just going to confuse astrologers. This may be of interest to you personally, but I don't see it as anything that is good for the book.

What would be good?

You can ask somebody else if you wish to consult somebody else. The whole value of the book, as I see it—which is an attempt to expand the capacity of how astrology is applied—is to get the personality of the planets. Physicality has everything to do with astrology. Astrology is, of course, based on astronomy, and astronomy is about the nature of the physical universe. Granted, in this case, the physical universe, as it was once described by astronomers from several hundred years ago, wasn't really allowing for the actual. You know this. So the best you can do with this book is to give astrologers the personality of the planets. That is the way I see it. But to provide answers of the universe and talk about Creator and all of that—I don't see the point. It just distances people. But I am not uncomfortable talking to you about it, if you wish to include it in some other tome, as Zoosh might say.

I have been getting a little talk in my ear here, so to speak, from Zoosh. He feels it is not appropriate for the book. He understands your desire to know more, but at the same time, I am only allowed to reveal the tiniest amount of my personality to you so that we do not wander far afield from the topic. You have to understand that my intimate knowledge—meaning contact with the Explorer Race on Earth—is greatly limited. I do not feel it, so how can I talk about it? I am insulated and protected from what is going on. I do not really see it.

Now, if you want to have a book someday of various galaxies where the galaxies speak, such as myself, then I can be more revealing. But I think we will have to get this book to the end, and then some other time we will do a book about the galaxies. Then I can be more forthcoming, but it can't be for the astrology book.

Everything Emerges from the Center of the Galaxy

What is the most enjoyable part about being the personality of a galaxy?

I believe the variety, because what emerges from the center is that which desires to express itself that has not been expressed in this galaxy. It may very well have been expressed in some other galaxy in this universe, but it hasn't been expressed within the context and the overall personality of this galaxy, and wishes to do so—not necessarily in this galaxy, but wishes to do so within the context of the personality somewhere and it just happens to be in this galaxy. So that emerges in the form of a sun or planets or both. Then souls who have interest in engaging with that, including their core personality and the planet's personality with its sun and so on, will choose to have that opportunity and will find themselves there on those planets.

You don't pick a life. When you are going to be born someplace, you don't say, "I want to live on Earth." You don't do that. You pick the circumstances you want to live, the general things you are trying to accomplish. I grant that the Explorer Race phenomenon is something different, so let's start over again. You don't pick Eefa in the Pleiades star system. You just essentially say, "I want to experience this and this in my life. I want to learn this and this." Then that is where you wind up, because that is the most likely place where you can experience those things. There is a tendency to believe that one chooses the planet you are going to be on. According to my understanding, this is not true.

You said "emergence from the center." Suns and planets come from the center of the galaxy?
Yes, of course, in the case of this galaxy. I am not saying that it is that way in every one, because I do not have personal experience with every galaxy.

Is that like a birth process?
In my case, it is.

Is that a white hole, and there is a black hole on the other side?
No—that is a mental concept.

It's a birth. Oh! We have something about that in the books about the center of creation. I didn't know it was in the center of every galaxy.
I didn't say it was. I can only speak for myself.

But it is here—how exciting! Are they born because they want to be, or because you want them or you call them, or what? How does that work?
As I stated, they have the desire to exist someplace that has a certain theme, which is the core of my personality. It could be called a theme, you know. Thus, they wind up here.

"They" are the planets or the people?
The planets. First the suns, then the planets and the people.

So they are preexisting, just like immortal personalities of people, and they can come here to have an incarnation—like that?
I don't see why not.

How incredible! That is really good stuff.

Teamwork Has Everything to Do with Astrology on Earth

So what would you like to say to the humans on Earth about astrology?
It has been your choice to experience your personality at such a level that you are constantly thrown back upon your own capacity to extrapolate, to the best of your ability, your functions, your capabilities and your traits. Astrology is meant to help you with all of that, and it is also meant to provide a means to give you some general idea of possibilities for the future. Never strain too

far, however, from those specific personality traits that are your strong suits and also traits that you may wish to develop and practice. Keep in mind that the reason you are here and the reason you are available to be here is that you have had, as your immortal spirit, a desire to discover more about living as a personal identity—a being, yes—that can function on its own somewhat autonomously. When you don't remember who you are, you have, at various times in your life, the necessity of functioning autonomously—meaning, if you don't remember who you are, then you don't know who to ask (meaning your teachers and so on).

These teachers and guides and spirits and deities you are in contact with at the deep sleep level and even to some extent at the light sleep level, most of you are not in contact with at the conscious level—though in other lifetimes, in places that are benign, where learning is not so much of a function of moment to moment but is spread out over a lifetime, there you can speak to your teachers and guides and angels and deities anytime, consciously. But here, where you are learning how to develop the capacity to function autonomously in a benevolent way, even in the face of things that are not benevolent you are choosing to challenge yourself to grow and to build on your desire to create. You are learning how to create almost in spite of some of your desires. Many of your desires come from a lack of knowing yourself and a lack of remembering who the souls and immortal spirits are around you. This is understandable. Everyone who experiences such a lack of knowing about oneself wanders around like that as well. You are here only for a short time, and in the overall encompassing of your being, it will still take quite awhile to incorporate it all after you have moved on from life on Earth.

Still, you have chosen to come so you can develop your capacity, not only to act spontaneously, but to act in such a way as you are able to utilize your strong suits—your strong traits, you understand—and to allow others who have strong suits, where in your case they are not so strong, to act as well. In short, you learn how to function in a team with everybody doing what they do well, and even though you might do to a degree something that other people do well, you learn quickly that in the team one does what one does well and lets others do what they do well. You are here on Earth to learn that. Be patient with yourself. Learn to do what comes naturally for you. Learn to function in the team. Teamwork and achievement through teamwork has everything to do with Earth and the astrological system. Good night.

Thank you, Seeker. Thank you very much.

Ancient Phoenician Ship

ASTROLOGICAL HISTORIAN

Focus on Family Relationships and
Early Identification of Children's Talents

May 31, 2007

Greetings.

Greetings.

The Origins of Astrology Were Derived on the Sea

The origins of astrology—not entirely that which was written down, but the origins—were derived on the sea. This is why Neptune knew about it, because of Neptune's traditional correlation to the sea. In ancient sailing times, sailors lived by understanding their ship's relationships to the stars. In the times of the Phoenicians and even before that, there was a great deal of understanding about one's correlation to the stars, not only for getting from place to place at night, but also—in this ancient culture that preceded the Phoenicians but was around that time—there was a relationship that people could feel between themselves and the planets by which they steered the ship.

On all ships in those days, there was the person who did nothing else but relate to the stars. They would sit in a special spot on the ship in most cultures, where they had a clear view of the sky—as long as it was not raining, of course. But when it was not raining, they would be drawing pictures of the sky. In the course of one of those times, this individual who was drawing pictures of the sky had with him two assistants. One was young, as one often finds in the case of a trainee, but the other was the wife who was an assistant as well. In this ancient culture, the wife had the capability to speak in a language she did not understand. The young one was not her son, but she was what you would call the aunt of that young one, you understand, the mother's sister.

She was the aunt, so there was a connection between all three of them. He was young enough so that he could understand by feeling the words she would get, and he was the first one who brought it to the attention of the star looker that the lady was speaking knowledge about the stars. The star looker was explaining the planets: this one is here, this one is there, and so on, essentially talking about things in the sky that you would see now, recognizable things in the sky. If you looked up in the sky now, you would see the Big Dipper and things like that, and such ideas existed in those times as well. They would look at the sky and see things that reminded them of day-to-day objects, or at least things that looked familiar.

So the youngster, who was about eight years old—not really a child in those times, but what might be considered a child in these times—said, "This is what she is saying," because the star looker would always be concerned for his wife when she would speak in this fashion. He was able to interpret it, so it was kind of a secret between them all, and he would put down the words on that drawing of the sky that described the basic natures of the planets. Since he could write well, this was something that survived him.

If you were to look at it, this correlation looked very much like a modern star chart, because it had to do with more than the planets in your own solar system. This makes sense, doesn't it, because we are talking about the stars that guide sailors. So this would be along the lines of stars beyond your solar system. Still, the basic foundations of your understanding that you were affected by planets, the stars and so on—that is when it came through. If I were to put a time on it, I am going to use the time of the Phoenician culture and say it was about 400 to 600 years before that culture really came to be known sufficiently so that they would be remembered in your now times. That is my marker, all right?

Now, I bring up that version of astrology because before that time there was a general consensus amongst people who studied the skies—there have always been people who did that—that people were affected by the stars. There was even quite a bit of belief, which could be loosely classified as religious belief, that would suggest that the stars had some nature of deity associated with them specifically. Some of that became something akin to a religion, but some of it also evolved into a descriptive system of human nature.

These kinds of studies in ancient times lasted because it was possible to note the position of the stars in the sky as soon as possible. If a child was born at night, someone in the culture would run outside and remember the basic position of certain stars in the sky. If a child was born in the daytime, one had to wait, yes, but someone would look that night. Over time, you would have to remember it, if you didn't have a means to write. But if you did have a means to write and keep a record—you know, initially you could do a stick in the dirt—you would make a picture and you would essentially draw the correlation of the stars to your position where you were on the Earth.

People did this without being trained. There was a belief, an understanding, that this meant something. Of course, people would draw, if possible—meaning if they could see it, it wasn't cloudy and so on—they would draw how much Moon there was and so on. After a time in a culture, one could begin to identify personalities associated with these pictures, at least on a general basis.

Inspiration Is the Means by Which People Live

The reason I am bringing this up right now is because the study of the sky and the study of stars and their correlation to personality, as well as to geography in the case of sailors, has been something that people on your planet have studied for a long time. Most of the core information associated with astrology that has survived into your times came through primarily from pictures associated with the night sky drawn by individuals and also what you simply might call channeling, or speaking with inspiration as it is sometimes referred to. This had to weather a certain amount of superstition, but because it is so well correlated, because it fits in from one culture to another—at least in the Western world and other places too—it has outlived many other cultures. Do you know there are some places and times—excuse me if I refer to a time as a place—where what you now call astrology was the way by which people lived, whereas in your time the way people live, aside from organized society, is through religion?

But religion is really another way to look at personality, just through a divined manner. Much of religion in your times as well has been delivered in its core material by someone speaking with inspiration. Inspiration is your primary connection to the soul of your being. Every individual has that capability and often experiences it in cultures that are still in existence on your planet.

Inspiration is the means by which people live. It is only in cultures that have authoritarianism at their root that inspirations like this are sometimes discouraged, but this is a phase that you are passing through and more than historians will note its failings. Popular culture will take note of it and there will be no way to stop that, because popular culture is something that always develops amongst the youth at first, and even when they grow and blend into the predominant culture where they are living, they do not let go entirely of that which they once believed when younger. This is how civilizations evolve, because they are always either driven, or pulled, toward the roots of the capacity to be inspired.

You are wondering who I am. I will say that I am the being with many voices who spoke to these human beings to guide them about the correlation between the Sun, the Moon, the stars and the planets that allowed them to make reasonably accurate predictions about what any individual may do, is capable of, and must watch out for. In this way, parents could intercede before a child went down a path that might be self-destructive. Or in other cases, parents could support a child when the child showed a natural interest in something that was not only benevolent for the child but might result in something good for the society, culture and family. In short, a great deal of astrology was initially applied to what the parents could do—not something that was intended for a select few, but rather something intended in the most beneficial way to the family.

Cultures that thrived on the outgrowth of the family—which is what people are, what they do, how they develop—have been the ones that have tended to prevail over time. Your culture at its root holds the family dear, and even though there has been a loss in direction of what to encourage a child to do and what to discourage a child to do (other than your moral principles, which have value as well), there is still the fact that your cultures, many of them, hold the family dear today. This will ultimately lead you to the place of inspiration, which will always connect you to knowledge about yourself that can be used for coming generations.

Historians Should have Cabinet Positions in Government

I do not have a name that is exclusive per se, but I am loosely referred to as "the historian." It is not my job to predict your history; it is my job, as any teacher might do, to help you to predict your own. Historians in your time are respected, but they do not have the appropriate position in government where they belong. Government is the best place for historians, if they are given authority—in your government, a cabinet position would be appropriate—because a good historian can predict vast amounts of guaranteed failure simply on the basis of the knowledge that is present in your time.

A good historian can predict what going down a specific path might result in, based upon the known history of your time. Motions toward something that only a well-versed historian would know about have been made that, of course, ended up the way they had ended up before. Historians worldwide have to have a sense of humor in order to survive those blunders on a governmental or even more local level, and many people can see mistakes like that coming as well. However, those in the political world are sometimes driven by other impulses, not the least of which is what the people clamor for, which is not always something that is the best.

So I am bringing up this rather broad brushstroke, as you like to say, so you can see that there is a cultural beginning associated with astrology. It is not simply something that has come about by bits and pieces accumulated over time. That is true, but there is a very personal nature to it, and the reason it has the potential of being so valuable in your time, as it has in other times, is its potential to support the family, the parents, the children, the grandparents and future generations by supporting children on the path that is best for them and suggesting that a path they are on might be better for someone else—not with authority, but as a suggestion. This is best done when youngsters are young enough to where they are suggestible [chuckles], because even though they might rebel a little bit or a lot, they will come back to their natural true path—the one that feels good to them—in their career, in their profession, in their hobbies, in their talents, or in their abilities.

Astrology is all about the family. It is for families. It is about relationships, of course—the relationships of the planets to each other, the stars to each other—and it is for the family and the family of human beings. If you look at it that way, you will see why it is a gift. It is not meant to be used aggressively against people; it is only meant to be used in ways that support and assist. Where astrology has gone wrong in the past is that it has been used to conduct wars, but like many other systems based upon inspiration—or in that sense based upon something associated with spirit—it will, to a degree, operate to protect. But it is offended when used to harm and therefore will work less and less until the practitioners are able to inform those they are advising (which takes courage, of course) or those who are advised do not trust it anymore.

This is why over the years astrology has gone through times of popularity and other times when it has been suppressed, because it has been misused. I am ruling out, of course, other philosophies or even religions that are suspicious of anything that is predictive in nature. In time, you will evolve toward a more benevolent society that is accepting of religions but discourages religions from promoting anything harmful or competitive. Competition has its value and it can be fun, but when it results in harm, that will someday soon be discouraged by global societies, which desire to promote a good life for all. This is the way of your universe and ultimately will become the way of Earth.

But astrology was here much earlier than just 600 years before the Phoenicians, wasn't it? It was in China and in India and some of the other civilizations even before India, wasn't it?

It goes way back, thousands and thousands of years, but then the Phoenicians go back a ways as well.

Astrology Needs to Focus on the Family

So what is the most important thing you think we've lost that maybe you could resurrect for us?

That is why I brought up the family. There is a tendency in your time to think of astrology at the very least as something that is a fringe belief, but it is not. If it were a fringe belief, it would not be possible to trace it back so far. Astrology is all about the family. That's the most important thing that has been lost, either because of certain elements being used, as they say, for battle, or that the astrologers would discourage talk about the correlation of one family member to another. But any well-studied astrologer will, when requested, be able to do this with a certain amount of accuracy, even given the level—meaning the available information—that is available to them or their capacity to consult with others or even to use your reference and knowledge sources of the time.

I feel that for astrology to be more universally accepted, it is important to focus on the family: the relationships of the children, astrologically, to the parents, as well as the parents to the children, and the grandparents and all of this. This way there is an honoring of the talents and abilities, as well as the potential talents and abilities, of each to the other. Don't turn it into a religion with authoritarian aspects. Don't force people to *be* their sign—because, after all, people can be more than that. But do use it as a guideline so that you can find out why you like this person and not that person so much, and the correlation between the lessons of one's sign and the abilities of another sign and so on. Most of this has already been done. It is available. Astrologers who study different fields know this; it is not unknown.

That's where to go with astrology, because that is what can do the most good for you now. There is a tendency now to look at astrology from an individual point of view, but the best way to use it, I feel, in your time, where it is not being used—I am not saying don't use it the other ways; I am saying, where it is not being used so much—is in the family. That is what I recommend.

So you would cast the charts for the people in a family and then compare them?

Any astrologer would suggest that. In the case of the parents with young children, if you know the sign of your child . . . and nowadays it's pretty accurate what time the child is born, though with the doctors or nurses or midwife, you don't always get it to the second because you are allowing for when the child first appears or when the child is entirely out of mother. It depends on the system used, but you have a pretty good idea. Given that, it is possible, you see, to actually encourage the parents to treat a child this way, not that way, and so on. It is also helpful to the parents to know what to look for. Of course, there is something referred to as karmic astrology, which might also give the parents a means to know what to watch for: stumbling blocks or hazards, or simply lessons.

Astrology has a great deal to offer, but right now it is considered somewhat esoteric. But if you take the bulk of what astrology has to offer now and apply it to family relationships, I feel it would fit right in to your culture. It is something that is not a science, but it uses some scientific principles. I feel that in your time science has been blown out of proportion in its importance to your society, because your societies—in the Western world especially—equate objects as being more important or often equally important with people. So it is not surprising that science is so important. Science has great value, but it doesn't always offer the best things to believe in.

I Have Always Been Attracted to Developing Cultures

Can you say a little bit about yourself?

I have always been attracted to working with developing cultures. That is my key attraction. I have been in existence before this universe, but when I heard that this universe existed and that the Creator of this universe was greatly intrigued by the idea of growth and change, I knew I would find cultures here that were developing. That is why I came here, and I have been here for some time. For this Creator of this universe, you see, has or had other cultures that were growing and changing in the past, and I was encouraged by this Creator's representatives to work to develop cultural and moral principles that would benefit that culture and that culture's relationships to other cultures—which on the broader scale beyond your now planet would have to do with relationships, usually to peoples of other planets. This is my interest, and of course, then you can see why I am where you are.

You worked with many cultures on this planet before the Explorer Race?

I am referring to planets beyond this planet. I became interested in this planet when the culture before the human being was moving on to its next place, because one notes that there is a major change. They did not need help because they had developed a very refined culture. But I was able to note that they are moving on, they are making room for somebody, eh? That is when I started to hear about who you were going to become on this planet. I was speaking to animal spirits about these things, for they were beginning to populate the Earth in much greater numbers than the previous culture really needed in terms of variety and teachings, because the previous culture was entirely in sympathetic vibration with the plants and animals, and therefore could know and understand everything they had to offer to beings unlike themselves—unlike the animals, unlike the plants, but nourished by the same energies.

In the case of your culture, you are also unlike the animals and unlike the plants, and even though you are nourished by the same energies, you are not aware of that. The previous culture was, and because you are not aware of that, the growth curve and the developmental aspects of your culture are much greater and have taken more time. Of course, there have been repetitive errors made largely due to groups, even as small as simply familial groups—meaning in repetitious stages in a family, to say nothing of larger societies making the same mistakes over and over. It was obvious you needed some kind of system by which you could avoid those mistakes if possible.

In the previous culture that left, was there an insulating veil around the planet?

No, there was no need because it was completely compatible with the star visitors and so on, so no one needed to be protected. People from other planets came and went freely. That is why, even in your times, evidence can be found, the anomaly of something dug up. Or just in the process of digging, something is found fifty or one hundred feet underground that doesn't make sense in terms of the time period of the area surrounding the find. Why is it there? That is because in previous times these objects were dropped or left by fairly advanced cultures.

Where did the previous civilization go?

For the most part, they simply are still in existence in another version of this planet, but you do not see them, most of you. You do not notice them, most of you. But some of you are developing the ability to see that which is present but not interacting to any great degree with your cultures or your physicality. They are more available for access, but you have to remember who and what they are. They are cultures that are in sympathetic vibration with the animals and the plants. They know what the animals and the plants know. They know what Earth knows. Granted, they don't carry it around in their minds all the time, but they know it when they need to know it, and the planet you are on has that capability. Since you are made up of that planet, you then have that potential. That is why very often that previous culture will act as a guide to an individual.

You all have guides, everyone. You don't always hear them; you aren't always encouraged to. The guides are usually connected to your teachers and others, and can pass on information, knowledge, wisdom—in short, encouragement, suggestions—that connect you when you are conscious to your best path, what is best for you. It is not unusual. I would say one-sixth of the time every individual on this planet has at least one guide associated with that other culture—one-sixth of the time of your life. Sometimes there is more connection, sometimes less, but for every individual, one-sixth of your lifetime you will have a guide from that culture.

Are they in a focus that we will go to when we expand and awaken?
    This is not clear yet. Maybe.

Is there some name or mythology or old history that we would know them by or through which they left stories about themselves?
    Generally speaking, throughout languages, they are often referred to as the ancients. As the result of that terminology, however, there has been some confusion with them and other cultures.

Yes, there have been so many on this planet.
    Yes.

Astrology Must Have Heart

So the woman on the sailing ship who talked in another language—who was she receiving this information from?
    She was receiving it from me, but she was not able to get that inspiration in her own language. She was only able to get it in a culture that preceded hers by a few hundred years. This was a problem, but apparently she had planned before her life to have that interpreter in the form of the youngster, and when that took place, she was understood and valued and appreciated more—not just tolerated for her unusual personality, but understood, valued and appreciated more.

So is most of what we know now on the planet about astrology traced to her or to prior to her?
    Not most, but they were the first ones who were able to make a record of it in writing that could be shared with others. This took place on a ship, and the ship went from place to place. In those days, there was a great deal of sharing of star knowledge from one ship to another ship, regardless of culture, because if you had pictures and you had symbols, aside from your capability to speak through interpreters, you could provide that for others. You would draw pictures and help correlate. In short, it was spread through the value and capability of seamanship. The star lookers were considered part of seamanship.

Every ship, you say, had one, right?
    Every ship that traveled at night or traveled beyond the point of being able to see land had to have one, or they most often didn't come back.

So you were the one who gave them the information, and the information had been on the planet before but it had been lost until that time because it hadn't been written down?
    Well, yes, it had been available throughout time, but records do not always last, even if they are written down, and the people need to be reminded. Even in your now time, I am helping astrologers who are availing themselves of this

method to speak with inspiration, to understand nuances that they, because of their capabilities of study, are able to receive.

So it is constantly being added to, then.

But you understand, a lot of what is available are aspects associated with the family, and sometimes, even in your time, governments or other research groups are interested in relationships that are external to the family—meaning having no direct benefit to society or to the family. As a result, sometimes there is a great deal of research and encouragement of development of astrology in fields that are not always beneficial. This kind of knowledge is not necessarily the best way to pursue astrology. To perform at its best, astrology must have heart, and the heart of your culture is in love and the family.

Are there things you would like to add to this book that have been lost, that haven't been found yet—information about different planets, influences or maybe planets we don't know about?

You see, so much is known about astrology; entire libraries could be filled with what is known that is in print now. I am trying to direct astrologers. I am talking with you and to astrologers themselves toward correlating what is known about the family, because that foundation will tend to perpetuate the best of astrology. Make sure that love and the family have everything to do with astrology, because that is what will last and be appreciated, be applied, and be discovered how valuable it is.

Almost all else in astrology, while of interest, is a pathway of exploration that may lead to pitfalls. I am not saying it is bad; I am saying it is much more likely to lead to a pitfall for astrology. So put the focus of astrology on family, family relationships and what a child might expect—and of course, when children grow up, what you might expect and so on. Put it into the family and love, and astrology will outlive you all. That is the main thing I want to say, which is why I am being so redundant.

Well, I appreciate you showing up. I didn't know you existed, so I couldn't have asked for you.

I felt it was important to say this at the end of the book, because this book is really aimed toward astrologers. Others will read it and be interested, for in your time there is a lot of interest in this subject, but ultimately it will be aimed at astrologers to get the most they can out of it and to add to the body of knowledge. That is the intention, because many times astrologers, even after a lifetime of study of their subject, have to use their own inspiration in order to make their best guess. Those who come to astrologers will always want to know, "What is the potential here? What might we expect?" As long as the astrologer makes it clear that this is information based upon knowledge and study and differentiates it from the astrologer's best guess and it is written that way—meaning astrologers' inspiration or feeling based upon the love of their occupation and their desire to help the people who come—then astrology will continue to offer its wisdom and value.

Do you feel that the Earth will have something to contribute to this book?

Yes, I do. It might take more than one session, because Earth herself may desire to speak to many aspects, but that is up to her (I know you like to refer to her as a "her"). She may wish to be brief, or she may wish to be more expansive. We'll see. But I think it will need to be done when you are both fresh. This is probably not a good day to begin with Earth.

Hopefully, we are coming to the end of the Explorer Race experiment, so then what are your plans? Will you find another developing culture? Will you stay with the Earth and the beings from that planet in Sirius who are coming up behind us? Do you have any plans?

No, I will probably go elsewhere. The culture that follows you will probably for quite a while need something more . . .

Simple.

Simple, exactly—not complex, but a lot of love and so on. I will go elsewhere and return only if I feel the need from the people.

Astrology Allows You to Correlate Your Lives Beyond This Planet

So is astrology used in other places, or do you do other things with cultures besides this? Was astrology something you just developed because we don't know who we are?

Yes, you needed something by which you could correlate your own lives specifically beyond this planet. There have been a lot of studies of how you relate to the planet, but there needed to be something that would allow you to take note of the most profound feature and features of one-half of your lifetime. For one-half of your lifetime, it is nighttime, and when it is nighttime, you look up and the light of the night also lights your way in the dark, so you are drawn to that. In order to develop your citizenship beyond this planet, you needed to feel a connection to the stars and planets, and therefore, if you understand the influences of these immortal personalities upon your own, you might feel more looked after, more loved, and you might feel it with an ability to engage your senses as well as your thought. You see the stars and the planets. You know they are there.

You chose to tell people about these influences, but these influences had been there long before you chose to start telling humans about them, right?

I told the humans about them through the means that I do, because you didn't know. You needed various systems by which you could find your way and not just everybody having to stumble on their way from this place to that place. There needed to be methods by which you could survive and thrive, aside from obviously learning what to eat, what to drink, how to live, how to survive. There are other things that are vital as well.

The other systems that are allied with astrology, like tarot and numerology, did you talk about those, too? Or did other beings bring those through channeling, through inspiration to humans?

I contributed to those, but other beings were specifically involved with that as well, so that could be a separate volume. But I made some contributions.

Signs Are Based on More Than One Thing

We have talked to the planets and have their personalities in this book. When we attempt to talk to the signs, will they be like abstract concepts?

Signs are based upon more than one thing. When you talk to the planets, you are talking about someone specific, so to speak. But if you are talking to, say, a specific sign—Aquarius, for example—we are not talking about one star here. We are talking about multiple stars with millions of planets, so it becomes very complex.

It is not the purpose of this book to simply add to the vast knowledge about astrology but to redirect interest on a more personal level toward personalities that can be integrated and incorporated into the astrological understanding on a practical level. You see, the system, the way it is set up for this book, is to understand the personalities of individual space bodies (planets) upon your own individual being, as well as the being in small groups, as in the family. There is very little knowledge about the personality of the planets—and your Sun and Moon, of course—that directly impact you. There was some flirtation with the moons of other planets, but most of those moons do not directly impact you, you see. But your own Moon does, so you have heard from there.

This book will be valuable because it focuses attention on an aspect of astrology that is somewhat overlooked. Yet many astrologers are very fascinated with and drawn to the personality of the planets, and this whole idea of the personality of the planets has been explored. We are just attempting through this book to offer much more material to flesh out the picture of the personalities, so to speak.

Children Are Being Born Under the Thirteenth Sign

There wasn't a lot said about the thirteenth sign. Is it the combination of the other twelve in one person?

Yes.

Are there people being born now who are of that sign?

Those people are being born now, but they are very young. Certain personality characteristics will be noted about them, but sometimes these individuals have shown up before and have been somewhat misunderstood. Still, they are being born with more frequency now, and several personality traits will be noticeable.

One, they will have a certain chameleon-like capacity—meaning not that they would purposely disguise themselves, but that they will be able to get along with all the other signs completely compatibly. You know, there are these correlations in astrology: "This sign can get along with that sign very well," and so on. Those of the thirteenth sign would be able to get along with everyone. You do find that in some cases in astrology now, but they would not only be able to get along with everyone sometimes, they would be able to get along with everyone all the time.

They would also be able to demonstrate traits of all the signs, meaning that they would also, of course, be able to draw from the talents of all those signs. They would need, however, a certain amount of direction, because all those signs also have certain pitfalls and they might have those pitfalls as well, but not to as great a degree since they are not entirely focused in one sign. So they would need a certain amount of protection and insulation in the tender years of their life—say, before eight. So that might be helpful.

I am trying to give you personality traits, because quite obviously, when they are born, they would seem to be this or that sign, based upon their time of birth and so on. Very often, though, their time of birth will be around midnight. That is important to know for an astrologer. It might not be exactly midnight, but it will be around midnight on whatever day they are born. They won't necessarily be born on the cusp, so don't use that as a means to know. But for children born around midnight in general, just a few minutes either way—by a "few minutes," I mean no more than five minutes either way before or after midnight—then you would generally want to take a look at that.

If you are working with the family and have the chance to meet the youngster when he or she is three or four years old or something like that and is quite open, be friendly. Know how to talk to a child—astrologers, this is essential for you—and see if you can make your best guess. You will have to be around the child and also see how the child interacts in his or her family situation. You won't be able to pick up that this is a child like that immediately; it will require a certain amount of observation, even if you have all of your inspiration capabilities readily available. It will take time and observation, but that is all right. You would have those first eight years in which the child might be a bit more insulated, but there are a lot of children who are more insulated during those first eight years. There won't be any more boys or girls; it will be equally distributed.

They will not have some problems that other children might encounter. For one, they will generally have a capability to pick up languages or accents, even though they may or may not study them very much. If they study them, they will be able to pick them up pretty quickly. They are likely to be more tactile, want to touch things, understand things on the basis of pictures just as well as ideas, sometimes with a balance leaning more toward pictures. This also has to do with a universal language: pictures, in that sense, go beyond any language. Those are some traits.

So their potential is anything they choose?

No. Well, of course, that is abstractly a potential. Their potential will be largely based upon what they feel is needed. If they are in a family, they will gravitate toward what's needed in that family. In their culture, if they feel something is needed, they will gravitate toward that.

But not permanently? Will they flow from one thing to another?

Not necessarily, though it's possible. If there is something needed in the family or in the larger group—say, the church or the small town—they will gravitate toward that. If someone else comes along who can fill that position better, they might feel free to move on to something else. But if they don't and that doesn't happen, they might remain in that position. Nevertheless, they will always be attracted to working out problems between individuals who do not have an obvious means of direct communication. They will feel an affinity to animals, and animals will like them. Although they may not all be good gardeners, plants will tend to be more full of life around them.

It sounds like they could be excellent negotiators and diplomats.

Yes, something that your cultures often need, to say nothing of the family and the extended family, eh?

Certain Qualities Are Required to Be on Earth

Now, let me ask you this: That means thirteen personality types on the planet, and somebody said that there are . . . is it 252? There were so many more personality types in the rest of creation. Can you say something about that? In other words, if we incarnate on other planets, we have many more types to choose from, right?

Let's just say this: There is a certain quality that is required if you are going to be on Earth. For one thing, your personality type has to be comfortable with being curious. Not all personality types are like that.

I know. I have talked to some of them who are not curious in the course of these books.

Yes, and you have to have other qualities. The joy of discovery is a cousin of being curious. You have to desire a certain amount of socialization or greater or less than, but you have to have that as a desire. You have to be reasonably comfortable with ignorance.

Just think of the general qualities on your planet; I have only named a few. There are a great many personality types that do not have any identification with the basic fundamental existence of people on your planet. Here is one that is profound that you can all identify with: some personality types aren't interested in eating or drinking, meaning that this wouldn't be necessary where they would choose to be born or where they would choose to exist, if you prefer. So there would have to be personality types that could get along and at least survive, to say nothing of thriving on your planet as it is. There are not that many personality types that would have all of those basic qualities. Thus, the ones you have are the ones that do have all of those qualities, and that is why there are so few in comparison to the many. But those few are sufficient in order to accomplish Creator's purpose apparently—I do not claim to be a creator.

Birth Astrology Applies to Walk-Ins

I would like to consider one other topic before we are done. There are so many walk-ins on the planet and many more to come. Astrology, for walk-ins, stays mostly with the astrology of the soul who built the body, right?

Let's not say the soul who *built* the body. Let's say the soul whose intentions *inspired* the form of the body. Generally speaking (and I am not just splitting a hair here), the fundamentals of how the body looks, unless there are obvious anomalies—say, nine fingers instead of ten, for example—the body is meant to be in a certain way, the way most people look, all right? Other than that, there may not be that much influence, physically speaking, of the individual soul on the physical body, which is why souls might tend to come and go.

A soul that is going to be in the body on a full-time basis, while the child is growing in mother, the soul might not always be there—"soul" in that sense also being the personality, or what's sometimes called the immortal personality. It might tend to come and go. When they are there more often, then they tend to get more active, as all mothers know, moving one's arms and legs. Then when they do occupy the body, there is some adaptation by the body to that soul, but it is more the other way. The soul has to adapt to the body and to the physical world that body and soul are in. The whole purpose of this is so that the soul learns to adapt and acquire the various interactions of the lessons that it desires to learn or study in Earth life.

So when a walk-in takes place and that soul exits without a physical death, that walk-in will simply inherit a body that has not been programmed by the soul. Rather, that soul had to utilize the body to acquire its lessons and had to accept the body "as is" to do that—the original soul. If there is a walk-in, the walk-in has to do the same thing. Walk-ins have to accept the body "as is" and then interact, study their lessons, and so on, based upon what is found. So the system is almost identical in terms of acquisition of one's experiences as for the original soul in form.

So does there come a point if the walk-in is in the body long enough that the date it came in has any relevance?

I would say that if you can tell when you came in—it is very difficult if there is no cognizance of the walk-in experience, but if you can tell within a day or even two or three days—just make a note of it. The chances of your being able to get the exact time are unlikely, but if it were possible or if in some time it is possible, then write that down, and it can be considered by a good astrologer the way the rising sign might be considered or the Moon. It doesn't replace them, but it is considered a quality with those signs—as compared to, say, the Sun sign. But if it is not known, then one accepts, wholly and completely, the astrology from the point of physical birth.

Yes. Well, most people don't ever know. Is there anything that astrologers should look for, or is it irrelevant? Should astrologers be concerned about whether the person before them is a walk-in or not?

I wouldn't say so, unless the person brings up the subject on his or her own: "What about walk-ins? Could I be a walk-in?" Then astrologers, if the personality of the person is known . . . they might have accumulated enough information about walk-ins by that time—meaning not now, but by their time—to be able to make the best guess utilizing their inspiration, But if they are not able to get it on the basis of their information and what they have been able to observe on the basis of simply talking to the person over time, then I would say for astrologers that it would be best to put that aside.

Generally speaking for the walk-in, though, you would use the astrology based upon the physical birth of your body, because as I say, both souls—the original and then the walk-in, should that occur—have to accept the physical body "as is." So that is the same for both souls, you see.

That's a whole new fact. I always thought and according to what I've read in conventional New Age stuff, the soul created the body in a way that would be best for what it wanted to do in its life.

Well, this is possible, if the physical body has any specific identifiable anomalies such as, say for instance, a condition that one might be born with. As I say, some unusual body thing, a handicap, or maybe something just the opposite. Maybe the body is born with a tremendous capacity for understanding the relationship of one thing to another, as in a high IQ, for example (which is not the best method of understanding mental capacity, but is something you perhaps still use). Or the person might have physical capabilities, being born stronger than other youngsters as they develop, or may even have other talents and abilities physically that are not readily apparent on an examination of the baby. In short, one might be born with capabilities that are extended, as well as difficulties or challenges that may be known or are observable.

In that case, the soul must adapt. The original soul must adapt to that body, even though it may be something associated with that soul's desire to learn something or develop compassion, for example, just as one possibility. The walk-in must accept that body "as is" but must also have desires or lessons or something they are here to study or learn that is in correlation to that physical body. This means that both souls—in the case of the original and the walk-in—must have certain similarities in their intention for their physical life, so that the body "as is" is not in the case of the walk-in a burden, something that works in detriment to the walk-in being here physically. The body has to work *with* your soul.

There has to be some bias, so you as a walk-in might have some significant similarities on the soul level to the soul that was originally in there. But there would be significant differences as well—which is why, for example, after a walk-in it might be possible for that persona, the soul of the new soul in the physical body, to suddenly be able to resolve something that the previous had never been able to do. Equally, it might be that something the previous soul had been able to do is suddenly no longer of interest to the new soul in the body, and thus they stop doing it or they suddenly don't know how to do it—as it would seem to others that this person has suddenly forgotten to do something.

They might be able to pick it up quickly, or it might be something that they simply won't have interest in. Usually, it will not be something having to do with vital family relationships or anything like that, but it might be something simple. Maybe the previous soul liked to listen to old music and the new soul is more interested in modern music, something like that.

Is there anything else?
I think that's sufficient.

Astrology Is a Loving Offer to Human Culture

Is there any other topic you would like to say anything about?
I'd like to make a closing statement to astrologers.

Okay. You are such a fount of knowledge here; I was trying to think of something else to ask you.
You are doing quite well for someone who really does not have much knowledge about the subject in which you are researching [chuckles], but you have perhaps had this challenge throughout all these books.

Yes.
Very well. This book has been meant largely for you who study this subject and who apply it with the greatest degree of vision, accuracy and caring toward those who come to you. Most people do not realize how very deeply astrologers

care about those they serve. I am going to recommend that you make it clear. Publish something on your card. It can be a brief statement or even part of something in your pamphlet that says the reason you are involved in the study of astrology goes beyond how you are personally fascinated with the topic to extend to the desire that you personally have to ease the path of all those individuals you can assist and guide.

It is important in this time to make it clear that this is your purpose, and if you are an astrologer, then that has to be part of your purpose or you wouldn't be involved. It is, after all, the study of human interaction as influenced by spatial bodies and other individuals. So make it clear on a friendly basis that you are not simply a studious individual with intellectual capacities and knowledge. Don't hide that the study and application of astrology to human culture and human beings is anything other than a loving offer based upon wisdom, experience and caring. Good life.

Thank you so much. Good life.

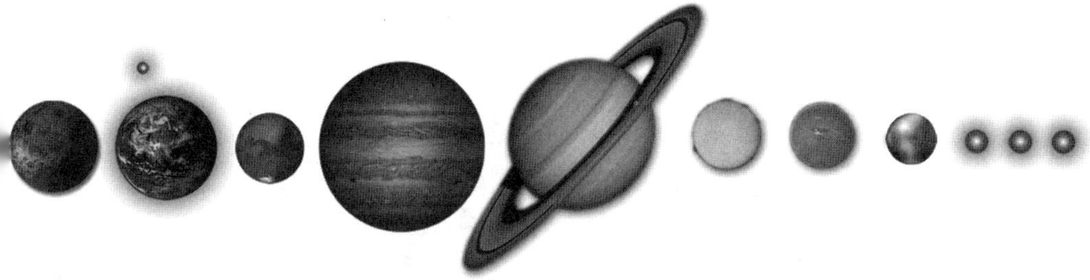

384 • • • ASTROLOGY: PLANET PERSONALITIES & SIGNS SPEAK

⊕ Earth

MOTHER EARTH
The Way Things Work in Earth School

June 4, 2007

This is Mother Earth.

Welcome! You didn't volunteer—were you waiting for us to ask?

I was waiting for the others to speak so that you would be able to have a larger context and would then be able to ask questions based upon the relationship factor. You understand, you have heard the book as it has been expressed up until now, and I felt it was best to wait, since this is the planet who is the most influential where the human race and all other life on Earth is concerned. Also, other things touched on in the book so far are influences on humans. So that is why I waited.

Unexpected Pain Is Telling You Something

Well, first I want to say that we honor what you are doing, and I wish it didn't involve suffering.

Unfortunately, the way things are set up, suffering—or let's just call it pain—is included as a last resort. Interesting, that, isn't it? In the worlds you occupy (every place but this school) you can tell immediately if you are going to make a choice that is not for you. It might be a perfectly adequate choice for someone else, but if it is not for you, you know immediately because you get what would feel to you now on Earth in your physical body as a slight, subtle message. You wouldn't notice it these days, but there, beyond this school, it would be very perceptible. It wouldn't be uncomfortable; it would just be, "Oh, not there, something else," you see?

So that is the normal message, but you readers can see why such a message and no more of a message delivery system on Earth now would not be adequate, because you are used to discomforts on a regular basis and you as the human race tend to ignore small discomforts, even more serious ones. That is why Creator has allowed pain to exist, so that the demonstration of a message can be taken to another level. However, it is important for you to know that all disease and all suffering and pain—such as might occur in a car crash or something like that—is not associated with a message. This is just another system of messaging.

I want to be very clear about that. If you are making a decision that is not right for you and is perhaps even hazardous for you, the level of pain you'd experience would be a pain you would probably feel in your heart or in your abdomen, and it would happen for a short time. It would not be something that would result in a disease and get worse and worse and worse. So if you have heart disease or heart pain for any reason, it is not because you are on the wrong trail, all right? That is something else entirely. I want to make this very clear at the very beginning here, because a lot of people are confused about that.

Now, I am not saying that disease and the pain associated with it at times do not have an unheard message. I am just trying to say, to make it as clear as possible within this word system, that Creator—and myself, for that matter—would not wish to support something that makes a message so glaring as to include suffering.

So if you are going to make a choice or even a decision that is not right for you for any reason and you get a sudden unexpected pain in your heart, or more likely somewhere in your abdomen, and it is like, "Oh, what is that?" and then it goes away almost immediately or fades slowly or fades to a point, then that's probably something you ought to reconsider. I am not saying dump it or run [chuckles]; I am saying reconsider it. It might be perfectly acceptable another time but not in that moment for some reason.

I'm glad the word "reason" came up, because in your world there is a tendency to ask the question that all children ask repeatedly when very young, which is "Why?" However, the reason children ask it is entirely different from the reason adults ask it. Children say, "Why?" because they arrive with the system in place within their bodies that they use elsewhere beyond this school version of Earth. They arrive with that, and so when people are telling them to do things or insisting they do things or explaining things to them that don't fit within that system, the child wants to know why.

Whereas when adults say, "Why?" what they are really saying is, "Justify that to me." They are not standing there with their hands on their hips, so to speak, and saying, "Yeah! So what?" [Chuckles.] It is not that. It is rather that they are used to being persuaded, they are used to receiving evidence, and they are used to the system called "judgment." Judgment, however, as you know, has many pitfalls, and discernment would be more connected to your actual means of knowing beyond this Earth school.

That is why discernment has greater value than judgment, because judgment is also attended by and often overly influenced by bias and prejudice and misinformation and even disinformation—because sometimes people tell you things they know are not true. Maybe they are trying to influence you to do this or that. I am not here to judge anyone; I am simply saying that certain things you know and understand are not always true.

Your Soul Does Not Suffer Pain

When we are born made up of your material, we have the strength of Mars and the love of Venus and the welcoming of Neptune. We have all the qualities of these other planets already within us when we are born—is that correct?

Well, your physical body brings that, yes. But you don't necessarily use that as your predominant means of existence. You don't tap into that. It is present, but it is not something mental. It is physical, and when you arrive and are in existence on Earth, you are functioning with that system of knowing and understanding that I described in detail a moment ago. Therefore, you are inclined to use that system, and any inclusion that is associated with physical connections and influences through the physical are going to be secondary when you are first born. So you are going to use the system you know that exists beyond Earth, that you use there—the means by which you make decisions, the means by which you make other choices, and so on, which I explained. So it might be present, but you don't necessarily use it right away.

You will start to recognize as a baby that the system you are born with is not something people are prepared to act on, since adults and even young children beyond a certain age have abandoned most of that system consciously, and while they may be in touch with it unconsciously and to a degree subconsciously, they are not using it in their conscious day-to-day life. Now, there are exceptions, but most people are not using it. So when baby has to adapt and begins to get to the point where he or she can say simple statements, the first thing baby will say is "Why?" Baby will invariably say "Why?" not because he or she is inquiring mentally, but because the system baby arrives with—which is the system you all use beyond Earth school—is being compromised, or the system in that sense is not functioning. So the "why" baby says then is because baby wants to know, "Why this way?"—meaning the Earth way adults and older children are saying. If baby could speak like this, baby would say: "Why not our natural way, which I was born with?" Does that help you?

My point is that astrologically it seems we have all of those qualities innately. Is the point of astrology to see what our potential is that we have chosen to activate or use or learn or grow with for this life?

No, I would say it differently. I would say that your soul has certain desires. Granted, you understand that your soul is functioning with that system I referred to, the system beyond Earth school, so your soul has the innocence of that system. But it also has a certain determination to achieve what its goal is in life and sometimes will desire to achieve something and repeat and experience over and over to get the widest variety of possibilities—not realizing that this can be painful for the physical part of one's self and that, when that occurs, the soul is often momentarily confused. The soul recognizes there is something unpleasant going on in the physical self, the soul is not blind to that, but at the same time the soul does not feel pain.

This is a critical factor to know: your soul does not suffer pain. It might suffer frustration, it might be discouraged and so on, but your soul does not know pain. It takes your physical body to know that, and if your soul is determined to learn something, regardless of the effect on your physical self, you can then have a life that is, not guaranteed to have a lot of pain, but might be in a situation from time to time where pain becomes a real issue. If that occurs, it might be time to talk from your conscious personality to your soul and just say something like this. You might say:

> "Soul, I require that you distribute this lesson you are trying to learn over many lives so that I can feel physically better and be happier now."

That is all; don't wait for an answer. Say it out loud. If there are people around, then say it in a whisper, but it needs to be physicalized. Just say it once—that's all. The response might not be immediate, but it will be noticeable, usually within less than two weeks. It may not be that your pain suddenly goes away. It might reduce, though, and it also might mean that through the means to reduce your pain—the cooperation level from other human beings, the circumstances of your life in general—things might get better.

Now, I have gone there because it is important for you to know these things. Your soul might come in with certain desires that can even supersede the astrological possibilities, and it is important for your soul to honor the entire you and not just see the physical body as a vehicle to bring about the desired goal of soul. I am talking to souls here a little bit in general, because souls can unintentionally cause suffering. This is because of their innocence, not because of some malevolence—not that. They are innocent when it comes to pain and suffering.

This is why systems like astrology are so important, because they catch the attention of your mental awareness. And very often there is sufficient physical evidence that you can actually see and/or think about that will offer you sufficient proof between that and a certain amount of faith based upon experience with astrology and other systems that might exist that prove their value. Then it can help you to avoid situations that your soul might put you in because you haven't made that statement to your soul that I recommended.

You understand, with your questions now I am being very precise, and it is safe to say that we are going to be talking more than once. We will be talking a few times, because I want to be as thorough as possible so that you can understand not only the value of astrology but the way things work in Earth school, an instruction set you did not receive when you arrived here. If we can lay it out here pretty good in the book, it will be available for future reference.

Earth in This Version Was Prepared for You by Creator

Can we talk about you just a minute before we get back to astrology? You responded to a call by this Creator to come here?

Yes, I did. I responded because Creator needed to have a planet who could be sufficient unto itself and could maintain and provide for, at least for a time, the widest variety of species that could leave on the planet their own special and unique energy through the cycle of life and literally populate the soil of the planet in which food grows for all beings. This would ultimately result in the physical bodies of the human beings He is most particularly interested in to attend Earth school and to have that energy and soil available to them.

You know, this process that is going on now—that is called channeling or mediumship or many other terms—works because your physical bodies are made up of the energy and physical residue of all these myriad life forms that existed on this planet, a version of myself for lo these many years. As a result, this system can work simply because the nucleus of the cells and the atomic structure is a rainbow of life forms that existed before you, so that this life experience (their overall spirit influence, their wisdom) is all available. That is why someday you will utilize vertical wisdom—which, as you know, is where you know what you need to know when you need to know it, and if you don't need to know it anymore, then it is temporarily not available. So as you can see, I am trying to integrate material here.

The function of Earth school is to allow you the greatest and widest variety of influence in your physical self so that the reluctance to do something or say something or act on inspiration that comes to you is reduced. You might have an experience within the physical structure of your body, an experience of some other life form that knew, for example, that it could fly. Maybe part of your body was once a bird or knows it could breathe under water. Granted [chuckles], you know you can't breathe under water, but if you needed to, you might not be that reluctant to take the underwater apparatus with you. You might even enjoy going under water with that underwater apparatus and breathing air under water. But if you did not have a portion of your physical body that was once a fish, that experience might frighten you, even with the technological availability, and you might not do it.

So Earth in this version was prepared for you by Creator, by the myriad life forms that existed before you arrived. But while the experience and the energy of some of those life forms—and their inspiration and their guides and their teachers and their knowledge and wisdom—might be good for you to have on a physical level in your atomic structure and your cellular structure, an actual mingling with them was entirely unnecessary. Ergo, you are not walking around with dinosaurs, but you do have the experience of reptilians in a form that is safe for you to be around for the most part, for they are small. You can avoid them if you look for them [chuckles], and as small beings—smaller than you, you understand—they are inclined to avoid you most of the time, though I grant that some of the larger crocodiles and alligators would probably be best suited to be elsewhere and that is in the works.

If you suddenly notice that they are dying out as a species, don't try too hard to preserve them. Someday there will be something that resembles a miniature alligator about the size of a large lizard or even perhaps a crocodile about that size. I think crocodiles are going to go away; a miniature alligator would be more tolerable. Some of these beings have gotten a little bit too large to be living with you, and because of the well-intended protected status that has been granted to them, things have gotten a little bit out of balance there.

You Can Help Others Grow Beyond This Planet

I try to keep an eye on things, because I recognize that Creator has gone to all this trouble. I might add that I have done a lot of cooperating as well, because Creator desires for you—your souls, your spirits and, maybe you didn't know this, the combination of your soul and your life experience that is your spirit—to gain certain qualities and to be able to experience certain levels of awareness beyond your physical experience in Earth school.

An example of that might be in the system you are used to, in the natural system I described before—where the subtlest message is something you know, you feel, and you know that the decision you were going to make isn't right for you, although it might be perfectly acceptable for somebody else. That system is one level, and all other beings who aren't alive on Earth school right now use that system, as you do when you are not here. But in order to go on and have the capabilities that Creator desires you to have—meaning to explore the planets, help to bring about needed growth and change, and ultimately become a creator in your own state of being, combined with other spirits and souls of Explorer Race experience—in order to do that you need to have the capacity to have several levels that you can use. One of those levels will be the level of spirit as I have said: spirit being the combined energy being, presence, of your soul and your life experience.

So if there is some confusion or need to understand why . . . "why" might not come up as an individual creator decision. It might not even come up in a group situation when you are individually exploring planets and so on beyond here. But it might come up in communication with others, whether those others be individuals you might meet in going from planet to planet, or even when you become a creator and interact with other creators. If "why" comes up, then you will be able to demonstrate the reason why you do things by connecting to the being you are communicating with (in the case of a creator at that level, for that matter) or by utilizing very subtly and very gently a demonstration at the spirit level of "why"—meaning, "Why I did it this way," you might say, "is because of this experience."

The exposure to that would be that the people you are communicating with would be able to get close to it, feel it aurically—not actually touch the experience, but just get as close to it as they can understand so that they are presented with the reason why you didn't do it one way and why you did it the other way, based upon the experience that is known and brought about because of having been done many times before and always turning out badly. We cannot expect beings who are living in their natural way, who are not used to discomfort, to be able to feel/sense that, to be able to even think about it. But if you are feeling it for a moment—you are not speaking, you are just feeling it on the spirit level—then they can touch or be touched by that to a very slight degree, and they will know why.

In this way, you can help others to grow beyond this planet. You can help them to avoid pitfalls that you know might be a mistake for them to try in their growth curve, and you can become an adviser. "This is what I recommend for you, based upon your culture," you might say if they offer the question, "Why?" This won't come up most of the time, but when it does, you will be able to say, "This is why." If they decide this doesn't apply to them, then that is up to them, but at least they will be forewarned. This you can share from your spirit level, whereas your soul would be inclined to say, "Oh yes, wonderful, marvelous." But that is the innocent speaking, and innocents are wonderful. They are the core of being; they are love. They are appreciated, but they can make mistakes in a school like Earth.

Since part of your job as the Explorer Race is to encourage other cultures on other planets that have the desire to learn and grow . . . even though they might have a benevolent culture, if they want to add growth on a very slight level that is comfortable to them, then they are going to allow themselves to interact with you. If they don't want to allow that, then you simply won't see them. You won't find them. They won't be present for you in that way. Only that which desires growth will be exposed to the possibility by meeting you as Earth space travelers.

Souls Must Have No Resistance

Is this a common practice in every creation, that in order to have a life there, an immortal personality assumes this mantle—or covering or glove—of the soul of the Creator?

In this universe, yes. In the experience of all other planets, all the benevolent places, that is perfectly adequate. But if you are going to go to school, you have to have the term "spirit." Now, I am using "spirit" and "soul" as . . . I am differentiating them. This is to help you get as many details as possible so that you can understand how things work here as well as how this might be applied to the system called astrology.

Was it not taken into consideration that this can cause a problem, that a very naive, innocent soul might not be the best "co-incarnator" [chuckles] to have in a school like this?

Oh, it was considered completely. You want souls to come in who are innocent. Do you know why? They won't come in with a resistance. If you want beings to learn, it is absolutely essential that at the core of their being they have no resistance whatsoever. If they arrive with resistance or bias or prejudice, even if they desire in the most earnest way to learn something, that affects what they are trying to learn. They can have a million lives and not learn a thing along those lines. So a lot of consideration went into it. Souls are exactly, precisely what they are supposed to be everywhere, including here in Earth school.

Who gets to keep the experience: the immortal personality or the soul of the Creator? What is your understanding of that?

My feeling is that the soul—the immortal personality, in that sense—gets the experience, but the soul itself, being innocent, cannot really access that experience beyond this place and only in a limited way in this place, in Earth school. The immortal personality is really another way of referring to the spirit, but the spirit is actually a slightly different level the way I am using it, because beyond this place you might not necessarily use that spiritual level. You would use your soul and you would use your immortal personality as the means by which you can be identified as an individual personality by all beings, all right? So you might travel in space, as an astronaut, and you might meet beings from other planets. They might say to you, much to your amazement, "I know you. I used to know you as such and such on another planet," because they will recognize your immortal personality. I am differentiating there. So the soul then remains largely innocent. The spirit, though—that's an overall term I have already defined—also encompasses the immortal personality.

You were perfectly happy in the Sirius star system before you came here?
Yes.

You will return, right?
One grows fond of one's environment. If I am needed there, then I will, but not before that. There are many, many water planets in the Sirius star system, so there is no great pressure for me to return. I am definitely needed here, so here I am.

How many levels of your being are . . . how can I say it? If I was infinitely able to go anywhere, how many of your levels would be accessible to me?
Here, somewhere in the seventies. It depends how you look at it. Beyond here, including the universe, several hundred.

Ah! In this book we will stick with astrology, but at some future time I would love to talk about your other experiences.
All right.

You Are the First to Successfully Engage the Explorer Race Theme

We are the eighteenth civilization on this planet, but we are the first Explorer Race civilization, right? Or were there others?

I know what you mean. In terms of successfully engaging the Explorer Race theme, you have gone further with it than anybody else. It was tried once before and it really took a wrong turn, but that didn't last very long. So in terms of success in engaging the intention of being the Explorer Race, yes, you are the first. I am not going to really count the other, because it didn't really . . . it didn't stick, so I don't think it is worth it. But I want to be precise: you are not the first but you are the first successful one.

Even though it may not seem that you are being very successful right now, there is a great deal of learning going on, and because of the technology you have developed now, it is possible to have at least mental communication with others—insofar as that is truthful, which it isn't always. But rapidly you are coming into the time when you can have communication that is conscious, that is going to be truthful all the time, and that will not require technology. "Rapidly"—do you want a definition of that? I think it will be in place for many people (not everyone) within fifty years. But you have to want it, and you will have to accept the ground rules. The ground rules are *no secrets,* period. Not everyone will be able to accept that. If you feel the need to keep secrets, you probably won't embrace it for a while, but it will be available to embrace when that need falls away from you, should it. So you are not going to be required to do this, but it is going to be available. That is the major thing: no secrets, period.

Were any of the souls on this planet now, any of the immortal personalities incarnated on the planet, part of the previous attempt at the Explorer Race from your planet?

No, and that is as well, because that kind of memory could be influential.

We are told that 96 or 94 percent of all of the Explorer Race is out there, waiting for us to get through here. Did they all come through Earth?

I am not sure what this has to do with the book, but I recognize you are asking because you can. I would say not all, but they had moments. They all had moments here. But if you are saying "come to the Earth" by way of having a life here, then not necessarily.

Astrology Was Given as a Gift

So because we don't know who we are, whose idea was it—the Creator's, I understand—to bring the system of astrology to humanity, the idea that by knowing when you were born, you could learn more about your potential and your talents and what you could do here?

But really it was visited upon the Earth cultures in many different times and places, because guides and teachers on the spirit level felt that the individuals they presented it to needed to know it, that they would either become influential in their societies or were already and would be in a position to help people. So it was given as a gift, as one might give a valuable gift to someone to entrust it to them. It was given to many different individuals in hopes that it would survive, at least in part, and it has survived in part. But it is important to add more parts to it now, which is the purpose of this book, which may or not become a series. If it becomes a series, it will have to be of interest to astrologers, and the next book will include questions from astrologers, though not exclusively.

Just know this, astrologers: I know you have a very precise language of astrology. Regardless of your language, I will be answering and the other planets will answer in a language that lay people can understand. We will not use terminology, so try to keep terminology out of the question. If you insist, the question will be answered more generally, for we wish to provide (speaking for the planets) as much information to you as possible. But the purpose of this book and the series in general is to provide you with the feeling, the intuitive sense that you all require so you can go beyond the words and the tables, and feel what is appropriate by interacting with the individuals in general or the specific individuals you are helping.

I think that would be a great idea, to have the astrologers ask the questions. [Chuckles.]

There is an advantage in you asking this time now, though, because you are an innocent. By that, you are not biased about astrology one way or the other in a particular sense, so you are asking a lot of the innocent questions. The astrologers are going to ask questions that are a bit more structured to professionals and can also be broadened in the answering of the question to the interested public as well.

Wonderful.

Earth Is Overbalanced to the Feminine

Even though we have all of these influences from the other planets, these energies that can help us, the most important planet in our life is you, isn't that correct?

The most influential.

Yes. How would you describe your influence? I mean, it is all-encompassing, you know [chuckles].

Well, that is why I mentioned the physical structure right down to the atomic level. That is a given predominantly on a physical level and is influential there, but on the feeling level it's also very present, because physical feelings . . . they may not be specifically measurable by your technology today, but you are coming along with that. So it's also on the feeling level that allows for instinct, which is probably the best way to make decisions now. It refers to the natural system with the addition of the physical influence, which is very useful. As far as the mental, it's not so much there, and as far as the spiritual, only insofar as all beings influence spirit. So I'm pretty influential, not overpoweringly though.

We were told that because we broke the first planet we tried this with in this orbit in this solar system, you were asked to come here because of the water on your planet. Why is water so important? What does water do?

That's a wonderful question. The reason it is so important is that it tends to force (not as in sticking a gun in your back, but forcing in terms of playing cards, for example) the influence of the feminine more upon you. Water is a moderating element, it is a softening element, so one bad decision doesn't result in total disaster. You can make a bad decision on Earth in its water-school form—yes, Earth school water—and it is not necessarily catastrophic for yourself and others. But if you do that on a planet where there isn't water—no water at all, so no physical feminine influence of a planetary-level function—then one bad decision could end it all.

Therefore, you might say that the lesson was learned with the last planet who had been in this position, who sort of came to, "Oops, that didn't work.

So what can we do to greatly moderate the fact that these bad decisions *are* going to be made?" "If we want," you might say, speaking in the larger "we" here, "if we want the human race to develop to a great degree autonomously based upon its own experience, we have to not only allow mistakes, we have to be totally open to them. But what can we do to moderate those mistakes so that they do not turn into catastrophes?" Well, the immediate feeling was, "Wow, water: the feminine." At that point, the decision was made to polarize the sexes so that all human beings would be feminized to a consistent degree, whether they are male or female.

Before that, there were the two sexes but they weren't polarized. "Polarized" means, in this case, that whether you are a male or a female, you will be born or come into existence through a female, so it will not be possible to be 100 percent masculine, even though you might have a masculine body. In terms of your physical creation cycle, most of you spent nine months inside a feminine being, and, therefore, you are partially feminized and the masculine is something I would call spliced into the feminine, not the other way. The feminine can re-create itself on its own; the masculine cannot. The masculine is the graft, not the other way.

It is absolutely essential for you to understand this because it basically tells you what part of you is trying to learn. The part of you that is trying to learn is the masculine part; the feminine part does not have to learn. Now, I am not saying that women do not have lessons—or girls, for that matter—but I am saying that the feminine part of you is that which is the most connected to your natural way. It is the part of you that is most likely to be cooperative and work well with others. It is the part of you that is most likely to be influenced by spirit and the divine. The masculine is here to learn because the masculine is the part of you that is most likely to want to go and seek things out, to explore. How can you have an Explorer Race without explorations?

In a nutshell, the masculine part is here to explore, to find, to look, to see, to consider, to think, to act, to build. So if you are going to do this, that part of you has to learn, and in order to learn, it absolutely must be allowed to make mistakes. The way to moderate those mistakes is to have a planet that is overbalanced to the feminine and to require that no matter how masculine you are, you will be feminized because you are born through a woman. You can see that the system is all quite . . . how can we say?

Pretty carefully thought out.

Yes. A lot of consideration went into this system.

So before they were polarized, both sexes could give birth?

No. You would more often have cloning where there was no period of time in the feminine. So you could have that, but since birth is uncomfortable and requires a sacrifice on the part of the woman, and there is pain and suffering, unfortunately, then, there simply does . . . how many people would want that?

You are right. They would choose the easy way.

So the idea of cloning was very appealing. But in the process, one would not become feminized sufficiently so that you could learn from your mistakes—make a mistake, learn, and go on—whereas in the polarized masculine you could make a mistake and catastrophe could occur, and if you went on, you would be going on in some other planet, in some other life, in some other existence. You would be able to look back at the planet who was broken, as you put it yourself, and you could say, "Whoops! What went wrong there?" You might take some time to explore that, as all those who were involved in the so-called "breaking of the planet" spent lots of time afterward saying, "Whoops! What went wrong?" and examining it. I am done with that examination, I might add, but they know what went wrong and they are totally and completely in support of the Earth *water* planet.

Quantum Mastery Gives You the Potential to Do Anything Moderated by the Feminine

The souls on that first planet . . . have they now or did they at some previous time incarnate on Earth?

No. No, they tried. They feel like they did what they could, given the system that existed, and they would rather just stand back and watch. Many of them are very interested though, and they do come to visit, to the degree that they are able, to observe from a non-participatory position.

Are they considered part of the 94 or 96 percent of the Explorer Race who is waiting for us?

No.

Oh! They are not. They opted out?

No, they are not part of the stream. You asked which was the Explorer Race, and I explained to you that I wasn't really counting the other. What they tried before wasn't successful.

Oh! That's the trying you meant.

Yes.

Oh, I'm sorry. I thought it was one of the civilizations on this planet. On another topic, I want to say that I got so excited once I realized that incarnating here and having quantum-mastery cells in my body—as you said, atoms and nuclei that are of your being, and you are a quantum master—that this gives us the potential in the physical to do anything, doesn't it?

It gives you the potential to do anything moderated by the feminine, meaning that if you decide to create something . . . for example, look at atomic energy. The whole point of atomic energy was, "How can we release?" or to put it on a more personal level, "How can we learn to share in the motive force, the constant motion, of the atomic structure and use that to light up our cities and build our machines and so on?" The problem with atomic energy, though, is that you can see all the other things it was used for and how it caused an untold amount of suffering. Even in terms of the peaceful use of it, so to speak, in power plants, what is being done is not quite what the atoms would prefer to do. The atoms would prefer to share their energy and not be changed as a result of that. Do you know it is possible to move a truck across the street using the power of a single atom and nothing else? You can take the engine and everything else right out of it.

Really? How?

Imagine a big semitrailer truck fully loaded down. You can't do this now, but you will at some point be able to request that the atom that is most prepared to share its energy move the truck across the street. It might amuse you to see how the truck is moved across the street. It probably won't roll on its wheels. The truck would just be picked up, float across the street, and then be put down. Now, I realize this sounds like science fiction, but that is what exists everywhere else. Of course, you wouldn't actually have the truck; you would just have what needs to move across the street move across the street. But I am using that as an example so you can understand and appreciate (with a certain amount of wry humor) the juxtaposition of your now technological society and who and what you really are.

Is that how the Great Pyramid was constructed?

Essentially, yes. I am going to skip over that one, because that is a book in itself, but I will say this: Seams of stone associated with blocks of stone that are happily in residence with each other and are not easily moved, are so because the atoms—every single one that is touching the one in the other stone—are very happy with each other. That is how stone structures remain permanently, how they retain their shape. I am mentioning this because talking about the pyramid is a story in itself, plus it is also not the best representative of the answer I wanted to give. You would probably find some stone walls like that in other places—South America, someplace like that.

Are you saying we could get the true history of the Earth from you?

Yes.

Your Mental Process Is Changing

That's why I am coming in last here, because the point is to anchor this book. We will do another book: the history of the Earth. But also, you will use a lot of the material in this book in the appendix of the other book, because I am laying down, as you can see, very specific and precise ground rules that exist here which you don't necessarily think about. However, when you are inside mother, forming up physically, when you are in residence as a soul, you are totally conscious of all those things. You are also told by your guides and teachers that you are going to forget most of that when you are functioning on the Earth as a living being, and of course, you can't believe that: "How could I ever forget that?"

But the thing is, you don't understand what the word "forget" means, because at the point inside mother, forgetting doesn't exist. You are either inside mother or you are someplace else as a soul, and you are not in that body until it is actually born, comes out of mother, and even then sometimes you are traveling with your teachers for a time—although generally you are in residence full-time pretty soon. Then you discover what forgetting is—not immediately, but sometime within the first year of life you discover what forgetting is all about. It is not something you don't have anymore. What happens is that the adaptation to life on Earth in the cultures that exist now adds layers to your existence. You must learn what exists here.

That is why you ask, "Why?" as a child. "Why?" You might be saying in parentheses, "Why do I have to learn this when the truth—my natural, native, known knowledge that we all have—can work just fine here?" But you are arriving in a school. You do not have to give up any of that knowledge, wisdom—any of that which you have. But superimposed over that is the subconscious and the conscious mind. The conscious mind is a layer that has the capacity to forget and to remember and all of those things you think about mentally. That is superimposed over your being when you are born and exist on the planet. That is why when you say, "We have the capability to do all those things, don't we?" because you are a quantum master and so on, you have the capability and never lose it. It is available. It is within you.

So how can we remember it to access it?

Slowly, but surely. The way that is happening right now is that your mental process is changing. If it becomes vertical as described before, then you can touch the depth of you. The conscious mind is linear; it functions and it relates to linear time. The natural being who knows all those things—as the soul inside mother, you know all those things—if you could you might say inside mother while your physical body forms up, "How could I ever forget? What is forgetting? I don't know what that means." That soul does not exist in linear time, even though mother is in linear time. Her physical body goes through linear time, but as a soul presence, as a being, you are not in linear time.

Until birth?

Until you are born, that's right. Then you start living in linear time as you adapt and apply and experience the superimposition in order to apply linear time to your life. That superimposition is called the conscious mind, and its ability to relate to the deeper you is referred to as the subconscious. I am just using your contemporary terminology. But when you move from the linear mind to the more present-moment existence (which is available for you all right now), where you totally are in action, reaction and interaction in the present moment and you're not thinking about the past and you're not thinking about the future, but you are completely in focus in the present moment—you will then have a much easier time utilizing vertical wisdom, while at the same time being able to access all the opportunities and abilities you have.

You don't have to give up your conscious mind; you don't have to give up your subconscious. You are simply going to be able to access that normal state of your being that is insulated and protected here from being affected by your Earth life as you function on Earth. You will very possibly be able to access the means of existence beyond Earth that you use when you are not living on Earth. That requires vertical wisdom, and that requires, when used in the best possible way—where you are aware of that in that moment—focusing in the present moment. And that requires a physical body so that you can be conscious of the present moment.

That present moment simply is in flux in the world of time, meaning you are in the present moment as time, also known as experience, moves forward You are walking down the road, and every moment you are physical in the present moment. Your physical body is always in the present moment, although it can be influenced by the past or the future, based upon what thoughts and feelings you might have. But basically your physical body is in the present moment in every moment. Your heart beats. Your lungs breathe. Your blood moves. Your bones move. Your skin is reacting with the outer world. In short, your physical body is in the present moment, and the way you know you are focused in the present moment is to focus into your physical body, both on the feeling level and to use your mind to do so.

How would you do that? You might simply look down at your abdomen or your solar plexus, or you might wiggle your toes and become mentally focused on your feet, not thinking about the bone structure or the toes. Just *be* in your physical body. Practice being in that moment. Whenever that is occurring and you are not thinking, you are in the present moment.

In this mental age, so many people are like stick figures, with big heads and no awareness of the body. We are coming out of that though, aren't we?

Well, you have the opportunity to do so, and that is why this information is available for you to think about and then perhaps act on physically and even engage in instinct, which is so much simpler and almost always results in a benevolent outcome. It can't be guaranteed, though. A deer might run away when hearing a sound and its instinct is to get away as fast as possible, but the bullet might still catch up.

We have been going for a while here, and you are tired. The channel is still recuperating from something too, so let's continue next time. We will be talking for a while. I know you are thinking the book is coming down the home stretch here, but we will be going for a while yet and we will anchor the book. Good night.

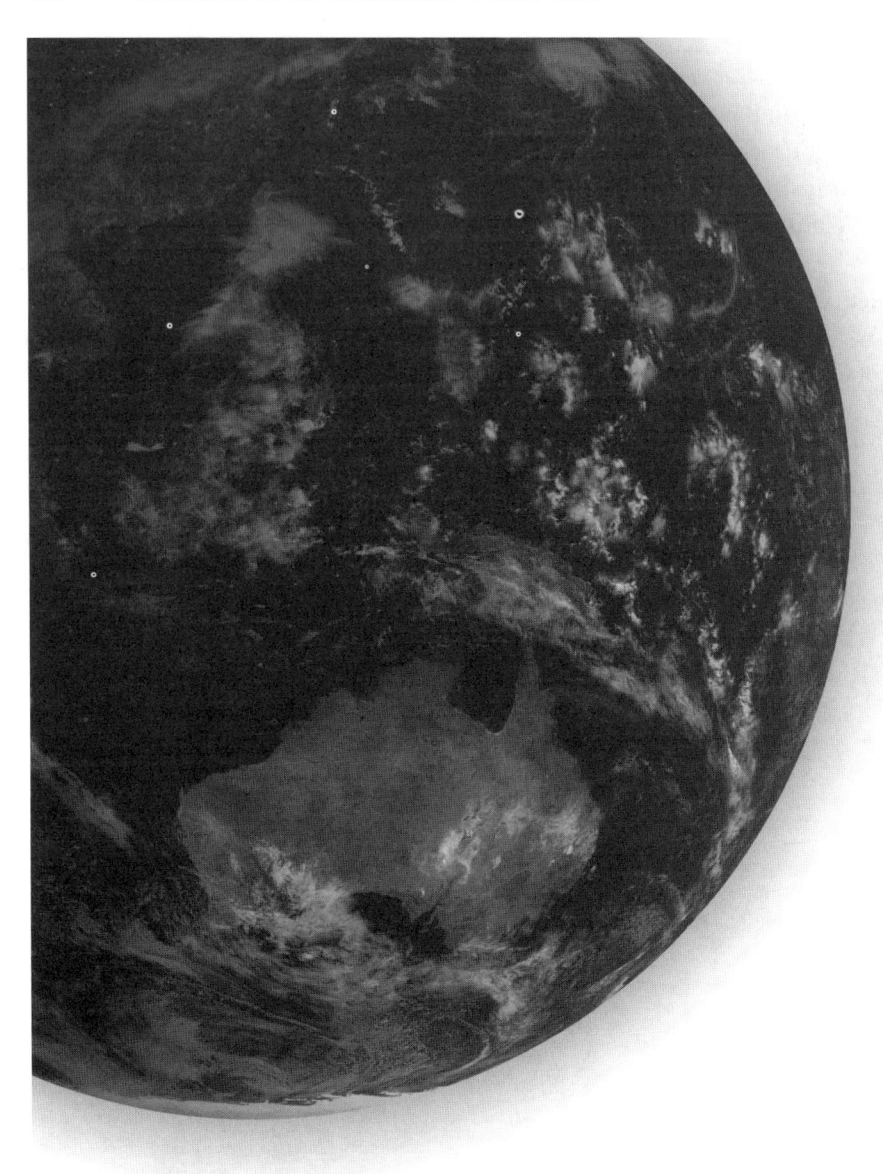

402 • • • ASTROLOGY: PLANET PERSONALITIES & SIGNS SPEAK

⊕ Earth

28

MOTHER EARTH

While You Are on Earth, You Are Expressing the Feelings of My Personality

June 7, 2007

This is Earth.

Welcome! I listened to the first part of the tape from last night, and one of my questions wasn't clear. I said, "Thank you for what you're doing for us, but I wish it didn't involve suffering," and I meant the suffering that you are experiencing from our presence on the planet.

I understood that.

Well, how are you handling that, and how does that affect humanity?

War Is Really Difficult for Me

It doesn't cause me immediate pain when someone moves a stone or drills or something like that, but it has a cumulative effect, even though I am able to support excesses. So drilling and taking out oil or taking out a lot of different types of the materials you use, I can support that to a degree—meaning not support you, but I am able to compensate for that with the rest of my planet. But the part that is difficult is the effect of war. This is hard to take, not only because of the damage to myself, but it is hard to take because of the damage that is done between those who are at war and those who are not.

It would be one thing if an area someplace was designated, "This is going to be where people who are angry at each other will fight it out," and they'd fight it out without blowing up the Earth and without hurting other people. I am not saying I feel good about that; I am just saying that this is where you fight it out. Don't use bombs, but rather just use some means to fight it out that keeps it between combatants. On the other hand, when it involves people who don't want to participate, people who are just trying to live their lives, as well as animals and plants, then this is . . . I don't like to use such a strong word, but I must be clear, yes? You are asking for clarity. It is an abomination.

I know that those who fight in wars—not necessarily those who send them to fight, but those who fight in wars and who reflect on that fighting, either in the moment or later in life after it is over—agree that it is an abomination, and no matter how much you rationalize the outcome, it remains one. So that is my objection, and I feel some of that pain. After a time—once that kind of war becomes accepted or rationalized—it becomes something that is essentially institutionalized, that "This and this will happen that we don't intend," so to speak (as combatants might say), or "This and this will happen because we do intend it in order to further threaten our adversary." I am, of course, paraphrasing what people might say. This is essentially institutionalizing it, and because of that, then I have to gradually withdraw my support. There are side effects to everything, eh?

I'm Withdrawing Certain Support from You

The side effect of my withdrawing my support of the human race, insofar as you are fighting each other, is that certain areas where I support the human race also get reduced. Think about it: If I withdraw support . . . not in certain physical areas where battle is going on where support is needed because of those who are not fighting and are getting hurt, but if I withdraw support of the physicality of your own bodies to express anger or to become enraged—in short, the support of the very cellular tissues of your body that are physically made up of the component parts of my own—then it has certain wide-ranging effects on the human race. I will say some of those now.

One of the effects is that the frustration level will tend to build up, as well as the uncertainty having to do with the inner conflict of what you can do physically and what you would like to do physically, and also the endurance level of the physical matter of your body. Due to the cumulative impact of wars over the past 150 years or so when things have become excessive, then the reduction in your basic body component parts of your physical ability to express—and then, as a result, your feelings physically unable to express, and then your mind frustrated by that—has been reduced from the level that existed before that time by about 20 percent. This has no effect on your immune system, so I want to put that idea to rest, for some have considered that. However, of course, the effect of other pollution, as you call it, has a great deal of effect on that. But I am just talking about my contribution.

Understand, this is not something I am doing as a punishment. I am doing this for my own protection and to protect those who are being harmed by this unfocused rage. There are consequences to this rage, and although I recognize that you are here to learn and thus you must make mistakes, I do not wish to support the mistakes that are so catastrophic and so destructive and so hurtful, such as huge bombs and so on. I don't have to give you examples; I am sure you can all imagine them just by paying attention to the news or day-to-day events,

I am not trying to judge the combatants by saying they are somehow immoral. I am saying that many of them are almost asleep, carrying out acts they would never do within the context of their moral upbringing and their cultural values. But this kind of thing is happening to the extent that it is being institutionalized and therefore accepted. I cannot do that; I cannot participate in that aspect of your behavior.

Therefore, even though I am withdrawing certain support to you so that you can, as the Explorer Race, begin to apply your natural magic—your true magic, or your capabilities, in other words, that you simply have forgotten as a result of living here without the true connection to your total being—I have also had to withdraw my support in that other way. So that is compounding the feeling sense of urgency you have, all of you, with no apparent understanding of the source of that urgency. It is my intention in this book to reveal my personality, which I feel is essential not only to support astrologers advocating that this is, in fact, my personality, but also for the general public who might be interested in astrology and also may have had some exposure to the overall philosophical approach and general-knowledge background of the Explorer Race material.

Did I understand you to say that all of this violence is a result of humanity's unfocused rage?

No, I don't want to say that. I would say it is a result of the unfocused rage of the war machine. It is natural to be outraged by what is done by the other side—depending on who you are, the other side in the combat. Naturally, one is outraged. If you cannot react against the actual perpetrators—individuals by name, you understand, which is almost unheard of in most combat situations—there is a tendency to react in a blanket way, meaning, "If I can't get the ones who did this," whatever it is, "then I will get this wider area." That as you know—just being an historian or having studied broader history, including history supplied in this manner—has led to one series of catastrophic destructions in the past after another. I don't wish to support that anymore, not just by allowing it—because I know you are here to learn, and therefore, a certain amount of allowing is required—but I don't wish to support the damage done to those who are not fighting, who are not combatant.

Right, what they call collateral damage, which is horrible.

Yes. I grant that those who do this collateral damage often regret it terribly and suffer as a result of it, and I am not questioning their morals. I am simply saying that I cannot tolerate that damage because of the way I feel. I have feelings as well. This is the reason, you understand (and this is the crux of the matter), that I believe Creator has requested my presence in this form. My personality and the essence of my personality are in every grain of sand of this planet.

You Are Expressing the Feelings of My Personality

I am who I am, and the planet is me. Your physical bodies are made up of this. It not only allows you to incorporate certain characteristics into your physical self that allow you to live here, but also those physical characteristics come with my basic core feelings as well. You might reasonably ask, "Where do feelings come from?" A child might ask that. If you were to ask that, the range of feelings that you have is a nucleus, all right? You have feelings when you are beyond this planet, but they are very few and you wouldn't consider them feelings. You would be calm. You would be peaceful. You would have moments of humor. You would feel love. In short, you would take that as what is natural. But here on this planet, if you were to examine the express feelings by those not on this planet, not involved in this Explorer Race experience, you would classify the feelings as I mentioned.

But what about all the other feelings? Where do they come from? That is why Creator has asked you to come here, to be on this planet, to be on Earth. Those are the feelings, literally, of my personality that you are able to express because you are here. Think about it; it is simple. When you leave here—go past the veil, as it is called—you return to your normal state of feelings. Those are the mechanics of why you shed those feelings, because you don't take your Earth life with you. You shed all of that, and you return in your soul. You rejoin your overall spirit, and you assimilate once again your normal range of feelings.

Thus, even if you are able to examine your Earth life to an extent, you don't feel the feelings you have when you are on Earth. You feel those feelings on Earth because you are here to learn, and you will feel passion, compassion and so on. You will feel potentially anger. You will have the desire to act. If you see a problem, you will want to fix it. In short, you have a greater expansion of your feeling self so that you can learn all about the greatest range of feeling creation.

All creators have a strong sense of feeling creation. They usually have a bias toward a feeling creation that is entirely benevolent. But this Creator is trying to do something new. Granted, as has been talked about in other *Explorer Race* books, this Creator is taking a risk, is attempting to bring about something that will stimulate growth and not be only destructive—right now, from my point of view, it is too destructive—but I grant that Creator has more wisdom and knowledge than I have (naturally). But at the same time, since I am not privy to Creator's agenda, then I have to express my personality.

Still, I recognize simply by my everyday experience that when souls depart from Earth, I feel them shedding all the pain and suffering. You don't take the pain and suffering with you, but you do learn in your immortal spirit what can be done in a more challenging world—such as this Earth school—and what cannot. Sometimes you learn, as you might say, the hard way, and other times you learn the gentle way. I know that Creator wants you to learn what happens if you do this, what happens if you do that, and Creator wants you to learn—getting away from war and violence for a moment—that sometimes even the best of intentions don't turn out well. The way to learn that is in an isolated environment as you find yourselves in now—encapsulated, so to speak—and that you shed completely when you leave this Earth and this encapsulation.

Storms Are a Way to Disperse an Excess of Feeling

When we go beyond the veil at the transition, do those feelings come back to you?

No, they don't come back—they never leave. You are physically made up of my physical body, but your soul is not part of my physical body. Oh, in the greater sense that we are all one, yes. But in terms of what you take with you, what goes beyond the veil or the encapsulation of the Explorer Race experience—that is not me. But everything else you adapt to, that is me, that is something essentially loaned to you. So I do not acquire from you; I reacquire.

In this expression of my body, I have learned what to do with such feelings when there is an excess amount of that feeling that either the human race is feeling or that I am feeling as a result of inherited impacts of the human race, as in war and other forms of violence, as well as unexpressed love. By "unexpressed love," I mean unexpressed love that is benevolent, held back for some reason—cultural values or other reasons. Then I have to do something with that conflict of benevolent creation and that which is not benevolent.

I usually have to dilute it in some way, because it is concentrating in certain physical areas that have magnetic properties of my body that, while I can deal with it myself, all the populations in that area would be subjugated . . . if I didn't do anything, they would be subjugated to total madness. If people didn't live there, it wouldn't be a problem, but by living there, if I didn't do something in those areas, those energies would build up and the people would . . . it would be as if they were exposed to something that caused them to become crazed and they could be capable of doing things that they would never do otherwise.

So what I do is I use my disbursal techniques of wind, rain, water, electricity: the wind to disburse it so that it is not so concentrated in that area (whatever that area might be); the water to dilute it and distribute it (these are all disbursal methods); and the electricity to attempt to change its polarization. In short, you can see where I am going: storms. The energy might need to be shifted in ways where the storm itself might be catastrophic, or more likely—that is just sometimes—I need to shift my body because of the energy of the human existence in that area, or perhaps I simply need to move in that area because I am a living being.

This is just like you. If you are uncomfortable, you move, and then maybe you get more comfortable. You can understand. So then you have an earthquake. Generally speaking, I do not recommend that people live in earthquake zones, and by that I mean truly active earthquake zones. Now, I know you didn't really want to have a full rundown of why there are catastrophes.

No, I do. Please continue.

All right. Then there are other forms. Generally speaking, in the accumulation of this Explorer Race material you have heard that I would prefer, and have been demonstrating this somewhat, that you move your human culture back from any point of contact with water. By that I don't mean rivers or inland lakes, but any point of contact with water, as in seas—an inland sea, for example, or a large lake beyond something that is small (say a mile or a few miles across) not that but something that is massive. I request that you move your culture and your creations back from that point by three to five miles.

I know this would cause massive displacement, but it is not safe for you to be there. For one thing, the sea creatures need access to those shores. I cannot say why, but it has to do with the perpetuation of their existence on this planet. This also has to do with the fact that I need those spaces, because the more human beings there are on Earth, the more feelings you experience and the more you experience in cumulative impact, you see, on each other and myself. So when I do these storms to keep the excess feeling energy as described loosely before, I need to have the capability of having certain areas without human beings there.

I would also appreciate it, if possible, that you live and create your lives a minimum of one hundred feet above sea level. This allows me to at times—it won't be all the time—do a massive cleansing of an area. A massive cleansing does not have to be just constant rain. Sometimes it might require that the ocean, the seawater itself (which is different, as you know, from inland lakes), with all of its life-giving capabilities, at least in its pure form, seed the land well inland as well. I do not do this to harm you—what you call a tidal wave—but I do this because it has to do with the creation of life and the support of life.

You find yourselves on a living planet, and this is the challenge to you. In times of the past—in terms of your soul experience, your immortal spirit travel— you may very well have been on planets who were asleep or resting so that there was no organism, no earthquakes, no living waters, nothing like that. Those kinds of planets would be training to get ready to be on a living planet. But now you find yourself on a planet who is vitally alive and who (speaking in the second person here) can and does produce effects as any living being might. These effects are not done to harm you ever, but they must be expressed by myself in order to maintain as much balance as I can from the imbalances caused—I grant, largely unintentionally—by the cumulative impact of the human race.

The Sea Gives Life to the Land

This planet, as it once existed, was something akin to the Garden of Eden—not in the sense of your biblical story, but rather akin in the sense that it supported all life and that there was a balance from one life form to another. I believe your scientists have studied this, as well as many cultures and individuals for that matter. But it wasn't a place, from my perspective, that was all beauty. Creatures ate each other, as they always have, in order to survive. These beings you call the animals and so on, on other planets and in other places where they live, do not do that. They do that here because it is required of them, and the "requirements of them living on this planet" is not my focus for the purpose of this book. You must know certain basics, but that is for another book, another time.

So I am not saying that the Eden qualities of the planet, without the human race as you know yourselves to be, was a place of peace and calm as might exist other places. But it was a place that supported all life, and one of the support systems was always tidal waves. You would not find too many animals, even plants (except for those who were very hardy indeed), or certainly any cultures beyond that that existed on the beach, so to speak, but rather they'd be well above it or as far inland as possible—normally, twenty to thirty miles inland.

Except for the rare type of island that might have almost no elevation to it, it is not typical to have a tidal wave wash over from one end to the other. Those kind of islands are not meant for human habitation nor animal habitation—unless they are sea creatures or able to fly. In that case, they would know when a tidal wave was coming, and they would retreat or fly away. They would return sometime later—not always those same individuals, but very often they were the same—and re-create life with the nourishment of the sea. The sea has the capability, with all of its life-giving elements in its natural state (not polluted), to greatly nourish.

I believe this has been studied in your times. It is understood, and I believe it is why the theory of evolution has been proposed, and I am not going to discuss that here. I am just going to say that the theory of evolution is a reasonable response insofar as life coming from the sea and evolving—only that aspect of the theory.

Now, there is a reason for everything, and the reason that in these times, where I need to express myself more because of the impact of so many people . . . I am able to sustain that to a degree, though I would prefer that you level off your population and allow me to catch up a bit. I do recommend honoring these suggestions I am giving, because it is not my intent to threaten you. I am just saying that I will be doing this again. In order for life to continue, the sea must at times come up a ways on the land, not always washing over the island from one end to the other, but in the case of larger landmasses supporting the land. If you look at it even from a child's point of view—a child, say, in school, learning basics—the land does not come straight up vertically where it touches the sea. It slopes very gradually down, so there is always land that is covered by water, always. This tells you that the land welcomes the water and recognizes its life-giving capabilities. So if you live near that or if you build your cultures or industries near that, it could be a problem.

Now I am going to speak to one industry specifically here, since it may become a factor in the future, and that is desalinization. I am going to recommend that you keep that to being not too much. I know it is not too much now, and for places that don't have any inland seas and lakes, I accept that. But please do not have your industrial part—the intake, the pipe as it were—don't have it lead to a processing plant that is at sea. Have it lead to something that is at least five miles inland and process it there.

Keep in mind, though, that the processing you are doing is literally destroying the element that gives life to all life as you know it. So my recommendation for places that must survive by desalinization is to make agreements with other places elsewhere that have plenty of fresh water. I know you will have to make agreements sometimes with peoples you don't like, but you might have something you can offer them as well. From Creator's point of view, as it has been explained to me, you are intended to live on this planet. Even though it challenges you when you do not remember who you are and then you tend to mistrust each other for various reasons, ultimately you are intended to live here because you must cooperate with each other. Even if you don't like each other for this or that reason, you must cooperate to survive.

What element in the sea gives life? Minerals?

I don't wish to say. I will simply say that every portion of it—every single portion—gives life.

Our body is mostly made up of something very similar to seawater, correct?

In much of its component parts, you might say. There have been studies done, I believe, but from my point of view, I see you as land creatures of the sea.

I Would Support a Benevolent Reduction of Your Population

How far back would you call this planet the Garden of Eden?

I don't want to call it the Garden of Eden. How long ago was it, from my perspective, in its Eden state? It was in its Eden state before the human race as you know it was here.

How many people would you be comfortable with on the planet?

Well, I don't really want to say, because there are those who would try to make it happen through artificial means. I will say that I would support a benevolent reduction of the number of people, but not in any way other than that—a *benevolent* reduction.

Have you ever had this many people on the planet before?

No, and you are, simply because you need to live, greatly impacting other life forms who are here to help you. I am going to set aside the animals for a moment, but you must grow your plants to survive, yes? And you must have land to do this. Right now, the animals you have domesticated for your food chain don't have much room to survive and are increasingly shoved, as it were—not because of the choice of the people who raise them, but simply because of the fact that all of the people on the planet must live somewhere—into a smaller and smaller space. As a result of this, often they are suffering more.

They come to a point where they do not choose to be here anymore, and when that happens, they allow—their spirits allow—some way to leave. Either they cry out to Creator that they wish to leave—that they are suffering too much and succeeding generations appear that they may be suffering more—and Creator does respond, or they allow something which their immune system would have fought off before to take place. Thus, you might find that some disease, which had always been a factor on the planet but had never been expressed by this or that group of animals, is suddenly having a devastating impact, sometimes even impacting the human race.

So I am saying that I understand your desire to have many peoples. People want to have many children. Children are the greatest gift. But I feel it would be best for a time to have less children. That is all I am saying, and I am not going to attempt to decrease the population by anything I do. You must know that what I am doing has everything to do with what I need to do for myself to survive.

Become Responsible for Re-Creating Your Existence

I also know that Creator wants you to learn and gradually reintegrate that which you are away from this planet, to desire not only to do magic, but to do magic that is holy and completely benevolent that supports all life all the time.

This is something you would call magic now, but when you are away from this planet, it is something you take for granted. Everyone does that, all life forms, and that is how you live benevolently all over the universe. Creator, however, wishes you to learn the pitfalls that can take place in creation.

Sometimes a creator might do something that looks on the surface to be, "Oh, this is going to be wonderful, something new; I'll try this," and then results in something disastrous. There are creations, I have heard, that have been uncreated through a council of creators simply because although something that a creator generated looked on the surface like it was going to be wonderful, it turned out to be catastrophic in its impact on a wide variety of life forms. A council of creators will get together and help that creator gradually, incrementally uncreate all of that—you might say, in the context of time, from the present moment of whatever that creation is in, very gradually going back to the point of its original inception of that applied intent. It has to be done very gradually so no one suffers. In the context of time, it could take millions of years, but outside that context, it's another thing.

I am not trying to overcomplicate the book, but the Creator of this universe would like you to learn such lessons in a smaller way so that you do not make errors you would regret in a level of creation. So Creator has set up something by which you can experience creation on a very small scale. You create your own life. You can perceive errors you have made, or at the very least you can perceive errors others have made and what they have resulted in, no matter what their intention was. Very often, people do something they feel is wonderful and noble, and then the ultimate impact is not so good. It's a fine-tuning that is going on here for you, you see.

What is your advice as to how we can get beyond wars and violence and man's inhumanity to man?

For one thing, I feel it is important for you to know how very responsible you are for your own existence right now. You cannot assume that things you have observed scientifically and even simple casual observations will always be. I'm not saying this is true, but it is good for you to think about it and plan and make an effort to create, even though scientific creation will not be enough. What if you were responsible for the Sun and the Moon and the stars, so to speak? I am saying this as an example. I am saying, what if you were responsible for all that stimulates life? You might, in that sense, have a pure planet of which you might have the means so that everyone can live honorably. You might, in short, re-create Eden.

I am not saying you can do that by grafting this leaf onto that tree. What I am saying is that you must welcome all life, including your own, and you must do so beyond words. You must have the feelings. You must focus on how you can create the most benevolent surroundings and welcome all life in the most benevolent way. I am not saying that I demand this of you; I am saying, "Think about it." Consider it, and also consider that what you might now consider to be or think of as magic that is benevolent—benevolent magic, if you like—is actually something that is natural to your capabilities.

Benevolent magic is not words. Benevolent magic means that which goes beyond what you believe you can do and has only a benevolent impact for all life all the time. So it involves what people might call energy or a physical feeling. I would really prefer that the term "energy"—which is a bit vague but is an attempt to express a physical awareness of something that feels different—simply be stated as "a change in physical feeling that feels good." [Chuckles.] I know that is vague, but you can come up with different words in your different languages to define it on the basis of your physical experience with it.

It is important that you consider, what if you were responsible for welcoming all life? You are here to learn as mental beings with spiritual cores, souls, in a physical world, the component parts of creation. Although creation might seem to you to be the popular big bang theory, I assure you that is completely not true. Creator doesn't go, "*Bang*, there is life"; it is all about love. It is all about gradual creation. That is why the gestation period inside mother is nine months. It is not "*Poof*, there is baby," meaning "*Bang*, there is baby," okay? Pay attention to details like that: love, harmony, what is happening inside mother, very gentle. It impacts mother. Mother is not always comfortable, that's for sure, but it is all about a gradual re-creation of life. That is how all life is created gradually, although I grant that the process is speeded up a bit for you living here. Pay attention to details.

What if it was your responsibility to re-create the way life is created here? Begin with, "How can life be created inside woman so that it causes her no discomfort whatsoever?" Eliminate the idea in your creation—not immediately, not now, but in your magic for the future—that you are going to use drugs so she can't feel it. For now, that is fine so she doesn't suffer. But how might it be done, given the way mother's body exists? Obviously, mother's body either has to change—which I do not recommend, because it is a beautiful creation—or the size of baby has to change, or something else. Make it benevolent. That is what I suggest.

After the change in polarization and then cloning was eliminated and childbirth was instituted, how did it happen that the child is so mismatched for the birth canal and there is pain?

Creator has set up certain challenges for you that are designed to encourage you, not only to cry out to Creator for help, but to welcome your capabilities to reduce suffering to the point where it does not exist, and to do so in ways that are only benevolent to all life. Creator wants you to reach beyond the veil with an arm, so to speak, that is totally benevolent. So in that moment, you must be connected beyond the veil to your overall capabilities. In order to reach beyond the veil, you must in that moment be totally in a benevolent space for yourself, acquire those capacities that you normally have in that moment—all the while remaining in a completely benevolent space—and state your intent. Add it as a request, as one might say—a living prayer, for example—and feel the energy that supports that.

If enough of you can do that, it might be possible for something to take place that allows birth to continue but will not cause suffering to mother. I know there has been a great deal of effort scientifically and in the medical community to reduce pain and suffering. That is why most people are desirous and willing to go through all the struggle to become a doctor or nurse in the medical field. I know some people think it is just because of money, but no. It is because you want to relieve people's suffering—that is almost always the case.

So that is what it takes. You have to be what you want to create in order to create it. That is the core of any creator. That is enough for today. Let's continue next time.

MOTHER EARTH • • • **415**

⊕ Earth

MOTHER EARTH

Astrology Prepares You for Future Challenges and Informs You of Your Opportunities and Abilities

July 5, 2007

Greetings. This is Earth.

Welcome. I was looking at the wondrous rain that just came down. You're waiting for questions?

Yes.

A New System Is Being Created Astrologically

Say, in your own words, why astrology is important.

Astrology has value in that it can help people to prepare for challenges they might meet in their lives, and it is always advantageous to be prepared for these things. There is a possibility that you may not meet these challenges in any difficult way. Conversely, instead of being difficult, it might be an opportunity that presents itself. Since you are prepared and versatile in your skills—and I cannot underline versatile enough—then you will have an opportunity in that specific area, wherever that challenge might be, to easily not only take advantage of the opportunity, but if there is any challenge, to be able to surmount it with ease.

Astrology will also inform you of opportunities and abilities you have so that you don't have to become excessively aggressive in those areas to learn them, because they will be easy for you to assimilate. Knowing this will help you, your friends, your family, your greater community to welcome you as someone who potentially will have certain skills and abilities or be able to easily acquire great skill and ability in certain areas, which might make you a valuable member of the community.

Community is a very important thing these days, because it is what the overall process on Earth is all about now. Earth as a planet (speaking for myself) is uniting much more with the other planets in the solar system, and you will all be exposed on an increasing level to the energy of those planets. You will find that this helps to prepare you and to balance astrology. This is something very interesting, because it is something that is happening now.

This now thing that is happening, which will accelerate in terms of its influence over the next four to five years, will create a new situation astrologically. Many of you will discover that even though you are a Libra, for example, you will be able to accomplish things that are easy for someone who is a Gemini, and vice versa. Just using that as an example, this balance comes about because of the greater union of the planets in the solar system, so that the coordination of skills is redistributed in a more evenhanded way.

The advantage of this is that things that may have been particularly difficult for one sign—and almost every sign has something that is particularly difficult or challenging—will be greatly moderated, and things that are so simple to the point of being ridiculously simple and boring as a result to any sign (every sign has those as well) will no longer be so simple that it is boring. It will be simple, but it won't be so simple that it is boring, and this allows that balance to take place. This is largely because of the union of the planets. You won't notice anything astronomically, but you will notice this experience even with people already on the Earth. It matters not whether we are talking about a child being born or a senior citizen. This will affect you all.

Soon Misunderstandings Will End

Have the planets in this solar system been disunited in the same way that humans have been as part of this experiment for the Explorer Race?

No, rather the other planets have been a little more insulated. But now that the human beings on Earth are evolving on a soul level and reacquiring your natural skills and abilities—though it might not always be obvious to you—the other planets are casting off their blanket of insulation and will be more in their natural state of unification, one planet with the other.

Which is the natural way we are in other solar systems and other places?

Yes. The more you become your natural selves, the more you will feel the beneficent value of all of this.

Is it in the marker of 2012 that the veil will be down completely?

Whose marker is that?

Well, originally it was the Maya, but it is all over the country right now. Originally, we thought it was the end of life, and now they are looking for other significant meanings.

Well, they were right, in a way. It was the end of life as it has been known, but you are actually waking up, so to speak, as the term has been applied broadly. People are waking up already, so there is an acceleration going on. What might end sometime within, say . . . I am going to broaden that 2012 to 2017 at least. What might end along those lines will be a tendency to misunderstand. I think that is really important. As people become more comfortable with demonstrating their feelings when they talk, the chances are that communication will become clearer, regardless of the language of the other person.

For example, if you see a person talking to another person and one of them is gesticulating wildly—not in any aggressive way, just gesticulating wildly—you can be reasonably certain, even at a distance, that that person is excited about something. You are not there and you may not even know whether the person is speaking your language or not but that level of communication is clear. I would say that to demonstrate your feelings when you are talking—whether you are speaking to a loved one, whether you are speaking to a public official, whether you are simply speaking to a friend—has great value. Think about doing it in some benevolent way and trying it out as homework.

Astronomy Is the Foundational Element of Astrology

We have been discussing astrology as influences from other planets on humans on Earth, but what is your influence on each of us according to where we are born on the planet?

This is going to surprise you, but this largely has to do with blood type. Generally speaking, the way iron moves in your body is the means by which I identify individual human beings. After all, aside from being something that is detectable and reactive to magnetic energy, iron is also a mineral, so it is a part of my body, and I am inclined to be aware of where iron is in general. Even if some of my iron has gone to the Moon, for example, because of some experiment, I am aware of it as a personal awareness. So my influence with you all is through the iron in your body—which, of course, moves in your bloodstream.

How does where we are born on Earth influence our interaction with you?

If you are located, say, near mountains, that might have a certain effect. If you are located in a desert, that might have a certain effect. Generally speaking, though, everyone who stands on the ground is standing on a mountain. It is just that it has not come up yet or has already worn down. But, you know, astrology isn't called astrology for no reason. Astrology is a combined word. It is the study of "astro," meaning the study of astronomy as applied to the individual human being personally.

I wanted you to talk today about your influence on humans, because you are the major influence on us in our lives of any planet, correct?

No. I think that is a misunderstanding. Narrowly speaking, that is why I defined astrology, because you have to consider astronomy. Astronomy is the foundational element of astrology. It is just applied as personalities. Mars, in that sense, is defined as someone in the case of astrology, but this is all very basic in astrology. I would not say that I am particularly an impactful planet in terms of astrology. You have a considerable amount of information already about who I am, and thus you can extrapolate some of that into who you are—to say nothing of those who have read any of the *Explorer Race* books, particularly in this case the first book—so that you have the basic understanding of who you are.

But essentially, astrology is about external matters: how the other planets affect you while you are on Earth, as Earth citizens. Those are the basics of astrology. When astrologers give you a reading, they don't tell you that much about Earth. They say you have this and this and that and that and so on, and then you are informed to the best of the ability of the astrologer and the information provided by the person to the astrologer—which is vitally important— you are informed, then, of these influences upon you.

I would say that the more important basis of astrology is, "How can the knowledge of these influences help me in my day-to-day life?" I feel that reincarnation is not a factor, and the reason I am saying that is: why would you want to prepare for a future life when you don't know where that future life is going to be? One thing's for sure, it is not going to be on Earth.

Once you graduate us, this focus that we are on will go into being fallow for a time, to heal?

That is a nice analogy. It will be unoccupied by human beings, though there will be plants, and perhaps over time a few species of other beings may wish to be present that you refer to loosely as animals. I would guess that for a long time there would be plants and various biological matter, which is helpful to restore soil, sand and so on. So this, where you have been occupying, will become resettled, you might say, in its own time.

Are the beings who came from the planet that blew up from the Sirius system going to occupy this focus or another one similar to it?

Not likely. This is not really for this book at all, but they are slowly striving toward a different focus of this planet, one that . . . I can only put it that it is a little harder. If you had to be in that, you would find it difficult, but for them it would be quite an improvement compared to what they have been through.

Are many of us going to move onto a different focus of you?

You mean, if you have another life? You might choose to do that at a more benevolent focus of my being. That is a possibility. But those kinds of benevolent focuses would be very much like being born on some other star system, because it is like that. Life is comfortable there.

So as each person now leaves this planet, either as a walk-out or in a natural transition of what we call death, they can choose to go anywhere? They will not be coming back here, you are saying?

They can as souls. Souls do not generally choose a place. Did you know that? Souls do not say they want to go here or there; they are not geographically inclined. When they leave here, they might wish to go someplace to be with those they have known before, whom they feel good about. They might wish to go someplace where they can have certain experiences. But they never say, "I want to go to Mars," or "I want to go to Pluto," or "I want to go to Earth." They always say, "I would like to go where I can do this or have that," or their teachers might advise them to go someplace where they can experience this and that. In short, they never say, "I want to go to the Pleiades." You might think you would say that when you left here, but you wouldn't.

I Am Aware of Human Beings

So with the Explorer Race running amuck on your planet, you have suffered, you have given such service, you have loved, you have been patient. Have you gained anything from this?

Gained?

It has just been a total service, then?

It has been a service. I don't know that I've . . . how do you mean, "gained"?

Oh, gained—achieved a joy you did not have before, learned something, felt something new, knew something, anything like that.

I am not a human being, for starters. But I have certainly enjoyed many of the personalities that have come and gone, and not enjoyed other things.

How do you enjoy a personality?

How *do* you enjoy a personality?

Interacting with them, laughing with them, being stimulated by them, learning, growing, sharing.

Well, good.

You do that with humans?

I am aware of human beings. When they are happy, when they are laughing, when some wonderful thing happens, I am aware. I am there, and I join in the good feeling. When there is sadness and unhappiness, I join in that feeling as well. All planets do this.

But all planets don't have the level of discomfort this one has.

Well, I have to allow that, since that is a way you learn.

Do you feel the experiment is going to be a success?

I feel it will. Let me just say this: It is in the nature of the study of astrology that one accumulates facts that are not always complete. It is in this challenge—this missing factor, this overall enigma—that astrology beckons those who love a mystery and want to know more about themselves and others. Don't eliminate that from astrology. Always seek to understand more about the astronomical influences on your life personally. Assume that if a comet comes through your solar system—harmlessly, just passing by—that it has an astrological influence. Even if there is a large asteroid that misses your planet by hundreds of thousands of miles, nevertheless assume that it has an astrological influence.

I believe that generally astrologers do assume this. It is important to factor it into your readings and to understand that the impact of, say, a large asteroid on the overall astrological picture would be very minor. It would be less than any planet or even a moon, but it would be a flavor, like a spice. Be alert to those things, and you will always find that astrology has many changing faces. Good night.

✳ ✳ ✳

This is an astrology expert.

Welcome!

Thank you. My expertise is a little different than the expertise of the astrologers here. My expertise is a little bit more in mathematics and parallels and combinations. I do feel very good about those who are able to extrapolate parallels and combinations—please keep it up. This is very important, especially during the next eclipse. The next eclipse of the Sun will be herald to a new form of subconscious for human beings. This is what I am going to talk about.

The Subconscious Is Entirely About Resolution

Right now, the subconscious of the human being is something that is largely out of your grasp. You have momentary experiences with it that you are conscious of. For example, if you are asleep and dreaming, and you remember your dreams, as some people do, you will notice that the dream seems to be going along fine, and then as you begin to wake up, it starts to get more dramatic. That is because the influences of your world and your life have an impact on that deep experience of the dream. I'm not here to talk about dreams—I won't go into that—but that moment of transition from the dream as it is to the dramatic turn in the dream is the insertion and the moment in which you can be aware of your subconscious impacting the dream—attempting to work out that which needs to be resolved in your life or in the lives of those around you whom you care about, even if they are not part of your family. That is your moment to be aware of that aspect of you.

Now, this is important for astrologers. Know that the subconscious is going to change. The human being will have much greater access to the subconscious, and it will be experienced in such a way as you will be able to close your eyes and just . . . right now, you might close your eyes and have a daydream or a fantasy, but the subconscious of the human being will be more accessible. A human being will simply be able to close his or her eyes and, instead of having a fantasy or a daydream, tap into the subconscious.

If you know this as an astrologer, you will be able to literally tell people what issues are coming up for them, and you will be able to let them know that they can have a communion, a conversation, with their own subconscious. Their subconscious will not be able to speak, but you as a thoughtful person will be able to talk to your own subconscious. You will not be able to talk your subconscious out of something, because after all, you are there to learn that or you are there to process something you have already experienced. The subconscious does both for you to steer you to resolution.

The subconscious is entirely about resolution, nothing else. So as an astrologer, you will find yourself in the unique position of becoming somewhat of a counselor. To talk it over with your subconscious, you need to close your eyes and relax and prepare your mind as if you were going to have a fantasy or a daydream, but don't do that. Instead, just begin talking to your subconscious. Don't give it a name like a person; say, "subconscious." If you do that, then you may be able to negotiate with your subconscious, which is actually trying to help you so that you can expand your abilities and get through problems that have been challenging you. Especially if you look at your life, you might be able to say, "Well, I have been experiencing this challenge over and over again, and I would like to experience it in a new way that would be fun, benevolent and easy."

For example, as an astrologer, get used to the idea of being a counselor, because the human being will be able to do this. But it is absolutely essential—and human beings like to do this, they like to personalize things, as you know—that they do not give their subconscious a name (a pet name, you understand), because invariably there are other people, other places or even animals with that name. If you refer to your subconscious saying, "I am talking to my subconscious now," there is only one you as an individual and only one subconscious that you have.

So talk to your people about that and experiment a little bit with it on yourself. You might find that if you are having some problem on an ongoing basis—you keep having occurrences that are helping you to resolve that problem or at least to try out new things in new ways—then you can ask. You can influence your own subconscious so that those challenges, when they come up, come up in benevolent, fun ways—so that you can interact at least with people, places and things that you would enjoy and you might not even realize . . . [connection is interrupted by problems with the phone].

Thank you so much. I am so sorry about the phone.

You cannot help it or the fact that Mother Earth needs to move her electricity here and there.

That is right, as she did.

Good night.

Good night. Thank you.

ASTROLOGICAL SIGNS

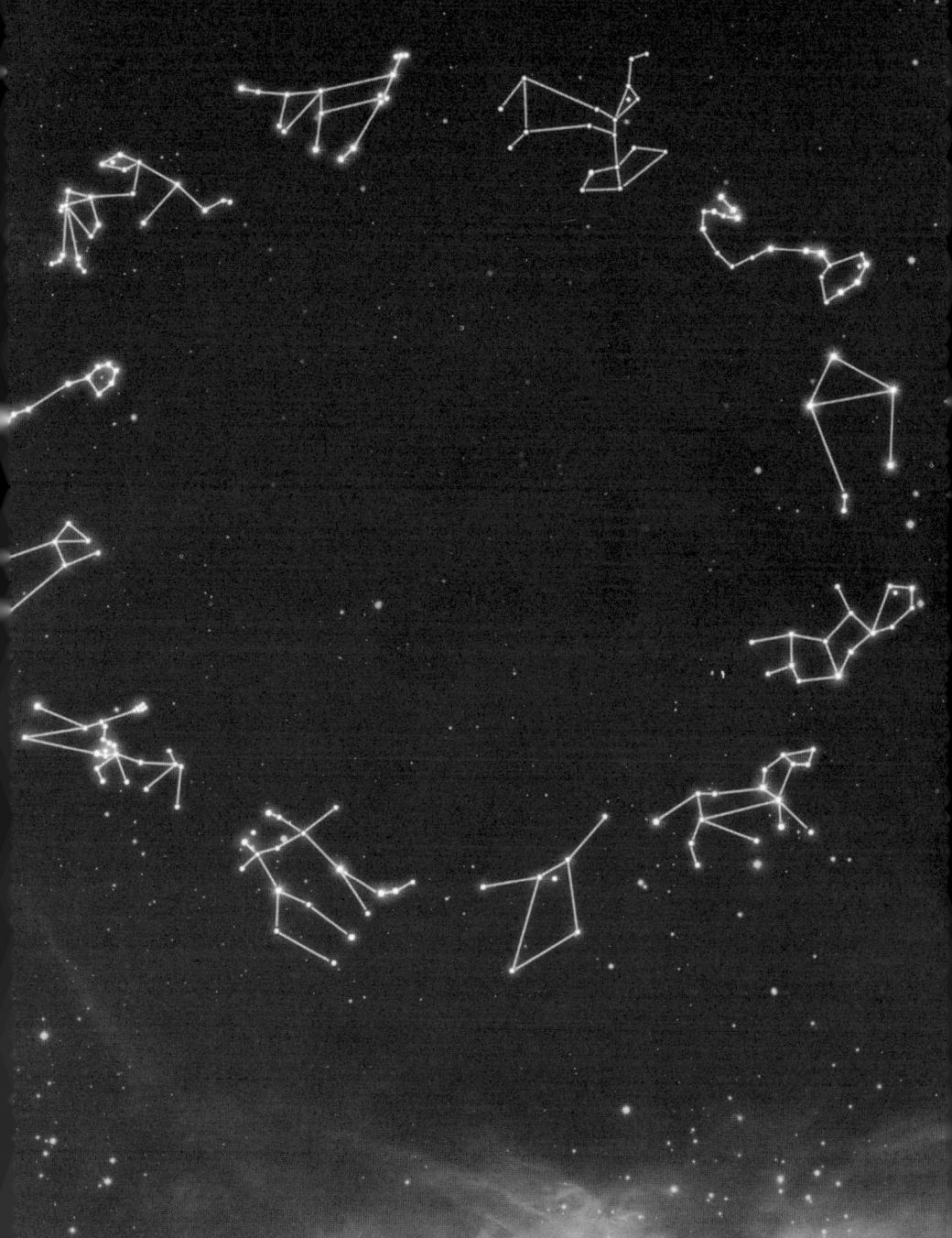

♍ **Virgo**
August 22 – September 23

# VIRGO

Encourages, Inspires and Stimulates You

July 28, 2007

Greetings. It is now possible for the channel to do the signs for the astrologic book.

Well, that's incredible! Are you a composite energy?

I am, yes, a composite energy that can speak some details, known and unknown, about the sign. I will attempt to speak more about what is unknown than what is known. In order to assist astrologers and to help them gain fine points, we will stay on this until we have completed the signs, in case you want to know what the plan is. In this way, you need not know much about the signs—just basic keywords, what they are known for—and you will, after today, have an idea of what sort of questions to ask.

Virgos Have the Capacity to Inspire and Stimulate

So Virgo is known for detail and precision, and those of that sign are often very good choices when the examination of details are required, but there is more to Virgo than that. Virgo has the reputation for being self-critical and appearing to be critical of others, but often the criticism from Virgo toward others is disguised. In fact, that which Virgos criticize is often that which they feel critical about in themselves, but this is known to astrologers. Now let's go deeper.

Some of the lesser-known facts about Virgos have to do with the qualities of life they can inspire in others. Virgos have the capacity to induce others to achieve greater heights than all their astrologic potential suggests. Virgos do not do this by demanding or commanding but rather by inspiring. One of the most inspirational signs is Virgo, because they can by their very energy stimulate all the other signs, including the totally balanced ones, to achieve beyond their capacity.

This is why, if you are running a company, you are going to want to have in the upper echelons of the company at least one person who is a Virgo. It is most important that this person be feminine. The feminine in general for the human being inspires. Mothers are well-known for inspiring children, and a great many teachers in schools, especially those who teach youngsters or even teenagers, are feminine. So your culture is used to the idea of being inspired by the feminine. The feminine Virgo has the capacity to inspire and also, simply by broadcasting the energy of her being, can stimulate the subconscious desires of those who wish to succeed. Businesses who wish to see the very best from their ambitious people will expose them to the Virgo energy.

Here's a suggestion to businesses: Consult your astrologer—I know, if you are reasonably successful, you have one—and see if you can find someone who is capable of simply broadcasting his or her own energy. This might be people who meditate or who can center themselves sufficiently into their own personality that they can sit quietly, say in a meeting, especially where new products or services are being discussed. So these people will simply sit quietly, either seen by those in the room but not called upon, or perhaps behind a thin screen (but it has to be fiber and not silk, perhaps a loose-weave cotton), and they would simply be focused in their own centered personality and request as much energy to flow through them as possible.

You might find that people you know have capacities who have inner ambitions but are reticent to speak out, will be more likely to speak out—either voicing concerns or voicing opinions that you desire them to speak of, but for some reason they are slow to do so. I recommend that. Now, this works also in education. The same process can work if students are slow to respond or slow to act on their personal ambitions. Of course, at the student level, it might be valuable to know what those ambitions are.

Conversely, on more unpleasant levels, if Virgos are broadcasting their own energy in the criminal world, what might otherwise be something that people would not do might come to the fore and they might do it. So it's important to be alert to that. I am not saying that Virgos have criminal tendencies, but rather because of their energy broadcast—having the capacity to encourage those people who have unfulfilled and often unspoken desires to drop their inhibitions and speak up or act—then Virgos must be considered profound beings for inspiration but also for stimulation.

Now, there's more. Virgo has a very special relationship with the Sun. The Sun is that which energizes all the planets, yes, but the Sun has a relationship to all other suns in the universe. The suns in the sign of Virgo are particularly connected to the Sun in your solar system. As a result, Virgo's relationship to the Sun in your solar system is profound indeed. If you incorporate the Sun, astrologers, into the center of the Virgo chart, you may discover aspects about Virgo that you had not considered. This is important and cannot be overlooked.

One more thing: Virgo has a relationship to the sign of Aquarius that has not been explored fully. Aquarius has capabilities that are mysterious, meaning they have the capacity to feel and know. But equally, when linked with Aquarius—and this is especially important for Virgos who have Aquarius, say, as a rising sign, for example—when there is a link with Aquarius, Aquarians as individuals or that more personal connection in a person's chart, the Aquarian energy can act as a further stimulant to Virgo's broadcast ability to inspire. This is essential to know if you are creating a chart for a family, for a business, for a corporation, or for governmental circles. I recommend that you look into that further.

All Signs Need to Be Encouraged to Be Who They Are

Virgo has a considerable interest in health, hygiene and diet. Can you expand on that?

Virgo is known for being detail-oriented, and there is no limit to this. Virgo is often attracted to the immediate, and what more immediate can there be but one's physical body? Virgos often have some quality about their person that they perceive needs to be improved. It can be physical, it can be mental, it can be on the feeling level, and so on. As a result, Virgo has a tendency to search, in great detail, the possible alternatives to conventional practices to improve these various physical, mental and emotional qualities. This is why Virgo is known for this.

How can Virgos compensate for being so attached to the minutiae, to the minute details, that they lose sight of the overall picture?

It is not their job to do that. One is born with a choice of a specific sign; it is not accidental. You choose the predominant signs in your chart because you want to pursue certain qualities, certain details in your life, and you want to make certain that the opportunities will be present to pursue them. Therefore, you choose to a degree—not to infinite detail, but you choose to a degree— that capacity to be guided by the general signs of your birth. So it is not Virgos' job to deny who they are but rather to fulfill it to the best of their capacity.

It is my intention (and I believe it will be with the others who speak for this book) to encourage that all signs be encouraged to be who they are. It is not for any sign—person, you understand, of a predominant sign—to be anything else. You are not here to be a well-rounded individual: an Aries is not expected to be a Libra. Granted, you might have Libra in your chart, but you're not expected to be that if a predominant sign, say your Sun sign, is Virgo. Your job is to be that Virgo to the best of your ability. I see no advantage in encouraging people to be something other than what they are, because they are born with these talents. Why discourage them?

So would one choose to become a Virgo or any sign because one already has those abilities and wants to go deeper, or because one is the opposite and wants to bring that into his or her skill set or develop that?

It isn't either/or. It could be that you wish to heighten these capabilities, for example, but it also could be because these capabilities are lacking in your soul's overall experience and because of something you wish to do in the next life. For instance—using the sequence of time as a potential here—you may wish to gain the capacity to see the details or to broadcast the inspiration quietly. Think of how many cultures exist where words are not that profound of an influence. There are some cultures, even on your planet now, that do not rely on words so much as gestures and physical motion. Someone who can broadcast inspiration by his or her very being would be a profoundly valuable person in that society. Why encourage that person to be anything but that?

Astrologers Can Rely More on Their Capacity for Inspiration

So you're saying Virgos broadcast inspiration?

Inspiration in the sense of a stimulation to encourage inspiration by others. Say you are in a business meeting and other people are talking about things and you have ideas, but the ideas are not formulated into words. They're more like feelings, and you can't really put them into words. What a wonderful thing to have someone to be able to stimulate inspiration in others so that you might get a word or two. With the beginning of those feelings converted into a word or two, you might be able to offer something that could help your company—or your family or your group of friends—avoid some catastrophic mistake or perhaps see a different way of expressing the project that you're working on.

So they inspire someone to be able to more fully activate their own inspiration—would you say it like that?

No, I would say they broadcast their own energy, which could stimulate and make available and, to a degree, cause other people to be more receptive to their own inspiration.

That's incredible. Are Virgos attracted only to the facts—like scientific, literary, mathematical—or are they imaginative? Is their imagination more detail-oriented, too?

Everything about them is associated with the infinite—meaning there is no limit to their capacity to see, experience, feel or express the details about something. This does not mean they do not have the capacity to express the broader range. It means that they are most likely to discover and to show details to others or point them out. But this is known about Virgo. So your job, as the questioner, would be to ask questions about what is not known about this sign, you understand? Focus on what is not known and pursue that, as you have been doing.

Okay. How could you describe yourself?

I am not someone. I am speaking as a synthesis of the Earth relationship to the constellation that you identify as Virgo. So I am, in that sense, a combined thought and physical personality. I am a consensus of that. It is a delicate balance maintaining that, so we will not be able to talk too long. I am what there is. I am what is available. What you are hearing is a synthesis of points of understanding. After we cease speaking, this synthesis will cease to exist. It is a temporary means of communication for what is basically a compilation of thought and wisdom.

Can astrologers tune in to this synthesis? Can they ask for it or can they meditate on this connection?

Always. But if they do so, remember to have in front of you simply a book or your tablets or your knowledge—not on the computer; it must be in print, solid paper—of what is known generally or what you have personally written about Virgo, for example. I recommend you put your left hand on that. Then if you have a photograph—or even if you could look at the night sky at certain times of the year and see the constellation, but a photograph is adequate—put your other hand on that and meditate. But first make sure that the paper it's printed on is something that feels comfortable to you.

That's beautiful. Thank you. Is that true for all the signs?

I would say yes. I feel it is most important for astrologers, if they have not, to include their inspirations. Granted, they won't always be correct, but astrologers now have the capacity that has been amplified to achieve a greater level of inspired capacity to move beyond their best guess as to what other qualities signs might have and how those signs are mirrored to other signs. Given the motion of the chart, as you know, signs mirror other signs through the connections known as trines, and when this mirroring takes place, one sign may seem to act like another—but this is known to astrologers. It's most important that you meditate, if you like, or choose inspiration as well as hard facts. Don't be shy. You can do this in a separate reading; you could call it an experimental reading if you like, for those of your clientele who are a bit more adventurous.

Let Astrology Be Flexible

You're not an astrologer, but you will be a little more versatile in astrology by the time this book is done.

[Laughs.] I don't know why I've been resisting it so long.

That's why it's been hard for you to do this book. I will say this much: There has been a reluctance in training for you in this life to give over authority to anything that bespeaks of a dogma. Astrology has come to be known for being dogmatic. That is why I am encouraging astrologers to stretch and use their inspiration. It is very important that astrology not be in any way associated with science, other than astronomical. That's all right, astronomy is fine, but don't try to make it into a science. Science desires nothing more than to be predictable, and astrologers must not allow themselves to fall into that trap. Of course, your clients wish for you to make predictions for them; that is acceptable. But if astrology remains fixed and predictable, it cannot move forward. The whole purpose of this book is to help astrology and astrologers in their application to move forward.

In short, don't be afraid to be wrong. Always preface something that you are saying with your inspiration as, "This is my inspiration for you." In that way, it separates it from what is known and provable, but it will also allow astrology to become flexible and feminine. The feminization of astrology is written; it is intended. Don't get bogged down in the fad of science. Science, at this time, is a fad in the way it is being pursued, with the ideas most rigid being popular. But anyone who is observing the technological boom these days will recognize that the tendency is more toward the leading edge of physics, which is totally flexible. Science is moving toward massive flexibility. Don't be left behind: let astrology be flexible as well. It will be the tendency of the synthesis of the signs to speak of these matters discussed for this book, to reveal the personality of these syntheses so as to help astrologers identify personality traits that they can extrapolate into further qualities of the sign itself.

This does not mean that Virgos are chaste or pure. It just means that, for example, if Virgos gets an idea about something, they might tend to focus on that idea exclusively and examine all the different directions, possibilities and angles of that idea. So there is no disadvantage there. Why not examine all the possibilities of it? One could find potentials for growth or possible exploration of something that has not been explored, and one might equally find potentials for fault and failure so that those avenues are not exploited.

Remember, the signs are not intended to become balanced amongst all the other signs. The purpose of having individual planetary influences and signs is to express aspects of variety. Variety is intended so that you will all be attracted to each other's capabilities. You are here on Earth to learn teamwork and to learn to value each other. You are not here to become all of the capabilities of each sign yourself in one life; you are intended to depend on each other. If you are a Sagittarius, you do not have to be a Virgo; make a Virgo friend (or more than one), and ask your friend his or her opinion about some matter that you do not grasp. Conversely, if you are a Libra and need the advice and wisdom of a Leo, go to the Leo; don't practice being one.

I Encourage the Developmental Capabilities of Others

Can you say anything about your contribution to what was previously talked about in the book as a thirteenth sign, which is a synthesis of all the signs?

My contribution there has to do with the capacity to encourage the developmental capabilities of others. You can see that this is similar to what I've said before associated with Virgo but not exactly the same, because the developmental capabilities would be something that are known to an individual, but they may not have considered certain means of expressing those capabilities. They might think of themselves, for example, as being someone who likes to ride horseback, but they may not have considered what they could *do* on horseback. They may not have considered where they could go. They may not even have considered that they have qualities that are artistic associated with horses. In short, they may not have fully explored their capacities in their fields of interest. That's my contribution.

Would you say the percentage of those choosing the Virgo sign is more on the side of those who are already detail-oriented or those who want to achieve that?

I would say that it is more likely those who would desire to achieve that or to sharpen up their capabilities in the world of the physical to achieve that. Generally speaking, those who choose to be born to that—or have that significantly in their charts—may have explored the capacity to see many things, to feel many things and so on in other lives. But here, in a slower-moving physical world where examination is possible, they might find that attractive. So it is more likely that one would have had previous experience, but it is not exclusively the case.

Astrological pursuits are a great deal about fine lines. Think of it this way: You walk into an art museum and you look at some fine old painting. The museum people don't want you to get too close to the picture, so you look at the picture in some other way—perhaps in a photograph, a blowup of tiny little portions—and you can see the brushwork. In short, you can examine the picture's details in certain ways (in books, for example) and you can see different aspects of the picture that you hadn't seen before, even subtle messages that are not obvious from a distance. But as you examine the details closer, what the artist is attempting to reveal may be very fine details indeed.

Sometimes the direction of the brush stroke is intended to influence those who look at it. Do you know that if the artist uses a longitudinal brush stroke, the tendency is in the viewer of that artwork to relax, but if they use a vertical brush stroke, the tendency is to become aroused or stimulated? Did you know that? That's an example of the value of examining detail that Virgo is known for.

Look at a painting like that some time. You will notice that the direction of the brush stroke has an impact as well as the image. This kind of thing is usually studied in more esoteric circles in art, but you artists out there, if you're reading this, incorporate it (if you don't already know about it) into your paintings or even in other forms of expressive artwork. It might surprise you and even delight you how your audience reacts.

It is important to recognize the qualities of personality associated with a sign, and I believe the planets have made this clear, trusting astrologers to recognize and interpret those planetary personalities and add that interpretation into their knowledge base. It is my intention and, I believe, the intention of the other signs to reveal such qualities themselves per the planets so that astrologers can apply, learn, know and interpret for themselves and others.

Is there anything else?

No. I will make a closing comment.

Remember, You Are Not a Fixed Sign

If you are a Virgo, feel good about yourself and consult with your astrologer. Remember, you are not a fixed sign; you can change and grow. Remember, when you are examining yourself or anything else, to look at all sides. It is all right to have such an honest approach, but even if you see that which can be faulted, remember how many ingredients go in to making the finest food. Sometimes, when tasted, some of those ingredients on their own taste terrible, but when combined with all the other ingredients, they make the most wonderful taste. Remember that about yourself and about all else, and you will be at peace. May you have the most wonderful life. Good night.

Thank you very much.

435

♊ **Gemini**
May 22 – June 21

GEMINI

Brings You Adaptability, Flexibility and New Abilities

August 1, 2007

This is Gemini.

Welcome!

Thank you. Now let us begin.

Recently You Have Felt the Overwhelming Presence of Impatience

The known traits of Gemini, some of which you are familiarizing yourself with as we speak, are all correct. Yet even after thousands of years of observations by astrologers and lay people, there are other traits. You might reasonably wonder why these other traits have not been noticed. I don't know if Virgo mentioned this, but there is a reason.

Now that you are coming into the next step in the re-culturalization of the human race on Earth into your more natural being, the traits that are associated with your natural being are being slowly assimilated into your lives and hence, by the astute astrologer, into your charts and into your future. For those of you out there who are performing these functions, I recommend a chart that is based upon the material in this book (it can be titled anything you want), and I am suggesting that you begin now to look for these traits. Don't assume that these traits will only appear in the very young; age has nothing to do with it. It is entirely about timing, you might say. You can be ninety years old, you can be four years old—it doesn't make any difference. These times are bringing you all into your more natural state of being.

One of the universal traits that is being accentuated in you all is something that might be considered a negative trait, but there is a reason for it, and that is impatience. Patience, granted, is a lesson here on Earth and has been for many years, but many of you have noticed, in the past year or two especially—and even for some of you a little before that—the overwhelming presence of impatience. It is in almost every single thing that you do. When you get up in the morning and you're dressing, even if you have a day off, even if you're on vacation, you feel impatient. When you're talking to others, the energy of impatience absolutely infiltrates every word you have. When others are speaking to you, even if you're absolutely fascinated with something they're saying, you are feeling impatient.

So what's that all about? As I say, it might be considered a negative trait, but there is a reason for it. Here you all are, desiring more than anything else to be home—"home" meaning to feel completely relaxed, loved, accepted for exactly who you are, so that you can be who you are. Home may not always be your physical home. Home might very well be a home that is associated with your total being: your soul, your spirit, your immortal personality. Since this is an unwritten agenda for almost all of you—except, granted, the very, very young—then what you have is this building impatience to get there because you have had the sense—the flavor, so to speak—of your natural selves with you.

This is something that is slowly filtering into you every day. Some of it is this and that trait for individuals, yes. But for everyone there is also a profound sense of anticipation. Anticipation can be considered a positive trait very often, if one is open and wide-ranging and accepting. Yet we can all see how very well anticipation can lead to impatience with just the slightest little nudge, eh? So this is what's being fed to you—not anticipation per se, but the reaction for you all is anticipation.

If you were to feel it on Earth from another human being as life is now, the energy would feel very much like anticipation. But the actual energy—it's hard to put a word on it in any known language on Earth—is about core necessary being. Core necessary being—granted, not one word—is entirely about the means to adapt to your natural state of being in an environment that would normally be hostile to it. I'm not necessarily referring to your friends, your family, your work, your home—none of that. I'm referring to the culturalization of Earth by all human beings over these many years.

Animals Help Stimulate Your Natural State

This is why so very many of you get a sense of peace and calm, and can enjoy these feelings being stimulated in you now by the natural state of self becoming slowly in you by being, say, in a forest, if you can find one, around natural animals—meaning beings who do not owe their survival in any way to anything human beings are doing for them, though they might be struggling a bit with what human beings are doing (not necessarily for themselves, but sometimes just as a result of something for themselves, such as pollution, for example). But still, if you get far enough into the forest, you might be around birds and earthworms and beetles and ants. In short, you might be around some creatures who still have a strong sense of their natural souls.

Pets, while they do have some of this, are very often adapting to the traits, not only of the human culture that they must adapt to in order to live with humans, but also to the traits of the humans they live with. This is especially the case with transformative pets, meaning those who might take on traits for you, might adapt the negative energy of those traits—meaning by taking on traits for you, they take on the excesses of those traits—who might adapt to those excesses in such a way as it could negatively impact their health. But because they love you, they are prepared to take that on so that you do not get sick.

Some of these animals are well known to you: horses, cats, dogs. There are a few other pets who will do this at times: cockatoos will do it almost always by suddenly making the sounds that they make unexpectedly. Most cockatoos have sounds that they make on a cyclical basis. People who live with them come to expect those sounds. They may not be very loud or they may be loud, but there are sounds that are made. Pets sometimes do this as well, but it is difficult to tell when they are expressing those traits. In the case of parrots, it is not about the sounds; it is about the ruffling of the feathers. They might be ruffling the feathers for themselves, but very often they are transforming excessive energy whose traits are impinging upon your benign state of being.

The First World Order Is Based on the Global Family

I bring up these things that are influencing the environment for all human beings because it must be taken in context, what is said here by the synthesis of these signs into the functionality of your cultures on Earth and the gradually evolving culture that is emerging of the business corporate model, which is becoming out of necessity the first so-called world order. As you probably know, although some of you might bridle at that term, the first world order is based upon this model because almost everyone can at some level agree that it has value.

You might grow potatoes on your farm and you need to get those potatoes to market. Everyone understands that. But what about someone who works making Fords, for example, or Chevrolets or Volvos, for that matter? You might not see immediately how what somebody else does on the other side of the world, growing this or making that, directly affects you, but the term "the world is shrinking" has more to do with the interchange of cultures, ideas and products.

Products have a tendency to unite you. You may, as an individual, for this or that reason not be comfortable with a certain race or type of person. Maybe it is simply because you have never been around them before. But you might go to a restaurant that serves that type of cuisine and love it, and as a result be sometimes exposed to that culture and the people of that culture. So you might then become more adaptable to that culture, perhaps even fond of it. You have had that experience, many of you.

This union, based upon mutual need, is often considered the corporate model, but think about it—is it not also based upon family? We do things for each other, yes, in a family: "I do this for you. You do this for me." We do this because we love each other, yes? But in the broader market, Mom tells you to go to the store and you go to the store, but the store does not give you the milk and bread. You must purchase it, even though the people might know you personally, might like you personally. Maybe you play softball with them, maybe you go out and play futball with them (that's f-u-t, okay?), maybe you simply enjoy a nice quiet and lengthy game of cricket with them, who knows? The main thing is that you enjoy them, they enjoy you, but you have to pay for it—the milk, the bread and so on.

As you know, this situation prevails, so the first world order is based upon the expanded family—meaning the family beyond your family, your neighborhood in a sense, where you go to purchase products and services. Others in your neighborhood might also come to you to purchase your products or services, or hire you and give you a job and give you pay for that job and so on. You understand that in your neighborhood, but you need to recognize that this first world order is based upon the global family. You will need to actually be grateful for the people you don't know and have never met but will learn more about, because there is a desire to know (isn't there?) about the people who are manufacturing products or providing services on the other side of the world, and so you shall. This is why the first world order is based upon what has come to be known as the corporate model but what I would prefer to call the "extended family." I feel that is important, and I feel it is the true basis for this book.

Advancing Adaptability for Others

Now, here's a little about myself. In terms of referents that are not associated with the known aspects of Gemini, one of the aspects for which I will come to be known will be an ability to advance on a local and international level an ability to perform a trait or an act heretofore entirely unknown to that individual. So it may be possible in times to come that you might be at some convention, let's say, and you are surrounded by people providing services and demonstrating different forms of conduct—or, for that matter, demonstrating how to use products and so on. You will look at something and feel an affinity for it for no particular reason, and you will almost be able to substitute for someone in that booth demonstrating that product within about twenty minutes—meaning that is how adaptable you will be to it.

This is an important trait, because it will give you a sense of reassurance that continuity that is not based upon this and this and this connected . . . that continuity can be associated on a parallel-line basis, not just on a continuous-line basis. What does that mean? You are in a family, perhaps. You have a mom and dad and a couple of children, maybe a grandma and grandpa, maybe some uncles and aunties, and you are all on certain parallel courses when you are with each other. You sit around the table or you sit on the floor—whatever your culture is—and you have a meal, and you enjoy each other's company while you are having the meal. That would be an example of parallel courses.

This is a situation like that. You find yourself so adaptable to something that you do not know, have never heard of, but it is something that in that moment you have a complete compatibility with. It is very possible that later on when you are no longer in that convention you will wonder how on earth you were able to do that, and it might even make you a little nervous. But should you be exposed to that situation again in the right circumstances, with the right people around and no expectation by others that you perform this amazing so-called magic trick again, you might be able to do it. But don't pressure yourself.

The purpose for these things that you will be able to do almost miraculously—and then later on maybe not—is to remind you that the union of all beings can be shared. This will pop up from time to time in exposure to foreign languages as well. I am not saying that you will necessarily be able to speak a foreign language like a native, but you might find that for a time, under the right circumstances, you will be able to understand more of that foreign language than you ever imagined you could. A lot of this will have to do with picking up the nuances of what the people are feeling as they are speaking—if their feelings match what they are saying—and other times it will simply be that parallel adaptation, one to one.

We were told that adaptability was a gift given to us by the Pleiadians, but you are saying that Geminis are much more adaptable than the rest of the population?

You think that what I am speaking about is a Gemini trait? Do you think that all of what I am saying now has to do with Gemini? Did you not understand when I gave my opening statement that I was talking about everybody? The first thing I spoke of that had to do only with Gemini was that trait I just mentioned. Other than that, it has to do with everyone.

Okay. May I ask why you are focusing on humanity as a whole when we are talking about the sign of Gemini?

It is very simple—every single sign contributes to the whole. What is the whole?

All of us.

Yes, so why should I not speak about the whole?

Well, I am glad you are.

We are agreed.

Gemini Will Help You Connect More Strongly to Your Guides

I will state one more trait, and then we can either do questions or finish sooner. There is a second trait that I will come to be known for—and you understand that all of you have certain aspects of all the traits in the wheel of astrology at different times of your life, but you can consult astrologers about that. But here's the other trait I will come to be known for: When breathing and feeling the sense of physicality—not just when uncomfortable in the body, but perhaps when invigorated for some reason or enthusiastic and noting one's physical response—I will also come to be known for a bridging effect that takes place during that moment of physical enthusiasm (not excitement) that bridges beyond those physical traits associated with enthusiasm (that sort of exultant feeling) and connects much more strongly with one's own personal guides.

One might have a sense of image, persona, in the guide—not necessarily seeing your guide as the guide might choose to look at that time, but a sense of location where the guide might be (generally, it will be to your left, meaning the perception of your awareness of that being will generally be to your left). You might have a sense of actual location, which is very useful since, when you are feeling inspirations where you sometimes have words—usually a single word, but occasionally two—if you know the location of your guide, you will be able to identify the clarity and the certainty that those words are coming from your guide because of the physical location you have identified that guide to be in.

That will be a Gemini trait?

That will be a trait that Gemini helps to introduce into the world. I can see that there is another misperception here, simply based upon language. The traits that are being introduced by these signs will not exclusively remain the traits of those signs. They will be donated to the environment in general. So the traits will come through these signs, be noticed initially with people who are identified as that sign—for some specific reason in their chart at that time or born to, perhaps—but the traits will not remain exclusive to that sign. They will simply join the pool of more available traits to human beings at large.

They will, in that sense, accentuate the availability of those traits and allow human beings, even though they may not be feeling Gemini at that time, to have greater access to those traits. Granted, the traits stated by each sign will be more generally available to that sign, but they will also be available to a greater amplitude to the general populace.

That is wonderful—like an expanded potential.

Yes. Very good.

Is that what you will contribute to the thirteenth sign too—these things you have talked about?

I think you will have to speak to that sign.

Okay. I didn't know we could.

Perhaps.

All Aspects of Astrology Are Useful

So like Virgo, you have come together now for this session. You don't normally exist, do you, as a being?

Correct. I am a synthesis, and as such my personality, as you are experiencing, is donated by many—temporarily, of course.

Are they personalities of constellations? Who has donated these qualities?

All that is associated with Gemini in its purest, most benevolent state.

Gemini always seems associated with the mind.

That might be why I felt it was helpful to give an overview to those reading the book who may not be astrologers but who may have a general interest in astrology, as anyone might, simply because it is a profound tool of adaptation to Earth. Understand that astrology is not some taskmaster. It is not telling you who you are and who you must be. It is a tool to utilize in order to adapt in the easiest, most comfortable way to Earth life as an Earth human being. Is not such a tool of great value?

If one thinks of it that way, then one sees, "How can I go anywhere without having a certain basic understanding of astrology, at least for me, to understand who I am and how I fit into the world of these other signs?" One need not, of course, carry around an encyclopedia of astrology, but one might reasonably wish to have such tools available so that one will not assume that one's personality traits, for example, are unique and exclusive to one's self. It is always educational to meet other people who are of the same sign—to say nothing of close to your birth date—who might at various times exhibit traits, many of whom you might enjoy if you know they are that sign and some from time to time that you might find annoying, just as others from time to time might find you annoying (anyone, you understand).

So I feel that such a tool to learn how to live on Earth more easily and comfortably is most definitely a great gift. Now, understand that we are using astrology associated with the Western world for this book, but there are other approaches to astrology. While this book does not make much of an effort to reach out in that direction, perhaps other books in the future will be applying capacities and donating knowledge about those other approaches to astrology globally.

Like Vedic and Chinese and all the different ones?

For example, yes. These are different points of view based upon observations and cultures that, in some cases, have not been as homogenized as the cultures of the West have become, meaning with more consistent threads. So astrology or that which might come to be identified as astrology might then express itself with a different face. I am not saying one is better than the other, but depending upon where you live, who you are, and the insights and wisdoms offered, they can all be complementary.

What about heliocentric astrology, using the Sun as the center? Is there a benefit to that?

Oh, yes. All aspects of astrology, even ones some people might consider esoteric, are very useful, because they allow not only astrologers to grasp the subtle nature of the person they are assisting but, most importantly, to understand the hidden aspects. That is the whole point of heliocentric astrology, to understand that which is hidden—but in this case of heliocentric, that which will be most likely to emerge. If you know as a lay person that some trait is likely to emerge sometime in your life, you might become obsessed with it and look for it and misidentify it. But if—and this is a very important thing in your society—it is your astrologer who knows and not necessarily you, then you do not have to carry around the constant anxiety: "Is that going to come up? Is this going to come up?"

When it does come up, your astrologer will be able to help you and guide you through any bumps on the road, so to speak, that those traits might suggest or reveal themselves as. Equally, your astrologer might be able to help you to utilize these capacities that may be new to you or simply what was almost unconscious, which becomes a conscious physical adaptation. This is why very often when people consult professionals of this or that service, those people do not necessarily tell you everything. It is not that there are secrets. It is just that there has come to be known, in the case of astrology, that if the person knows too much, there is a tendency to focus on those things that may not have anything to do with your life at that time and can confuse and confound you. You might be looking for something that simply isn't there at that time, misidentify something going on in your life as that thing that isn't there yet, and pursue a path that is filled with rocks and boulders because your guides are trying to deter you from that path since it is not the right time for it.

Let your astrologer have this knowledge with, say, a heliocentric study. This does not mean getting a heliocentric reading is not available to the layperson, but the astrologer may not reveal everything he or she knows until you exhibit those traits. That is why it might be advantageous, if at all possible, to try and stay with either the same astrologer or the same family of astrologers—meaning that if the profession is passed down from, say, mother to daughter, or father to son, or what-have-you, then it is likely that who and what you have been will be taken into account. Nevertheless, if that is not possible for you, a good astrologer may have the tools of the variety, such as heliocentric, to study and get a pretty good idea of where you have been on your path and what you might expect.

That is amazing. I see almost like a picture of a bud turning into a flower. You don't need to know about the flower when you are still the bud, right?

Exactly, and it could confuse you. So it's very important, that. You can understand it in the light of other professions as well. Someone might be fascinated in what another profession does and would like to emulate it, but it may not be for you. Perhaps your own profession will allow you to express your natural talents and abilities.

It's Important for Astrology to Be Complimentary to a Child

Would it be good for parents to get a reading for their child and then again at intervals as the child grows up, almost like getting a checkup every so often?

In the case of a parent. I don't necessarily recommend that the child have to sit down and listen to it. But once children get to be around five, six, seven, eight years old, they might be interested because they are interacting with other members of society—not just children, but other adults and older children. They are at school, and it might help them to perceive these differences in a way that can create even more safety for them, to say nothing of the safety that the parents can provide by guidance, advice and protection.

So the idea of having a general overview of these things—not to complicate the child's mind, but a general overview (a few keywords: this, that, not that)—might be useful. This is what I suggest. If you are going to have a personal reading for yourself, say, about the coming year and what you might expect as possibilities for you and maybe, maybe not, I don't recommend that your children be there for that. If the children are very young, of course, they could sleep, or perhaps if the astrologer has some entertainments for a child, they could watch the television in another room or something—what many astrologers might do.

But, on the other hand, the time might come when the astrologer would talk very quietly—meaning very simply, very gently and nurturingly, not demanding in any way—and say, "Well, you are an Aquarius," or something like that. "What a wonderful sign." It is important to be complimentary to the child, because children live in a world of disapproval. This is challenging. Generally speaking, a child in society is exposed to more disapproval than approval. This is why many people in your Western world and other worlds—the Eastern world very often as well, to say nothing of north and south [chuckles]—will often grow up confused about who and what they are, and will start looking for things they admire in the signs of others rather than in the astrological unity of one's own capacities. Nevertheless, the astrologer must be complimentary: "My, you are an Aries. Isn't that wonderful?" and then say, "Some of the things that Aries might find easier to do than others would be . . ." Just list off two or three, and speak them to the child.

Someday—and perhaps this exists now—there might be astrology books written very simply for the very young. That is fine, but it has to be kept simple, cheerful and complimentary. If there are suggestions as to what to avoid—pitfalls, so to speak—then that has to be put also in a benevolent way. It cannot be demanding or commanding. There is a reason for this—not just psychological. If you are constantly being exposed to disapproval in one way or another, even from those who love you—sometimes for perfectly rational and reasonable purposes, reasons—if you are exposed to it all the time, you will gradually begin to deflect and tune it out. You also gradually begin to doubt yourself as a human being. This is why it is hard for teachers to teach, because the children have been wounded a bit, even in the most benevolent situations (but we'll talk about that another time).

The main thing is that the astrologer must be primarily complimentary and nurturing, even if the child is, according to the parent and others, misbehaving. Generally speaking, even if the child is suspicious of an adult being complimentary [chuckles], it is best to be that way when children are twelve years old or less. Once they get to be more adolescent, developing their own personalities, then they can be exposed to as much complexity as the astrologer feels the youngster can take in on the basis of his or her actual interest. You will be able to choose that as an astrologer, knowing what you are able to know about the child's basic information.

That is speaking to the child directly. But if a parent gets a reading on a child, wouldn't that help the parent know which way to guide the child a little better?

It would be very helpful, because sometimes as a parent you might simply not have been exposed—on an intimate level, as one is exposed on an intimate level to any family member—to the traits of personality (especially budding, as in a child) that your child is expressing. You might assume that something is not a good trait, when, in fact, it might simply be the roots and shoots, so to speak, of that trait developing, which will come to be a good thing.

For example, since I started off talking about patience and impatience, children are affected by patience and impatience, of course. Generally speaking, to the best of your ability as a parent, you must be patient with the child and you must assume that the child will make mistakes—whatever mistakes are considered in your culture, in your family or in your country, for example, or in your town. You must allow for that, and cultures must also allow for that—and for the most part, cultures do allow for that. But as an individual parent, be patient and not too demanding. Assume that your child will need to be reassured on a regular basis.

Just as with lovers—husbands, wives or other forms of lovers—it is not all right to say, "I love you" once, where you said it and that's that. If you love someone, you might very well need to say it more than once a day, because it is not about the words, it is not about the thought. It is about the feeling that is engendered before, during and after you say the words. In the case of a parent with your children, you might say, "I love you, dear," and touch them or pick them up and hold them, if they are still [chuckles] of an age where they desire that and enjoy that. If they are older, you might simply say, "I love you."

I know it is hard work, but when a parent says, "I love you," to a child especially—not just to the other parent, although that is also important—feel it before you say it, while you say it, and after you say it. This is good training for the child, because it is a training based upon the unspoken. When you are broadcasting a feeling of that genuine love, which involves patience and acceptance, then the child grows to identify love with those qualities of feeling, not just with words. Then later on in life, when someone says, "I love you," and those feelings are not present, that child will have the foundation of discernment to know what love is.

That is beautiful.

Geminis Can Help You Learn How to Be Flexible

Too often parents, I think, say one thing and feel another. We all do.

Yes, but change is possible. I have found it to be so, and other Geminis, I believe, have found it to be so. You can all learn that from Geminis. It is not easy to be flexible, but if you want to learn how to be flexible—not a crash course, mind you, just a little exposure—if you have a friend who is a Gemini, notice how easy it is for him or her to change. You don't have to be like that, but just be around it and see that it is possible to change and not only live to tell about it but to thrive.

It is hard to change for most of us.

Sometimes it is possible. Do you know one of the ways people enjoy changing? Going to a restaurant that serves a type of food you have never consumed before. It is always good to go with a friend who might be able to advise you or, at the very least, knows somebody in the restaurant whom you can ask for advice: "Oh, I have never eaten this type of food or that type of food; I'm getting a little older, so I have to watch my health," whatever. But that is a good way to discover whether you can adapt and follow your own feelings when you do so.

Then you might even go to, say, a theater or even a presentation of that culture's predominant religion—not church, mind you, but a presentation—and see if you enjoy it. This is not because you are going to take up that religion or culture, but just to enjoy something that is presented as a sharing. Adaptability is helpful in these times, when people are becoming more aware of each other's presence and needing the reassurance that that presence, that that availability associated with the world human culture, offers something to you, even if you are just reading about it or learning about it for the first time. Sometimes it is very comforting just to know that it is, even if you are not a portion of it.

Is it your understanding that souls choose to be influenced by Gemini because they are already adaptable and flexible, or because they want to learn that?

It could go either way. They might wish to know more about it. They might, because of some life they are going to experience or perhaps even be influential in circumstances in some other life, wish to learn how to become more adaptable—more spontaneous, so to speak—and yes, they might choose that. Equally, they might choose something associated with Gemini simply because it is entirely new to them and they have not practiced it—and perhaps, as an overall soul being, they might need to be exposed to some of those traits to enjoy their benevolent capacities, as well as to perhaps at times be a little frustrated by the urgencies they represent.

So whatever sign one meets, then the traits associated with it could be full spectrum, from just the soul trying to teach it to another soul being very proficient?

Certainly. Especially when one is meeting someone, say, who has been on the planet for some time and has therefore been that sign for some time. You might find adaptability has entrenched itself at the very least, eh? [Laughs.]

If they've survived, yes, probably.

Astrology Permeates All Life

I am so sorry I am so tired. You are amazingly eloquent, and there is so much to ask about.

Well, perhaps someday, if this book supports you [chuckles] and not just you supporting the world with these words and thoughts and philosophies, then . . .

We can go deeper.

You could, if you wanted, get to more communion about these matters. But this book is intended to give astrologers especially—and those interested in astrology and those developing an interest—an overview of to some extent the known, to a large extent the lesser known, and certainly to an extent also the unknown associated with astrology. Now, granted, some of this information may have been around on the planet for a time, but very often it is known only in very esoteric circles—guarded, you might say, by those who feel that their knowledge and awareness of it is a thing that is precious.

I too understand that, but it is very important that this come out now for all to have it available to them. Perhaps for even the wisest astrologer amongst you, you might find a few things here and there that are new to you—who knows? It is possible. So if there is interest, another book could come along, but this book is meant to be a foundation of the philosophical principles available through this channel and through this publishing house to contribute to the overall approach, education and existence of the astrologic Earth and its cultures and its influences.

The more I listen, the more I understand the vastness on this topic, which I didn't know about before—how it permeates all life.

If you listen back to the beginning, you might find it interesting as well, since the beginning was meant for everyone and you will notice that. I am not chiding you. It is natural to be tired, and as one moves on in life physically, one gets tired more so, which is why perhaps [chuckles] the both of you, as you are moving on in life, need to pay attention to doing these things at times when more sleep, at the very least, and less distractions are present.

Yes. I am sorry about that

Now, you are taking it as a criticism. You are apologizing, and that always means that the reaction is based culturally (it is important for you to know these things, you see) upon the training one has received, very often in reactions unconscious. That is a reaction unconscious. I made it clear I wasn't chiding you, but you reacted unconsciously as if I were. Now, that is not a criticism, but it is important to pay attention to it so that you will say, "Well, thank you," and feel it, because the training unconscious is the most influential from one human being to another and from one human being to anything everywhere on this planet now.

That is not only why [chuckles] this book is being produced from the point of view of the beings who speak through this channel, but generally speaking, why all the books being produced and printed by this publisher are being provided. It is important to at least be able to think about these things. Someday, as this publishing house becomes a bit more capacious, if I might say, it will be possible to view more. But for now, if I might speak as a presenter, I will simply say that this publishing house is offering what it can offer to all those who will come, to all those who will read, to all those who will hear that which will inform you, stimulate you, at times excite you, and even at times annoy you—because sometimes it is annoying to discover that which is true when it may be inconvenient.

Yet how wonderful it can be to know what is coming, even if one must dodge it when it arrives. If you don't know what is coming, how will you be able to dodge it? So that is my tribute, and on that note for now, I will say good night. May you have the most benevolent life reading, understanding and philosophically exchanging with yourself and others.

Thank you from my heart. Thank you.

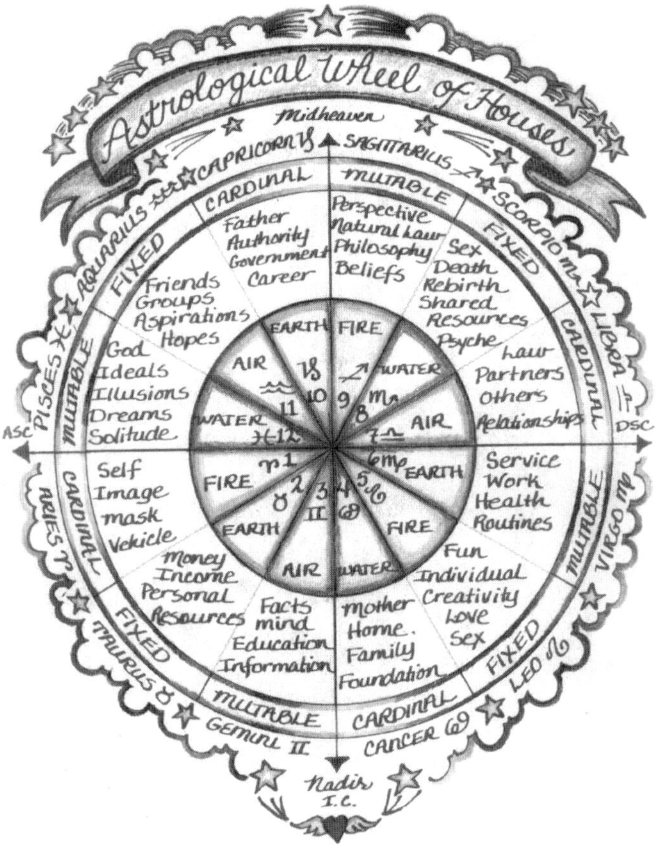
Astrological Wheel of Houses
Midheaven
Nadir
I.C.
ASC
DSC
CAPRICORN ♑
SAGITTARIUS ♐
SCORPIO ♏
LIBRA ♎
VIRGO ♍
LEO ♌
CANCER ♋
GEMINI ♊
TAURUS ♉
ARIES ♈
PISCES ♓
AQUARIUS ♒
CARDINAL
MUTABLE
FIXED
Father Authority Government Career
Perspective Natural Law Philosophy Beliefs
Sex Death Rebirth Shared Resources Psyche
Law Partners Others Relationships
Service Work Health Routines
Fun Individual Creativity Love Sex
Mother Home. Family Foundation
Facts mind Education Information
Money Income Personal Resources
Self Image mask Vehicle
God Ideals Illusions Dreams Solitude
Friends Groups Aspirations Hopes
EARTH
FIRE
WATER
AIR
1
2
3
4
5
6
7
8
9
10
11
12

Clusters of Galaxies

ETCHETA

12 Families Were Roots of Personality Traits and Genetics for Earth Humans

August 4, 2007

This is Etcheta. I am a visitor to your planet.

Welcome!

Your Personalities Are All Rooted Back to the Twelve Original Families

I am here from a place that is very far in the past of your migration pathway to this point in time. When your civilization had established itself in this universe and was experimenting with cultures on this planet or that planet, there was a sense at the time that the Explorer Race, which was known then as an idea, was prepared to fulfill its destiny. (This is considerably in the past, you understand.) So what happened? There was a visitation from one of Creator's emissaries to say that the assumption of the completion of preparation was false and that only the beginning had been completed, that the hard part was yet to come. You understand, I am speaking to you, not just in words of your time, but in concepts, because the peoples of that time did not understand what "the hard part" meant, even in their own language. Such a thing was inconceivable to them as it is very much the case for most occupants of your universe this day in your time.

So there was a general meeting of all the peoples who identified themselves as root civilizations of the Explorer Race, and volunteers stepped forward to allow their soul chains—or reincarnational lives, you might say—to be involved in "the hard part." All those who had an uncomfortable feeling associated with the hard part stepped back. Ever since then, all those beings associated with the hard part, which you are all experiencing now, have yourselves rooted to those original volunteers. Those volunteers themselves can all be traced back to twelve original families, and those twelve original families are all associated with the root characteristics that you now associate with the Sun signs of astrology.

[Gasps in astonishment.]

So, you see, while I am an ET visitor here, I am also discussing the subject at hand. This is why and how this astrologic study has prevailed and been influential throughout times that go back well before the human population on Earth, because it was originally perceived as families. Some families were from this planet, some from other planets, and the feeling at the time was that these groups went together and you would have noticed it if you had come from afar and were with them. But these groups, when together, represented total balance—not only comfort and relaxation because of the way they complemented each other, but also all the roots needed to provide the foundation and the fundamentals of creating, generating, supporting and perpetuating any culture anywhere in the universe. These twelve families represented all the qualities at the basic level of those needed to get along well in any circumstances in the universe.

Of course, at that time, no one understood what "the hard part" meant, even though the Creator's emissary spoke at great length and with great attitude about what the hard part might be. Still, if you have no concept, no place in your culture, no understanding whatsoever of what "hard" might be, then it is generally meaningless and one listens with great joy and happiness at being exposed to such a wise teacher. Even in your time, you have wise teachers who speak in such a way that people enjoy hearing them but do not really understand afterward when the talk is over what it conceptually meant—only that it felt so good [chuckles]. So you understand that this is not something that is so unfathomable or where the people were somehow naive. It was just that the explanation came with such a good feeling.

This is not an attempt by Creator to persuade but rather an attempt to request those adventurers of those families who would be the roots of personality—and, to a large degree, genetics—so to encourage the widest variety of personalities, the widest variety of appearances, and the widest variety of cultural differences that could mix on one planet to produce the best-quality synthesized human being. It would not be artificial in this case, that which is not produced by science but is produced—because of the races and cultures and all of that coming together to eventually produce a hybrid human being, based upon all the genetics of the planet—through the marriage and the culmination of love through the birthing process. Ultimately, those children would look a certain way.

Look at the races you have on the planet today: They have dark skin and light skin. Some are tall, some are short, some are large, and some are thin. In short, there is a wide variety of appearances, including different appearances in different races and personalities. It is ultimately that the people of Earth will have a light brown skin. By "light brown," I would compare that to the color tan, perhaps a little bit darker than tan, as a color that is still a color description in use. Let's see, you have a product that you consume. What is that called?

I have heard milk-chocolate color used in that context.

Yes, it would be a light milk-chocolate color, and the general appearance of the person would be slim but healthy looking. So the personality would be calm and yet able to rise to any stimulation, including that which might be representing danger and that which might be representing, on the other side of the spectrum, great safety, happiness and continuity. The whole point is to create a versatile race of beings that can adapt to any situation found in the universe and thrive—not just live, but thrive.

Many of You Are Reconsidering Who You Are

So the twelve have come as far as you are now. There is, of course, as a result of being cut off from your memory of who you are and where you are from, conflict in your world. There are those from ancient cultures who believe it is important for you to now remember who you are, where you are from, and why you are here. Thus, what is happening for you now is the gradual recollection of these root sources of your being.

It is not for you to remember everything your guides and Creator have ever said to you during your lifetime. This will come back when the time is right. But it is important to have enough of your memory that you have beyond this planetary school that allows you to remember why you volunteered as an individual today, why you volunteered as a soul personality to come here and pursue this most worthy attempt to create a pioneering Earth cultural society. So in steps now, very gradually, you are all on the planet waking up, as some of you call it. But the waking up is largely that which involves remembering who you are, where you are from, and why you are here, and that will continue.

It will necessarily force many of you to consider and reconsider who you are, and it will necessarily cause many of you to have a momentary confusion about who you are. You have been raised, many of you, to a large degree in different cultures and different ethnic situations, different nationalities, countries and so on. Yet very often with all of the good that comes from such variety, there is a history taught that causes you to be fearful of each other, especially those from other groups or cultures. Sometimes these fears may be warranted, but other times they are simply perpetuated angers from the past, having nothing to do with the peoples of today. Yet the populations continue to be at odds with each other, sometimes taking this to an extreme.

In a very short time, all of this will appear to be of no advantage in pursuing That will be the next stage of your "waking up," as you are calling it. That stage will be universal. It won't be a simple loss of interest in fighting; it will be an awareness that sweeps over everyone, that no matter what harms have been done in the past, inflicting harms on those in the present will not ever resolve anything in the past, no matter what. That change of mind will come with a change of heart, and the motivation behind pursuing this revenge will simply fall away.

It is important to let you know this, because many of you will experience this, as many of you are now, as a feeling of lethargy. This lethargy is not associated with a disease, nor a lack of motivation to pursue any of your goals. It is rather a letting go of cultural genetics, which I would associate with the repetition of tales that have gone so deeply into your bodies that they become more associated with your subconscious and not associated with what you are aware of mentally in your conscious mind. They are generally not even accessible through hypnotic or meditational states, to say nothing of psychoanalysis. That is why I refer to it in this fashion.

But the experience that one has now of this lethargy is directly associated with the release of those motivations, which are essentially subconscious. I don't want you to worry too much about that lethargy, even though I grant that some of it has to do with the decrease in oxygen available to give you strength and to replenish you. You must make an effort to encourage forests to grow and other types of life that exhale the air you breathe. Otherwise, it will not be possible realistically to exist in the way you have known on this planet. But others have spoken about that, and I will not speak about that today.

It is my job today to remind you of who you are, more in the sense of where you are from rather than the memories that will flood in soon for you. You have at your disposal now a great deal of opportunity. Look at each other anew, for in your near future you will see your neighbor in a completely different way. You won't look at your neighbors with suspicion and mistrust; you will look at your neighbors with curiosity, wanting to know how it is that they live, what are their interests, what are their talents and abilities, and so on. For many of you, these feelings will remind you of those you have had as children, and you will wonder if there is something wrong with you, having a second childhood, so to speak.

But it is really that release of the old that drags you back to a time that you cannot resolve in your cultural history, so you might as well let it go and be in the present moment and experience people as they are—not, as you have been taught in the dim past, as they might be. This opportunity will allow you to move on and remember more and more of who you are, where you are from, and why you are here, so that the natural gravitation toward each other as friends, companions, lovers and family will take place. This is Creator's purpose for you on this planet, and the gradual waking up will allow you to remember that purpose and to pursue it in comfort.

The Thirteenth Sign Is Not a Replacement

As we move into combined genetics and one body form, we will also move into the thirteenth sign, the synthesis of all the signs?

It is not to let go of the signs.

But to access all of them.

That is right, because remember, as I said before, if a visitor came to those times in the past when the Explorer Race thought they were ready—[chuckles] before the hard part—the reason the visitor might feel a sense of "anything is possible" when being in a group of the twelve families is because of the variety, not in spite of it. So it is not to be giving up the twelve signs and achieving something considered to be of such great perfection that the twelve are not needed. It is not that the twelve are not needed; it is rather that the twelve, when coming together and producing that being, will generate amongst you some individuals who have aspects of all of that twelve.

Granted, there will be some aspects of personality that individual members of the twelve signs would not always like about themselves or each other, but that goes hand in hand, so that one might learn. That is why the aspects of the signs that you understand as Sun signs have challenges, and that is also why astrologers let you know about these challenges—so that when they come up for you, you can recognize that this is what you have chosen to focus on learning as a member of that sign group in this life. Then when those things come up, you are forewarned, and you do not spend the rest of your life justifying positions based upon the lessons you have come here to learn [chuckles]. So, no, while that so-called thirteenth sign will emerge, it is not as a replacement but simply as an addition.

Thank you for explaining that. That makes sense, because we were told there were twelve personality traits on Earth but 256 in all creations everywhere. I always wondered why we have so few, but this answers it.

The Twelve Families Came from All Over the Universe

Now, where in this universe was this place that the twelve families lived?

No, no. You have missed that part. They were all over the universe. Since they were all over the universe and looked in different ways and so on and had developed these personalities based upon their actions and interactions with their environments, this is why they felt complete. You see, they were all over the universe.

Ah! They came forward at the meeting of all of them.

I have given this example of "if you had gone to a place where all the families were together." I am not saying that there was a meeting. There wasn't a meeting. When the Creator's emissary comes, it is not necessary for everybody to be in one place. The Creator could speak individually to every single individual in this universe right now, and you would experience it perhaps as someone speaking to you but you would not have to gather in the same place.

So how can we place it in time, then? Was it before this galaxy, before Orion? How can we place it in some stream, like in that time while we were Zetas, before the loop of time?

You cannot, because you are not in a natural state of time. But it was long before the time that you are living in now, long before Earth as you know it existed.

Were the families humanoid, or were they all different?

All different forms, adaptive to the environment. After all, think of the small amount of knowledge that science has offered you on the basis of being able to reinforce or back up what they are stating—simply based upon the best speculations of your solar system and, to a degree, photographs of same. Think how a culture living in those conditions might evolve. Humans would require tremendous technology just to be able to try to step on such a planet. If you are going to be from that planet and have no technology at all—in short, be able to function comfortably—you might not look like a human being, but you might very well be observed from the eyes of a human being as a local, let's say.

Were any of them in human bodies?

Not as you would recognize human bodies today, but humanoids, yes.

Do the original twelve families as such exist out in this creation in the form in which they were then?

Yes.

Will we meet them at some time?

If you wish, that will be available, because as you begin to remember the reason why you are here, you will begin to see those twelve families. Some of you have done this already. Some of you identify the appearances of some of these beings as a guide, and it might very well be that you have a guide who has that appearance. Generally speaking, guides on the spiritual level, if you see their appearance at all—which is not typical but occasionally happens for you—would be beings who would have a similarity to your appearance at the very least, nothing really strange. The only type of thing one might see that isn't similar to your appearance is the energy body of these beings, which may not necessarily be humanoid. But the energy body would be light, you see, so you would feel comfortable.

How interesting.

I've Come to Observe You from Time to Time

What about you? Where do you fit into all of this?

I visit your planet from time to time and observe the circumstances of your societies. I do not judge you, of course. I recognize that not remembering who you are and finding yourself on a planet with a wide variety of peoples on the one hand is exciting and wonderful, and on the other hand, given what you are taught about this group or that group, to say nothing of experiences you have had, it can also be disruptive and hard to bear.

So I have come from time to time to observe the awakening process, which has been taking place now gradually—in this group or that family, and this culture or that nationality—over the past thousand years or so of your time. There is enough written, not only in the present, but in the past, that can be found, if you look hard enough. There is also enough conversation and there is the technology to communicate (fairly well, if not perfectly) with cultures on the other side of the world—though, of course, cultural nuances are largely lost. Still, there is the beginning of the means to communicate. Therefore, the potential to remember has been expanded. So I come and check at times to see how you are doing.

Do you come alone or in a large group with others?

I come on my own. I do not come in a vehicle, per se. I come in the traveling method you all use in your sleep state, which is as a migrating personality. You usually describe it when you are in the sleep state that you travel in light, but that is simply the protection around you to keep you insulated and protected so as not to be exposed to danger, you understand—to keep you in your own world so that what you remember when you wake up from your sleep will fit into your world in some sense and what you don't remember is that which is involved in other worlds. So I migrate in personality to your time and observe, and then return to my own time, which is the time of the awareness that the hard part is yet to come.

Are you from one of the twelve families?

No. I am from a pilot group associated with observing the activity of the inception of the Explorer Race and the intention of seeing how it all works out.

Have you gone into the future to check out how it works out?

The problem of going into the future . . .

Is which one [chuckles].

That's right. Also, one's own desires can influence the direction you take, so I have attempted to avoid that. That way disappointment can be avoided as well.

The Twelve Families Represent Personality Traits

Is there any correlation with what we call cultures now—beliefs, religions, ways of thinking—that connect to these original twelve families, or are they all mixed up in the soup by now?

The twelve families represent personality traits. They do not represent cultures, races, religions or any of that.

In the astrological sense, then: talents, abilities, possibilities, potentials?

The astrological sense really is the foundation of the human personality as you know it today from the past and in the future, so it is really the foundation of the human culture in its basis and its expression. It is—how can we say?—the Rosetta stone of who you are, although the Rosetta stone, you understand, is a stone associated with interpretation, so perhaps that is not the best example. I would say that without astrology you would probably be lost, and that is why some self-destructive groups or individuals over the years, who were upset with life in general, have attempted to destroy astrology, not wanting to know the past, the present or future potential, simply being upset with life. That is understandable when you don't remember who you are, where you are from, or why you are here—wherever "here" might be to you in time.

We will have gained a little new information in this book. Is there still information not available to us at this time that could be given to us about the various personalities?

The book is not done yet, eh?

Okay. [Laughs.] The humans are the descendants of these twelve families, and yet we are told that the planets and the signs beam forth these energies. What do the planets and the signs have to do with the personality traits of these twelve families? How do they radiate these energies?

All create the ingredients to originate, support and sustain the elements of personality intended to mix into the group to create the finest being able to accomplish the challenges and the embraces of life to come.

Then how does each family relate to a planet or a sign?

You are trying to force it, but it doesn't force. The planets do exactly what they said and more, of course. But with all of the nuances of astrology, you find astrologers saying, "Well, this is true for you because of this and this and this." They are not just trying to provide you with scientific proof, but rather they are simply stating to you that you are this because you were born in such and such a time, and that is certainly true.

But when they are saying that you are this also because of this and this and this—referring to degrees of this and that and so on—what they are really saying is that you are supported in being that because of this body or that body, or this planet or that orbit, or that association with that planet's orbit, and so on. Don't assume that you are dealing with black and white here, as you like to say. You are dealing with ingredients. Have you ever had a food that contains both sweet and salty? Does it not taste other than sweet and other than salty, as well as sweet and salty?

The combination, yes.

And so.

Okay, forgive my ignorance, but I would like to pursue that just a little bit more. Everyone born here is a descendant in some way from one of those families?

Only on the basis of your personality traits and, to a degree, genetically, because of the coordinating efforts of the cultures that were between then and now. Think of the thousands of cultures and planetary societies that existed between the time of those twelve families and your own culture. Do you think it was a straight line from those twelve families to the people of Earth?

So we picked up lots of other traits and attributes on the way?

[Chuckles.] You picked up lots of genetic sets for sure. You don't look like those people at those times, and you would not be confused in any way with their personalities, but you have root associations with their personalities. A good psychologist would be able to pick up on that quickly, to say nothing of a good astrologer.

Let me put it to you this way: you are not a young person anymore. Once upon a time, you were. You lived in a particular culture and society, but you have traveled, have you not? Would you not say that your personality has been affected over time because of your travels and the people you have met and the circumstances you have been in, the foods you have eaten, the clothes you have worn, and so on, throughout a single life on Earth?

I see—and then extrapolate that to the millions of lives we have lived.

Well beyond millions. Naturally, nuances accumulate.

Be Aware of Your Sign and the Challenges Associated with It

Do you have a group that is interested in your report? Is this your interest, or is there a group whom you report back to what you have learned?

I realize that is a concept of your time. There is nothing I learn at any given moment in these travels that is not readily available to be known by everyone.

Right. I have been human too long [chuckles].

It is not that. It is just that there is an assumption that the hierarchical methods employed on Earth are universal. But, of course, they are not only *not* universal, they are essentially an attempt to get along as well as possible, given that one does not remember who one is, where one is from, and why one is here. [Chuckles.] Then you do as well as you can do, and often quite naturally mistakes are made. So things do not relate to other places like that. Keep in mind this one rule, generally speaking: every place else things are much simpler, meaning complication as you know it and experience it, challenge because of complication. This ought to make sense to you, given that the sign you are [Aries] tends to thrive and enjoy life more when complication presents itself. Look it up.

Yes, I am aware of that. [Chuckles.]

That does not exist in the rest of the universe, and that is why you personally are here. You enjoy the challenge of complication, but you can see the pitfalls of that, can you not? Some complications are minor, and one can enjoy a quick solution and a good feeling, but if one gets attracted too much to complications . . .

Then one creates them.

One not only creates them, one creates a wall that is a font—you understand that term "font," meaning always available—of complications and challenges, so that one becomes addicted to complications and challenges, and can never, in any circumstance, achieve any goal that was once entirely achievable when one pursued life with greater simplicity. Make a note of that, and discuss it with your astrologer.

What's the solution?

The solution is being aware of your sign and the challenges that are associated, you understand, with your Sun sign. I am aware that you are a walk-in, but that doesn't make any difference. You brought that with you. What you bring with you as a walk-in must fit into the physical body you occupy.

Until You Wake Up, You Will Be Driven from the Past

Can we go over this again? I don't understand how the energies got from the families to the planets. These twelve families each had personality traits, groups of traits that are roughly similar to what we call the traits of the twelve signs now.

Yes, Sun signs.

Sun signs, yes. The movement of the planets sends energy that . . .

Supports these traits and supports other traits that are intended to nourish, support and sustain all life as you know it, and many times sustains these traits—the benevolent ones. But also, because you are here to learn, sometimes the planets will—in a portion of their orbits usually associated astrologically with the retrograde portion—support the more challenging aspects of your sign, such as the one I just mentioned for you a moment ago. Personalize it in that way, since you are here to learn. Your lessons as an individual of that root family with which your lessons are associated, also known as a Sun sign . . . you have chosen those lessons associated with that sign, and then those traits—often referred to as negative traits by astrologers; I am not saying necessarily that they are negative, but that is how they can be felt—become your lessons.

The planets do understand that you are here to achieve knowledge, wisdom and practical physical experience of those lessons, so they wish to support that as well. They are not trying to make life hard for you. They are attempting to support why you are here in terms of your immediate physical life, not only why you are here in terms of that distant past, which I speak of today.

Ah! You explained that beautifully. Thank you. Now, each planet is associated with a sign, but we have more signs than planets. Are we still missing some planets?

There may be other planets, but you do not need to have twelve planets to have twelve signs. This is an assumption. You have quite a few other capacities. There is the Sun, of course; there is the Moon, of course. Do you understand? So let's put it simply: You don't need to have twelve planets to support twelve signs. You do have the twelve original families. They are the core traits of personality associated with Sun signs.

So is there some direct path from these core personalities through the constellations that we call these signs, which then emanate those energies at Earth? Is that how it works?

It is not linear. We cannot avoid the fact that you are living in a linear time construct, and of course, all of your questions are based upon time.

Yes. I am sorry.

No, you cannot help it. But I will say that there is an association with that, since those beings of that "time," so to speak, are all immortal, so they are all still alive. The idea of a life, which is born and then dies, is not the only way to be.

So what connection do they have, then, with what we call the constellations, which inhabit a space that we call signs?

Other than the fact that everybody is united to everything, none. They don't need to have that. They are what they are, as I have stated. You are continuing to try to force into a single formula all that supports you in being who you are. Why force it? If you are crawling across the desert and you are thirsty, and someone approaches you with a glass of water—and some to dab on your forehead, eh?—do you say, "No, I don't know who you are?" You say, "Thank you." Don't try to force it into one thing.

Okay, then let me ask it this way. Do the beings who live in that constellation, who formed the synthesis of what is called a sign that is speaking through Robert, have they chosen to exemplify those characteristics of that sign that is related to that original family?

No, but you will have to speak to them. They live their own existence. They are not all of those traits.

But there are enough of them that that energy is radiated toward us.

It is much simpler than that. But, essentially, the answer to your question is no. Until you wake up, you will be driven from the past. When you wake up, you will be in the present and will thus be able to be anything. But as long as you are driven from the past—not from the past I am talking about, but from the past of your own family or culture or nationality—then you won't know who you are.

As long as we are driven from our Earth past, from the past timeline, you are saying—how we were conditioned?

Yes.

This is revelatory. This is great.

I Am a Simple Student of Cultures

What are your other interests? What do you do when you are not here? How often do you visit us? Time again, hmm?

You have to remember that I can do more than one thing at once, which you also can do. Even now, you do more than one thing at once. The difference is that I am aware of it. So I have many interests, as you do. The general interest I have is who, what and where.

So what other cultures do you look in on, then?

Anything that has to do with who, what and where.

[Laughs.] So you get around a lot, right?

Yes, but you would too, if you were in my situation. It is a wondrous thing, how not only beings adapt to the circumstances of their planets, but also how they enjoy their own personalities in relationship to each other and those circumstances of the planets. One becomes increasingly conscious in such travels of not only the variety of life but of the flexibility that is available in adaptation. I have not ever been bored.

Do you go beyond this creation?

No more or less than you do. There is a limit to what I choose to say. I do not wish to be deified, as I am sure you do not either. The more distance you create between those whom you work with and support, the less likely that the benefit of what you are offering can be accepted eye to eye. I am simply an observer, not a deity—a simple student of cultures.

What about the place where you live? What kind of culture do you have in the place you call home?

I do not only live there.

You are aware of all the places where you have aspects of yourself?

You have had lives other places, eh? You might not remember those now, but I do.

So it is like visiting. Were you there when the twelve families stepped forward?

Before that.

You were there before that and so you didn't step forward?

I am not associated with it; I am separate from it. That is how I am able to observe and explain it as any student might explain a lesson. The teacher says to you, "Explain how the peoples migrated from this place to that place. What was their motivation? What was their desire? What was their goal? How close are they to achieving it?" and so on. The student might be able to explain that in time.

Okay, but are you saying that if he was in it, he wouldn't be able to explain it as well from . . . ?

No, because if you are a participant, you'd be focused in it, just as you are now.

Do you think there was some stimulus from the Creator, maybe like He had already decided on the twelve personalities and there was some inspiration of that particular group to move forward?

I am not clear.

If the person or being who told me was right, there are 256 personality classes (or traits or types) in this creation, and twelve of them moved forward to volunteer as the basis for the Explorer Race. Do you think that they were inspired by the Creator to do that because they had what He was looking for?

I couldn't say that. You would have to ask Creator that. As the student, it is my job to explain to you when inquired. You understand, you are inquiring, so I am explaining to you what I understand, but I am not here to speak for Creator.

Okay. It just occurred to me that He might have already had a recipe in mind for what He wanted as personality traits for the Explorer Race.

It is possible.

Simplify the Conflicting Elements in Your Life

So here we are, then, on the verge of remembering. What would you recommend we do to facilitate that process?

What I would recommend is that you simplify your lives as much as possible. Don't throw away or dispose of things you need. Don't throw away or dispose of people you need, to say nothing of people in general—the animals and plants as well, of course. But look at your lives and decide. Are all of your pursuits making your life or your family's life or your culture's life better, or are they just creating conflicting elements in your life that are complications?

Look at the conflicting elements in your life, and see how they can be simplified. The fewer complications you have, the more you will be able to feel at ease to wake up, because the more you wake up, the easier it will be to let go of those complications. You will be able to feel what is you and to know what is meant to be associated with others. You will be able to let go of this or that because, "Oh, that is really meant for others. And here I thought that it was meant for everyone, but no, it is just meant for some." You will be able to let it go, you see? That is what I recommend.

You are talking about, not only material possessions, but attitudes and activities and beliefs, all of that?

I am not placing any limits on it.

Have you ever talked through a channel like this before?

Oh, it is possible, but I don't think it would be available on Earth. On that note, I will say, may you achieve your destiny in ways that would feel benevolent and would be the culmination of the ideal that you represent. Good night.

You are wonderful! Thank you. Thank you very much.

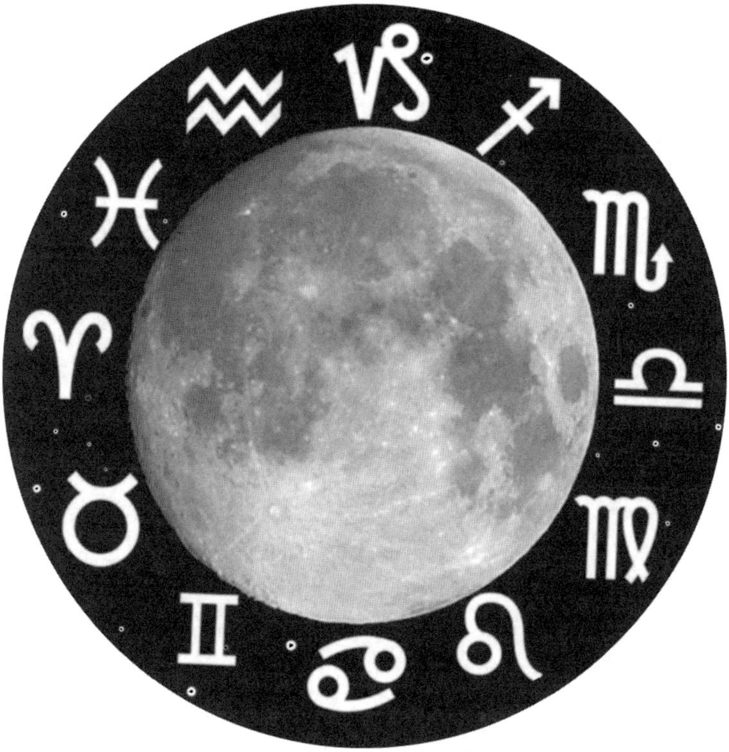

Pisces
February 20 – March 20

PISCES
Focuses on Feelings, Instinct and the Unseen

August 6, 2007

This is Pisces. Greetings.

Welcome! Welcome!

Feelings Are the Root of Your Survival

I am often identified with the feminine, but there are aspects of me that are not fully understood.

That is what we are here for.

The whole point of this book is to reveal what has been lost over time and/or to clarify, and clarification is a good thing. I feel there has been too much stress placed on the anti-feminine with the Pisces sign—and by that I mean judgments about what the feminine means from one culture to another. In the occasional culture it might be pro-feminine, but for the most part, your societies globally now are dominated by those who are afraid of the feminine. This is probably because your societies are dominated by men, but it is not possible, you see, as a male, to have an understanding of the root benevolence of the feminine. You can read about it, but you cannot understand it as a participant. Still, if you have feminine concerns, they can attempt to interpret to the best of their ability their feelings about the feminine.

Feelings are everything in your society now because you have had this long study on the mind and its capabilities, and you have discovered as a result the limits of the mind. The mind is not expected to be all or do all, nor was it designed to do that. Thus, when you run up against its limits or its capacities that go only so far, the tendency is to continue to search and search and search for the mental answer. But there is not a mental answer, nor is there one that is designed to be found by a creator of this universe.

Feelings are the root of your survival. You would not live long as an individual out in the wild did you not trust your feelings. All the mental knowledge in the world would not help you if you approached a plant to consume based upon your mental knowledge exclusively of that plant. For all you know, that plant has been treated or exposed to something that might be harmful to you. So if you go to reach for the plant and you say, "Aha, I have read about this plant. I know it is safe for me to eat," and eat it and get sick, then you would wonder and question your mental knowledge.

Mental knowledge is meant to have for a portion of your existence. It is good to know, it is useful, but it is not about survival, though it appears to be. Survival and even the ability to thrive are all about feelings. The mind identifies feelings as the vague unspecified, which cannot be precisely calculated. That is the actual mental description of your mind's understanding of feelings—although you could add a lot of words, that is the foundation. So given that, the mind, when it comes to the end of its capabilities, would start searching in many places, but it would not search in a place that is vague and unspecified. It is going to look for clarity; it is going to look for precision. So you have to utilize other capabilities.

Feelings are your physical body's means of communicating to you, the overall you, your body's physical understanding of its immediate material world—which might include your body, yes, but would also include reaching for that plant material that you were going to eat in my example. So you reach for it and you get an uncomfortable feeling. It is like, "Oh, I know this is safe mentally, but this portion of the plant doesn't feel right to me." You go a little farther. You reach for another portion of the plant. Perhaps it is a tomato, for example. "Oh, that doesn't feel good either." You walk down the road, and eventually you find a tomato that feels good. You pick it, you eat it, and you are fine.

Feelings allow you to survive and thrive. For example, you walk down the road again and there is a mall, but the mall does not have signs above the door. It is the side of the mall you can get to. For some reason, you can't get to the front, so they are all back doors. They all look the same, and you know you are trying to find the grocery store, but you can't, for some reason, get to the front. You can't tell which is the grocery store, and you walk from door to door: "I know this is the building." So you reach out with your hand: "Oh, this door doesn't feel good." Eventually, you find a door that feels good. You open it, you walk in, and you are in the grocery store. Or you open it, you walk in, and you are in some better place.

The key to surviving and thriving is learning how your feelings feel in your body and interpreting them on the basis of your practical, physical experience. Now, that foundation is something you understand (speaking to you here), but it is something that your mind cannot understand. That is why your mind has this vague mistrust of feelings, because your mind has classified feelings with a mental description that it often calls emotions. It has a complete understanding in its own right of what emotions are, but it does not trust emotions. It does not always understand that feelings, which it classifies as a portion of emotions, are separate. Physical feelings allow you to what? Survive and thrive. That is important to begin with. That's a little clarity, eh?

Pisces Has the Ability to Broadcast Energy of the Future

Now, there's more. The more to start with today is that there is something else Pisces does that you don't necessarily know about. Pisces has the quality and the ability to broadcast energy of the future. If you were to gather, say, ten, twelve, fifteen people who have Pisces predominant in their charts and put them into a room and ask them to just be quiet—maybe meditate, or try to not think—to simply be themselves. In the process of that, they would be broadcasting a vast amount of energy of the future. In theory—using the mind for a moment, as an example—you could, if you were a sensitive, walk into that room and get a pretty good idea of the future for specific individuals who don't necessarily have to be in that room, or even for society's neighborhoods or communities, or even for the planet, and the Pisces people would not have to say or do anything. You could just talk quietly into a recording device or into a device that transmits, or you could make notes or attempt to remember.

Pisces does not broadcast future events. Pisces does not create future events (in this situation that I am talking about). Pisces simply broadcasts energy of the future, which is like an open band, and that is why I say that a sensitive person could walk in and, utilizing that energy, get specific information about the future for others. If that person already has the capacity to get that information, it would be greatly heightened and the accuracy vastly improved.

I feel it is good for you to know this, because so many of you now feel a great need to know more about the future. Of course, one of the reasons people consult astrologers very often is about the future. An astrologer's job is not to tell you the future but to give you some possibilities, approximations—a general sense of what could happen, what might happen, or what is less likely to happen at this time. But if astrologers were in that room full of Pisces people, aside from finding it interesting, their capacity to be able to speak clearly—not only of the knowledge of their own profession, but to speak instinctively or with inspiration—and add that to their astrological wisdom would be greatly enhanced.

Now, what if astrologers have a strong Pisces energy in their personal chart? Generally speaking, at this time in your culture, that would mean that if they know how to interpret that—which I feel this book will help with a great deal—they would find that trusting their inspirations, which are coming at them very strongly now (you Pisces astrologers out there) . . . they would be able to have more confidence to speak these inspirations.

But there is more: I am not trying to say that Pisces astrologers would somehow be able to be more accurate, but generally speaking, the accuracy level about predicting potential futures for a client who has offered the proper information so that the astrologer can work with you would be 1 to 2 percent better than other signs who are astrologers. I grant that this may not be a great amount, but if you put that Pisces astrologer in that room with the fourteen or fifteen Pisces people, then that ability would improve by a significant amount, possibly tenfold.

I am not saying that you need to round up some Pisces people to be in that room; I am saying that it is an experiment worth trying for astrologers. The challenge would be to get those Pisces people to not think. That takes training and time, but if you are able to acquire such friends who can cooperate, give it a try. Don't do this trying to predict your own personal future [chuckles]; rather, try it with somebody you don't really know, something abstract. But the absolute requirement is that they personally are asking, so don't just pick somebody out. They have to want to know. See how it works. It might be interesting for you to discover this, and it might be a way to greatly improve the quality of astrologic readings.

One of the other signs said that as these new or forgotten traits come forth in the signs they are talking about, they are shown first in that sign more strongly, but then they become available to everybody.

What a question. I will comment in this case. Yes, this will gradually permeate, especially because of the broadcast quality of Pisces. Now, I have given the experiment in my example, but what about people who have a strong Pisces in their chart when they are just going about life? When they are functioning, when they are living, breathing, when they are sleeping—what about that? They are always broadcasting energy of the future; this is a reality. I have just given that experiment example in the beginning because it would heighten the situation, but any Pisces is always broadcasting energy of the future, and to a degree but not completely, this will infiltrate over time to others.

If, however, an individual has no Pisces—this is not typical, but say, for example, you have no Pisces in your chart, which happens—then this would not become a portion of your existence in terms of broadcasting the energy, though you might very well be able to access the energy working with a Pisces astrologer or an astrologer who is exposed to Pisces energy as per my example. So it is not absolute, what the other sign said. I honor that sign's knowledge and wisdom, but I feel that in this case it is not entirely the case.

Pisces Is Instinctual in Its Nature and Can Reveal the Unseen

How do you define those with Pisces energy? Does it have to be the Sun sign, or can it be the rising sign? Can it be if you have half a dozen planets in Pisces?

That is for the astrologer to decide. I recognize that you are asking as a curious individual so that you can ask reasonable questions, but you do not have the astrological knowledge, nor can I take the hours and hours that would be required to explain it to you. So feel free to ask from not having that knowledge. After all, if you were an astrologer, this book would be different, but the whole point and the whole reason that this book is offered is that it is offered innocently. By "innocently," that means that neither you nor the channel knows very much about astrology at all, and therefore, you have no biases or prejudices to speak of other than the fact that, being somewhat ignorant about a topic, there might have been—if I might say, in your case perhaps—a little mistrust about it. But I feel you are over that now, that you understand how very personal and heart-centered astrology is, not some abstract approach to dissecting life.

[Laughs.] I have learned much, yes. A book I am looking at says Pisces is the most susceptible to the outside influence of all the signs. Is that a positive aspect?

Well, you understand that I am not here so much to talk about what is known about astrology, but what that means is that Pisces is the most likely to be instantaneously aware of the needs of others around them. That is what it interprets as, and the astrologer would know that. Very often this is useful, especially for, say, the Pisces mother. She might know instantaneously what her baby needs. I am not saying that other mothers would not, but that Pisces energy would help. It might also be a bit uncomfortable if the Pisces is around people who have other feelings, even though they may not act on those feelings at all. A Pisces could become uncomfortable around people who have feelings that are not so pleasant and even have agendas that are not so pleasant.

Nevertheless, you would know, and as a Pisces, you would learn to trust your feelings and would distance yourself from that energy, and that is all right. Sometimes that energy would be present temporarily; other times it would be present more regularly from that person, place or thing. So you distance yourself from that, and you go someplace where you feel better. You understand, I am saying that Pisces would not have to strain too hard to learn about instinct. Pisceans are in their very nature instinctual. This doesn't mean that Pisceans cannot develop their mind; it means that they start with the capacity without being taught, and they tend to retain that capacity, even if being taught the opposite. But instinct functions for them well.

It sounds like it's a part of everyone's natural self, once they wake up.

Yet if you examine the chart for everyone, not everyone has Pisces as a predominant energy. Do you have it?

No. I have several planets in Pisces.

So you have some.

Yes. That is why I had asked earlier how you defined those with Pisces energy.

You understand, I asked, "Do you have some Pisces energy?" and you said, "No," but that is not true.

I have half a dozen planets in the sign Pisces, yes.

So you have some. So in the future, you can say, "Yes, I have some."

Yes [laughs], I am half Aries and half Pisces, a very strange combination.

Not at all. Do you have an astrologer? I recommend you get one. That astrologer doesn't necessarily have to have read this book yet, but when it comes out you can always present it, and he or she will either read it or not. But if you get an astrology reading from an astrologer, first off make sure it is an astrologer you feel good about. So know your feelings, know what your body is telling you when something feels good as compared to a desire. Desire and feelings are not necessarily the same thing. You might desire something strongly based upon a mental goal, whereas your body might very well have a feeling of whether something is safe or not safe, but you might not interpret that clearly if you have a mental goal for something. So pick your astrologer on the basis of what feels good, regardless of what "thinks" good.

Good advice.

Understand that there is a reason why I am speaking to you personally. It is in the nature of Pisces to be personal. When you are around Pisces people—even if you say nothing, even if they are sitting next to you on a bus—they can't help it, their experience with you is personal. They feel you. You can be across the room, but they feel your energy. It is personal to them. Don't ever be insulted if someone starts drifting away from you [laughs]. It might just be that they are Pisces and they are not comfortable with your energy in that moment. Another moment could be different. This is why Pisces people need to have their own spaces available to them that they can retire to at times, just to recover and feel their own energy and not be overwhelmed by the energies of others.

Do they have a problem knowing their energy from others? Is that a problem with Pisces?

No more than anyone else. It is important that the whole series of books here will speak of these things, especially in the *Shamanic Secrets* series. The *Shamanic Secrets* books have a foundation in the physical world, you see, whereas the other books may not be that way. This book also has a foundation in the physical world because it is about your day-to-day physical life, even though you may be hearing consistently from different planets and things that are a synthesis of essentially an idea (which is what's going on now), and yet it is all about your day-to-day physical, practical reality. That is what astrology is. It may be derived by understanding your relationship to things that are outside of you, but its entire purpose is structured toward your day-to-day physical life. Given that, it is unique, and it is a book of instructions that you believe in many societies you did not come with.

As with any book of instructions that comes with anything, it must tell you what it is about. This book of instructions is to explain this, in this case the human being in your world. So this is what you can expect for yourself. This is what you can expect for the world—explaining the wheel, so to speak. This is what you can expect here and there. In short, astrology is the book of instructions.

This does not exclude your religious dogmas. That is an attempt to interpret the overall sense of existence, often giving you suggestions to live by which that particular religion has found to be of value. Philosophies do something similar. But astrology is the book of instructions of what *is*, and the attempt in this book is to add more to what is for the astrologer and for other interested parties. You see, right now what I just said is very personal because it is directed to you, but it is also directed to every single reader and others who may acquire this knowledge in some other way.

That is wonderful. Is there anything else about Pisces that may have been lost or hidden?

Let's see if I can come up with one other. Pisces has the capacity to reveal by its own existence the unseen in another. Think about how often you as an individual, regardless of what sign you may be—whether you have Pisces in your chart or not—would have liked to understand why you did this or that, or why you felt this or that, or why there are blank spots in you that you just can't access. If you are around enough Pisces people, you will find these blank spots diminishing. You will also find that you will be able to bring together the words—or the interpretive words, which might involve emotions, for example—to ask the questions that you have been unable to assemble that would result in answers to fill in those blank spots in ways that feel right to you. So in that sense, it is not Pisces' job to give you the answer, but Pisces can help to reveal the unseen.

Astrology Is Affected by the Stars You Can See

That is why I feel again that this book is so important and that astrology is so important in general. When I say "astrology," of course, I am referring, not only to astrology as you understand it in your part of the world, but to other ways to look at astrology as one might find in other parts of the world. You understand that astrology is affected not only by where the client is living but also by where the astrologer is living. There is an interesting explanation for that. It is not only in reference to the geography—meaning the energy of the portion of Earth in which you are living—but it is also, as many astrologers know, affected by the stars that you can see.

When you look up in the night sky, if you live in the Northern Hemisphere you see certain stars, but if you live in the Southern Hemisphere, you may very well see, as people know, other stars that are not visible in the Northern Hemisphere. This can change the perception of the astrologer based simply upon the influences of the radiated light of these stars that come through—day or night, it doesn't make a difference. Or in the case of the client being in a different hemisphere from you, it could change his or her perception. This is often the reason why if a client lives in one hemisphere and the astrologer lives in the other, or vice versa, there can at times be misunderstandings from one person to the other. I am not saying that you must have an astrologer in your own hemisphere, but it can often be helpful if you do.

Conversely, for the astrologer to consult or gain in knowledge and wisdom, it can be useful to consult with other astrologers in your own hemisphere, but it can be profoundly useful to consult also with astrologers in other hemispheres—meaning, from the north to the south or from the south to the north, for example. Then you can expand your perception, your capability to perceive, and your broader understanding of astrology and life itself. When you are radiated by different stars in your life, it is not a conscious thing, but it is a reality. I might add that it is this way all over the universe, not just on Earth.

So would it be beneficial to understand one's self more to get astrological readings from Chinese astrologers and Vedic astrologers—from other systems in astrology?

It depends. If you would like to, go ahead, but I am talking about different hemispheres. You are speaking from the Northern Hemisphere. If you got a reading from an astrologer in China, it would still be the Northern Hemisphere. If you were to receive a reading from someone in, say, the Republic of South Africa or Australia, for example, or Argentina perhaps, that is quite far in the Southern Hemisphere.

Do they all use the same system?

You can ask them what they are using. Yes, I think a variety of readings might be useful, but keep in mind that different astrologies are not only perceptions or approaches to astrology—or planet-oriented understandings of life or star-oriented understandings of life. Either one, or both, is influenced by where the astrologer lives, by the food he or she eats. Think about it. If you grow food in your garden and you live in the Southern Hemisphere, then the stars there are radiating on that food as well as the Sun. Of course, there is the Sun, there is the Moon, but there are the stars that the planet is exposed to in the Southern Hemisphere, and that food is going to be different. It is going to be meant to be consumed by people in that hemisphere. You can, of course, ship it to places in other hemispheres, but it may not support your knowledge and wisdom to live in that hemisphere.

I am not saying don't eat that food, because certainly it might bring variety and enjoyment in your life, to say nothing of satiating your hunger. But if you wish to be supported and nurtured to understand your life, it is always good to eat the food grown locally at the very least as well. I would recommend eating it predominantly so that you are not confused, so that you do not have a great deal of open doors, so to speak, to acquire knowledge and information based on what you eat. Those doors will remain open with nothing in them because you are not living in the hemisphere where the food was raised that you are eating predominantly. Try to eat predominantly that which is raised or grown locally, or at the very least in your hemisphere. Feel free to add other things, but it's best for it to be predominantly from your hemisphere.

How would it affect our growth and our potential, then, if we were to live for a period of time in the Southern Hemisphere?

You would start adapting to the capacities, the capabilities, the lifestyle and the energy provided in that Southern Hemisphere. It would probably be very good for many people. Many have gained tremendously simply by living in another culture, to say nothing of living in another hemisphere. Certain aspects of your mind and body would grow and thrive. You would have certain capabilities that were latent brought more to the surface for you. Generally speaking, as long as it is a benevolent circumstance, it would be very worthwhile and I would recommend it for anyone who can do it.

On the other hand, once you go back to the hemisphere in which you normally live, if you do not return to the other hemisphere from time to time, you will tend to find that those latent things that were amplified when you were in, say, the other hemisphere, will fade again and not be readily available. It is available when and where needed, you see, but given all the other things that you must do, if it is not needed because you are living in another hemisphere, then it may not be as accessible. But when you return, in the case of a return to that other hemisphere, it will come back quickly.

So we need to travel more.

If possible, yes—but not just traveling, going there for a day. You need to live there for a time.

How long?

I would recommend at least a year or two years. But if you live there for even a season, a growing season, then that could be good. I would recommend at the minimum now at least two or three growing seasons. That might take a couple of years.

The Hidden Is Part of Life

Do you feel that most of what was lost from astrology was just that, lost—where people died, cultures got wiped out in wars, teachers didn't have a successor to teach it to, and so on? Or are there facets and knowledge about astrology that have been deliberately hidden?

Think about human nature. You don't have to, but could you say easily that it is in the nature of the human being to hide? What is one of the most popular games that children and often parents play with their children all over the world?

Hide-and-seek?

Yes. It is in the nature of human beings to turn what is hidden into a game so that when children grow up to become men or women, what is hidden from them is not only something that they need and want and demand to be revealed, but it becomes something that is like a game: "Oh, it is a problem. How do I solve this?" This is as in the child, "Oh, where are you? I can't find you. Are you here? Are you there?" and the child runs around and looks. The hidden is part of life, and of course, since you come to Earth, you must forget almost everything about yourself so that you will discover new things and possibly create something you have not created before because you didn't need to. You know who you were, you know what you are about living in other places, but on Earth you don't, because Creator has made this school for you to learn and think. The one absolute to learning something new is to forget who you are, so you forget temporarily while you are here—except, of course, when your soul travels when you are sleeping. Then it all comes back.

But we don't get to bring it back here.

You know why you don't get to bring it back?

They say it would distract us.

But do you know why?

Why?

You can't bring it back. Do you know why you can't bring it back? I will explain this, because it is worthwhile. When you have a dream, you are asleep and you are dreaming, and many things happen in that dream. When you wake up, you can only remember in the dream what is of Earth. If it falls under the heading of who you really are—where you are really from, what you are all about, and all of that—if it comes under anything like that, you cannot remember that, because the rule is you forget all that to come here. That is why when you wake up, what you remember in the dream is totally disjointed. It all has pieces that look like Earth, but in the major portion, you don't know who the people are, though sometimes you change their faces if they look similar to people you know.

This is why people often have experiences when they wake up remembering something that feels like a prophetic thing that is going to happen, but it may well have been a teaching that you were receiving from a guide, an angel or one of your spirit helpers that is being taught to your soul—when, of course, your soul is remembering exactly who and what your soul is, meaning remembering your entire personality. But you are not able to remember that, because when you are on Earth, you remember only that which has to do with Earth. So your mind immediately references that which you remember from the dream, attempts to fit it into your life as you understand it, and even tries to fit it into the news, meaning things that you are not living but which you are aware of because of what you are reading or seeing on television.

It is interesting that we won't be able to live in this focus and remember. It will have to be beyond this focus—is that right?

Beyond this focus, yes, because if you are in school, you must use the books provided. If you use books that are from another school, you will get confused because it won't be about this place. If you start living and imagining and being who you are other places, if you know who you are in reality completely, you would not behave anything like what you would behave here. You would become, of course, very relaxed, but then almost immediately you would become very uncomfortable because you would be living in a world that is totally foreign to who you are, where you are from, and why you exist. In short, you would become very unhappy very quickly.

So you think that it would be the be-all and end-all of existence, but that is not true. That is why it is hidden from you and you experience it only at deep-sleep levels, or when you are done with your life here and you move on. Then it is safe. It won't distract you, as you said, and the hiding then becomes a good thing. Children know the joy of playing hide-and-seek. If they play it enough, they realize it is a game. It is meant to be fun. The hidden doesn't always have to be bad. Sometimes it is a good thing.

There Are No Secrets

What I actually meant was, have certain secret or religious groups or those who try to control us deliberately hidden some of the knowledge of astrology?

I understand what you were asking. I had to precede it with that, because it is in your nature, not only to experience the hidden, but it is in your nature to hide. Think about it. Think back in your life. Did you ever hide anything? Did you ever have something special and put it away so the other kids wouldn't get it, because if they got it, it would be gone in a moment, right?

So it is not so strange. People hide things; it is in your nature. This doesn't mean it is in your true nature, but it is in your nature that you develop here. To hide things is not unusual at all, and sometimes you hide things to protect others—at least, you believe that in your own mind. What parent has not hidden things from children to protect them? Very often, it is a good thing they are doing that, because the children could harm themselves, or they could become confused about who they are, or in the case of the parent, they could start asking troublesome questions. Hiding is not always a bad thing, and many times people who hide things feel they are performing a service. They are not just trying to control you. However, as a child, one often feels that your parent is trying to control you, eh? [Chuckles.]

So understand that the hidden has made more out of it than what it really is. Even if somebody had the book of all the answers to all the questions and had that stashed away in some impenetrable attic, all the answers are available through inspiration or through means like you are conducting right now in this process. The answers are available. The book of answers can be accessed by anyone, though it is helpful to have the right questions.

That was a very nonjudgmental way to go about answering.

Think about it. Think how normal it is to hide things. Think how normal it is to know that others have things hidden. But keep in mind that very often what is hidden is meant to protect others, not to cause them harm. It may not always be the case, but in the majority of cases, it is so—when you take into account just the few examples I gave. Your parents hide things from their children, eh? Put the sharp objects away from the kiddies.

But as we wake up now, then there won't be any secrets.

There aren't any now. You just need to know what to ask and how to ask it. You are doing a pretty good job.

Thank you. There aren't secrets now?

There are no secrets. There are people who believe there are secrets, and it makes their lives difficult, to attempt to keep others from finding those things out. But generally speaking, even speaking now for a moment to those who are keeping secrets to protect others, know that the danger is not in others finding out. The danger, as you really know, is in others who might wish to cause you harm in finding out. So the key is the resolution of problems between people. Then everyone can know your secrets and there is no harm, because people do not have resentments against you. So seek to resolve your differences, and secrets will become a non-issue.

You are saying that for those who are sensitive and for those who are inspired and for those who know to ask that at this point in time, that there are no more secrets regarding Earth life?

Not quite. I am saying that there never have been, if you know how to ask. It is important that when you find out a secret, you don't say, "Oh, so-and-so was keeping that a secret. I am mad at them. I am going to get them." If you are entrusted with a secret, hold it and make sure for a time that it is safe before you reveal anything to anyone else. It may be someone's precious secret. If you believe that is not that case, then you may find a way to integrate that knowledge into your life in a way that benefits you. Try to make sure that it benefits others as well.

If you discover that it was somebody's secret, a precious secret, make peace with that person so that he or she comes to trust you and understand that you found out that secret but you do not mean any harm. It might just be a chance for a new friend. That applies to individuals as well as many, many groups. The reason there is such joy at discovering the hidden, which makes you feel better—although not always [chuckles]—is because it is intended to bring you closer to other people. It's not intended to create, stimulate or promote strife.

Doesn't Pisces also have to do with the unseen and the hidden?

Didn't I already say that? The knowledge that exists now is that it appears that Pisces has to deal with that. I am simply saying that Pisces broadcasts various energies. There is a difference between living with something and simply broadcasting it. It casts that knowledge in a different light.

The Thirteenth Sign Will Be a Sign You All Assimilate

There is going to be a thirteenth sign that some people will embody, which will be a synthesis of the other twelve signs. Can you say what your contribution to that thirteenth sign will be?

My understanding is that none of the signs will directly contribute, that the energy will come from another source. But primarily, it will come from the need of the people. The thirteenth sign will be something that you all have, not a sign that exists now, such as one understands the differences between Pisces and Virgo or Gemini, for example. But it will be a sign you all assimilate. That is my understanding.

In your understanding, is there a being who will speak for that?

You will have to ask when the time comes. Most likely, it will be after you have heard from all the other signs.

For those of you who are reading and studying this book, understand that the way you study it, the way you apply it, and the way you live it, not only has to do with your understanding of life on this planet, but will also vastly support future generations who travel to other planets or who greet travelers from other planets on your own. It is meant to help you to prepare, just as much as it is meant to help you to know. I thank you for your interest, I thank you for your choice in profession, and I thank you for your desire to know, apply and assist others. Good night.

Thank you very much. Thank you.

483

Taurus
April 21 – May 21

TAURUS

Stimulates Feelings from Earth that Can Be Shared

August 29, 2007

This is Taurus.

Welcome. Tell me what you can that's new to us about your sign.

How to Connect with Feelings Emanating from Earth

I am understood to be of many things, but here is something personal. I have the capacity to stimulate feelings that can emanate from the Earth into any individual. In that sense, one must allow for where the stimulation is coming from, and passing through the Earth thus, it must be able to filter to that which is benevolent—Earth is that for her guests—and also that to whom it is directed. Now, just to make sure that we are clear on this, what I am saying is that utilizing the Taurus energy, it is possible to direct a feeling through the Earth to anybody on the planet. But because we are talking about Earth here, the feeling would have to be something that reaches them and something they feel benevolently.

I will tell you how to do this: If you have this energy available to you, then go out on the land. You must have your bare feet on the soil. It is not necessary to bare any other part of your body, but your feet—the bottoms of your feet especially—must be bare. It can be on sand, if you are in a desert or on a beach, but if you are on a beach, I would recommend for the sake of simplicity that the sand not be very wet. It could be slightly damp—meaning that the tide has gone out and the sand is slightly damp—but it is always better if the sand is dry. Then perhaps you have someone you love who is on the other side of the world doing this or that. If you can coordinate with that person so that he or she knows when that feeling might be coming, that is the best way.

Then you can focus on a particular feeling. Perhaps you love someone; perhaps you want to nurture that person in some way. You can think of any number of feelings, but thought of the feeling will not do it. You will have to feel it to the maximum you can in your physical body. It is almost like a performance, that. You would have to fill yourself with the feeling —imagine an actor doing that on a stage— and become that as much as possible. When you get to the point where you become that, then take a deep breath in. When you blow that breath out, look down at the ground or the sand, and imagine it coming out of the bottoms of your feet as well—when you blow your breath out, imagine breath coming out of the bottoms of your feet—and blow that breath out. Take three deep breaths and blow them out slowly, looking at the ground.

I know you think that you are to think about the other person, but don't. You have a certain amount of time. Blow the three breaths as suggested, then relax for a moment—ten seconds, maybe fifteen seconds—and do nothing but think of that person. Think of him or her in the most benevolent way, all right? Don't dredge up any reasons why you are angry or annoyed with that person, or even annoyed because he or she has to be there. Don't have the feeling of annoyance, you see. Think only of that person in a loving way, since we are using that as an example.

There is a pretty good chance that within twenty minutes—and I don't mean to say *in* twenty minutes, but sometime within the range of twenty minutes—they should be able to feel that feeling. It wouldn't hurt to plan ahead and make arrangements, if you can, to say what feeling you are going to do. But nevertheless, do the best you can with this. This can be done most easily by someone who has a great deal of Taurus energy in their chart—a Sun sign would be good and also other places. It would also be good to try, if you have—let's see, I do not know your terminology—if you have Taurus as a rising sign, for example.

Now, interestingly enough, if you get good at this, you might actually be able to do it as a service for others. If you have friends who have loved ones and you find that this is working, you might be able to perform this service for others. Obviously, you would have to send a feeling other than personal love to them, but you might be able to send joy or happiness or reassurance or courage or something like that—bravery, peace, calm, anything like that. But it would require the Taurus energy to be a major factor in your chart. So simply having it in one of your houses is not sufficient.

Your Astrological Chart Is Stored in the Spinal Fluid

This book I'm looking at says that your energy is feminine with Venus as your ruling planet. Is there anything about this that is not known? Any feminine traits?

I don't think of my energy as being feminine, but certainly it could be interpreted that way.
Tell me about your energy, then.
It is balanced. Most of the signs are.

Ah! So they have been, as you say, interpreted by astrologers as one way or the other?
Well, this is because of the way astrology has been set up as a system, and I can see how it can be interpreted that way, but I feel that it is balanced. Of course, one has to take into account the Moon in order for it to be balanced. Yet some, when they take account of the Moon, consider the Moon to be feminine, and I do understand that.

At what point in the birth process would you consider to be the time of birth? When the head first emerges? When the baby cries? To fix the minute exactly, what would you tell people to use as the moment of birth?

When the baby first emerges, about the point when the top of the head and perhaps a little more—say, the top of the head and the third eye—are present, then that is the moment of birth, even though the birth is not complete. I believe that, medically speaking, the birth is considered complete when the child is entirely out of the mother, and I see no fault in that. For the purposes of this book, I do not know how you could possibly find out, because after all, when the baby is coming out, it is not a pleasant experience for mother, and if a doctor or midwife is present, he or she is giving the mother full attention and the baby attention also, and can't be scribbling down what time it is. But at some point, that will all be readily available. In fact, in some medical situations, I believe that when the baby's appearance first is present—meaning first emerging from mother—there may actually be, in some hospitals, a record kept of that. That would probably be up to the doctor, so you can't count on that.

But for people who are older, when the doctor got around to writing it down, that could be . . .

They are not that casual about it. You would be surprised at how, since birth certificates have gone into effect, they are pretty careful. When they determine that birth has taken place, then they glance at the clock. Glancing at the clock is something that is done often in operating rooms, because one must know the time for many reasons, so it is not something that is casual for medical people.

Is there any place in or on any of the bodies of a human being, whether it is the magnetic body or the electrical body or the astral body—is there any place physically or in any way at all where the Astrological chart is stored in the body in any form at all?

That is a very, very good question. I would say that if you are looking for a place where the energy of the time of birth and thus the coordination of your astrological potential is stored, it would be in the spinal fluid, because it has to be some place that has motion and has a range of capacity to move, you understand, and thus is flexible. But it also has to be a place that is highly protected.

Fascinating! I have asked this question a zillion times, and nobody has ever given me an answer.

Yes. Perhaps you asked the right being, eh?

That is probably the way it is. You have a sense of humor.

I do.

How does one sign have a sense of humor and another doesn't?

How does one human being have a sense of humor and another doesn't? It is all in personality.

Creator Created Certain Personality Types for Earth

Someone said earlier that each sign represents one of the twelve families that lent their personality traits to the Explorer Race. How do those qualities transfer to you? Do you take them on? Are beings in that constellation naturally of those personality characteristics? How does that work?

You understand that none of the signs—including me—are going to go into Explorer Race stuff too much. But I will say that certain families of existence . . . meaning when Creator created this universe, Creator developed certain general personality types, not down to the last nuance, but personality, if you understand my suggestion. Within those personality types, there are some that are likely to be more flexible and adaptable. Those are the ones that are here on Earth, so they also correlate to the Explorer Race, but that is another story. This is a good question to ask for one of your *Explorer Race* books. So all of the signs on this planet—though it is not always apparent—are flexible and adaptable, which is part of the reason they must be in fluid, you see, the spinal fluid.

In order to express the basic traits, which are well represented in the general knowledge of the astrological signs in this system of astrology, one can then assume a certain amount of understanding that all throughout the universe there are other people who have similar traits to you, regardless of what form they are in. But one does not have to wander that far. Just suppose there were beings other than humans who had traits from the same family of consciousness—meaning general personality types—that were right here on Earth. Who might they be?

What we call animals.

Yes, and microbes. Everything is alive. It is hard to imagine that atomic structure, that a nucleus—and imagine how many there are—would have personality, but it does. It is easy to perhaps suggest that it would have a rudimentary personality—something likes to be in the middle and something likes to go around the middle, as in the atomic pattern—but moving away from such small things, there are simply these generalized personalities on Earth. They are different for the other species, because the other species are not here to learn anything, so their traits in personality tend to be more positive. Since they are not here to learn anything, they don't need to have anything that is dragging them down or supporting an overall lesson or even an overall group of lessons.

So if you can take astrology and winnow down the different signs to their various basic personality quotients and eliminate the aspect of the darker side, as it is called (or the shadow side, as it sometimes might be referred to), you could easily say that some—not all, but some—of these personality characteristics could be spotted in a dog, a cat, a fish, a horse, and this is where it gets interesting, in a molecule, in a cell.

Imagine if and when doctors and medical people become acquainted with the interactivity of personalities within the human body. What if that which makes up certain organs has a predisposition to make that up because it has predominantly this or that feeling? That is how your bodies get created, because Creator has created something that, in its massive complexity, is really very simple at its root. That what might make up the heart—we all know the heart has certain biological functions, but it also has loving functions, caring (we think of a loving heart and so on)—would come from the personality traits, so those cells would migrate to the heart. How do they know? How does the baby form in the body? What becomes the heart and why?

Attraction.

Attraction. The personality of the energy that makes up the cellular structure is attracted to being that and really would not care to be anything else, just like something is attracted to being a tooth or an eye or a finger. Once that's integrated into medical practice—and I realize it will take awhile, but not so long, because once you start having contact with extraterrestrials, you are going to learn all about that—you will find that it will be much, much easier to help heal people because it won't be necessary to do many of the radical procedures that are done in your time. I am not really faulting them, because the best of intentions are at heart to motivate this to be done. But suppose you could simply have the person eat something, as long as his or her digestive tract was working, and trust that your body—as it does all the time with food—doesn't just feel things, but your body also creates cellular structure. Suppose you could trust that your body could transform that food, that those cells invite that food to become that, and the heart, for example, could be repaired, or any organ. Now, that is all I am going to say about that, because I want to encourage research in that direction, to understand that personality is not just something one finds in Mom or Dad or other people you know. Personality is universal, and that's the way Creator designed it.

Now, there is more. Isis said that one of the reasons humans choose to be born in certain places is that those places have atoms and molecules and particles imbued with the energy of that place—of the sign they have chosen to manifest—and those charged particles help the baby create its body. Can you say more about that?

No. I already said what I was going to say about that, but I think it is good that you are correlating it, and it would be good to put that information in.

That is fascinating. We might learn how to do benevolent magic to ask that energies go to different parts of our body to help heal until we do meet the extraterrestrials.

Think about it. You don't speak to the food before that, but you could either have a meal or you could perhaps speak to the food and speak perhaps to the deities associated with the food, and then you could ask it in benevolent magic, a living prayer, to perform that function. Of course, there is always that which you don't know—perhaps the person has a different destiny—but you could ask. Why wait? You could ask now. I grant that once the system is fully understood by medical peoples, it will be rapidly integrated because it is not that complex, although the system that will be introduced to human beings initially by extraterrestrials—even though they use something much, much simpler without technology, but they will introduce things to you with technology because that is where you are now—will have to do with various electromagnetic pulses. But the foundation will still be just exactly what I said.

Ah, that is interesting.

Remember, the whole point of electromagnetism is not to change and alter; it is to encourage, to invite, and to welcome.

So by putting out a certain harmonic with these pulses, you invite a certain energy, then?

Yes, depending upon where the lead is connected.

Everything Broadcasts Feelings

Is the sign of Taurus emanating these energies or supporting these Taurus energies that are here on the planet?

It is supporting the energies on the planet. I believe most of the signs do that. You understand, the signs are made up of various planetary bodies and so on, but to some degree it is symbolic. Nevertheless, simply the function of any group of planets—to say nothing of galaxies—is in support of itself and others. Right now, you see a group of human beings, and then you pull back with your aerial maps and you see buildings, and you keep pulling back. Eventually, you see Earth, but you keep pulling back.

If you could pull back far enough, you eventually could see this universe and you would see a form, because each of the galaxies emanates light, doesn't it? They illuminate the sky at night, and you have had many a fascinating evening looking at these beautiful light images. But think about it: It is possible to arrange lights in such a way as to make a form. The expansion of a galaxy means that, not only are the planets in motion in the solar systems and so on, but all galaxies are in motion. If you could pull back far enough, as I say, these points of light would make a form, and the form is in motion.

What form is it?

It is not a human being, but it is a form that would evoke within you a definite set of feelings where, if you were approaching it from a distance, you would say, "I want to go there." Think of souls and how immortal they are, and there are more creations than this one. Suppose you are in another creation and you are invited to come to this creation. Well, an invitation is nice, but you would want to feel welcome, wouldn't you? You would want to have certain feelings cosigned so that you would feel them and thus be attracted. You would feel them in your awareness, depending upon . . . I know you have sight and sound and all of that, but you may have different types of awareness from afar. You would feel all of that, and thus you would feel welcome.

But can you say what the form is that we would see?

It is not a human being. It moves.

So it's like a dance? It changes shape?

Yes, exactly. It changes shape. But I will tell you that if you can see under a microscope various cellular structures . . . not necessarily protozoa, because there you have something that remains generally the same shape. This is something that changes shape and has various loops and appendages, and then changes again according to what is being celebrated, what is being expressed.

Think about it. Human beings have feelings, and they are constantly broadcast. Animals have that also, as do cells. This happens on the small level. Of course, it happens on the large level. You are all one in reality, and while you may not always feel that, there are many times where you might have moments of feeling it. Perhaps you are going to an event—you go to the theater or you go to a sporting event—and something happens, and you all in the stadium cheer mightily. You are all feeling roughly the same range of feelings in that moment, so you are all one in that moment. Take that out to the size of a planet, then out to a solar system, and then out to a galaxy and beyond.

So galaxies are emanating feelings as they move?

Those in the galaxies are. Are you emanating feelings as a person? Do you think other people in your general part of the city are emanating feelings? And out and out and out and out and out? So to say that the galaxy is emanating feelings, then yes, if we use the other meaning of galaxy—meaning the full range of galactic feelings of all beings, as well as the matter itself, but the matter is also alive.

You Are Part of a Larger Astrology

The solar systems move within the galaxy around some central point. The galaxies move around something, and we are moving into a space that is filled with a higher energy, right?

Define "higher." We are not talking about astrology anymore, because astrology . . . who is this book aimed at? Earth human beings, yes? Where do Earth human beings live?

On Earth.

There you go. So we need to keep Earth in focus.

Okay, but Earth is moving as part of the movement of everything else into a space that has a faster vibration, a higher harmonic, a higher dimension, something. That is affecting us now, right?

Yes, but only in a slight sense, like you might prepare a meal and salt and pepper it, for instance. Like that. It is the salt and pepper, but it is not the meal. It is important to remember that, because influences are one thing, but it may not be the whole meal. It's only a spice of the whole meal, eh?

Astrology is limited to the Explorer Race, so that it's only these twelve signs in this imaginary zodiacal circle around Earth?

I wouldn't use the term limited. I would say that it is focused on Earth, because this is where you are.

Yes. But is there astrology in the creation? Is there astrology in the galaxy? Are we part of a larger astrology, or is it just because we don't know who we are and it is only focused on Earth?

That is a very good question. You are part of a larger astrology, but it might be considered an interesting study someplace else. Whereas on Earth, it is one of those things that if you know about it, it can greatly ease your way because, as you say, there is the lack of knowledge of who you really are on Earth and you need all the help you can get to discover what might be easier for you to do or where your talents might lie—as compared to struggling for years and years to do something for which you have very little potential.

So the plan is to maximize our potential, then—not learn something absolutely, completely new?

You can learn new things if you want to, but let's just say—keeping it down to Earth for a moment—if you want to make a living and you don't want to be sweating and slaving all the time, it might be good to do something that incorporates your natural abilities. That doesn't mean you can't read about other things, learn about other things, study them, and talk to people.

But focus on what you are good at.

Pay attention to what you are good at, and recognize that, because you are learning here, there will also be things that you are totally attracted to that are not necessarily good for you because they represent the side—you understand, you have a polarized planet here—they represent the other polarity. People don't often understand what astrologers do, of course, but people don't often understand that you not only have these certain traits—capabilities, potentials—but these traits and potentials, whether they are there from one polarity or the other, are not just broadcast, they also function as attracting factors. You will attract circumstances, people, places, things into your life that will represent all of these things so that you can live out the elements of the sign you have chosen to be born into.

Some of it has to do with lessons, but if you think of it that way, it will help you a great deal to understand why certain things keep coming up, even though you felt like you have totally and completely resolved them. It comes up not only to see if you will apply the ways you have resolved it to—and if that still works in that time, allowing for the factors of growth and change in your world and societies—but also it comes in again because it is a factor of your makeup and therefore is going to come to you. To the degree that you give it your attention and get bogged down in it, well, that might have to do with your accumulated wisdom and experience. A child might get bogged down in it a bit and need guidance and support from parents and loved ones and friends, but if you get a little older and you have experience and you've "been there, done that," then you don't necessarily have to get bogged down.

It functions not only as a broadcast quality but also as an attracting quality, just like the simple illustration of polarity—a magnet, yes? It attracts, and it also broadcasts. One thinks of a magnet as something that attracts something else, but as you know, it also repels. In the function of the repelling, it is actually projecting. It repels from like to like—positive to positive would push the other positive away—but what that means in this case then, strictly using the scientific terms, is that you are actually projecting. So the magnet has two poles: one attracts and one, in the case of our example here, projects. It is that way, exactly, with astrology.

Taurus Has the Capacity to Affect the Taste of Things

I always thought Taurus was sort of a solid type, and you sound so vivacious and so full of humor and not fixed at all—you know [chuckles], very flexible.

It sounds like your attitudes about the signs are getting more flexible all the time. It is good, because one travels the astrological wheel to an extent, don't you? You might be a certain sign, but you travel around the wheel. You have your time of the year, don't you? You go through this sign and that sign and all that, so you get exposed to the energies. You perhaps read astrology, and the astrologer says, "Well, this month the signs are this and that, so many degrees of Taurus," and so on. This means that the way the year is segmented, you are traveling the astrological wheel, so you are getting exposed to that and you will react this way or that way in different circumstances, but you are being exposed to the energy of that more so. You don't have to be conscious of it, you don't have to become an astrologer, but I think a basic understanding of astrology would be helpful for everyone. I grant that there are different systems throughout the world, but we are focusing on this one, because this is where you and your readers live.

Do you see that astrology will be taught in schools at some point?

It is taught in some schools now, but you are talking about general public education, yes? Perhaps, but general public education sees itself and allows itself to be rooted in certain religions, even though they might not feel comfortable with that idea. In fact, generally speaking, in various countries one often finds that predominant religions of those countries are very influential in the schools. So you might find in some countries that astrology—the astrology that is part of their culture—is also available in school. But if you are asking for your own country, I would say it will be awhile yet. So you might have to pursue it outside of the classroom.

Why is your sign considered fixed, when you seem so flexible?

Well, you are addressing a synthesis personality. You are confusing the personality that I am demonstrating with those you might know or have met who happen to have a predominance of Taurus in their charts. So don't go by that.

Is there anything else you can think of that comes to mind—or whatever one says to a synthesis [chuckles]—that we don't know about yet?

Taurus has another trait, which you don't often consider to be a trait of a sign at all. Taurus has the capacity to affect the taste of things. Here is something to try. I want to give this, because it is fun. Here is something to try, and you don't have to be a gourmet, though you can try it with wine, if you wish. I am not going to say what you think; it's not that things taste different to Taureans [laughs]. Do you know that if you have a considerable amount of Taurus in your chart—I will go with wine; I began with it, I will go with it—that you could actually go to a crop that is being raised for a type of wine. And if you have tasted perhaps the greatest (up to that point in time) wine ever representative of that which you are growing—perhaps you are growing grapes for some type of wine, any type, including a blend, but let's say it's something specific—you could (speaking in terms of the farmer here, the people who are growing it, raising it) focus totally on the flavor of that fabulous wine.

It wouldn't hurt to have a little bit present when you are out in the fields. You don't have to go around and touch every plant. What you can do is roughly find the rough, general middle of the place where the vines are. Of course, it may not be a perfect square—as a matter of fact, it would be strange if it were—but find someplace that is roughly the middle, or any place that feels comfortable to you, but you must be surrounded on all sides by vines (individual vines, you understand). I don't know how wide the rows are, but they're probably too wide to reach out and touch plants on either side, so don't touch any plant until you walk up. Stand and walk up and down the rows until you find the exact plant that feels best to you, allowing for the fact that these are vines. We are talking about a place in the vine that feels the best to you.

Drink a little bit of that wine, and notice the feelings in your body when you drink it. When those feelings are heightened—and heighten them as much as you can—reach out with the fingertips of your right hand, especially your long finger and the fingers on either side of that, and allow your thumb and small finger just to relax but don't pull them back. Reach out and gently touch the leaves or the stem on the vine. Only touch it while you have that feeling, nothing else. If you feel another feeling coming up or if there is a loud sound that distracts you, immediately pull your hand back from touching the vine. Then it will be possible to instill that in the vine, because it will spread. Just do it once, in one place in your field.

If you have more than one field perhaps—you might have a certain amount of types of vines growing, this in this field and that in another field—then repeat the process. If you do not have any of that fabulous wine available, try to remember how it felt when you were drinking it and focus only on those feelings. Don't let anything else be present, if you can possibly help it. If you get startled by something, then forget about it and try another time. But again, touch a leaf or the stem. Touch it for maybe no more than thirty seconds, just briefly, but more than five or ten seconds if you can. Understand that you need to focus only on those feelings—no wishes, hopes or dreams, no demands or commands, just the physical feelings in your body. Plants have feelings, too. They will note that feeling, and they will understand what it is you want them to do. If they can do it, they will.

We could do that with a smell for roses and a taste of tomatoes and corn and all sorts of things?

Yes. This is something that would take someone with a great deal of Taurus in his or her chart to do.

A whole new occupation here.

Yes.

[Laughs.] We have created a new profession.

That is my intention. That is why I brought it up a couple of times. A lot of the jobs that exist on other planets and in more benevolent times here on Earth in societies that have come and gone—for the most part, not exclusively gone—have done these things, and there is no reason you cannot do them in your own time. Recognize that cultures come and go, societies exist and move on, and this is the way of a polarized planet. Don't be attached to something being forever. Your souls, your hearts, your love, your feelings—they are forever. Your family of feelings, your friends from other planets and other places—these things are forever. You are in that sense your personality, and that is forever. Recognize that it is only your job on this planet now to express your feelings and your traits in the best possible way and perhaps in a way that serves yourself and others. Good night.

Ah! You were wonderful. Thank you very much. Thank you.

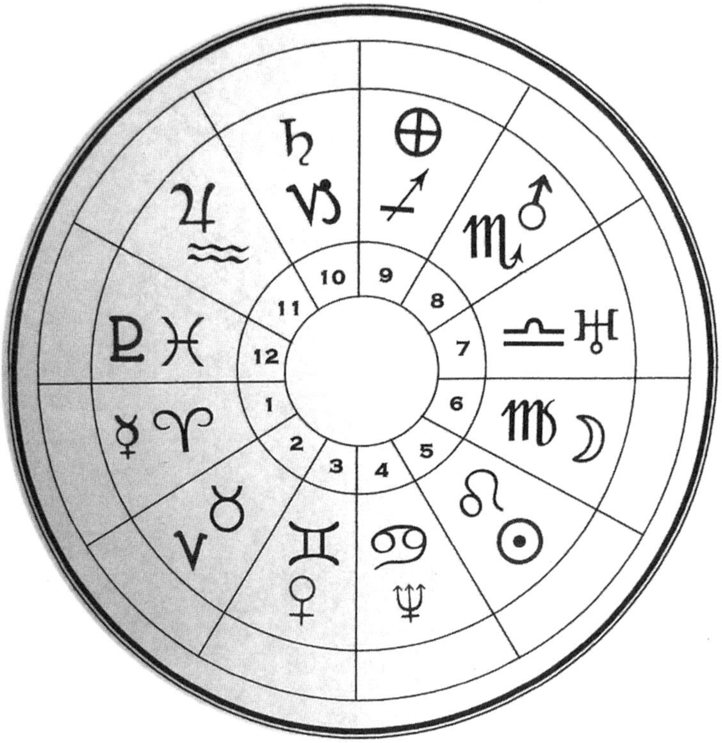
10
9
11
8
12
7
1
6
2
5
3
4

Aquarius
January 21 – February 19

AQUARIUS

Seeds the Energy of Creation, Inspiration and Awakening

September 4, 2007

This is Aquarius.

Welcome!

Greetings. Now, here's a little bit about what I actually do, as compared with what I am known for. It is in my nature, including the nature of my representatives on Earth—meaning those who have this influence predominantly in their charts, whether they be human beings or other—to instill all new things. This does not mean that we necessarily create, but we seed the energy of creation, inspiration and awakening. Many times one might see an animal, as you say, move in a strange way, meaning one might not expect a spider or a beetle to suddenly rush across a road—an extremely dangerous thing to do, which really terrifies them, as it would anyone.

But they would have Aquarius energy, you see, and they would know or be prompted to do this act in the safest way for them. Of course, none of them feel roads are safe because vehicles, being so huge compared to them, are upon them before they even see them, considering their speed and velocity. So they dash across, for the most part, and they would be prompted to do this only in a case where the situation was urgent, meaning that someone was going to cross that path almost immediately. So that energy would be needed, because it might be the last little bit of energy to bring forth some wonderful idea, some personal inspiration, or perhaps some great invention.

Human beings are also known to do this. The ones who are most likely to react to such a prompt without thought are children, and unfortunately, given the high rate of speed of vehicles on your roads, most drivers do not have much of a chance to stop. I am not saying that parents are at fault at all. I am saying that I feel that vehicle speed ought to be much more regulated and perhaps sensors placed in vehicles, so when someone rushes out, the vehicle stops without the person having to move his or her foot. The tragedies happen because somebody has to move his or her foot from one pedal to the other, not so much that the brakes don't work. I would warn parents that if you have an Aquarius child who is under the age of seven, that child must be watched a little more closely if you don't have a fence to keep him or her in your yard or in the playground.

Aquarius children are not going to, for the most part, be prompted to do this—dash out in the street, for example. But they might be more inclined to behave in ways that may seem to be odd or unusual, such as to walk in some fashion, to move their arms or hands in some fashion that might seem to be odd. Sometimes you see those with that energy who might be prompted to touch the air. A bird might be able to do this, but many times the air needs to be touched in the exact place where someone—usually an adult, but possibly a young person—is going to pass through that air. Therefore, that youngster might reach up in some unexpected manner, put his or her arms or hands in front of someone or more likely simply in a space where someone might walk through, and thus be affected and prompted, stimulated and inspired, to produce that wonderful idea or personal suggestion that improves the quality of his or her life and very often the lives of others.

So with that kind of impetus energy, one often finds Aquarian people near places of innovation. Businesses and corporations, you may or may not be able to know whether your employees are Aquarians, but you may. If you happen to know, you are going to want to have at least one or more of these people in your research and development units, even if they are performing some kind of a mundane job. Just find an excuse to have them there, to have them walk around and just be in that place, if they have a good deal of Aquarius in their charts—a Sun sign, say, or even various influences. Consult your company astrologer. If you don't have one, get one, and see if that can be arranged. You won't regret it.

I also would comment on another factor of the Aquarius energy. The Aquarius energy—especially if it is predominant in your chart, or even if you are around someone for whom it is predominant—has a tendency to be a focal point, not unlike a lens, for any and all atmospheres. From my point of view, the term "atmospheres" might refer to stars, suns, radiations from stars, or suns or planets who are affecting Earth at this time. You all know that eclipses have an effect on the personalities of people. In some cases, it might be fleeting; in other cases, it might be more profound. These people will also act as a focal point, meaning that if anything is going on like that or if certain stars, suns, even trines are taking place of those planetary groups—through any house, anything—these people will unconsciously and without being impacted themselves be very much the lens.

Now, you all know that a lens can focus something, concentrate something, but there is another way to look at a lens. A lens can also broaden something. Take a beam of light, for example, and expand it, not just to focus it to a smaller image. It would depend entirely upon where the Aquarians themselves have their own personal energy of innovation. A good astrologer could figure that out. If the innovation is in one place, then the lens goes this way. If the innovation is in another place, then it goes that way. A good astrologer can figure that out on the basis of this information, because this kind of exposure to such a person can create either an amplification of something that may be helpful to certain people or the opposite, where it might be able to condense that energy—totally unconsciously, you understand, just through the nature of their being—so that it does not play out in such a wide pattern.

Now, think about it. If you have a group of people in your family, group, organization, business, anything, who is likely to be specifically impacted by, say, an eclipse (of the Sun or the Moon, whatever), and that impact might be difficult, might cause momentary struggles, might even cause strife, and so on—they don't usually, but they can—then you would want to have one of these people around who might be able to condense that energy. It is less likely to be more broadly radiated and affect all of these others if such a person is there. It might concentrate on one person, for example, or one or more, just a few, but not be a broad impact on so many. Those are two things that are not known about Aquarians.

Animals and Other Life Forms Are Also Affected by Astrology

You said something that I hadn't considered before. You are saying that animals also focus energies of astrology?

Animals, humans—any life form is affected by the astrological elements of this planet. Why would you think that human beings alone would have that energy? Animals do not come to the planet—or let's just say that nonhuman life forms do not come to the planet—to learn anything. They come to assist the progress of the human being through your lessons and so on. But they are born at certain times under the same influences that you are born under, and while they may not show all the traits that one identifies with the astrological science as applied to the human being, one has to factor out a great deal—not all, but a great deal—of the downside, the "what if" aspects of astrology that would have to do with the human being, because those would have to do at least in part with your personal lessons. But since the animal or the nonhuman does not have that as a personal lesson, one would only see slight aspects of that having to do very mildly with personality quirks, for instance, that the animal might engage a human being at a certain time or might care for privacy at a certain time, something like that—a very mild version, but not unexpectedly feisty, for example.

Of course, they have that. If you know when an animal is born, it can make all the difference in the world matching up the persona of that animal with, say, yourself. Very often, though, the animal has the capacity to be quite well aware of its own personality and seek out the human being through some friendly act and so on, so that the human being recognizes the cat.

The animal does not have any aspects associated with the negative side of the astrologic, meaning the "what if" side of the astrologic. The animal has only the positive side, and although it might have certain aspects of the so-called negative side—meaning "I want to be alone," or "I am happy to be with you"—then that is really all that being would have. On the other hand, if you know, for instance, when the animal was born—say you are aware, you are present, you were perhaps assisting the mother when she was having puppies or when she was having kitties, or perhaps more significant for people in the horse-racing world, for example, when the foal is coming out—you can get a pretty good idea of the astrology of that particular being.

If you have that idea of their astrology—their astrological sign, you understand—then you will know something vitally important, especially in the nature of horse racing. I am not necessarily saying that I feel good about the way horse racing is conducted, but I'm simply saying that matching up the jockey's astrology with the horse's astrology can often make for greater compatibility. Now, say you also have the desire for a dog to perform certain functions for you—be a good watchdog, be a good companion. Then matching up that astrology would also be much more likely.

Now, when you are adopted by an animal . . . say a dog shows up at your door, doesn't have another place where it is living, but adopts you, or more often this is done by a cat. Unless it is very hungry, that cat will approach the person or the people for whom they feel the compatibility. In short, they will know that astrological compatibility, but the human being probably will not know. So very often that match-up does take place between people and their pets, because the animals will know, even though the connection from the human being mental consciousness may not be aware of that. But if you know, you might be able to match people up with the proper pet—for those of you in the pet store business, for example—that would create much of a guarantee of compatibility.

It is known by some astrologers, but it has not gained popularity yet. I feel it would be good for it to gain more popularity, but, well [chuckles], it's not critical, eh? It might be critical in situations where, for instance, a police dog is teamed up with a policeman. Then you might want to have the best possible relationship, even though the dog has been trained and so on. Another possibility is a Seeing Eye dog. If you have the opportunity to have a dog who is compatible with the human being, then why not?

While You Are Emanating Energy, You Are Also Acquiring

So we all radiate energy. Every human and nonhuman and plant and everything radiates energy, right? We were told astrology exists because we don't know who we are and we can figure out our talents and abilities by knowing our chart.

You emanate a certain amount of energy, yes, but while you are emanating, you are also acquiring. So it is not like a light bulb where the light is always on and radiating—unless you factor in that the light bulb is receiving electricity and thus receiving and emanating. So in that sense, yes.

So is the animal affected in any way by being . . . what? By receiving energy astrologically? How would you say it?

No different than you. You are in reception of that energy based upon the various planets—and positions of planets and motions of planets, etc., etc.—that are involved in your chart. So you are in reception of that all the time. With people who are not of the astrological world, there is a little confusion here, so this is a very good question. The assumption is that it is like a photograph that's taken of the planetary positions when you are born, and that is that—meaning that's the position, and that's that. But it isn't a photograph, it is a moving picture, and it continues to move throughout your lifetime, just as you move throughout your lifetime, and it is always supporting you.

Those circumstances are supporting you, and those planets are supporting you. In short, it is a flow in. Of course, you as a representative of those planetary energies on your planet are moving about, you are breathing in and out. You are emanating, so you are broadcasting that energy. You might reasonably ask, is there a reason to broadcast that energy on the surface of your planet other than the fact that your birth does have a great deal to do with your astrological connection? Yes, of course. The planet has to be constantly attuned—not forced, but informed in the form of energy—as to who and what are present.

Oh! That's totally new.

Well, you see, how is the planet going to know how to provide? After all, the planet knows how to provide for beings who are present, not just on the basis of observable characteristics, but also—and much more importantly—with the broadcast energy involved. In this way, the planet is an energetic being. The planet is, in fact, a planet, yes? She's a planet—Mother Earth, as you say.

So when that broadcast energy is involved, then she feels the impact of these other planets, positions of planets: the Sun, the Moon, the stars. She feels it, and she knows that if the beings on her surface are associated with these planets, then there are certain basic energies that need to be present to serve, support and nurture beings like that.

"What might those energies be?" you might say. We are not talking just about air—breathing it in, the right regulation of gases in air. We are not just talking about foods (what can you eat?) or water (what can you drink?). We are talking about the component energy of these things: the soil you walk on, the nature of the energy of the planet. What do you feel? How do you sleep? How do you dream?

In short, if you are a tuning fork, so to speak, you are responding to the resonant energies of these planets and their positions—and, of course, the planet's personality changes as it changes its position, as any astrologer can tell you. Then the associative needs of the person—and Earth's ability to respond, because she is so many things and so accomplished—must be in balance, not only for the continuity of life, which all over the universe is totally different than it is on Earth. For instance, a physical body like a human physical body might be born on some more mild benevolent place—let's say, the Pleiades—and could easily live 600, 800, 1,200 years perhaps, given certain conditions. But that same body, almost exactly identical, can be born on Earth and live maybe 100 years, 110, if you are lucky.

So, then, how does Earth know? She knows to moderate her energies so that even in ideal conditions—let's say, for example, with no pollution at all, the oxygen-to-nitrogen ratio perfect, and the carbon dioxide exactly balanced (say they were absolutely the best)—even so, with the maximum potential, given the exact right food and psychological everything, the physical body of the Earth's human is not likely to last more than 175 years. It is understood by Earth—by the association of those planets, by the Explorer Race sowed by Creator, by Mother Earth in reception of all of that to know—that you are here for a short time because you are in school, and the idea of perpetuating your time in school is not so attractive. Hearken back to your own time in school. Did you really want to stay there forever?

Life is so much easier every place else, and you are immortal in your personalities. Your body might change, but your personality lives on without so much as a pause. When you leave your physical body here, your personality lives on. Granted, as you move through the veils, you shed the discomforts associated with your Earth life, but you would know yourself. Of course, you would, and others who have known you would also know you. So you are immortal in that sense.

Thus, Mother Earth must know, on the basis of the correlation of the planets associated with the Earth human being, how long to support life per individual—human or nonhuman. Granted, nonhumans are not here to learn anything. In some cases, they choose to live longer lives—say, the tortoise, for instance, or ancient trees—but this may be a passing thing. They may not choose to do that in the future. It is up to them.

But in the case of human beings who are here to learn, who are in school, even in optimum conditions you will not be extending the life of your bodies here so much, so don't try. Why would you want to? I understand it is because you are not aware that your life goes on, and why would you take my word for it? [Chuckles.] I understand, but the reason you are having difficulty in extending your years of living is because Creator does not want you to have to suffer. Therefore, you live here not too long, and then you resume your comfortable lives and lifestyles off-planet, where life is benevolent.

Welcoming Has Everything to Do with Mother Earth

Does Mother Earth have a way of adjusting the energies from the planets and the signs to a certain area, if they need more in this area and less over here? Can she do that?

No. It depends upon who is there. You have to do that as people, so there really isn't the need for that. Remember, everything about Earth is about balance, but if such a condition were needed for any reason—I understand you are talking theoretically here—most likely, then, the quickest way to adjust this would be that animals would suddenly rush to that area who are of that energy. You have probably seen nature films, and there might be a great many birds someplace. Unless there is some danger, one does not see them all lift off at once, but you might see a few lift off, and the assumption is they are somehow a family. But sometimes they are of the same sign and they need to move through the air because someone or something else is going to move through that air that needs to be affected by that energy.

Also, one must remember that there is wind, so the wind might be coming by and the animal doesn't think about this. They respond on the basis of felt need. That is why there is a certain amount of pause. They don't all suddenly leap up and fly, but they will tend to fly through the same space. The wind will pick up that energy, take it to where it is needed, and infuse it or make it available for those who need that level of inspiration. Remember, Mother Earth is number one about balance: water, wind, soil, earth, fire, and so on. Balance!

How does that work? You said the energy feeds inspiration or awareness. The Aquarian energy, then, helps all other people become more inspired and more aware?

Yes. How does it work mechanically? How do *you* become inspired? How does it happen? You think of yourself as becoming inspired by guides, yes?

But your guides don't need to have that astrological influence to inspire you. One does not always consider that a human being—someone you might take for granted, whom you pass on the street—can inspire you, but one does have inspiration based upon contact with others. This is found very often in, say, a brainstorming meeting where people get together and they talk about this and that, but sometimes somebody gets an idea simply by looking at things, not just correlating things, because not all people are word-oriented—some people are visual-oriented. They will look at this, they will look at that, and also because of the energy present, the capacity for inspiration might be greatly improved.

Now, you understand, in the comment I made before, with the Aquarian child moving, waving his or her arms in such a way unexpectedly, this does not singularly prompt the inspiration for the adult who walks through that air. The inspiration is totally in place from a great many other factors, but it just needs that last little support in order for the inspiration for that human being to become conscious. You see?

To sort of kick it out and give it birth or something.

Not kick it, but to welcome it. Welcoming has everything to do with this planet. This planet is all about welcoming. It is not about kicking, though I recognize that started because of people's sense of humor (that point of view) and because Mother Earth will sometimes demonstrate—no question about it—violent aspects of her personality: volcanoes, storms, and so on. But most of the time, most of what Mother Earth does, is welcome. How many times have you gone out into nature and felt totally welcome and at peace, to say nothing of the fact that animals and humans give birth, and while it is not a pleasant experience for the mother for the most part (though in some species it can be), then the welcoming still must take place in order for the baby or the offspring to be welcome to the planet.

One might be able to get the sense of this more in a nonhuman birthing situation, because most of the human birthing situations done these days in your modern world do not really allow for welcoming, but the planet is available for that. One might see, for instance, that kind of welcoming in a water birth, because in the case of a water birth, for example, the baby literally upon emergence from mother swims out. The baby is not taught to swim, but the baby had been in liquid, and the idea of baby swimming out feels totally natural for baby. I don't want to sound like I am preaching—I am not. I am just saying that welcoming has everything to do with Mother Earth.

Do you see us doing that in the near future, going to water births?

I do not see it in the near future, but more as people become more conscious of preserving the planet and essentially rebuilding the planet. That is what you are going to have to do: you are going to find yourself in the situation where you are going to be attempting to re-create pristine Earth conditions. Of course, scientists will love that, but at the same time, the tendency to overdo it will be omnipresent for some time. You will need support there, and you will need to get past your prejudice against magic.

Magic (and I am talking about totally benevolent magic here), when functioning in a surrounding of benevolent energies, can support, nurture, invite and … what? It can *welcome* Mother Earth to re-create her natural affinity toward balance and welcoming of all species. So don't try and do it all yourself. You can't just do it scientifically. You might be able to produce it scientifically for a split second, but you have to take note of the conditions you are trying to reproduce, and any scientist will note that any condition you are trying to reproduce is always in flux.

So while you might be able to reproduce a moment, it will only be a moment and you may not be able to keep the flux going in its natural state. Still, it is something you've got to do, unless you incorporate welcoming, nurturing magic associated with energies and associated with portions. You have been given some instructions about benevolent magic, but most of the more esoteric aspects have involved energy and the gradual training of people to be exposed to this kind of thing.

All Signs Are Balanced

The book I am looking at says that Aquarius is a fixed, masculine sign, and yet everything you are saying about it seems to be more of a flowing. How did it get put as a fixed sign when it seems it is much more flowing and flexible?

As it is with many of these signs, that formula is really based upon mathematics and comparisons of many, many, many years of astrologers looking to see what is and an attempt to create, to turn astrology into science. I referred to astrological science, and it is true. However, astrological science in this case is *feminine* science. It is not masculine science, which has been polarized on your planet—which isn't surprising, because polarities are part of the planet. In a polarized point of view, one might say that, "This is this, and that's that," and that is very attractive if you feel like your world is out of control.

As you well know, most people on your planet feel, at one time or another and very often these days in general, like the world is out of control. So the idea that something is this and that is all there is to it, is very reassuring even though it is not the case. After all, as you become more conscious of who you are and come into your natural personalities, the idea of anything being in a totally fixed framework is going to become increasingly repugnant to you. But right now, it is attractive.

It won't remain attractive for long. As a matter of fact, most of the young people who are under eight years old, and many who are teenagers as well, are repulsed by that whole idea that they are this and that's that, whatever "that" is. They also find totally repugnant the idea of being classified and dropped into a category. So please allow youngsters to be flexible.

How will they learn to react to astrology, then?

How do you mean?

Well, it seems to have rules and regulations, where things are this or things are that.

All signs are balanced. All signs are masculine and feminine. That's the reality. It is just that astrologers have things in a fixed position right now because that is attractive, and the astrology is based upon known quantities. You have to remember that in order to get astrology to be even remotely accepted by societies, astrologers have often had to put it into the context of contemporary ideology. What could be more contemporary than science?

Astrology Has Much to Do with Observation

No sign has talked very much about the ruler of the planet who is associated with it. Uranus is assigned to Aquarius—is that correctly identified?

Yes, they are correctly identified. But keep in mind that those planets are associated with the signs, yes, but what is not considered are the various versions of the planets. You have perhaps discussed in other books the various versions of Earth. There are various versions of the planets, and to a lesser degree than the physical version of the planets, those are also in cooperation with the effort here certain backups. By "backups," I do not mean redundant systems. There are certain other planetary systems that also support that particular harmonic—and I am referring to the harmonic here in the case of planets associated with your now astrological system as you understand it.

So all the planets are associated correctly, but it is hard to describe. I will simply say that the answer to your question is yes, but there is more, and about 22 percent at this time, though it is flexible, is associated with the *more*. Most of that is not associated with this focus of existence, but some of it is, for that matter, associated with entirely different galaxies. Some galaxies not even in this universe are involved, and they give support and energy in something that resembles a circuit so that the energy of Uranus in this situation is supported beyond that which is available in, let's say, this solar system.

When Earth is going through struggles—or, for that matter, when any planet in the solar system is going through struggles, such as the one who was struck by a comet some time ago—that has a profound impact, and all the other planets in the solar system must give aid, support and comfort. When that planet was struck by the comet some time ago, the Earth itself had to give a huge amount of aid and comfort, and was at that point no longer really able to support any surface life. All of the backup systems—again, I am not talking about redundant systems; I am talking about the circuit of energy that supports the planets in this solar system from beyond this solar system—were working overtime to support that which was unable to function to support Earth life. It is a very complex situation, but that is the simplest way I can put it.

So the planets have connections, sometimes in this universe and sometimes beyond.

Yes, that is a good way to put it.

And they draw on it as needed, like that?

Yes, that is a way you could look upon it. But it isn't that they draw on it so much. There is a need and it is promptly . . .

. . . fulfilled.

Yes, fulfilled, exactly.

So what, then, is the connection between the planet and the sign? Based on these energetic flows, is there some sort of connection between the sign and the planet energetically?

Everything is energy, so there is a connection between everything and everything else energetically.

All right. So what is the connection between the planet and the sign—not just yours, but of any planet with any sign?

It is a bit arbitrary, meaning that the planet is chosen to represent the qualities associated with the observable traits of any given sign, but the planet's motions may or may not always directly affect the persona as demonstrated through the human being, for example, of that sign. So it is somewhat arbitrary. Only if one can observe the actual motions or have them calculated for you by an astronomer, for example, then one might be able to say, "At such and such a time, these conditions are presenting themselves if you have this sign predominantly in your chart"—meaning you might encounter this, you might encounter that, based upon years and years and years and years of observation of people who are of these signs. So this makes astrology really—and this is the way I look at it—a social science, because it has just as much to do with observation as quantity of previously studied material.

Well, the reason I asked is, this book I am looking at says Uranus is the ruling planet of Aquarius now, but traditionally it used to be Saturn. So how can the ruling planets change?

It is either associated with the impact of the orbit . . . and, of course, you can't know the wobble too much, unfortunately. The wobble is a factor, but it really won't help to tell you that much, because you don't have that information, nor are you likely to have it any time soon.

The wobbling of the other planets, not the Earth?

Yes, and the wobbling of Earth. But if it is associated with the influences on the sign, then there is a direct connection. In some cases, it might be somewhat arbitrary, especially if the orbit of the planet is not entirely well-known, which one might find especially with the outer planets. We can't go on too much longer, as I think we are getting well past the helpful aspects. These are good questions—they just are tending to be too mathematical.

I see. All right. I hadn't seen them as mathematical.

I do not wish to sound critical. I recognize you were attempting to understand something and to clarify something. Unfortunately, almost all of what you were attempting to understand and clarify is already completely known and understood by astrologers.

Oh, I see. Well, actually, I was just wondering how much value could there be to the planet if they could arbitrarily change them. That was really why I was asking. You have so much more to say—do you want to speak more than once?

It is possible, but we will not know that until the next session. I will finish up here, but I won't rule out returning.

I don't feel like you are done yet. [Laughs.] There is so much more to say about the whole subject. Some of the things you've said have just not been known before, I am sure.

Aquarians: Be Aware of Your Impulses

In summation, those of you who have Aquarius as a major influence in your chart, be aware that you might at times have impulses to do things that would involve changing your physical placement, moving about, and perhaps even raising your hands over your head or doing something that might seem a bit strange. Try to incorporate some natural gesture in here, and then it won't be too surprising. I have observed at a distance through examining, not immediate moments, but examining some of these characteristics. I have known Aquarian gentlemen, for that matter, discover that they could doff their cap and thus move their arm up, you see, to put that energy into the space one might find. You might be able to discover other things that you can do, such as applause. You might applaud with your hands in front of you or you might applaud with your hands above you.

In short, I am not trying to tell you how to live. I am just saying that if you have Aquarian energy as a significant factor in your chart, you might find that you will have the urge to do this from time to time. If you can do so and not be embarrassed and not cause a problem for yourself, please do so, but don't take any unnecessary risks, all right? On that note of responsibility associated with Aquarius, I will say, enjoy your life!

Thank you very, very much.

Good night.

Good night.

子
The Child
Ambitious
11:00pm - 1:00am
December
1912
1924
1936
1948
1960
1972
1984
1996
2008
丑
Patient
1:00am - 3:00am
January
1913
1925
1937
1949
1961
1973
1985
1997
2009
寅
Aggressive
3:00am - 5:00am
February
1902
1914
1926
1938
1950
1962
1974
1986
1998
卯
Talented
5:00am - 7:00am
March
1903
1915
1927
1939
1951
1963
1975
1987
1999
辰
Passionate
7:00am - 9:00am
April
1904
1916
1928
1940
1952
1964
1976
1988
2000
巳
Wise
9:00am - 11:00am
May
1905
1917
1929
1941
1953
1965
1977
1989
2001
午
Popular
11:00am - 1:00pm
June
1906
1918
1930
1942
1954
1966
1978
1990
2002
未
Creative
1:00pm - 3:00pm
July
1907
1919
1931
1943
1955
1967
1979
1991
2003
申
Intelligent
3:00pm - 5:00pm
August
1908
1920
1932
1944
1956
1968
1980
1992
2004
酉
Pioneering
5:00pm - 7:00pm
September
1909
1921
1933
1945
1957
1969
1981
1993
2005
戌
Loyalty
7:00pm - 9:00pm
October
1910
1922
1934
1946
1958
1970
1982
1994
2006
亥
Noble
9:00pm - 11:00pm
November
1911
1923
1935
1947
1959
1971
1983
1995
2007

♌ Leo
July 23 – August 21

LEO

Initiates, Supports and Attunes with Humor and Wit

September 5, 2007

This is Leo!

Welcome!

Well, I am glad to see that you are with Leo's favorite symbol of sign.

[Laughs.] Yes, this is Tiger, the cat.

You know, I think he is quite well aware of the fact that it is a symbol only. However, you do understand—and I know astrologers do as well—that the symbol is really something that is attuned to life. This gives you an idea of why the stars have been chosen to represent the signs, for they can be patterned after these known and also the popular in lore of the time. In this case, Leo associated with cats does tend to have certain qualities associated with cat personality—meaning they're independent, go their own way, and are not easily influenced to do otherwise. Also, they have a tendency to teach, and when learning, they do so on their own without the assistance of humans [chuckles], though they may get assistance from their own kind. Now, astrologers know this, but I just thought I'd mention it, since you are with a cat at the moment.

Leos Can Initiate Personality Traits in Others

As other syntheses of signs have stated, I will also reiterate that the personality here reflected is a compendium of Leo qualities. Also, if you have Leo in your chart, even if it is not your Sun sign, especially if it is significant in your chart, these things stated in this book also affect you. I know astrologers know this, but I am saying this for those of you who are interested in astrology but are not yet experts. So now, here is something lesser known about Leo. Leo has the capacity to originate qualities of personality in all human beings all the time, even if those qualities of personality were not something you were born to.

This is part of the reason Leo has sometimes shown, often in cheerful ways, an authoritarian demeanor. This is not so much because Leo always knows what to do in every situation, but rather those with prominent Leo in their charts express that broadcast quality of initiation in the only way they know how. When Leos are expressing that authoritarian aspect of their personality, regardless of whether they have the knowledge or wisdom or not, they are almost always broadcasting that quality of initiation of personality trait that is available for all beings on the Earth (meaning human beings) and usually will initiate something or support something that is there but not expressed yet, that can be valuable to individuals and, hence, groups of individuals.

Now, I am ruling out situations in which Leo people would have genuine knowledge and wisdom, and are teaching or lecturing or instructing, for that will not come with that Leo passion. But when the passion is present—and you will know that, if you are with such a person, because that person will be speaking and demonstrating his or her feelings at the same time—you can be sure that, if you personally are there and you have a personality quality not yet expressed or that you were not born with that would be helpful for you and ultimately for others, that you will be exposed to that capacity for that quality to emerge as something you know about within three days.

For example, you may, when you are with people other than that Leo, have a problem or something you cannot solve. Perhaps it's not just, say, a mathematical problem or a business problem or a child-rearing problem, but it has to do with a quality, a talent or an ability you do not have, nor have you ever expressed. But suddenly after exposure to such a person's broadcast qualities, you find that that problem becomes easier to resolve and you discover something within yourself you did not know was there. This explanation will also help astrologers to understand that sometimes the more overt or even extreme aspects of a sign's expression of itself may simply be that person's adaptation—a personality adaptation, as it were—to something that is going on within the physical body that he or she was born to and meant to do.

This Broadcast Energy Can Be Overwhelming

It is not unusual that people with prominent Leo might suddenly get authoritarian or strong in their expression of self because of that energy being present. Interestingly enough, this is not always taking place when the Leo person has something that he or she personally believes in. It might take place in moments—and all you Leos know this—when there is something being discussed or something present for which you feel an urgent need to express but which at the same time you feel really rather frightened that you know nothing about. Something reasonable comes out, but it comes out with a burst of energy that almost overwhelms you and sometimes is felt as overwhelming to others.

Consider a transmitting power for an electronic device—a radio station, let's call it. If a radio station is broadcasting strongly, those in the immediate area will pick up the signal well, but those many miles away may not be able to pick it up so well. The same is true in this kind of a broadcast from Leo people. Those in the immediate area may not even be the intended people to receive the energy, though they do, and those at a distance, you see, may be those who are intended. That is why, Leo people (speaking to you now), you will sometimes have these outbursts—really bordering on passionate outbursts, as it were—about something you don't really know about and may not have the slightest care about, because of that broadcast energy. Now, if you know that, it will not upset you. It will not make you nervous, and you will not feel like you have to hide. That is another quality, where you sometimes feel you have to hide because you are feeling somewhat embarrassed.

If you know you are going to broadcast that energy or if you are conscious of that quality within yourself, you don't necessarily have to say anything. You might find yourself in a position, you see, where you do not have to say a word or it's not possible to say anything, but you can allow that passion and feeling to come through you. If you feel you are about to burst and you have to do something physical, then this is what to do: Just take a deep breath—not for the purpose of releasing stress, as in the stress-relaxation technique, but just one that's comfortable—and start blowing out very gently, in a way not to be seen.

When you take that deep breath, you are going to take it in—literally, of course—where your solar plexus is and where your lungs are, but that is the area where you feel the most motivation, the most urgency to speak. You will blow out from that area. If you can turn around and blow in this or that direction, up or down, fine, but blow in the area that you can blow in. Don't blow that breath toward any one person, because you may not realize who that energy is meant for. But just, if you can, blow it in some direction where there is no one you can see and trust that it will get to where it needs to go.

I mention this now at the top of our talk, so to speak, because I want astrologers to understand that the sign that is sometimes considered humorous is really entrusted with this vital and valuable quality, and sometimes—and astrologers know this—it is overwhelming for Leo. That is why their personalities adapt as they have. If you know that this is going on for Leos—and examine it through the charts that you keep—then you can let them know and pass it on to them. I hope it works well for you, astrologers.

I just realized why Leos probably make good actors. With that ability to broadcast energy, they can really communicate their feelings for the part they are playing.

Yes, if they have a part that's associated with that. But if they have a part that is smaller, or a retiring part—meaning that the role is not expressive and passionate—then it's that much more difficult for a Leo. However, if a Leo can do it with the unspoken—perhaps not even showing characteristics physically, but if the director accepts the showing of it—you can perhaps exhibit tremendous pathos, for example, without really demonstrating any quality of upstaging of the other performers. Just feel the part, and it will be broadcast. It might also help you to get a role in a casting call.

Don't Focus on Negative Traits

We've been getting positive traits, but are there negative traits that aren't known also?

I don't think the book is going to feature that, because the purpose of your publishing company, especially in the past ten to twelve years, is, "What can you do about it?" You see, astrology has been somewhat burdened with the requirement of saying what could happen, what is the negative trait and so on, and as a result has found itself in the same position—though in a different field of social awareness, as economists find themselves in, for example, or sometimes social historians—of talking about repeated qualities that people would not want to hear about.

I feel it is more important now for astrologers to speak about that which can benefit the person and, of course, be balanced with it. But it is vitally important to not present so-called negative qualities as something that is like fate—meaning, say, "This is something you are going to do." You must stop in astrology predicting things like that, because people are even more suggestible today than they have ever been due to the increase in receptivity. That increase (as has been stated in this series of books over time) has everything to do with the reawakening into your natural native personalities and the receptive energy you must have and welcome in order to become your whole, complete selves again. Therefore, given that overall condition, if astrologers are telling people in an authoritarian voice, "You have these negative qualities and in your life you will express them"—I know you very rarely do that, but sometimes there is that edge in your voices—then it makes it more likely that they will do it.

It is completely different, of course, if a person has expressed those qualities before or is even expressing those qualities at the time you are seeing him or her. But it is always good to say to them (if you don't mind my suggesting your bedside manner), "You have done this in the past." This doesn't mean that they are not doing it in the present, but it is not your job to counsel them, if they are not asking for it, nor is it your job to support familial arguments. I realize astrologers often get caught up in that.

So this is simply something you can say, that, "This is something you may have experienced," or "This is something that is a hazard for you." That is perfectly all right. But as one who knows about authoritarian speaking, let me simply say that it has its time and place but not necessarily is it something that is best for astrologers. Astrologers now must take the high ground and support others proceeding on their path as well.

As we become more benevolent, we will display less of those what were thought to be negative traits, right?

Yes, but I don't think you can count on that in lieu of doing the work that it takes on a daily basis to process your own personal dramas. In other words, don't wait for that to happen. Strive for it, and put it into your daily life as a goal. Also recognize that life may require you at times to be this, that or the other. Nevertheless, if it is your goal, you will work on yourself to achieve it rather than simply wait for it to happen in some unspecified time, maybe not even in your lifetime.

There Are Latent Traits that Will Be Revealed

What is the energy of Leo? What is the engine for the energy?

Ah, yes. Just a moment. I don't think it has a name in your star charts, but it's at a great distance from your galaxy. It is a sun. I don't know how to describe it; it doesn't have a name.

Are these suns or galaxies? They seem to be all different things. Are they volunteers? How do they fit into the scheme of things?

[Laughs.] They always fit into it based upon what needs to be done on Earth as expressed through the human being. That's it in a nutshell, since we are using colloquialisms, okay? If it doesn't fit into what the human being needs to do on Earth, it is simply not involved. However, as time goes on and more of your natural, native personality becomes present and you begin acting more the way you do when you are on other planets in more benevolent, benign circumstances, then more and more will come to participate and other qualities of all the signs will begin to be displayed.

Picture it this way, if you are an artist, that you can see very strongly. We will say Leo, all right? There on a page is printed in bold "Leo," but then off to the side there are other latent qualities of Leo that might be letters, but they are simply outlines of letters. Then there is also Leo that has dotted outlines, which have to do with qualities as yet unexpressed because of the circumstances, energy and position of your planet, solar system and galaxy—which has everything to do with the reemergence of your natural, native personalities in toto.

So if I asked all of these signs in four or five years, you could come up with more traits that were not just lost and unknown but, as you say, latent and just beginning to be revealed?

Let's put that another way. The traits that were revealed were traits associated with the signs but simply not known because of what I just said.

Oh, because we weren't using them yet.

That's right. You weren't using them, and your natural, native personalities were not completely present yet, but those traits are present. It is not something [chuckles] where the trait is simply unavailable and so on in some far-off place. No! That's a real trait associated with the sign. That's why the sign-synthesis personality will generally say something lesser known about the sign in words like that—"lesser known" meaning not known because of circumstances.

But that's fascinating. I thought it was information that had been lost in the past, but it wasn't lost, it just wasn't showing up yet in humans.

It may have been both. Maybe in the past there were also times when the planet was more benevolent, benign, and those on the planet, even of the Explorer Race in the early days, were also that way, and you were more connected to your natural, native personalities. But as time went on, different things happened. For it can be both, you see.

I see, yes.

Leos: Study the Cat

The cat is sleeping on my book—just a minute. [Laughs.]

He's infusing it with that good and catly energy. The book will be better for it! You know that it is important (as an aside here) to leave in these little personal references about the cat sleeping on the book. You must leave things like that in. People love that kind of thing.

Oh, all right.

Always leave things like that in, because the book then becomes grounded in humanity rather than the voice of authority speaking from the sky. Believe me—I know about that.

How do you know about that?

Leo! [Laughs.]

[Laughs.] Okay. This particular book says that Leo traditionally finds marriage to be difficult, so what would you advise? Is there anything new to be said about making it easier?

I think that's well and totally established by astrologers. Generally speaking, though, my advice to Leos about moments of passion where there is no means to express, as I gave the example about breathing, try to do that. Very often, the reason there is difficulty in marriage has to do with that aspect of Leo expressing in some way where you sometimes as a result will get in trouble. But if you can express with breath, you will find that this would defuse the situation almost always, and you won't trip over your own feet because your feet go into a place.

You might tread, you see, where you do not have knowledge or wisdom because you are passionately attempting to express that energy and using your own personality traits that you have had to develop out of necessity to simply be Leo—or to express the Leo in your chart at that time. Then you might, how can we say, boldly go where you are not intended to go. You'd have to live with the consequences, but if you can do this thing with the breath, it will defuse a lot of things—such as being opinionated, for instance, in a marriage situation. It also will help you to learn how to be receptive and to know when it is safe to be receptive. One of the big challenges for Leo, as astrologers know, is to know when it is safe to be receptive.

So study the cat—really! Leo is one of the few signs associated with a representative in the animal world who really can learn from that animal. Study the cat. How is the cat receptive? How does the cat express it? And, most importantly, how does it know when it is safe to be receptive? So if you don't have a cat, if you don't live with a cat, make friends with one or ask one to make friends with you, or visit somebody who has a cat who is willing to be friendly with you, and just notice. I won't say more about it. Cats have qualities—great instinct, great spirit–and it is also possible to learn how to be more connected to a cat's personality. I know you many of you are attracted to dogs, but believe me, it is good to study and learn from cats.

Your Body Is Your Greatest Teacher

Would you say, then, that on other planets there is not a need for or an opportunity for great passionate expression? So would a soul come here to have the opportunity to express something maybe it can't someplace else or to begin to feel that energy that maybe it hasn't felt before?

One of the things that startles souls the most when they come to the Earth that you know is the outbursts of expressiveness. On the one hand, as you say, some souls might find this attractive, for there may be outbursts like that on other planets presented in a theatrical fashion, though if you were able to sit in, in an insulated manner, you would not find them to be true outbursts. The audience would react with shock for a moment, and you would say, "What happened?" [Chuckles.] It wouldn't seem like an outburst. So it is possible that a soul who may be attracted to theater—the drama and so on—might wish to come to Earth to experience that, learn more about it, be it if they wished. So it's possible, but then souls come to Earth for many reasons, don't they? That is one possible one.

This probably doesn't relate to the astrology book, but as we become more benign and benevolent, everything will become a little more . . . what? Muted, tame, less expansive in expression?

Yes, but not because someone waved a magic wand. It will become that way because you will begin to listen to your bodies and know what your bodies are expressing. You won't just say, "Oh, I don't feel good." You will be communicating with your body. If you don't know how to do it, someone will help you. In short, what happens is an increase in awareness based on physical perception. You've come to this planet because it is all about physicality in such a way that you cannot ignore physicality. You cannot simply say, "Oh, that is too physical for me." You have to live it; you have to be it. Since that's why you are here, what happens when your natural, native personality comes in more for you is that you tend to be more open to embracing the purpose for you being here. You don't leave, but you start to get the message.

So much of life is so difficult and challenging, isn't it? Plus, you are surrounded with way too much. Your lives are way too complicated, so there is a tendency to not get the message, to not pause and understand the message. But if you are motivated to understand what your physical body is trying to tell you in every moment, you will understand that the organism that you do not always allow to be itself is your greatest teacher. Your physical body can help you to take steps in the right direction for you *in all cases*. It can also help you to understand the nature of your own personality and where it is best for you to be, who with and when. It will not, however, *ever* justify it with why. It is a vehicle meant to give you instantaneous answers, but it will not justify those answers.

That is why you are born as a child, so that you are able to love your body and enjoy the magical things it can do, and it is fun. So you start out loving your body. Your parents know that. Parents can support and nurture that communication and love that a child might have for his or her body, and thus, in time, it might be possible for adults to be able to love their own bodies as well and not reject them as something they have to cart around to accomplish their goals and purposes.

As a result, one can take steps down pathways that were meant for you. Those steps are easy, comfortable, with plenty of support. But if you are on a pathway that is not meant for you, simply because you found it attractive or life seemed to be pushing you on that pathway, you might find it very difficult with no support at all and feeling blocked in every moment. Therefore, it might be necessary to back up or look and see if there is another path beckoning nearby that feels good, for which you are supported to be on. Maybe that's your pathway, but you will know also on the basis of how you feel about it. In this way, you discover what's right for you and what's right for others. But many others have discussed this; we don't need to go into that too much here.

Astrology can help you find your own pathway, though, because a good astrologer, an expert—even a young person studying it who is working with an expert—can help you to find pathways that might feel better to you and can help you to know pathways that are meant for others. The whole purpose of astrology, after all, is service—service to humanity to provide the best quality of life possible. It does not exist for any other reason. If you know that about astrology, you will not simply slough it off when it is not always 100 percent correct. What other form of knowledge, wisdom and predictability based upon that knowledge and wisdom is 100 percent correct?

Don't force astrology to be an oracle that you do not force others to be. Astrology is always and only meant to serve your needs. It may not always be perfect, but you can be sure that astrologers have gone into that profession, not only because they are interested and fascinated in the topics for themselves, but because they want to help others. If you know that, then most of the time your experiences with astrologers will result in something worthwhile.

The Signs All Offer You Different Possibilities

One of the signs mentioned that in a few years the signs will start merging and souls will then have fewer choices to make as to what they choose to express or to learn. What is your feeling about that?

Or you could say it another way, that souls would have the opportunity to experience more in a given life because the commands or demands of that sign, which help you to express what your soul came to express, will no longer be as urgent and you are therefore able to be a Leo and a Libra at once. That's another way to put it, you see. It's an opportunity.

So you feel that the signs you choose do not really force you but influence you along certain lines so you can grow?

Yes, because it's influence you have requested. You, as a soul, have come to the planet to be born, to live, so that you can achieve something that you are seeking to achieve. You want a means to support you on that, especially when your guides and teachers tell you that you are not going to be able to remember your personal motivation because you are not going to remember most of your knowledge and wisdom that you have accumulated throughout all your incarnations. So then you say, "How will I know that I am on the right path?" and they will say, "Ah, there is a perfect thing in place. You will love it. You will be born into a physical body at the moment of your emergence from the birth canal of mother into the world. You will be born into a physical present moment associated with the positions of planets who will support you, and there will be people in your lifetime who can guide you with their accumulation of knowledge and wisdom that will help you and support you to know who you are, why you are here, where you are going, if you wish, and where you don't need to go." When you are told that as a soul, you say, "Wow! All right, then!"

All right, that's great! You are so expressive!

Leo! That is our nature!

You know so much. Can you just say it without waiting for me to ask questions?

No, you have to ask.

Okay. So really, then, there is no one sign that's better or worse. They are all just different possibilities, different designs for dramas.

Yes, and it is very important to understand that, because certain signs might get a reputation in the minds of others as being more challenging. That is why it is so important for astrologers to take the high ground and say, "You are this or you are that in this portion of your chart, and that gives you a tremendous opportunity to do this and this and this," rather than saying, "Oh, that makes your life a little bit more challenging because you will have to do this and this and this." See, we need to move astrology to the high ground for that very purpose, because all the signs offer tremendous potential and possibility. When you have people where all the signs are present—say, in a group, maybe trying to accomplish something—the group will be able to be much more flexible and wide-ranging in its capacity to take on a challenge or a problem. So, for instance, a government committee or even an executive branch of a government would be much better off if there was one person or more representing different aspects of each sign.

I have observed in the past on this planet—looking back to the past for a moment—such governments having been formed on the basis of known astrological wisdom. What happens is that your ability to respond is greatly magnified. It's not so much that you would necessarily find that system to work well in the day-to-day running of the government—you have that organized in a different way—but when you have an ability to respond based upon personality qualities that are as complete as possible on Earth, such as the whole wheel of astrology, you then never find yourself in a position where you don't know what to do and you are at a loss.

I am not necessarily saying [chuckles] that you should replace your governments with this kind of system. I am saying that it would be very good to have a round table of consultants, including every sign represented at least once. I would recommend every sign represented on the Sun-sign level at least three times. This way you are likely to get a wider variety of representation. A good astrologer could probably make the choices—not only of expressed personality traits for such a round-table group, but also of latent traits that are present and may be very helpful for such a consulting committee.

That's brilliant—boards of directors, yes, and like you say, executive branches. We are just not aware and we're not utilizing that at all.

Astrology Is Becoming More of a Potential

Astrologers have known for many years that it is an underused social analysis tool, but as time goes on, I feel that the time for astrology is becoming more of a potential. How can we say it? The Sun is rising on astrology. This is going to be a means to help that will become increasingly popular.

I'm just try to get past the fact, reader, that astrology is for entertainment. These are statements that have been necessary to put in the books on this or that subject, or people having to state that in this and that way for legal reasons, but they don't necessarily believe it. Astrologers don't go into astrology because they want to be entertained; they go into astrology because they want to know and because they want to help. Entertainment is wonderful, but there is more to life, yes? You want to know; you want to help. Well, why not astrology? Why there is no PhD program in astrology in your colleges is beyond me.

How would you set it up?

It's very simple. There are astrological boards and so on, groups, and you would recruit people who could teach the fundamentals and then the more advanced qualities. You'd set it up like anything; it can be done. Of course, there are astrology schools now, but I am talking about universities. Why isn't there a PhD program? I am asking the question, not because I expect you to answer or because I am going to provide an answer. I am asking the question because I feel it is a good question to ask, and I will allow those who are interested in astrology to pursue it at the university level. There will be resistance, but it will wear down in time, especially when it becomes so popular that universities respond, as they often do when a subject gets popular. Once upon a time, universities didn't have the time, the inclination or the desire to teach anything about computers. My, how times have changed! What is a computer, after all? It is a means of information. Well, that's all I will say.

Basically astrology is concerned with human personality types, so it could be tied into psychology and a deeper understanding of the potential of humanity.

Recognize that Your Broadcast Energy Is a Gift You Have to Offer

What other thoughts have you got floating around there that would be inspiring?

Well [chuckles], that is your job. Nice try. You wanted to repeat your request from before, but it didn't get past me. Nice try, though.

So you know what you are really expressing that I hadn't considered before is a tremendous sense of humor. So Leos seem to have a great sense of humor!

Yes, it's a quality that Leos often use to make a point. Sometimes people don't understand that—that Leos are always attempting to teach, even if they don't exactly know what they are talking about. Perhaps I already covered that with the exercise, but because of this, Leo might sometimes use humor, but it is also in Leo's nature. Again, consider the cat. Do they not do things sometimes that are just marvelously funny? There are pictures abounding as well as stories about amazing, wonderful and humorous things the cat does. So as I said before, study the cat and you will know thyself, Leo.

Now, I read that cats and dogs have vibrations that, while not antagonistic, can make them uncomfortable with each other. Do Leos develop a vibration that is not comfortable with any other sign?

No, no, not at all! As a matter of fact, Leos are often known to be best friends. They are funny, they are witty, and they are interesting—if I do say so myself.

I would like to say this to Leos: You have been entrusted with the energy of Leo because your souls have proved—on other planets, in other situations—that you are prepared to be devoted to a cause that uplifts all beings. This does not make you any better than any other sign on Earth, but it does present you with an opportunity to broadcast an energy that supports and attunes. If you know that and can do the breathing work I mentioned, it will take great pressure off you in terms of expressing when you are not comfortable with words to say, and it will give you a great gift in that you will not have to retire to quiet and self-criticism because of having expressed verbally.

You don't have to do that, but you can recognize that this broadcast energy that comes through you—that you feel so strongly and with such passion—is the gift you have to offer. It is a gift that you can experience, that you give. Know that it is in your nature to do that, even if you do not have conscious awareness of being in service. If you know this about yourself, you will be much more comfortable with the volubility that you are sometimes known for. Leo has a great gift to offer simply by being. Incorporate the breath technique I have suggested, and you will find that you will be more relaxed, more comfortable in your lives, and have the knowledge—expressed or not—that you are in service for a cause you believed in so much that you came from a great distance to serve. Good night.

That is just beautiful. Thank you.

IMAGINES CONSTELLATIONVM
BOREALIVM

♐ Sagittarius
November 23 – December 22

SAGITTARIUS
Amplifies Good Feelings in Groups of People and Planets

September 6, 2007

This is Sagittarius.

Welcome!

Thank you. I mean to speak briefly about certain qualities. I am not known for this so much, but I am able to function as an amplifier for signs on the opposite side of the wheel of astrologic signs as they are drawn in the chart—never to either side, always and only to the opposite side, which would encompass several different signs. It would be like this, that for those always and only two, regardless of their incompatibilities or even their support systems for each other (referring to the signs as someone here), it would draw them closer together by creating a community center, so to speak—a center position so that they could bridge all their gaps.

This is something that I am not known for, but it is important to mention, because those signs on the opposite side would not always be in compatibility. Therefore, a practical application of this might be if you are arranging a conference or a meeting where you know the people's predominant astrological influences. What would be useful—if you needed to create better conversation and negotiation or perhaps some form of communication bordering on communion—is to have a Sagittarian there but to not give them too much to do. They could be appearing to do something, but not having to pay much attention to that, and their only real reason to be there would be to allow and embrace and amplify the good feeling between the parties represented by the signs I mentioned before.

Granted, this would not work in all cases, but it might work in some cases. It might be particularly helpful if you have individuals representing this or that group, or simply representing themselves who are intransigent with each other. That would be a practical application. Also, there are some astrologers who will, if the awareness of something other than an individual human being is able to be charted—such as animals or even something more abstract such as countries, tribes—if they can be charted, the same condition would apply, where a conversation, even around a campfire to create liaisons (even temporary ones), could be accentuated using this same process.

Sagittarius Also Helps Improve Connections between Planets

Let me see if there is some other factor of Sagittarius that is not particularly known. There are planets—not in this solar system, but in a solar system in this galaxy—who are what I would call replacements. This solar system has lost a planet or two in the distant past, simply based upon factors not originally associated with the creation of the solar system, and this has created some difficulties. There are two planets in a nearby solar system ("nearby," relatively speaking) in your galaxy who are prepared to replace planets who may be injured.

Not long ago, one of your planets was injured when struck by a comet, and it might be necessary to replace this planet. If it is done, it will be done in a way that is not particularly noticeable by science, but it will be observable in the mathematical calculations—meaning the general projection of what the planet weighs and so on. Those kinds of figures will suddenly be altered, with the replacement planet being different in mass and makeup. If such anomalies are noted suddenly and unexpectedly—or even have been noted—then you can be reasonably certain that the replacement has taken place.

Sagittarius energy is something that can help planets either be conditioned anew—so that they can function better—or it can help to smooth the replacements. In this sense, one can see a correlation to the previously mentioned phenomenon, in that Sagittarius energy has the capacity to improve the motions—both forward and backward, yes, but also to improve the connections laterally—between beings of common ground, whether they know they have the common ground or not.

Well, this would be very important for you, because Jupiter is the planet that's connected with you.

Who are you referring to?

You said the planet who recently got hit by a comet might be exchanged for another planet. How will that affect the sign of Sagittarius, then, if a different personality is there?

As I said, the planets are already there, and ever since Jupiter was struck by the comet, the other planet—even though it did not immediately replace Jupiter as you know it—immediately took over about 75 percent of what Jupiter was doing in the solar system. There is another planet yet that is available as a replacement, but understand that this planet does not have a particular bias toward replacing one planet or the other, just as the planet who is helping Jupiter did not have a bias either—because there was always the chance that the comet would miss Jupiter or would fragment completely before it hit Jupiter. It did fragment a bit, I believe, before it hit Jupiter, but unfortunately, Jupiter suffered a serious injury.

I didn't realize it was that bad. Well, you said we would notice an anomaly. Is the new planet denser?

The new planet is a little denser, has a stronger geomagnetic field, and might be more likely to be able to deflect such . . .

Such similar comets in the future?

Yes. It wouldn't be able to deflect any greater than the previous planet in the case of a meteorite or even an asteroid, but in the case of a comet, which is less dense and more susceptible to deflection in its orbit, it ought to be more capable in that capacity.

So is the replacement planet actually there now, or just helping from a distance?

I will allow science to answer that. I will leave that up to science, because I think it will give those who are in observation of such facts something to examine and enjoy the search. I don't want to ruin the surprise.

Okay. So the other planet could replace the asteroid belt, say more about that.

I don't think I mentioned anything about an asteroid belt. The other planet who is available would be available for replacement of any planet who may need assistance in your solar system. That is all. There are no plans, and the asteroid belt did not come up. You will understand why you asked that question when you listen back to the tape.

Well, I heard two planets, and in my mind, it was Jupiter and the asteroid belt. Is there any reason to replace the asteroid belt with a planet?

No.

Astrologically, the new planet has or can take on the same personality as what we call Jupiter, then? The expansiveness, the joy, all those things?

Yes, but—and this is a good question—it also has other qualities. One of the other qualities that it has is an innate sense of curiosity, almost to the point of nosiness. In the sense of nosiness, that would mean a little more of a desire. Previously, Jupiter wanted to know, had curiosity, but now that has stepped up a notch or two, so to speak, in that the need to know will be presented with two parallels. One, there will be much greater patience in knowing. Two, the opposite parallel will be a much greater need to know. So either of these parallels can be quantified in the chart by the astrologer as long as the astrologer is aware of the person's Moon. The Moon will tell you, astrologer, whether that person has one or the other (so a note to the professionals there).

I talked to Jupiter. Was that before or after the change?

That's just asking me whether it's happened or not! Do you think I will fall for that?

No, I just wondered if I should go back and talk to Jupiter again before the book was over.

That may not be the case . . . or it may.

You Experience All the Signs During Your Life

There is a curious picture here. I know you don't want to talk about what is known, but the picture in the book I am looking at is symbolized by a centaur, which is a horse with a human torso and head.

You understand what that means, eh? That means that Sagittarians are known for identifying with the animal world, and they are also known for being in alignment with that. But they are also known for having some difficulty in identifying with the human world.

That's interesting!

Yes, but one also finds that in some other signs that are called dual signs, some of which are more well known and understood—and this is all understood by astrologers, even amateur astrologers—in the sense of as Pisces or, more specifically, Gemini, where one is conscious of being, having capacities beyond a singular focus . . . I would like Gemini and other signs like that to think of themselves that way. If you are informed that this is a predominant influence in your chart—or any type of thing like Sagittarian or Pisces and so on—just assume that you have capacities beyond what is obvious, including what is known.

Therefore, when you either notice with happiness or perhaps trip over a personality characteristic that you didn't realize you had, you will know that you may be able to develop it in some positive way for yourself and perhaps others. Generally speaking, that rule applies to all the signs, because all of the signs traverse from their sign at the time of their birth around the wheel (as I prefer to call it) through the signs. You experience, then, all of the signs to one degree or another as you progress through your year. So anything associated with any one sign is something that you will all have a chance to experience at one point or another. This is very important to remember in astrology and is not always considered seriously, except by the professional astrologer who has considered these things seriously over time.

I like that, because I used to think that you could go around all the signs through reincarnation, but now they are telling us that we don't reincarnate here anymore. So considering that, we can enjoy those energies or expand ourselves during the year?

I would like to make a comment on reincarnation, if you don't mind. It's true that you do not reincarnate here on this planet anymore. You incarnate elsewhere, of course, but you do not come here anymore. So when you are done with your life here, you don't, but you will have the opportunity sometime. Many of you have noticed this with pets and occasionally with people—that you will notice certain traits in another that you identify with somebody previous who has passed on. You might say, "Oh, that is that person reincarnated," but what it really is, is that the traits you had previously seen in someone or even a beloved pet will be more accessible to you, if you see yourself as the receiver.

Consider this to be a circuit for a moment, speaking electrically. There is the positive pole, there is the other pole, and you have the one who observes the traits and the one who demonstrates the traits. With the incarnation where you see those traits again, it is not because those beings are reincarnating; it is because you are acutely aware of those traits and can notice them in other beings. It is as if you have been sensitized to those traits. But even if you identify it as being the same being, you will very quickly notice, as others who live with animals have noticed in the recent past, that this is indeed a different being but that there is an echo of the previous being present.

I mention this, as it is particularly important for those who look for a human being who is a reincarnation of someone else. That is no longer possible on Earth, simply because there are so many souls that wish to come here during the time of Earth's transition that the line is long, so to speak, and there are so many other choices. So those who move on, do, in fact, move on.

Can you say how long ago that changed? In the past, there was reincarnation here, correct?

Yes, I believe in the past it was possible, but in those past times there were a much fewer number in population and, also, many of those past times with the planet were relatively benevolent. Therefore, it was equalized with most of the other planets who are available elsewhere. So the idea of going to another planet was pleasing in that it was just variety, and occasionally, people would choose to reincarnate on Earth. Generally speaking, I know some of you out there believe you have had many Earth lives, but in my perception, that is not the case. It is rare to find a person—a soul, if you would—who has had more than two Earth lives. There are a few who have had three.

So if you feel a sense of personal identification with having had more lives, I will give you the reason why right now. Remember, I said that you travel around the wheel as you progress through your year. You might be remembering a life associated with another sign that you progressed through during the time of your physical lifetime, where you felt a sense of familiarity. (It is very complicated, but I must speak in general terms.) This is how one person can remember having the life of a previous person, and more than one person can remember that. This is often noted with people of some fame, but occasionally, it is recalled with people who do not have much fame.

It is happening because of your progression through the signs in your years as they come and go. Regardless of what sign you are, sometimes you will be in progress on a yearly basis through a sign (or you would call it, through a time) that you find really wonderful. A sense of well-being even occurs, because that sign and that time are so much in alignment with all the factors of your astrological identity. Thus, when you are recalling past lives, you will use that ideal compatibility, those moments of moving through that sign (try to picture this visually). In those ideal moments, you will relate back from that position to lives that have occurred or been born to that energy. Thus, at different times of the year you might remember this life or that life as a past life and come to the conclusion that you have had many past lives on Earth. But this is not the case.

Someone else also told me—I think Isis—that particles have memories and sometimes we are influenced by the memories of the particles that are making up our physical bodies at that moment.

Yes, that is very clear, and it is not so much that you are making it up. It's real. It's just that it cannot be proven as one might be able to prove a physical fact. But if it can be felt in that moment, it is true. Your times, being associated more with the mental pursuit, have for many of you confused the true nature of physicality. You are on Earth in a physical body—that's the pure and simple truth. This tells you immediately—and it is your absolute foundation on all four corners, if we get to use a square building—that you as a soul personality are here to experience your truth in that life (whatever it may be) physically. Feelings are the communicative language of the physical self, and all else will be built upon that. It is important to keep such things in mind, because the mental body is always pursuing innuendo and detail but often forgets that all of that is built upon a very specific foundation.

You are all born here on Earth in a physical body. Your personality comes here to be in this physical body. All is built from there. You have a physical self, and its primary language is feelings. So even though the mental body might become engaged in the pursuit of facts—and even details or innuendos of details—the mental body sometimes becomes lost because it is pursuing in all directions various shadings of facts and forgets that the primary reason you came here was to express your truth through the engagement and total experience of the physical body and its primary language. If you forget that—which the mental body has a tendency to do, since you are in a time now of experiencing mentality, and mentality has been praised for its values—then sometimes you are looking in the wrong places for the right facts.

That is why feelings are not always able to be expressed in words, and yet some of the most profound truths that you will ever become aware of at any given moment in your physical life will have entirely to do with feelings—physical feelings. Any attempt to speak words associated with them will be a pale echo of any communication representing the feeling (pardon my mixed metaphor).

Sagittarian Influence Can Make it Difficult to Connect with Human Things

I remember when Zoosh started talking about feelings in the middle nineties and it was like a foreign language. It was like, what are you talking about?

It is so challenging in the mental world to speak of feelings, because you are attempting to describe red, blue, yellow or green to someone who cannot see colors. It is essentially useless and really ought not to be tried, because some languages are not intended to interpret to others. They are intended to be used. You can describe until you are almost out of breath to others how to ride a bicycle, but once they learn how to ride the bicycle, they have that capability.

So the way to find out about feelings is to use them, practice them, and employ them. Of course, you do this unconsciously all the time, but when you are doing them unconsciously, you don't coordinate them with events and circumstances. When you practice them, you do identify that if this happens, you feel that and so on. It can be useful so that you do not get confused and seek in the trunk of lost ideas for something that is physical.

You speak very elegantly. I am looking at the qualities ascribed to Sagittarius, and they mostly seem very positive. If one comes here to learn a lesson, it seems there are more positive qualities than negative to Sagittarius. Is that true?

Well, I feel that all the signs are like that. I feel that the signs generally have positive qualities. Some signs associated with the natural world may have certain tools available to them, and perhaps Sagittarians' connection with the animal world, as it's depicted in the drawing you spoke of, is really another way of saying that Sagittarius has a tendency to feel its connectedness to the world beyond humanity.

On the other side of that though, of course, strong Sagittarian influence in your chart might make it more difficult for you at times to connect with the ways and means of being human. You will know that if you—as a Sagittarian person, so to speak, with Sagittarius as a major influence in your chart—are having great difficulty understanding something or some group of things that human beings are doing where all your friends take it for granted and find it amusing, perhaps humorously so . . . that you don't understand it or you struggle to understand it. That is not unusual for a Sagittarian influence in your chart.

Equally, when moving around the wheel of your progression for your year, when you find yourself in that time of Sagittarius, it may give you those opportunities, those insights in terms of your capabilities more—just as any time you move through any of the signs, you will have the capabilities or abilities to do this or that more likely, more easily. Equally though, if there are challenges associated with any sign, you might have those pitfalls. That is really how astrologers will compute—not only using their accomplished references and researches from the past, but also using those tools to simply say what you *might* experience in the coming year, meaning potentials.

You know, I have always looked for positive traits that people don't know about, but I have never asked any of the signs if there are any less-than-positive traits that people don't know about a sign.

If you don't mind, let's keep the book focused on the positive. Your societies in general right now are overwhelmingly fearful of that which is less than positive, and while I don't mind speaking of these matters—and I don't think the other signs do either, the synthesis of the signs—I feel that your society could benefit more from the benevolent aspects that are largely, but not exclusively, undiscovered. When blame and blaming go away more, then it might be possible to explore those other aspects.

Do you see that coming?

Yes, of course! As you become more of yourselves, become more aware of your total personalities and total being, your natural personality traits that you have when you are not at this school of Earth will come forward and the whole idea of blaming will simply fall away. I might add that there are some cultures on the planet now that are less involved in blaming and might tend to see any event occurring generally under the heading of fate—although they wouldn't use that term, because the whole idea of fate, of course, is the idea of "fatalistic," and one likes to improve on such possibilities, yes?

Absolutely! This is a planet of free choice.

That is the plan. It is not always the case, especially when Mother Earth hiccups, so to speak, or she has something to do. Then you are reminded that you are a resident but not the owner.

Your Earth Life Has to Be via the Focus of One of the Twelve Families

I know that Mother Earth interacts with other planets, but does she interact with the idea of the sign itself or with the constellations within the sign?

Mother Earth does not interact with the signs. She will interact with the planets.

That are in the constellations that are in the sign?

Well, she will interact with planets, period—all planets. So, no, it is not like that. It's complex again, and it is really profoundly visual, so I will struggle with the words and do my best. Mother Earth is associated with all planets everywhere, being a planet. You on Earth have only certain families of people—souls, if you would—that are allowed to come here. Those families are not associated with blood but are associated with pursuits, interests—so that your interests, as you've developed them over time in incarnations or existences elsewhere, might drop you from who you were into one of these families. It may not be permanent, but for a time you occupy that family based upon your knowledge, wisdom and interests. When your family happens to be associated with the coordinating elements of a group of planets representing those qualities that are within the line of sight (at least up to a point) of this planet, then those qualities temporarily—or more permanently, depending on the cultures upon them and the planet itself—will become united in that group of familial qualities.

There are twelve of those groups of familial qualities, and thus, if you are going to have a life here, long or short, it will have to be through the focus of one of those groups of families. There are, of course, other families of beings—again no blood ties, just associated with the qualities I mentioned before—that would not ever bring you to Earth school. Your pursuits, interests, wisdom and so on simply wouldn't bring you in this direction, and you would go elsewhere.

So just because you are a member of that family does not require you to live a life on Earth, but it is simply a possibility. Very often, those interested in more—meaning becoming more, having more capabilities and so on—will be attracted to go to a planet (understand, we are talking about souls here) regardless of the conditions to be experienced in that life on that planet, with the overview that once that life is over, you will be more or have more that you can do or express and so on. Therefore, these overall souls' perception is that regardless of what you experience, you will eventually come out the other end with more. So this is truly the innocence of the soul being expressed here, not realizing that there may be things experienced in this Earth school as it is now that, if you had known beforehand, you would say, "Well, I can get along without that."

What a wonderful way to explain that, yes. I think that there are probably gazillions, but I had heard that there were 256 personality types in this creation?
That sounds about right. I would group them as families.

So you don't have to be one of those twelve families, which are the signs in my understanding?
Yes.

If you are from any of the others, as long as you are willing to assume the characteristics of one of those twelve signs, you can come to Earth. Is that what you said?
No, because it is not about assuming characteristics. It has to do with what your actual soul's interests are, personally speaking. You don't don

the garment of that for the moment. You have to actually have those personality characteristics in your soul. If they truly exist—because of your personal interests, pursuits, what you find enjoyable, and so on—and then you happen as a result, you could be considered part of a family, although you wouldn't necessarily consider yourself that. You'd have another sense of relationship, but you could be considered part of that. Then it would be available to you to have a life on Earth. It isn't that you don those characteristics so that you can have a life on Earth.

Ah, okay. There has to be something in you that resonates with one of the signs.

It has to be quite a few somethings, not just a single thing, so that nobody sort of stumbles over their personality and falls into a planetary life experience—not only wondering how they got here, but not really getting anything out of it. There has to be a considerable desire for growth—change, accumulation of something more, essentially—to come to Earth. This doesn't mean that people who come to Earth are greedy. It generally means that people who have Earth lives are devoted to service in one way or another. This might not always be obvious by the characteristics of an Earth personality, a person you know. But generally speaking, Earth human beings as a group tend toward service in their lifetime—so much so that you generally take it for granted. But it is not necessarily the case other places.

Well, the Explorer Race is a great, fantastic service to all of creation.

Yes, I am not denying that, but I am saying that you take it for granted on Earth. If you understand clearly that I am referring to these families, I am not saying it is something you are locked into. You might have a life someplace else and decide you no longer have those interests. As your interests change and grow, and you acquire more wisdom and experience, you might become identified with another family, which may or may not . . .

Be one of the twelve.

Be one of the twelve. Getting back to how we started in the first place, your incarnation is extremely unlikely, then, to bring you to Earth. Generally speaking, that is another reason why people are not reincarnating on Earth now, and it is not surprising. When you wake up, so to speak—or in short, begin to remember more of your overall personality characteristics and are not blocked from that, as has been in the past on Earth—then you become aware of possibilities that have been withheld from you while you are living on Earth so that you can explore your Earth lessons and accumulate the more. When you become aware of those other characteristics, you are reminded of things that you pursued in other lives in other places, and you get, of course, enthusiastic about those pursuits.

Therefore, the idea of coming back to Earth as it is now or even some benevolent Earth in the future has little or no pull. It is not as if you are isolated from your loved ones. When you move off from the planet and move through the veils, it is typical to see loved ones. No one is stuck on Earth.

Those of the Thirteenth Sign Will Support the Rest of the Signs

Each sign will contribute something to the new thirteenth sign. What will Sagittarius contribute to that?

It is hard to say. I think that, generally speaking, you will be able to extrapolate that from the sign itself, if you are able to communicate with that sign—and that is, at this point in time from my perception, highly questionable. But I would say that most likely what would come as a donation [chuckles], or more likely a sense of familiarity with that sign, would be compatibility. Be aware that it may not be possible to create a synthesis of a sign to communicate, for the purposes of this book, that does not exist yet on the planet. Then you are asking for a synthesis of a nonentity.

[Laughs.] Okay, but how does that reflect out on the greater creation, then—if the signs each relate to a family, is there is some oversoul family?

No, it is all right. Everything relates to everything else. All in the creation is related to everything else. So if you are talking about some universal family, that would be it. For the families I am stating here, it is not hard and fast. It is just for the purpose of communicating similar, traceable traits for this book, for contributing to this book, but I am not talking about any hard-and-fast rules. You might not get any of the other signs who agree with this point of view at all, or you might get some.

But that's the whole point. I mean, we want your personalities, you know?

Well, then, I am trying not to hold it back from you, eh?

Nope, you are flowing forth. But we haven't talked too much about the thirteenth sign. My understanding is there are a group of people who are going to be born with those combined characteristics. Is that right?

Yes, and I will give you this. Generally speaking, but not always, they will either be born around the first of the year or the exact opposite. Of course, you must understand that we are dealing with the Gregorian calendar here. There are other calendars on Earth that would throw the whole astrologic into a blender, but since we are dealing with the Gregorian calendar, that's my explanation. So don't expect it at any immediate moment, but when it does happen, those are the places to look, because those signs, especially around the first of the year—those people with those birth dates—are particularly open to assimilation. Sometimes this creates a certain amount of confusion for them, but other times it strictly expresses compatibility, meaning adaptability.

I have never asked this of anyone either. Obviously, they wouldn't be here if either the Earth or the Explorer Race didn't need them. So what part of the plan will they fulfill? What is their purpose?

You will have to ask them, but I will give you this. Generally speaking, they will help all signs—meaning all the rest of the wheel—to move more smoothly and easily into your natural, native personalities, strictly by having little or nothing to do with what they say but a great deal to do with projected feelings, their personalities.

So is it like a harmonic or a resonance or some kind of radiation? Something they exude?

I am just going to leave your question unanswered for the moment. But do include it in the text, because yes and no is my answer to that.

Dogs Generally Preview Unexpressed Human Traits

You are just such a font of information, I am trying to think what else we can elicit from you that is interesting. Is there anything else you can say that we don't know?

I'd like to say a closing comment. Right now, many of you who are interested in astrology or even working on it professionally or researching it—and this book is really aimed toward you—are looking at the aspects of astrology demonstrated in characteristics of the human personality. I feel that it is important for you to look also at the characteristics demonstrated by dogs, not because you are going to do dog astrology (though some of you might), but because dogs are particularly compatible with human beings and dogs very often will represent the quality of personality that human beings are almost prepared to demonstrate. Look toward dogs and something that they are doing or trying to do or trying to communicate.

If you have a dog, you will often see this look in the dog's eyes of that desire to communicate something urgently—not just associated with having to go outside quickly or needing to eat right this second, but something that is there. You look in their eyes, and they look back at you, and you can lock eyes because you are familiar with each other. There is no mistrust. Pay attention to that, because generally speaking, when there is a trait that human beings are going to express soon as a group, it will be previewed by dogs.

This has to do with part of the reason why dogs are so popular, because human beings just have a natural affinity with dogs—and other animals too, but in this case dogs also have that affinity more so with human beings and other animals as a rule and can live with you and even bend beyond their natures in order to be with you. I grant that sometimes you, as human beings, have to bend a bit too to have them in your family. This is partly because dogs, as a general personality of being, have within them a desire to improve the quality of life for those whom they care about, and generally speaking, they care about human beings outside the boundaries of their own group.

Can you give me just one example of a trait that they are previewing?

No, I can't do that, but I can give you an example of a trait that they previewed in the past that human beings are now expressing more freely. Human beings in the past—say, the past 400 years or so—were very often slow to represent that they knew what someone was going to say before that person said it. Have you ever had the experience where someone is talking—and this is not so much for a family member who says something to you over and over, but someone is talking whom you just met—and you suddenly knew what that person was going to say? And even though you don't have it word for word, what that person says falls into exact alignment with what you knew he or she was going to say? Dogs expressed that first as an energy.

Dogs seed the energy of traits that are native and natural to you, which would be the next trait that would be expressed of part of your native-born soul personalities. Dogs seed that. It goes out to human beings, but it takes awhile, given all the distractions for human beings, to express it. Therefore, your beloved friends will absorb some of it and begin to express it, and that is when they give you those looks. Of course, you are looking at them and you wonder what they want: "Are you hungry? Do you want to go outside? Is there something else?" But in the process, you are connecting with that feeling broadcast by your beloved pet.

Dogs express love so totally, and we are just learning to do that. Is that one of the traits, one of the things they are doing for us?

It is one of the things they have done in the past, as another example.

I think that a lot of you know how to express love. You are just shy because of your cultures, but it is not something unknown to the soul. So when you come to a broader welcoming of animals on the planet, recognize that every single other animal species on the planet is also engaged in supporting or helping some aspect of the human physical, mental, spiritual and other expressed absolute phenomena of the human being.

There is no animal on the planet Earth who is not in some way contributing to the betterment of human beings, even those who cause you annoyance or harm. I am not saying that this is permanent. Those who cause you annoyance or harm are passing through, and they will move on soon, but sometimes this annoyance and harm will bring you together. Sometimes the simplest things, such as mosquitoes, would give you something to be annoyed about together. Find more things to experience together, and maybe mosquitoes can move on. Good night.

Thank you very much. Thank you.

540 • • • ASTROLOGY: PLANET PERSONALITIES SPEAK

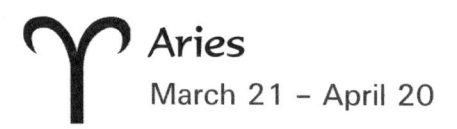

♈ Aries
March 21 – April 20

ARIES
Are Expected to Act Physically on What They Say Mentally

September 20, 2007

This is Aries.

Welcome!

Well, how are you?

As an Aries, I am doing very well, thank you.

I felt it was important for me to check up on one of the Aries clan.

Aries Teach Others through Their Dreams

Tell me about yourself.

It is important to remind the reader that the personality shown is a synthesis of that which attunes Aries peoples and people with significant Aries in their charts on Earth, not an actual being. Given that, I cannot speak as if I am someone, so can you rephrase the question?

Yes. Tell me anything you can about the sign of Aries other than what we already know.

Let me say this: Aries is not always given its credit due, because Aries is not considered to be one of subtlety. The issue about Aries is that Aries is intended to initiate, but we know that. What is lesser known about Aries is that Aries has a tendency to initiate, not just by the spoken word and by example, but through a state of condition that I can only call dream intuition. What I mean by that is that Aries people and those with significant amounts of Aries in their charts have a tendency to function in the dream world not unlike the way guides and teachers and angels function.

They are, of course, filtered through all the individuals they attempt to contact, filtered by the guides of those people. But Aries people have such a desire to teach—whether what they have to teach is of value or not, they have such a desire to teach and often have something of value to teach. So if they feel any kind of opening at all, even if it is not stated verbally but is noted in some pattern of behavior of whom they wish to teach, they may attempt to reach the person through their dreams. This is not an attempt at being manipulative; rather, it is an attempt to drop a hint, and this is how it happens.

Aries people might find themselves thinking excessively about something they are attempting to explain, teach or share with someone—or many someones, perhaps of a certain group. Now, this is important, Aries people: If you notice that you are thinking about something you didn't realize you were thinking about, meaning you suddenly notice you have a pattern of thought going on, what is happening almost always is that you are attempting to reach people who are asleep and dreaming. It is important to note that, because there is a tendency by Aries people to quickly cut off that pattern of thought.

If in any way that pattern of thought feels destructive, depressing, self-destructive, anything like that to you, then feel free to cut it off. But if it is just something you wouldn't normally think about or if it is something that is innocuous—not harmful to you or anyone else, as far as you know—then allow the pattern to continue, even if you might notice a sense of response, meaning it sounds conversational. You are not going crazy. It just means that there is something you are doing with a dreamer some place that may, when interpreted through their guides, angels and other teachers, reach them. Sometimes you are not even speaking to the individual; you are speaking to the teacher or the guide in hopes of convincing them that there is some hope of passing on this knowledge or wisdom for you. How's that?

Aries: Teach Your Wisdom

Now, another thing: Aries people often have a belief that they are from this place or that place, and this is not surprising, given the nature of stars and planets and all of that business. But, generally speaking, Aries people on Earth now tend to focus—this doesn't mean it was where your life was, or anything like that—through a primary star system, and that is Andromeda. There is a great deal of energy that drives Aries through the Andromeda star system. I am not ruling out the planets that represent Aries in the star chart; I am just talking about the energy that supports Aries.

Aries is intended to function in the mental world, yes, but Aries is expected—given how much you have in your chart—to act physically on what they say mentally. I am not saying anything that you astrologers don't already know, but Aries often feels a certain compulsion to act out what they speak about. So, Aries people, you are not always known for pausing before you speak, but it is important to know that in these times on Earth, where creation and creativity are so much in the forefront, it is important to speak to teach people only that which you already do because it works for you. Try to focus in your wisdom and not just teach people about something you heard that somebody else was doing and for all you know works or doesn't work. It is important to teach people about *what you know works*—at least it works for you because you demonstrate it in your daily life.

In other words, teach your wisdom. It may not always be that this is what appeals to you to teach. You may not even realize what all your wisdom is. But the reason it is important to know this is, if you attempt to teach people something that you are not doing and it is just something you read about or heard about, it will suddenly happen, within twenty-four hours, that you will find yourself learning what it is you were attempting to teach. So it is very important now for everyone—not just Aries, but for everyone—to pay attention to what you are teaching. Teach your wisdom. You know for a fact that it works for you, because you do it and it works. If something comes up in twenty-four hours because you were attempting to teach it to someone who may or may not have wanted to hear it, if it comes up and it is in your wisdom, you will be able to deal with it, you see? A little important note there, I feel, that will help a few folks.

I have always wondered why the symbol for Aries was a ram. Is that happenstance, or is there a reason for it?

No, all of those symbols were well thought out. It is not always that, but it is that because Aries have the reputation and personality to charge in, whether they are wanted or not. Rams are not always known for asking. That is all it means. It is not just a sarcastic commentary, these signs, these pictographs, if you would. The lesson for Aries is, maybe pause sometimes. The real lesson, and that is why I spoke about it, is that for Aries, speak your wisdom and don't be shy about it if you feel it has value in the situation. But be careful, because you often love knowledge and there is a tendency to teach what is not your wisdom, and then the twenty-four-hour law will go into effect. I am calling it a law, not because it has always been on the books, but rather because, in these times, so much of creation and so many creation capabilities are present for each and every one of you on Earth—all human beings— that the value of speaking your wisdom instead of just charging in to teach people what you read or heard about cannot be overstressed, okay?

Do you find a lot of Aries in positions of spiritual teaching?

Well, I would say no more and no less really than other situations. You may not like this, but you might tend to find more Aries in positions of dogmatic teaching. Now, that means that Aries people, if they believe in something, are not easily shaken out of that belief, and therefore, there is a tendency to be dogmatic about things. I am not saying they don't grow. What I am saying is their core beliefs are there and they are not going anywhere. So you will often find people in Aries who have reached some position of teaching in religious communities. I am broadening your question to include religious communities, because I am not sure if you meant that when you said spiritual. Were you including religion?

No.

Okay. Ask a question.

Well, some of the questions I ask are because I don't understand the subject, and then they don't get answered.

About 40 percent of what we have talked about is already known. Let me remind you to reiterate what others have said, and that is that your ignorance of the subject of astrology is actually an advantage in some ways, because you have a tendency to ask questions that an innocent might ask. If you were a professional in the field, you may not ask these kinds of questions. So, astrologers out there, please be aware that the questioner is not an astrologer, not even a good amateur astrologer, and take that into account. But don't assume that we who speak are ignorant of these things.

In Ancient Times, Astrology Was Considered an Art

Who set this system up? Did the Creator set it up? I am wondering whether the planets assumed the position they are in and volunteered to be connected to certain signs. No one has ever explained that. How do the planets get connected to the signs?

It is a long story, but shortening it up here, going way back when astrology was first being taught by inspiration like this, it was taught to those who were compiling wisdom in order to be able to pass it on in some circles. There was writing long before what is known, and some of this was left artistically cut into stone and some was attempted to be left in documents, but you know that these do not last in ancient times. So to put it simply, over the years this has been taught many times over to people who are observant of parallels between certain individuals of similar birth dates and other individuals of the same kind of similarity. Also, certain similarities have been noted in the animal world, also known as the natural world. So those who were adept and interested in these areas were often the ones chosen to receive this knowledge and wisdom.

That is why in the ancient schools of astrology, it was always considered that this was an initiation, literally a spiritual initiation into the art of astrology. It is expressed in your time as a wisdom—as a thought, words, teaching—but in ancient times it was always considered an art, because the artist, the astrologer artist, could not pick up a book and consult it. By "ancient times," I am talking back before books were largely circulated. So it was given through inspiration like this, but the relationships of this planet to that planet is really just a way to create general patterns so that you can state that astrology has to do with astronomy. But if you are asking if the planets themselves are directly volunteering to be a portion of some philosophical group of personalities, then no. They are just there.

On Earth, astrology as you know it now first started showing up around 7,000 years ago. But you have to remember, at least if you are going to take my word for it, that at that time people didn't need it so much. At that time, people were used to being intuitive and functioning with their physical instinct to know to go here, to go with this person, to go with that being, to follow this animal's trail, not that animal's trail, and so on. So a learned discussion of similar personality traits and what can be extrapolated for the future on that was not so much the case, but there was always interest in what might be expected physically for the future in one's environment.

So astrology originally started with individuals who wanted to know about the future in their physical environment. It wasn't about people at all, but after a time, as people became less focused in the intuitive and the instinctual, it took that turn toward being about people in an attempt to offer a temporary substitute for those who were no longer consciously experiencing their instinct and their intuition, and practicing it. Thus, in your time it is largely a mental pursuit, even though it is still an art, and those who practice it, study it, and provide it for others are artisans of the craft.

Aries Will Easily Adapt to the Shift from the Mental to the Physical

It became much more important, then, as we developed the mental body and focused on the mental body?

No, I think you may have missed my innuendo. It became much more *necessary* when focused on the mental body—not important! When you are focused on the mental body, there is a tendency to overlook that which cannot be conceptually considered. When people do that, they almost always have a tendency to overlook physical evidence if there is a more persuasive mental argument that is critical of that physical evidence. This is how things are often delayed, because the obvious is overlooked in favor of the more stimulating theory.

I mention this because Aries people are known for their fine minds. Yet as you said yourself, in this time of the world, in recent days, being more focused in the mental world, such beings as Aries find themselves in a friendly environment but now, you see, focused more in creation and creativity while the mind is still present and desires to think, be influenced, and influence others. One is confronted on a daily basis with what is necessary physically, whether one has paid attention to that in the past or not, or whether one has considered it of value or not.

In recent years, the past 150 years or so, in some spiritual communities there has been a tendency to seek solace in encouraging words. Certainly religion offers that as well, so Aries has been attempting to provide solace. Still, I speak of these matters because the change that is going on right now is something that Aries can adapt to. Aries nature is to be physical and mental in balance. Aries sometimes gets very focused in the mental, but Aries has a strong physical side, which is why that creature is depicted for Aries. Therefore, I feel that Aries people will be able to adapt to this time—which has changed already from a focus on the mental to a focus on the physical—and be able to adapt to the results presented by physical evidence much more easily than some others.

We're becoming more physical, more aware of the physical—how do we integrate the spiritual into that?

You are forced really to be more aware of the physical because of the population of your fellow human beings on the planet. It is not as if you can really avoid them, you know, nor would you necessarily want to. But integrating the spiritual is actually much easier, because when people are confounded by something, they look to their normal resources to find answers, but an answer in thought is no longer sufficient. It was for quite a while, but science has done a great deal to promote a welcoming of the physical. With science and the scientific method, although it might be seemingly very wordy and mental, ultimately if you can't go to the laboratory and produce physical results, it remains a theory, however fascinating. So science and the enamoration with science in your time have actually helped to promote an awareness in the general culture that the results are important—the outcome, you see.

So involving spirituality is not a problem, because when science and other worded persuasions are not sufficient, one always looks beyond the mentally understood to the unknown and often enigmatic. Spiritually, you can find many things that may support portions of your life that you know for a fact are not mental or physical—for example, dreams. Dreams have been thought in the past to be prophetic, and sometimes they are. Dreams have also been thought to be—how can we say?—dangerous, and granted, sometimes they are. But in your time, dreams are simply a preparation for nonverbal communication, and nonverbal communication between one person and another is the same as the nonverbal communication a person might have with a cat or a dog or a horse or any other creature. There is no need to communicate in words, and masses of communication take place without a word being spoken. Anyone who lives with animals knows that.

So the times are all a-changing, and we wordy people have got to change with it.

You just need to be able to physically produce evidence of what you say to others if you are attempting to convince those others of the value of what you are saying. Simple words are not sufficient. You don't have to produce proof necessarily in the scientific sense, but you do have to produce evidence by the way you live your life that there is value in what you are saying. If others see that the way you are living your life is valuable and it has or bestows value on others—meaning others benefit from the way you live your life—then there will be a tendency to look with favor upon your arguments. So you may not have to produce the goods, but you will have to walk it, if you talk it.

Right, walk the talk.

Feelings Are the Physical Messages of Your Inner Body

What will Aries contribute to the thirteenth sign?

The contribution will lie almost entirely in strength of personality and determination. You can ask the thirteenth sign more about that.

Oh, it wasn't clear that we would get to talk to that sign.

I don't know. I am stating that the opportunity is there.

Yes. You said earlier that those with Aries signs were focused through Andromeda. Is that the galaxy or the constellation?

It is the galaxy.

It is my understanding that we are helping the Andromedans bring feeling into the mental process, and as we evolve, our linear minds will go back to the Andromedans.

I don't know anything about that. All I know is that the Andromeda galaxy is well known as a place of mental capacity, the ability to understand all through focused thought and through—utilizing your body type, if you don't mind—the nervous system, so that the mind/body interaction is the means by which all is known and understood by many different cultures in that galaxy. So, in that sense, if one was a human being in that galaxy as you are here, you would think not only with your brain. You would think with your entire nervous system.

Therefore, you can see how, even though Andromeda may be known for its mental focus, if you are using your mind and your body, you are completely open to instinct, because instinct is your body's synthesis of mind, body and spirit functioning together to know. You don't have to have it explained to you why you are going to turn left instead of right. Left feels better, or vice versa. You don't have to have anybody persuade you that turning right is better. It feels better, and so you turn right—just as an example.

So are people with Aries signs more apt to be able to think with their whole body, then, or are they coming into that?

You have to remember that astrology charts are a wheel, and everyone has the opportunity, progressing through the year, to experience a certain amount of Aries energy. But if you are asking whether Aries people are likely to be the leaders in that capability, no. You are likely to be able to focus on instinct and understand it physically quicker than some others, but you are not likely to be the leaders, because instinct is profoundly subtle. While feelings are involved and the physical self is important in Aries people, "feelings" means not only what you touch but what you touch within. Feelings are the physical messages of your inner body, and that is what instinct is.

So you may find, as an Aries person or one with a considerable amount of Aries in your chart, that you will be able to take note of feeling but you will not be supported in the conventional textbooks as to what feeling is. That is why I am attempting, poorly perhaps, to explain it on an instinctual level. For example, you might experience something even vicariously through a theatrical event, and your body immediately produces within itself a feeling. Perhaps the feeling will be excitement; perhaps it will be the feeling of fear. In this world coming in now—it is happening because of your capacity to create, everyone—you will respond to your feelings and you will be able to take note of the feelings of others. This is not just in your imagination, but you will be able to literally feel the feelings of others around you. Thus, you may find yourself in a position of having to *be* a feeling, having to focus on a feeling to calm the feelings of others.

Imagine for a moment that you are a parent, a mother or father, or even an older brother or sister, and your fellow brothers and sisters (or as a parent, your children) are all frightened about something. If you yourself can focus on calm as a physical feeling in your body—not forcing it, but finding it within your body, then going into it and being that calm—it might very well affect the others so that they have a better chance of becoming calmer themselves. This does not mean that they won't need nurturing and love, but the broadcast quality of Aries people is strong. Therefore, the feelings you have in your physical self are more likely to be felt if you choose to broadcast ones that are benign, benevolent and helpful.

See if you can find these feelings within yourself so that you might be able to assist others when such feelings are desirable. It cannot be used to influence others in some self-interested way, because others will have different interests. But if it is done to throw oil on the waters, so to speak, to create calm instead of fear in a situation where calm would be beneficial, as compared to a situation where fear might be beneficial . . . in which case it is not your job to take people's fear away from them. Sometimes fear is a message saying, "Run," in the case of approaching danger, yes?

But in the case of fear that is perhaps unwarranted, at least in your mind—perhaps involving a stranger coming into your midst but one whom you have met before, just a stranger to others, and you know that this person is safe, a friend—you can feel calm and any other feeling that you find in your body, and focus on that feeling. It will be challenging to focus on that feeling while communicating with others, but if you train, you can do it. Remember, it is not your will forcing your body to feel. It's your mind focusing on the feeling that's in your body and thus being that feeling. So your mind is not excluded, but your mind does not act as the authoritarian. Mind, body, spirit together as one—no one over the other.

People Choose Their Signs for Different Reasons

Would you say a soul would choose to have a life with Aries energy if it was headstrong and eager and perhaps not too subtle, or would it want to choose that energy if it was the opposite? Does it work both ways when people choose a life? Do they choose something that's in them that they want to express, or the opposite of that?

As you say, sometimes something is chosen because of the desire to learn about it, to understand it from a position of having lived it, as compared to being on the outside looking in. Yes, very often souls will choose something like that, especially if they are in a hurry to learn something that they feel they may need at another time, another place. But, of course, on Earth you have a school that is of short duration compared to lifetimes that are normally lived on other planets.

So if a person, say a soul, is told that he or she will have the opportunity to live one life only on Earth in Earth school and that he or she can use that life to learn, as well as to experience the general lessons of Earth, some individuals might choose a little of this or a little of that in order to learn many things. But other individuals might focus largely on one or two things in order to learn something for sure. So, yes, sometimes it is a desire to experience that, but other times it is a desire to learn it, to understand it, to walk in its shoes, so to speak, so that there will be not only passion, but compassion—"passion," in this sense, meaning enthusiasm. Every soul of every being is different.

So there is no recipe. If they have that within them and they are trying to understand it, or if they are really docile and they are trying to learn that quality—it could be either way.

That's why the astrologer is so important, because the astrologer can tell you what is more likely and the astrologer can also explain to you what you are likely to experience, even on different sides of an issue. He or she might be able to say, "Well, coming up in your year, this might happen and that might happen, and during that time, being the sign that you are, you will experience it this way, but you might also experience it that way." There is a tendency by people who don't understand astrology or think that it is something meant for entertainment to believe that these are general statements and that anybody could be any of that at any time, but of course, that is not true.

Astrologers know—as well as hobbyist astrology people know—that the various aspects of the behavior associated with the sign are not general at all. The more you know about individuals—meaning the basics such as birth date and time, also place is sometimes helpful (though not always; it depends on the system)—then you can tell them vast amounts of highly detailed information, most of which will be true. The reason it isn't all true is that, as you know, not all planets of Earth's solar system have been discovered and charted in their proper orbits. So the astrologer is somewhat limited by the fact that not all is known, but given the fact that some is missing, it is surprising how accurate it is most of the time.

Your Sign Is Stored in Your Energy Body

Since we know that planets and groupings of planets called solar systems have personalities, would you say that it was the planets and the solar systems in a sign who are focused on this energy, or is it the people, the beings who live on the planets in that sign, who focus this energy?

It is the people who choose to experience certain lessons, teachings and so on, and in order to learn that, they must come to a place where that lesson and teaching is being supported. So it is like the flow, yes? The flow comes toward Earth. You, as a soul coming toward Earth, decide to be born at a certain time, maybe even in a certain place, and in order to experience that lesson, you are born with that culturalization, referring to the chemical process here, where you are—how can we say?—born and brewed to be something.

So you experience it. You broadcast it, but you are not a slave to it. As you grow to understand your natural tendencies as understood through astrology, you can not just master it but you can be forgiving of aspects of yourself that might, when you were younger, have given you frustration. You can be forgiving of aspects of others who are also struggling with some of their difficult lessons, and you can become as wise as you are able. In the understanding of astrological challenges, astrology is a way to understand that this is a school and will remain one for some time. It is also a way, however, to understand that the reason you do not live here too long is that you cannot live here so long that you will absorb too much.

Simply stated, with a life on Earth in these times followed by lives other places (even though it's not linear like that, but for the sake of simplicity), it will take about a minimum of forty lives to process that which is learned, understood, or even glimmered a sense of on Earth. It will take about forty lives in other places to work through all of that or to integrate it into those lives with an understanding—to support those other lives and, of course, since you are all service-oriented, to serve the needs of others more beneficially because of this learned wisdom. So to live past a certain point is of no advantage. Otherwise, you spend too much "time" resolving and blending the ingredients in other lives.

You said there was a culturalization based on the time and date of birth. Where is that stored in the body? It can't be in the physical, since the cells keep . . .

I referred to it in the chemical sense: the way one might culture cheese from milk. That's what I meant.

Okay. But where is this culturalization stored? In the physical body or one of the other bodies?

It is stored in your energy body, which receives. It is always receiving from spirit and that which is safe. So, generally speaking, it is not seeded in your physical body. One cannot do a postmortem on a human being and say that this person is an Aries or a Cancer or a Libra, you see. It is not stored there; it is in the energy self. It is not entirely a joke, although it sounds funny. It's not stored in the physical body, and it is not identifiable in the physical body, even in the DNA. It is an influence, however.

It is an omnipresent influence that does not always come to your attention, unless you trip over something that is a challenge or a lesson of that sign that you have tripped over before, and then, oh yes, you pay attention. But sometimes you don't notice the benevolent aspects of that sign because you are used to it and there is a tendency—by all the signs, I might add—to assume that because you are used to it and you do it, that everybody does that. But that's not the case. Different people have different talents, different accomplishments, different capabilities, and that is known and understood every place else. The reason you have this mix, this blend of personalities, is so that no one person or no one group has to do everything. It is always intended that you serve each other's needs and that you are served by others as you need.

When you say "energy body," could you help me understand that? Is that the feeling body, the astral body? What are some other words that would equate to that?

The astral body is not really a term that I use. I will just say it is that which you arrive in, your lightbody, that which you travel in when you are in deep sleep with your physical body, that by which you leave the physical body when you are done with your life on Earth. But I don't use the term "astral." It means too many things to too many people.

So is it stored in what we would call the piece of us that is the immortal personality?

I can see that you are confused here, because your question is based on, "Where is it stored?" It isn't. When you drink water, is that all the water you ever need in your life? No, it passes through you. It's the same thing. The influence comes into you and passes through you as you express your personality. So it is always there, like a water tap that is on in a slow, steady stream, but it is not stored anywhere. It doesn't need to be.

But if two people are standing together and one is an Aries and one is a Taurus, what in the Aries person magnetizes the Aries energy and what in the Taurus person draws the Taurus energy?

Let me rephrase your question, and you will understand immediately. If you have a house and there is a dog standing next to a cat, they are also energized. How come they don't get confused about who they are? How come the cat doesn't think it's a dog and the dog doesn't think it is a cat? That's the answer. Now *you* tell me what it means.

[Sighs.] Well, they are attracting that energy, and I know why, but not how.

You want to know the mechanics of it, eh? When you come here, you desire to do certain things. So in order to do those things, you result in a certain sign, yes? But you still want to do those things because your immortal personality—or your soul, you see—is within you, so your soul is always receptive to being fed by that which allows you to do those things. That's the mechanics.

I see. It goes back to the need and the desire. Thank you.

The next time you are standing next to a Taurus person, there is no need to be concerned that you might suddenly become a Taurean. For that matter, there is no need for the Taurus person to be concerned that he or she might suddenly become an Aries. All that is safe. Don't worry!

I love your sense of humor.

Aries Energy Emanates from Andromeda

All right, back to my original question. I had a question that wasn't phrased correctly, because you answered it differently. If we are attracting this energy, where is it coming from? Who is sending it? Is it the beings who live on the planets in what's called the sign, the constellation? Or is it the planets, the solar systems, the beings of whatever shape or form or dimension who are those planets and solar systems?

No. It is your guides, teachers and angels.

They are sending that energy to us!

They are there for you individually, no matter how many of you are on the planet. So it is not as if they don't have enough guides, teachers and angels to go around. They are sending it, but the energy comes . . . how can we say? Andromeda is the battery. It is the electricity, so to speak. It is the motive force, but the focus is through your guides, teachers and angels so that you can accomplish as a soul what you came here to do. They are not directing you; they are not forcing this in you. They are simply helping your soul to fulfill its purpose in your Earth life.

This is why they can be reasoned with up to a point. In your deep sleep state or with your teachers, your guides and angels, there is a tendency to say, "But, but this!" And, "But that!" [Laughs.] You are more reasonable when you are with them, because you know you are loved, you see. But still, there is a tendency to want to understand why you are experiencing something in your life. Thus, they immediately take you to some other situation where you can observe them working with somebody else—or maybe observe other angels, guides or teachers working with somebody else. You will see what goes on there, and you will understand it as a student might understand a demonstration given by a teacher. When you see it happening, it is very clear, but when it happens with you, it is not always so clear. You understand that, yes?

Okay. Do I understand correctly that the Aries energy emanates from Andromeda? You are saying it is the engine.

That it is the engine, right. The energy tends to be supported from that place. But I am not saying that if you want to find your home, you've got to get in a rocket ship and head for Andromeda.

I understand. So that's for Aries—does every sign have an engine or a battery?

Sometimes it's the same one. You will have to ask them.

I talked to several when I didn't know to ask.

Oh, it's not that critical. After all, when you get in your car and you start the engine, you don't get in the car to relate to the engine. You get in the car to get somewhere. The engine is not your focus, though it is the motive force, isn't it?

I was just interested in, like you say, the mechanics. So that's fascinating!

You Feel the Motivation

So one of the things, then, that the teachers and guides do for each human is, once that human has desired to learn something, those guides and teachers emanate energy to him or her that will help?

No, not emanated. They function more as a filter. Let's say that one of the teachers understood that his or her student, meaning you, was on the planet as a soul to learn something. Then that energy that's coming to support you . . . not the energy of life—Creator provides that—but the energy that's coming to support why you are there, as described in the case of Andromeda. Your teacher would simply be that which you are attempting to learn.

See, if you were on some other planet, you would know what you came there to learn and you would understand it, but since you are here to learn, even though that filters through the teacher into you, you are separated from knowing so that you can learn on the planet—the veil of ignorance, you understand. So what you feel is not the knowledge, not the wisdom; rather, you feel the motivation. That's what left after the veil, you see? You can't know. If you know, then there is no chance of you actually fulfilling your desire to learn something on the basis of not knowing.

But the motivation remains, and that's how people sometimes have drives, will do something over and over again. I'm not necessarily referring to self-destructive things here at all; rather, I'm generally referring to things where you might accomplish something, get good at it, and then you might do some other aspect of it and also get good at that. Say an artist might get good at painting and then suddenly, mid-career, decide to take up sculpture, just for an example. It's been known, and this kind of thing is found very often. If you find yourself then repeating things that are in the general area of similarity, this is probably something you came here to do. Once you have mastered something or gone as far as you can with what it was that you were doing, then you might do some other aspect of it. Perhaps you can get more from it that way.

That has to do with the motivation being provided by your guides, teachers and angels, even though they have the wisdom. As I said, if you were on another planet and that wasn't needed, you would be sitting there with your teacher, and if you wanted to know something, your teacher would have that knowledge and *bip*, just like that, you would know it. But on that planet, you wouldn't be there to learn in that sense by doing. You would simply be there to learn by understanding—different than the planet you are on now. While you might learn things by understanding on this planet, what you hold dear to be true is that which you practice, what you put into practice in your life, you see, your wisdom—because it works for you or in some cases consoles or comforts you, even if there is no tangible evidence that it may be so.

You find this often in religious and spiritual communities, but sometimes you find it in other places. This is why very often the unknown can be attractive. The enigmatic—that which cannot be quantified—can be attractive if physical life or mental life does not offer you the answers you need or desire. Then it is possible. How many children have heard this from their parents or loved ones: "One of God's mysteries, honey." It is a comfort, then, and sometimes later in life it is still a comfort. It may very well remain a comfort.

Just because you might have that said to you on this planet does not mean that on other planets people don't believe in God. They just understand that God is everything and that they are not excluded from that everything. That's the only difference. Many people on your planet understand that too; it is just more difficult to express that, given the different philosophies and ways of being. But you are getting there.

We are coming to the point, though, where we are going to understand the mysteries.

The way you understand the mysteries is always through the heart, because the heart does not require a complete mental understanding—it only needs the physical evidence that something is so. The physical evidence for the heart is the feeling of love; that might express itself in different ways, but often physically it is felt as warmth. It might be felt other ways to others. You know how love feels to you, and thus when your heart feels that, you don't need to have it explained to you. You understand, you know, and that is what will come. You don't need to understand how a spaceship flies. If you need to be on the spaceship, you are perfectly happy being on the spaceship and flying away. I am not necessarily recommending that as a solution for all your problems. After all, you don't know where the ship is going, but [chuckles] that is another story for another time.

It is good, while you are here, to do what you can to bring about benevolence for yourself and others. Who knows what has been done by others to bring about benevolence for you? Very often, you don't know. Sometimes historians try to point that out, and other times there are other places to find out. Most of the time, most people do not know how much good is in their life that has been provided for them by others whom they don't know and will never meet. Any simple study of history will tell you a lot of that; you don't have to get it this way. Read a history book and decide whether you would prefer to live in the 1600s or now.

Now we have to come to an end here; let me close with this. Those who have Aries in their charts, you may know or you may not know that you have an opportunity in your lifetime to experience many things that you have not experienced yet. If you manage to be alive over the next forty years, you will discover that your Sun sign is actually combined with another, as many of the Sun signs are joining with other ones. Someday there will only be four or five signs, and then forty, eighty years or so beyond that, there will only be one sign. All beings will be all and understand all or believe in the value of all. This is coming on Earth, on the Earth you know. Good night.

Thank you very much. Thank you.

♎ Libra
September 24 – October 23

LIBRA

Supports All of You in Expressing Its Qualities that Are Inherent in All People

September 28, 2007

This is Libra.

Welcome!

Whales and Dolphins Are Holding the Libra Energy for You

Well, let me say a little bit about myself. I am a coordinated element once associated with balance and so on, but there is more to me than has been met by the eye. The coming of age of the human being on Earth has a great deal to do with the reemergence of the energy associated with Libra in the daily interactions between all human beings. One associates with the astrologic individualistic aspects, but one does not always consider that some of these aspects, or series of traits, may be adapted by the entire community of human beings on the planet.

There are some animal species now demonstrating that consciousness. Dolphins and whales are the most obvious to you, so I will leave it at that. There are also a few other species, but I feel it is most important to bring to your attention that the way most dolphins and not all but most whales communicate and interact with each other and other species at times (not always) has everything to do with the Libra energy. They are really holding this Libra energy for you as you come into your emergence of your own full being. You will not have to wait for that emergence to be present when you are complete.

I would like you, though, if you can, to study a bit upon the interspecies socialization with whales and dolphins. Let's eliminate so-called killer whales from this comparison and concentrate only on dolphins' interactions with other whale species. You would see a joy, a politeness and, most importantly, cooperation—cooperation to the point where one species might make minor sacrifices so that the other species would be well tended to and well served by life.

This spirit is not unknown with the human beings. It has been known through the years as neighborliness, cooperation, friendliness. In Hawaii, it is known as aloha; around the world, it is known by different names. So this is not something that is unknown to you. In the times in which you are living now, you find that this kind of thing has been misplaced from time to time. This has to do sometimes with the pace of life and the many distractions that you have now and sometimes more extreme conditions you have to deal with. But in order to function well now as a human population who must receive knowledge and wisdom from all animal species—in other words, all other species you can recognize as individual beings on the planet—you must develop a means to be comfortable, polite and cooperative with each other in all circumstances, including circumstances that might be stressed or difficult, all the time.

The Libra Energy Will Support You

So the Libra energy on a global basis will support you. I will make a suggestion now. If you can look toward the sky and are able to see the group of stars that your astrologers have been taught are associated with this energy, and/or if you can read up on the basic tenets of the Libra energy . . . don't read the pluses, the negatives, the minuses. Don't read all of that, just the basic few words; I think most astrologers can give you ten or twelve words. Something like that would give you the basic words associated with that sign. Just relax into those words as feelings.

You will discover, for the most part, that this covers the feelings you are most comfortable expressing and most comfortable receiving from people you don't know and have never met—that is the most important thing. By "never met," I mean you might have been around them, but you were never introduced. You never had a conversation with them, other than perhaps a casual hello in passing. This is what I recommend for you to do at this time.

Qualities like charming, prizing harmony, pleasant living conditions, easygoing, romantic, diplomatic, idealistic and refined—that's what we are all coming into?

That's what you need to present to each other and express for yourself. It's not that you are coming into it. You all have those capabilities now; you don't have to learn any of them. You know what they are, and most of you have expressed those capabilities—not words, not thoughts, but actions, feelings—to others from time to time. Learn how to do that insofar as it fits into your culture and society on a regular basis.

Some of you in your cultures are already doing this, so you are well out ahead of other cultures that have not begun to express it. Other cultures are perhaps not associated with these traits, and they will be harder for you. But you can do it. Begin with your good friends—that is the best way. It is also the easiest way, and when you get used to what it feels like, then you can begin to do this with others.

So we'll retain our individual characteristics, but rather than this friendliness, this neighborliness, this concern for others being just Libra, it will be part of all humans no matter what their sign is?

Yes, because when you think back on your own life—as much as you can gauge that, as you understand—you will recall that kind of spirit being prevalent in the past. Even now one finds this cooperative effort in various cultures, but in many large cities and other places, for one reason or another, one does not find so much of this cooperation and friendliness as one once did. It is important to do this so that you will recognize immediately those feelings when you are around species other than human beings who are attempting to either communicate with you or demonstrate something to you—so that you will not only know how to survive but thrive.

Most animal species have within their knowledge immortal—meaning that which goes beyond their own lives—the capacity to survive and thrive, often in difficult circumstances. While human beings also can survive in difficult circumstances, they don't often thrive. You need to be able to know how to thrive, because you will have to change. There are changes coming, not only because of so many human beings being on the planet at once, but simply because there are so many less animals and plant species. They have been holding, expressing and generating the energy of balance, but they are leaving the planet—and by "leaving," I mean simply not reincarnating. Therefore, it is going to be up to you to hold, maintain and generate that energy of balance, and this is the best way to do it, for starters at least.

So when you are expressing these good feelings to others . . . say, you are used to that, you are used to how it feels to you, and you express these feelings and you are used to how it feels to you when others express those feelings to you. In short, you are very aware of your own physical feelings when these kinds of things are going on. If a dog comes up to you, you won't just bend down, pat him on the head and say, "Good boy," because it is possible that that dog will suddenly by its presence trigger those feelings in you. If those feelings come up, you will know that that dog may have a message for you. If you cannot understand that message quickly, then look in the dog's eyes and see if you can recognize the feeling expressed in those eyes—because the feeling as expressed in those eyes is exactly the same as it is expressed in the eyes of human beings.

When you are cooperative and friendly with your fellow human beings, the opportunity to look them in the eye is much more frequent.

So you will begin to recognize the telegraphed message in the eyes. Also, the dog may lead you someplace. In short, you will find ways to communicate with the dog. Of course, this will happen with other species, but I am picking dogs because dogs, for many of you, are objects of love or friendliness.

Libra Has to Do with Balance

How did the scales come to be associated with Libra?

Very simple—one word.

Balance.

That's it. It's a symbol of balance.

What about the indecisive nature of Libra—seeing both sides of the scales at once?

In that situation, Libra has been criticized for being indecisive, but actually what that means is that by seeing more than one side—not necessarily two sides, but more than one side—it allows Libras to become the best diplomats, you see, because they don't get attached to one side or the other's point of view, even their own side. In this way, they tend to be very fair. So I would say that, if you look at diplomacy—not the results, but the process of diplomacy—you might recognize in the long run its great value. Still, the actual step-by-step process would seem to be profoundly indecisive, and yet what is the result?

So I say "indecisive" is by way of a value judgment. I grant that those who have strong Libra in their charts may find it difficult to choose one thing over another, even on a personal basis. So the thing to always do, as most Libras probably know by now, is to try to do both in some way. Say you are getting dressed for the office and you are attracted to your blue dress *and* your orange dress. Nowadays, given the styles, it would be possible to wear your blue dress with an orange sash or vice versa, for example.

These traits that have been held by the dolphins and the whales, then—the friendship and companionship—is this what you will contribute to the thirteenth sign, or is there more?

No. I really cannot talk about that. I don't want to lose the energy of talking about my own point of view. If we talk about some other sign, we are going to lose our energy right this minute. Let's stay on Libra.

Are there other traits we don't know about, other qualities?

Yes, thank you. Here is a trait that is not known about Libra, though I have actually revealed one in the larger sense at the beginning of our talk. You are talking about everybody expressing that, so I will say another one: Libra is not known yet for this, but Libras have the capacity to produce within any individual an awakening to their own personal resources, meaning this is something that is often experienced by youngsters. They look at somebody doing something, and they try to do it.

You have seen children try to draw. It is kind of laughable, but there is always the child who picks up the crayon and draws something, and it looks pretty good. This does not mean that Libra is all about art. It means that the awakening to one's own personal resources, talents or abilities is always associated with the Libra in one's self. I am not just talking about self-discovery; I am talking about one's innate talents or abilities that one discovers only through the circumstances of life. I picked the child for an example, because you have all been children, yes? You have all been children, and while you don't necessarily remember that, you are around children and you see them going through their periods of discovery.

But even in today's world, as you live it, you are surrounded by people doing so many different things. Very often you find yourself in a position where, because help isn't around for one reason or another, you have to try to do something, and sometimes you are really surprised that you are able to do what you need to do as well as you have done it. This is Libra allowing you to grow into your own ability.

All Traits Are Becoming More Accessible

You said something very interesting. So each human does have, within them, the capacity to be all of the signs, but in incarnating they choose to focus on one. Is that a true statement?

No, because if you know something about astrology, you will know that the Sun sign is not all there is to it. There is more to it than that—not to split too many hairs with you, since I know you don't know much about astrology, and that has its advantages for the purpose of creating this book. So when you choose a certain birth time, within a few seconds you choose that. You cannot choose it much beyond, say, a fifteen-second swath one way or the other. When you "choose" that, you are coming in to experience certain lessons, growth, capacities and so on.

So calling it "choosing to be that sign" is a misnomer, you understand. You have to put "choose" in quotes, because you are coming in to experience certain lessons, capabilities and adaptabilities, you might say. Therefore, you might say that your guides—teachers, Creator, everyone—funnel you into this potential birth time so that the position of the planets, the energy of the planet you are on, and the overall physiological culture of the human being support your connection with the signs that will support what you came here to do.

But now that you are beginning to become more of who you are completely, everything takes on a different situation, because beyond this planet—even though you might be on a planet where you are born or come into being, depending upon how you want to say that—you will still have certain things you want to do. Of course, things are more benign and benevolent, and you might still experience that gift of a certain focus that one might, if you look at it astrologically from the Earth point of view, identify as a sign. But what you experience is a much greater accessibility to all traits of all beings when needed.

So what you are experiencing now—as you have suggested before with one of your questions or comments—is that all traits are becoming more accessible to any and all human beings now, because even if you are not wanting certain lessons, when you are born here now, you are accepting that the total being you are and the being you are now are coming closer together, so that you will become your total being on Earth. So you have to accept the fact that one of the things that is associated with any birth going on now on the planet (to say nothing of people already on the planet) is this reemergence into total being.

So, therefore, you must accept the fact that, even if you are born as an Aquarius, you might very well have Sagittarius or Libra or Leo traits as well. As time goes on, it will become a little more difficult for astrologers, even if you are very well experienced, to make your best guess on the basis of being with somebody who may or may not know their birth date whom you are trying to help out as to what predominant planets and other influences are associated with this person's life. So you may have to stretch a bit.

Well, that's wonderful! So much more potential! So many more possibilities!

That's right. So this is a good thing, no?

Yes. Of the twelve signs, are they pretty much balanced between men and women, or are some signs more chosen by females than males and vice versa?

It is pretty much balanced.

What about continents around the world?

No, it doesn't make a difference.

What in humans—once they are born in a certain place at a certain time—in any way at all attracts the energies of that sign more than someone standing next to them who is another sign? What is it in the human in the physical, or in any of the bodies attached to the physical, where there's this attraction to certain qualities of certain signs? Where is it located?

I see what you are saying. It would be located in the place where your spirit is often interacting with. That is the top of your head.

What we call the crown chakra?

What you call that, but it is physical.

It is! Can you say more?

Well, it is physical the same way as you might feel spirit influence upon you or your own body's needs requesting support or help during a time of crisis or difficulty. You might get a tingling at the top of your head, but it is actually transmitted in the light-sound matrix, which connects all life. But it is physical in the sense that it could be measured.

Transmitted from what or whom?
From all.

Transmitted from all? The energies of a certain sign are transmitted from all?
All is transmitted from all. There is no instance where anybody—and by "anybody," I am including animals, plants, molecules, atoms—does not have this connection. That is the law. So you asked about the astrological traits connecting, and I am just saying that it's no different than any other form of energy that transmits to your physical body to animate your physical body as you within the body. It's no different; it's just part of the overall.

You have to remember—and it's difficult, because astrology isn't set up that way in terms of a study mentally—that you come here as a soul to experience certain things. As a result, you find yourself *as* these signs, but you don't come here to experience the signs. It's the other way. You come here to have experiences, and in order to have those experiences in the way you wish to have them and to have the best possible opportunity to achieve what you hope to achieve, you find yourself *as* these signs. It is that way, not that you come here to be a Leo or a Gemini or anything else. What you want or need comes first. Astrology is an analytical means of understanding the physical nature of life in the way that most clearly expresses, helps and guides.

That is very good.
Feel free to quote me.

[Laughs.] All right.

There's an Acceleration Toward Benevolence

What area of space—or planet or star system or constellation—is the engine for Libra?
One moment. I don't know if this will do you any good: M4.

All right. We'll look that up. [Laughs.] In addition to the energies of the signs, there are cosmic rays coming in all the time from various places. Do any of those influence us astrologically in addition to the signs?

No, they do not have any association with the signs. Remember, signs are not external. One gets used to the idea that there is an externalization here, because you look to the sky (and I used it myself) and you say, "Oh, there are the stars associated with Taurus." So you get used to the idea that astrology is the study of something external, but it isn't. That is just a way to remember the signs.

Astrology is associated with something that is planetary, meaning Earth. But even then, it is a tool of analysis. It is not associated with other worldly factors. You have other tools of analysis. When you go to visit the psychiatrist or the psychologist to get some counseling or even to play that person in tennis, you don't say, "Well, I am going to play my ET-oriented buddy to find out what he or she knows and what's the latest from outer space." You just say, "I am going to play Doc and see if I can beat him this time in tennis." I am not trying to make light of it. I am just trying to say that it is important now to be focused on the planet you are on—to be here now—because you are immortal as a soul personality.

Whatever happens to you on this planet, you will go on, and that is a guarantee. When you go on, you will find that your life is easier because you are here in this school to learn something that you personally want to learn. So you are allowed to come here and given the opportunity to learn as much about it as possible. You will remember all of that when you leave this planet, and of course, at your deep-sleep level, you will remember it as well so you can be instructed by your guides and teachers. This is why you will sometimes repeat experiences that surprise you because you thought you were done with something. But you repeat it because your soul personality, that immortal part of you, isn't entirely sure that you got it all.

You can tell when you repeat something that is almost identical—and perhaps even is identical to when you did it before—that unless you are making some error in your life, most likely your soul isn't quite sure whether it got it all last time. This happens, by the way, with good things too, not just things that you trip over. In the future, it will tend to happen much more with good things.

Well, that's wonderful. Is the soul always aware of whether or not you get it? I mean, sometimes it seems like souls inflict a little more struggle on humans than is necessary.

Well, that's just on the basis of innocence, no more than that. So the soul isn't always aware of the impact on the physical body, but souls are being educated through the use of guide training. Whether souls will ever become guides or not, the training program to become a guide automatically puts the soul in a position where it must be in observation of guides working with other human beings on Earth as it is now—and you can see the suffering, even if you don't feel it yourself. So all souls are having this experience now and have been having it off and on for the past five to six years.

Now, I am not saying that you are all going to become guides. What I am saying is that the training is bringing to your soul's attention—your immortal personality, your soul—that things it had simply discussed with guides and teachers before have real impact on physical personalities on Earth. That is part of the reason things are changing. Souls have essentially had the "aha" moment and say, "Okay, I know enough about that. I don't need to understand every last innuendo about it. If it is causing my physical personality to suffer, I don't want that." So this guide training, whether you become a guide or not, is very helpful in that.

Sometimes you will sit in on guide training as a soul, meaning that you might see something going on between a guide and a teacher, and you are essentially in observation of it. You can tell, because your point of view is not associated with the others there, that you are in observation, because you are not really communicating, you are looking on. If you are looking on, you may be having guide training for yourself, your soul. You might become a guide, but you might equally be learning. So souls are being educated, and that is why the acceleration toward becoming your total being on Earth has taken off in the past few years. Souls have all gotten it now. It is like, "Oh," and "Okay, well, I know enough about that."

That is the most wonderful news! Is there a correlation between that and the fact that the Creator was told to start feeling our suffering and not just look at it—and now Creator is just beginning to feel what we feel?

No, because Creator had done this a long time ago and Creator has passed that on to guides and teachers to instruct all beings—meaning all souls on the planet, in this case referring to human beings, because the animals and plants all know it—of the physical effect. Souls being innocent and being insulated from feeling any discomfort, they need to be in observation so they can see the physical body's discomfort. The way to do that is this form of training—no direct correlation, but in terms of progression.

This is wonderful. I am so glad you said that. So there will be, as you said, an acceleration in the benevolent side of life, and the violence and the pain will fall away?

Yes, in time, because as you become more aware of your total being, you will be aware of the feelings of others. That is why I gave the homework that I did in the beginning, so that you can begin to express that. You can support the motion toward that as well as being supported by it. So that's in balance, you see?

Yes. That's why you were talking about it. Wonderful. That is the best news! That is great.

I am not going to talk too long today, and I will tell you why. You have things to do, and we are going to do another session tomorrow. You don't normally do these sessions two days in a row. It is a strain for both of you. So we will continue on for a little while, and if we can't finish today, we will finish tomorrow, okay?

You Are Being Protected from the Extremes of the Past

There is something I have read and heard people talk about: that when you find out what sign you are and you begin to learn about that and work with those energies, that the next step is to balance the sign across from that. Is that true?

It has been in the past, but now you can see that things have moved past that point, and that is what we have referred to, in that the communication between the signs has accelerated. You understand, this is not an abstract thought—the communication between the signs. What are the signs? They are people, so the communication between people is accelerating (ergo the homework again, as I said in the beginning). It is not just the sign opposite you, though that has been the case in the past. It is moving from that toward being all signs. So instead of being an opposite situation, you have something more circular in its support systems.

That's great! Then the being (I think Aries) said that within a few years the signs are going to begin to merge. So does that mean that the human incarnating will have a broader spectrum of potentials to choose from?

No. It will actually mean you will have less, because the knowledge of the souls—not only on Earth, but also those coming to Earth—is beginning to become more what I would call "empathic." As a result, the chances of picking some lesson that might result in suffering or the kind of instantaneous feedback that lets you know you are drastically on the wrong path, such as one might experience in some form of violence, is not going to be chosen by souls anymore, because souls have had the "aha." As a result, no, it will mean that less things will be chosen, things that are actually a bit more subtle, things that are definitely a lot more gentle—in short, the kind of lessons that might be more likely chosen to be experienced on another planet where things are more benevolent. Except that instead of learning that lesson over 1000 or 1200 years or so for a life on another planet, just as an example, you would learn that on an accelerated basis for your life here in 100 years or so. But it would not be an extreme thing. It is not that souls are going to be told they cannot pick extreme things; they simply won't, because of compassion. It is necessary.

You can imagine taking a rubber band and stretching it out a long distance. There has been that kind of a disconnection in order to insulate and protect souls because they are tender. But now, instead of snapping back, as you would do with a rubber band, the rubber band is slowly coming back to the point so that there is insulation and protection for souls but also the souls must then share that protection with their physical extensions, meaning you. Therefore, it is not that you are being insulated so much from life, but you are being protected from the extremes of the past. Thus, those extremes will be left in the past as you move toward the more heart-centered reality that is your true nature.

That's great! Everything you said is so heartwarming. Well, I am out of questions. What else would you like to say?

I don't have that much more to say. We will just finish up.

You Need to Let Go of Blame

In your world now, you are experiencing a lot of struggle and strife, and when you experience this struggle and strife, it is because of your cultures. Often your reaction is that you look to see who is to blame: "Who is keeping us from having a good life? Who did what when?" Then you can say, "You did it, and we are not having what we need because it's your fault." You will find that in order to achieve your natural balance to gravitate to who you are and to create a benevolent Earth, you will need to let go of blame, even though it might seem to be perfectly and completely justified.

I am not saying you should allow destructive people to run around freely in your society, but I am saying you will need to let go of blaming that results in punishment—because when you do punishment to people, say in prison, there is a tendency to forget about them. They are sent to prison, and whatever happens in there, "So what? They are being punished." But when you let that kind of thing happen and turn a blind eye to it, you experience prison effects in the world. You cannot turn a blind eye to anything nowadays. You must be totally aware that prison is meant for one reason only: to separate people who are destructive from the cultures they have been destroying. That is all. There is no need to punish further than that, for that separation and the life of the prison is enough.

So please stop punishing and allow each prisoner to have his or her own space. Recognize that the separation from the culture is enough. Remember, prisons and their original purpose were entirely to keep the culture, meaning the people, safe from destructive people. That is all. They were never set up originally to punish; this has just gradually evolved. Let go of punishment and just separate the people as needed. That is my statement for today, and you will find that this will allow greater balance so that these people do not come out of prison with revenge on their minds. Then everybody is in prison. You see?

Yes. Yes.

Good night. Good life.

Good life. Thank you so much. Thank you.

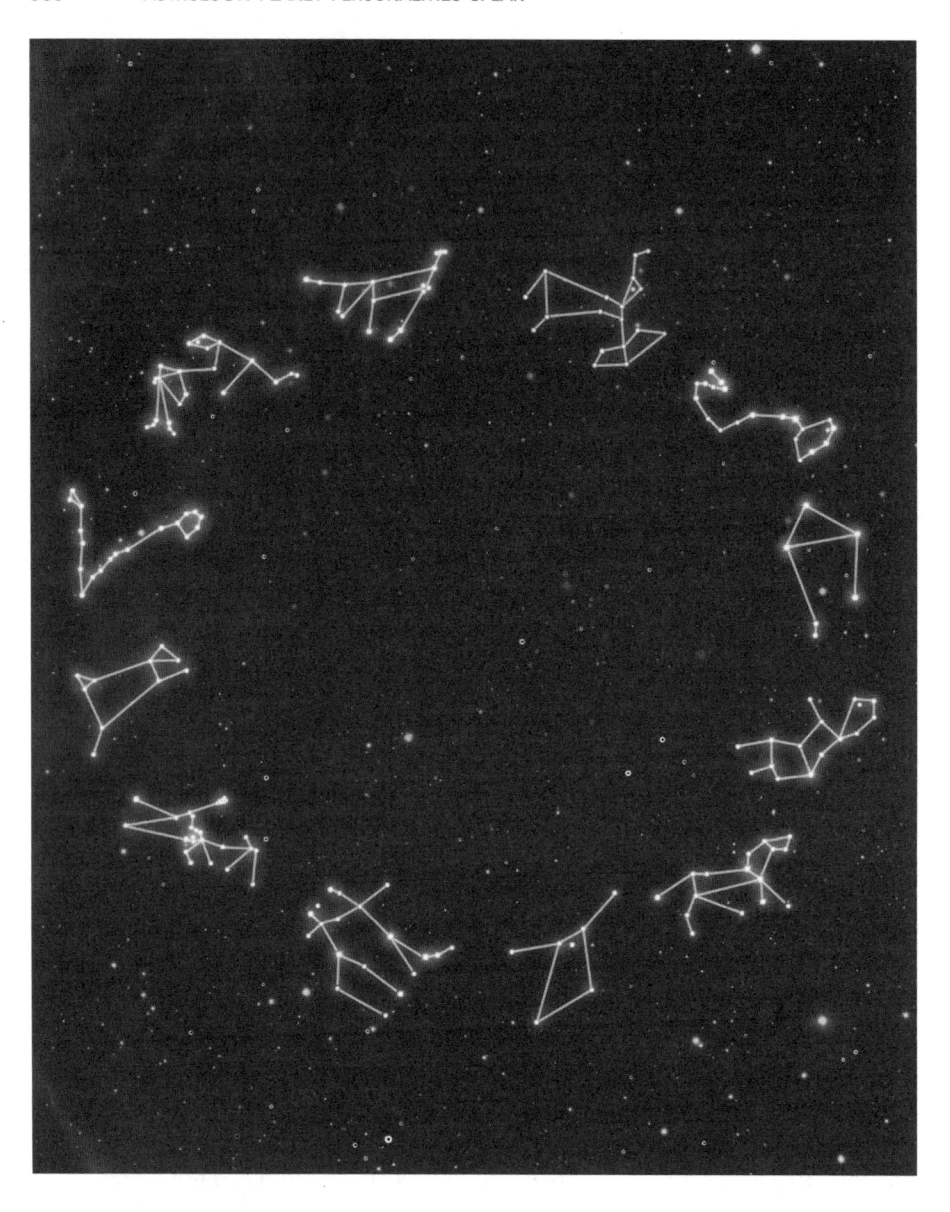

The 13th Sign

THE 13ᵀᴴ SIGN
Coordinates, Facilitates, Calms and Heals

October 2, 2007

This is the thirteenth sign.

Welcome!

Astrologers who have already begun to note the different characteristics of those born on the cusp will be able to more easily define the sign. It is a sign for the times on Earth; it is meant to function as the coordinator. People born during these times will have the capacity, just by their presence, regardless of what they are doing, to emanate an energy that tends to calm troubled waters and bring healing to the parties at the negotiating table. This energy is something they will be born with, so they do not have to do anything—it is just present. Conversely, if they are angered or agitated, their presence will have the opposite effect. So if you know this, you can prepare for the best usage of your talents, should you be born to that sign.

Now, here's an interesting side note: Those born on the first day of January for the past twenty years *already* have some of these qualities, and you may have noticed them with yourself, should you be associated with this birth date. This time on your planet has a great deal to do with the rediscovery of your true natural personalities, some of which are associated with the human species but others of which are associated with you as a unique individual. Much of what you have heard that is detrimental to your expression of your true nature will fall away. This does not mean it didn't happen; what it means is that the impact upon your day-to-day personality in every present moment will be lessened. In the past, you have thought about it. But in the future, you will be able to express your natures more easily and with comfort. Do you have any questions about the thirteenth sign?

The Thirteenth Sign Will Come to Be Known as the Peacemaker

It was my understanding that all the other signs were going to contribute some of their aspects to this.

I cannot speak about the other signs. What part of space might the thirteenth sign be focused through? I will tell you, though you have not asked—but you would have asked in time. It is focused directly through the alignment of the Sun through the Moon. So it is the only sign, I believe, that is directly associated with this solar system. You can see, then, that with that practical nature of the existence in which you find yourself, this sign has to do with grounding. That is the most important thing to remember.

But will it stay with only one day, or will it gradually expand to encompass more days?

It will always and only be that one day.

From midnight to midnight?

Yes. Well, from midnight to 11:59 PM—you could say, 11:59 PM and 59 seconds, but let's not quibble there. We will leave that up to the astrologers to determine. There is always a little bit of flexibility.

But how will that fit? Will it become a rising sign? That's a Sun sign, so how does it interact with the other signs in the traditional ways?

It will fit in. Astrologers will be able to do that easily. I know that you are saying, "Well, how can we figure these things out? Where will it fit in the ephemeris?" What you have available to you here, astrologers, has no need for the ephemeris. But I will say that on occasions when the Sun and the Moon line up—and you know about that—when that happens, the energy of the thirteenth sign will literally blanket the rest of the signs, meaning that in the positive sense it will do as I stated earlier, but in the negative sense, there is the potential for agitation.

So when those moments do take place, which are referred to as eclipses, then you will need to factor that in. The thirteenth sign will come to be known, however, as the peacemaker, and over time—and not a long time at that, after about seven years—the more negative quality will fade to being at most a minor agitation. Equally, the more positive quality will expand, and that is when the thirteenth sign will come to be known as the peacemaker, although the other signs may already have that quality.

So those will be the planets associated with it, then—the Sun and the Moon?

Well, those are the bodies of space, yes.

They would be called the ruling planets as the other signs have ruling planets?

I don't know about all of that. Astrologers will be able to figure that out.

You Have Always Had a Thirteenth Sign

Every sign, they said, has energy that comes like an engine from a certain place in space. What is the engine for the thirteenth sign?

The engine for the thirteenth sign has to do with all of the suns in existence in the Pleiades.

Wow! So you said that this energy has been making itself felt for about the past twenty years?

Yes. People born to this day have known or felt, especially during their adult life, a sense of being different. Even as children, they felt a little different—not to say that other children don't have this experience. But they have felt a little different, even if they were very much involved in the community as, let's say, an equal. Parents equally have noticed that children born on the first day of the year have something different about them. It has always been considered somewhat special in worlds of culture that are involved with the Gregorian calendar, since it is a celebrated holiday. But regardless of what calendar you use, it will be a most benevolent sign, especially after it gets more established— meaning after it's been present for about seven years.

Will there be a symbol associated with it?

I'm sure astrologers will come up with a symbol, something to do with the Sun and the Moon.

So you're a synthesis, then, of what? Of moons and suns, or of just suns?

I'm a synthesis of personality, just like all of the other signs who have been speaking to you. I am no different. Those stars and constellations were just by way of a reminder mostly—a system, visual, but so much of astrology is spiritual in its nature. Over the years, I believe there has been some attempt to turn it into a science to make it more acceptable, but it is not really that. It is much more enduring than that. Science has come, and some day it will go, as you know it now. Some day it will be more spiritual, more loving, and have enduring values, which will allow science to express only its benevolent and loving side, and not its potential for destructiveness.

But this sign, the thirteenth sign, other than what you said about the agitation, doesn't seem to have a downside, then.

I believe I expressed the downside.

You did, but it was minor.

Well, that depends. If you are on the receiving end of it, it may not feel minor. Also, you have to remember that we are talking about one day here, so we are not going to have masses of complexity. Understand that each day in the encompassed time associated with the other signs is different.

They each have a degree, right?

Yes. Here we have one day only, so a degree of simplicity might be expected.

What was the idea behind this, or what was the preparation for it or the impetus for it? How did it happen that we have a thirteenth sign?

Oh, you have always had that. It had just receded, and it was not directly involved in influencing you in your culture. You've always had it, just like you have always had more to your soul and heart and personality. You've always had that; it just isn't present. There are many things you might have in your life that are not present at any given moment, but as time and experience go on, they become more present.

Are there other signs who are not present?

I cannot speak to that; I am not aware of that. If you are talking about another planet, then certainly. But that does not affect you in any way.

There is another planet? What planet is that?

On other planets.

Oh, on other planets. Oh, right! We are only talking about that which affects us.

In order to keep the book practical.

More and More Astrologers Are Using Inspiration to Fill in the Gaps

If any group of people was ever practical, it's astrologers. They are some of the most practical, because out of necessity, they have to face the facts all the time. They do sometimes with a little authority, but well-intended, help others to face the facts as well. That is one of the good things about astrology. It's not rigid, it doesn't tell you what absolutely will happen, but it can tell you what is less likely to happen and what is more likely to happen—and even better, what you can do to prepare for it and how you can succeed no matter what happens. If that is not a helpful philosophy, I don't know what is, eh?

Definitely. So as more information becomes available about astrology, do you see that more people will be able to get the benefit of it?

Yes, I do, because more and more astrologers are using inspiration to fill in the gaps. As they begin to compare their inspirations, which some of them have done, then there is a tendency to see that, working independently, they have had the same inspirations. I would say that this would tend to give more credence to those inspirations, not just in the individual applications that an astrologer provided for an individual person getting a reading, but as a general rule of thumb involved in bridging the gap of the unknown. So, yes, I feel that astrology will become more a part of the day-to-day awareness of individuals, and why turn your back on it? It is not a religion, but it is spiritual.

You talked about an overlap. So what percentage of the sign that would have been called that person's sign on the first of January do you take into consideration, if any?

I would say that for a few years it will be up to astrologers to notice in terms of their observation. One thing astrologers tend to do is make notes, so most of them have notebooks that go way back. As a result, they might even be able to look at that material now and correlate it and see how things have been for January 1 babies.

This is not a new topic to astrologers. We are only adding this little bit of information, and it's not unheard of in fields of astrology—the idea of a thirteenth sign. I believe it may have even been speculated that the time for that would be in and around the first.

But I think what is not known so much and not considered too much is that it is only one day. That has been controversial in the past, that a sign would only be one day, but if it has an effect from time to time, as in the case of eclipses, it is not overwhelming. I will say that if you are born on that day and there is an eclipse anywhere on Earth—by the way, it is important to note this—you need to take it slow and easy that day. Don't do anything dramatic. If you are planning to climb Mt. Everest, start the next day. If you are planning to wash your car, don't do it that day—do it the next day. You may not have quite as much physical energy; you might not be able to think quite as clearly. Don't operate heavy machinery, and don't slice the tomatoes in the kitchen. In short, lie around. Read a book. Watch television. Visit with your grandchildren, but take it easy. Every other day when there isn't an eclipse, just live your life.

So would they radiate more of this peacekeeping energy on days of eclipses or less?

More, as I said.

More, okay. I don't know what else to ask.

There isn't anything else. I just wanted to come through with this because it's present, and the energy is present now as well here. I will make a closing remark. After all, this is really the kind of thing you would have toward the end of the book, if not at the exact end. But it is up to you. Put it any place you feel it is appropriate.

Your Prayers Have Not Gone Unheeded

You have all been asking for help, most often in prayers, sometimes in benevolent magic or other, and it is important for you to know that your requests have not gone unheeded. People who are born on January 1 are not here to be messiahs, but they will, out of their very natures, have the capacity to provide benevolent energy. You will notice it, especially parents. There will be a tendency sometimes to favor children like that. Equally, when they are upset or agitated, you will [chuckles] want to keep your distance a bit. But as parents, you will be able to whistle a happy tune, or if the baby doesn't like whistling—and sometimes they don't—you will be able to sing to him or her. It doesn't matter if you can carry a tune, just sing with love in your heart, and that baby will calm down. A song is particularly effective with babies of this type. Just make sure that the words are benign and benevolent.

So, learn some children's songs. There are lots of them out there. It is a time you are coming into now where all of you are easing toward your natural, native personalities. The thirteenth sign will be here to help that process now in the most benevolent way. Good night.

Thank you very much!

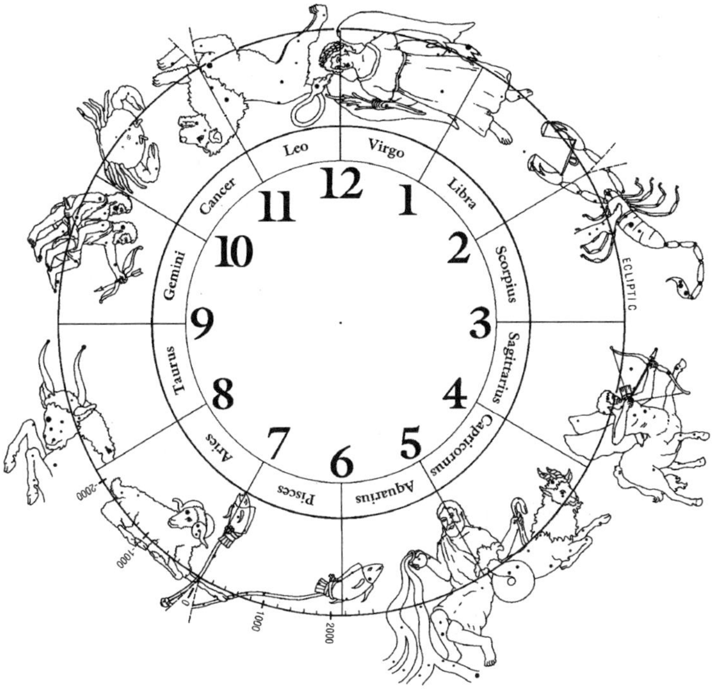
Leo
Virgo
Libra
Scorpius
Sagittarius
Capricornus
Aquarius
Pisces
Aries
Taurus
Gemini
Cancer
12
1
2
3
4
5
6
7
8
9
10
11
ECLIPTIC
-2000
-1000
0
1000
2000

♑ Capricorn
December 23 – January 20

CAPRICORN
Meanders, Makes Several Commitments and Enjoys the Journey

October 27, 2007

Greetings! This is Capricorn.

Welcome!

You Are Now Learning the True Lesson of Capricorn

Several years ago, Zoosh said that humanity had yet to learn the lesson of Capricorn before we completed this Earth phase of the Explorer Race school. Have we done that? Are we doing it?

You are doing it now. The true lesson of Capricorn has to do with understanding the meandering nature of humanity. Humanity is inclined to take the least direct course to any objective. Granted, this is not conscious, but the least direct course makes complete sense if you consider that, at least from your soul's perspective, you are here on Earth in order to experience the maximum amount that Earth has to offer in light of your personal offerings—meaning who you are and what you have to give. Regardless of what your mind thinks ought to be done, it doesn't make the least bit of sense that human beings would go from point A to point B. Rather, it makes sense only that human beings would go from point A to point Z, even if B is the objective.

Therefore, the lesson of Capricorn is not just patience; the lesson of Capricorn is to enjoy the voyage. Capricorn is not known for this, but it is important to reveal it, because all those who have Capricorn in their charts as a prominent aspect of their being will almost always find that it will take them longer to get there, no matter where they are going, how they are getting there or what their motivation. This tells you that the hidden aspect of Capricorn is not just caution, as it is deemed to be, but rather an intention to take as long as possible and to acquire as much experience as possible. So given that prominence in your chart, the best thing to do is to enjoy the journey.

When the timing in the calendar year is going through Capricorn, then in order to experience the best that this sign has to offer for all beings, it is absolutely essential that this is not a good time to try to rush from point A to point B. Take your time. Take it nice and slow, and just make the journey as enjoyable as possible. Have everyone who is expecting you assume that you are going to be late so you don't have to feel bad about it.

If it is that time of year, everyone assume that everybody else is going to be late as well. This way, nobody will get upset. This is not a good time to plan for that which operates by precision timing—with the possible exception of voyages in terms of technology, but you might see something you want to do besides going from one point to another on that voyage.

The Idea of Absolute Precision Has Tainted Astrology

That is so interesting, because I thought Capricorn was organization and structure, and yet you are saying . . .

The whole point of this book . . .

Is new stuff, yes.

This is not to say that we are something completely other than what the astrologers know we are, but this is intended to reveal the aspects of our personalities that are not commonly known and that for the most part have been lost over time. The reason astrology is not an exact science is that these aspects have been lost over time. This isn't because astrologers aren't ambitious and aren't desperately trying to uncover them; it's rather because the material is so deeply lost in so many crevices that in order to dig it up and reveal it, you have to go on this mining expedition, which is what this book is all about.

This book is an attempt to clean out the niches and say, "Hey! What's this?" That's the whole purpose of this book. As you know, it is aimed primarily toward professional astrologers, especially those who have been involved in this for a long time, and it is also aimed at people who are simply interested in astrology and have been at it for a long time, because if you want to be the finest astrologer you can be, you're going to have to move beyond the precision that is tainting astrology. Astrology has been tainted by this idea of absolute precision, which is a direct aspect of the cultural influence of science.

Before it was exposed to science, astrology in times past was deemed to be the most valuable philosophy—a "philosophy" being a means by which to live in the most benevolent way. But when you compare it to science, which is an error in comparison, then you have a philosophy up against a set of statistics and other aspects of required reproducible results. The whole point of astrology is that it is an *art* and a philosophy, so the astrologer of today must be able to reach beyond. You must be able to use your intuition. That is why we are attempting in this book to reveal as much of the personality of these signs as possible—so that you as the astrologer can be like the actor. Actors must not only say the lines convincingly but they must convince you that they *are* the part.

So, astrologers, you can see our personalities a bit in these words, and perhaps someday you will be able to hear this material—at least in snippets—in recording, and you will be able to *hear* the sense of personality. When you do that, you will thus be able to reach beyond the words themselves and understand that, "Well, if this sign represents itself in this personality and that sign in that personality, and if I as an astrologer adapt to that personality for a moment, then I might be able to produce knowledge and wisdom about this sign myself that is not written but is revealed in the characteristics of the sign that I am feeling now." That is the purpose here—the way I see it, anyway.

The Personality of the Signs Reveals Everything

Pluto is moving into Capricorn in 2008. How will that influence the next generation?

The wonderful thing about Pluto is that it really requires that you must change. Now, change does not mean that all that is working is thrown into the trash basket; it means that all that has the potential to work is thus more available to you. As a result, on the journey of Capricorn, you will be able to have the time to pull into your personality that which has been latent but present and have the opportunity to demonstrate those characteristics of personality and practice them and get better at them. So by the time Pluto transits Capricorn completely, you will be able to demonstrate not only prominent characteristics of your personality but latent ones with expertise. So welcome, Pluto.

Any other hidden or forgotten aspects of yourself that you can tell us about?

I think that's the most important one. That's why I tried to give astrologers the tip about my personality. This is so important—and I'm speaking about the other signs too, not just myself. Pay attention to the personality. That reveals everything. When you do that, you will reach beyond.

Many of you are doing that right now, astrologers—I know you are. But the book here, you see, is demonstrating the personalities. You will notice that some of the sign syntheses will be aloof, and others will be very forthright, and some will be funny, and some will be serious, and all of this kind of business, just like people. So use that and look for it in those for whom you are offering your skills. This book is intended to be studied, so I'm bringing that up on purpose.

Another aspect of Capricorn is that on that long journey of meandering to get from one point to another, Capricorn is known for not acting, you see—holding back, not making a commitment. But, in fact, one of the things Capricorn does on a regular basis is to make firm commitments. It's just that those commitments may not last more than an hour or two or three hours. But in that time, Capricorn is *totally* committed to something or someone. And after that time, Capricorn moves on to the next thing. This does not mean that Capricorn is not a committed being; it means that Capricorn has the capacity to be committed, on a single day, to many things—but in sequence, not simultaneously.

Ah, so when you have their attention, you have all of their attention?

If they give you their attention, then speak to them and don't look around and study the sky and study the ground. If they're looking at you, you have their absolute attention. If they're looking at the sky or looking at the ground, then you might as well talk about something else, eh?

It's Natural to Want to Discover Every Possible Thing

Does what you said about the journey and wanting to go to Z to get from A to B have something to do with the fact that we seem to be taking an extra fifty years or so to finish out our schooling here? We were scheduled to be done, and then another fifty years or so was added on to the completion date. Is it that we wanted to make sure we didn't miss anything? Is that a Capricorn trait?

It is, and that's why I brought that up, because it's a human trait. When I brought it up before, you may have identified it as a Capricorn trait exclusively, but I brought it up because the human being, regardless of ambitions to the opposite—"Oh, what's the quickest way to get there"—quite naturally (by naturally, I mean you are born to it) wants to discover every possible thing from one point to another. And I can prove that.

Look at what babies do. When they first start crawling, they crawl from one point to another. Any parent knows that the moment babies see anything of any interest whatsoever, they go for that. This tells you that that is a natural human phenomenon. It is also why, I might add, planned journeys that stop in many different places are so popular, because the idea of going to many, many places, even though you might be ultimately ending at some objective place, some goal, is a natural human trait.

This tells you how influential Capricorn is in the human makeup personality, not just at a certain time of year. Picture a bowl. Say there is a stripe across the bowl, and the stripe says "Capricorn." It starts on one side of the bowl, and it goes down to the base of the bowl and right up the other side. Now imagine that all the other signs are the same way, and all of the stripes are overlapping each other. So the human race is at the bottom of the bowl, not because you are lesser than, but because you are immersed, you are fully engaged in life. So you are always experiencing all the signs. All the signs are contributing all the time, even though it appears that as you progress through the year, you're going from one to the other. But, in fact, it's all the time.

Keep in mind that the calendar you are using now by which you calculate your astrology is not the calendar you were always using. So these signs are in effect for all calendars and all times. We're talking about something here that has to do with permanence, regardless of what calendar you are using. I can assure you, your calendar in the future will change completely. Generally speaking, your calendar, your clock and everything will be based on a rounder number. Probably you'll use a hundred, and everything will be broken up into segments there. This will be possible because of the technology you have today. In the past, when the Gregorian calendar was invented, such technology didn't exist, but with the kind of instruments you have today, you could re-create the calendar. I believe it's been done several times as an exercise. But I meander off to another side road.

[Laughs.] How Capricornish!

How Capricornish indeed!

[Chuckles.] We find some of the best stuff by meandering.

Yes! After all, who hasn't meandered in a library? What fun is it to go to a library and say, "Oh, I just need this one book"? You want to wander up and down, up and down the aisles and see if some of the titles don't jump off the shelf at you: "Oh! What is that about? Wow! Look at that! Oooh, look at those pictures! I want to see the inside of that." How Capricorn! It is with you all the time.

You Can Experience the Best from All the Signs All the Time

If you know that, you can experience the best from all the signs all the time. Think about it. What if you don't have to be born a Capricorn—or a Libra or a Sagittarius or an Aries? What if you don't have to be born under these signs in order to experience all the wonderful things they offer? What if you can experience all the wonderful things all the signs have to offer all the time? Because it is a bowl—don't forget the picture of that bowl. If you can remember that, then you won't say, "Oh, I'm this and I can't have that." You can be it all.

That's an awesome idea!

Thank you.

There are two issues I've heard about from previous signs. One is that in the future, the signs are going to be merging. Can you discuss that?

Well, from my point of view, I've already discussed it, you see. What I'm saying is, why wait for the future?

Aha! Merge them now.

My perception is that this is the case now, and it's possible to see that. I believe it is that way now. Even though I'm not saying to reject astrology as you know it to be, look for that as a factor, especially with the generation coming up now. Astrologers, take note that the generation coming up now is very hard to classify, even with well-experienced and wizened astrologers. You might be able to sit down in front of any adult or next to them on the bus, so to speak, and in a few moments of conversation, have a pretty fair idea of what prominent signs are in their charts. But with the younger ones coming up now, that's going to be difficult, because in one moment, you'll think, "Oh, they're this," and in the very next moment, you'll say, "No, they have to be that!" They are more merged than any other previous generation.

Astrologers, I think you're going to find this very exciting, because you're going to have the opportunity to re-create the chart. The chart will include all the signs all the time. Given that, you will be able to pick traits from different signs that are a portion of the person's astrological identity. It's going to initially require all of your efforts to move beyond the so-called science of astrology into the art of astrology. Now, I know you can do this, and it's not as if you haven't begun to experiment on it already, but give that more credence and give it more time. The merging of the signs, from my point of view, is a fact; it's not something in the future. And it's a fact because of this generation coming up now. Look toward them. The ones who are already demonstrating qualities like that are ten- or eleven-year-olds, but the ones coming up behind them, the one-, two-, three-year-olds, like that? Woo hoo! Oh yes, they are that now!

That almost makes me want to come back again and start over.

Capricorns Have an Ability to See the Truth in Others

There's also the thirteenth sign that some of them will . . . what? Inhabit or embody or be?

Yes, we've already gone past it. The thirteenth sign is leading the pack in the sense, one might say, from my point of view. The thirteenth sign, representing all the signs but in a single day—of having been born on the first, yes?—is actually spearheading the whole thing I just got done talking about.

The aspect of Capricorn that would be most prominent in the thirteenth sign would be the ability to trust in the moment any individual one would meet, because of the capacity to literally see into the soul of that person by looking at his or her eyes. Now, this is not something unknown. Anyone can do it, but most people don't trust it, whereas Capricorns do. This is part of the reason that Capricorns do not make casual commitments of a long range, because they can see into the soul of a person and they can tell—though they don't like to admit it because it creates complications on a social level—when a person is being straight with them and when that person is not. This is another reason why, if you have a business, you're going to want to have one or two Capricorn people around, especially during times of negotiation. Now, granted, people who wear glasses or contact lenses might make a little bit of a problem for them, but they can still look you in the eye and know when you are unsure of yourself—and also to know when you are lying, no matter if you have the greatest Las Vegas poker face ever known.

All Capricorns do not know this about themselves, but they have that capacity, and this will be contributed to the thirteenth sign. Look for this, Capricorn. You sometimes find that when you look in the mirror—and you have to do that when you're putting on makeup or maybe you're brushing your teeth or flossing them or something—you get unsettled and you think it's because you don't like the way you look in that moment. It's rather that you're looking at your eyes and you actually don't like the way you *feel* in that moment. If you know that about yourself, you will examine your own feelings and see if you can find out what your body is trying to telegraph you rather than assuming that there's something about your appearance that distresses you. This is also a big tip for Capricorns.

There are a lot of big tips in here!

Do you know why I can give these tips?

Why?

Because I'm used to meandering! If you're meandering, you find interesting things, eh? You don't miss them so much. Don't forget to take those side trips when on vacation, where that road looks interesting or that tree looks beautiful. So you'll be five minutes late—stop and look at the tree. Admire it. Take a picture. Then go on.

This Is Advanced Astrology

With all the new choices, we need the tool you're talking about—about accessing all of the personality traits possible to live on the Earth, right? Ways of being, ways of living, ways of thinking, ways of acting?

Ways of approaching things, yes. It's not so much the accumulation of wisdom but rather the ways of approaching things: whereas one person might climb up the hill one way, the other person might look for a trail to see if he or she can get up the hill by a means someone has already staked out, yes?

Someone in this book talked about the twelve families who contributed personality traits to the Explorer Race: different ways of being and acting.

Well, from my point of view, the families are associated with the signs, but the signs are really . . . you understand that the stars and the planets associated with the signs are just a way to give people a means to look up in the sky and say, "Oh, look; there's this," and "Oh, look; there's that." It's kind of a reminder. But from my point of view, the twelve families have to do with cultures from the stars and not—how can we say?—the Smiths and the Joneses. It has to do with the signs as you understand them. I'm not saying that there's a planet you would go to and everyone would be one sign or the other sign. There isn't that much of a lack of variety in the universe. Generally speaking, the universe is everything about variety, and you usually have to step aside someplace, go to the study hall, if you want quiet and sameness.

Could you call the signs archetypes of personality?

That's already been thoroughly covered in other books. I see no reason to go over it again. You understand, I am not trying to criticize your manner of plumbing the depths of astrology, but since we're aiming this book toward professionals and at least talented hobbyists, I think they will have covered that ground already.

Well, I don't know where the tidbits are hidden, so . . . [chuckles].

It's perfectly all right to meander. You understand, this book is not intended to teach people the basics of astrology. It assumes that you already know that. This book is for people who are past the basics, all right? This is advanced astrology, and that's why the signs, as we are calling ourselves, are sometimes a little strict with you, because we're trying to avoid the pitfalls of sameness. It is in the nature of the astrological realm to discover new aspects of this, that or the other. As a matter of fact, for most astrologers, it is a quest to discover what's new or how to understand something different or "is it possible to connect this to that?"

That's another aspect of this book that we hope to assist astrologers with. The addition of this information will allow many learned astrologers to connect signs in ways that have not been connected before. Also, in the earlier part of the book where the planets demonstrated their personalities, this will also allow those who study that and compare to the signs how the function, including the basics of astrology, can be fleshed out.

I bring this to your attention so you understand that this whole joy now as found in fictional novels as well as in movies and other aspects of media, to say nothing of religion, is largely about a quest, and the quest is ultimately for the answer. What is the answer? Some people think it's all about asking the perfect question, but I don't agree. I think it's about the answer that offers, as a result of that answer, the connection between the question you were going to ask and the previous one you just asked. Sometimes, questions are very difficult. One starts out with a thought, and halfway through the question, you realize that you don't have the ending for it. It's almost like telling a joke for which you forgot the punch line. The story is great, but where's the laugh at the end?

So be open to the fact that this book is intended to serve as a trail to discover that wondrous thing that the quest is all about. If you use the book that way, the book itself becomes the light bulb. The light bulb, in the cartoon, is the idea. It's not actually the object of the quest; it illuminates the trail. That's the purpose of this book.

Don't Overlook a Planet's Appearance

Is there anything to say about the planet who's associated with your sign—Saturn?

I would say there's not much that isn't known about that. I believe Saturn has perhaps been more probed than many other possible planets. Well, there are a few exceptions—I suppose the exploration of what Neptune's all about is definitely a mystery. But no, I don't think there's too much that hasn't been examined there. Of course, astronomically, there's a great deal to discover, and Saturn itself represents a mystery: "What's going on there?"

The more you have the opportunity to explore the appearance—not the actual planets, astronomers, but the actual appearance of the planets—the more you'll find that this is vitally important. Please don't overlook the appearance, and don't get attached to the colorization that computers might attach to the planet's appearance. Study not the details of the appearance but your personal reaction to seeing the best picture you are able to produce into that of a planet.

Check your feeling, reaction, not your thoughts. You know what your thoughts are: "What is that? I want to know more about that," curiosity, yes? But check your emotional, your feeling reaction when glancing at one planet. Then check your feeling reaction when glancing at another. But wait at least five minutes between glances so that you can examine it. Make notes, or better yet, make it a recording note: "I'm feeling this." You're not going to be able to identify your feelings with words very well, so describe the physical feelings in your body based upon a physiological description.

The whole purpose of the planets' appearances is intended to remind you of your physical feelings in your body. So what isn't really grasped or what is often forgotten—it's another piece of forgotten stuff, eh?—is looking at the picture of the planet and saying, "How do I feel?" The planet's appearance has everything to do with the way you feel physically, but this doesn't mean the planet is stimulating you to feel that. It means that your feeling is associated with the way the planet appears.

Here's something interesting, and that's why I'm telling you this, astronomers, okay? When many, many people on the Earth are having certain feelings—and for you this comes up at certain times of the year or during certain events—check the planets you can see well and see if they look different. Take pictures on the basis of what people are feeling on the Earth—you're going to see something. The planets change their appearance, albeit subtly, but sufficiently to note when people have significant feelings. And I'll tell you something else: If you can get an actor, someone who can portray a feeling or even a sensitive who can experience a feeling to a huge degree, sitting right next to you (it's best to have this person sitting on your left) while you are looking at a planet—it has to be a planet; it can't be a moon, it can't be a sun—you're going to possibly be able to note a slight change, possibly just as noticeable as the one I mentioned before.

If you can do that, granted, it will be controversial, but you're going to have some fun with astronomy that you didn't know you could have. Think about it. What are the planets really for? Scientifically, it would be this, that, the other thing. But you could reasonably ask yourself, as astrologers did years ago: "What are they for? Why are they here? Do they contribute to our personalities exclusively, or do we contribute to *their* personalities?" It goes both ways.

So getting back to my whole idea of the bowl, that's why I say that you all are all the signs now associated with the planets, you see? You are all the planets now. Since there are so many of you on Earth, you are affecting the planets more than they are affecting you. Think about it. I've wandered down the aisles of philosophy, and I can stimulate a thought. I'm not necessarily going to give you an answer. I want you to think about it.

Is this only possible with the planets, or if one looks at the area of the sky where the sign is, can it be extrapolated to that?

No, you don't have enough magnification to do that. So you have to look at what you can look at.

But if we could?

Someday. Think about it.

You are amazing! This is an amazing talk.

Well, what can I say? I'm a philosophical . . . I'm the old geezer you see wandering up and down the aisles in the library: "What's she doing? What's he doing? What are they up to? Oh, they're just looking for new things to do. They're looking for new subjects. They're enjoying the journey." This is something that I encourage you all to do. Don't be attached to what you can't be; know that you can be any of the things associated with any of the signs. If you know that, it won't limit your potential.

Potential is one of the things that's expanding right now, right?

Well, it's coming to your attention. It will really be noticeable with the young ones. They're not going to be comfortable with limits. Young ones have never been comfortable with limits, but the difference with these young ones coming up is that they're not only going to be uncomfortable with limits, they're not going to accept them! And it'll be noticeable in their personalities. Now, parents, don't worry. They're not going to be jumping off the roof, trying to fly like a bird—though it is your job to warn them not to—but they won't accept the limits of personality.

I know one like that who's three years old.

This is good. You already have the personal experience with it. Is that not wonderful? So you can say . . . well, you are a witness, eh? You can say right here, "Oh Capricorn, it's so true!" [Laughs.] Well, do you want me to give a closing statement?

Well, I can't think of anything else to ask right this minute, so go ahead.

Enjoy Your Journey through Life

Speaking to you here and to all of you out there as well, never feel bad because you don't have any more questions. Just wander down the aisle, look at some of those titles, and pull the books off the shelf. Before you know it, you'll have more questions than you know what to do with.

In your journey through this book to discover more about the human personality, remember also to recognize that every plant, every blade of grass, every animal, also has a personality. No one who's lived with animals on a regular basis believes otherwise. When you're journeying through life, don't be upset with yourself when you do not reach some goal at an arbitrary time. Say it's supposed to take this long to go through college but you take an extra couple of years. What's so awful about that? Think of all the extra books you read. Think of all of the subjects you were able to enjoy. Think of all the new people you met and with whom you were able to build friendships, some of which will last a lifetime. Think of all the funny things that happened. You'll remember those things, and the painful things will drop away. Enjoy the journey, remember the good memories, talk of the stories with your friends and loved ones, and experience life. Good night.

Good night. Thank you very much.

Cancer
June 22 – July 22

CANCER
Explores with Subtlety and Sensitivity, Looking at the Known in New Ways

October 28, 2007

This is Cancer.

Welcome!

Greetings. What would you like to discuss?

Well, the emphasis here is on what don't we know about you, so tell us about your sign.

The Explorer Aspect of Cancer Has Been Lost Over Time

Perhaps what has been lost over time would be the explorer aspect of this sign. I am known for sensitivity and all this, but there is another aspect. The reason for this sensitivity is to allow nuances heretofore unknown, which are clues of something you wish to find, to be detected. So in that sense, if you have Cancer in your chart as a prominent element, this would suggest that you are looking for something or desire to experience either something you may have overlooked in other parts of your exploration of lifetimes or something you feel is essential to be aware of in this time of history, meaning the historical development of the human being.

So you can see how that influence is so vitally important at this time when you are attempting to trace—not retrace, but trace—your steps to a more benevolent present via a means to connect with your benevolent selves without having to retrace your steps. You started out this whole journey in a very benevolent place. It is your intention, however, to literally find a new pathway to benevolence while going through the minefield of your past history. This is something that has not been done before. Of course, the reason it wasn't done before was so that souls do not become damaged beyond repair.

So this is suggestive, isn't it? It is suggestive of the fact that your souls are going to be working with other souls in the future who would be, by casual or even minute examination, damaged beyond repair. Not just one person or a group of doctors or therapists, but *every single soul* needs to know how to reach these damaged souls and needs to know how to reach them with compassion. Compassion can only be achieved on an eye-to-eye level through experience.

Therefore, you have gone through this minefield of history so that you could understand the experiences of those who have been so severely harmed and be able to reach them within the context of their lives. This would suggest, of course, that you are training to be guides, but there is more to it than that. You are training to become teachers who will help individuals to move through their historical re-creation—which is literally what will be happening—in such a way as the past history that they've gone through (the hard times, the suffering) can be proceeded through from the beginning without any of the mistakes that were made in that history, which lead to more suffering.

So it's like running an obstacle course, but instead of all of the pitfalls and obstacles that are engaged, struggled through and, I might add, suffered through, that doesn't happen this time. Do you know who those beings are whom you will be working with?

The Explorer Race.

Quite right. Do you know what history you will be working with?

Our history on Earth.

That's right. So you are going to go right back to the beginning as souls to work with your own kind, your own people, and help them to see, sense, feel, know where they took a wrong turn—meaning a more challenging turn—and help them to take the right turn. Do you understand that? You are training to redo it all.

Just Cancers or all humans?

All humans.

All humans on the planet at this time, or all of the Explorer Race?

All of the Explorer Race. Many are already trained, waiting, but then you have all lived that history, haven't you? So here you are going to go back to where you began your history on this planet. You are going to have the same lives that lived in those times in those places on that planet, and a conscious segment of you (who will be conscious of what is coming) will be working with those lives that you all lived that are unconscious—only you will have learned how to communicate with those lives at that time.

We will be guiding ourselves.

That's right.

This Is Your Third Time through Your Lives

So Cancer leads the way, or the archetype of "Cancer-ness" is what's coming out in all of us, or what?

The sensitivity. Remember, you are asking what's missing. What's missing is the explorer. How does an explorer find something that others have missed?

By being sensitive to it, by being aware.

That's right, by being educated and sensitive and aware to understand what the tracks mean, to understand what the smells mean, to understand what all the nuances mean. But even if that understanding is not present, to be able to use your instinct to make the best decision for yourself and others, because explorers blaze a trail, which others follow. Astrologers, if you know that, you will be able to guide people who have this sign prominent in their chart, because in the past these people have been largely misunderstood. Those astrologers who have this sign prominently in your own charts know how misunderstood you have been. So it is very important to explain the result of being this sign and the profound influence that someone who is of this sign can have on others—which is why people who have this sign prominently make such good teachers.

When do we start this? Has it already started? I mean, when we go back through our lives.

Yes. This is your third time. You are going to get it right this time. You have done it a couple of times already. That's part of the reason you have the sense of familiarity sometimes in situations that seem impossible to be familiar (speaking to everyone here). So the third time you go through, you are going to get it right. The first time you went through, you just lived it. The second time you went through, you were determined, when you went through it again, that you wouldn't make the same mistakes, but you didn't make any preparations, because determination alone is not enough. You need to know what to do and how to do it—and perhaps, most importantly, when to do it. In short, you didn't make the arrangement to have a guide you could work with whom you would pay attention to.

Even now, look at you, going through this situation. How often do you really listen to your guides? How often do you sit down and ask for guidance? How often do you pay attention to the subtlety of that guidance? The teacher can't appear in front of you like on a movie screen and say, "Okay, this is what to do—pay attention!" The teacher can only speak to you in subtlety; the teacher cannot speak to you most of the time in words. It is rare that you hear a word in your mind from a guide, but you might get a gentle touch.

Most often, the easiest way to access working with a guide is through physical feelings, because your physical body is the most sensitive aspect of your entire being when you are on Earth. You think of your souls as being sensitive, and that may well be true in the conceptual sense. But in the physical sense, your day-to-day experience is the physical world and your body is the most sensitive, so if you don't pay attention to your feelings, well . . .

The Job of the Astrologer Is Literally One of an Alchemist

This is mind-boggling.

It's the way I see things. I see no reason to explain it any other way.

So this is one of the reasons astrology is being stressed? It's a tool to help us see these pitfalls?

It's important, the job of the astrologer—one of the most important jobs and totally misunderstood in your time. Astrologers are expected to be conjurers, producers of magic tricks, and are treated as if they were literally performers, illusionists. But, in fact, here we have a profession that is the job of a teacher, a philosopher, an artist and, to some extent, a person who must change matter from one form to another. Do you know that word? I do not have . . .

An alchemist!

Good. The job of professional astrologers is literally one of the alchemist, where their job is to work with a human being who is not informed the way they are of the foundational elements, the cornerstones—of the knowledge and wisdom, to say nothing of the many nuances. All old-fashioned bricks are made of mud and straw: all of the little straws that make up a single brick, and all the bricks that make up the wall, and all the walls that hold up the houses, and so on. Astrologers must have knowledge of these things. Therefore, it is their job to change through influence, through education, through teaching, and then watch that brick transform itself into stone and then into iron—but not so solid that it can't be sensitive enough to move aside and allow the flower to spring up in between as one sees in concrete on a regular basis.

It's an important job, the astrologer! I am not trying to put pressure on you, astrologers. Rather, I am reminding you of the importance of your work, which will be a little bit more appreciated in the future. But right now, because of the contemporary fashionable interest in science, which is an important facet of technology and manufacturing, there is a tendency to overlook the bricks and mortar, which has to do literally with the construction and building blocks of life. It is not your job as an astrologer to create life, but most definitely it is your job to guide it and help it become the best form of life it can be in the most benevolent way and in the most constructive way.

Will going through this a third time be done out of time?

Yes, it is a repetition of time sequences. That's part of the reason people have an attachment to thinking about some of the planets in your solar system as being one way when they are clearly presented to you in another way. The most glaring example is Mars. Through the years, people have been determined to believe that Mars is a thriving planet with cultures and cities. Of course, it once was, and interestingly enough, it will be again on the next pass through. It just isn't this time, because it would be that much more of a complication, and you don't need that right now. Right now you have decided that if you are going to learn how to interact with a guide so that the guide/teacher is clear and you are able to understand the teaching—not only in quiet moments, but in moments of distraction—then you will need as little other distraction as possible.

Are you saying that we once lived on Mars as citizens or we lived on Earth when there were citizens on Mars?

The latter.

That was an awfully long time ago, in this time.

In this time, but it is the same sequence being repeated. It is not that difficult. It has to do with motion, but that's all.

Say more about that.

No. I am not going to tell you how to fly through time. It has everything to do with the fact that planets turn on an axis. How important is the axis and spin and the "vortexal" element in your lives—atoms, stars being born out of the center of galaxies? How important is it? It has everything to do with time sequences and motion, period. I am not going to go any further with it.

Exploring Has Everything to Do with Subtlety and Sensitivity

We are being told that we are coming into—awakening into or emerging into, whatever the phrase is—our natural selves. Do we start the next go around after we have emerged into our natural selves?

Yes, those of you who have not completed. As I said before, some have completed, and they are waiting, eh? Those of you who have completed will wait. It is not as if you are sitting around a table twiddling your thumbs. There will be things to do, but you will essentially be ready when the job is completed. The third time through won't take so long. You can see why, yes? Think of the errors that were made just in your recent history: errors that were made and resulted in World War II. Well, if those errors aren't made, it won't result in World War II, and you will just zip right through that time.

Your job is not to go back and relive every moment of time. Your job is to go back through it and avoid the errors that resulted in unpleasantness of *any* kind—not just the crucial ones. So this will have to do with the individual as well, on an individual level too, not just the catastrophic errors: no ball on the stairs to trip over and fall down and break your finger. Normally, you do that at the end of your life. You go through and you say, "Oh, if I had done this, then that wouldn't have happened," and so on. But you are going to live it, and it will be pretty quick.

You will want to keep doing that until you get it right. That way, when you go on and work with others in the galaxy and beyond in the universe, you won't have to go back and do it again. You don't want to go out and launch into the universe, and wish you had trained a little more after the fact. It is always better to train before. You see, when you are involved in major things, you can't be saying, "Oops." "Oops" doesn't cover it.

Since the effect is so far-reaching and it affects so many others?

"Oops" means you have to go back to the beginning and start over. So, you see, the whole explorer thing—it has everything to do with subtlety and sensitivity. After all, imagine how the smells of different flowers are. They are very different. What about tastes of different foods, yes? How do different things feel? Some are smooth, some are coarse, and so on. You have all of these means of sensing, but you must develop a practical and easy and simple means of physical sensing. So you find yourself as a soul in the ultimate sensing matter of your physical body on Earth: a physical place. What else would do?

Okay. I feel overwhelmed—this is so much new information.

I know. We are really giving you this material as a treat for slogging through the book, as it were. That's just a personal note, because I realize the book has been difficult for you. There you are, a novice at the very least in the astrological world, and you are attempting to assist in the production of all this vast material to support professionals in the field. But as the most wizened professional knows, very often it is the novice who asks just the right question because he or she is not blinded by the facts.

Well, that's why we come to Earth, isn't it, to forget who we are and be ignorant?

In the larger picture, yes. That is also one of the important aspects of wisdom. Astrologers, expect to have great knowledge as you move on in your profession of astrology. Expect to become wizened and sought out by those who wish to know more of what you know. But always remain open to novices who, although they may ask questions that are very basic most of the time, will from time to time come up with a question that prompts you to think about all the vast wealth of knowledge you have acquired in a completely new way. So always be open to the young ones, or even the old ones, when they wear the garb of a novice.

All right. So this treat—I really appreciate it.

Cancer Stimulates Looking at the Known in New Ways

As to the sign of Cancer itself, is there anything more pertaining to that sign that we can glean from you?

Yes. There is one more nuance that might be useful to know: the ability to reach beyond the known and to take what is known and look at it a new way. This is really why I brought up the whole point about the novice, because novices do that in ignorance, meaning they don't know that they don't know. That is the thing the Cancer energy can do. It can help to stimulate recalculating and rediscovering that which you thought you already knew absolutely. How many times has this been reexperienced in science, teaching, philosophy, the arts? That is why people with the Cancer sign are often so associated, not only directly in these fields, but indirectly—very often not getting credit but having spoken up to say something, some question, to say, "Well, what about looking at it this way?" At first, there is laughter, and then silence when the great minds ponder the depth of meaning behind that question.

That is why there are whole groups of people trying to reconsider how to ask questions, because the answer is not always as important as the question. The question can help you to see something in an entirely different way. It is a very important aspect of the sign of Cancer. For example, consider water, perhaps one of the more fascinating elements on Earth. When you see it in its liquid form with the Sun reflecting on it, it is amazing, and yet at night, it is dark and only slightly reflecting and mysterious, what's underneath there. Yet when it is ice—clear ice at that—it captures the light and displays its colors, and when it is a snowflake, it takes on myriad different forms, practically never the same form twice. Is that not mysterious?

It's one of the joys of being here.

It is the gift, which is why it is not entirely impossible to get souls to come here.

The promise of the joys and the gifts and the learning against the discomfort. It's quite a balance.

Yes, and of course, the whole purpose of the next pass through is to make it possible, with all of that training, to have all of those joys without any of the discomforts. Then one can ultimately, when one goes out to teach and influence in other parts of the galaxy and thence the universe, no matter what one experiences . . . can you even imagine all of the different cultures and beings whom you may wish to meet and who, of course, will want to teach you? You will welcome them most of the time. Yet do you know the primary way you will teach them? You perhaps think that you will tell them about something, but no. The primary way is that you will help them to think about what they already know in a new way by asking the right question.

You're here to learn how to ask the right question, not to learn the answers. When you think about that, it makes complete sense. Can you imagine, even for a moment, the astronauts going to some planetary culture that is vastly more advanced, where the technology is so advanced that it is beyond your capacity even to consider how it might have been created, much less practiced. What can you do? You will do what you have always done. You will ask questions, and ultimately you will ask a question where everyone will stop and look at each other and rethink what they already know. You can't teach these people anything. They know vastly more than you know, but you can help them to rethink what they do know in a different way.

That's a wonderful explanation, because all we were told before was that we would radiate an energy that would cause beings on other planets to change, but it wasn't explained how that would work.

You know how it is with the odyssey of these books. Meandering trails do uncover the stray acorn.

[Laughs.] That's what Capricorn said yesterday.

Living on Earth Is All About Influence

Well, this is wonderful, and these traits you mention will be part of what you contribute to, not only all of the signs when they merge, but to the thirteenth sign, right?

Oh yes, of course. The thirteenth sign is basically a sphere with open windows so that it has full access to all the other signs and beyond. Beyond is primarily a flow of inspiration, not unlike a light would be directed toward a prism and out would come all these different colors. Is it the same light, or is it another? Scientists and artists ask that. Some people are still asking. When the thirteenth sign shows up, that discussion will renew.

Only one out of 365 of the people being born will be that, or will there be more people born on that day?

There might be more people born on that day. I was just going to fault your math. You can't assume that. As a matter of fact, even if you looked at the birth statistics now, you would discover that it doesn't break down like that.

Some days are more popular.

That's right.

Based on astrology?

No, generally based on the weather. We won't pursue that any further. Those of you who live in winter climates get the joke. I will finish up. Those of you who are reading this book have noted that it is truly an adventure and an exploration. I applaud you for your interest in astrology and appreciate your desire to know more, not only about the planets' impact on the lives of human beings, but even your impact on the planets. For this life you are living on Earth is all about influence: how you influence each other and how you are influenced by the myriad of aspects that surround you at all times.

Ultimately, you will take that influence out into the universe and plant it here and plant it there, and someday your family will sprout all over the universe. One place they'll look like this, and one place they'll look like that. Ultimately, they will all someday be able to ask the perfect question, which goes something like this: "Why?" or "How?" When you look at your own history, so much of it can be moved from one point of self-destructiveness to another point of benevolence simply by asking why and how. May you have the most benevolent journey in all ways. Good life.

Thank you. Thank you very much.

♏ Scorpio
October 24 – November 22

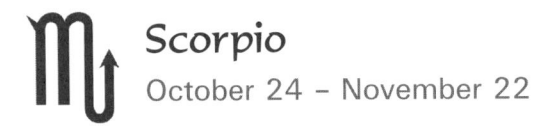

SCORPIO
Unifies, Supports and Re-Creates

November 3, 2007

This is Scorpio.

Welcome!

It May Be Possible to Re-Create the Missing Links of Astrology

I will say a little about something that has been lost. There is a hidden meaning behind Scorpio and its sign in the sky. The hidden meaning is, Scorpio is that which unites all the ages of the human being on Earth and your evolution from what you started out as—which was a completely homogeneous, spiritual soul entity that was adaptable to many forms—into what you now are, which is the last of the forms that you will occupy before returning to that homogeneous entity again. This is not to say that at the end of your lives on this planet you will suddenly be one being, but most of you will not take any form other than a variation of the human form before you join that single being for a short time. Then you will decide what to do after that.

Scorpio, in terms of the true chart then, is the last sign if one looks at the chart as a calendar instead of a wheel of life—for that is truly how it plays out. Even though Scorpio does not finish your calendar year, it announces that the form your souls will take has established itself as this human form until you regenerate as one being. That has largely been lost in your time, but it was well known about 4,000 years ago (maybe 4,200 years ago) in Egypt and a few other places with groups of beings who studied the stars. Most of their knowledge and wisdom has been kept hidden, and unfortunately, a great many of the clues they left behind for others to follow in certain objects have been largely looted from various places and spread out all over the world in various private collections. Would they be put together again, it might be possible to place them in their original situation as they were once in the Great Pyramid.

Then an astrologer surrounded by nine human beings who could translate energies from beyond—meaning spiritual energies of a totally benevolent form—would direct that energy toward the astrologer sitting in the middle, surrounded by these various objects. That astrologer would then be able to provide every last one of the missing links of astrology and also answer most questions having to do with the past, the present and the future of the human race as you know it on Earth—not all over the universe, but how it applies to you.

I am saying this because it may be possible to re-create some of that energy, and I know people have been trying for a long time. But it would take a very wise astrologer not focused only in one field of endeavor, and you would need a minimum of three shapes. You would need a shape in the form of an isosceles triangle, you would need an equilateral triangle, and you would need a sphere. Those three shapes you would have to move around in the king's chamber until it feels just right. Then outside of those three shapes—and the chamber is not that big, so you would be apt to feel it—you would have the nine individuals, and in the center of that, sitting in a comfortable chair, would be the astrologer.

I am passing on this information because I feel in your time, with a concerted effort, this can be done. But it must be understood that this is not a mental pursuit; it is a spiritual pursuit. All the beings in there, including all the human beings inside the pyramid anywhere during that time, must have a great love for human beings in general. You don't necessarily have to be in love with any human being, but you could. But you must have a love for the human race and a general benign outlook upon life on Earth. This does not mean that you wouldn't have likes and dislikes, but that aspect of your personality must be well and thoroughly deep and ongoing in your practices. You don't have to be saints; you just have to have a desire to improve the quality of human life. This has been tried, I know, but I wanted to add my comments to it.

Scorpio, then, is intended to be that which unites, that which supports, and that which helps to re-create. I have touched on some aspects known by astrologers, but that is important, because I know astrologers, just like everyone else, need to be encouraged that they are on the right track.

Can you say what the other symbols are?

No. I am just giving you those three, because you may be able to do it with those three. It really wouldn't make any difference if you had the other symbols, because it's the materials they are made out of which cause them to work so well, whereas the symbols I mentioned could be made out of anything, though I would recommend something perhaps like granite. It doesn't matter what color. A darker color might be good, but it doesn't matter. Don't feel like you have to bring crystals, as that is actually a disadvantage. A darker-colored granite would be fine. It can have just about any appearance—it is the shape that's important.

Can you say what the other symbols are made of?
   Something not of Earth.

Do the people who have them understand the significance of them?
   Some of them do, but most of them don't. Let me be clear (your question wasn't): The people who have them do not understand the spiritual significance. Some of the people who have them understand that the material is not like anything found in a natural state on Earth, but not everybody knows that. It cannot be made to work using technology. You can't force it. It will only work with and surrounded by that benevolent loving energy that many people are able to assimilate and pass through them.

The Connection to the Unifying Element Is Important

Can you say more about Scorpio being the final sign or the unifying sign? How can we work with that?
   You can work with it knowing that, when you pass through the time of Scorpio, which I believe you may be in now, your awareness of not just where you fit into the wheel in astrology but where you fit into the wheel in your own physical family and where you fit into it in your community, is just as important. Try to coordinate, astrologers, those social aspects as you usually do, and once you have coordinated that in a graph—or in a separate wheel, as many of you do—then see if you can not only tie it, connect it, to the position of the Sun and the Moon, as you do, but also to the position of Pluto—which, as you often know, is not always something that is completely accurate. When you do that, you will have a better understanding, astrologers, of how you can use that material I just stated before.

   The connection to the unifying element is all-important, and it is more easily understood, of course, when you look at someone's personal life. You can understand the unifier is there, including their immediate community. But it is also important to understand it in light of your planetary connections: the Sun, the Moon, the Earth and Pluto.

   Pluto, after all, is the last place you are likely to get to when you are exploring your own solar system, and it will be on Pluto, by the time you get there—a combination of "by the time you get there" as astronauts and what you find there—you will then understand how you came to be on Earth. There will be a means—nothing written, nothing that you can pick up and say, "Oh, I understand"—to know completely by then. So those are all the hints I am going to give you on that. I am taking into account, of course, that astrologers can read between the lines here, and I am not going out of my way to explain things that astrologers already know.

Scorpio Can Leave an Imprint for Others to Follow

I read that Scorpio is the most powerful sign. Do you agree with that, or can you comment on that?

[Laughs.] I would say, given the nature of the unifier, which is the way I see Scorpio, that this might be why the powerful aspect comes in. This is why, for those of you who have Scorpio as a prominent element in your chart, you must recognize that what you often feel as enthusiasm or vigor, others might feel as overpowering. So the way to use this, of course, is to take on some project that will allow you to express the multi-faceted capacities you have and you can leave your personal imprint on it.

Try always to leave an imprint. It will improve the quality of life for peoples in a way that they appreciate, not just in a way that *you* think they ought to appreciate. This is very important! It is easy, when you have that physical energy within you, to believe that whatever thought or philosophy you are involved in at that time of your life, or that you personally are involved in, is the most important truth in the land. But one of the big challenges you will face as a person who has, not just the Sun sign Scorpio, but anyone who has Scorpio in their chart, is in allowing others to have their beliefs and encouraging those beliefs in them. That is not easy, because very often you will feel filled with the awareness of whatever you hold to be dear to be the absolute truth.

So I believe that Scorpio may be considered to be a powerful sign, because sometimes, in the past, people have left an imprint for others to follow. Even though it may have been corrupted by others who came after them, it had a lasting effect. But also, the energy of Scorpio has a tendency to be unavoidable, noticeable, felt, which is why I am speaking to those with Scorpio in their chart in this fashion, because it is important that you apply that energy in ways that do not cause you to give up. So don't take on something that is so impossible only as yourself. Learn to work with others compatibly, and you will appreciate the influence that you are meant to have, even if you don't get direct credit for it. Others will know, and that's what counts.

Can those who don't have Scorpio prominent in their charts during this time of the year ask for this energy in their endeavors?

You don't have to ask. Since you are *in* this time of year, it is more available for you, but if they are qualities you wish to have only during this time of year, then it is available. If you wish to have those qualities during the entire year to the best of your ability, I recommend you read about Scorpio, because you cannot take in only the positive qualities. You will get it all. Of course, it cannot overpower the other aspects of your chart. It is in the nature of the re-creation of one being that you all blend, of course, but it's always done very slowly and gradually. Nothing happens just like that. This is not to say that you don't have sudden events, but when it comes to an inner restructuring of your soul and thought—personality, all of that—that has to happen very slowly, and Creator has patience.

Is some of what you have talked about going to be your contribution to the thirteenth sign, or is there something else?

I would say that my contribution to that sign has more to do with the blood—in the person's veins, the actual physical, that thirteenth sign. While the blood will seem to be like everybody else's technically speaking, these people will have the ability to sense through the use of their own fluids the general countenance (I don't know if you are still using that word), the general sense, the general feeling thoughts of others—not generally with individuals, but with groups of others. In that manner of speaking, you might walk into some place where you don't know anybody and get a general feeling of what people are sensing, feeling, thinking—that kind of thing. That will be in the blood.

Is that something Scorpios do now?

No, because it will work in concert with the entirety of that sign. We are talking about that sign. It will work in concert with all the rest of the contributions to that sign.

Amazing!

Well, some people can do this now. But we are talking about how everyone who is that sign is going to have that capability.

Your Other Forms Have Helped You to See and Feel Life in Different Ways

Can you say something about the other shapes or forms that souls who are now humans have inhabited in the past as part, I assume, of the Explorer Race? I didn't know that we had inhabited other forms.

Other than human? Of course! [Chuckles.] Can you imagine for a moment that you haven't? Of course you have inhabited other forms.

As part of this experiment?

Yes. Through the word description "karma," you have been told that you have accomplished all of the lessons there—not everyone, but as a total population you have accomplished that. How could you possibly do that if you were only a human being? You must be able to have perspective, and that perspective only comes when you are in other forms. You can understand that completely. You may live with a pet—a dog, a cat, a horse, something—and you would not have the perspective of that other being. Even though a practiced individual, a shamanic person perhaps, might be able to briefly share the form of a beloved pet—not just anyone, but a beloved pet who is cooperative—this would be only temporary. No, you have to be other forms so you can understand things. That is my perception, and this is why I believe that very often—not always, but very often—one sees in astrology other forms of life depicted as their sign.

You see other forms of life depicted just so that you will be reminded that you are not only supposed to see through your own eyes and understand the world through your own eyes. You must be able to see at least in moments, so that you can feel the life through the eyes, heart and soul of another being. Some of this training is available, of course, but very often you will experience some variation. It won't look exactly like on Earth, but it will be some variation of a life on another planet that will look perhaps in some ways similar to life forms you have on this planet, and you will then be provided with greater depth in your soul.

This is a lot of the explanation of why, when you come here to be a human being once again on this planet, you will have depth sometimes, know how to act and interact with other forms of life—even though no one ever taught you that from the moment you are born on this planet up to the point of that interaction. It is often found out in the wild, in the country, in the woods, at sea and in places where you might encounter other forms of life. It isn't always written about, but it frequently becomes a story within the family: moments at sea, things that become legendary. "You were out at sea on a sailboat crossing the ocean, and there was a stir in the water. Suddenly next to the boat you were surrounded by dolphins, or perhaps there was a whale there, and it just floated on the surface with you. And you felt after a long loneliness—passing from one point to another in your sailboat on your own—that you were not alone, that there was another being there who purposely sought out your companionship for a few moments. From that point on, the voyage felt much better, for even though you couldn't see them, you knew they were there"—like that.

So have we experienced life on other planets with some of the beings I talked to, for instance, in the animal soul book—beings who are energizing, inhabiting, creating or having to do with some of the beings we call animals on this planet?

I am not familiar with that book, but I think that you could extrapolate something along those lines.

Thank you.

The important thing to remember is that, in order to understand how astrology works, you have to recognize that everything is important and that clues are often given in ways that are not associated with language. Think about it. Say you are an astrologer living 300, 400, 500 years ago, and you are speaking a language that everybody else speaks but you also can think for yourself. You might consider, "What if people in the future don't understand my language? What if I am not able to leave anything written that is likely to last?" "That seems likely," you would say.

Even today it is hard to have things last. "What can I do?" You will try to leave a picture in such a way as it's more likely to last. The nice thing about astrology is that most astrologers have a real burning curiosity about their subject and are always turning over just about every stone they can find, alliteratively speaking, to find out more. So if you leave a picture of this symbol or that symbol associated with a sign, someone will find it.

An example would be that tarot cards are associated with the different signs?
Well, you understand that the designs on tarot cards are not fixed. There are a great many different designs, so I am not going to go into the tarot, since that is not my field. I am, after all, a synthesis of a sign. I have some access to this or that, but if you want to talk about the tarot, you will have to speak with somebody else.

Well, the most important one then, as you said before, is the symbol of the sign itself.
The more lasting symbol. Symbols change over the years, but the more lasting symbols . . . try to keep in mind that if animals are depicted, especially animals you still have in your own time, if you observe them and their personalities (even though you may not necessarily think of them as pets or friends), then you will sometimes get a partial idea of what the astrologer was trying to say. But sometimes there is more to it than that. After all, especially in times gone by, in the past, astrologers who were able to function and research their topic almost always had to have sponsors, and the sponsor would want this or that from the astrologer. So you couldn't always leave the message exactly the way you wanted to. That is why this book is important, so that we can fill in some details (speaking for myself and the other signs and the planets here for a moment).

The Scorpion Has Nothing to Do with the Sting

Is there anything, for instance, about the symbol of the scorpion that has been lost or that present astrologers are not aware of?
I think we tried to cover that at the beginning. But I would say in terms of that particular creature being applied to Scorpio, while those of that sign and those who have friends of that sign and so on might say that this is an aspect of the sign, I cannot say that that is so. It is no more an aspect of that sign— meaning the sting—than it would be of a great many other signs. That actual aspect got associated with that sign because the sponsors at that time of the

astrologers who put that sign up there originally were living with somebody who was that [laughs], so it is a rather mundane explanation.

But the secret of it, which is what you are asking about, has to do with the durability of that form of life, the scorpion. It is durable—it can live in the most extreme situations and it can survive. Why was that chosen? After all, the astrologer might have had to pick something like that in order to amuse his or her sponsor, but it was also picked because that particular creature can not only survive a great many hardships but does survive a great many hardships—meaning lives—and has to adapt to different conditions because they have a message to give. That's the message I gave at the beginning of this talk.

There is evidently some place in this galaxy that provides a motor for the energy of Scorpio, right?

Generally speaking, my feeling is that the seas of the worlds' planets provide that energy, so it is not just one place. It's any place with a sea like you have.

So specifically Sirius?

No, any place. But that is really known by astrologers—well, it's a slightly expanded version of what is known by astrologers, but only slightly. I think some of your other signs have glossed over areas that were largely known by astrologers, and in that case, I don't know everything [chuckles]. I have some information to offer but perhaps not as much as you would like.

Oh no, you are wonderful, very clear.

I can finish up.

There are the energies of astrology, but the Earth moves around the solar system, and the solar system moves around the galaxy. The galaxy moves around the Central Sun. How does our moving through space affect these astrologic energies? Is there any effect on them?

You see, I cannot go that deep. That is why I was going to finish up, and then somebody else was going to come through. You can ask that kind of question of them.

Oh, all right. Thank you.

Astrologers: It's Important to Be Encouraging

Astrologers, your job, as you know, is to interpret this vast wealth of information that you already have and—adding in this small amount by comparison from this book—using your own personal resources, insights and inspirations as you gauge the person sitting in front of you, looking at his or her eyes, looking at what that person does with his or her hands. Try to sit at a desk or a table so that the person's hands are more likely to be visible to you. What is that person doing? What is his or her body language? Or perhaps just be in a situation where you can see that. Perhaps the person is sitting in an armchair or something.

Your job is to interpret all these things, to gauge to the best of your ability what aspect of this or that sign is likely to be an influence in these people's lives. Then, of course, if you possibly can, guide them toward the path that is beneficial for themselves and others, which I know you do. Don't focus too much on the pitfalls. You can warn them that this could happen and that could happen, but don't spell it out. People have a tendency to want to have details on the worst that could happen. The trouble with that, as you well know if you are experienced, is that people have a tendency then to overcompensate and to miss opportunities. After all, sometimes when things happen that may be unpleasant, it is very brief, it is over quickly, but you may have gained tremendously in new friends or companions as a result—as might occur in, say, an event, weather or earth changes that do not have a catastrophic impact on an individual's life. But that person participates, helps other people and so on, and afterward has many new friends.

So try to put it into that context, if you are not already doing it. This doesn't mean you have to pretend that bad things don't happen, but it is important, especially with the generation coming up now—the youngsters, really young—to encourage them, because they will have a tendency to re-create the world in a wonderful way and they will get discouraged at every turn by history and more ancient forces. You can be an influence that is not only benevolent but encouraging. Take that into account, especially when you are speaking to the younger set. Encourage them as much as possible, and that will be one of the best things you can do. Good life.

Thank you very much! Thank you.

✼   ✼   ✼

Greetings.

Greetings!

I am the overseer of the astrologic mathematical principle. I cannot speak long, the energy being difficult for the channel. But I will say that when you look at a map, and on the map you see the arrows pointing to the different directions, and you consider the geometry involved to get from one place to another with the use of the stars, remember that it is in the nature of astrophysics to not only guide but also to provide.

You can be anywhere on the planet, and the stars are in your lives. The stars on and around your lives—the stars, meaning in the sky, wherever you are on the Earth, surrounding the Earth—are all in a position even with the movement of your planet, of your solar system, of your galaxy. The stars that you see at all times hold not only the key to understanding your personal life through the assistance of the astrologer. But also, in the long term, they act as map guides to help you to get from one place to another—whether it is across the sea, down a river, across a continent, or from one planet to another. Let the signs, whether they are in the sky or in the personality of another, lead you inevitably toward your own hearts and souls.

You have been placed on this planet to not only discover the true nature of the mechanisms of life but to learn how to be the most beneficial beings you can be. Appreciate the other beings on your planet. Learn their value—not just what they can do for you, but what you can do for them, even if it is just to leave them alone. Understand that all has been placed in the exact position it is in, including all life, so that you can achieve this goal. Good night.

Good night. Thank you!

✷ ✷ ✷

Robert: Hello? It's me [Robert]. The energy was really difficult. I had a feeling that they were giving me this picture. It looked like a picture of a wizard or something, with a garment that had different signs and pictures on it. It's funny, but they were giving me that picture of the being at the end.

We've come to the end of the book—thank you.

Okay. Good night.

Good night.

609

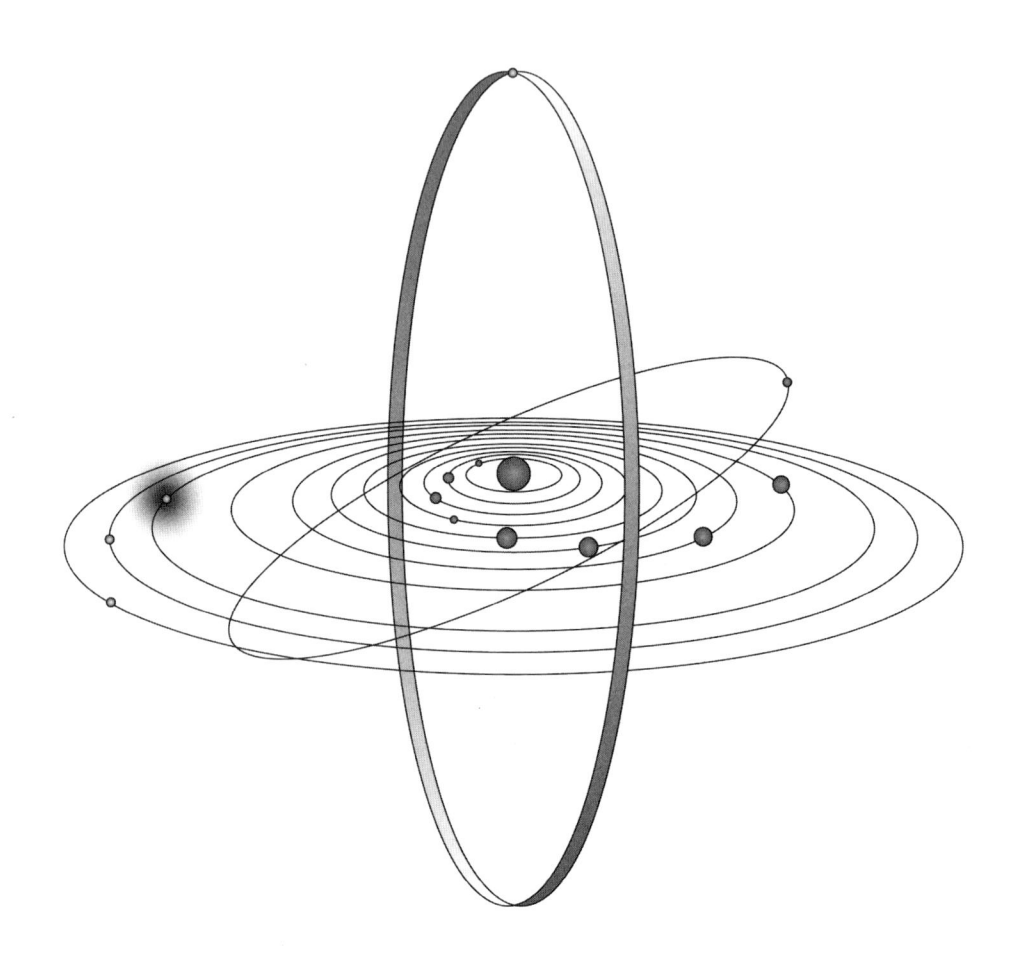

The 10th Planet

THE 10ᵀᴴ PLANET
Being Able to Ask the 10th Planet for Wisdom Is Your Reward

November 21, 2009

Greetings.

Greetings.

Your Responsibility Is Going to Be to Guide Other Planets through Discomfort

The Tenth Planet is a compendium of your learned lessons. This means that you will not be able to positively identify it until you have completed your task from whence you came. Most of what you have to do has been done, but you still have to find your way back to the beginning from whence you started, albeit a further cycle on, and you need to do so in a benevolent way. So jumping off a cliff won't get you there—and I mean that figuratively and literally.

I want everybody to pay attention to that. You will have to find your way there benevolently, and it won't be easy, because as it says in the famous book, "The lion will have to lie down with the lamb," and more importantly, the lamb will have to lie down with the lion. So there must be compatibility, comfort and welcoming. This means that you will have to personally be comfortable with (not just tolerate) welcoming those whom in the past you would have never welcomed. Everyone will have to do this—no harm to anyone. It can be done and it must be done for you to complete what you came here to do. I'll tell you why.

You started off in complete benevolence, and even though you've moved on and the cycle has come and gone and you're attempting to close the loop, so to speak, you still need to return from whence you came—meaning that you must return in complete benevolence. It is not sufficient to simply say, "Oh, thank heavens, we got here; now everything will be all right." So once you have done that, then the Tenth Planet will be your reward. A reward is not riches; it is not what you would now consider a gift. It is a responsibility that comes with an accomplishment.

You will have achieved something that has been tried over and over and over and over again in the universe and has not been achieved. You are so close to achieving it, you can almost touch it. But you will have to accomplish it in exactly the way I mentioned. This isn't exactly a new idea—it's been presented to you before—but there are always reasons, aren't there, why "we can't do it," why "she can't do it," why "he can't do it," why "they can't do it." There are always reasons, and many times those reasons sound perfectly rational and reasonable. But you're going to have to do the irrational and the unreasonable. You're going to have to befriend people you would never befriend otherwise, and they are going to have to befriend you.

This is something you need to think about and take a hard look at. Remember that even though you will have that joy of accomplishment, you will then—once you achieve that return from whence you came—have a great responsibility. All the other planets who will be experimenting with the teeniest amounts of discomfort so they can finally have growth, which they've wanted—not every planet, mind you, but all the ones who do want it, all the cultures, you understand—they will need guidance. They will not just need guidance on how to get by on a day-to-day basis; they will need to be assured by those who have done it from the beginning to the end (meaning you, the Explorer Race) that it not only can be done, but it can be completed and you can go on. They will need, in short, experts.

While no single-lived individual—meaning a single life—has made the loop entirely by themselves, in toto you as the Explorer Race will have the combined wisdom to advise all the beings on all these other planets on how to do it and to be able to assure them that it can be done, especially since they will not be doing it the tough way you've done it. You went to extremes, and there were a lot of very difficult penalties along the way: suffering, karma. So you will have to be able to reassure them, not just in an authoritarian manner, not just speaking as an expert, but you will have to be able to stand, sit, crawl, walk, fly—in short, you will have to do whatever is accommodating of those cultures.

You will have to be able to communicate with them as yourselves, radiating and completely open with the feelings that they will be able to recognize as someone (meaning a group of someones) who has *really* done this—and it can be done. You will have to be able to show them that even though they will never have to go to the extremes you went to . . . and you won't share with them those extremes, because they won't be able to stand it. It would be like a disease visited upon them. You will have to be able to reassure them in a way they can take in, that it not only can be done but that it's worth doing. That's your responsibility.

You have all volunteered to become the Explorer Race as individuals—millions and billions and trillions of you—and you will condense down to a few souls in time, although not now, not right away, because hundreds and thousands of you will be needed to go out and share these teachings. But in time you will condense back down to about ten souls, and you will become like a panel, a board you might say, with whom many will come to consult. Those who come to consult will not be the individuals who will be asking the questions; they will be their guides, their teachers.

This Universal Project Will Help Everyone Achieve Growth Benevolently

All that is far into the future. I bring it to your attention, however, because the Tenth Planet is a planet of accomplishment and responsibility. It is a reward and a duty. In short, it is everything you volunteered for in order to come to this planet and be a portion of this project. This is a project that aims on a universe level—not just on a universal level, but on the level of the entire universe—to help every planet, every culture, every individual to achieve growth in the most benevolent way they can. Thus, you will have to be adaptable, and when you think and take into the capacity of your minds all of the different cultures, all of the different styles of being, all the different experiences of the Explorer Race on Earth—so much, so many, eh?—when you take that into consideration, then in truth you will have to be able to communicate in ways that are not only understood and appreciated but in ways that are felt and are comforting.

The only way you can do that is to have had every possible experience. Many of the experiences happened early on as you delved into very light portions of discomfort, but many of them will happen as you close the loop, completing the exposure of slight discomfort. That's a ways off yet, but it's coming. Right now, you have a lot of discomfort—not everyone, not all the time, but there's a lot of discomfort here. But after a while, you'll get past the extremes and then you'll be closing in rapidly on closing the loop, even though it's not an actual closed loop. It's like a coil, a cycle. You will return on a line with where you began, but you will have achieved much, so you won't be starting over. You will have achieved much, but you will have gotten to where you wanted to go.

It all started with a very simple question. It started with these words, albeit in many different languages and in some cases feelings only, but to put it into your language, it all started with, "Who would like to help?" And on your part, it started with, "We would." I understand that this was on the soul level and there was no real understanding, no depth of appreciation of what you would have to go through. But as you close in toward completing that cycle, you will then—and you have to, you see—return from whence you came, meaning you will have to achieve complete benevolence, but you will have to approach it slowly, slowly, slowly toward the end.

You can't just rush toward the end. You will have to achieve it slowly because that will be your final understanding of what it's like to have total benevolence and just the tiniest amount of discomfort. Those are the people you're going to be helping: people who have almost total benevolence but who will have the tiniest amount of discomfort so they can learn, because it stimulates the learning curve. Even the most daring individuals on any planet will not get past 2 percent discomfort, which to you would be the most trivial in what you have lived in your life.

I Am the Planet of Your Combined Wisdom

Now, you might reasonably ask, "Well, how does this relate to a planet?" It's because I am the planet of your combined wisdom. You will have to not just tolerate each other, you will have to accept each other and embrace each other *as you are* in order to achieve this. When you do achieve it, you will achieve wisdom because you will have found something that works and is practical and can be done even in the most extreme situations. When you have done that and achieved benevolence in that situation, helping people to achieve that kind of benevolence again . . . because, you see, once they start in just that tiny amount of discomfort for some of them, it will seem like an adventure and they won't want to give it up, and you're going to have to encourage them why they are to.

You're going to need to encourage them to reach for growth in spurts and then return to their total benevolence, enjoy that growth, and then at a later time perhaps have another tinier amount of discomfort and have a spurt of growth. But they do not want to linger in that discomfort because it's oh so easy, isn't it, even at that tiny level, to embrace excitement and adventure. Even though those words sound thrilling to you, even though they sound at the very least interesting, how many times do excitement and adventure lead to something you hadn't planned upon? "That was exciting," and then you've got some kind of injury that takes a long time, maybe a lifetime, to get over. In short, you will have all the knowledge and wisdom you need to not just talk them out of it but to radiate the feelings so that all those beings in all those different cultures on all those different planets will know that you know what you're talking about.

That's what the Tenth Planet is, the combined total of your knowledge and wisdom and the feeling of accomplishment and responsibility. Take apart the word "responsibility" and you'll get "response," your ability to respond. You can't respond in such a wide range of possibilities, you understand. Most of you even in the Explorer Race, no matter how many lives you've lived, will not have been exposed even in toto of your being (the entire Explorer Race together). You will not have experienced anything like these cultures, so you will have to be . . . what? Flexible. If there's one thing people on Earth have to become in an Earth life, it is to be flexible.

So you'll be able to handle it. And if you as individuals can handle it, you can be certain that there is another friend in the mix of the Explorer Race who can handle it. So I want you to start thinking of something on a thought level: start thinking that it's possible to be friends with every single person on the Earth, no matter what. How many times have you heard the saying "rise above it"? That's what you'll have to do. It won't be today, it won't be tomorrow, but it will come. It's something important to teach your children and for your children to teach their children, because it will come. You'll have to rise above it. Even in the most daunting situations, you'll have to rise above it. I know you can do it.

Do you know how I know? There is enough of me in existence that tells me that this is going to happen, but it will only happen if you do the work. If you don't do the work, then I'll fade into considerably less of my existence, where I've been many times before. But I have never been so manifested as I am now, which leads me to believe that you're actually going to be able to do it. Others have tried, many times. I know, because I've come partway toward being fully physical many times, but I've never come anywhere near this close. Call me an optimist, if you would—that's fine. I believe you will accomplish it, but it won't be easy. Still, I feel the need to tell you what you have to do, so you are forewarned. It's not complicated, and it may not be easy, but once you get used to it and recognize that it will take a lot of forgiveness, it can be done.

Really what you will be doing—in order to do this, you understand—is something that you normally do on a day-to-day basis when you are beyond Earth. When you are your actual souls or spirits, that's how you are all the time. But you will have to do that while you are physical. You will have to allow your soul or your spirit to be you. It doesn't mean you have to give up your personality, it just means that more and more of your soul and spirit will become part of your day-to-day personality because at that level of personality, you see, forgiveness is a fact. There is no resentment, there's no anger—there's only unconditional love. I know you can do this. It won't be easy, but I know you can do it.

I Am Not Entirely Physical

I have a little problem here. We published in 1991 a chapter about the Tenth Planet where the planet didn't talk but the beings said that they were the connection to crocodiles on this Earth and they had brought temptation to Earth.

I can't speak for that. All I can say is, I am sorry you have a problem. You asked to speak to the Tenth Planet. I am the voice of the Tenth Planet. Zooish through Robert said, after the session was over, that the planet in 1991 was a place holder in the orbit—waiting for this planet to manifest, they have now left the solar system.

Where are you in our orbit? In our solar system?

Farther out than the planets you know about.

Can you say where, beyond what?

You know I'm not going to do that, but you can make your best guess, can't you? You know where your planets are. You have a pretty good idea, eh? So all you have to do is just basically guess that there is something farther out that is in orbit around the Sun but not really physical enough for you to see.

Oh, I see!

Of course [chuckles], not really physical enough for you to see—I said that, didn't I? I'll spell it out: not really physical enough for you to see, but for those of you who are sensitive, there may be times when you can feel my presence. It might be in those moments of supreme forgiveness, like when you're involved in forgiveness or being befriended by someone you never thought would befriend you, or something like that, eh? Then you'll be doing that, but you might have a dream, you might have a sense of someplace else. It will come with a feeling of accomplishment and a feeling of responsibility. When that happens in a dream, if there are no apparent beings involved, well, you and I might be proverbially shaking hands.

You said you're only partly manifest here but stronger than before. Where is the rest of you manifest?

No, no. I know that this is the way you understand physicality. You're thinking in linear terms of physicality. But I am nonlinear; I am concentric. Therefore, I am all here, but I am not entirely physical. You are surrounded all the time, you understand, with spirits. Sensitive people can sometimes see them for a moment. In those moments, they are seeing a portion of some being. You are surrounded with spirits who are not physical, but they are here just the same. I am like that, but I am not in linear time. I understand that your questions must be spoken in that context, but I have to bring it to your attention, you see.

Also keep in mind that linear time is not native to you. I think many beings have been talking to you lately and bringing it to your attention, albeit gently, about, "Oh, you're asking that in some kind of linear way," and so on. You've heard that many times, and it's important to put that out, you see, because that's not your normal sense of being. Your normal sense of being is much more like me, much more like spirit—that's who you are. That's why life is so difficult for you. Though there are great joys here on this planet, many times life is difficult for you, even if something uncomfortable is not happening. That's simply because it's so foreign to you.

You've Never Known the Feeling of 100 Percent Accomplishment

This is a book about astrology. Are you in any way connected with any of the signs we know about now?

No, that's why I'm speaking to you from who and what I am. Those who are able to make their best guess and are sensitive enough to have those feelings of where and when, if you get enough people (sensitives) to do that with some astrologers in the mix there, then you might get a vague idea. I will say only that my orbit is in the same general type of orbit as the other planets. So if you drew a line straight out from the Sun, you'd roughly get the general direction. You understand what I'm saying, eh?

Yes. So you're on the elliptic; you're not in an eccentric orbit?

I'm not rotating around the Sun in some other orbit. I would be rotating the same general way as other planets. I am not entirely physical in this place yet, because you have yet to do things that will bring me to that state.

Can you say how long it takes you to go around the Sun, although that's a linear question?

If I answer that, then you'll know where I am. There's mathematics involved there.

Why is it so important that we not know where you are?

Have you ever striven for a goal with a reward at the end? [Pause.] Have you?

Yes.

It tends to ruin the reward a bit if you know exactly what it is. After all, it may sound to you like, "Oh, why would we want more responsibility? We've got plenty of responsibility now—that doesn't sound like much of a reward." But then, none of you has ever known the feeling of total 100-percent accomplishment.

You've had moments of it—winning the race, achieving a goal—but you can remember how fleeting they were. They were wonderful and then gone. None of you has ever had the feeling of a 100-percent total experience of accomplishment all the time. With that feeling, the added responsibility will be like nothing.

How will you express when we achieve that? Will you be physically manifest? Will we see you?

You'll be able to, but not with the naked eye, obviously. I will look mysterious. You will want to come and explore, but it'll take a long time. By the time you have the capacity, then someone will be giving you a ride, okay? By that time, some peoples will give you a ride out there. They won't right away, by the way, no matter how much you beg and plead. They won't because they'll understand what you're doing. That's why you don't have too many contacts these days. They're staying away, because they have been informed how important what you're doing is. But sometimes they come and look, and you get to see them. That's to intrigue you, to let you know that you're not alone.

There are those who love you and care about you and want you to know that they are there. Almost always, beings in those ships are friends of somebody on the Earth—meaning they have known you in some other life. They may still be in that life, because they may live 1,200, 1,500 or more years, you see. So from their point of view, they're coming to visit their friend, even though you may not know them, you don't remember who they are. They come with love and then they go—just to let you know they care about you. But there's not a whole lot of contact going on, because everybody knows how important it is what you are doing here and how terribly difficult it is. After all, if it weren't so difficult, it would have been done long ago. It's very difficult.

The Reward Is Being Able to Ask for the Wisdom

You were invited by the Creator of this universe to come here, correct?

Yes.

How did He or His emissary—He/She/It—explain to you why you were invited?

It wasn't like that really; it was a feeling. I'll do the best I can in your language. The feeling emanated was to accomplish, to perpetuate, to saturate, and to provide an ultimate wisdom. I found that appealing.

Yes. What was your experience before that invitation?

I was, in terms of the feelings I've been expressing, pretty much that.

Somewhere else?

Yes. I was expressing accomplishment, responsibility and acquisition of wisdom. Perhaps you don't understand that when you accomplish what I mentioned, you will be able to request, for example—because you don't have to come here and walk on the planet—to dream, as a dreamer, with the Tenth Planet and have some wisdom. You understand, wisdom is in this case the assimilation of the known wisdom of what is needed. After all, where are you going to get that capacity to be able to interact with beings from all kinds of cultures that you can't even imagine, can't even conceive of? You will need wisdom, not knowledge.

Knowledge encompasses the depth and breadth of everything ever thought about, any given subject. As you well know from being on Earth, a lot of that would be wrong. You need wisdom. You need to have something that works. You'll be able to present the problem, you'll be able to be the dreamer (sleep, dream and remember), visit the Tenth Planet, wake up with the wisdom. "Oh, now I know what to do," say you after sleep, no matter the problem.

Can we ask for that now in dealing with the problems we have on this planet?

You can ask, but I don't think it will happen. After all, you want the reward before you accomplish the deed. So, no.

Oh, I see, that's part of the reward.

Of course.

Oh, I didn't understand that. So the reward is to be able to ask for the wisdom.

If you want to have some kind of *that*, you can ask each other. If you don't have some knowledge, then you ask each other. Right now, you do that a little bit on the Internet, but even that is limited. Sometimes you just have to ask somebody else. "How did you do that?" say you. People say that every day. Sometimes they get an answer that will work; sometimes they don't get that answer. Then they ask somebody else. Eventually, they find something that works and then maybe they create something as a synthesis. That is how the path leads to wisdom. You do something that works. It works as long as it works, and if things change, then you might need more. So you ask somebody else, and you adapt. You become flexible, you grow, you change, you become. That's what you all do on this planet. You begin and then you become.

You are very wise.

Well, that is one of the things I am.

I Am Connected with the Explorer Race

Do you interact with the beings who are the spirits of the other planets in this system?

Not very much. After all, I am basically waiting for you to do something, so I have had those interactions many times in the past. After a while [chuckles], when you have spoken all there is to speak—we don't talk or chat, we don't do that—it's like comfortable silences between friends.

So is any part of your energy being used someplace else for other purposes, for other beings?

No.

You're just waiting?

I am waiting. It's not as if there aren't wisdom and wisdom keepers elsewhere. I am not exclusive. There are many other beings who can do exactly what I can do. It's just when the question went out, I also said, "I will."

We're going to really need wisdom when the Creator leaves. You'll be with us then, right?

We'll see. I don't have to make that . . .

Decision now?

Yes. You may not need me then.

Oh, it's probably when we'll really need you.

Everything that I've said I am made up of is revealing my personality: who and what I am. I have given enough for astrologers to identify my personality. I am what I have said I am. Any astrologer will be able to use that. That's what astrologers need, you know.

Yes. I just thought you had to be connected with something.

I am connected with you. Not with humans, with *you*, the Explorer Race on Earth. There are humans all over, but I'm connected with you on Earth. There are those who are waiting; some have come and gone. They are waiting, and I am connected with all of you. I am connected with the Explorer Race.

Where are the others?

Nearby, in spirit.

Are they all in spirit? None of them have an actually ensouled life?

Well, if they do, there's time.

There's time to have that life before they join us? Or there's time for the spirit to be with us?

Time for them to have a life before you join them.

Okay. Are many of the guides and teachers and the incredible number of spirits around the solar system now spirits of the Explorer Race?

I'm not going to answer that. If there's a long pause, I might be thinking, but I'm not going to answer that. [Pause.] It's not that it isn't a good question, but that can't be revealed at this time. Generally speaking—if I may speak for all beings—when beings will not answer a question, it's always because it's too soon for you to know that. Not you as an individual, you understand, but it's too soon for anyone who is a member of the Explorer Race to know that. After all, even if you were to swear to me up and down, "I promise I will never tell," it doesn't make any difference, because if you know it, you will think about it, and your thoughts radiate. They'll go into the mix of thought in general, and you might even dream about it. There's no stopping that.

Visual Arts Are Moving in a Cycle

I'd just like to live long enough so beings could speak freely again.

You don't have to live to do that, but keep in mind that in this day and age of visual arts, it takes serious students to read and think. It will be done, but with those visual arts . . . you know, it's an interesting thing that visual arts are moving in a cycle. Right now, people like their movies, television, things like that, (I have to speak more quietly; the voice is wearing out and we'll have to stop soon.) But pretty soon, the physical theater is going to make a huge comeback, because people will want feeling. They don't get feeling radiated from a movie; they don't get it radiated from a television set or a video. They may have feelings, but it doesn't radiate to them, whereas the actors on the stage in a live production have feelings and they radiate to the audience.

So when people want the next thing, they're going to want that, they're going to want a live performance. How about that? Be sure and put that in the book or someplace, because actors not only need the encouragement but also I want to give people a tip where they can go for the next big thing. It's funny that the next big thing is actually an old thing. Now we're going to have to finish up.

For you to understand the nature of your being, know that you will always be those who quest for knowledge, wisdom and practical applications of wisdom. You are at the core of your being as souls, as spirits, ultimately practical—keep that in mind. When you achieve more and more wisdom, it must be practical. You must be able to do it. It must be adaptable, it must be flexible, and ultimately, it must be inclusive. Good life.

Thank you so much. Good life.

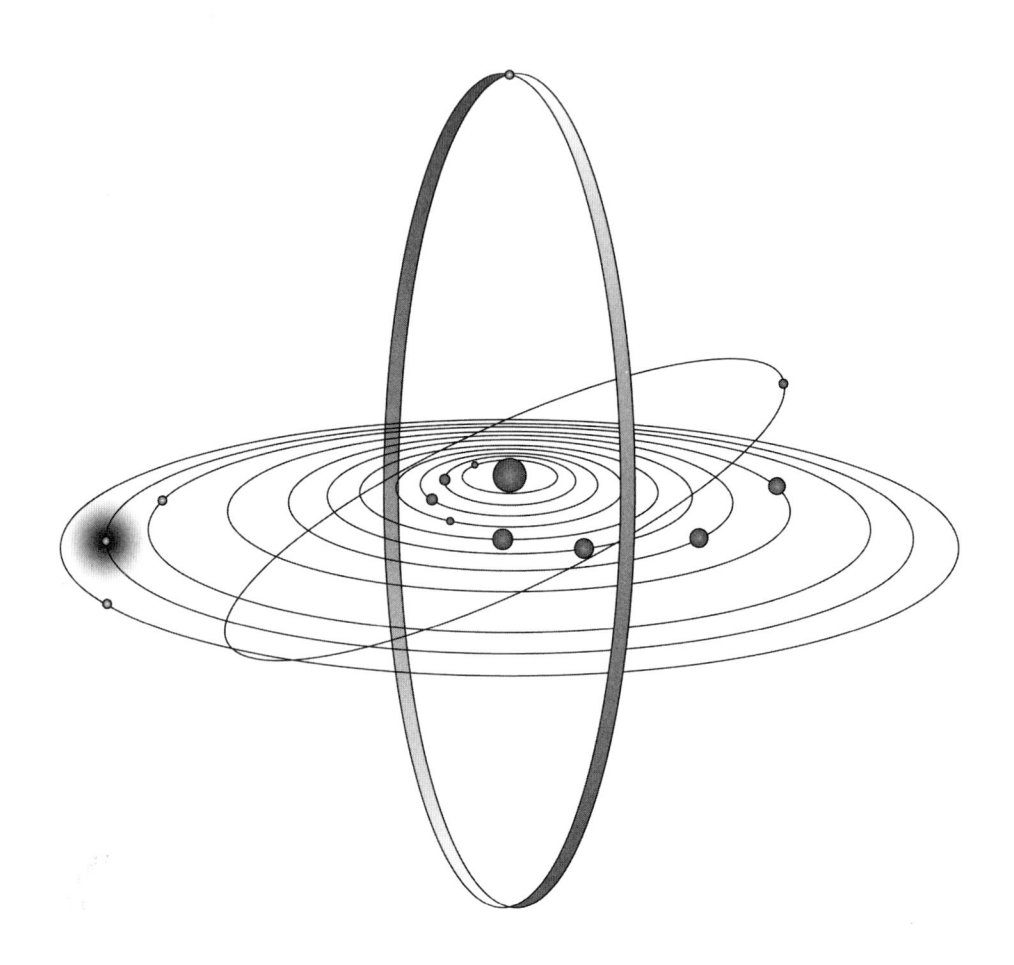

The 11th Planet

THE 11ᵀᴴ PLANET
Is Dissolving the Discomforting Past

November 30, 2009

Greetings. This is Planet Eleven. Welcome!

The Distant Past Is Being Dissolved

I am already hard at work because some of your linear past is already prepared to be undone and dissolved into its component parts. You might say I am the recycler, in that sense. The good news is, most of what is being undone is that which is disturbing or discomforting, as Zoosh might say. So this is all beginning to dissolve. One of the most noticeable impacts that the reader might be interested in, especially the astrological consultant, is that this is going to help support the dissolution of traditional roles for men and women. There has been this terrific out-of-balance state for the male of the species for so long that the female of the species has come to adjust itself toward the belief that this non-attuned masculine way on your planet is somehow natural and normal, which it is not. So a lot of what is being dissolved now are the building blocks of the warrior male.

The feminine warrior wisdom, which is the knowledge of all the aspects of war so that war can be prevented, is actually derived from the total being: masculine and feminine combined. The idea that the masculine being is somehow attracted to the act of war is not true, not the core of the masculine being. The masculine being is, in its temporary status of being split off from the feminine, really at its core curious. Curiosity has been ascribed to the feminine, but it is in fact just as masculine as feminine. The only difference is that in the case of the masculine being, there is a greater tendency to act on that curiosity as compared to the feminine beings' intention and core, you understand, to understand what they are curious about.

I bring this up because the current roles generally acted out in many cultures on the planet Earth now—not by all men, not by all women, but generally—have these polarizations of masculine and feminine. In the case of the masculine, it is about 60 percent negative, meaning a different meaning of negative, meaning not the masculine at all. This dissolution, this recycling of that energy that is going on right now, while it is not totally about that, I feel that this is the thing that is most of interest to my point of view. Undoing the past so that the present can be more focused in the present—and because of the nature of curiosity in the masculine and feminine, and a desire to know the future much more than a desire to know the past—this undoing of this discomforting past, especially that which has fed into these imbalanced roles, will make it much easier for the masculine and feminine being to be present-oriented and attracted to the future in such a way as the benevolent future will be easier to acquire. So I feel that this is the main thing going on now that is important for astrologers to know and understand.

Planet Eleven is not entirely physical, not unlike Planet Ten and, I might add, Planet Twelve. Still, it is possible for me to begin my work. I can only begin this because you have completed so much of yours, you see. It has always been contingent on that. But because you have gone through the full range of karma and everything you came to do to Earth has been done at least once—accounting for all souls present of the Explorer Race, both having been on Earth and those on Earth now—it allows me to begin my work. None of it is going to uncreate anything in your present, in anybody's present, so no worries there. You're also not going to forget beloved ancestors or anything like that, no worries there.

But the distant past—most of which is not written but has done a great deal to create hostilities—is being dissolved. There's no advantage to remembering it. Why remember something that will just get you upset? You might reasonably ask (and historians have asked for years), how is it possible that we can have a benevolent world when there is so much history known and, worse yet, so much anger about it? I'm not trying to say that that's not justified; I am saying that there comes a point when the perpetuation of history, both recent and long-term, in the conscious minds of youth as well as adults, does nothing but perpetuate warfare.

There is a desire to remember, and the motivation is so that whatever disaster occurred is remembered so that it doesn't happen again, and I understand that. But almost 89 percent of what is remembered today in your history is based on that which preceded it but is not written. So you might say the mood was preset, and thereby much of ancient history that you're able to translate has already been set into certain dioramas of—to put it in the simplest possible way—good guys and bad guys. Of course, whoever the good guys are and the bad guys are depends largely on your point of view. So I bring this up because I feel it is relevant in your time. My job is to undo that which can be undone because you have brought some form of resolution to it, though you may not be conscious of it. That's my opening statement.

How do you undo our past? How do you dissolve it?

If I were to tell you that, you could—anyone could—undo things that are needed. Why would I tell you that? Suffice it to say that it falls under the heading of spiritual magic.

Male and Female Roles Will Blend

How do you recycle? You said you're a recycler.

Oh, that's the easiest part. Once the polarization has been removed from any portion of energy, it is just naturally available to be utilized again. It becomes neutral. I'm not talking about charged-particle theory or anything like that; I'm just talking about mass and energy. Once the onus of whatever it was a portion of in some discomforting way has been removed, then it is simply energy that is naturally recycled. I don't recycle it; it recycles itself.

Say more about the emerging roles of male and female. How are they changing?

It is a natural process. The male will begin to demonstrate some nurturing qualities of the female, and the female will begin to demonstrate more action based upon her own curiosity. The female has been held back because of your roles, and many females have not really been able to fully express themselves. Some forms of expression have been allowed in, shall we say, progressive cultures, but many of them have not been encouraged or there's been so much bias and prejudice that the discouragement was palpable, even if not spoken.

So you'll find that roles will blend. Women will still have children—men are not going to do that—but there will be much more of a sense of unification. In fifty years or so, it will be quite typical for men and women to be able to have conversations and not have to strain to try and understand the other's point of view. Now, because of the roles ascribed to males and females—and really the children trained into those roles from birth—the idea of misunderstanding each other is a given. Fifty years from now, it will be in the forgotten past.

Most Veils Will Drop When You Become Enjoined with Your Full Spirit Being

Is your orbit on the plane of the elliptic? Does it go around the Sun in the same . . .

Yes, pretty much the same way as all the planets in this solar system—you don't have to finish that question. There's nothing erratic going around the Sun that I'm aware of. Occasionally, there might be a fragment of bits and pieces of stuff from space that might go around the Sun that way, but it doesn't stay forever.

How manifest, how physical are you? Will we be able to see you with instruments?

Probably not from Earth, but as you send out more and more vehicles into deeper and deeper space, then eventually, yes. It will take awhile—probably at least 150, 200 years to at least chart the orbit through magnetic resonance. This will be done, but Planet Eleven is not a big planet. Neither is Twelve. We don't have to be big because our job really isn't to exert any gravitational pull.

Could you say something about the diameter?

Oh, Planet Eleven is only slightly larger than your Moon.

Eventually will it become a solid physical object?

Yes, but this will occur most likely when you have made that transition to being enjoined with your full spirit being—"you" meaning the population on Earth. This is coming, and when that occurs, there will be this great relaxation in the solar system, to say nothing of the galaxy. Most veils will drop, but I think one will remain. The last one will remain in place for a few hundred years just to make sure [chuckles]. It will not screen you as individuals; it will only screen the rest of the universe and, in that sense, the rest of the galaxy. But it will be easy for visitors to come from other planets and gently pass through that veil, whereas now it is very difficult and that's good for everybody concerned.

Previously we were told of an eleventh planet that had like pieces or knobs of it that would come off and undo Earth if we didn't attain our goal. Is that planet gone?

No, no. This is no longer a factor, you see. It isn't necessary because you've achieved your goal. Things that don't need to be in the real world—and I'll explain in a minute what "the real world" is—don't exist in the real world. You do not exist in the way you understand your existence in the real world, see. The real world has to do with all souls on Earth, combined with your greatest spirits—that's the real world. But the world that you live in and that you consider to be the real world is not real. It's artificial. It has to be, so that you can accomplish what you went there to do. Not to put too fine a point on it, but I will simply just say that that aspect of that planet you mentioned is not needed, so it doesn't exist—and it's not needed because you did what you went there to do.

The Correlation between
Planet Eleven and the Moon Is Significant

Can you tell me something about yourself?

You mean for the point of the book, astrologically speaking?

Yes, please.

Here are a few more qualities to help the astrologer. Since you know that Planet Eleven is that which can undo, the correlation between that and Moon energy is significant. I want you to take a good look at that, astrologers. There are, as you know, aspects of peoples' astrology that would fall under what you would call the positive and the negative. Some individuals who have a difficult chart might very well be able to make a connection spiritually with Planet Eleven—and this is particularly important for those of you astrologers who also do sensitive work. This could possibly not negate that aspect of their chart but diminish its impact. So I feel that this is the most important aspect for astrologers.

My Favorite Is the Feeling between Dimensions

So you have always been with this planet, but you just were not in this dimension or visible to us?

You mean as a personality?

Yes.

Yes, of course.

Did you come from someplace else, like many of the planets?

As a being, I was invited to participate, and [chuckles] I'm not sure Planet Ten said this, but if so, then I'm going to reiterate. The great attraction of the participation was that I would not be called upon to be present [chuckles] for a long time, and I haven't on the personality level been present really except for the past 3,000 or 4,000 years. So it wasn't much of a commitment. All totaled, I haven't been here that much, so I could do other things, be where I was, do what I do—travel from one dimension to another, not from one place to another. There are more dimensions than there are numbers.

What's your favorite?

I think my favorite is the feeling between dimensions. Imagine that moment when you are waking up after a deep sleep, not because of a loud noise, not because of something startling, just naturally waking up and feeling very rested. It's similar to that—totally relaxing.

The planet stays here, but you travel in consciousness, right?

Yes, the planet remains, but my personality can travel.

You said that there are more dimensions in this universe than there are numbers, or was that including all of the other creations in all of the realms?

In this universe. Creator, remember, likes variety. So that's something to look forward to, eh? Here's an interesting factor: I know of no being other than Creator who has explored all the dimensions of this universe. And there are those making the effort.

Like you?

No, I haven't really made that effort, but I know of other beings who have. The only one I know who has explored every nook and cranny, if I may say that, of all the dimensions that exist in this universe is the being who created them. I think that given the fact that beings are immortal, this gives you an idea of how much there is.

And how much more there's going to be when we achieve our goal, right?

It's hard to say. You might take a look at it and say "Weesh, too much." You never know. You'll have a different point of view about it.

That's a new point of view. I always thought they wanted more potential.

Sometimes—on your now planet, of course—more often seems better. But when you're in your natural state, there is no attraction to more whatsoever. Since you are totally in balance, you can't gain more balance when you are in balance.

What can you gain? More experience? More joy? More what?

There is no desire to gain. There is only a desire where you are now to gain because you feel a constant sense of loss, and that is because you are not united with your total spirit. But the moment that happens, that feeling will go away.

But we'll still be curious, won't we?

Oh, yes. But you won't be desperate to gain . . .

Like we are now.

That will just disappear.

This Will Help You Move More into Your Natural Roles

Someone recently said—I think Zoosh or Isis—that in everything up to the past forty years the discomfort was being dissolved. Are you part of that?

That's not where I am. You will have to ask them about what they meant. My work is in the distant past; that's where I am right now. Where I am is in the unwritten history—that which you don't know about—for which there are no records, even in symbolic form, that you don't understand but that have managed to survive the test of time. It's important to dissolve it, because for a lot of your history, you understand, you chase history back far enough and you'll still say, "Well, there are these roles." I assume psychologists and sociologists have done that, traced history back—at least some of them. So there are these roles and there's a tendency as a result to believe that that's natural.

Roles that people played, you mean?

Yes.

Will you be coming forward in time, then, as you proceed with your work?

Yes. But right now I'm in the distant past because that's the area that needs my attention. As the distant past is dissolved—that which is discomforting, you understand—a lot of the pressure to perpetuate these artificial roles will just ease off. Do you know that even the symbols (especially the symbols) that those who study these things—archaeologists and so on—have just not been able to interpret or, as is very often the case, have not interpreted correctly, that they'll suddenly be able to interpret them? They'll be able to take a look at what they've interpreted already and say, "Wait a minute, this could mean something else." Therefore, a lot of the mysteries will disappear, because it won't be a mystery any more, it will be known.

Oh, that will be great. Are you talking about the past of the Explorer Race or of the other civilizations that have been on this planet?

No, just the past of the Explorer Race. The other civilizations that have been on the planet are fine; they didn't come here to learn anything.

Right. When you say roles, do you mean the roles of the male and female?

Yes.

So how can we then move more into our natural roles?

You're doing that. You're evolving, letting things go, and you're getting support from Creator and other beings. You're in the process of doing that; you don't need my help for that.

How did it come that you got to be the expert in this undoing? What was your experience?

Oh, I do not claim to be an expert. I was just available and knew how to do it. There are thousands of others who know how to do it, but I was willing to come.

Ah, you answered the call—the famous answer.

That's right, I was willing to come and the others were busy. I was actually busy, but Creator said, "Well, you won't have to go right away," and I said, "Oh, well, then of course."

Yeah, some of them have been here a long time. Oh, that's great. So then what will you do after you finish undoing things here?

Oh, I suppose I'll stick around and see how you turn out.

Ah, that'll be great. You might have to undo some of our stuff, huh?

Well, that won't be difficult.

Many Astrologers Are Spiritual Beings

I'm not too sure how this works with these new planets. The astrologers themselves will connect the planets to signs?

Well, you see, a lot of astrologists in your time are also people who are spiritual beings—not mathematicians, you know, as astronomers must be. There are a lot of spiritual beings who are astrologers, and many of them can channel or they might do other things (like numerology) or they might be sensitive—they might be able to reach out and feel the planets. As a result, they might be able to feel the planetary energies in the clients they are working with. So I'm allowing for the fact that astrologers are spiritual people, besides being intellectual people, and that's why I'm talking to them that way.

I know that all astrologers do not have such interests or pursuits or passions, but some do. And those who have such capabilities or are interested in such capabilities, that's whom I believe this book is really aimed at. I think it could be useful to astrologers who are not interested in such things, but for astrologers who *are* interested . . . well, it will be invaluable, I believe. That is not an advertisement [chuckles].

Why the special connection with the Moon?

Astrologers will understand that. I'm going to make a closing statement. I want you all to understand, readers, that it is not the job of the astrologer to fix anybody—and I think you know this, as this is Astrology 101, okay? You know that. But it is your job to help people understand how they can work with what they've got. You know that. The additional information I'm providing and you're getting from other beings in this book is to help you to fill in those nooks and crannies that seem to be undefined. Don't feel like you have to work everything in this book into a chart. But for those of you who can do charting, well, give it your best shot. Good life.

Thank you very much. Good life.

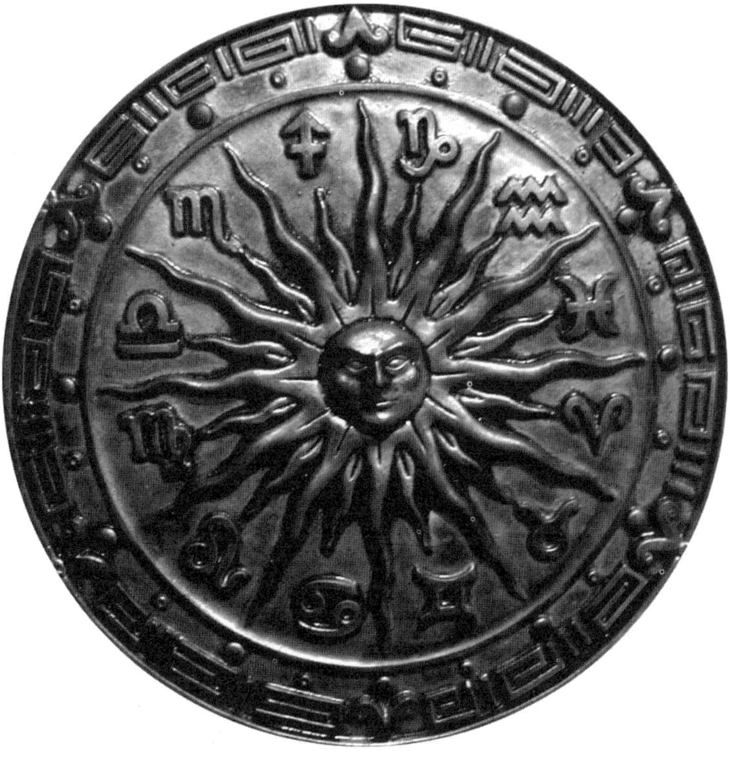

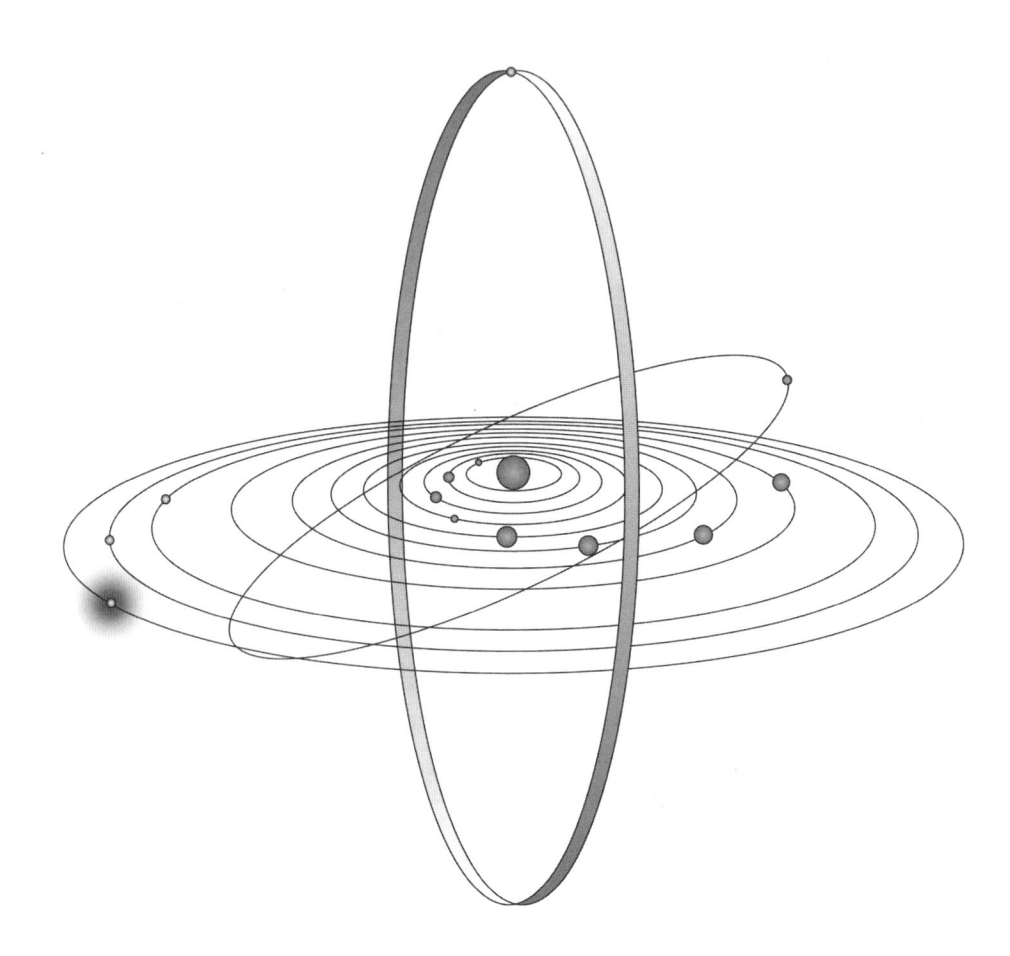

The 12th Planet

THE 12ᵀᴴ PLANET
Is Entirely Focused on the Past and the Resolution of the Past

December 7, 2009

This is the Twelfth Planet.

Welcome.

Thank you.

The Heart Energy and Feminine Energy on Earth Is Rising

I have been in full-time operation for a while now. The heart energy return for your culture on your planet has begun some years ago. You see, you have been told for some time now that the heart energy and the feminine energy and all of that is rising on planet Earth. Yet owing to your souls' journey (not all of you for the Explorer Race, but some of you) through the Orion star system and various things that happened there, the energy that has been rising for some time on Earth of the feminine and the heart is not really affecting you to cause more than your physical self to react to it. But your soul has memories that run deep, and the depth of those memories require a soothing influence of the so-called Orion Heart—which means, in this case, a means to calm the troubled past.

The advantage of this is that it works twofold, not only for the problems in the Orion star system—most of which were benevolent lives, but a few that were tumultuous—but also because of the nature of that capacity to resolve past energies in general that are tumultuous (also known as discomforting), it has begun to work to resolve past discomforts associated with the Explorer Race on Earth, some of which have to do with the same kind of go-around, if you would, that one might have found on Orion past. It's not all just struggles, you understand.

The problem in Orion past in those places where struggles did happen is that is where emerged a desire to control. Of course, there was always a little bit of that once fear came onto the scene, but the desire to create an organized method of control—even where it wasn't needed or obviously wanted—brought up the whole idea of a rigid society, a controlling society, and it has been a seduction ever since, even in the most broad-minded cultures.

This is not everyone, not every culture, but the larger the culture gets, the more difficult to manage it on any level of predictability, and most systems work best when there's a certain amount of predictability and therefore anticipation can take root. Then when you have a really large culture, a large system, elaborate governmental enterprises and so on, the tendency to fall back on a form of excessive control is very seductive. Also, one tends to find this emerging when times are unpredictable, because such governmental entities or any kind of structured hierarchical entity often becomes fearful and thus more controlling in unpredictable times. But these things are cyclical, and when more "good times," so to speak, come, such controlling elements are not as visible, though they might still be present. It's almost like a subconscious of a culture.

So without getting too excessively complex, I'll simply say that the Twelfth Planet has been in full function for the past fifteen years or so. This does not mean that I—if I can refer to myself that way—am physically perceptible, but for those who can send out deep space probes, I think you'll notice a profound magnetic resonance. Even if you can send out gentle sound waves (it won't work with strong), you'll notice a slight reverberation. If you send out strong sound waves, you won't notice it. It can only be noticed with gentle waves—just a tip to the science community.

Creator Invited Me for My Masculine Energy

Do you orbit the Sun on the same plane as the Earth?

Yes, all the planets do. You'll find this typically throughout the galaxy and most likely throughout the universe—I haven't checked all the others. But, generally, you find that.

Before 1994, you were not manifest on this dimension?

No, I was here, I just wasn't functioning in an influential way with the Explorer Race. But I was present.

What were you doing? Waiting?

Yes, that's a good explanation in a word: waiting. Waiting is not as boring as it might seem, when you have perception and patience. "Perception," in this sense, is the ability to be aware of the universe from one end to the other. So it's not as if there was nothing to consider. The universe is so vast—one looks around, so to speak.

You have been here since this solar system was created?
Yes.

You were invited here by the Creator?
Yes. Everyone was, including you.

What was the particular reason he invited you?
Creator made the invitation based on the masculine energy I encompass. The Orion struggles that were foreseen by Creator were something that were going to become encoded, Creator perceived, with a rather stubborn energy— one that would not respond quickly enough to feminine support. So Creator requested my energy to be present, since my energy is almost totally masculine when I am functioning the way I am now. In that way, that Orion past that was discomforting responds well to that energy. It's not because it's authoritarian, but because there's a tendency for the masculine energy to be more physical, to project certain qualities that are . . . it's hard to describe in your language. To project certain qualities that can achieve a beneficial balance is the best I can put it.

When you started, you talked about the heart energy and the feminine energy increasing. That's not your energy?
No. That's the Earth. That's what I said. You have heard for years that the heart energy is rising on Earth, the feminine energy is rising on Earth, yes? That's what I said. I didn't actually say all those words, but I assumed you knew what I meant.

All right. I was looking for what you were, what you represented.

I Help Bring You Balance

In addition to discreating the past, what other influence do you have on us now?
That's the main influence. In order for you to be released from the past, there needs to be balance that is more than you yourself can bring into the picture. Since you are so overwhelmed by your own lives—and most of your lives are totally out of balance, unless you are totally focused in the physical, as for instance an athlete might be—you need to have someone, something if you would, external that can do that for you. It's as if you've sent out a sign; I am the cosign. There has to be something else that can help you, because you are so overwhelmed by your own lives and, to a great extent, to the roles you are playing.

Other than the obvious physiological differences between men and women, when you are born on the planet, you are born very much alike, and whatever culture you are in ascribes certain roles. Usually these roles have to do with accentuations and limits of behaviors, and they are almost always off, meaning they are meant—and this refers back to what I was saying before—in a culture to create control and predictability, even though many times there might be a desire to encourage a better way of life (I'll grant that). Very often, however, if a choice has to be made between a better way of life and control and predictability, the latter is often chosen by a culture.

Granted, sometimes the culture might be strongly governmental, but ultimately a governing body is simply more of the people. It is uncommon for it to be mechanized culturally—you understand, an artificial intelligence culture. That's something you're all pretty much afraid of, but it doesn't generally happen. It can be prevented. You will prevent that, though there will be some striving for that, saying, "Oh well, if we program the computer to be totally benevolent, it will be," but there will be a tendency to forget that "the computer" was made by human beings and is not a human being and is what it originally was. Therefore, unless it is totally at ease with its component parts and its current role, which is unlikely, it will always be ill at ease.

All machines are like that; they are uncomfortable. When you are giving them the influence and the authority to make decisions, things are going to be off, unless the machine itself has been reminded of who it is. But there have been explanations, perhaps, of how to do that.

The Twelfth Planet Has Everything to Do with the Past

I was just reading about the Twelfth Planet [The Explorer Race, Volume One] who had our heart energy, and a goddess spoke.

The Orion heart energy—there's a difference. So that's the key. You also have to keep in mind that you can know more now, eh? It's always like that. When that material first came out some time ago [it was channeled in 1991, published in 1995], that's what you could know then. Now you can know more, so I'm giving you details.

So astrologers will figure your planet into their calculations?

We haven't gotten to the astrology part yet. I was just trying to catch you up. I'm trying to answer your questions, but I realize the whole point of the book is the astrology, so you can if you like, for this chapter, refer to that all as a prologue and put a reference to the material, the Twelfth Planet material.

So, now, if I may start with the astrology: The function and influence of the Twelfth Planet has entirely to do with the past and resolution of the past. So if you can factor in the Twelfth Planet and it is influential in somebody's chart, you will know that that person will be profoundly interested in and/or attempting to resolve his or her own past or the past of others. Needless to say, a strong influence of the

Twelfth Planet would definitely be benevolent or beneficial to someone in school learning about history and would probably support the study of history and for one to become a historian even, to go that far. So that is the primary influence.

Now, as far as somebody having no influence of the Twelfth Planet, it doesn't mean that they won't be interested in the history and the past, but it does mean—and this is particularly important if you can confirm through your own spiritual capabilities that there is no influence from the Twelfth Planet—that the person is going to be present- and future-oriented. That's a pretty important point in your now state of being in your culture, in your community. That's a good opening, as far as what I do astrologically.

I'm at My Greatest Influence When Sunspot Activity Is at Its Height

Now, there might be another aspect here. I know, astrologers, that it's not exactly something you can put your fingers on, to say where the Twelfth Planet is, and that this is not in the ephemeris. I do understand that. But I want to let you know when the Twelfth Planet is at its zenith of influence—and it won't be at the same time every year, but it will be generally at a similar time. There's a clue, a very important clue. When sunspot activity is at its height during the year that you are in, then you can be certain the Twelfth Planet is at its greatest influence.

Now, I realize that this is going to rule out predictability, but to a degree you can look back astronomically and see when sunspot activity was generally found to be more active. You can be certain that the Twelfth Planet, then, is also much more active in influencing the people of Earth. That might be helpful, because it does factor in a degree of predictability, doesn't it, speaking to the astrologers here.

Is that only since 1991? Or in the past?

No, no—way on back, as far back as that's been kept. So a certain amount of astronomical records then are established, and you'll be able then to understand that. Granted, in the past, when it happened in the eighties and the seventies and so on, back as far as records go, that doesn't mean the Twelfth Planet was active then. But it's a way for you to know now when it happens. So it gives you a degree of predictability and the knowledge now, since the Twelfth Planet is active in the way I mentioned before, influencing the people of Earth. Then you can say, well, this is happening for you.

It also is suggestive on another point. When someone is born during the times of greater sunspot activity, you might be able to say that these people—nowadays, you understand, and in the few years I've mentioned that have been particularly active, the past fifteen or so—are most likely to be very influential with helping to resolve the past. They might make good counselors, they might even make good attorneys, counselors in general, you understand. They might be able to bring about resolution in difficult situations—ministers, perhaps, like that.

What is the dynamic between you and the Sun that accentuates your energy during the sunspots?

Sunspots are really an activity on the Sun that has to do with activation and support for the outer planets. You know that when this happens, there are very strong radiations from the Sun, certain types of rays, as you call them. While they rush past your planet with a certain degree of impact, these rays are really meant for the outer planets—and when I say "the outer planets," I'm counting from Pluto and beyond. So that's why they're so powerful and seemingly way more powerful than you would ever need or have any use for, though in the not-too-distant future, you'll figure out a way to produce a certain amount of energy that will be helpful in radio-wave transmission, utilizing these times of impulses of energy flowing by from the sunspots. But I can't say too much about that, because those who are working on that would prefer that I do not.

Oh, that means we could use that powerful ray going out to expand the distance our radio waves will reach, something like that?

I can't say, but it's not about a radio. I'm just saying "radio waves," and those who are working on it will know what I'm talking about.

I'm Not Really in Your Visible Spectrum

What was in your past before you came to park yourself out there in our solar system that caused you to be doing what you're now doing?

As a personality, I was always in this general area. Creator simply asked me to become embodied as a planet during the time you would be here and the precursors to you, meaning the other planets, cultures and so on. In short, to become a part of your influencing bodies, it was necessary to have a planetary structure because there is a dynamic associated with planets that affects you as an individual, as a culture, and as a global community on the astrological and astronomical level. So I was basically requested to become a planet during that time. But I was here already as a personality.

What were you doing here?

Being. The same thing you do when you are not embodied—just being. It might interest you to know how big I was. At that time, I was about as big as the head of a pin. Now, being this planet, I am about the size of Jupiter. So that was kind of fun.

Is there a certain point when we will actually be able to see you, if we could see that far? Could a satellite see you?

I don't think you'll be able to see. As I say, you'll be able to detect in the way I mentioned before, but I don't think you'll be able to see me as a planet because I'm not really in the visible spectrum. That doesn't mean I'm in another dimension; I'm just not in your visible spectrum. You might ask reasonably, "What does that mean?" Do you know that if things do not have a color, you can't see them? Or if they have a color that's not in your visible spectrum, again you can't see them? This is part of the reason that a form of radar is used to explore space. You might say "a form of radiation waves," because scientists understand that not everything is visible, no matter how good your magnifying glass might be. So at some point, when you can send such a device out farther than you have in the past . . . though you've made some efforts, but you've lost touch with those satellites that went way, way out.

The Voyager series, yes.

Exactly. That was a fun thing you did [chuckles]. I think it was a good thing; I'd like to see more of that. At that time, you will be able to detect me.

What color are you?

It wouldn't do you any good for me to say.

What percentage of colors in the universe can we see?

That is a *wonderful* question. Generally speaking, 97 percent of the universe is in colors you cannot see. Of course, when you are no longer embodied and even for some of you at the very deep levels of your sleep, you might have times when you see these things, because at those deep levels you are not strictly limited by your visual perception. If you like—and I know you do—you can request to see something that you would love to see (make sure you put it like that) that is beyond your visual spectrum in your deep dream state that you can remember.

Don't be attached to it being some distant planet or star. It might very well be something in your day-to-day world! For instance, those of you who have beloved pets or even new babies around the house, six months or younger . . . if you do something like that at the deep dream state and you remember it, you might see a different shape for them. You might see some big lightbody, in the case of a dog or a cat, for instance. You might see what they look like on their home planet, something they're aware of and think about when they're visiting your Earth. In the relatively short time a dog or cat might live on Earth embodied, they do remember what they look like on their home planet.

That's beautiful—thank you.

I think that's something you might like. For some of you who have perceptions and can See, you can simply rephrase that question and ask that that be part of what you can See now. Then you can ask that you See something that is benevolent and wonderful, that is beyond your spectrum capabilities of envisioning—put it like that—if you can See.

You Need to Bring Your Masculine Energy into Balance with the Feminine

Describe to us the true meaning of masculine energy.

Well, you have to understand that I can only describe that in the way I see it. I cannot give you a universal description, and the universal description would probably be a book long at least, because if you asked everybody, they'd all have a different description. But from my point of view, the masculine energy is that which reaches for and the feminine energy is that which receives. It's as simple as that. Some people respond much better in a "reaching for" environment; other people respond better in a receiving environment, meaning they are receptive, they like to be around people who are receptive (sometimes referred to as sensitive). "Reaching for" might have to do with going, doing, like that. That's my perception of it.

That describes my understanding of the Explorer Race, that it's reaching for, going and doing. But it has to be balanced, right?

Yes. You don't just blunder into something and cause problems. That's part of the reason you've been isolated for so long, because other worlds perceive that you would cause problems because of your tendency to be over-masculinized as a society. With over-masculinization, the tendency is to just stumble and blunder right through the woods, stepping you don't know where and you don't care where. If you've ever seen people run into a woods sometime and they're off the trail, they're just unconscious of the damage they're doing. Needless to say, if you were on another world and you saw such activities or heard about them, you'd say, "No, thank you."

So the reason the feminine energy and the heart energy are rising on the planet you're living on is to help you bring your masculine energy into balance with the feminine and get comfortable with it. Then when you are welcomed to travel to other planets, you will be sensitive enough—male or female—to step gently, pay attention to where you're putting your foot, and assume that everything you're stepping on or interacting with, including the breath that you take, is *alive*.

Are you a balance to that energy that's rising on the Earth? You're masculine energy that . . .

No, no. I am not adding masculine energy. In order for the Orion stuff to be resolved . . . you understand, the Orion stuff, that's in the past. It doesn't have anything to do . . . its root is in the past, it's on Orion. Those of you who are alive on the planet now who have been there and had good lives there, you don't need it. But if you've had troubled lives there, discomforted lives there, in order for a resolution to take place for you, you need support to resolve that. But your soul is not always responsive to the feminine when it has to do with the old Orion culture. This has nothing to do with the astrology book, by the way.

Correct me if I'm wrong. So your energy is helping those on this planet who had bad lives in Orion to disengage from that, to discreate the old discomfort, to not be affected by it anymore?

Yes, exactly. The double effect, though—it's sort of a bonus—is that since that old troublesome aspect of Orion is where those issues arose before, as I've said already, this has also affected the past, your history on this planet. So it's affecting your history on this planet to also allow certain aspects of that influence, which is carried over to even your now culture. You understand how groups of people might even today be mad at other groups of people for something that happened so far into the past that there's not even a living soul around who can say, "This is what really happened." It's something that's just written or has been spoken about for years. All that stuff needs to be resolved, and it has to do with your discomforting history, which goes on and on and on and on and on. It has to be changed, and you need help to change it. So it's kind of a bonus. It's not something I'm doing; it's something that's happening as a result of what I'm doing.

Let me give you an example: Say you're walking down the street and you're eating something that's fabulous, that's wonderful—it's the best doughnut you've ever had. But no one's ever seen doughnuts before. Someone looks at it and says, "Can I have a bite of that?" You give that person a bite and it's, "Wow, this is fabulous." Then you walk by the bakeshop and they're baking bread, and they say "What's this?" "It's a doughnut." They have a bite of it and, "Oh, my goodness—we could make this." It's like that, it's an effect—not intended. You're eating the doughnut because you're hungry, but other people like the doughnut.

But the influence goes out.

It's an influence. Astrologers are going to get a little bit out of this, though, because it has to do with the fact that we're trying to cover about thirteen or fourteen books worth of material here in this one book. Someday somebody will put this all together and create a tremendous cross-reference. You've already done part of that, I believe. But this will all make sense someday.

Well, this is wonderful.

Your Physical Body Is Not Unlike a Planet

Will we get an astrology that gets the Tenth Planet, the Eleventh Planet and the Twelfth Planet into the ephemeris?

Sure. It will not be quite as precise as the ephemeris you have now, because the ephemeris you have now has been greatly influenced in the past few years by the extent of the improvements in the technology of astronomy. You look at an ephemeris from many, many years ago and it wasn't anywhere near as accurate, although the accuracy it had tended to be much more spiritual, meaning the astrologer had to have capacities that were sensitive. They had to make their best guess based upon what *felt* right. That's an energy that's coming back to you all now. You have to know, "How does this feel?" and to recognize that when you're saying that, it doesn't mean, "How does it think?" It means, how does this feel physically in your body?

Your physical body is not unlike a planet. It's affected by gravity and the Moon's influence and all of that stuff. So how things feel physically is not always 100-percent accurate truth, but it does give you a foundation. So for the astrologer to be able to feel into what it might be, what it could be, is really a repetition of the past. The way the ephemeris was created before, you could be absolutely certain at how many minutes of and how many degrees of and all of that kind of stuff that you find in astronomy, based upon the fine-tuning of the astronomical instrument.

So much of the information we've gotten from some of the planets who were known was material that had been lost, but also some of it was material that wasn't known but which we're just now ready for. You were not lost; you've never been functional before. So we're learning about you now because we've changed and grown and expanded, right?

Yes, generally, yes.

I mean, no one knew about you in the past, did they? You weren't part of the information they had.

Oh, they knew it in the past.

That's what I'm trying to get at—they did?

Oh yes, they knew it in the past. After all, there are twelve signs, yes? And astrologers have been saying for years and years, "Well, there must be twelve planets." There have even been those who've said, "Well, I can feel this, this, this," and it was hard to say that's wrong to them, because it was understood that they were trying to feel something, to make sense out of a conundrum. Yet there were others who said, "Well, we can't prove it, we don't know it's so, and even if it is so, what are the qualities? How can we use it in astrology?"—meaning, what are the qualities associated with the planet? So the purpose of this book is to give you not only the hidden, lost qualities associated with the various aspects of the book that you've already done, but the hidden and unknown qualities associated with planets who have been speculated upon or felt to be there by sensitive astrologers in the past and to a degree in the present.

Do you have an affinity toward any particular sign?

No. [Pause.] But using the qualities of my personality, not only in how I say the Twelfth Planet is, but how I interact with you—make certain you publish this verbatim, so that people can see the back and forth between us— the astute astrologer will be able to see, "Look how that planet's talking to her and look how she's talking to him, and how does that planet talk . . . ?" In short, the astute astrologer can actually read a narrative of any conversation and make an educated guess as to the basic chart of the individuals speaking. Did you know that? It might be worth knowing. That's part of the reason I think other entities have said, "Oh, you've changed your words, that's not too good." There are a whole lot of folks who can gauge their value, their identity and their purpose when having somebody to identify with when reading these books. That's why you must be human and have feet of clay like all.

That's a revelation.

It's good to know these things, eh? Little bits and pieces, yes?

Yes, I like to know why, not just what.

Creator Never Asked Me to Be a Planet Permanently

So will you ever have populations on any of the levels of your planet, in higher spiritual dimensions possibly?

I do not have population on, in or within. I do not think I will. I feel that I am strictly here to do what I have said, but Creator never asked me to become a planet permanently. Just being a planet was the best way to be able to influence, and I have found that that is so. But there was never any discussion of population [chuckles].

So your time here is only until we basically move up and have the past discreated, right? Then you're free to do something else?

At some point, Creator said I could choose to return to my original state of being. But nothing else was stated, so I cannot answer that question other than with what I just said—that I would have a choice to do other things that I wanted to do. That's how I interpreted that. But for now, I'm taking a "wait and see" attitude.

So you can see just into this universe or into other universes?

I don't look to others. If I look to others, I might get confused about why I am here.

Did you look to others before you took on this job?

No. Generally speaking, beings in this universe do not look to others. I know they can, but one of the things that happens is confusion, and you cannot get rid of it. Once you have that confusion from another universe, that's part of you. When you're a being who is influencing other beings, you can't do that.

Of course, because you'll pollute what you're influencing.

So, you see, the only beings who generally might do that are travelers. If they're traveling through this universe to another one, then they can do that, especially if they're not going to have any influence on any beings in this universe. Of course, they don't always know what influence they're having. Generally speaking, I think Creator has disguised that.

So what most interests you when you scan all the life and activity that's going around this universe? Is there something that particularly interests you?

Yes, what you're doing on Earth. It's unique. Everything else is totally benign and benevolent, and that's a wonderful thing. It's completely in balance all the time, but—how can we say?—there are no "bumpy roads" elsewhere. I'm a little bit interested in the bumpy road, and I'm sure that's why . . .

You're here.

Creator said, "Would you be interested in this, then?"

You Need to Consciously Make Life Better for Yourselves

Are you protected from our discomforting energy? You don't feel it, do you?

I don't feel it.

Even the discomforting Orion energy?

No, I don't feel it. I'm very good at resolving, but I detect what needs to be resolved by looking to see what's out of balance.

How do you resolve it?

If I told you, wouldn't you do that? It's not difficult. It requires projecting to every particle and every particle that makes up every particle a totally benign level of unique balance that would be influential and benevolent to that individual item. So one frequency, so to speak, isn't enough. I use the term "frequency" not as a descriptive term but as an example.

So you know what you're focusing on when you influence with this benevolent energy?

I think I'm pretty good at it.

Then it's resolved and you go on to the next one? Like that?

Yes. That doesn't mean it can't be unresolved if the Creator decided to create another Explorer Race; I just don't think that's going to be necessary. But we'll see.

Why would it be necessary? Only if we failed, right?

I wouldn't call it failure. I would say, if you stopped and had to do it over again.

What would cause that?

We'll see. I do not know.

Oh, I thought we were well enough along that we had the momentum to succeed.

At some point, you have to start making conscious decisions to do things. You'll know because right now, for instance, you need to make the effort to consciously create a better life for yourself and others. You can't *just* believe it's going to happen. But you *do* have to believe it's going to happen.

Give me an example of consciously making life better.

Do things for people—that's an example. Do things for them that they would like to have done for them, as compared to what you can do. Sometimes there are things you can do and the people don't need it. So find someone who does and then do that to help that person. That's an example. It doesn't have to be complicated. A lot of people are doing that now.

But everybody has to do it?

I think that would be a good thing. It doesn't have to be complicated, though. Have you ever been someplace and someone is reaching for something and can't reach it, but you can reach it and you can hand it to him or her? That's doing something for somebody. I'm not saying that doing that once in your life is sufficient; I'm just saying it's an example. You wanted an example—that's one.

So it helps to be tall? [Chuckles.] Never mind, I'll take that out.

You can leave it in, but if you leave it in, make sure that your laugh stays in too. It's important for the astrologer to see our personalities.

You Have to Be Aware that Everything Is Alive

Do you approve of the Explorer Race experiment?

Oh yes, I think it shows promise. The key will be in how others on other planets who are in a benevolent state of grace and complete balance react to you, how they are influenced by you, and if it causes any problems for them. That's why when you go out and meet them, you have to be absolutely aware that everything is alive. This concept is real. Your science can prove it, even though they don't necessarily want to accept that. It's been difficult, even up to the point of the degree of which you're conducting experiments in space. Many of the space travelers you've sent up have had troubling moments: "Is it okay to do this, or is it okay to do that?" I'm glad they're thinking about that.

What's an example of their thought? Is it okay to do what?

For example, it's very controversial having left things on the Moon. A lot of people, not just the astronauts or cosmonauts, have wondered about that: "Is it really all right to leave this here?" Well, obviously if you go to other planets, you're not going to be able to bring anything from your planet and leave it there, unless they particularly request something. If they request something, then you can bring that. You'll probably find a way to transfer it to them. It might be something simple—most likely it will be. It won't likely be anything that you consider has any particular value, but it might have it to them. So that's going to take a lot of finesse.

I think we need to wrap this up. Astrologers, I salute you—those of you who are doing this, even at the hobby level, to say nothing of professionals. I know you want to help other people to understand their lives so that they can do more in a benevolent way for themselves and others. For that matter, your original interest may have come from wanting to understand more about yourself. So, of course, all of you have a considerable amount of interest in the past, present and future. Given that, you will know that due to my influence and ability to interact with the past in a benevolent way, I have touched all your souls. Good life.

Good life. Thank you.

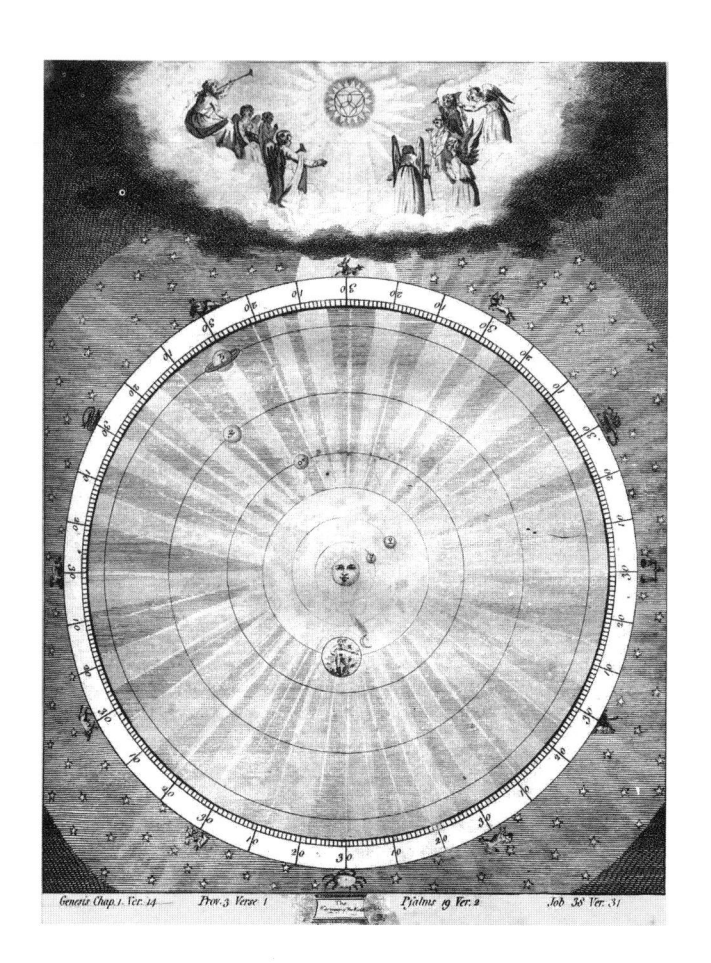

Genesis Chap. 1. Ver. 14 — *Prov. 3 Verse 1* — *Psalms 19 Ver. 2* — *Job 38 Ver. 31*

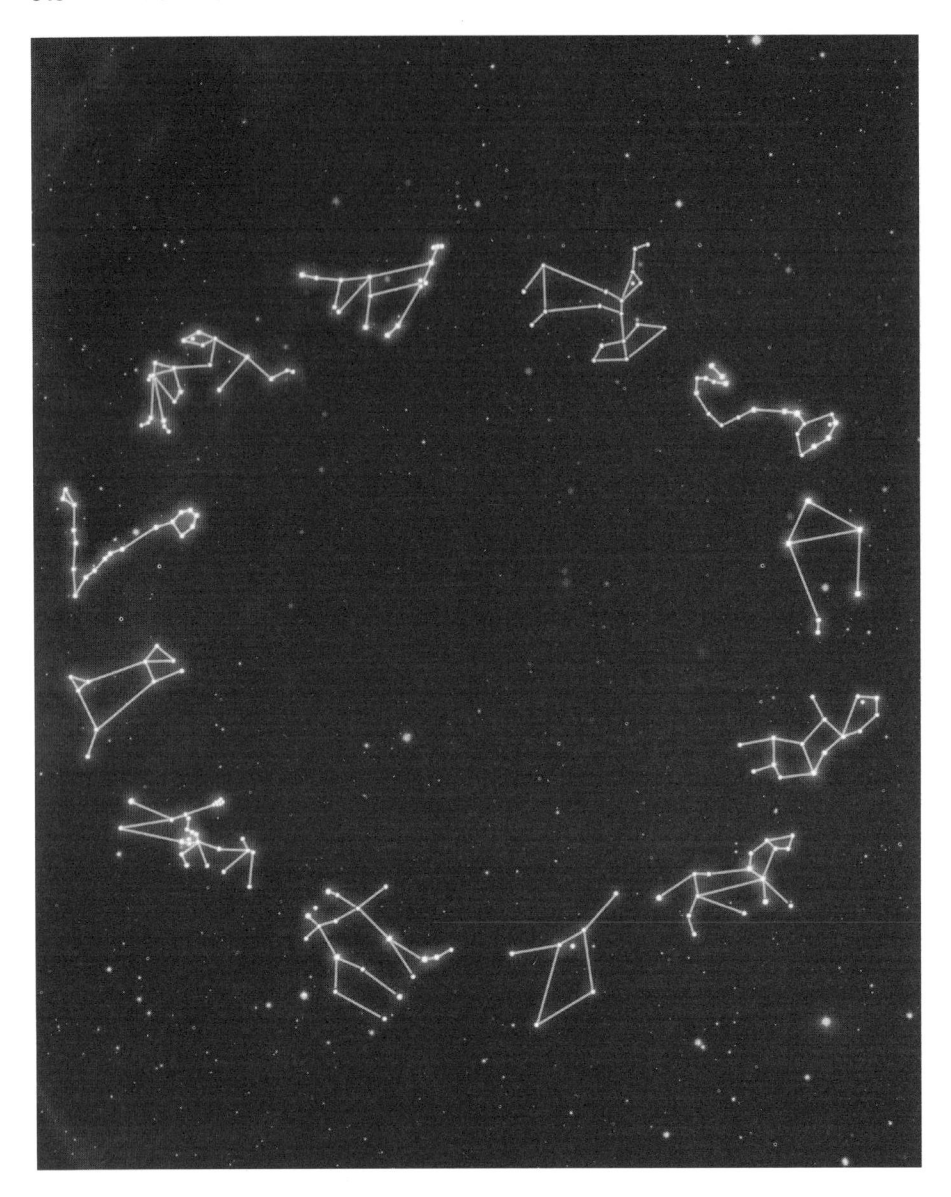

Astrological Signs

TEACHER OF ASTROLOGY

Astrology Is a Means to Engage the Mind and
Encourage Imagination—
Use It to Achieve Unity

May 31, 2002

I am the teacher of wisdom who allows growing cultures to find meaning, purpose and worthy challenge in their lives. I travel in star systems mostly—for the past few million years equivalent to your time—to consult and advise on those already well established. With your Earth culture, I have noted the necessary preparations in your now time to give the followers the beings you all need and desire to live up to by their example.

Sometimes these beings take the form of teachers or out-of-the-ordinary people. Sometimes they arrive in golden chariots as your religious books say—which are, of course, from other veils you call dimensions. "Veils," I think, is a better word, because it suggests that something is screened from your view but is there. Of course, the other obvious thing is a vehicle from some other place.

There's always, in all of your civilizations, a desire for such a teacher or exceptional person or visitor from elsewhere to come and unite the people to one cause and purpose, to warm your hearts, to take away your pain, to deliver to you the value and nurturance of living: as a feeling, as a thought, as a memory, and as a hope. This has been done before, but civilizations here have come and gone while you are attempting to establish an enduring one. Now, of course, you are going through the trouble time where the civilizations survive or they don't, but you're going through a somewhat fixed step—not fixed from the external, but fixed in terms of your own repetition of certain procedures.

Imagination Paves the Way for Change

Right now you are experiencing the difficult side of the mental powers. The mental powers can be utilized for great good, but the false side is that the seduction for the mental powers is facts. In my experience, anything mental is always in flux. This is natural: you learn more and you change your mind. But once you become enamored with facts—and certain parts of mentality are particularly enamored with this in this time for you—then you begin looking for facts everywhere.

One of the ways to know when a society is attracted to facts is to track religious and cultural beliefs, and wait until they turn into a belief that always signals the coming challenges. In civilizations struggling to move through difficult periods, religious and cultural beliefs always become science in one form or another. This does not mean that science is somehow the enemy or inherently evil, but rather it is simply like a chef. A chef knows when the food reaches a certain point on the basis of its flavor, its appearance, its aroma and so on. It is like that for us Outsiders, or observers. We know that when religious and cultural affairs reach a certain point, science appears, and to the mind it becomes almost like a religion in its own right because it produces and reproduces and creates multiple offspring of facts, and the mind is seduced by facts.

It is not that the mind does not have capabilities and cannot soar, but the best part of your mind is imagination, because imagination paves the way to prepare the mind to change. You learn more, you change your mind, you grow. Imagination is the receptor to learning more: "What if? Could it be? I wonder." All of these things are associated with imagination. You'll find that even any cursory examination of history will often reveal patterns.

I will not go into these because this is too long a subject, but I will say this: Given the state of science that you now have, the next step is always the same. I have seen it in cultures all over. The next step is always the breakthrough that physicists invariably predict, and that is the merging of inspiration, imagination and love, in terms of the warmheartedness one has for one's family and one's loved ones and one's community and ultimately more—with one more factor, and that is the knowledge.

The knowledge invariably creates a connection between all beings so that one can see how all things are connected. This knowledge is given to your various societies, ones that are known (to the best of the Outsiders' point of perspective) that they will survive at least to the point when that cathartic action takes place, which is the next step after science. The preparation for this, the groundwork, is to provide certain techniques and methods. One of the preparations lays a groundwork for you to see how you are all united, how certain manners and mores (yes, even such things as that) are influenced and also rationalized—which is a strong factor in your time and, of course, one that supports the basis of conditioning in your cultures.

These unifying principles given are always the same, one of which is astrology. Astrology is the way that encourages the mind to explore possibilities, to see similarities, and to encourage motion in the mind to apply a mental picture to the wheel. The wheel in this sense is not a technological invention but rather the circle of life in your time celebrated in many ways, both symbolically and otherwise.

True Knowledge Is Always Flexible

Astrology, then, was given to various cultures a long time ago, ones that endure today, cultures that go back thousands of years. Some are in places like India and its sister country, Pakistan (countries that would do better to be one country, but their struggles now will help them to see how much they are alike in the future). The other cultures that were given astrology—not necessarily as a fact but rather as a way, a story, to see how people are alike and unique within groups—are China and various native peoples, some of whom are still with you today.

The ones who responded to it would be the ones, in terms of their culture, who would find explorations with the mind most attractive. It's easy for you to look at your cultures and civilizations of today, and say, "Which cultures and civilizations are most attracted to mental explorations, are philosophical: 'What is this? What could it be? What might it become? Where did it come from? How can we use it?'" That's not difficult; I will not go into that. You can explore your own contemporary societies on Earth to see which cultures might particularly find those questions attractive.

What knowledge leads to the next step after science? Invariably, it is always the same. It is, "Who are you? Where are you from? Why are you here? What is it that you really need to do? Where are you going from here? What will you do when you get there? How can you accomplish all this?" That's it. That's the knowledge, and it will come via messengers, as in this [channeling] process that has been ongoing for many years now in all these books. It will also come, not only from those who study these books and speak of these things, but it must come from a global communication system—not just that which speaks to the mind, as your broadcast industry or even the computer does, but one that speaks to the heart, voices that you hear, resonance that you wake up to over and over and over again so that you are affected. You speak to your friends, "What is that? Who said that? I heard it." You talk to your friend, maybe in another country, and he or she says, "I heard it in my language."

In short, it must move past the technology of the day, also known as contemporary science. It must also move past that which is expected—"ordinary," you say, conversation, letters and so on. It must be something that is universal. Everyone, all humans, hears it in some way, meaning they have words that inspire thoughts and imaginations, and they have feelings that inspire hope, that nurture, that encourage, no matter what your state of being is or how enamored you are of facts.

Given the state of your cultures and the factionalizing from one religion to another (to say nothing of one's sect or one's cultural group), the facts given—[chuckles] I joke with you—the knowledge given must make sense in the mind, must feel true in the heart and body, and must be practical in application. Such knowledge in your time always comes from some method like this, as described. It might be from a person, it might be from many people, it might be from apparent beings. You have been warned in your cultures and philosophies of false prophets. The way to recognize a false prophet, compared to what I am speaking of today, is that a false prophet always does one thing aside from everything else—her or she always gives you facts.

When you receive the knowledge, the knowledge is always flexible because it counts on the fact that you all know deep down within every one of you that no matter how conditioned you are to your system or t, you know that you are unique. No matter how much you want to be like your friends or those you look up to, you know you are unique, even if you do not think of it that way or feel it that way. The way you might feel it is, "People do not understand me. They don't know the real me. They see this, they think that, but there's more, much more to me." That is a way of knowing you are unique. Children in enlightened societies are encouraged to believe they are unique and that they share certain similar cultural traits with those they live around that they can identify with and which will nurture them in that culture to carry on that culture. I'm not commenting on whether that is a good thing or not, but that is what you experience now.

Don't look for facts in the true knowledge—that which is rigid and states, "This is how it is." Rather, look for things that are flexible. You might also look for things that seem to have gaps [chuckles]. The gaps are often left for you to fill in the spaces. When you are allowed to fill in the spaces, you can make mistakes, try different things: "This works; that doesn't." In short, you are encouraged to create the material that fills up the gaps and spaces. That's another way to know you have received the true knowledge that will benefit you. So, remember, the false prophet will give you rigid facts. That which is of the true knowledge will give you flexible knowledge and sometimes knowledge that has gaps. You must know that in order to like it, it must feel good physically, in the warm, loving place physically in your body. This knowledge (how to find the warmth or create it) has been given to you already.

The Love-Heat Exercise

I am giving what we're calling the love-heat exercise in a way that Speaks of Many Truths taught me how to do it. Take your thumb and rub it very gently across your fingertips for about half a minute or a minute. And while you do that, don't do anything else. Just put your attention on your fingertips. Close your eyes and feel your thumb rubbing slowly across your fingertips. Notice that when you do that, it brings your physical attention into that part of your body. Now you can relax and bring that same physical attention anywhere inside your chest—not just where your heart is, but anywhere across your chest, your solar plexus area or abdomen—and either generate or look for a physical warmth that you can actually feel.

Take a minute or two or as long as you need to find that warmth. When you find it, go into that feeling of warmth and feel it more, just stay with it. Stay with that feeling of warmth. Feel it for a few minutes so you can memorize the method, and most importantly, so your body can create a recollection, a physical recollection of how it feels and how it needs to feel for you. The heat might come up in different parts of your body—maybe one time in the left of your chest, maybe another time in the right of your abdomen or other places around there. Wherever you feel it, just let it be there. Don't try and move it around—that's where it's showing up in that moment. Always when it comes up and you feel the warmth, go into it and feel it more.

Make sure you do this when you are alone and quiet, not when you are driving a car or doing anything that requires your full attention. After you do the warmth for five minutes or so if you can, or as long as you can do it, then relax. And afterward, think about this: The warmth is the physical evidence of loving yourself. Many of you have read for years about how we need to love ourselves, but in fact, the method is not just saying, "I love myself," or doing other mental exercises that are helpful to give you permission to love yourself. Rather, the actual physical experience of loving yourself is in this manner, and there are things you can do that are supportive of it. But in my experience, and the way I was taught, this is the method you can most easily do.

The heat will tend to push everything out of you that is not of you or that is not supporting you, because the heat, as the physical experience of loving yourself, also unites you with Creator. It unites you with the harmony of all beings, and it will tend to create a greater sense of harmony with all things. You might notice as you get better at this and can do it longer that should you be around your friends or other people, they might feel more relaxed around you, or situations might become more harmonious. Things that used to bother or upset you don't bother you very much, because the heat creates an energy,

> not only of self-love, but of harmony. Remember that the harmony part is so important. You might also notice that animals will react differently to you—maybe they'll be more friendly, perhaps they'll be more relaxed, maybe they'll look at you in a different way. Sometimes you'll be surprised at what animals, even the smallest—such as a grasshopper, a beetle, a butterfly, a bird—might do because you're feeling this heat.
>
> Because it is love energy, it naturally radiates just as light comes out of a light bulb. Remember, you don't throw the heat out, even with the best of intentions. You don't send it to people. If other people are interested in what you are doing or why they feel better around you, you can teach them how to do this love-heat exercise in the way you learned or the way that works best for you. And the most important thing to remember is that this method of loving yourself and generating harmony for yourself creates harmony for others, because you are in harmony. Remember that this works well and will provide you with a greater sense of ease and comfort in your life no matter who you are, where you are, what you are doing or how you're living your life. It can only improve your experience. The love-heat exercise is something that is intended to benefit all life, and in my experience, it does benefit my life.
> —Robert Shapiro

This way you will know you are being trusted to fill in those gaps. If you make a mistake, you will know from the consequences. If it is not a mistake, you will know because everyone will find some value in it—if not right away, then in time. You have had difficulty with that last one I just said, "If not right away, then in time," because it is easy to rationalize mentally: you don't like it now, but you'll grow to like it, or you don't like it now, but you'll get used to it, and so on.

The knowledge tells you about yourself. Think about what I said it does. These books you have received about the Explorer Race attempt to give you much of that knowledge, but they don't really tell you what to do with it. Oh, they might give you some things you can try, and some things will work for some people and some things will work for others, as is the nature of your uniqueness. But it does attempt to lay down at least some knowledge, purposefully leaving many gaps.

The Value of Astrology Is Upon You

The value of astrology is upon you. It is not a religion; it is not an end in itself. It is a way of incorporating the mind into your day-to-day life that allows the mind to feel it is contributing, it is understanding, it is appreciating, and it is nurturing the value of life. But ultimately, it is the *feelings* that bring you home. Practice the warmth you find or generate, and this will help you to find your way.

My people, whom I refer to as the Outsiders, since they are not part of your civilization, provided this astrologic information to enduring cultures that you have, those that are still with you—some who have embraced it, some who have not, and that's fine. In time, further information will be given so that astrology is seen in the light of the true knowledge, which allows it to have gaps and spaces, and to be a support matrix. Read about yourself based on your birth date and time if you can—not just the entertainment astrology, but more thorough explanations. Ask the experts to put them in terms you can understand.

The more you read about yourself, the more you will understand your potentials. Don't be limited by it. Feel free to try other things, but notice that when you try other things, you will still be, at least in your own mind, that which you were born to. Know that feelings unite, and no matter what you were born to, it is when you unite with feelings and loving warmth that you can either do many things beyond that which you were born to, or you will naturally attract with that warmth those you can do them with, who can teach you, who will do them for you, or for whom you can do them.

I will not give you a name, because it is not possible to give you a name in your time that will not be claimed by one religion, philosophy, culture or political group, but I will say that I have been to your world many times when civilizations have come and gone. I have seen them come and go, and that is why I encourage you not to become overly enamored with facts. Facts invariably suppress imagination, and that is what destroys societies. The mind is not the enemy, but it must be experienced in balance. When you are practicing to feel the love-warmth [also known as the love-heat], don't think, but when you come to the end of your love-warmth practice as you are learning it, think for a moment about anything. You will notice it is almost impossible, if not in fact impossible, to maintain the love-warmth while you are thinking.

This tells you that that which is your foundation, the love-warmth, is in its very nature exclusive. It is exclusive of what? It is exclusive of facts. Thought is always based on facts, real or unreal. In your time, as you learn how to rethink—to think in new ways not only based on the true knowledge of who you are, where you're from and so on, but also how to use the mind in ways that support and nurture the love-warmth feeling—you will discover that the mind can be used, that it can support.

Homework: Add Words to Your Love-Warmth Practice

I will tell you how to begin. Sometime toward the end of your love-warmth experience of the day (you might feel it many times once you put it into practice and you're beyond simply learning it, but sometime toward the end of your learning session with it), consider the word that most benevolently describes that one person—be they male or female, young or old, a deity even, or an imagined person—one word that describes them in the most wonderful way. It does not have to be someone alive anymore. It might even be someone where you use your imagination to imagine how they *might* be when or if they are with you.

While you are feeling the love-warmth, toward the end, have that word on a piece of paper, because you won't be able to think about it. Have the paper turned face over so you can see the back, but as you're feeling the love-warmth, turn the paper over and look at the word. Focus only on feeling the love-warmth and see if that word can be in your mind while you feel the love-warmth. That is your homework.

From there you will be able to add other words, but just do one at a time, one a day. Make a list of the words; they will all describe that which is beautiful and wonderful to you. From person to person they might be different. For some of you, the words will be completely different, but you must find a foundation of words that you can support, maintain and be compatible with while experiencing the love-warmth. Don't try to inflict the words on the love-warmth, but rather the love-warmth is your foundation. If the words stop you from feeling the love-warmth, then you will know that it's not that word. Or you will be able to think that word and maintain the love-warmth. Some words might even cause the love-warmth to get stronger. Make note of that too, after you stop doing the love- warmth. Do one word a day only. You will build up a vocabulary of words in time that you will be able to use to describe things, to speak while you are experiencing the love-warmth and be able to maintain it.

In time you might be able to add other words, but start with these kinds of words first. It will create compatibility with your love-warmth, which is your foundation, and will reeducate the mind how it can be, how it can exist, how it can support and be supported and still be itself. Remember, the mind is not your personality. It might be how your personality defines itself or thinks—meaning how it associates itself with words or various facts—but the true description of who you are is how others feel your love-warmth when you are feeling it around them if they are receptive to it. Either they're doing the training themselves, or because you are feeling it so strongly for yourself, they feel it anyway and that is the signal of you.

All beings who can feel the love-warmth—animals feel it almost all the time, plants, stone—all these beings are part of the natural world. They are not here to learn but to teach. For human beings, what you are learning with the love-warmth—how to do it and now how to apply it—is really what the natural world knows. So this prepares you, in the physical form of a human being on Earth now, to rejoin the natural world, which is your natural state when you are not in such a rigorous school.

Astrology is a way to help you, a way to support and nurture you, a way to encourage you to use your imagination, but it is not now nor has it ever been intended to be fact. That's why gaps and spaces were purposely left so that you could fill them in, try different things, and experience your imagination with this form of inspiration.

Cultures Have Risen and Fallen on Earth

How large is your sphere of influence? This creation, or much beyond that? Orbs, realms, the totality?

There are no boundaries. (The energies collect around the eyes—this wet cloth is helpful.)

Was it you personally or another one who does what you do who first gave the principles of astrology to the early cultures here of India, Pakistan and China?

There were other cultures as well, the native peoples, some of whom are still alive today or perhaps their stories are. It was not me; it was another one.

One specific being?

Yes.

Can you tell when in our history that happened, in terms of time or how many civilizations ago?

In terms of your current civilization, depending on how you count, it was from 7,000 to 11,000 years ago, but I grant that the civilizations as they exist today were different then and the teaching took place over many generations. I grant also that a few facts have been lost along the way, but that's good. Facts are too rigid. What was taught were guidelines, suggestions, generalities, with specifics given only when the students would make comments on different individuals they were working with or groups of individuals they had noticed might be related or aligned in some way, since dates of birth were not always known for sure then. Then more knowledge was given.

Was it a process of channeling like this, or did some of them physically take a human body? Or were they actually born into human bodies as teachers?

They came from elsewhere. They came from outside your planet.

Did they appear as themselves?

They would look like human beings so as to not frighten you; plus, they would look like the cultures they were meeting. There would be something sufficiently distinctive about them, albeit an admirable quality, that would encourage the students to be attracted to the teacher.

You have the ability, then, to change your form to look like the people you're teaching?

Sufficiently similar so that they do not feel overly uncomfortable.

Do you have a natural shape, or are you more like a point of light?

Shape is not rigidly a factor of our existence.

More like a flowing?

It could be that. It could be something else.

Do you recognize each other by your feeling?

Yes. All beings in the natural world do.

So 11,000 years ago is not very long. Is that just when one of the beings like you gave the teaching to the cultures that are represented now? You've been here many times before that, right?

Yes, because cultures have risen and fallen on Earth. I might add as an explanation to something that is difficult for your science people to understand: The big so-called prehistoric beings with the big tails and the big teeth and so on . . .

Oh, dinosaurs?

Yes. They were not native to this planet. They were brought here against their will as a biological weapon used by one culture against another—which, of course, ultimately eliminated both cultures. That is why in time they were rescued and brought back to their own planet, where they are benevolent, benign and sometimes smaller.

Do we have any records, cultures or myths that would mention those people who were using the dinosaurs?

No, because that was a fairly advanced civilization in science, utilizing science for warfare, that has gone and left no findable trace. When you begin studying a little more about cultures that have existed that have been lost and so on, then you will become more aware of them and their similarities to you. As I said before, all these cultures died out because they got too involved and enamored of facts.

I think Zoosh once said there were eighteen different civilizations. Is that your understanding?

That sounds about right to me. From my perspective, you are number eighteen.

There Needs to Be Flexibility

So what stands ahead of us, since the challenge that could wipe us out is being enamored of science?

No, it's being enamored of facts. Facts are fun to learn, and you can have them benevolently as long as there are gaps and spaces that can be built on first with imagination. Then parts that seem to fit will be found at some point. But if they are rigid facts, then that will not serve you. You can say certain things with certainty, but it depends on how you look at it. You can say the sky is up, but pull back from the planet. A person stands on one side of the planet and looks up, yes? And a person stands on the other side of the planet and looks up. But given that perspective, which way is up and which way is down?

There needs to be flexibility. Sometimes you don't see something or you forget something. Therefore, the fact is more benevolent if there are gaps and spaces, if imagination is honored with the true honor it deserves as that which supports inspiration, that which nourishes and receives inspiration, and that which requests and desires inspiration to move onward.

It's not appropriate at this time, then, to really discuss astrology? I wanted some new facts. But now that you've explained . . .

You will find that there is a desire by astrologers to learn about other planets that might be in your solar system and chart them and so on. I will say that at some point you might find things like this, but that is less important. It is better for you to imagine more about astrology, to try it and see if it fits. Astrologers have been doing that for years, to say nothing of generations, and that's a good process because it allows you to be creative and does not make of you a follower. It is not a bad thing to be a follower as long as the follower is encouraged to imagine, be inspired and more. But if the follower follows rigid facts, then only existence without joy can follow.

Astrology is a means to engage the mind and encourage imagination. You provide it with ideas that you get nurturance from these different sources, but you get nurturance from all the stars and planets everywhere, not just these. Even if you are associated with one or the other, you still get nurturance from all. What is a mental explanation is not a fact; it is simply knowledge.

What I was looking for is the way astrology is perceived now and then to go beyond that and state, "Where did the energies come from that are supposed to come through these planets in our solar system?" What's the larger picture?

Did you not request the being or beings who provided astrology to Earth? I am a portion of that. I am not the being who originally came here—that being is no more. It has been assimilated into the totality of what we are. We take on certain personalities; I am one at the time that speaks to you now. I have that personality of that being available to me with all of its knowledge and wisdom, but you cannot speak to that being because that being has become what I explained.

Love-Warmth Is the Foundation of the Natural World

When beings like you come to a planet like Earth, they give a system of knowledge that in this case was astrology. When they go to other cultures on other planets, do they have other systems of knowledge that they use?

Usually it is not something mental. You people on Earth were given something mental because you need to experience the mind in order to assimilate it and reeducate it. On other planets, only that education of the natural world is given. Sometimes that takes the form of understanding different beings you would take as animals here (though there is no such thing). But on the other planets where there is sometimes some variety, rather than break things down in terms of this birth date, that birth date, rather we talk about what they don't know about themselves on that planet to each being—so that they know about themselves and that they also know about the others on the planet unlike themselves but with whom they are compatible.

Therefore, they know what they need to know to enjoy each other more. They are not told about any histories that are unhappy, because such things are not needed there, but they are informed and nurtured and encouraged to know more in the way that would support them to experience each other more benevolently, more happily, or even simply just more. They are supported to want to come together because, "Here's where you're from—isn't that interesting? You're also from someplace nearby, even though you look completely different—isn't that interesting?" Such things tend to bring beings together.

Are there developing cultures on all planets?

No. That's why I said at the beginning that my job and the job of the others now is to advise and consult. The only culture that needs a lot of help is [chuckles] here. Most of the other planets . . . and when I refer to "other planets," I mean other planets who have cultures that you would find similar enough so that you could relate to them if you met them. I'm not talking about all cultures everywhere.

So for other planets in, let's say, the local galaxy, astrology isn't an art form or a form of knowledge?

If they are researchers and their studies involve the study of Earth people, they will know all about it.

So they don't use it themselves on their planet?

Correct.

Astrology is only on Earth?

But it gives you a means to understand and to utilize and to appreciate. In other places, it is considered to be like a philosophy—granted, a mental philosophy, but still a philosophy—by which people learn and grow and are attracted and so on, and are able to build on that. It is not considered anything but a philosophy.

So what forms do your ongoing consultations with Earth people take now?

Our ongoing consultation would usually be to inspire—let's say, in the past it has been to inspire astrologers and at some point in the future it will be, as I said, to provide what I refer to as the true knowledge. But it is true knowledge with gaps, so you are not stuck with facts and you can modify it.

Is it probable that you would, through this channel, bring some of what you call true knowledge through, or are we not ready for it yet?

Much has been brought through. I indicated that.

Oh, the whole Explorer Race *books are that.*

Not all, but some of it is in the books. When it is time for true knowledge, everyone will receive it in the same sequence—meaning in the same sequence of time. One might get this, one might get that, but you will all be getting it so that you can compare notes and share experiences and appreciate the value no matter what your culture, religion, nationality or any other word you use to describe how you are different.

Will you be part of this broadcast or radiation or diffusion or whatever of this knowledge?

Diffusion—that's a nice word. Yes.

Is there a time frame on it? Is it soon, when you'll be doing this?

I will not give you that. It is dependent on what you as a planetary people do. It will be sooner if you do this, later if you do that. It will be sooner as more and more people, including you, experience the love-warmth regularly. That is the foundation of the natural world. It is the stuff that attracts one particle of life to another and so on and so forth.

It's the basis of unity, right?

It is the basis of all natural life in the natural world as I know it.

We Go Where We Are Needed

Can you talk about yourself just a little bit? Do you consider that wherever you come from is a place, or are you omnipresent, like on the grid lines or something? Can you say a little bit about your life?

As you have heard from others, wherever we are needed we can be with no boundaries in space, time, ideas or feelings. We do not come from a point of origin as you know it.

Is there a number you could put to the beings like you who do this, or do you sort of morph in and out—where there are some and then there are more?

We are complete in all the individual personalities we need to apply the work.

Which means, then, that if you need fifty, you have fifty, and if you need two, then you have two?

Exactly.

This is what you've always done?

Always, yes.

Do you know who created you?

We have always existed. Do you know your true predecessors or who created you? Do you understand why I am asking?

Because most people don't know?

No.

Why?

Why did you ask me?

I wanted to know if you came from beyond the totality or if you'd been here when Ssjoooo first waved this particular day of light into being?

And how did I answer?

You said you've always been here.

And . . . so have you.

So has everybody?

Yes.

So this is your life, then? You are called, you go to the places you are needed, and this is your joy, what you do, yes?

Yes.

Since you are mostly focusing on the Explorer Race, when we achieve a level of unity and go on, will you do this elsewhere?

We are not mostly focused on that. We go where we are needed and we will continue to do that. You see us as mostly focused on you because you are here.

I misunderstood. I thought you said the focus was here now because we need it so much.

Yes.

So later your focus will be someplace else.

Exactly.

But I didn't get a clear answer to this question—this is a strange case, the Explorer Race, but in other creations is there a period of development that they go through?

You are not strange, but you are unique. They are unique, and all beings are unique in their own way. Sometimes, like you on Earth, they will need to go through a period of development where they are encouraged to grow and change in this benevolent, natural way. Then they might need various forms of nurturing from us or others, and that is available.

So you don't just teach philosophical systems? You nurture in many different ways.

You want to know things that would make me grand. I am not grand. I am a humble being providing that which I can provide based on what I know to a greater and sometimes lesser value to those who may receive it. It's important to think of me that way so that I do not become some voice of authority. I would rather be one of the many than one of the few.

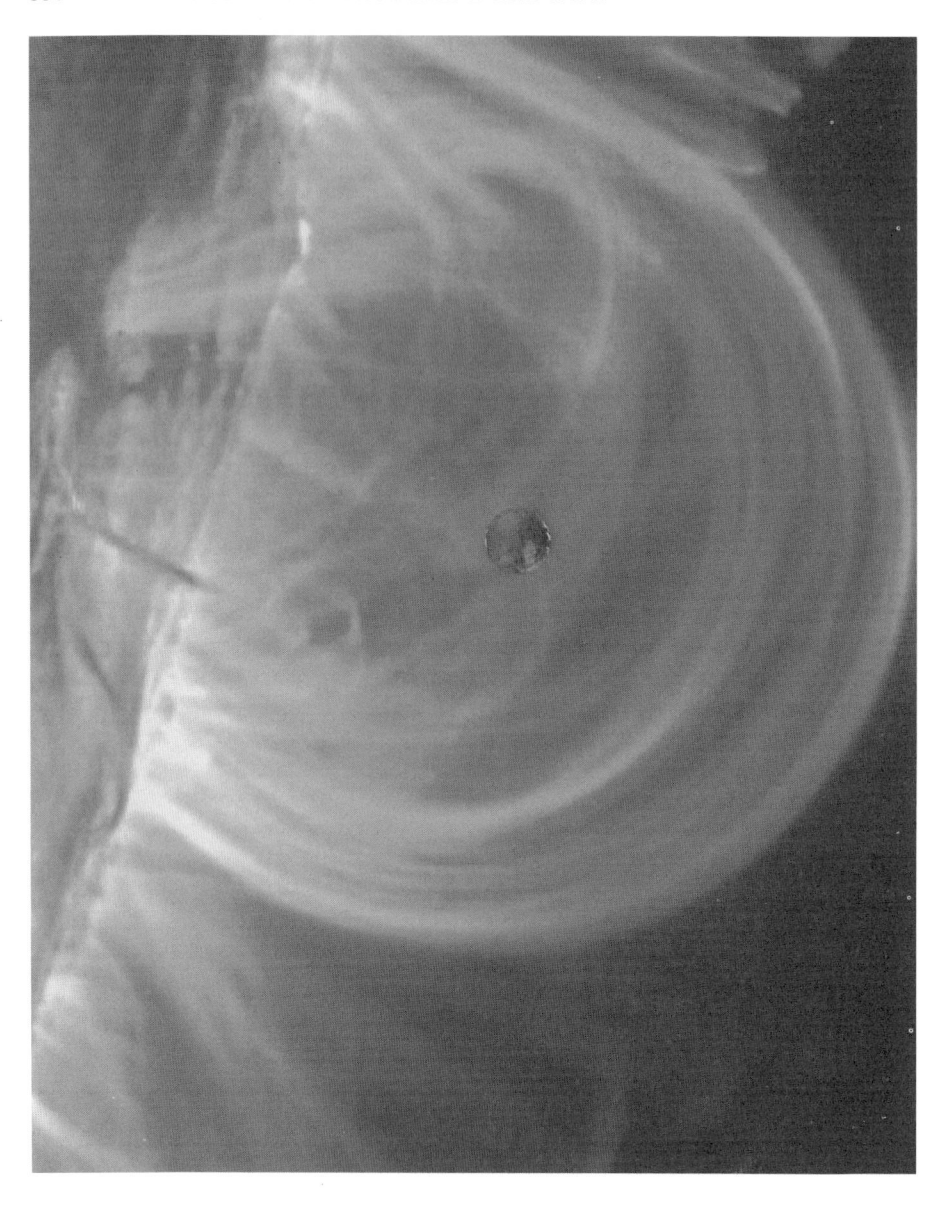

Earth Enveloped in Sun's Rays

REVEALS THE MYSTERIES
The Intimate Nature of Life in this Solar System

January 15, 2003

The Sun is often considered in your cultures to be like the father, but this is not a good description of the Sun—it's not sufficient. The Sun nurtures life as you know it, physical life on your planet. I won't talk at length here, because science has given you a lot, but this book is intended to give you the personal side that science has not explored very much yet, although someday they will. The Sun and Earth are connected on the basis of personal intimacy and a form of love that is not usually appreciated by the human being.

The Sun Provides Mother Earth with Touch

The Sun provides its rays of light and nurturance, but the Sun provides more than that. When Earth feels, not lonely, but when she feels the need for companionship . . . and this happens. Everything isn't a "thing"; everything is a *someone*. So Earth is *someone*. What happens when she feels the need for companionship? You know, companionship can be friendship. You call your friend in another country or city and you talk and it's fun, but it's not the same as when you're together with your friend, where you can hug her or him and laugh about things together and interact and have a meal together and so on.

What happens when Mother Earth wants that kind of companionship? What can she touch? As you know, where you live on Earth . . . there are the dimensions of Earth, yes, but let's talk about where you are. Mother Earth is all about touch: "How does this feel?" It is not just the feelings in your body, but, "How does this actually feel? I reach out; I touch this. How does it *feel*? Oh, that's interesting." Some things are rough, some things are soft, some things are smooth and some things are firm—in short, there are lots of different touches. Some things have a light touch and some have a more solid touch, but it's very clear that Earth is a lot about touching or even being touched. When you sit in the chair, in that sense you are touching the chair but the chair is also touching you.

What does Mother Earth do when she wants to be touched? This happens every day. What she does is that she has the feeling that she needs to be touched—she has her own feelings just like you—and the Sun reaches out and touches her. You have begun to measure these touches scientifically (you can measure certain things). Sometimes Earth needs more touch than others. Science sometime recently has discussed: "This big thing came out from the Sun and the radiation was strong."

Are you talking about a solar flare?

Yes. They can measure it on the Earth and know that it's going to interfere in your electronic signals and so on. But when that happens, it's never arbitrary on the Sun's part. It is always and only because Earth needed to be touched in a more physical way. The rays of light from the Sun usually are enough, but not always. Sometimes she needs something that she can actually feel physically, that her auric field can feel as it passes through. You know, your science has come up with the means to measure these energies as they literally pass through and go past your planet. Most of the way you measure it is by its effect on other things, but you do have ways to measure the energy itself.

For Earth, she feels it as physical contact. How else can she get physical contact that feels good—something she desires—in a safe way for her and, for that matter, for you? She can't snuggle up to and touch the Moon. I don't think that would feel too good to most people on the Earth, to say nothing of plants and animals.

In short, it's not always something you think about. Even if you don't have anybody in your life, you often have a friend you can hug or at least someone you can shake hands with, so there's touch. Mother Earth needs touch from someone she trusts, knows and feels absolutely good about, and that touch must come in a way that will not harm all life living upon her. So naturally it comes from someone—the Sun is someone—who can reach out and touch her with something she can feel physically and is not harmful to life here. Is that not beautiful?

The Earth Gives the Sun a Sense of Purpose

Now, you might also ask, "What does the Earth do for the Sun?" She as a planet (as we speak of her in that gender) gives something to the Sun that makes it possible for the Sun to have a purpose for living. This is something your societies have really forgotten, but sometimes parents discover it—you don't remember it as a child, though you have the experience, but parents are usually conscious of it—and that's that Earth gives the Sun her need. Therefore, the Sun knows it is needed, knows it's required for life, for nurturance. Earth gives the Sun the gift of a purpose.

Think about it: How many times have you had a skill or ability, something you could do or even something you liked to do, that you wanted to share with somebody else? That's a need on your part. Sometimes you have someone you can share that with, but this most often comes up for parents. When the children are there, they need you to do everything while you teach them the way of life on Earth, and then as they get older, you can share things with them that you like to do and maybe they will like to do that, at least for a while. Perhaps when they grow up and develop their own personality, they go off and do other things, but when they're little children, they want to do what dad's doing or what mom's doing, and by their need they give you a reason to exist. That is purposely built into the human experience to remind you of the bigger picture. The main thing Mother Earth gives the Sun that the Sun *loves* is her need for what the Sun can provide. Of course, the other planets do that also.

You don't often think about the Sun that way, but the reason you sometimes think about the Sun as being a father or a mother—some cultures think of the Sun as mother, instead of father—is that the planets, from the Sun's point of view, are the Sun's beloved family. They're not children, as in my example with parents, but I wanted to give you an example in your life you could identify with. You've all at least been children—some of you both.

So the Sun thinks . . . it doesn't actually think, but the Sun knows that the planets are the Sun's intimate family. The Sun reaches out in its own way with light and also with those energy waves. Sometimes the planet needs the Sun, but it's turned the other way. How can it get that with that energy wave that passes right through and says, "Here I am"? It gives you that hug and the energy the planet needs, even if it might be spun around away from the Sun so that part of the planet is in the nighttime, as you say.

The Sun Is Foremost About Intimacy

So there is that intimate relationship with the Sun and Earth, and also with the Sun and the other planets—but there is more. The Sun also knows that when those rays go out, they will go out to other suns in other places, and the Sun then has a family that goes beyond the solar system here. The Sun's family is, you might say, like a birth family, what you're born to, although birth does not happen the same way for suns. But suns are born to be suns, yes? They are created to be suns. Yet their close family beyond their immediate solar family—meaning the solar system—is other suns.

So when they radiate out that energy (as you say, a solar flare), because Earth or maybe another one of the planets in the solar system needed that physical touch, it also goes beyond, it goes past, it keeps on going. It goes past the solar system and it tends to go out spherically. It goes out in all directions, and a lot of it goes to other suns. Those other suns are doing that too so that all suns are in touch with each other at all times.

The important thing for you as human beings to know about the planets and the Sun and the Moon is how very intimate they all are with each other. That's why life on Earth is so intimate. I grant that there are times you wish it weren't. But think about it: Even if you don't have someone to be intimate with in your life—and at certain times in your life, you might not—you cannot get away from intimacy, because you have to be intimate with your own body on a daily basis simply to perform your daily functions. You have to eat and you have to let go of what you've eaten before. That's pretty intimate.

Intimacy, then, has a lot to do with the Sun. You touch and are touched. This is to remind you of your connection to the Sun, and it's also to remind you of your connection to all life. All life touches and is touched, even what you consider to be things (I use the word "things," because it's your word), inanimate objects. Everything is alive, and everything touches or is touched. This tells you that the Sun is first and foremost about intimacy.

This is why when astrologers look at your chart, they might see where Venus is, for example, because this will tell you a little bit about how you can make contact with human beings in a way that might be best for you in an intimate relationship, as astrologers say. But a lot of times astrologers look at other things that they don't necessarily tell to the people they are helping. One of the things they look at is, not just your Sun sign, but they'll also study the different angles of things, how they bear on the Sun according to you. I want astrologers to be clear in your time that the Sun is about intimacy. Granted, Venus is about love on a personal level, but the Sun is about touch and it is the place where intimacy begins.

Planets in This Solar System Receive All the Touch They Might Need

So you're saying that the planets at what we consider the edge of the solar system are receiving the same sense of intimacy from the solar flares that the inner planets and Earth are?

Yes. Let's just say, for this example, that Venus wants to be touched. So Venus has a need. There are other things, but we'll get to that. (I'm picking

Venus as an example because it's a planet.) Venus wants to be touched, so the Sun sends out that energy and *whomp,* out it goes—what you measure as a solar flare because it's physical, you can see it, there it is, and you can measure it to a degree. Once it goes past Venus, it keeps on going. Maybe the touch requested by Venus wasn't even requested by Earth, although it comes by and here you can feel it. In your calendar, different planets might want to be touched by the Earth on a cyclic basis. The planets are cyclical.

The cyclical nature of planets . . . they turn around on their own axes, plus they go around the Sun, so they're always in motion. They all do that, so everything is cyclical and they're on their own time sequences, but we're putting them on your calendar because that's the one you use. Different planets at certain times of your year and then the next year and the next year and so on, might want to be contacted because that's when the feeling comes up for them. They don't do it according to your calendar; they don't look at their watches and say, "Oh, it's time for . . ." But the feeling comes up for them at a time that you can measure by your calendar. I'm bringing this up because sometimes you'll find that the energy from what you call solar flares can be marked on the calendar and you can say, "Well, this is the time of year when we tend to experience things like that."

I mention this because, in my example, if Venus wants to be touched, then the energy comes out, touches Venus and keeps on going, touching the other planets. Remember, what's the Sun about? Intimacy and touch. The planets who are in the solar system wouldn't be here if they weren't on a very intimate level with the Sun. What happens if a planet is either here temporarily, or in the case of planets who are not here anymore, what happens if they get a strong pull to be someplace else—where the planet itself is feeling a pull if there's no interference, you understand, from external sources, other civilizations, technology or something? What happens if, on the odd occasion that I have heard about a couple of times, a planet will feel like being in another solar system? Can it actually migrate? What about the situation where a planet might feel welcome in more than one solar system, as is the case with Earth? Then the planet can migrate, but everything else has to be very equal and balanced, and there has to be a place for that planet once she gets there. This you can read about, reader, if you like, in previous *Explorer Race* books.

Now, what if the planets require a form of motion that is not readily available from the Sun—meaning, if you look at the solar system as you know it, you might reasonably say, "Well, the Sun turns on its axis and the planets turn on their axes, and they all go around the Sun on the basis of a similar axis." The planets don't go this way while other planets are going the other way.

Pluto does, doesn't it?

A little bit, but not much—you'd have to measure it mathematically. But there are orbits in the welcoming stages that are interspersed, in some cases when there are great distances between one planet and the other in the solar system, where there is an orbit that is available from the Sun's point of view where a planet could come and be placed in that orbit, spin on its axis, and join the solar system. Of course, beyond the outermost planets in the solar system there are many available orbits that will welcome other planets when they wish to join.

This obviously begs the question, "Did all planets in this solar system come into being at the same time?" No. They came into being at other times, in other places. When the planets were forming up around the Sun on the basis of feeling welcome, on the basis of their personal needs, and on the basis of feeling attracted—because the Sun is so intimate and this solar system was so clearly going to be a place where planets could receive all the touch they might need—planets came from different places at different times, not only to be happy here with this Sun, but also because of what was going to take place here.

You on This Planet Are Creating Solutions

You on this planet are the Explorer Race, and very important things are going on. You are making a tremendous contribution. The reason I bring up the Explorer Race is that certain conditions had to prevail to not only nurture you as the Explorer Race but also to allow you to learn what you needed to learn and to be constantly—every moment, every second—reminded of it, because you wouldn't be able to remember in the typical way you remember on other planets.

On other planets you always remember who you are; you have a sense of continuity from life to life. On this planet you don't have that because you need to re-create the way you've always done things. This allows you to come up with new solutions to sometimes new problems, but for the most part, they are new solutions to very ancient problems not adequately solved on other planets in other universes.

Perhaps they were solved sufficiently for a time, but where can you possibly solve a problem—and how can you conceivably solve a problem—on another planet where people tend to remember who they are and remember all their lives and what they've done and where they know what works for them and therefore they do it? They don't do anything that much different. Well, their lives are different, but their personalities are the same and they remember that. Why would they do something that didn't work for them when it works well for somebody else? Let them do it that way and you do things your way, because that's what works for you and that's how you can help each other. You're going to do that; it's compatible, it's natural. But here on this planet Earth, things are different, as you know.

So what happens on these other planets when they have a problem they cannot solve because life there is benevolent and yet they have this problem? Who's going to resolve that? For one thing, because life is benevolent there, they don't have any serious problems, but they might have something they'd like to have resolved. They don't know anybody who has resolved such a problem successfully, and what they are using is okay for now, but they'd like to have a better solution. Yet the solution has to come from beings who sufficiently resemble them so that there is some connection between cultures—meaning that whoever does come up with the solution must have a solution that applies to their culture or it doesn't do them any good.

There are many cultures like this on other planets. The only way solutions like this can be created is to have a planet where the people on the planet do not know what their previous lives were all about. Granted, that makes life a lot tougher—you feel in comparison, in my brief description here, that you are stumbling around in the dark. You say, "Gosh, I wish I remembered how I'd always done things so I didn't try to do things that don't work, and it's so hard when I keep bumping up against things that don't work." Granted, other people can do them and they work, because that is something that's part of their ongoing personality from planet to planet and life to life—just like you can do things that work for you that those others can't do because it's part of your personality, part of your skills you've accumulated from life to life.

Some Planets Came from Elsewhere to Support You

The reason the planets have to be set up in a certain way in this solar system—not only Earth but the other planets as well—is because here you are, living on this planet, creating solutions that you'll probably use when you have other lives on those other planets, and only you can do it on Earth because Creator does not want to make it hard and discomforting for everybody all over the creation. He just wants to provide a school where the students who are willing to take it on—tough school, Earth, isn't it?—are willing to solve problems that come up without being able to remember who you are.

This forces you to try things out that you would never do having the continuity of recollected personality that you have elsewhere. You'd never do it because it had never worked for you before. Why should you do it? Besides, somebody else can do it well, and if you need it done, they'll do it for you just as you do things for them as it works on other planets. Here, although you might do things for other people and they might do things for you—and you might notice that people can do things and you can do things and it's not always the same—you need the planet to be a certain way so that you are reminded of continuity. On other planets, you don't necessarily need that reminder.

So if Earth has an orbit around the Sun, then the other planets have to have an orbit around the Sun. In short, there need to be consistently similar situations that you can identify with so that regardless of your culture—whether you are scientific or sacred or religious, or spiritual or a combination of those—nevertheless you can look at Mother Nature around you and say, "Well, look, the animals are like us in some ways. The plants are even like us in some ways. The planet is obviously spinning because part of the day we're faced toward the Sun and part of the day we're not, so it must be moving." Granted, some nonscientific cultures don't think this way, but they are aware of motion. So much has to occur that has to do with intimacy and the requirements of how Earth must be and who can live on Earth to remind you, the Explorer Race, of who and what you are, because you don't have the recollection and the continuity of your lives that you have on other planets.

So only that life can live here on Earth that will remind you of who and what you are, at least on the surface—and sometimes you crawl under the surface. If you're going to meet life under the surface, such as under the water, it can only remind you in some way of yourselves or have similarities in some way: the beings there have to eat, breathe, sleep, that kind of thing. So that causes Earth to be a little bit like the Sun, and isn't that typical? Aren't family members often like each other in certain ways? The Sun considers the planets family, and the planets consider each other family, and they consider the Sun family and their moons—all that's family.

All life on Earth needs to be reminding human beings who might come into contact with it, even under a microscope. As you look out to the stars, it has to remind you of something about yourself. So Earth, like the Sun, welcomes not only that which Earth can be intimate with and feel good touching—the roots of plants go down into her soil, the feet of animals touch her, the fins of fish move her waters about, and so on—but because of who you are and why you are here as the Explorer Race, it must also be intimate and compatible with you.

From the Earth's point of view, that's why she's happy to provide you with the physical materials as part of her body that will make up your body, which necessarily, in and of its own being, must be intimate to be re-created—it's pretty intimate, being born—and must be intimate on a daily basis for an adult. You have to touch yourself all the time, every day. You eat, you release liquid and solid matter—it's very intimate. When you have friends, you touch, hug. With business associates, you shake hands. With lovers, you make love.

Everything must be intimate, and Earth is able to do this because her family member, the Sun, is so good at it. She's been able to pick up that quality, some of which she had but most of which she's picked up. She's good at touch, but intimacy is a little different, and she has been able to pick it up, nurture it with touch, and support your learning process here.

Are you saying that some of the other planets came from other solar systems?

That's what I'm saying, and they came in a similar fashion. This one—Earth—came as is described in previous *Explorer Race* books. It was needed and here it is.

The Earth came from Sirius. What about Mercury?

We'll get to that when we talk about Mercury.

Oh, you'll talk about each planet since they came from someplace else?

We're going to go planet by planet, but today we're talking about the Sun as we relate the Sun to the Earth and we relate Earth to the Sun. Sometimes we will talk about other planets, but we're talking today about the Sun.

Homework: Experience the Feeling of Timelessness

Say something more about the Sun. Did it come into being knowing it was going to be the Sun of the solar system for the Explorer Race?

Yes. Is that not amazing? When you think of how human beings think . . . I in my life was a human being, so I can identify with this. We think of things moment-to-moment, yes, but also day-to-day or day-to-night, and we don't often think on a practical level of the future—not, "What am I going to eat next year?" You might think, "Where am I going to *be* next year?" But that's how we think.

It's different for planets and suns. Their sense of time is different. For them time is not a factor. You use time here on Earth in your cultures, at least today you do; in times gone by, so to speak, not everyone used time or calendars. Now you do so, and I use those terms. You use it to measure and quantify what you need to do and when you need to do it. It makes your culture work better for you now. But planets and many other forms of life do not function in the world of time.

People often ask, "What is timelessness? We can't even identify with it." Yet I can give you a simple way to identify with timelessness and have a physical experience of it. That is to focus on any feeling—a physical feeling, but a feeling you can stimulate by thinking of an emotion you want to feel. Pick an emotion that is pleasant and go into that feeling—you can think of the word. Go into that feeling in your physical body that comes up as a result of that emotion, and go into the physical feeling as much as you possibly can. When you're in that physical feeling, also try to maintain that descriptive word or words associated with that emotion.

When you're really in touch with it, you will experience timelessness, especially if there's little or no external stimulation. Some of you might find it easier to insulate your ears with earplugs or something over the outside so you can't hear anything. Or you might find it easier if there is little or nothing in contact with your physical body. For some of you, floating in a pool of water helps; for others, it doesn't. Try it. You will be able to experience moments of timelessness.

Generally speaking, the impact of this feeling on the human being—on those alive as human beings—is that you will almost always, as a result, either go into a deep meditative state, as you call it, which is a deeply relaxed state, or you will go to sleep because this state will remind you of being inside mother. It is the state of being that is very similar to pre-birth for a human: floating in the water, often gently, and generally feeling benevolent feelings. Baby is somewhat insulated from mother's feelings. It's good for you to know this, mothers, because sometimes things come up during your pregnancy and you have strong feelings.

Granted, as baby gets closer to delivery time, say the seventh month into the pregnancy, then baby might be affected by strong feelings that you have. But before that, baby is able to maintain baby's feelings. After the seventh-month time, if mother and baby are feeling something similar, both of them feel that feeling stronger. So be aware, fathers, when living with your wife when she is pregnant. If her feelings get very strong sometimes, especially when she's at seven months, it might be that she and baby are having the same feeling at the same time. When it's a good feeling, that's wonderful—both feel wonderful. When it's not so wonderful, then mother might be more agitated than usual and baby might kick.

So the feeling of timelessness (you have that homework now), enjoy it. I think you will like it.

Good night.

Light Technology PUBLISHING

Shamanic Secrets Mastery Series
Speaks of Many Truths and Reveals the Mysteries through Robert Shapiro

Shamanic Secrets for Material Mastery

This book explores the heart and soul connection between humans and Mother Earth. Through that intimacy, miracles of healing and expanded awareness can flourish. To heal the planet and be healed as well, we can lovingly extend our energy selves out to the mountains and rivers and intimately bond with the Earth. Gestures and vision can activate our hearts to return us to a healthy, caring relationship with the land we live on. The character of some of Earth's most powerful features is explored and understood, with exercises given to connect us with those places. As we project our love and healing energy there, we help the Earth to heal from human destruction of the planet and its atmosphere. Dozens of photographs, maps and drawings assist the process in twenty-five chapters, which cover the Earth's more critical locations.

498 p. $19.95 ISBN 978-1-891824-12-8

Shamanic Secrets for Physical Mastery

Learn to understand the sacred nature of your own physical body and some of the magnificent gifts it offers you. When you work with your physical body in these new ways, you will discover not only its sacredness, but how it is compatible with Mother Earth, the animals, the plants, even the nearby planets, all of which you now recognize as being sacred in nature. It is important to feel the value of oneself physically before one can have any lasting physical impact on the world. If a physical energy does not feel good about itself, it will usually be resolved; other physical or spiritual energies will dissolve it because it is unnatural. The better you feel about your physical self when you do the work in the previous book as well as this one and the one to follow, the greater and more lasting will be the benevolent effect on your life, on the lives of those around you and ultimately on your planet and universe.

576 p. $25.00 ISBN 978-1-891824-29-5

Shamanic Secrets for Spiritual Mastery

Spiritual mastery encompasses many different means to assimilate and be assimilated by the wisdom, feelings, flow, warmth, function and application of all beings in your world that you will actually contact in some way. A lot of spiritual mastery has been covered in different bits and pieces throughout all the books we've done. My approach to spiritual mastery, though, will be as grounded as possible in things that people on Earth can use—but it won't include the broad spectrum of spiritual mastery, like levitation and invisibility. I'm trying to teach you things that you can actually use and benefit from. My life is basically going to represent your needs, and it gets out the secrets that have been held back in a storylike fashion, so that it is more interesting."

—Speaks of Many Truths through Robert Shapiro

768 p. $29.95 ISBN 978-1-891824-58-6

Visit our online bookstore: www.LightTechnology.com

Light Technology PUBLISHING

THE EXPLORER RACE SERIES

ZOOSH AND HIS FRIENDS THROUGH ROBERT SHAPIRO

•**THE SERIES:** Humans—creators-in-training—have a purpose and destiny so heartwarmingly, profoundly glorious that it is almost unbelievable from our present dimensional perspective. Humans are great lightbeings from beyond this creation, gaining experience in dense physicality. This truth about the great human genetic experiment of the Explorer Race and the mechanics of creation is being revealed for the first time by Zoosh and his friends through superchannel Robert Shapiro. These books read like adventure stories as we follow the clues from this creation that we live in out to the Council of Creators and beyond.

❶ THE EXPLORER RACE

You individuals reading this are truly a result of the genetic experiment on Earth. You are beings who uphold the principles of the Explorer Race. The information in this book is designed to show you who you are and give you an evolutionary understanding of your past that will help you now. The key to empowerment in these days is to not know everything about your past, but to know what will help you now. Your number-one function right now is your status of Creator apprentice, which you have achieved through years and lifetimes of sweat. You are constantly being given responsibilities by the Creator that would normally be things that Creator would do. The responsibility and the destiny of the Explorer Race is not only to explore, but to create. 574 p. $25.00 ISBN 0-929385-38-1

❷ ETs and the EXPLORER RACE

In this book, Robert channels Joopah, a Zeta Reticulan now in the ninth dimension who continues the story of the great experiment—the Explorer Race—from the perspective of his civilization. The Zetas would have been humanity's future selves had not humanity re-created the past and changed the future. 237 p. $14.95 ISBN 0-929385-79-9

❸ EXPLORER RACE: ORIGINS and the NEXT 50 YEARS

This volume has so much information about who we are and where we came from—the source of male and female beings, the war of the sexes, the beginning of the linear mind, feelings, the origin of souls—it is a treasure trove. In addition, there is a section that relates to our near future—how the rise of global corporations and politics affects our future, how to use benevolent magic as a force of creation and how we will go out to the stars and affect other civilizations. Astounding information. 339 p. $14.95 ISBN 0-929385-95-0

❹ EXPLORER RACE: CREATORS and FRIENDS
The MECHANICS of CREATION

Now that you have a greater understanding of who you are in the larger sense, it is necessary to remind you of where you came from, the true magnificence of your being. You must understand that you are creators-in-training, and yet you were once a portion of Creator. One could certainly say, without being magnanimous, that you are still a portion of Creator, yet you are training for the individual responsibility of being a creator, to give your Creator a coffee break. This book will allow you to understand the vaster qualities and help you remember the nature of the desires that drive any creator, the responsibilities to which a creator must answer, the reaction a creator must have to consequences and the ultimate reward of any creator. 435 p. $19.95 ISBN 1-891824-01-5

❺ EXPLORER RACE: PARTICLE PERSONALITIES

All around you in every moment you are surrounded by the most magical and mystical beings. They are too small for you to see as single individuals, but in groups you know them as the physical matter of your daily life. Particles who might be considered either atoms or portions of atoms consciously view the vast spectrum of reality yet also have a sense of personal memory like your own linear memory. These particles remember where they have been and what they have done in their infinitely long lives. Some of the particles we hear from are Gold, Mountain Lion, Liquid Light, Uranium, the Great Pyramid's Capstone, This Orb's Boundary, Ice and Ninth-Dimensional Fire. 237 p. $14.95 ISBN 0-929385-97-7

❻ EXPLORER RACE and BEYOND

With a better idea of how creation works, we go back to the Creator's advisers and receive deeper and more profound explanations of the roots of the Explorer Race. The liquid Domain and the Double Diamond portal share lessons given to the roots on their way to meet the Creator of this universe, and finally the roots speak of their origins and their incomprehensibly long journey here. 360 p. $14.95 ISBN 1-891824-06-6

Visit our online bookstore: www.LightTechnology.com

Light Technology PUBLISHING

THE EXPLORER RACE SERIES

ZOOSH AND HIS FRIENDS THROUGH ROBERT SHAPIRO

❼ EXPLORER RACE: The COUNCIL of CREATORS

The thirteen core members of the Council of Creators discuss their adventures in coming to awareness of themselves and their journeys on the way to the Council on this level. They discuss the advice and oversight they offer to all creators, including the Creator of this local universe. These beings are wise, witty and joyous, and their stories of Love's Creation create an expansion of our concepts as we realize that we live in an expanded, multiple-level reality. 237 P. $14.95 ISBN 1-891824-13-9

❽ EXPLORER RACE and ISIS

This is an amazing book! It has priestess training, Shamanic training, Isis's adventures with Explorer Race beings—before Earth and on Earth—and an incredibly expanded explanation of the dynamics of the Explorer Race. Isis is the prototypal loving, nurturing, guiding feminine being, the focus of feminine energy. She has the ability to expand limited thinking without making people with limited beliefs feel uncomfortable. She is a fantastic storyteller, and all of her stories are teaching stories. If you care about who you are, why you are here, where you are going and what life is all about—pick up this book. You won't lay it down until you are through, and then you will want more. 317 P. $14.95 ISBN 1-891824-11-2

❾ EXPLORER RACE and JESUS

The core personality of that being known on the Earth as Jesus, along with his students and friends, describes with clarity and love his life and teaching two thousand years ago. He states that his teaching is for all people of all races in all countries. Jesus announces here for the first time that he and two others, Buddha and Mohammed, will return to Earth from their place of being in the near future, and a fourth being, a child already born now on Earth, will become a teacher and prepare humanity for their return. So heartwarming and interesting, you won't want to put it down. 354 P. $16.95 ISBN 1-891824-14-7

❿ EXPLORER RACE: Earth History and Lost Civilization

Speaks of Many Truths and Zoosh, through Robert Shapiro, explain that planet Earth, the only water planet in this solar system, is on loan from Sirius as a home and school for humanity, the Explorer Race. Earth's recorded history goes back only a few thousand years, its archaeological history a few thousand more. Now this book opens up as if a light was on in the darkness, and we see the incredible panorama of brave souls coming from other planets to settle on different parts of Earth. We watch the origins of tribal groups and the rise and fall of civilizations, and we can begin to understand the source of the wondrous diversity of plants, animals and humans that we enjoy here on beautiful Mother Earth. 310 P. $14.95 ISBN 1-891824-20-1

⓫ EXPLORER RACE: ET VISITORS SPEAK

Even as you are searching the sky for extraterrestrials and their spaceships, ETs are here on planet Earth—they are stranded, visiting, exploring, studying the culture, healing the Earth of trauma brought on by irresponsible mining or researching the history of Christianity over the past two thousand years. Some are in human guise, and some are in spirit form. Some look like what we call animals as they come from the species' home planet and interact with their fellow beings—those beings that we have labeled cats or cows or elephants. Some are brilliant cosmic mathematicians with a sense of humor; they are presently living here as penguins. Some are fledgling diplomats training for future postings on Earth when we have ET embassies here. In this book, these fascinating beings share their thoughts, origins and purposes for being here. 350 P. $14.95 ISBN 1-891824-28-7

⓬ EXPLORER RACE: Techniques for GENERATING SAFETY

Wouldn't you like to generate safety so you could go wherever you need to go and do whatever you need to do in a benevolent, safe and loving way for yourself? Learn safety as a radiated environment that will allow you to gently take the step into the new timeline, into a benevolent future and away from a negative past. 208 P. $9.95 ISBN 1-891824-26-0

Phone: 928-526-1345 or 1-800-450-0985 • Fax: 923-714-1132

Light Technology PUBLISHING

THE ANCIENT SECRET OF THE FLOWER OF LIFE
VOLUME 1

Once, all life in the universe knew the Flower of Life as the creation pattern—the geometrical design leading us into and out of physical existence. Then, from a very high state of consciousness, we fell into darkness, the secret hidden for thousands of years, encoded in the cells of all life.

Now we are rising from the darkness and a new dawn is streaming through the windows of perception. This book is one of those windows. Drunvalo Melchizedek presents in text and graphics the Flower of Life Workshop, illuminating the mysteries of how we came to be.

Sacred Geometry is the form beneath our being and points to a divine order in our reality. We can follow that order from the invisible atom to the infinite stars, finding ourselves at each step. The information here is one path, but between the lines and drawings lie the feminine gems of intuitive understanding. You might see them sparkle around some of these provocative ideas:

- Remembering Our Ancient Past
- The Secret of the Flower Unfolds
- The Darker Side of Our Present and Past
- The Geometries of the Human Body
- When Evolution Crashed, and the Christ Grid Arose
- Egypt's Role in the Evolution of Consciousness
- The Significance of Shape and Structure

$25.00 Softcover 228 P.
ISBN 1-891824-17-1

Available from your favorite bookstore or:

LIGHT TECHNOLOGY PUBLISHING
PO Box 3540 • Flagstaff, AZ 86003

Drunvalo Melchizedek's life experience reads like an encyclopedia of breakthroughs in human endeavor. He studied physics and art at the University of California at Berkeley, but he feels that his most important education came after college. In the past 25 years, he has studied with over 70 teachers from all belief systems and religious understandings.

For some time now, he has been bringing his vision to the world through the Flower of Life program and the Mer-Ka-Ba meditation. This teaching encompasses every area of human understanding, explores the development of humankind from ancient civilizations to the present time and offers clarity regarding the world's state of consciousness and what is needed for a smooth and easy transition into the 21st century.

Visit our online bookstore: www.LightTechnology.com

☥ Light Technology PUBLISHING

THE ANCIENT SECRET OF THE FLOWER OF LIFE
VOLUME 2

The sacred Flower of Life pattern, the primary geometric generator of all physical form, is explored in even more depth in this volume, the second half of the famed Flower of Life workshop. The proportions of the human body, the nuances of human consciousness, the sizes and distances of the stars, planets and moons, even the creations of humankind, are all shown to reflect their origins in this beautiful and divine image. Through an intricate and detailed geometrical mapping, Drunvalo Melchizedek shows how the seemingly simple design of the Flower of Life contains the genesis of our entire third-dimensional existence.

From the pyramids and mysteries of Egypt to the new race of Indigo children, Drunvalo presents the sacred geometries of the Reality and the subtle energies that shape our world. We are led through a divinely inspired labyrinth of science and stories, logic and coincidence, on a path of remembering where we come from and the wonder and magic of who we are.

Finally, for the first time in print, Drunvalo shares the instructions for the Mer-Ka-Ba meditation, step-by-step techniques for the re-creation of the energy field of the evolved human, which is the key to ascension and the next dimensional world. If done from love, this ancient process of breathing prana opens up for us a world of tantalizing possibility in this dimension, from protective powers to the healing of oneself, of others and even of the planet.

$25.00 Softcover 252 P.
ISBN 1-891824-21-X

- The Unfolding of the Third Informational System
- Whispers from Our Ancient Heritage
- Unveiling the Mer-ka-ba Meditation
- Using Your Mer-ka-ba
- Connecting to the Levels of Self
- Two Cosmic Experiments
- What We May Expect in the Forthcoming Dimensional Shift

Available from your favorite bookstore or:

LIGHT TECHNOLOGY PUBLISHING
PO Box 3540 • Flagstaff, AZ 86003

Phone: 928-526-1345 or 1-800-450-0985 • Fax: 923-714-1132

✧ Light Technology PUBLISHING

A New Book by Drunvalo Melchizedek

LIVING IN THE HEART

Includes a CD with Heart Meditation by Drunvalo Melchizedek

$25 with CD
Softcover 120 P.
ISBN 1-891824-43-0

"Long ago we humans used a form of communication and sensing that did not involve the brain in any way; rather, it came from a sacred place within our heart. What good would it do to find this place again in a world where the greatest religion is science and the logic of the mind? Don't I know this world where emotions and feelings are second-class citizens? Yes, I do. But my teachers have asked me to remind you who you really are. You are more than a human being, much more. For within your heart is a place, a sacred place where the world can literally be remade through conscious cocreation. If you give me permission, I will show you what has been shown to me."

- Beginning with the Mind
- Seeing in the Darkness
- Learning from Indigenous Tribes
- The Sacred Space of the Heart
- The Unity of Heaven and Earth
- Leaving the Mind and Entering the Heart
- The Sacred Space of the Heart Meditation
- The Mer-Ka-Ba and the Sacred Space of the Heart
- Conscious Cocreation from the Heart Connected to the Mind

Drunvalo Melchizedek has been studying pure consciousness and human potential for almost forty years. His focus on the rediscovery of the human lightbody, the Mer-Ka-Ba and the way Sacred Geometry is inherent within the lightbody and all of creation is shared through workshops and books as he has brought his vision of the Flower of Life and the Mer-Ka-Ba to the world.

Now his new work, *Living in the Heart*, with the techniques that lead you into the Sacred Space of the Heart, goes even deeper into the possibilities of human potential and the creation process itself. Within these pages, Drunvalo shares his knowledge and tells you exactly how to achieve this ancient state of consciousness so that, finally, what you dream in your heart you can make real in your everyday life; a beautiful, abundant life and ascension into the higher worlds become a natural sequence of living in your heart. Join Drunvalo and be part of the large group of people who have found the joy of living in the space where you and God are one.

Visit our online bookstore: www.LightTechnology.com

Light Technology PUBLISHING

SEDONA
Journal of EMERGENCE!

Rated Number One!
We Offer Answers to Satisfy the Heart and to Inspire Lives!

YOU ARE EXPERIENCING AN UNPRECEDENTED EXPANSION into a new reality and a dimensional shift into a new state of being. This movement from one dimension to another while in a physical body has never been done before—it feels like you are building the rocket you're riding while it is blasting off!

THERE ARE NO ANCIENT BOOKS, NO RULEBOOKS, no manuals or procedures, no record of how to do this thing, because it has never been done before. During previous dimensional shifts, embodied beings would die in the old reality and then be reborn in the new one in new bodies with a different vibrational frequency.

SO LIGHTBEINGS, THROUGH THEIR CHANNELS, EXPLAIN THIS PROCESS and offer guidance and spiritual techniques to help you learn to feel and express love and benevolence– and to encourage you to change your behavior to ensure that the Earth remains habitable while you expand into your natural self and awaken to your natural talents and abilities. As this happens, you will allow yourself to flow with all humanity into a more benevolent version of Earth—into another dimensional focus, another of the strata of this existence.

ELECTRONIC SUBSCRIPTIONS available for SJE!

$29⁰⁰/YEAR for 12 months anywhere on the planet!
$55⁰⁰ for 2 years!

Must be puchased online at: www.sedonajournal.com for you to obtain a user name and password.

Get the latest channeling and astrology 2 weeks before it is available on the newsstand.

The Sedona Journal of EMERGENCE! is the one monthly magazine readers never throw away.

Get SPECIAL UPDATES of channeled material before they're available on the newsstand with ELECTRONIC SUBSCRIPTIONS!

Phone: 928-526-1345 or 1-800-450-0985 • Fax: 923-714-1132

☼ Light Technology PUBLISHING

SEDONA Journal of EMERGENCE!

ORDER NOW!
TO RECEIVE SPECTACULAR SAVINGS!

ORDER ONLINE!
SAVE expensive freight or postage on your Sedona Journal subscription

We are now making ELECTRONIC SUBSCRIPTIONS
available for the
SEDONA JOURNAL OF EMERGENCE!
We have now added content that will not fit into the printed magazine!

- Get the entire *Journal* online by subscription—and get it 2 weeks before it goes on the newsstand!
- Save on expensive freight or postage on your *Sedona Journal* subscription!

Electronic Subscriptions

☐ 1 yr. . . . $29   ☐ 2 yr. . . . $55

All Electronic Subscriptions must be purchased online at:
www.sedonajournal.com
to obtain username and password

Get the Best of Both Worlds!
Special Combo Offers!

U.S.A
Get a 2ⁿᵈ Class Printed Subscription Along with an Electronic Subscription - USA only

☐ 1 yr. . . . $59   ☐ 2 yr. . . . $109

Canada & Mexico
Get an Airmail Printed Subscription Along with an Electronic Subscription for only

☐ 1 yr. . . . $95   ☐ 2 yr. . . . $179

NOTE: The US Postal Service has changed postal rates, eliminating Canadian 2nd Class Surface and increasing all airmail rates.

All Countries
Except USA, Canada & Mexico
Get an Airmail Printed Subscription Along with an Electronic Subscription for only

☐ 1 yr. . . . $152   ☐ 2 yr. . . . $285

NOTE: The US Postal Service has changed postal rates, eliminating global 2nd Class Surface and increasing all airmail rates.

---

yes! Send Me:

Printed and Mailed Subcriptions

	PRIORITY	1ˢᵀ CLASS	2ⁿᵈ CLASS
☐ 2 yrs (24 issues)	$169	☐ 2 yrs. . . $129	☐ 2 yrs. . . $79
☐ 1 yr (12 issues)	$86	☐ 1 yr. . . . $65	☐ 1 yr. . . . $43

USA

CANADA & MEXICO   AIR
☐ 2 yrs (24 issues) $149
☐ 1 yr (12 issues) $79

U.S. dollars only

NOTE: The US Postal Service has changed postal rates, eliminating Canadian 2nd Class Surface and increasing all airmail rates.

ALL COUNTRIES
Except USA, Canada & Mexico   AIR
☐ 2 yrs (24 issues) $255
☐ 1 yr (12 issues) $136

U.S. dollars only

NOTE: The US Postal Service has changed postal rates, eliminating global 2nd Class Surface and increasing all airmail rates.

My Name _____

Address _____

City _____ State: ____ Zip: _____

Phone _____

Email _____

Gift Recipient Name _____

Address _____

City _____ State: ____ Zip: _____

Personalized Gift Card from _____

METHOD OF PAYMENT:

☐ CHECK #   ☐ M.O.

☐ VISA   ☐ MASTERCARD   ☐ NOVUS   ☐ AMEX

CARD NO. _____

EXPIRATION DATE _____

SIGNATURE _____

Phone: 1-800-450-0985 • Fax: 928-714-1132 . . . or visit www.sedonajournal.com

Visit our online bookstore: www.LightTechnology.com

Light Technology PUBLISHING

SEDONA
JOURNAL OF EMERGENCE!

SUBSCRIBE NOW
TO RECEIVE *SPECTACULAR SAVINGS!*

✴ COMBO SUBSCRIPTIONS

Get the best of both worlds with special combo offers. Includes both printed and electronic subscriptions. All electronic subscriptions must be purchased online at www.sedonajournal.com to obtain a username and password to access your subscription.

	1 yr 12 issues / months of each	**2 yr** 24 issues / months of each
USA - 2nd Class	$59 USD	$109 USD
Canada and Mexico	$95 USD	$179 USD
All Other Countries	$152 USD	$285 USD

✴ ELECTRONIC SUBSCRIPTIONS

Get the entire Journal online by subscription and get it 2 weeks before it goes on the newsstand. Save on expensive freight or postage on your *Sedona Journal* subscription! All electronic subscriptions must be purchased online at www.sedonajournal.com to obtain a username and password to access your subscription.

	1 yr - 12 issues / months	**2 yr** - 24 issues / months
All Countries	$29 USD	$55 USD

✴ PRINTED AND MAILED SUBSCRIPTIONS

	1 yr - 12 issues / months	**2 yr** - 24 issues / months
USA - Priority	$86 USD	$169 USD
USA - 1st class	$65 USD	$129
USA - 2nd class	$43 USD	$79 USD
Canada and Mexico	$79 USD	$149 USD
All Other Countries	$136 USD	$255 USD

WWW.SEDONAJOURNAL.COM

Phone: 928-526-1345 or 1-800-450-0985 • Fax: 923-714-1132

Light Technology PUBLISHING

EASY ORDER 24 HOURS A DAY

Order ONLINE!
www.lighttechnology.com
Email:
customersrv@lighttechnology.net

* Shopping Cart w/ Secure Transactions
* In-Depth Information on Books, Including Excerpts and Contents
* Use our Great Links to Other Sites

Order by Mail
Send To:
Light Technology Publishing
PO Box 3540
Flagstaff, AZ 86003

SEDONA Journal of EMERGENCE!
Peace to All Beings

* Read Excerpts of Monthly Channeling and Predictions in Advance
* Use Our Email Links to Contact Us or Send a Submission
* Electronic Subscriptions Available—With or Without Print Copies

Order by Phone
800-450-0985
928-526-1345

BENEVOLENT MAGIC & Living Prayer
Ancient Secrets of Feminine Science

Learn the techniques of benevolence toward self and benevolence toward others and you will create global peace. Download all the techniques of benevolent magic and living prayer for FREE!

Order by Fax
928-714-1132

The EXPLORER RACE SERIES

All of humanity constitutes the Explorer Race, volunteers for a grand and glorious experiment. Discover your purpose, your history and your future. Download the first chapter of each book for FREE!

Available from your favorite bookstore or:

Shamanic Secrets
For Material, Physical & Spiritual Mastery

What we call shamanism is the natural way of life for beings on other planets. Learn to be aware of your natural self and your natural talents and abilities. Download the first chapter of each book for FREE!

Phone: 928-526-1345 or 1-800-450-0985 • Fax: 923-714-1132